The Interface of Orality and Writing

Biblical Performance Criticism Series

David Rhoads, Holly E. Hearon, and Kelly R. Iverson, Series Editors

The ancient societies of the Bible were overwhelmingly oral. People originally experienced the traditions now in the Bible as oral performances. Focusing on the ancient performance of biblical traditions enables us to shift academic work on the Bible from the mentality of a modern print culture to that of an oral/scribal culture. Conceived broadly, biblical performance criticism embraces many methods as means to reframe the biblical materials in the context of traditional oral cultures, construct scenarios of ancient performances, learn from contemporary performances of these materials, and reinterpret biblical writings accordingly. The result is a foundational paradigm shift that reconfigures traditional disciplines and employs fresh biblical methodologies such as theater studies, speech-act theory, and performance studies. The emerging research of many scholars in this field of study, the development of working groups in scholarly societies, and the appearance of conferences on orality and literacy make it timely to inaugurate this series. For further information on biblical performance criticism, go to www.biblicalperformancecriticism.org.

Books in the Series

Holly E. Hearon and Philip Ruge-Jones, editors
The Bible in Ancient and Modern Media

James A. Maxey
From Orality to Orality:
A New Paradigm for Contextual Translation of the Bible

Antoinette Clark Wire
The Case for Mark Composed in Performance

Robert D. Miller II, SFO
Oral Tradition in Ancient Israel

Pieter J. J. Botha
Orality and Literacy in Early Christianity

James A. Maxey and Ernst R. Wendland, editors
Translating Scripture for Sound and Performance

J. A. (Bobby) Loubser
Oral and Manuscript Culture in the Bible

Joanna Dewey
The Oral Ethos of the Early Church

Richard A. Horsley
Text and Tradition in Performance and Writing

Kelley R. Iverson, editor
From Text to Performance:
Narrative and Performance Criticisms in Dialogue and Debate

Thomas E. Boomershine
The Messiah of Peace
A Performance-Criticism Commentary on Mark's Passion–Resurrection Narrative

The Interface of
Orality and Writing

Speaking, Seeing, Writing in the Shaping of New Genres

Edited by
Annette Weissenrieder
and
Robert B. Coote

CASCADE *Books* • Eugene, Oregon

THE INTERFACE OF ORALITY AND WRITING
Speaking, Seeing, Writing in the Shaping of New Genres

Biblical Performance Criticism Series 11

Cascade Books
An Imprint of Wipf and Stock Publishers
199 W. 8th Ave., Suite 3
Eugene, OR 97401

www.wipfandstock.com

ISBN 13: 978-1-4982-3742-0

Cataloguing-in-Publication data:

The interface of orality and writing : speaking, seeing, writing in the shaping of new genres / edited by Annette Weissenrieder and Robert B. Coote.

xvi + 438 pp. ; 23 cm.—Includes bibliographical references and indexes.

ISBN: 978-1-4982-3742-0

1. Oral tradition—Congresses. 2. Bible—Criticism, interpretation, etc. 3. Bible. O.T.—Performance criticism. 4. Bible. N.T.—Performance criticism. I. Weissenrieder, Annette, 1967–. II. Coote, Robert B., 1944–. III. Title. IV. Series.

BS522 I584 2015

Originally published by Mohr Siebeck 2010 in the series Wissenschaftliche Monographien zum Neuen Testament 260. Published under license from Mohr Siebeck.

Table of Contents

Preface

"[…] so was erudition: for, in the treasure handed down to us by Antiquity, the value of language lay in fact that it was the sign of things. There is no difference between the visible marks that God has stamped upon the surface of the earth, so that we may know its inner secrets, and the legible words that the Scriptures, or the sages of Antiquity, have set down in the books preserved for us by tradition. The relation to these texts is of the same nature as the relation to things: in both cases there are signs that must be discovered. […] [T]he Ancients have already provided us with interpretations, which we need do no more than gather together. Or which we would need only to gather together, were it not for the necessity of learning their language, reading their texts, and understanding, what they have said. The heritage of Antiquity, like nature itself, is a vast space requiring interpretation; in both cases there are signs to be discovered and then, little by little, made to speak."[1]

In *The Order of Things*, Foucault describes a relationship among visual images, oral sources and written texts which may well be foundational. He addresses various aspects for which an interpretation of sources could be central, such as the relationship among visual images, written texts and speech, the necessity of gathering these sources together and learning their particular language, as well as understanding images as both objects of interpretation and indeed acts of interpretation of speech and written text.

Our programmatic title, *The Interface of Orality and Writing: Hearing, Seeing, Writing in New Genres*, takes into account the role that images, texts and oral sources played in the production and reception of early Christian ideas. The basis of the interface of orality and writing has always been communication. Image, text and speech are part of culture and hence also part of a symbol system, and it is with the help of such symbol systems that people communicate.

To some extent the present volume of essays engages longstanding issues and perspectives, insofar as its studies in the area of oral tradition are linked with the historical-critical exegesis of texts. But we extend such exegesis in terms of further methodological facets. It is not just exegesis of texts and their possible oral precursors that are discussed. In addition, the exegesis of ancient iconographic schemes and the role of visual media – indeed the treatment of communicative intermediation in general – are brought into play with biblical ex-

---

[1] M. Foucault, *The Order of Things. An Archaeology of the Human Sciences* (London/New York: Routledge, 1989), 37.

egesis for the first time in this volume. Moreover a central role is played by the
question of the forms of memory and their *Sitz im Leben*.

The key term in the phrase "interface of orality and writing: hearing, seeing,
writing in new genres" is "interface." In this investigation, several perspectives
come together which accentuate the line of questioning suggested above and
which are brought to light by the contributions.

The essays in this volume point first to our understanding of the notion of *text*
and how it has been used. Indeed the question immediately arises whether
ancient biblical or non-biblical texts even distinguished between, as it were, oral
and written text. While some contributors to the volume attempt to demonstrate the oral character of texts as such (for example Antoinette Wire and Roger
Nam), others set out to show that texts entailed no such distinction (e.g. Susan
Niditch, John Foley).

In order to avoid prejudicing our understanding of text in terms of our
present experience, we must factor in the cultural differences underlying the
ancient notion of text. In the first place, in Greco-Roman antiquity to read a
text meant simply to read it out loud. As an abundance of scholars have convincingly argued, reading written text aloud was the common practice in Greco-Roman antiquity.[2] This is shown by passages in Plato, e.g. in Phaedo[3] and
Theaetetus[4], and in Theon[5], and by passages on the theme of "hearing," as in
Pliny the Younger[6], as expounded at length in this volume by Teun Tieleman
and John Foley. What is true for pagan antiquity is equally evident from biblical
texts. Kristina Dronsch points to Acts 8:26–40: Philip hears the Ethiopian read,
which requires that the Ethiopian was reading out loud. The practice of oral
reading is particularly manifested by manuscripts written in *scriptio continua*.
These give no indication of paragraphs or verses, and thus make no distinction
between what is visible and what is audible, a fact to be kept constantly in mind.
There was in antiquity no reading without hearing. In his more recent work,
included in this volume, Werner Kelber has turned to aspects of written texts in
antiquity which – consistent with his concept of "mouvance" – acknowledge
the performative character of ancient written processes. Here interestingly a
media adjustment of the written text takes place, to the voice with which Kelber
characterizes the early scribal tradition of Jesus sayings.

Is reading therefore a process "which is based on how the letters reflect the
sound of the speech?"[7] If so, reading a text would be an oral performance

---

[2] P.J. Achtemeier, "Omne Verbum Sonat: The New Testament and the Oral Environment
of Late Western Antiquity," *JBL* 109 (1990): 17–19.

[3] Plato, *Phaed.* 97β: ἀκούσας μέν ποτε βιβλίου.

[4] Plato, *Theaet.* 143b.c.

[5] Theon, *Progymnasmata* 61.

[6] Pliny, *Ep.* IX, 36.

[7] J. Penny Small, *Wax Tablets of the Mind: Cognitive Studies of Memory and Literacy in Classical
Antiquity* (New York: Routledge, 1997), 24.

"whenever it occurred and in whatever circumstances."[8] With regard to the reception of texts, this implies that "effective communication" (Antoinette Clark Wire) is inevitably tied to someone reading out loud who can make the "vocal effects"[9] audible, and therefore tied to the sound of the voice. Susan Niditch shows that in antiquity hearing was a function of written communication in writing: "Oral-related considerations suggest [...] that the Hebrew Bible, even in written form, was meant to be heard and spoken." Does this then mean that for a text to be understandable it had to be audible? This momentous question is discussed here in the essays on performativity (David Rhoads, David Trobisch). But the question has a further implication especially in form criticism: Speech has to do in principle with communicating the gospel, a process in which speech is assigned the function of supporting the written word. Does this mean that speech in the text is not to be taken as a rhetorical figure serving to hide the fact that there is in fact no speech in the written medium (Trevor Thompson)? And as Ruben Zimmermann demonstrates, form-critical questions within the orality debate are closely tied to the question of forms of memory.

The essays in *The Interface of the Orality and Writing: Speaking, Seeing, Writing in New Genres* point secondly to questions of methodological foundations, which are in a way inseparable from questions of the nature of texts. At first glance it might appear that the medium of pictorial or visual representation would have little to do with understanding texts: in the one case the emphasis is on making something audible, in the other seemingly different case, visible. Three considerations speak against such a demarcation: First, behind this assumption stands a methodological decision. In the current methodological discussion in archaeology and art history – which views iconography as one of its sub-disciplines – the questions raised by semiotics have become the main focus of attention. If one understands culture as a symbol system, then it is logically consistent to understand images both as a part of culture and as elements of each valid symbol system. Common among many, very different "image theories" is the idea that images cannot be viewed as simple visual reproductions of reality. Theoretical reflection upon this often-implicit assumption is offered by constructivism. Constructivist theories ask *how* knowledge is produced. According to the basic thesis, visual sources do not represent mere reflections of reality, but are rather to be interpreted in relation to the typical behavioral roles of people (in antiquity), their philosophical-medical knowledge of the human body, their mentalities, and their structures and conflicts in social groups and society as a whole. Thus artifacts must always be matched with the sources of general structural history,

---

[8] Achtemeier, "Omne verbum sonat," 17.

[9] W. Shiner, *Proclaiming the Gospel: First Century Performance of Mark* (Harrisburg, PA: Trinity Press, 2003), 162.

i. e. with further visual and textual sources regarding the general circumstances of a particular age. Yet on this basis one thing has changed fundamentally: through such social contextualizing, the categorical separation on the one hand between text and speech and on the other hand between image and category of work of art has had the ground knocked out from under it[10].

The second consideration is this. In ancient times, objects of art had a peculiar liveliness of their own, especially those artifacts which through accompanying inscriptions evoked an act of speech. The philosopher and art historian Horst Bredekamp has recently presented an interpretation of this quality: the inscription makes viewers move their lips and thus lend their voice to the object. Image and speech act are connected with each other.[11] A person sees the inscription "Roma" on ancient coins and understands and voices its message: this object is affiliated with Rome. Or sees the inscription "I am Hermes the Kyllenier" next to Hermes on an amphora. Hermes is shown as a stately bearded man with screen hat, staff (*kērykeion*), and winged shoes; he conveys a message which is directed to us, who read the text with the painting. We receive a message from Zeus directed through his messenger Hermes. Visual images combined with written texts require that we interpret them as a comprehensive phenomenon.

The third reason to hesitate to demarcate the audible from the visible is that David Balch has opened up a new discussion in New Testament studies by raising the issue of the relationship between the experience in antiquity of rooms, replete with the visual, and the performative forms of orality; for of one thing we can be certain: both public and private rooms were frequently decorated with numerous paintings of mythological subjects and subjects from nature.

The contributions in *The Interface of the Orality and Writing: Speaking, Seeing, Writing in New Genres* point thirdly to the concepts of communication, tied variously to theories of media, prevalent in the orality debate. Most share with one another as point of departure Kelber's contention that dialogue is the unqualified guarantor of successful communication and intersubjective connection. Dialogue flows in "oral synthesis" between the dialogue partners.[12] Hence Kelber's media theory is based on a model of successful dialogical *face-to-face-communication* (*Nahkommunikation*). This concept has a momentous consequence: a written text may no longer be categorized as a part of the only guaranteed form of successful communication. A disconnection between orality and written text becomes obvious. Using the Gospel of Mark, Kristina

---

[10] Cf. A. Weissenrieder and F. Wendt, "Images of Communication," *Picturing the New Testament* (eds. A. Weissenrieder, F. Wendt and P. v. Gemünden; Tübingen: Mohr Siebeck, 2005), 43.

[11] H. Bredekamp, "Theorie des Bildaktes," unpubl. paper; Gadamer-Professur at the University of Heidelberg 2005.

[12] Kelber, *The Oral and the Written Gospel*, 19.

Dronsch und Annette Weissenrieder show that the notion of face-to-face-communication *Nahkommunikation* is not inevitable. The failure of face-to-face-communication can be shown in an instructive way in Mark 6:1–6. This story reflects above all the failure of communication in dialogue between Jesus and interlocutors in his hometown. In light of the work of the media ethicist and theorist Raffael Capurro, philosopher Sybille Krämer and communication scientist John Durham Peters, Dronsch and Weissenrieder propose a change in perspective, namely that dialogue based on "a continuous process of adjustment of language to communal expectations, of social to linguistic realities"[13] forms the exception rather than the rule. What is required instead is a concept of communication[14] that takes seriously non-reciprocity as "ein Strukturmerkmal der Kommunikation unter den Bedingungen von Differenz."[15]

In sum, the title of this volume of essays expresses its program: in the investigation of the interface of the oral and written, across the spectrum of seeing, hearing, and writing, new concepts of media theory and mediality may emerge.

The greater part of this volume consists of a selection of papers delivered at a conference held at San Francisco Theological Seminary in San Anselmo in March, 2009. These papers appear here in revised form. In addition, we have invited a number of other authors further to explore issues that arose in the context of the conference.

The main ancient text considered, but not the only one, was the Gospel of Mark. Several addressed the complexity of the relationship between orality and writing in the foundational Hebrew Scriptures (S. Niditch, A. Schellenberg, A. Schuele, R. Nam) and in rabbinic Scriptures (C. Heszer and Daniel Boyarin). As indicated above, speakers presented many aspects of the competing and complementary roles of memory, performance, and writing, of literacy and popular culture in the composition and transmission of narratives, as well as visual media (gesture, images in text, decorative art, coinage). The conference brought together biblical scholars, experts in early Judaism, classicists, art historians, and specialists in oral literature in lively interdisciplinary conversation.

The conference was held to honor Antoinette Clark Wire and her research in oral tradition, both ancient and modern, exemplified by but far from limited to her work on the Corinthian women prophets and on modern Chinese women singers. The conference was designed to draw particular attention to her most recent book, *Holy Lives, Holy Deaths: A Close Hearing of Early Jewish Storytellers.* Inspiration came from her interest in capturing the voices and mindset of story-

---

[13] Kelber, *The Oral and the Written Gospel*, 92.

[14] See Durham Peters, *Speaking into the Air. A History of the Idea of Communication* (Chicago, London: University Press, 1999), 7 for an instructive definition of communication.

[15] S. Krämer, *Medium, Bote, Übertragung. Kleine Metaphysik der Medialität* (Frankfurt: Suhrkamp, 2008), 104.

tellers who engender and continue to surround the written texts we have from antiquity, and in attempting to comprehend the contexts in which stories were communicated. It is thus most appropriate that the written texts in this volume are largely echoes of and commentaries on a conversation.

* * *

Several people contributed to the development of this work, and we want to thank them here.

We are especially thankful for the support of San Francisco Theological Seminary, which contributed both practical help and financial support that made possible the funding of the conference and the visual images used in this volume. A special word of thanks goes to Petey Thornton, Holly Woolard, Kyung-A Park, Naomi Nakaoka, and Kazuhiko Nakaoka for invaluable administrative assistance in organizing and running the conference at San Francisco Theological Seminary.

For the final structure of this book, our thanks go to Prof. Dr. Jörg Frey, who has been helpful in the completion of the plan of the book, and the editorial staff of Mohr Siebeck, especially Dr. Henning Ziebritzki and Tanja Mix, for their assistance in preparing the manuscript for publication.

We are particularly grateful to Prof. Dr. Polly Coote (SFTS), Assist. Prof. Dr. Rossitza Schroeder (PSR), Prof. Dr. Barbara Borg (University of Exeter), Prof. Dr. Brigitte Kahl (Union Theological Seminary, New York), the faculty of SFTS esp. Prof. Dr. Jana Childers (dean of SFTS at the time of the conference and thereafter), Prof. Dr. James Noel, and Prof. Dr. Christopher Ocker, and to our doctoral students at the Graduate Theological Union in Berkeley who provided thought-provoking questions and suggestions in conversation on the topic of the interface of orality and written text in Old and New Testament and Rabbinic Studies, at the conference and afterwards.

We would like to thank Prof. Dr. Polly Coote, Douglas Olds and Lucas Walker for their assistance in preparing the manuscripts.

This book is dedicated to Antoinette Clark Wire, in honor of her scholarly work, especially as regards orality, and in recognition of the personal esteem in which many of us are privileged to hold her.

Annette Weissenrieder
Robert B. Coote

Part I: Introduction:
Speaking, Seeing, Writing in the Shaping
of New Genres

Hebrew Bible and Oral Literature:
Misconceptions and New Directions

Susan Niditch

This contribution to the conference on orality and writing in antiquity explores past applications and new directions in approaching ancient Israelite literature as traditional-style literature that is richly informed and framed by an essentially oral culture. Specific topics addressed are: the sometimes misunderstood contributions of Albert B. Lord; the way in which the field of oral literature has interwoven with the field of biblical studies in the past; some of the misconceptions that have informed and continue to inform biblicists' approaches to oral literature and oral literary studies; and some brief case studies from the biblical book of Judges that point to the continued relevance of oral studies in our efforts to appreciate and interpret the culture and literature of ancient Israel.

Brief quotations from the foreword and introduction to *The Singer of Tales* reveal much about the presuppositions and goals of Lord's classic work.

> We believe that the epic singers from the dawn of human consciousness have been a deeply significant group and have contributed abundantly to the spiritual and intellectual growth of man [...] This book concentrates on only one aspect of the singer's art. Our immediate purpose is to comprehend the manner in which they compose, learn, and transmit their epics. It is a study of in the processes of composition of oral narrative poetry.[1]

Lord goes on to describe how Parry's work with formulaic epithets in the Iliad and Odyssey had convinced him that "the poems of Homer were traditional epics" created in oral composition and that he "turned to the study of Yugoslav epics" that were still being created by bards in extemporaneous settings to see how such a process of composition worked within a cultural context and to apply his observations "to learn how (the ancient poems) may have been composed.[2]"

The purpose of the work was structural with its interest in the formulaic construction of narrative; it was ethnographic, seeking to understand the way literature was produced by human beings in cultural settings; it was comparative

---

[1] A. B. Lord, *The Singer of Tales* (New York: Atheneum, 1968), xxxv.
[2] Lord, *Singer of Tales*, 3.

and anthropological using living models to shed light on worlds now preserved only in the archaeological remains of material culture and the literary artifacts themselves. Comparisons with the field of biblical studies, of course, come to mind: form-critical interests in content and structure and in life settings plus the use of more fully preserved neighboring ancient Near Eastern traditions to shed light on ancient Israelite social worlds and literary products.

Lord concludes that the Iliad and the Odyssey share with Balkan epic material certain key markers of oral composition; a high degree of formulicity, a formula being "a group of words which is regularly employed under the same metrical conditions to express a given essential idea";[3] metric regularity/line length; a lack of necessary enjambement: the thought is complete at the end of the line even if the sentence continues. Thus orality affects and reflects what Alan Dundes has called the texture, text, and context of a work:[4] "texture," its style, which in the case of oral literature reveals repetition, economy of language in the words chosen to portray images and ideas; "text," its very content or plot or structure which will also be highly formulaic, composed of recurring themes as in the musical "themes" of an opera or other musical genres; and "context," its life setting or social world, and Lord would emphasize in particular the illiteracy of the creators and the audience as well as the training of the singers and the expectations and participation of the receivers of the performance, aspects of the oral world explored by John Miles Foley.[5]

Lord himself approached these matters of texture, text, and context complexly and deeply. The formula he reminded us is not a mechanical wooden device for making lines of proper length and rhythm but a meaning-rich component of characterization, tone, and message, a means of thematic emphasis, and a reflection of aesthetics. Repetition is richness if one understands the register, nor is there just one oral register. There can be switches of register in one work to reflect content, character, and message. The choices made in the use of these flexible compositional devices matter; he wrote of formula patterns that could be filled in various ways.[6] He was attuned to the artistry of composers some of whom were more gifted than others. Variations matter and what is not repeated is as important as what is. Lord's work has often been misrepresented by his critics and inflexibly applied to various works of traditional literature by his fans.

---

[3] Lord, *Singer of Tales*, 30.

[4] A. Dundes, "Text, Texture, and Context," *Interpreting Folklore* (Bloomington: Indiana University Press, 1980), 20–32.

[5] J. M. Foley, *The Singer of Tales in Performance* (Bloomington: Indiana University Press, 1990); idem, *Immanent Art: From Structure to Meaning in Traditional-Oral Epic* (Bloomington: Indiana University Press, 1991).

[6] Lord, *The Singer of Tales*, 44.

In a wonderful little 1996 work, classicist Gregory Nagy lists the ten most misunderstood things about Lord's theory of oral composition, some of which we have alluded to above.[7] These include, for example, the notion that "the poet has only one way of saying it"[8] or that "meter makes the poet say it that way"[9] or that the Iliad is so unified, it cannot be oral[10] and the related idea that Homer must have been able to write[11] or the suggestion that there is one simple "world of Homer" (ignoring the rolling quality of the development of the Homeric tradition and the on-going nature of the ancient tradition).[12] Nagy notes that oral works can become quite fixed, and written works can be quite open to variation, while scribes engage in performance like activity in the very act of writing – what Paul Zumthor calls "composition-in-performance" as a work, quoting Nagy, "is regenerated in each act of copying."[13]

Lord's work has led to a host of useful perhaps inevitable and necessary, but I would argue (and I think the authors would agree) less than satisfying searches for "oral roots" of biblical works. William Whallon,[14] William J. Urbrock,[15] and Robert C. Culley[16] carefully explored the possibility that the poetry of the He- brew Bible exhibits oral-compositional roots. John R. Kselman wrote an essay, "The Recovery of Poetic Fragments from the Pentateuchal Priestly Source."[17] "Oral" was synonymous with "poetry" and associated with a "past" to be recovered. David Gunn looked for oral roots of the biblical battle re- port.[18] The authors virtually all expressed disappointment with their results. The degree of formulicity was not high enough to "prove" oral composition. But the work of all these excellent scholars was very valuable in revealing the tradi- tional style textures and texts of Israelite literature. The aesthetic is indeed

---

[7] G. Nagy, *Homeric Questions* (Austin: University of Texas Press, 1996), 19–27.

[8] Nagy, *Homeric Questions*, 25.

[9] Nagy, *Homeric Questions*, 23.

[10] Nagy, *Homeric Questions*, 26.

[11] Nagy, *Homeric Questions*, 27.

[12] Nagy, *Homeric Questions*, 20.

[13] Nagy, *Homeric Questions*, 69.

[14] W. Whallon, *Formula, Character, and Context: Studies in Homeric, Old English, and Old Testament Poetry* (Washington, D. C.: The Center for Hellenistic Studies, 1969).

[15] W. J. Urbrock, "Formula and Theme in the Song-Cycle of Job," *SBL 1972 Proceedings* 2 (ed. Lane C. McGaughy; Missoula: Scholars Press, 1972), 459–87; idem, "Oral Antecedents to Job: A Survey of Formulas and Formulaic Systems," *Semeia* 5 (1976):139–54.

[16] R. C. Culley, "An Approach to the Problem of Oral Tradition," *VT* (1963): 113–25; idem, *Oral Formulaic Language in the Biblical Psalms* (Near East and Middle East Series 4; To- ronto: University of Toronto Press, 1967); idem, "Oral Tradition and the OT: Some Recent Discussion," *Semeia* 5 (1976): 1–33; idem, "Oral Tradition and Biblical Studies," *Oral Tradition* 1 (1990): 30–65.

[17] J. R. Kselman, "The Recovery of Poetic Fragments from the Pentateuchal Priestly Source," *JBL* 97 (1978): 161–73.

[18] D. Gunn, "The 'Battle Report': Oral or Scribal Convention?" *JBL* 93 (1974): 513–18; "Narrative Patterns and Oral Tradition in Judges and Samuel," *VT* 24 (1974): 286–317.

related to matters of worldview and cultural context. It turns out that the issue of provable oral composition is a bit of a red herring, as is the sharp divide that Lord himself imagined between oral worlds and literate worlds, oral composition and works created in writing. Lord himself later wrote of "transitional works" somewhat refining the notion of a great divide between literate and illiterate, composition in writing versus oral composition.[19] Admittedly, however, Lord still retained a somewhat dated, evolutionist view of works that are written but seem to have so much in common with the formulas and themes of provably oral works. Perhaps his categories worked better for the particular genres he studied with their set line length and metric patterns – again there are various oral registers.

Biblicists have partaken of their own view of the great divide and have expressed a rigid view of the evolution of written from oral works. The form-critical approach is grounded in the notion that early, oral, simpler works are eventually written down and complicated by literate sophisticated writers. The former are primitive, the latter complex. We find this point of view in the writing of Gunkel and in a host of other biblicists' work.[20] This orientation leads to a pastoral romanticization of early contributors to the traditions, picturing them sitting by the fire, the sound of bleating sheep in the background.[21] It also leads to a distaste for the notion of oral world backgrounds to the Hebrew Bible as too unsophisticated and demeaning of the great writerly tradition.[22] In fact, orally composed works can be long or short, created by people who can read and write or by those who can read but not write. Written traditional-style literature can be meant to be read aloud while orally composed works are set in writing by means of dictation or recreated in writing through memory. Writers can imitate oral style. Written works, their plots and characters, enter the oral end of the spectrum and visa versa. Once writing and reading are available in a culture or nearby, even if only practiced by elites, the two ways of imagining and creating literature influence one another and belong on a sliding scale or continuum as Ruth Finnegan has shown.[23] Nor does oral style serve as a certain marker of

---

[19] A. B. Lord, *Epic Singers and Oral Tradition* (Ithaca, NY: Cornell University Press, 1991), 25.

[20] See, for example, H. Gunkel, *The Folktale in the Old Testament* (trans. Michael D. Rutter; Sheffield: Almond, 1987; originally published in 1917), 33.

[21] H. Gunkel, *The Legends of Genesis* (New York: Schocken, 1966), 41.

[22] See R. Alter, "Samson Without Folklore," *Text and Tradition: The Hebrew Bible and Folklore* (ed. S. Niditch; Semeia Studies; Atlanta: Scholars Press, 1990), 47–56; Y. Zakovitch, "From Oral to Written in the Bible" (in Hebrew), *Jerusalem Studies in Jewish Folklore* 1 (1981): 9–43.

[23] R. Finnegan, "How Oral Is Oral Literature?" *Bulletin of the School of Oriental and African Studies* 37 (1974): 52–64; eadem, *Literacy and Orality* (Oxford: Blackwell, 1988); eadem, "Literacy Versus Non-Literacy: The Great Divide?" *Modes of Thought* (eds. Robin Horton and Ruth Finnegan; London: Faber & Faber, 1973), 112–44.

relative chronology. That is, the more oral-style a work in terms of Lord's criteria may have been composed later than a work which varies its language, speaks in lengthy subordinate clauses, and so on. It is a matter of register. These issues in texture say a good deal about authors' interests, settings, about ethnic genres and audiences, but relative degree of "orality" is not a simple matter of chronology. Oral works and oral-style works are created and re-created even when writing is common. It is moreover no simple matter to distinguish between the orally composed work and the written work imitating orally composed works. Indeed in Hebrew Bible it is impossible to do so. All is now written and yet all, I would argue, evidence the use of traditional-style registers of varying kinds and degrees.

If one reads John Foley's many works[24] or the essays published in the last decade in the journal *Oral Tradition*, one sees this scholarly orientation to the interplay between oral and written. Increasingly scholars emphasize the role of memory in the oral-literate interplay as it affects the composition, preservation, and reception of traditional-style literatures. This approach is exemplified by David Carr's recent book[25] and the set of provocative brief review essays contributed by scholars in various fields to Volume 18 of *Oral Tradition*.[26] A number of excellent recent works, in fact, grapple in various original and complex ways with the relationship between the oral and the written in the genesis of the biblical tradition: Raymond Person,[27] William Schniedewind,[28] Martin Jaffee,[29] and David Carr[30] all explore this complex interplay. A word on some of these newer works.

Ultimately, Carr and Schniedewind have certain notions about ancient Israelite education and the centrality of elites in the composition of the Bible that, to me, seem to open the door to new misconceptions that regard biblical traditions as reflecting a rather fixed virtual canon. Their interests are more in the Bible as a book whereas mine are in the ways that the book or rather the anthology we call the Hebrew Bible reflects an oral word mentality, even in its

---

[24] See, for example, J. Foley, *The Singer of Tales in Performance* (Bloomington: Indiana University Press, 1995); idem, *Immanent Art: From Structure to Meaning in Traditional Oral Epic* (Bloomington: Indiana University Press, 1991).

[25] D. M. Carr, *Writing on the Tablet of the Heart. Origins of Scripture and Literature* (Oxford/ New York: Oxford University Press, 2005).

[26] *Oral Tradition* 18 (2003).

[27] R. F. Person Jr., "The Ancient Israelite Scribe as Performer," *JBL* 117 (1998): 601–609; idem, *The Deuteronomic School. History, Social Setting, and Literature* (SBL Studies in Biblical Literature 2; Atlanta: Society of Biblical Literature, 2002).

[28] W. S. Schniedewind, *How the Bible Became a Book* (Cambridge: Cambridge University Press, 2004).

[29] M. S. Jaffee, *Torah in the Mouth: Writing and Oral Tradition in Palestinian Judaism, 200 BCE–400CE* (Oxford/New York: Oxford University Press, 2001).

[30] D. Carr, *Writing on the Tablet of the Heart. Origins of Scripture and Literature* (Oxford/New York: Oxford University Press, 2005).

obviously written form. Whereas Schniedewind writes about "How the Bible Became a Book," I am interested in how unlike a book the Bible is, even in its written preserved form. Carr and Schniedewind really seem to be resisting a new paradigm, instead tucking notions of orality more safely under some of the old assumptions about documents and intertexuality. Person, whom I will mention later, and Jaffe who works so beautifully with Rabbinic tradition, in my view, take more seriously the oral-traditional qualities and contexts of the literatures they study. Jaffee's work is especially interesting in that the Rabbis are so scholastic and yet they valorize oral composition and transmission. The tradition in which they participate and corpus that they create, transmit, and preserve, like the Bible, reflects the textures, content, and presuppositions that underlie orally composed works.

We should also mention the important contributions of John Miles Foley. Foley seeks to understand the ways in which traditional style works create meaning. He points to the "metonymic" quality of certain recurring phrases or images.[31] These parts invoke a whole. That is, a simple recurring phrase or motif has the capacity to bring to bear on a scene or characterization a full range of associations invoked by it. Such traditional elements have this capacity because the composers and receivers of the narrative or description are familiar with the wider range of associations invoked by the epithet or formula, the color, or the image. They share the wider tradition of which it is a constituent part.[32] An Israelite example of such an "aesthetic of traditional referentiality," to use a phrase of Foley's,[33] is provided by the epithet for Yhwh, "the bull of Jacob." It brings to bear on a Psalm or a legal text the full range of notions of Yhwh as virile, macho, fecund creator. The victory-enthronement pattern is implicit in the phrase with all that implies. Traditional style literatures in this sense are quintessentially economical and telegraphic in communication. Thus Foley entitles one of his books "Immanent Art."

Having explored Lord's theories, misconceptions about them, old ideas about orality and the Bible and new approaches which emphasize the interplay between oral and written rather than evolution and the great divide, we come to applications. Do we notice and appreciate certain features and qualities of the biblical book of Judges because we are sensitive to the oral-traditional qualities of these written works? How do we interpret, what do we see that we might have otherwise missed were we unaware of oral-literary studies? We provide examples under each of our headings, texture, text and context, and begin with context.

Judges itself provides a variety of models for the contexts in which actual oral tradition might have been experienced by Israelites, and the genres presented

---

[31] Foley, *Immanent Art*, 7, 11, 13.

[32] Foley, *Immanent Art*, 33, 133, 217, 252.

[33] Foley, *Immanent Art*, 95.

have numerous ethnographic parallels in living traditions. First, of course, is the scene in Judges 5:10–11 which, if we are translating correctly, suggests oral performance accompanied by music.

> Riders on tawny donkey-mares,
>> those who dwell near Midian,
>> those who walk on the way,
> tell one another!
> With the sound of tambourines between watering holes
>> there they recount the justice-bringing acts of Yhwh,
>>> just acts for those in his unwalled towns in Israel.
> Then the people of Yhwh subdue the gated cities.

Perhaps even more interesting for issues of genre and sociological context is the use of proverbs and riddles. The riddling contest with its verbal jousting is supposed to safely play out animosities between opposing, in-marrying groups. In tales of Samson (Judges 14–15) no such amicable resolution occurs, but it is awareness of the form and function of the traditional medium of the riddle that makes the scene with the Timnites come alive.

The proverb in Judges 8:2 is another good example that captures performance context. The author beautifully understands and portrays the occasion for a *mashal*. The Ephraimites are angry at Gideon for having gone to battle without them thereby denying them a chance for additional honor and glory. He responds "What have I done now compared to you? Are not the gleanings of Ephraim better than the vintage of Abiezer. Yhwh gave the chieftains of Midian into your hands, Oreb and Zeb, and what have I been able to do compared to you?" The form of the proverb has the typical pattern "x better than y" as found in Prov 22:1 and Eccl 7:1.[34] The saying is set in the syntax of a rhetorical question. The author portrays a typical setting for the deploying of a proverb or *mashal*, in Hebrew. This brief speech act draws a comparison between a present situation or event and some metaphorically relevant motif, scene, or story in order to reduce tension in an interaction between groups or individuals who are protective of their status.[35] The proverb deflects anger and prevents overt confrontation or violence. In a self-effacing way, Gideon graciously compliments the Ephraimites, their superior valor and accomplishments. He states obliquely through the saying and then overtly in its interpretation that the Ephraimites have, after all, captured the greatest prizes of battle, enemy leaders. This accomplishment makes his own conquests pale by comparison. Thus the "gleanings" gathered by Ephraim, the grapes merely left behind after the harvest, are better

---

[34] For international examples of this pattern see A. Dundes, "On the Structure of the Proverb," *The Wisdom of Many: Essays on the Proverb* (eds. W. Mieder and A. Dundes; New York: Garland, 1981), 54.

[35] On the "*mashal*" as genre see S. Niditch, *Folklore and the Hebrew Bible* (Guides to Biblical Scholarship; Minneapolis: Augsburg Fortress, 1983), 67–87.

than the "vintage" that is, the best that Gideon of the clan of Abiezer could accomplish. Hearing what they want to hear about themselves, they depart, anger abated, and the disagreement does not lead to blows. Context has to do thus with status, the deflection of anger, and peaceful resolution; it is attention to the traditional style, form, and setting of the proverb that underscores these important shadings. We could also discuss Jotham's *mashal* in 9:8–20 in which a traditional form provides a means of social critique for the powerless. If I were not attuned to oral-traditional contexts of such material and to their qualities of texture and text to which I have also alluded, I would not appreciate the full meanings, messages, and cultural settings of this material.

Regarding the text, the story itself: Is Samson a fool? The story about Samson and Delilah, the plot or pattern of its content, has Delilah betray Samson three times before his honest revelation about the source of his power. Repetitions are not tedious reminders meant to keep illiterate listeners abreast of the plot but have critical thematic implications. Often, again, it is not the repetition but the repetition with nuance that counts. That Samson actually hears Delilah call upon the Philistines repeatedly ("The Philistines are upon you" vv. 9, 12, 14, 20) strikes many commentators as proof of his folly. Similar comments are frequently made about folk characters such as Snow White. How could she possibly be seduced by the witch's deception a third time? On the one hand, folktale heroes and heroines always do engage in these patterns of repetition. In traditional literatures, the repetitions create thematic emphasis, shape characterization, and build tension, for those within the tradition know where the stories are headed. It is the process of getting there that counts. In Samson's case, each instance of the frame and the line about the Philistines draws an essential contrast between us and them, while showing Samson growing bolder and bolder, convinced finally that his power is unassailable, hair or no hair. Alter suggests with insight that Samson is addicted to taking chances.[36] One might also read vv. 9, 12 to suggest that the Philistines remain hidden in the inner chamber while Delilah refers to them, waiting to see how the hero will react. Perhaps Samson does not believe that Delilah has actually betrayed him and thinks that she is merely testing the veracity of his admission, which adds to the pathos of the account. The repetitions also trace patterns important to Samson's characterization and the tale as a whole from nature to culture, from deception to truth, from male control to female control.

While the first exchange involves rawhide strings, the second exchange involves ropes (16:11), a somewhat more culture intensive product, having undergone some process whereby fiber is cultivated, harvested, treated, and woven. The ropes are new and unused but not raw. Samson's reference to

---

[36] R. Alter, "Samson Without Folklore," *Text and Tradition: The Hebrew Bible and Folklore* (ed. S. Niditch; Altanta: Scholars Press, 1990), 50.

taming his hair in the third exchange involving weaving his hair in the loom (16:13) comes closer to the truth. Weaving is "typically women's work" in ancient Near Eastern village culture, a cottage craft undertaken at home.[37] Thus talk of looms suggests a metaphoric link between the conspiratorial webs and designs of women such as Delilah and the actual feature of women's material culture. The tale comes full circle as Samson's revelation to Delilah that the source of his strength resides in his uncut hair (16:17) echoes the divine messenger's repeated instructions to his mother in ch. 13. And finally, one sees through these repetitions that Samson is not afflicted by stupidity but by hubris, the source of heroes' fall, for the writer adds to the repeated framing language a new element, "And he awoke from his sleep and he said, 'I will go forth like other times and be shaken free, but he did not know that Yhwh had turned away from him.'" An attentiveness to oral-style repetition is thus critical to our capacity to interpret.

Finally we turn to texture. We have already alluded to the texture of language in Samson's riddle and the description of his downfall. The use of formulaic language in Judges 5 is also illustrative of traditional style in the book of Judges. Lord's emphasis on formula patterns and compositional technique attunes us to the delimited vocabulary, the role of refrains, to the oral-traditional-style language in this beautiful ancient piece. Notice for example, the call to attention in Judges 5:3:

> Listen, kings!
> Lend an ear, potentates!
> I to Yhwh, I will sing.
> I will make music for Yhwh, god of Israel.

The verse is built of formulaic expressions. The synonymous pairs "listen/lend an ear," "kings/potentates," "sing/make music," "Yhwh/god of Israel," which are found in chains of parallel items elsewhere in the tradition, are made a part of common formula patterns. The first of the two patterns is "listen term + source of power (natural, figure of state, cosmic)," the second is "a term for song or praise + 'to the deity.'" For the former, see Deut 32:1; Isa 1:2; the chain in Jer 13:15; and the variants in Isa 49:1, Mic 1:2, 3:1. For the latter, see Exod 15:1; the variants in Ps 57:10, 68:5, 105:2, 138:1; and the chain in Ps 27:6.

Even more interesting is the catalogue of warriors in vv. 15(end)–17 which I think has often been mistranslated:

> In the divisions of Reuben,
>   great are the stout of heart.[38]
> Verily you dwell between the settlements

---

[37] Ph. J. King and L. E. Stager, *Life in Biblical Israel* (Library of Ancient Israel; Louisville, Ky: Westminster, 2001), 152–8.

[38] From the root חקק, with the nuance of resolve.

> to hear the whistling for the flocks.
> Concerning the divisions in Reuben,
>   great are the stout of heart.[39]
> Gilead in the Transjordan plies his tent,
> and Dan, verily, he resides in ships.

Most modern translators, like their ancient counterparts, Vat and OL, choose "why," for the word I translated "verily." Frank Moore Cross suggested that this word *lmh* is best read not as "why," as is most common in BH, but as an example of the "emphatic lamed extended by –ma known from Ugaritic" and so translates "verily."[40] Verse 17 is thus seen to be a formulaic, traditional catalogue formula, "tribe + location + tenting/residing," and serves a critical cultural function in asserting group identity (cf. Gen 49:13; 16:12; Deut 33:18–19). It says essentially, this is how we are constituted, who our ancestor heroes are. Here is a slice of our history as we understand it. In Judges 5, various groups are described, where they dwell, what their occupations are, and how brave they are.

Attention to the qualities of the oral-traditional deepens and enhances the reading of Bible and the way in which I teach it to others whether in the classroom or in books. I have tried, in fact, to frame my new commentary on the book of Judges with attention to qualities of the oral-traditional. In this final portion of my paper, I would like to address briefly the way in which attention to orality leads to a different sort of commentary touching upon format, text-criticism, and translation.

Every translator of Scripture must, at the outset, face the question of format. Ancient Hebrew had no commas, no capital letters, no semi-colons, and no paragraphs. Contemporary translations of Judges such as the NRSV or JPS Bible generally lay out the literature in prose paragraphs, reserving cola or lines for pieces such as Judges 5 that seem and sound more like "poetry" to contemporary readers. Even the cautious translators of the NRSV occasionally feel the need to employ a format that reflects "visible song," as Katherine O'Brien O'Keeffe calls the continuing presence of oral style in the written works of traditional cultures.[41] These modern translators are guided largely by inner biblical "headers," the ancient writers' introductory phrases to pieces of tradition. Thus at Num 21:14, after a reference to what is said in the "Book of the Wars of the

---

[39] MT reads the root חקר, "searchings (of heart)." Given the refraining style of the poem, it seems likely that the same phrase appears here as in v. 15. See n. 38.

[40] F. M. Cross, *Canaanite Myth and Hebrew Epic* (Cambridge: Harvard University Press, 1973), 235, n. 74; idem, *From Epic to Canon: History and Literature in Ancinet Israel* (Baltimore: Johns Hopkins Press, 1998), 54–55, n. 7; see also B. Halpern, "The Resourceful Israelite Historian: The Song of Deborah and Israelite Historiography," *HTR* 76 (1983): 383.

[41] K. O'Brien O'Keefe, *Visible Song: Transitional Literacy in Old English Verse* (Cambridge: Cambridge University Press, 1990).

Lord," the NRSV translators set up a list of place names in cola. But the actual syntax of each of these examples from Num 21:14–15 is no more or less poetic than many portions of Numbers that are set in prose paragraphs.

Concerned to highlight "the spokenness of the Bible," Everett Fox more boldly prints his entire translation of the Pentateuch "in lines resembling blank verse."[42] Influenced by Martin Buber and Franz Rosenzweig, he states that these "'cola' are based primarily on spoken phrasing."[43] But where should each colon end? Fox notes that "(c)ola do not correspond to the traditional verse divisions found in printed Bibles." They "arise from the experience of reading the Hebrew text aloud and of feeling its spoken rhythms. The specific divisions used in this volume are somewhat arbitrary; each reader will hear the text differently" (xv).[44]

Another who has wrestled with such issues in format as they relate to the sound, texture, and meaning of Scripture is Phyllis Trible, whose insightful analyses of biblical texts are influenced by rhetorical criticism. Trible, like Fox, sets up texts in cola. The breaks between lines frequently emphasize repetitions in syntax or content, calling attention to the traditional style of ancient Israelite literature.[45] Sometimes indentation is used or semicolons or periodization to create subtle shadings that Trible perceives in the ways in which language reflects message or imagery. Trible notes that the process of laying out the text is somewhat subjective.[46]

My own approach is influenced by the work of Phyllis Trible, Albert Lord, and Frank Polak, who has posited a link between oral tradition and a classical style of Hebrew in which short clauses, finite verb forms, and a rarity of subordinate clauses or long strings of nouns are typical.[47] Lord points out that oral-traditional literatures avoid "necessary enjambement," meaning that the thought is complete at the end of the line, even when the sentence continues. Of South Slavic song he writes,

Very rarely does a thought hang in the air incomplete at the end of a line; usually we could place a period after each verse. The absence of necessary enjambement is a characteristic of oral compositions and is one of the easiest touchstones to apply in testing the orality of a poem. Milman Parry has called it an "adding style"; the term is apt.[48]

---

[42] E. Fox, *The Five Books of Moses: Genesis, Exodus, Leviticus, Numbers, and Deuteronomy: A New Translation with Introductions, Commentary, and Notes* (New York: Schocken, 1995), xv.

[43] Fox, *Five Books*, xv.

[44] Fox, *Five Books*, xv.

[45] P. Trible, *Rhetorical Criticism: Content, Method, and the Book of Jonah* (GBS, OT. Minneapolis: Fortress, 1994), 102–3, 151.

[46] Trible, *Rhetorical Criticism*, 230–33.

[47] F. H. Polak, "The Oral and the Written: Syntax, Stylistics and the Development of Biblical Prose Narrative," *Journal of the Ancient Near Eastern Society* 26 (1998): 59–105.

[48] Lord, *The Singer of Tales*, 54.

A scholar of socio-linguistics, Dell Hymes, has pointed to a similar phenomenon.[49] I do not seek to prove or test "orality" in the case of Judges, but it is significant in appreciating its texture to note that the work frequently displays an "adding style" with its disenjambed cola. My commentary thus formats Judges in lines, as does Fox in his translation of the Torah. Non-indented cola usually have the requirements of a clause, a subject and a verb; they constitute a complete thought or begin a thought. As Polak's work might predict, much of Judges can be arranged well in self-contained cola, indicating the strong presence of classical style. The layout of the translation thus allows for blurring the distinction between prose and poetry, revealing a genre of "poetic prose" that does not fit neatly into modern Western categories, but which seems to characterize the style of so much of biblical literature.

Attention to orality also affects my text-critical approach. I am not interested in finding the best readings or Ur readings or in the reconstruction of an original or earlier form of Judges. Rather, I am interested in the variants preserved in the manuscript traditions and in the way in which extant manuscript traditions functioned in context. One need not merely speculate about some of the variants that existed in the tradition. Within the MT of Judges, there is evidence of variation that has been embraced rather than edited away. Judges 1 contains, for example, three differing notices about the disposition of Jerusalem (1:7, 8, 21) and two different implied versions of the conquest of Hebron, one involving a leadership role for Judah at v. 10 and another for Caleb at v. 20. Joshua plays the role in Josh 11:21 and Caleb in Josh 15:13–14. Basing his work on the form and content of LXX Josh 24:33b and the Qumran Damascus Document (v:1–5), Alexander Rofé has suggested that an earlier version of the book of Judges lacked 1:1–3:11, beginning the narration with the tale of the judge Ehud (1982: 29–32).[50] The existence and circulation of a shorter "Judges" is certainly a possibility.

A work such as Judges no doubt existed in multiple versions, even once its various stories were combined along the lines with which we are now familiar. Oral versions of larger or smaller portions of Judges would have existed side by side with accounts that were written down. Versions preserved by Deuteronomistic-style writers who held to a certain view of history might have differed from versions preserved and told by others in the tradition. Such oral tellings and written portions that may have been preserved in a family archive or the like are all lost. When exploring the preserved and transmitted written manuscript traditions of Judges, one rarely encounters radically different versions; rather, the relatively set content exhibits more subtle variations in terminology and phrasing and differences in relative length.

---

[49] D. Hymes, "Ethnopoetics, Oral-Formulaic Theory, and Editing Texts," *Oral Tradition* (1994): 331.

[50] A. Rofé, "The End of the Book of Joshua according to the Septuagint," *Henoch* 4 (1982): 17–36.

My commentary on Judges takes the position, however, that even variations in manuscript traditions, which are essentially set in this sense, reflect an oral world mentality in which different versions exist side by side in the tradition. A model for this phenomenon of multiplicity is offered by the Qumran corpus which contains two editions of Jeremiah, two editions of Exodus, variant editions of Numbers, and two possible editions of Psalms.[51] Scholars point to the richness of "textual plurality" at Qumran where "there were multiple editions of many of the biblical books … but the specific textual form was not a consideration."[52] The attitude is typical of a traditional world in which variant texts are deemed valid and authentic. Similarly, Talmon writes of the "'liberal attitude' towards divergent textual traditions" at Qumran.[53]

As a student of the place of manuscripts in largely oral worlds, I am less inclined to reconstruct a whole text, to build it, however judiciously, from the limited number of available manuscripts. I worry about the artificiality of such a process and believe it more true to life to assume that there were always multiple versions of the tradition before the Common Era. One can never know if a reconstructed text ever lived in a community, nor can one recover an original version, if there is such a thing. With a vital interest in religions as lived, I would like to know that an extant manuscript was meaningful to a group. Variation among manuscript traditions, however, is of lively interest and important to the study of literary and religious tradition, for these various texts may reflect different ways in which communities of Jews and Christians understood the tradition. Scripture was heard in different words, and the medium was important to the message.

Some of the differences between readings make for genuine differences in the plot or in characterization. For example, Achsah in Judg 1:15 emerges somewhat differently as a woman in the various traditions, plucky and less plucky, for the Greek and Latin traditions have Achsah's husband Othiel initiate the action, whereas the MT leaves the action to her. The manuscript variants of 1:18 disagree as to whether Judah is successful in battle. At 1:22, MT has Yhwh assist Joseph, whereas OL has the help come from Judah. The traditions differ for 1:22 as to whether or not the enemy is conscripted into forced labor. It is useful to ask how differences in the texts may reflect the different impression

---

[51] E. Ulrich, "The Bible in the Making: The Scriptures at Qumran," *The Community of the Renewed Covenant: The Notre Dame Symposium on the Dead Sea Scrolls* (ed. E. Ulrich and J. Vanderkam; Notre Dame, IN: University of Notre Dame Press, 1993), 75.

[52] J. Trebolle Barrera, "The Authoritative Functions of Scriptural Works at Qumran," *The Community of the Renewed Covenant: The Notre Dame Symposium on the Dead Sea Scrolls* (eds. E. Ulrich and J. Vanderkam; Notre Dame, Ind: University of Notre Dame Press, 1993), 92, 108.

[53] Sh. Talmon, "Aspects of the Textual Transmission in the Bible in the Light of Qumran," *Textus* (1964): 97.

received by particular groups concerning the activities of a Samson or the outcome of a particular battle. Text-critical variations, like contradictions in content within the same manuscript tradition, may mark or effect differences in
worldview.

Other differences are more subtle. Variant readings called "synonymous readings" by S. Talmon[54] – that is shorter, expanded, or alternate phrases that convey
a particular image or piece of content – can be viewed as versions of the same
dābār, literally, "word," in Person's terms, as oral-style variants of the same
essential meaning unit.[55] One might then inquire why one form of the *dābār* has
been preferred by an author to another – matters of aesthetics, taste, message,
and thematic emphasis all come into play. Person is building on Milman Parry
and Albert Lord's observation that for their informants, epic singers of the
former Yugoslavia, a whole phrase was considered a word or unit.

Some of the variants reflect differing textual traditions as discussed above; the
stories were told with certain variations that are still reflected in ancient textual
traditions. Other differences have been introduced into the traditions through
scribal errors. Sometimes, however, differences in the translations may not be
due to differences in the Hebrew *Vorlage* but to translation decisions and creative
composition.[56]

The attempt to make sense of a difficult reading (which in some cases may
have arisen from a simple scribal error) often also leads to creative translations.
As James Kugel has suggested about the phenomenon of Rabbinic midrash and
other modes of Jewish interpretation of Scripture in antiquity, the "ambiguities"
or "rough edges" of a text occasion commentary or gloss.[57] Translations may also
reflect midrashic techniques that Isaac Heinemann has called "creative philology,"[58] for example, when the reader takes his cue for meaning from one
Hebrew root rather than another or when a root is over-literalized. These ways
of reading result in variant traditions, and each variant conveys a set of meanings
to a believing community in a process akin to midrash. Hebrew is based on
triliteral roots, and such nuances in meaning may be achieved with the shift of a
vowel, whether by mistake or purposeful wordplay. Here one encounters the
border between translation and transformational composition in the style of the
Jewish targum, a form of translation that allows for gloss and elaboration. My
text-critical notes point to such variants.

---

[54] Sh. Talmon, "Synonymous Readings in the Textual Tradition of the Old Testament,"
Studies in the Bible (ed. Haim Rabin; Scripta hierosolymitana 8; Jerusalem: Magnes, 1961),
335–83.

[55] R. F. Person Jr., "The Ancient Scribe as Performer," *JBL* 117 (1998): 601–9.

[56] See H. Gzella, *Cosmic Battle and Political Conflict: Studies in Verbal Syntax and Contextual
Interpretation of Daniel 8* (Biblica et Orientalia 47; Rome: Pontifical Biblical Institute, 2003), 19,
26–7, 47.

[57] J. L. Kugel, *The Bible as It Was* (Cambridge: Harvard University Press, 1997), 3–5, 18–23,
28–34.

[58] I. Heinemann, *Darkhei ha-Aggadah* (Jerusalem: Magnes, 1954), 4–11, 96–107.

In other instances the ancient translator may not be working with a variant Hebrew tradition, but has felt it necessary to expand, to gloss, or to fill out the "true" and "full" meaning of the Hebrew, thereby creating an alternate tradition and participating in the compositional process, all allowable in the anonymous oral world of writing, as shown recently by Deborah VanderBilt concerning Anglo-Saxon translations of Latin works.[59] The lengthier version in OL of Ehud's escape and the allusion in OL to Samson's being beaten by captors, which assimilates him to Jesus, may be examples of such techniques of "filling out" and "glossing." All these instances point to the border where translation decisions, textual variants, targum, midrash, inner biblical variants, and intertextuality meet on oral–world terms.

Translation. This is a lively time in biblical translation. Like Everett Fox who has produced an exciting new translation of the Torah, I am interested in oral and aural aspects of the text that convey biblical rhythm, syntax, wordplay, and sound. I do not claim that all of the Hebrew Bible was orally composed, though some works possibly were, but suggest that qualities of the oral enliven and infuse the written works of Scripture. Traits such as wordplay on a shared root or upon roots that sound alike, repetition of key terms or formulaic phrases within a piece or across the tradition, and repeated frame language reflect an economic use of language whereby the same language is often preferred to variation for conveying an image or idea. In the Hebrew Bible as in other traditional literatures, webs of meaning and connotation envelop certain terms and phrases, linking one usage with another. John Foley refers to this variety of traditional usage as a kind of "metonymy" in which the part stands for and invokes the whole.[60] By attending to root meanings and attempting to use, when possible, the same English term to translate the Hebrew, I hope to highlight rather than hide these qualities of interconnectedness in the tradition.

Oral–related considerations suggest, as noted by Fox, that the Hebrew Bible, even in written form, was meant to be heard and spoken, and, like Fox, I have tried to take this spokennness seriously in rendering the Hebrew as closely as possible into English. I am also sympathetic to Robert Alter's desire to convey the sense that the Bible uses special and elegant language. The formulicity of the Hebrew Bible, for me, is part of that specialness. The Israelite composers of biblical texts employ, as he notes, "a conventionally delimited language" that is "stylized" and "decorous," using "a limited set of terms again and again, making an aesthetic virtue out of the repetition."[61]

---

[59] D. VanderBilt, "Translation and Orality in the Old English Orosius," *Oral Tradition* 13 (1998): 379.

[60] J. M. Foley, *Immanent Art: From Structure to Meaning in Traditional Oral Epic* (Bloomington,: Indiana University Press, 1991), 13; see also G. Nagy, *Homeric Responses* (Austin: University of Texas Press, 2003), 16.

[61] R. Alter, *The Five Books of Moses: A Translation and Commentary* (New York: W. W. Norton, 2004), xxv.

Even though Alter emphasizes qualities of the written and literary over the oral, he and I make some similar translation choices. He defends his translation of "*waw*" as "and," an element that repeats frequently in the Hebrew syntax, but which in modern translations is often finessed to convey not a meaning of conjunction but subordination.[62] Alter counters that the "*waw*" was spoken and heard as repeated, important metrically and syllabically. I tend to agree. My goal throughout is to capture both the meaning and medium of the Hebrew, paying special attention to its heard qualities and to be as literal and rooted in the Hebrew as possible without sacrificing the economical elegance of the traditional language.

The field of oral studies, which has its own history and development, has made and continues to make important methodological and theoretical contributions to the study of ancient Israelite literature. Engagement with a range of oral-traditional literatures and with the ways in which scholars have approached them enriches the study of Hebrew Scriptures and enlivens the understanding of the cultural settings that frame and vivify its varied compositions.

---

[62] See, for example, Th. O. Lambdin, *Introduction to Biblical Hebrew* (New York: Charles Scribner's Sons, 1971), 108.

Orality and Writing in Ancient Philosophy:
Their Interrelationship and the Shaping of Literary Forms

Teun L. Tieleman

1. Introduction

Far-reaching claims have been made about literacy as the key factor explaining the emergence of Greek philosophy[1] in the 6th century B. C. E.[2] It has been assumed that written texts, indeed the very characteristics of the Greek alphabet, stimulated the Greeks' capacity for abstract thought; that the new technology of communication shaped their very way of thinking.[3] Moreover, textualization involves the reification of the word, that is to say, the text becomes an object

---

[1] I am referring in particular to the speculative yet empirically based cosmogonies of the Ionian or Milesian physicists (Thales, Anaximander, Anaximenes) that were clearly developed as alternatives to cosmogonic myths. One may feel that 'proto-science' is a more apposite appellation in their case. However, what they engaged in was to become part of philosophy, i. e. natural philosophy, and was recognized as such. Aristotle, *Met.* A was and still is influential in having philosophy start from them as the discoverers of what he saw as the material cause. The rationalist attitude taken by these earliest philosophers is also found in contemporary medicine as is witnessed by the earliest Hippocratic treatises. Its hallmark is a causal framework that appeals to natural processes instead of arbitrary interventions by gods. Further, the process of self-definition and self-articulation of 'philosophy' ('love of wisdom') as a term denoting a particular intellectual enterprise we still know today is more or less concluded by Plato. Plato, it may be recalled, again added natural philosophy to its agenda after it had been renounced by Socrates.

[2] See esp. E. A. Havelock, *Preface to Plato* (Cambridge, Mass.: Belknap, 1963), vii and *passim*; idem, *The Muses Learn to Write: Reflections on Orality and Literacy from Antiquity to the Present* (New Haven, Conn.: Yale University Press, 1986), 98ff. Idem, *The Literate Revolution in Greece and Its Cultural Consequences*, (Princeton, N. J.: Princeton University Press, 1982), esp. 220–61; Havelock's ideas were largely accepted by anthropologists such as W. J. Ong, *Orality and Literacy: The Technologizing of the Word* (London–New York: Methuen, 1982), e. g. 27–8; cf. J. Goody, *Literacy in Traditional Societies* (Cambridge: Cambridge University Press, 1968), 3f. But cf. idem, *The Power of the Written Tradition* (Washington, DC: Smithsonian Institution Press, 2000), 138 for a more nuanced view of Havelock's thesis. For reverberations of Havelock's ideas among classicists see *Language and Thought in Early Greek Philosophy* (ed. K. Robb, Hegeler Institute: LaSalle, Ill., 1983). Cf. also the critical comments made by G. E. R. Lloyd, "The social background of early Greek philosophy and science," *Methods and Problems in Greek Science* (CUP 1991): 121–40, esp. 121–27.

[3] According to Havelock (who was influenced by earlier work by Milman Parry and A. B. Lord on oral poetry in relation to Homer), the writing or poetry as a formulaic medium is

separated from its author, an object whose relation to reality, or truth, can be considered critically and regardless of distances of place or time.

Today most historians of ancient thought do not question the significance of literacy for *le miracle grec* including philosophy. But they do adopt a more nuanced view about the extent and nature of its impact: other cultural factors have to be taken into account to do justice to the differences that existed between Greek society and its Near Eastern neighbors, who after all were literate too.[4] Moreover, among the Greeks the spoken word continued to enjoy a prominent role and status quite unlike what we are led to expect by our knowledge of literate societies in later periods including our own. In fact, orality and literacy co-existed, and interacted, in unexpected and unfamiliar ways.[5] In the present study I will show how this situation explains certain features of Greek philosophy, including the shaping of particular literary genres.

2. Literacy and the Origins of Philosophy

Let us first consider the following testimonies dealing with the earliest philosophers, the so-called Presocratics. Of Anaximander of Miletus (*flor.* c. 550 B. C. E.) it is said:

(1) [A.] was the first of the Greeks whom we know who ventured to publish a prose account (*logon*) of nature (Themistius, *Or.* 36, 317 C = fr. 12 A 7 D.-K.).

---

suited for narrative only. It still represents an oral mode of thought. In consequence, those Presocratics who expressed themselves through verse could never successfully advance to abstract and hence truly philosophical ways of thinking. The decisive turning point occurred much later and is represented by the work of Plato (which given this story makes Plato's notorious comments on the value of the written work remarkable, to say the least; but he did banish the poets from his ideal city, though not for the reasons required by Havelock's thesis; but Havelock argued that this must have been what motivated Plato at an unconscious level): see the works quoted prev. n. Of course some Presocratics wrote in prose: see infra, pp. 20–1. Subsequent research on Presocratic philosophy has by no means borne out Havelock's claims about the supposed conceptual limitations of philosophical poetry. Besides, it is not as if poetry gradually became obsolete as a recognized medium for the expression of philosophical ideas; see infra, n. 6.

[4] In addition, the special characteristics of the Greek alphabet are no longer believed to be capable of effecting the changes in outlook attributed to them by Havelock and his followers. The syllabic and hieroglyphic scripts of Near Eastern cultures no less involve abstraction; see J. Assmann, *Das kulturelle Gedächtnis. Schrift, Erinnerung und politische Identität in frühen Hochkulturen* (4th ed., Munich: C. H. Beck, 2002), 259–64.

[5] In legal contexts, for example, written documents were not considered adequate proof but had to be accompanied by oral testimony until well into the fourth century BC. R. Thomas, *Literacy and Orality in Ancient Greece* (Cambridge: Cambridge University Press, 1992), 3. For the relation between the written word and oral communication in various contexts see esp. chs. 4 and 5.3.

It had been, and for some time continued to be, customary to choose hexametric verse, the meter of didactic poetry, for this kind of subject, in the wake of mythological poets such as Hesiod. Thus the Presocratic philosophers Parmenides (late 6th to mid 5th cent. B. C. E.) and Empedocles (c.492–432 B. C. E.) employed verse. Others, however, followed Anaximander in writing prose.[6]

A few fragments from Heraclitus (*flor.* c. 500 B. C. E.) throw light on his literary activity as well as that of his contemporaries:

(2) The book said to be his is entitled *On Nature*. He dedicated it and deposited it in the temple of Artemis, as some say, having purposefully written it rather obscurely so that only those of rank should have access to it, and it should not be easily despised by the populace [...] The work had so great a reputation that from it arose disciples, those called Heracliteans (Diogenes Laërtius IX, 5 = fr. 22 A 1 D.-K.).

The use made by Heraclitus of metaphor, riddles and an allusive style in general earned him the reputation of being the 'obscure' philosopher, a feature attributed by our source, Diogenes Laertius (c. 200–250 C. E.), to his desire to address his message to the aristocracy only and avoid divulging it among the common people, who, being incapable of understanding it, would only despise it. Here as elsewhere a biographical fact is construed on the basis of what is to be found in the extant sayings of the philosopher, for lack of real biographical information. Thus Heraclitus in certain fragments complains about people's lack of understanding and speaks like an aristocrat, with contempt for the lower classes.[7] The desire to be exclusive and secretive about one's philosophy is a recurrent motif, which is sometimes connected to the decision not to commit one's (deepest) thoughts to writing at all.[8] In the case of Heraclitus it is invoked to explain his opacity of style. The fact that he deposited his book, i. e. one scroll, in the temple of Artemis, is not implausible in itself but probably motivated by his wish to secure the survival of a certified specimen, just as other valuables were stored in temples. People would come and make copies, for which they may have had to pay, but they could not take the mother copy. At any rate a relatively large number of fragments of Heraclitus' book have been preserved, not least because most of them can stand on their own feet: individually they are memorable,

---

[6] The ethnographer and geographer Hecataeus of Miletus (who is on record as having been Anaximander's pupil) and other precursors of Herodotus are called *logographoi*, i. e. prose-writers; cf. Hdt. 2, 143; 5, 36, 125. Although prose became prevalent in philosophical writing poetry was by no means superseded; one may think e. g. of texts from the Hellenistic period such as the poems (including the well-known *Hymn to Zeus*) composed by Cleanthes (c. 330–230), the second scholarch of the Stoa (who even went as far as stating that poetry was better suited for the clear expression of philosophical ideas: *SVF* 1. 487; cf. ib. 486) and of course the *On Nature* (*De rerum natura*) by the Epicurean Lucretius, an admirer and emulator of Empedocles.

[7] Frs. 22 B 1, 29, 33, 39, 49, 121 D.-K.

[8] Compare for instance Plato's so-called 'unwritten doctrines', see *infra* n. 27 with text thereto.

evocative and so highly quotable, whatever their role may have been in their original context. Diogenes' point about the Heracliteans in this connection is interesting: they became followers in virtue of the book's strengths, without having known the man himself. Heraclitus was traditionally known as a sporadic philosopher, one without his own pupils. Diogenes then seems to imply that later Heracliteans such as Plato's contemporary Cratylus must have been converted by the book rather than by a teacher who stood in a line of successive teacher-pupil relationships going back to Heraclitus himself. But this point too may reflect something said by Heraclitus in one of the fragments, viz. where he says that one should not listen to him but to his exposition.[9] His contemporary Parmenides of Elea took a similar attitude. The goddess who in the poem introduces Parmenides to the structure of things encourages him to examine the consistency of her *argument*, an examination that is hardly imaginable without a written text.[10] The passage concerned is all the more remarkable since it is part of the revelation a divine figure who clearly fulfils a role similar to that of the goddesses, i.e. Muses, invoked by the great poets Homer and Hesiod. Early thinkers such as Parmenides, Xenophanes and Heraclitus compete with established cultural authorities such as Hesiod and Homer as well as with one another. They develop their own position in conscious and explicit opposition to these others and in a way that presupposes the availability of written works. Compare the following fragments of Heraclitus:

(3) Heraclitus fr. 22 B 40 D.-K.: The learning of many things (*polymathiē*) does not teach intelligence; if so it would have taught Hesiod and Pythagoras and again Xenophanes and Hecataeus.

(4) Heraclitus fr. 22 B 129 D.-K.: Pythagoras, son of Mnesarchus, practiced research (*historiēn*) beyond all other men and, making a selection (from) the relevant literature, he made for himself a wisdom of his own, polymathy, malpractice.

To know about and criticize the ideas of cultural authorities of different generations and places presupposes the availability of books written by them. Heraclitus uses this fact against his competitors by pointing out that their case proves that a lot of learning does not guarantee true insight. That this involved what they had learned from books is especially clear from text (4), which is concerned with Pythagoras (c. 570–490) alone. In fact, as Jaap Mansfeld has shown, this fragment parodies a so-called seal (Gr. *sphragis*), i.e. the standard opening sentence of a book or scroll: name, patronymic, protestation of the importance and reliability of what will follow in the book.[11] The enjoyment of this parody

---

[9] Fr. 22 B 50 D.–K.

[10] Fr. 28 B 7, ll. 5–6 D.–K.

[11] J. Mansfeld, "Fiddling the Books: Heraclitus on Pythagoras (DK 22B129)," *Ionian Philosophy* (ed. K. Boudouris; Athens: International Association for Greek Philosophy, 1989) 229–34; repr. as Study nr. XVI in *Studies in the Historiography of Greek Philosophy* (ed. Jaap Mansfeld; Assen, Neth.: Van Gorcum, 1990).

presupposes a readership that is able to recognize it. In sum, a fair degree of literacy and bookishness emerges from this handful of fragments about the earliest philosophers.

Clearly, the written word played a crucial part in the emergence of the typically Greek phenomenon of philosophy. At this stage, it appears, Pythagoras was exceptional in that he wrote nothing. Although text (4) makes clear that at least Heraclitus believed Pythagoras had made use of existing literature, it cannot be inferred that he wrote himself. In antiquity opinions differed as to whether or not he had but those denying it appear to have been a majority.[12] But later on, as we shall presently see, lack of literary legacy was not unusual and put Pythagoras on a par with many later philosophers including the great Socrates as well as others.[13] Writings bearing his name did appear, of course, but none were accepted as authentic. The well-known Pythagorean phrase 'He said so himself' (see e. g. Diog. Laert. 8. 46) indicates oral instruction.[14] But Pythagoras' project was different from that of Parmenides and Heraclitus in that he founded a community of followers. Here oral communication and personal example and authority were crucial. Other Presocratics such as Heraclitus and Parmenides were not interested in creating a sect or community. As we have seen, they explicitly renounced personal authority as distinguished from the truth and cogency of their arguments. But theirs was a project of an intellectual kind; this was not yet 'philosophy as a way of life' in the sense this would acquire in the Hellenistic period, when the phenomenon of the school or sect (*hairesis*) came to dominate the philosophical landscape.[15] Many Hellenistic philosophers had be-

---

[12] See Josephus, *Contra Apionem* I, 163 (= frs. 14, 18 DK); cf. Plut. *De Alexandri fortitudine* 328a, Posid. ap. Gal. PHP 5. 6. 43 De Lacy; cf. Porph. Vit. Plot. 57. The minority view is reflected by e. g. D. L. 8. 6; see further H. Diels and W. Kranz, *Die Fragmente der Vorsokratiker* (Hildesheim: Weidmann, 1989), vol. I, 14. 17–19. Walter Burkert, *Weisheit und Wissenschaft. Studien zu Pythagoras, Philolaos und Platon* (Erlanger Beiträge zur Sprach- und Kunstwissenschaft vol. 10; Erlangen: Nürnberg, 1962), 106, 203–5, accepts the prevalent tradition that Pythagoras did not write. C. Riedweg, *Pythagoras. Leben, Lehre, Nachwirkung. Eine Einführung* (Munich: C. H. Beck, 2002), 61–2, 72, 75, however, credits a report that Pythagoras practiced the Orphic poetic genre of *hieroi logoi*.

[13] Thus Diogenes Laertius in his *On the Lives and Opinions of the Distinguished Philosophers* even presents a list of those who wrote nothing (1. 16): "Again some philosophers left writings behind them while others wrote nothing at all, as was the case [...] with Socrates, Stilpo, Philippus, Menedemus, Pyrrho, Theodorus, Carneades, Bryson; some add Pythagoras and Aristo of Chios, apart from a few letters. Others wrote no more than one treatise each, as Melissus, Parmenides, Anaxagoras. Many works were written by Zeno, more by Xenophanes, more by Democritus, more by Aristotle, more by Epicurus and still more by Chrysippus."

[14] His precepts were accordingly called *akousmata*: things heard ("Hörsprüche").

[15] Heraclitus' teaching is universal and also extends to the moral and social sphere, but – for reasons which need not detain us – in a way that does not lead to the formation of a community bound by common rules whereby to live. He is known as a 'sporadic' philosopher, i. e. one without pupils. Parmenides' teaching was defended by his younger associate Zeno of Elea by means of the famous paradoxes but was not designed to start a school either. Of course these

fore their eyes the example set earlier by the life and death of Socrates, to whom we now turn in connection with a few immensely influential passages in the work of Plato.

3. Socrates and Plato

Many of the 5th century B. C. E. professional teachers known as sophists wrote extensively and on a broad array of subjects (e. g. rhetoric, literature, linguistics, cultural and intellectual history), part of which certainly belongs in the history of philosophy. Socrates (469–399), by contrast, and famously, wrote nothing – at least nothing philosophical.[16] This appears to be related to his method of *elenchos* ('refutation', 'testing'), i. e. his method of questioning interlocutors with the aim to bring to light their true beliefs.[17] It proceeds on the basis the interlocutor's admissions, with the aim of delivering him from the insights with which he is, so to speak, pregnant. Thus Socratic midwifery virtually excludes written discourse as a means of attaining or bringing about insight. It has been remarked that Plato's (427–347) choice of Socratic dialogues as his literary form should be seen as the closest literary approximation of the Socratic conception of philosophy.[18] How far he was influenced by anything Socrates himself had said in

thinkers want to change the outlook of their readers, whom they consider deeply deluded. But to call this 'transformative' and even 'salvational' is potentially misleading insofar as it suggests that their purpose was to change people's way of life in a fundamental way (the alternative would be to take this in the rather trivial and diffuse sense that reading their work makes an impact on us): *pace* A. A. Long, "The Scope of Early Greek Philosophy," *The Cambridge Companion to Early Greek Philosophy* (ed. idem; Cambridge: Cambridge University Press, 1999), 13. Heraclitus' teaching provides a justification for the social and political status quo; as to religion, it is acceptable to take part in ritual provided one brings the correct insight into the divine to it. In the case of Parmenides it is even more difficult to seen how his view of the experiential world as the infelicitous product of a strictly forbidden mixing up of Being and Not-Being could entail a new way of life to be shared by the members of a philosophical movement or school.

[16] According to Plato, *Phaedo* 60c–d, he wrote a hymn to Apollo and versified the fables of Aesop in his last days in prison. Of course, spurious Socratic works existed, see A. H. Chroust, *Socrates, Man and Myth: The Two Socratic Apologies of Xenophon* (London: Routledge–K. Paul, 1957), 279 n. 791.

[17] On the *elenchos* and its purpose see G. Vlastos, "The Socratic Elenchus," in *Oxford Studies in Ancient Philosophy* 1 (1983): 27–58; reprinted in *Socratic Studies* (ed. M. F. Burnyeat; Cambridge: Cambridge University Press, 1994), 1–38.

[18] It may be recalled that *Sōkratikoi logoi* were also written by others and so became a literary genre. A number of Plato's dialogues (especially those belonging to the earlier group traditionally called 'Socratic' and 'aporetic are more genuinely dialogic in character than other, later ones. Whereas the former class preserves an impression of the workings of the Socratic elenchus, the latter are in fact often monologous in that they hardly proceed on the basis of the admissions made by Socrates' interlocutors (and sometimes the main speaker is not even Socrates). The two styles come together in the *Republic*: book I offers a typically Socratic,

justification of his refraining from writing is impossible to tell. Given the value accorded to the spoken word in Athenian society, there may not have been so much need for a justification – and in the later ancient tradition concerned with Socrates' life this well-known fact passes almost without comment.[19]

Still, Plato in the *Phaedrus* has Socrates pronounce upon the relative merits of spoken vs. written discourse in the philosophical context. Plato's well-known 'Critique of Writing' is found at 274c–278e. Here Socrates tells the *mythos* ('story') about the invention of writing by the Egyptian god Teuth, who proudly presents his invention to king Thamus. Thamus however responds as follows:

(5a) 275a2–b3: Your invention will produce forgetfulness in the soul of those who have learned it, through lack of practice at using their memory, as through reliance on writing they are reminded from outside by alien marks, not from inside, themselves by themselves: you have discovered an elixir not of memory but of reminding. To your students you give an appearance of wisdom, not the reality of it; having learned much, in the absence of teaching (*aneu didachês*) they will appear to know much when for the most part they know nothing, and they will be difficult to get along with, because they have acquired the appearance of wisdom instead of wisdom itself.

And a little further on:

(5b) 275d8–e6: [...] written words [...] point to just one thing, the same each time. And once it is written, every composition is trundled about everywhere in the same way, in the presence both of those who know about the subject and of those who have nothing at all to do with it, and it does not know how to address those it should address and not those it should not. When it is ill-treated and unjustly abused, it always needs its father to help it; for it is incapable of defending or helping itself (tr. Rowe 1986, slightly modified).

As Socrates had taught, true knowledge comes from the inside; it is not transmitted by someone else, or it would all be a matter of authority. But it can come about in a process of questioning – the answers one has to conceive oneself. Hence the crucial role played by dialogue in education (*didachê*). Clearly Plato reacts here against a use of literature whereby the presence of the author himself is considered dispensable. Consider also the following passage from the same context:

'elenctic' discussion, which equally typically fails to produce a positive definition of what the interlocutors are looking for in this case, justice. After the sophist Thrasymachus, unable to beat Socrates in the latter's game but unconvinced that he is wrong, has left, Socrates' friends at the beginning of book II challenge him to provide a constructive theory of justice of his own, which is what Socrates does in the subsequent books, hardly interrupted by the remaining interlocutors. Here then the Socratic elenchus has been abandoned.

[19] Thus Diogenes Laertius in his life of Socrates (2. 18–47) simply substitutes a few remarks on the scope of Socrates' conversations for the survey of writings he usually gives at the end of a philosopher's life, or *bios* (*ibid.* 46). Socrates features in the list of philosophers who refrained from writing (alongside a list of those who did write, sometimes copiously), *ibid.* 1.16: see *supra*, n. 13.

(5c) 278c4–d6 (on an author such as Homer, Solon, or Lysias): [...] if he has composed these things knowing how the truth is, able to help his composition when he is challenged on its subjects and with the capacity, when speaking in his own person, to show that what he has written is of little worth, then such a man ought not to derive his title from these, and be called after them, but rather from those things in which he is seriously engaged [...] To call him wise seems to me to be too much and to be fitting only in the case of a god; to call him either a lover of wisdom (*philosophon*) would both fit him more and be in better taste (tr. Rowe 1986, slightly modified).

If the philosopher-author knows the truth of what he wrote about, this will be become apparent in a conversation about his text. Moreover, what he has to say is superior as compared to what he has written (which is said to be 'of little worth'). For this reason the philosopher's reputation should not depend on his writings. This is the educational point that is made: we are not dealing with a wholesale rejection of writing but rather with a reminder of its limitations, which require the presence of the author. Plato confines the written text to the limited role of an *aide-mémoire* for those who already know.

Both knowledge and the written word can be referred to in Greek as *logos*. In fact Plato throughout *Phaedrus* 274c–278e operates with a distinction between three *kinds* of *logos*:

1. Internal *logos*, 'written inside', i. e. thought and knowledge;
2. *Logos* as spoken discourse, i. e. thought externalized;
3. *Logos* as written discourse, 'external marks'.

This represents a descending order of value based on the familiar Platonic original/image analogy.[20]

Some of ideas expressed in this *Phaedrus* passage recur in the seventh letter preserved under Plato's name:[21]

(6) Plato, *Seventh Letter* 341c: I can say this much about all those who composed treatises and those who will write them and who all lay claim to knowledge of that with which I am seriously concerned. It is in my view impossible that they understand anything about this...There does not exist nor will there ever exist any written treatise of mine dealing with this; for it can in no way be communicated like other teachings but, as a result of prolonged intercourse and communion with respect to it, it suddenly comes into being in the soul as light kindled from leaping spark, and thenceforth it nourishes itself.

---

[20] Cf. Assmann, *Das kulturelle Gedächtnis*, 265, who compares Aristotle's similar distinction at *De interpretatione* 1, 16a3–5: "[...] spoken sounds are symbols of affections in the soul, and written marks symbols of spoken sounds."

[21] Today the majority of Plato scholars tend to consider only the seventh letter as possibly genuine. But even if one does not accept letter's authenticity, one cannot but acknowledge that this passage is closely modeled on the *Phaedrus* passage we have been discussing. This is exactly how one expects the author of a pseudepigraphic letter to go about; the original works are used to enhance the impression of authenticity. Apparently, this author(s) aim was to present Plato's short-lived involvement with the politics of Sicily in a favorable light.

Once again we come across the Socratic idea that philosophy turns on conversation, as a result of which insight may be kindled in the mind of the pupil.[22] The passage has stimulated far-reaching speculations about Plato's so-called unwritten doctrines (*agrapha dogmata*)[23] as constituting his true or core teaching (with the dialogues written by Plato at best preparing the mind for the real thing).[24] Insufficient attention has been paid to the context of this passage, however. It must be noted that Plato (or the author impersonating him) responds vehemently to the claim of Dionysius of Syracuse that he knew all or the most important part of Plato's teaching on the basis of a single *conversation* he had had with the philosopher in addition to what he had heard from others. Dionysius had even published a book on what they had talked about, presenting it as his own teaching (341b; cf. 338c–d). Given this context, Plato's purpose is not to discard the written word as unsuitable for philosophical teaching in favor of oral instruction. Rather he makes it clear that Dionysius (or whoever else is making similar claims) cannot possibly have grasped his teaching on the basis of either his writings *or oral communication*: this requires prolonged communion of the kind Dionysius was not interested in.[25] In fact, the references to Dionysius' sources of information on Plato's teaching all concern oral communication, i. e. conversations with Plato or others. This having been said, it is clear that the passage agrees with the one from the *Phaedrus* (on which it may in part have been modeled) in stressing that genuine insight is gained through a process of prolonged communion between teacher and pupil. In other words, the presence of the master is required.

As we have observed, when Plato did write he chose the genre that represented the closest literary approximation of the Socratic oral tradition. His pupil Aristotle (384–322) too published dialogues (his 'exoteric' works) but, it may be recalled, what apart from fragments has been preserved are not these but his 'esoteric' works, i. e. what may be called his *Arbeitspapiere* (rather than lecture notes, as has often been said) not intended for publication, texts which evince proximity to oral discussion between him and his entourage.[26]

---

[22] Cf. Pl. *Theae.* 150d: Socrates, while disclaiming wisdom, attributes the progress in his pupils to their conversing with him.

[23] For which see Arist. *Phys.* Δ 209b11–17 and the doctrines ascribed by Aristotle to Plato elsewhere (e. g. *Met.* A chs. 6–7).

[24] E. g. by Th. A. Szlezák, *Platon und die Schriftlichkeit der Philosophie. Interpretation zu den frühen und mittleren Dialogen* (Berlin: De Gruyter, 1985); cf. the critical review by D. L. Blank, *Ancient Philosophy* 13 (1993): 414–26.

[25] Similarly R. Thurnher, *Der siebte Platonbrief. Versuch einer umfassenden philosophischen Interpretation* (Meisenheim am Glan: Hain, 1975), 94–100.

[26] For a survey of Aristotle's literary output see e. g. Jonathan Barnes, "Life and Work," *The Cambridge Companion to Aristotle* (ed. J. Barnes; Cambridge: Cambridge University Press, 1995), 5–15. On oral features in Aristotle's preserved writings see S. Föllinger, "Mündlichkeit in der Schriftlichkeit als Ausdruck wissenschaftlicher Methode bei Aristoteles" *Vermittlung und Tradierung von Wissen in der griechischen Kultur* (eds. W. Kullmann and J. Althoff; Tübingen: Gunter Narr, 1993), 263–280.

4. The Hellenistic and Imperial Periods

The example set by Socrates and its reception by Plato go some way towards explaining the position taken by later philosophers on the written vs. oral discourse issue. In the history of philosophy the Hellenistic period is marked by the emergence of schools led by a head who stood in a succession leading back to the school's founder. The scholarch not only explained the teaching of the founder through oral and written instruction but was also supposed to set a personal example, i.e. to embody the school's teaching through his whole demeanor. What he wrote was primarily meant to function within this educational or pedagogic setting. But he could also decide not to write at all and leave it to some of his pupils to write down what he said, that is to say to make lecture notes. But the schools do show a certain difference as to the value placed – and effort spent – on writing. Epicurus (341–270) and the important third head of the Stoa, Chrysippus of Soli (c.280–204)[27] were quite prolific as authors. Some of our sources even give the impression that a long list of publications lent prestige to a scholarch and, in consequence, became an issue in the polemical exchanges between the schools. Thus Diogenes Laertius presents the following report that goes back to the Academic Carneades (214–129/8):

(7) Epicurus was a most prolific author and eclipsed all before him in the number of his writings: for they amount to about 300 scrolls without containing a single quotation from other authors; it is Epicurus himself who speaks throughout. Chrysippus tried to outdo him in authorship according to Carneades, who therefore calls him the literary parasite of Epicurus. For every subject treated by Epicurus, Chrysippus in his contentiousness must treat at equal length; in consequence he has frequently repeated himself and set down the first thought that occurred to him and in his haste left many things unrevised. He has so many citation, that they alone fill his books.[28] Nor is this unexampled in Zeno[29] and Aristotle (Diog. Laert. 10. 26–7; transl. Hicks, modified).

The Academic attitude to literary production was decidedly more ambivalent and restrained. Arcesilaus, founder and head of the so-called Skeptical Academy, was out to reinvigorate the Socratic tradition of open-ended debate. An

---

[27] [Suetonius], *Life of Persius* (p. 33, 1. 38–9 Clausen) reports that the Roman poet Persius (first cent. C. E.) left his fellow-Stoic Cornutus "about 700 books [i.e. scrolls] by Chrysippus". Diogenes Laertius (7. 180–1) specifies a total of 705 books and appends a catalogue of titles (*ibid*. 189–202). Of this catalogue only the logical part (119 titles) has been preserved in full; the ethical section breaks off after 42 titles and the physical section has been lost in its entirety. From other sources further titles can be added raising the number of attested titles to 217. See T. L. Tieleman: s.v. 'Chrysippus', in *The Encyclopedia of Classical Philosophy*, (ed. D.J. Zeyl; Westport, Conn.: Greenwood Press 1997), 136. Of this vast output only fragments – many of them small – remain.

[28] For similar criticism about Chrysippus' repetitiveness, sloppiness and rampant quotation see the parallel at Diog. Laert. 7. 180.

[29] I.e. Zeno of Citium (c. 334/3–262/1), the founder of the Stoa.

important philosopher and opponent of the Stoics, he is on record of having refrained from writing, quite in line with his admiration of Socrates. That one biographical tradition has it that he, like Plato, did not shrink back from burning books appears to be a fabrication but the story may be taken to reflect a critical attitude.[30] Likewise Carneades wrote nothing. Many of his arguments were however recorded by his pupil and successor Clitomachus of Carthage (187/6–110/9).[31] That only lecture notes were taken is a practice we encounter more often in the history of the Academy and other schools.[32] It accords with Plato's stipulations in the *Phaedrus* we have been discussing, viz. with the written word firmly embedded in the (interactive) teaching context.

This situation presupposes a school in an institutional sense (however weak as compared to present-day institutions of higher education) at one particular location. Indeed, Athens remained the main centre of philosophy, where all the main schools were for much of the Hellenistic era, until, roughly, the first half of the first century BC. From then onwards philosophy and philosophical teachers spread – to Italy, Asia Minor and other parts of the Roman Empire. Athens lost its role as centre of the schools and home to the leading philosophers.[33] The decentralization of philosophy made the presence of the head of school, the direct experience of his conversation and personality, an ideal impossible to maintain (and indeed brought an end to the very institution of the scholarchate). It was a situation that could only lead to a more prominent role for the written word. But literary forms emerged that still reflected the previous situation, with its emphasis upon personal contact between teacher and pupil. An example is provided by the emergence of the philosophical letter, the most personal and intimate form of written instruction.[34] In fact, ancient epistolary theorists class the letter as a term of dialogue (see Demetrius, Eloc. 223–5; cf. 227).

---

[30] See Diog. Laert. 4. 32: "According to some, one result of his suspending judgment on all matters was that he never so much as wrote a book. Others relate that he was caught correcting certain works of Crantor, which according to some he published, according to others he burnt. He appeared also to have held Plato in admiration and possessed his works." Cf. 4. 47 (Bion burnt the books he had inherited and then became a philosopher), 9. 40 (Plato wished to burn the works of Democritus).

[31] Diog. Laert. 4. 67.

[32] Cf. Porph. *Vit. Plot.* 4: Amelius took notes while attending Plotinus' lectures for eighteen years.

[33] For this watershed, which is connected to the political developments in the years 88–86 B. C. in particular, see (with special reference to the Stoa) D. Sedley, "The School, from Zeno to Arius Didymus," *The Cambridge Companion to the Stoics* (ed. B. Inwood; Cambridge: Cambridge University Press, 2003) 24–32.

[34] Cf. also the *topos* that the letter is a substitute for the living presence of the philosophical educator: Sen. *Ep.* 45. 2, 78. 28; cf. 14. 8, 55–10–11; [Plato] *Ep.* XI 358d–359c 9a (letter that is devoted in its entirety to the problem that Plato cannot come over to the addressee who is in need of an educator), Paul, Col. 2. 5; cf. ibid. 1.

The genre of the philosophical letter goes back to the early Hellenistic period, in particular to the letters of Epicurus. As a teacher does in person, Epicurus presents an impression of his personality, concern about his pupil (i. e. the formal addressee), personal relation with him and other associates, etc. In addition, the letters present a summary of his teaching and thus an instruction as to how to read the more extensive treatises where the doctrines are expounded in detail.[35] This will have been important when the school's founder could not be present: already in Epicurus' own day there were Epicurean communities outside Athens. But apart from geographical separation, the letter also represents the founding figure after his death, Thus the genre of the philosophical letter provides both the biographical element and a reading instruction for the pre-served treatises. This appears to be the case with the letters ascribed to Plato, which are to be dated to the Hellenistic period and justify Plato's involvement with politics (or perhaps rather the lack of it). Thus they are also meant to put a particular complexion on the political theory to be found in the relevant dia-logues.

Much the same purpose is served by another genre that emerges in the Hel-lenistic period, viz. the philosophical *bios* or life. This too was motivated by the wish to produce reading instructions for those who were preparing themselves to read the original treatises of the founders of their school. It could fulfill this function in virtue of the assumption that a philosopher's personality accords, or should accord, with his teaching. To fully understand the great philosopher's text one should know what kind of person he was, how he had led his life and how he had faced death – the ultimate test of his philosophy's value. It was another surrogate way to ensure the author's presence even long after his death. Moreover, just as pseudepigraphic letters were written to enforce a particular interpretation of the canonical works by the founder(s), so too biographical narrative served to guide the reading process. It is this type of philosophical biography we encounter in the pages of Diogenes Laertius' *Lives and Opinions of the Distinguished Philosophers*, which although written around 200 CE largely depends on the work of Hellenistic biographers.[36] Another example is provided by the *Life of Plotinus*, which serves as the preface affixed by Porphyry to his edition of Plotinus' *Enneads*.

I may add as a third genre that arose in the later Hellenistic period as a result of the canonization of the works of the founding fathers of the main schools (notably, Plato, Aristotle, Epicurus), that of the philosophical commentary.

---

[35] See *Ep. Hdt.* 35, at the beginning (but cf. also 45, 83), *Ep. Pyth.* 84.

[36] On the work of Diogenes Laertius as so-called prolegomena literature, i. e. literature that served to prepare students for the reading of classical philosophical text, see esp. J. Mansfeld, *Prolegomena: Questions to be Settled Before the Study of an Author, or a Text* (Leiden: E. J. Brill, 1994), 179–91; on Diogenes' Hellenistic backdrop see J. Mejer, *Diogenes Laertius and his Hel-lenistic Background* (Wiesbaden: Franz Steiner, 1978).

Being a reflection of the oral explanation of the classic texts, this genre too functioned within the classroom context.[37] It arose in large part because of the increasing difficulty of the texts for ever new generations of readers including philosophical teachers. It may seem remarkable that no commentary literature in the strict sense arose within the Stoic school in connection with the writings of Chrysippus, the paragon of Stoic orthodoxy. But we must note that successive Stoic authors were in the habit of starting from the definitions and arguments of their predecessors; in a way, then, their treatises were commentaries already.

Finally, the dialogue form persisted: the Socratic dialogue Platonic-style, the dialogue between teacher and pupil, or between well-educated gentlemen. Lucian (120–c.180) calls the dialogue typical of Cynics in particular but this cannot be accurate.[38] Even some Neoplatonic commentaries were written in dialogue form. There is also an Epicurean example from later antiquity.[39]

But what happened in the actual classroom situation? How far did these literary genres play a part there? The most important form of transmission was the lecture (*akroasis, diatribê, logos, scholê*).[40] Obviously this could take different forms aimed at different audiences. Epictetus (c.50–130) may not have been a typical Stoic philosopher in all respects. But his extant discourses offer a few glimpses of the workings of his school in Nicopolis (in what is today North-Western Greece). that he offered separate classes for long-term students in which treatises by Chrysippus and Platonic dialogues (mainly because of Socrates' presence in them, it appears) were read and discussed and held lectures for a wider audience, some members of which may have just been dropping by on their way to or from the Eastern parts of the Empire.[41] It is these more general discourses that have been preserved thanks to one member of Epictetus' audience, Flavius Arrianus – yet another example of a teacher leaving it to one of his pupils to commit his lectures to writing. In this regard too Epictetus modeled his approach to philosophy on Socrates.[42]

---

[37] See Porph. *Vit. Plot.* 14: "In his classes he read the commentaries, perhaps of Severus, perhaps of Cronius or Numenius or Gaius or Atticus and, among the Peripatetics, of Aspasius, Alexander, Adrastus and others that were available. But he did not speak straight out of these books but took a distinctive personal line and brought the mind (*nous*) of Ammonius to bear on the investigations at hand." On Ammonius see *infra*, p. 32.

[38] Lucian. *Bis accusatus* 33.

[39] Diogenes of Oinoanda Fr. 63 Smith. On the role played by the dialogue as a form of instruction see further J. Mejer, *Überlieferung der Philosophie im Altertum. Eine Einführung* (Copenhagen: Det Kongelige Danske Videnskabernes Selskab, 2000), 61

[40] On how to lecture see e. g. Epict. *Diss.* 3. 23 ('To those who read or conduct dialogues for the purpose of display.'). On Epictetus' teaching programme see also B. L. Hijmans Jr., *ΑΣΚΗΣΙΣ: Notes on Epictetus' Educational System* (Assen: Neth.: Van Gorcum, 1957), 41–8. Another source of information is Plutarch's tract *On the Correct Way of Listening to Lectures* (= *Moralia* 37B–48D).

[41] See Arrian. *Epict. Diss.* 1.4.3–10, 3.9.12–3, 3.23.19–21, 3.23.27–9; cf. A. A. Long, *Epictetus. A Stoic and Socratic Guide to Life* (Oxford: Clarendon Press, 2002), 10ff., 98ff.

[42] A feature of Epictetus' Stoicism brought out well by Long in his *Epictetus* (see prev. n.).

Stoic teachers and schools were to be found throughout the Empire for another one and a half century but around the middle of the third century they disappeared rather abruptly. Platonism became dominant on the philosophical stage. Around 300 C. E. the Neoplatonist Porphyry arranged the discourses of his master Plotinus (204/5–270) into *Enneads* (i. e. sets of nine) and edited them, prefacing his edition with his *Life of Plotinus*, in line with a wider practice (see above). This *Life* affords invaluable glimpses of Plotinus' personality and style as a teacher including his attitude to writing.[43]

In ch. 20 Porphyry quotes a long passage from Cassius Longinus' (c.213–73) *On the End* where two types of philosopher are distinguished: those who have left writings and those who have contented themselves with the oral instruction of their pupils:

(8) Some of them undertook to set down their doctrines in writing, so as to give posterity the change of deriving some benefit from them; other thought that all that was required of them was to lead the members of their school to an understanding of their doctrines (transl. Armstrong, slightly modified).

In the following context Longinus presents examples of each category from three different schools: Platonism, Stoicism and Aristotelianism. Among the Platonists he mentions Plotinus as one who left philosophical writings. It is noteworthy that he also mentions certain Stoics and Peripatetics (whose schools seem on the whole to have been more bookish) among those who were more committed to teaching than to publishing works of professional philosophy. There is no hint of criticism of this attitude, which is presented as perfectly respectable.

But Plotinus' decision to commit his thought to writing was not one he made at an early stage in his career. In fact, he started out as firm believer in the oral approach to instruction, using what he had heard from his own teacher Ammonius Saccas:

(9) Erennius, Origen and Plotinus had made an agreement not to disclose any of the doctrines of [their teacher] Ammonius, which he had revealed to them in his lectures. Plotinus kept the agreement and, though he conversed with (*sunôn*)[44] with people who came to him, maintained silence about the doctrines of Ammonius [...] Plotinus for a long time persisted in writing nothing, but began to base his lectures on his studies with Ammonius. So he continued for ten complete years, admitting people to study with him but writing nothing. Since he encouraged his students to ask questions, the course was

---

[43] For what follows cf. M.-O. Goulet-Cazé, "L'arrière-plan scolaire de la Vie de Plotin," *Porphyre: La Vie de Plotin, vol. I Travaux préliminaires et Index grec complet* (eds. Luc Brisson et al.; Paris, Vrin, 1982) 231–327, esp. 231–80.

[44] Note the emphasis upon (educational) intercourse (*sunousia*) as in Plato, *Theae.* 150d (see *supra*, n. 22), *Ep.* VII: 341c8–9 (*supra*, p. 26); or "reading together" (*sunanagnôsis*) for which cf. also Mejer, *Überlieferung der Philosophie*, n. 183. By Plotinus' time *sunousia* has come to mean 'class', 'meeting in a school'; see e.g. infra text (11); cf. also *LSJ, s. v.*

lacking in order and there was a great deal of pointless chatter (*Vit. Plot.* 3; transl. Armstrong, slightly modified).

The decision of Ammonius' pupils not to disclose any of his tenets adds esotericism to the abstention from writing they all shared.[45] This esoteric behavior has been related to Platonic passages, most notably our text (6), but is in fact found more often. The core doctrines are to be communicated to an inner circle of advanced pupils only.[46] Apparently, these three students considered only themselves to be in this position in regard to what they had heard from the venerable Ammonius back in Alexandria. The same motivation lies behind intentional obscurity in written discourse. We may recall that this motivation was, no doubt wrongly but still interestingly, imputed to Heraclitus (text (2) above) but this is just one example.[47] Note that Plotinus in starting his own teaching career in Rome also behaved in a manner befitting a Platonist by encouraging his audience to engage with him in dialogue, with the undesirable consequences against which Plutarch had already warned.[48]

Porphyry recounts how Plotinus only started, hesitatingly, writing down his thoughts in his fiftieth year. When Porphyry joined his circle ten years later his output still did not amount to much:

(10) Porph. *Vit. Plot.* 4: From the first year of Gallienus Plotinus had begun to write on the topics that came up [scil. in the meetings of the school]. In the tenth year of Gallienus, when I, Porphyry, first came to know him, I found that he had written twenty-one treatises, and I also discovered that few people had received copies of them. The issuing of copies was still a difficult and anxious business, not at all simple and easy; those who received them were most carefully scrutinized (transl. Armstrong).

Note that even by this time the esoteric reflex was still in place. In what follows Porphyry makes it clear that it was thanks to his encouragement and exhortation that Plotinus eventually wrote as much as he did (i. e. the writings tailored by Porphyry in his edition so as to form 6x9 separate treatises). About Plotinus' use of language Porphyry has a few remarkable things to say:

(11) Porph. *Vit. Plot.* 8: [...] in writing he did not form the letters with any regard to appearance or divide his syllables correctly, and he paid no attention to spelling. He was

---

[45] For other discussions see Th. A. Szlezák: "Plotin und die geheimen Lehren des Ammonius," *Esoterik und Exoterik der Philosophie. Beiträge zu Geschichte und Sinn philosophischer Selbstbestimmung* (eds. H. Holtzhey and W. C. Zimmerli; Stuttgart–Basel: Schwabe, 1977), 52–69; M.-O. Goulet-Cazé: "L'arrière-plan scolaire," (see supra, n.), 258ff.

[46] Thus Chrysippus stipulated that Stoic theology should be taught as the last subject when the soul has already become strong and knows to keep silent towards the uninitiated, comparing the philosophical curriculum to the initiation process of mystery religions: *SVF* 2.1008. For (alleged) Academic esoterism see Cic. AC. 2.18.60; Sext. PH. 1.234; august. C. Acad. 2.10.24, 3.17.38.

[47] On the phenomenon in the Epicurean school see M. Erler, "'Ἐπιτηδεύειν ἀσάφειαν," *Cronache Ercolanesi* 21 (1991): 83–8.

[48] Plutarch, *On the Correct Way of Listening to Lectures* 42F–43A.

wholly concerned with intellect [thought, *nous*] [...] 13 In his classes (*sunousiais*) he showed an adequate command of language and the greatest power of discovery and insight into what was relevant to the subject at hand, but he made mistakes in certain words: he did not say *anamimnesketai* but *anamnemisketai* and made other slips which he also constantly committed in his writing. When he was speaking his intellect visibly lit up his face (*prosôpou* [...] *to phôs epilampontos*; cf. [Plato] *Ep.* VII. 141c: above (6)) (transl. Armstrong).

I submit that Porphyry models this idealized portrait of Plotinus closely on key passages concerning the respective roles and merits of thought, spoken discourse and written discourse in *Phaedrus* 274c–278e, i. e. on the Plato's threefold distinction between *logoi* found there (see above, p. 26).[49] In addition, as we have indicated, the lighting up of his face may reflect the related passage from the seventh *Letter* (above text (6)). As such, this passage from Porphyry attests to the lasting influence of Plato's stipulations concerning speaking and writing in philosophical education and to that of the *Phaedrus* passage in particular.

5. Conclusion

In the preceding pages I have been surveying attitudes towards written as opposed to oral discourse to be found in the writings – or what remains of them – of the philosophers of classical antiquity. The first thing we have noted is that these attitudes should be considered against the wider background of Greek society with its striking and persisting appreciation of oral communication in various social and cultural contexts. This having been said, there can be no doubt that the spread of literacy was a major factor in the emergence of Greek philosophy and science from the start. Even so, it was of crucial importance that Socrates set an immensely influential example of the philosophical life – one that excluded (philosophical) writing. In his immediate wake, Plato responded to the spread of literacy by pointing to the limitations and dangers involved in doing philosophy on the basis of written discourse alone, that is to say, without the author being available in person for explanation and dialogue. The role accorded by subsequent Greek philosophers to the spoken word, to direct and personal contact between teacher and pupil, not only led to the esoteric role often played by philosophical writings but was also decisive in the shaping of specific genres of philosophical literature. Plato in shaping the Socratic dialogue had fixed conversations in writing. But as we have noticed, he also insisted on the presence of the author at the reading of a philosophical text. In the Hellenistic age this presence could no longer be taken for granted for various reasons: Athens

---

[49] Cf. L. Brisson, "Plotin: une biographie," in *Porphyre. Vie de Plotin*, vol. II (eds. L. Brisson et al.; Paris: Vrin, 1992) 22f. who compares the references to *nous* in ch. 8 to *Phaedrus* 276a.

gradually lost its role as sole centre of philosophical teaching but this was also the age of the emergence of philosophical schools with a founder and a set of distinctive doctrines that needed to be defended, explained, summarized and transmitted. Epicurus shaped the genre of the philosophical letter: in his letters he summarized the main lines of his teaching in a way preparatory to the reading of his more demanding and technical writings. In the absence of the author a letter from him represents the most intimate and personal literary substitute. The author's absence need not be due to distance in place only but of course will be often due to his death. If the school's founder had not written letters during his lifetime, these could be fabricated under his name – letters that likewise served as reading instructions for the genuine works of the founder.

A third 'surrogate' literary genre is the philosophical biography: a philosopher's life provided the clues as to how to read and fully understand his works. While much of this literary activity can be studied on the basis of Diogenes Laertius' work we found important additional information on the actual teaching practices in the work of Epictetus and Porphyry's *Life of Plotinus*. As we have seen, this last work in portraying Plotinus as the ideal Platonist teacher attests to the persisting influence of the critique of written discourse delivered by Plato in the *Phaedrus*.

The Platonic thesis that the written word cannot replace the spoken word but actually calls for it fixates and sanctions a particular stage of historical development, viz. of the spread of literacy in the Greek world. But, as we have seen, it, perhaps paradoxically, led to various new forms of the literary expression of philosophical ideas.

From Oral Conversations to Written Texts: Randomness in the Transmission of Rabbinic Traditions

Catherine Hezser

Scholars of rabbinic literature nowadays agree that rabbis taught and discussed their legal opinions and biblical interpretations in an oral cultural context.[1] Yet their teachings and discussions came down to us in written form. How can we explain the development from oral discourse to written texts? And, most importantly: how were rabbinic "traditions" generated and transmitted? It seems that rabbinic views were expressed on various incidental occasions rather than being restricted to formal "school" or "court" settings. Rabbis gave their opinion whenever certain situations and circumstances caught their interest. The further transmission of these circumstantial utterances was governed by a large amount of randomness. Therefore we must assume that many views would eventually have been lost and those which came down to us would have been changed, adapted, and reformulated during the long process of transmission from one occasional tradent to the next.

Rabbinic documents do not provide us with explicit descriptions of how they were created. We lack any direct ancient evidence of the reasons why documents such as the Mishnah, Talmud, and Midrashim were created, of who created them and how they came about. In his letter to the Jewish community of Kairouan Sherira Gaon, head of the yeshiva in Pumbedita in the tenth century C. E., deals with the authorship and composition of the Mishnah, Tosefta, and Babylonian Talmud, but his explanation cannot be taken at face-value as a historically reliable account of the literary development of these works.[2] He

---

[1] See C. Hezser, *Jewish Literacy in Roman Palestine* (TSAJ 81; Tübingen: Mohr Siebeck, 2001), 94–109 and 190–209; M. S. Jaffee, "The Oral-Cultural Context of the Talmud Yerushalmi: Greco-Roman rhetorical paideia, discipleship, and the concept of Oral Torah," in *The Talmud Yerushalmi and Graeco-Roman Culture*, vol. 1 (ed. P. Schäfer; TSAJ 71; Tübingen: Mohr Siebeck, 1998), 27–61. See also idem, *Torah in the Mouth. Writing and Oral Tradition in Palestinian Judaism, 200 BCE to 400 CE* (New York: Oxford University Press, 2001), 126–52.

[2] For a survey of past scholarship, synoptically arranged German translation of the two recensions, and commentary on Sherira Gaon's letter see M. Schlüter, *Auf welche Weise wurde die Mishnah geschrieben? Das Antwortschreiben des Rab Sherira Gaon, mit einem Faksimile der Handschrift Berlin Qu. 658 und des Erstdrucks Konstantinopel 1566* (Tübingen: Mohr Siebeck, 1993). See also Yaakov Elman's review of Schlüter's book in *Association of Jewish Studies Review* 20 (1995): 180–186.

obviously wrote many centuries after these documents were created and did not have more information than rabbinic literature itself. He mainly based his reconstruction on Babylonian Talmudic references which are not themselves historical and which can be interpreted in many different ways. His tendentious reconstruction must therefore be viewed within the context of medieval Babylonian Jewish culture, as Margarete Schlüter has shown.[3]

We shall therefore leave this medieval account aside and try to reconstruct the development of written rabbinic documents on the basis of rabbinic literature itself and the Graeco-Roman cultural context in which it emerged. Since rabbis never explicitly state how they created these works, any reconstruction has to remain hypothetical and gaps remain. The argument is also necessarily circular, since the very texts which stand at the end of the development serve as the basis of our reconstruction. This circularity is a problem of any investigation of the *Sitz im Leben* of a certain text and hard to avoid if no outside evidence exists. Comparisons with Graeco-Roman and Christian culture can at least provide some indirect external affirmation of our hypotheses.

As will be evident in our reconstruction, orality and writing were not mutually exclusive realms; we rather have to assume that significant interaction existed between these two modes of transferring information and knowledge. Starting with rabbinic oral teaching, we shall trace the various stages of transmission, collection, redaction, and writing, with the oral study of the written texts and the writing of commentaries at the end of the development.

1. The Oral-Cultural Context of Rabbinic Teaching and Discussion

Like ancient philosophers, rabbis promoted oral discussions and the memorization of teachings while being opposed to the use of books and notes. The only book whose use they recommended was the Torah, but Torah scrolls were costly and rare and therefore could be owned only by the wealthy and by local communities. We may assume that most rabbis had only occasional access to Torah scrolls and recited the Torah from memory in their discussions. They also urged students to memorize their own teachings so that they would become a repository of their master's learning, a memorial of and testimony to his expertise, available to later generations of scholars. In this way, rabbis' halakhic and exegetical views lived on in the mind of their disciples rather than being fixed once and for all in written form.

---

[3] See M. Schlüter, "Der verlorene historische Kontext der rabbinischen Literatur und Versuche einer Re-Kontextualisierung in gaonäischer Zeit," *From Narbonne to Regensburg: Studies in Medieval Hebrew Texts* (eds. N. A. Van Uchelen and I. E. Zwiep; Amsterdam: Juda Palache Institute, 1993), 44–61.

Torah scrolls were probably mainly or almost exclusively available in synagogues and study houses, which did not exist in every small town or village,
especially not in the first three centuries C. E. Permanent Torah niches – that is,
cavities built into the walls – are evident in the later Roman-Byzantine synagogues of the fourth to sixth centuries exclusively. Only with the innovation of
the apse in the late fifth century C. E., "the Torah shrine became an integral
element in the synagogue building."[4] Even then, not all synagogues had this
architectural feature, and especially those in the Galilee and the Golan were
lacking in this regard.[5] The Torah ark was probably often made of wood and
carried into synagogues on the Sabbath and holidays only, when Torah reading
services took place.[6]

The study houses (*batei midrash*) mentioned in rabbinic sources are much
more elusive to research than the synagogues, since no building that could be
identified as a study house has been excavated so far.[7] They could have been any
public or private rooms or houses in which Torah study was customarily practiced.[8] Some were probably local institutions open to anyone, whereas others
were associated with certain rabbis and may have been restricted to their students and sympathizers. To what extent Torah scrolls were available and actually
read at these places remains uncertain, since "study" could also refer to the
discussion of religiously relevant material on the basis of memorized Torah
portions only. On the other hand, one can imagine that especially the houses of
those rabbis who owned Torah scrolls and made them available to others, as well
as those public spaces where Torah scrolls were kept and used, were called "study
houses." If so, these places would provide access to the written text of the
Torah, but even in such a case the number of Jewish males who could read the
Torah would have been very limited, as I have argued elsewhere.[9] Therefore we
must assume that even at places where Torah scrolls were available, only a few
men could directly access them. The rest of the Jewish population would have
had mediated access through others' reading and interpretation only.

The main occasions by which rabbinic traditions were generated were rabbis' encounters with community members, other rabbis, and their close circles

---

[4] R. Hachlili, "The State of Ancient Synagogue Studies," in *Ancient Synagogues in Israel: Third-Seventh Century C. E.* (ed. R. Hachlili; Proceedings of a Symposium at the University of Haifa, May 1987; BAR International Series 499; Oxford: Archaeopress, 1989), 3.

[5] See ibid.

[6] See L. I. Levine, *The Ancient Synagogue: The First Thousand Years* (New Haven and Lon-don: Yale University Press, 2000), 328.

[7] Merely a lintel inscription mentioning the "study house of R. Eliezer ha-Qappar" has been found in the Golan; see Joseph Naveh and Shaul Shaked, *Amulets and Magic Bowls* (Leiden: Brill, 1985), 25.

[8] See C. Hezser, *The Social Structure of the Rabbinic Movement in Roman Palestine* (TSAJ 66; Tübingen: Mohr Siebeck, 1997), 202–14.

[9] See Hezser, *Literacy*, 451–73.

of students. According to rabbinic sources, fellow-Jews would approach rabbis and ask them for advice concerning their legal cases and personal problems on a wide variety of issues ranging from family matters and religious observances to property issues and quarrels with their neighbors.[10] These questions and answers resemble Roman jurists' function of *respondere*, the granting of legal advice to all those who approached them.[11] Whereas Roman jurists responded to their clients' queries on the basis of their legal knowledge, rabbis responded by applying their Torah knowledge to the situations they were confronted with, but they are unlikely to have checked Torah scrolls before providing answers. Their halakhic decisions' relationship to the Torah is often very general only. As personifications of traditional knowledge rabbis seem to have taken certain liberties when applying this knowledge to daily life.

Knowledge of the Torah also constituted the background of rabbis' halakhic and exegetical discussions with their colleagues. Again, the presence and consultation of Torah scrolls was not necessary in these settings. Rabbis did not have regular gatherings to discuss halakhah. They rather met a few of their colleague-friends informally, when meeting them incidentally or visiting them on social or professional occasions.[12] Rabbis are rarely said to have visited colleagues for the explicit purpose of studying with them. Halakhic discussions, which concerned matters of daily life, arose incidentally, when rabbis were involved with ordinary things such as dining together, showing each other their trees and gardens, or going to bathhouses together. In such situations, they would probably quote the Torah from memory, if they quoted it at all.

Like halakhic discussions with colleagues, the teaching of students was integrated into rabbis' daily life. Disciples, who were expected to render certain services to their masters (*shimush hakhamim*) that resembled the tasks of slaves in Roman society, would live in their master's home and accompany him wherever he went. They could therefore observe his practices in daily life and listen to his views on a variety of matters initiated by everyday situations and occurrences. In addition, certain study sessions (student "X was sitting before Rabbi Y") seem to have taken place whenever rabbis' work schedules allowed them. Like Graeco-Roman philosophers, rabbis taught their students orally during such sessions, by expressing their views on legal and exegetical matters, answer-

---

[10] See C. Hezser, *Form, Function, and Historical Significance of the Rabbinic Story in Yerushalmi Neziqin* (TSAJ 37; Tübingen: Mohr Siebeck, 1993), esp. 292–303, where the so-called case stories are discussed.

[11] See C. Hezser, "The Codification of Legal Knowledge in Late Antiquity: The Talmud Yerushalmi and Roman Law Codes," *The Talmud Yerushalmi and Graeco-Roman Culture*, vol. 1 (ed. Peter Schäfer; TSAJ 71; Tübingen: Mohr Siebeck, 1998), 581–641, esp. 583–88.

[12] See Hezser, *Social Structure*, 228–31; see also C. Hezser, "Rabbis and Other Friends: Friendship in the Talmud Yerushalmi and in Graeco-Roman Literature," *The Talmud Yerushalmi and Graeco-Roman Culture*, vol. 2 (eds. P. Schäfer and C. Hezser; TSAJ 79; Tübingen: Mohr Siebeck, 2000), 189–254, esp. 216–29.

ing students' questions, and making them memorize their answers.[13] They did not write and circulate their views in written form and were opposed to students taking notes during teaching sessions.[14] The lack of written study material would make the students entirely dependent on their masters. For the students their master incorporated all of the knowledge they could wish to learn. By memorizing his teachings they themselves would become a living – though temporary – memorial of their teacher, a chain of tradition which would continue from one generation to the next.

Few rabbis would have been wealthy enough to own Torah scrolls, and even if they did, they would hardly have bothered to unroll them to search for particular verses or passages in a text that lacked page numbers, chapter headings, and punctuation. In any case, rabbinic literature gives the impression that rabbis interpreted the Torah quite freely and quoted from memory rather than from written texts. Rabbinic legal and exegetical views are usually detached from the plain meaning of the Torah. In halakhic discussions the Torah is only occasionally cited. In their exegesis rabbis divided the text of the Bible into more or less tiny segments which they associated with each other in a liberal way, for example, through keyword connections. Biblical figures and stories were used and combined in innovative ways. None of this points to a continuous and systematic commentary on a written text that was read during these sessions.

2. The Circumstantial Expression and Transmission of Rabbinic Views

Rabbinic views were initially uttered locally on various everyday life occasions at many different places within Roman Palestine. Some of these locally expressed views would reach other places within Palestine or Babylonia by the travelling rabbi himself or through mobile intermediaries such as his colleagues and students. Amoraic documents of the third to early fifth century also sometimes mention letters which rabbis sent to their colleagues to request legal information. Only when individual rabbis' views were confronted with the different and sometimes opposite opinions of other rabbis could disputes emerge. Such disputes would either be generated through actual discussions amongst contemporary rabbis or they would be constructed theoretically at a later stage, when editors were confronted with different individual opinions and arranged them in dispute form for literary transmission.

---

[13] On the oral cultural context of Graeco-Roman philosophical teaching see L. Alexander, "The Living Voice: Scepticism Towards the Written Word in Early Christian and in Graeco-Roman Texts," *Journal for the Study of the Old Testament Supplement Series* 87 (1990): 221–47.

[14] Notes and notebooks are only rarely mentioned in rabbinic sources; see the discussion of such references in Hezser, *Jewish Literacy*, 96–7.

Rabbinic documents transmit numerous stories about rabbis who travelled to more or less distant locales and met colleagues. The references to travel usually introduce stories which focus on certain halakhic teachings. Such stories are already transmitted in the Mishnah and Tosefta, but they are especially numerous in the Palestinian and Babylonian Talmuds. For example, the Mishnah transmits the following story:

"It happened that R. Yehoshua went to R. Yishmael to Kefar Aziz, and he showed him a wine which was trained over part of a fig tree. He said to him: May I put seed under the remainder [of the tree]? He said to him: It is permitted. And he brought him up from there to Bet Hameganiah and showed him a wine which was trained over part of a branch and a trunk of a sycamore tree in which there were many branches. He said to him: Under this branch it is prohibited [to put seed], but [under] the rest it is permitted" (*M. Kil.* 6:4).

The first sentence of the story sets the scene: a second-generation tannaitic rabbi went to visit his (younger) colleague who lived at a different locale and that colleague took him into his garden to show him his trees. On that occasion a discussion over the issue of mixed seeds (*kilayim*) ensued. The focus of the story is on the halakhic issue, whereas the reference to the visit merely constitutes the setting. Irrespective of the historical reliability of this narrative setting, the story suggests that rabbis learned of other, more distant rabbis' halakhic views incidentally, on the occasion of meetings and visits to their homes.

Another Mishnaic story suggests that the observation of practices could be as important as the verbal transmission of teachings:

The House of Hillel said to the House of Shammai: Did it not happen thus, that the elders of the House of Shammai and the elders of the House of Hillel went to visit R. Yochanan b. Hahorani, and they found him sitting with his head and most of his [body] in the *sukkah*, and his table [was] in the house, and they did not say anything to him? The House of Shammai said to them: Is there evidence from there? Also they said to him: If you have been practicing thus, you have never fulfilled the duty of [dwelling in] the *sukkah* (*M. Suk.* 2:7).

Elders of the conflicting pre-70 C. E. schools of Hillel and Shammai are said to have visited a fellow-scholar on Sukkot here. They observe him sitting in the *sukkah* with most of his body while his table was located inside the house. This practice might violate the rule that during the Sukkot festival all meals should be eaten in the *sukkah* rather than in one's home (cf. Lev. 23:42: "You shall dwell in booths seven days"). The *sukkah* was a temporary structure which seems to be imagined here as having been built adjacent to the house. The House of Shammai, which is generally associated with stricter rules than the House of Hillel, first questions the validity of the precedent ("Is there evidence from there?") and then criticizes the rabbi's practice as a transgression of the biblically prescribed holiday observance. As in the previously mentioned story, a visit to a colleague's house is said to have occasioned the expression of a halakhic view which conflicted with the visited rabbis' practice.

Such stories are especially numerous in amoraic documents such as the Talmud *Yerushalmi*. Only a few examples can be given here. According to *y. Ber.* 2:1, 4b, "R. Eleazar went to visit R. Shimon b. Abba [...]" R. Shimon b. Abba is said to have told him that he was weak and used to fall asleep when reciting the *Shema*. He wanted to know whether he had fulfilled his obligation when continuing the recitation after temporary interruptions. R. Eleazar confirms the validity of this practice. According to *y. Ber.* 6:5, 10c, "R. Yona and R. Yose went up to the banquet of R. Hanina of Anat. He brought before them bread which comes with nibblings [or: deserts] after the meal [...]." The rabbis allegedly discussed whether a benediction was necessary before and after eating this bread. *Y. Sanh.* 3:7, 21b relates that "Rav went out to stay in the neighborhood of R. Hiyya the Elder. He passed a certain place and found R. Yochanan [who was] sitting and raising a [halakhic] problem [...]." The story continues to deal with this halakhic issue only, which Rav is said to have been confronted with incidentally, when passing R. Yochanan's house on his way to R. Hiyya the Elder.

3. Randomness in the Transmission of Rabbinic Opinions

The confrontation with the views and practices of other rabbis could lead to a support and confirmation of or to a conflict with one's own views. Rabbis who had direct or indirect knowledge of one particular halakhic opinion might seek confirmation by contacting other rabbis. For example, R. Ilai is said to have heard a certain teaching from R. Eliezer. "And I went around amongst his disciples and looked for a partner for myself [in having heard and memorized this teaching] but did not find [any]" (*M. Er.* 2:6). To be the only tradent of a particular view was obviously considered unsafe. Especially in the context of oral teaching and transmission, one could easily have misunderstood a view and transmitted it wrongly to later generations. This is also evident from another Mishnaic tradition:

R. Aqiba said: When I went down to Nehardea to intercalate the year I found Nechemiah of Bet Deli. He said to me: I have heard that in the Land of Israel they do not allow a woman to [re]marry on the basis of [the testimony of] one witness, except for R. Yehudah b. Baba [...] And I answered him: That's right. He said to me: Tell them in my name: [...] I have received [a tradition] from R. Gamliel the Elder, that they permit a woman to [re]marry on account of one witness. And when I came and recounted the words before R. Gamliel he rejoiced over my words and said: We have found a fellow for R. Yehudah b. Baba [i. e., someone who transmits the same view as R. Gamliel the Elder]. (*M. Yeb.* 16:7).

This text is particularly interesting with regard to the transmission of traditions between Palestine and Babylonia and the twisted ways in which rabbis learned of other rabbis' supporting views. The story relates that when R. Aqiba went from Palestine to Babylonia a fellow Palestinian scholar, Nechemiah of Bet Deli, confronted him with the allegedly exceptional view of the Palestinian sage Yehudah b. Baba, who allowed a widow to remarry on the basis of one witness's testimony of her husband's death. Nechemiah also possesses information about another Palestinian tradition which supports this view, namely that of R. Gamliel the Elder: when certain men were killed at Tel Arza, R. Gamliel the Elder allowed their wives to remarry on the testimony of one witness. Only when R. Aqiba returned to Palestine and told R. Gamliel the Elder's grandson what he had heard, did the latter become aware of the fact that support for his grandfather's opinion existed.

The story suggests that the oral tradition of rabbis' opinions remained precarious after those rabbis' deaths. It seems to have been difficult to find later-generation rabbis who remembered particular traditions and even more difficult for rabbis to become aware of shared views. In this case both Nechemiah of Bet Deli and R. Aqiba are said to have functioned as intermediaries through whom R. Gamliel the Elder's and Yehudah b. Baba's similar views could be identified and used as confirmation for R. Gamliel's view. The Palestinian sages Nechemiah and R. Aqiba are said to have met in Babylonia, and discussed Palestinian practices there. Nehemiah had migrated to Babylonia whereas R. Aqiba stayed there temporarily. Their mobility eventually brought them together and made them aware of the similar views.

We do not claim here that the story is historically accurate and transmits reliable information about these particular rabbis' encounters. It nevertheless gives us important insights into the random ways in which rabbinic views were transmitted. Even if later editors constructed the story, these editors were aware of the unpredictability of finding supporting opinions in a culture in which such traditions were transmitted orally at many different places. Sometimes a Palestinian sage had to travel to Babylonia to hear of Palestinian opinions that supported certain views he knew of at home. Another hazard of oral transmission was the indirect evidence one had of certain views. In the just quoted story (*M. Yeb.* 16:7) R. Aqiba functions as an indirect transmitter of R. Yehudah b. Baba and R. Gamliel the Elder's view to the latter's grandson.

In *y. Shab.* 1:1, 3a direct and indirect modes of transmission are compared and confronted with each other:

Gidul said: Everyone who says a teaching [lit.: something that was heard] in the name of him who said it should see the authority of the tradition as if he was standing before him [...] R. Zeira said to R. Yose [*y. Sheq.*: Assi]: Does my master know Bar Pedaiah that you say traditions in his name? He said to him: R. Yochanan said them in his name. R. Zeira said to R. Ba b. Zabeda: Does my master know Rab that you say traditions in his name? He said to him: R. Acha b. Ahava said them in his name.[15]

---

[15] The text has parallels in *y. Sheq.* 2:7(6), 47a (entire text); *y. Qid.* 1:7, 61a (first part); *y. Shab.* 14:4, 15a ("R. Zeira said to R. Yose / Assi [...].").

In this text direct personal transmission of traditions from master to disciple is presented as preferable to indirect transmission through second degree witnesses. The longer the chain of traditions, the more errors and changes to the original statement could occur. Yet indirect transmission could not be avoided once the original generation of students had died. Indirect transmission and changes to original statements would have been the order of the day in an oral society that was prone to transmitting rabbinic traditions over centuries, long after the original "author" had died.

Another example of the uncertainty involved in orally transmitted views is provided in *y. Shab.* 7:1, 9a:

They asked before the son of R. Yose: What have you heard from your father, from R. Yose [in this regard, see context]? He agrees with R. Yochanan. R. Hezekiah said to them: He did not say so. Rather, R. Shimon b. Zabeda was studying with the son of R. Yose. And he heard from him [that his father shared] the opinion of R. Eleazar.

In this dispute between anonymous rabbis and R. Hezekiah the specific halakhic issue is irrelevant for our purposes. What matters is that the text suggests that already a generation after R. Yose rabbis were divided over this rabbi's opinion and held differing testimonies from his son. Whereas anonymous rabbis had testimony from R. Yose's son that R. Yose shared the opinion of R. Yochanan, R. Hezekiah relies on R. Shimon b. Zabeda who allegedly studied with R. Yose's son. According to R. Shimon b. Zabeda, the son stated that R. Yose sided with R. Eleazar. Both anonymous sages and R. Hezekiah were one generation removed from R. Yose and obviously did not have direct information about his views on a particular matter. R. Yose's son serves as an intermediate tradent here. In the case of R. Hezekiah, R. Shimon b. Zabeda is introduced as a second tradent, that is, R. Hezekiah is even three degrees removed from R. Yose. The dispute concerning R. Yose's opinion remains unresolved here.

Halakhic opinions of earlier generations could be transmitted in different versions or be lost altogether. In such a case a reconstruction would have been difficult if not impossible. According to *y. Pes.* 6:1, 33a, elders of Batera had lost a certain halakhic tradition and therefore did not know the answer to a halakhic problem. They allegedly sent for Hillel the Babylonian, who had studied with Shemaya and Abtalion and might know the answer. In order to consult contemporary rabbis at distant places, amoraic documents refer to intermediaries or letters that were sent in quest for information. For example, *y. A. Z.* 1:9, 40b reports that "[…] R. Haninah son of R. Abbahu said in the name of R. Abbahu: Father had a case and he sent [and] asked R. Hiyya, R. Yasa, [and] Ammi and they instructed him to rent [fields to gentiles] in accordance with R. Yose's opinion […] [cf. *M. A. Z.* 1:9]." R. Abbahu allegedly did not know how to decide a certain case and consulted three fellow-rabbis in that regard. The commonly used formula "sent and asked" may imply that a messenger or letter was sent.

Sometimes written notes and personal visits were combined, as in the following story: "R. Yaqob b. Idi in the name of R. Yehoshua b. Levi: An event [*maaseh*] that elders entered R. Dosa b. Harkinas' [house] to ask him about the co-wife of his daughter [...]" (*y. Yeb.* 1:6, 3a). They allegedly asked him whether he was the one who permitted co-wives to enter levirate marriage. He said that this was the view of his brother, Yonathan b. Harkinas, rather than his own view (elders obviously knew of "b. Harkinas'" view only). When they went to visit the brother, Dosa warned him beforehand by writing a note: "Be careful, for the sages of Israel are coming to you." When they arrive, they argue with him, but he does not accept their view. "He [Yonathan b. Harkinas] sent [and] said to him [to his brother Dosa]: What did you send me? [These are] people who need to learn and you tell me that they are sages of Israel?" The story presents anonymous elders in a very bad light: they are mistaken about the identity of the rabbi who held a certain view. The rabbi then refuses to be convinced by their apparently different opinion and questions their learning altogether. Whereas the elders' mistaken knowledge is based on oral transmission and personal contacts, the b. Harkinas brothers are able to outwit them by exchanging written notes.

The examples show that no organized and systematic preservation and transmission of rabbinic traditions existed in antiquity. In an oral cultural context the transmission of traditions from one locale to another and from one generation to the next was always governed by a large amount of randomness and could easily lead to forgetting, changes, and mistakes, despite the value that was given to memorization in rabbinic society. Rabbis could instruct their disciples to repeat and memorize their views, but there was no guarantee that a student would actually remember an opinion (exactly) or that he would eventually become a rabbi himself who would transmit his teacher's views to later generations of students. On many occasions no disciples would have been present at the time when a rabbi expressed his view. If this was done in the presence of a colleague, that colleague may have held a divergent view and would therefore not have been interested in transmitting his colleague's opinion. There was simply no control with regard to which views would still be known to later generations and no guarantee that even the memorized views reflected the earlier rabbis' actual opinions.

Earlier rabbis' views could be lost, remembered in different versions, or mis-attributed. Individual rabbis became aware of the views of other rabbis at more or less distant places only if they took the effort to travel there themselves, if they sent messengers or letters of inquiry, or by mere chance, if they happened to meet a colleague who had knowledge of a certain tradition which supported or conflicted with their own. This means that halakhic discussions and confrontations between different opinions could only happen at the local level and amongst colleague-friends who used to meet each other occasionally. If a rabbi became aware of a distant rabbi's diverse opinion through hearsay or transmission by colleagues or students, he could simply dismiss that opinion and refuse to change his own. It is rather unlikely that he would have bothered to travel to meet the dissenting colleague and discuss his views with him. Although rabbis would sometimes have discussed controversial issues, the dispute form as we find it in the Mishnah and Talmud must be seen as a literary form constructed at the editorial stage, when dissenting views became more obvious and contradictions emerged.

The significance of randomness in various areas of daily life has recently been stressed by sociologists, economic historians, and philosophers of science.[16] By applying the mathematical probability theory to different aspects of the everyday life experience, a large amount of randomness can be detected which is usually not acknowledged or even noticed by most people. One is usually "fooled" by the assumption of order, direction, and rationality and unaware of the fact that most processes are governed to a large extent by chance and randomness. According to Taleb, "we underestimate the share of randomness in about everything" and tend to read order, regularity, and systematic progression into things.[17] Especially common is the mistake to judge something on the basis of its outcome, that is, to assume that a more or less orderly arrangement at the final stage was preceded by a regulated development.[18] Scholars are especially prone to read meanings into things and to try to detect patterns and regularities in processes that actually lack them.[19]

It is difficult if not impossible to determine the degree of randomness involved in certain processes.[20] The links between specific rabbis and between rabbis and particular students were not random but probably based on mutual attraction, appreciation, and support. Within the rabbinic network certain hierarchies developed in which some rabbis had a higher status than others and some students succeeded whereas others did not.[21] The opinions of those rabbis

---

[16] See, e. g., N. N. Taleb, *Fooled by Randomness: The Hidden Role of Chance in Life and in the Markets* (New York: Random House, 2004); D. J. Bennett, *Randomness* (Cambridge, MA.: Harvard University Press, 1998).

[17] Taleb, *Fooled by Randomness*, xli.

[18] See ibid. 22: "one cannot judge a performance in any given field (war, politics, medicine, investments) by the results [...]", and ibid. 56: "Our mind will interpret most events not with the preceding ones in mind, but the following ones." Thus, for example, the eventual "triumph" of Christianity in the fourth century C. E. should not overshadow the persecution of Christians by Roman emperors in the preceding centuries.

[19] See ibid. xl.

[20] See Bennett, *Randomness*, 83 and 131. In the twentieth century some mathematical definitions of randomness emerged and some scholars reckon with different degrees of randomness, but the amount of randomness involved in certain processes can hardly be measured precisely; see ibid. 161–6.

[21] On hierarchies amongst rabbis see Hezser, *Social Structure*, 255–306. On hierarchies within social networks see also A. Lázló Barabási, *Linked: The New Science of Networks* (Cambridge, Mass.: Harvard University Press, 2002), 58.

who had a higher status and more connections than others are more likely to have survived than those of lesser known rabbis with fewer students, yet even in the case of prominent rabbis such as R. Gamliel and R. Yose (see above) a large amount of their teachings would have been remembered by no one and therefore be lost. One might assume that rulings on those issues that became relevant again later would have been more likely to be remembered than rulings in rare and exceptional cases. But it is difficult to determine a hierarchy of significance in a culture that deemed every aspect of daily life religiously relevant.

It is important to acknowledge the role of chance in rabbinic transmission within an oral cultural milieu that persisted for centuries. As Deborah J. Bennett has pointed out, "When chance determines the outcome, no amount of intelligence, skill, strength, knowledge, or experience can give one player an advantage, and 'luck' emerges as an equalizing force."[22] The role of chance and randomness in the transmission of rabbinic traditions may be one of the reasons why rabbinic documents present many different rabbis' opinions side by side, making all of them seem equally relevant. According to Fuller, "To the untrained eye randomness appears as regularity or tendency to cluster."[23] Scholars of rabbinic documents may therefore assume that a regulated transmission process took place in the tannaitic and amoraic period when, in reality, transmission was random, as the examples discussed above suggest.

4. The Collection and Editing of Traditions

Was the collection and editing of traditions an ongoing process that happened simultaneously at different places and lasted for two centuries? Or was it the outcome of a conscious one-time decision by a group of rabbis who wanted to preserve the "classical" rabbinic tradition in a more lasting format? Can we distinguish between several stages within the editing process, and if so, how did the "final" editing of the larger rabbinic documents differ from the earlier stages? Were the "final" editors of one document located at one place or was the editing process partitioned amongst rabbis at different locales? All of these questions are still open and controversial amongst scholars.

Usually the editing of rabbinic documents is not discussed in a general way but focused on particular works such as the Mishnah or Talmud *Yerushalmi*. We shall deal with the *Yerushalmi* here. According to traditional opinion, the *Yeru-*

---

[22] Bennett, *Randomness*, 12.
[23] W. Fuller, *An Introduction to Probability Theory and its Applications*, vol. 1 (3rd ed.; New York: Wiley, 1968), 160, quoted in Daniel Kahneman and Amos Tversky, "Subjective probability: A judgment of representativeness," *Judgment Under Uncertainty: Heuristics and Biases* (eds. D. Kahneman, P. Slovic, and A. Tversky; Cambridge: Cambridge University Press, 1982), 37.

shalmi was edited in Tiberias at the beginning of the fifth century, shortly after
the death of the last generation of named rabbis mentioned in it. Only tractate
Neziqin was considered to have been edited earlier, in the fourth century, and
perhaps at a different place than the other tractates, namely in Caesarea, as
Lieberman has suggested.[24] According to this theory, the creation of the Talmud
Yerushalmi was a deliberate decision taken by rabbis at a particular time and place.
Scholars have also suggested that the Palestinian Talmud was edited hastily and
left incomplete, because Jews were persecuted by the Christian emperors at that
time.[25] The theory of a hasty compilation is based on the allegedly simplistic
editing of the *Yerushalmi* in comparison with the *Bavli*, and on a "lachrymose"
theory of Jewish persecution in early Byzantine times.

A very different theory has been suggested by Hans-Jürgen Becker ten years
ago.[26] According to Becker, the development of the *Yerushalmi* was not based on
a conscious decision; it rather came about in a continuous process of adding
material which began in the amoraic period and lasted until the emergence of
the first printed edition in 1523. In this theory, no proper distinction is made
between the editors and copyists: both merely added material here and there
without following a wider program.

As I have shown elsewhere, both of these models are unsatisfactory.[27] Becker's theory of a random agglomeration of material is unable to explain editorial patterns and consistencies that are evident throughout the Talmud, such as
the use of particular technical terms. The theory also lacks a proper social-his-
torical basis, for how could a large number of rabbis add to the same "work"
over centuries unless one reckons with a central archive or library for which no
evidence exists. The traditional theory, which usually reckons with only one
redactional stage that took place in a relatively short time period, does not pay
sufficient attention to the possibility of earlier collections and redactions of parts
of the material (such as story collections, collections of traditions pertaining to
one particular rabbi, or pre-edited *sugyot*) and simultaneous redactional processes at different locations. Only a combination of both theories is able to properly
explain the development of rabbinic documents: some material will have been

[24] On the editing of the Talmud *Yerushalmi* see Z. Frankel, *Einleitung in den Jerusalemischen
Talmud* [Hebr.] (Breslau: Schletter [H. Skutsch], 1870), 2–7; on Lieberman's theory of a Cae-
sarean origin of tractate *Neziqin* see Saul Lieberman, *The Talmud of Caesarea* [Hebr.] (Supplement to Tarbiz II. 4; Jerusalem: Azriel Press, 1931); Gerd A. Wewers, *Probleme der Bavot-
Traktate. Ein redaktionskritischer und theologischer Beitrag zum Talmud Yerushalmi* (Tübingen: Mohr
Siebeck, 1984); Hezser, *Form*, 362–77.
[25] See L. Ginzberg, *On Jewish Law and Lore* (New York: Atheneum, 1970), 27.
[26] See H.-J. Becker, *Die grossen rabbinischen Sammelwerke Palästinas. Zur literarischen Genese
von Talmud Yerushalmi and Midrash Bereshit Rabba* (TSAJ 70; Tübingen: Mohr Siebeck, 1999).
See also P. Schäfer, "Research into Rabbinic Literature: An Attempt to Define the Status
Quaestionis," *Journal of Jewish Studies* 37 (1986): 139–52.
[27] See Hezser, "Codification of Legal Knowledge," 626–29.

pre-edited, that is, transmitted as collections of narratives or combinations of halakhic opinions, but at a certain time the conscious decision to create a larger work in the form of the Talmud was taken by a group of anonymous editors who agreed upon certain editorial conventions which they imposed upon the collected material.

The first step which these "final" editors would have taken would have been the collection of oral and written material. They may either have collected whatever they could find or made a conscious choice at this stage already, by contacting the students and tradents of particular rabbis only. What is immediately obvious, however, is that this group of editors must have been well connected – that is, they must have been sitting at the nodal points of the rabbinic network in order to be able to collect the traditions associated with the many rabbis mentioned in the Talmud by name. They would have collected material from different locales throughout Palestine, especially from cities which had a major rabbinic presence such as Tiberias, Sepphoris, Caesarea, and Lydda. While the majority of the material would probably have been preserved in oral form, some of it may have been transmitted in writing. The editors may have contacted possible tradents directly, and they may have sent messengers or letters to others. Through first, second, and third-degree connections a large amount of material could have been amassed.

At the same time a large amount of material would have been left out and lost: some rabbis' chain of transmission may not have lasted until the fifth generation of amoraim but ended long before that time, so that their teachings were forgotten; other tradents were not friends with the editors or could not be contacted by them; tradents in cities may have been easier to contact than village rabbis; the editors may also have decided to leave out material which they considered inappropriate, for whatever reason. A large amount of material from amoraic times is transmitted anonymously or collectively, in the name of "rabbis of Caesarea", "*chavrayya*" or other groups that cannot be properly identified.[28] We also have to reckon with wrong attributions based on wrong recollections or faint memories of the origin of a rule.

What would have been the nature of the material that was collected this way? In the Talmud *Yerushalmi* we find tannaitic material as well as traditions of five generations of amoraim, that is, material from a number of centuries. Despite rabbinic emphasis on memorization, it is highly unlikely that the traditions of a first- or second-generation amora which reached the editors orally hundred of years later would reflect a particular amora's *ipsissima vox*, as scholars of the past have often assumed. We rather have to assume that the longer the chain of

---

[28] On these groups see especially St. Miller, *Sages and Commoners in Late Antique 'Erez Israel: A Philological Inquiry into Local Traditions in Talmud Yerushalmi* (TSAJ 111; Tübingen: Mohr Siebeck, 2006), 31–178.

transmission and the larger the number of tradents the more a tradition would have been changed in this process, even before it reached the editors. As we have seen above, even one generation after a rabbi's teaching on a particular subject only one tradent could remember it or different tradents remembered different versions of the opinion. Since each rabbi seems to have had a relatively small circle of students, not all of whom may have become rabbis themselves, the number of tradents of a particular rabbi would have been quite limited. The rabbis' students' students would have focused on their own teacher's views rather than cared much about memorizing the older views of their teacher's teacher. Therefore literal transmission of oral traditions over many generations is very unlikely and constant changes and adaptations would have taken place.

The editors eventually combined individual teachings, collections, and ag-glomerations of material into a more or less consistent whole. Different editors probably worked on different parts of the *Yerushalmi* at different places but agreed on certain editorial procedures concerning the combination and arrange-ment of the material. They would have taken certain liberties themselves when formulating, adding to, commenting on, and harmonizing material. These edi-tors decided to remain anonymous and obviously distinguished themselves from the earlier amoraim whose names they mention. Like the editors of other early Byzantine collections such as the Codex Theodosianus, Codex Justinianus, and Christian Florilegia, they probably had antiquarian reasons for creating a col-lection of traditions of the past: the preservation of a "classical" body of material seems to have been their goal.[29]

5. The Writing and Copying of the Documents and the Study of the Written Texts

On the one hand, the production of large written documents would have been a radical change and innovation in the oral-cultural context of ancient Judaism. On the other hand, some of the material that came down to the editors would have been composed in writing already and written works and collections ex-isted in contemporary Graeco-Roman and Christian society. Although rabbis stressed the importance of orality and memorization in the context of teaching their disciples, they would have eventually realized that a large amount of ma-terial could be properly preserved and made available to later generations in written form only. The written works that circulated in Graeco-Roman and Christian society could have served as examples of the advantages of written transmission.

---

[29] See Hezser, "Codification of Legal Knowledge," 634–38.

Scribes would have been responsible for the actual writing of the documents. Some of the editors may have been able to write themselves, but in general, the composers were not identical with the actual writers of ancient texts. The former rather dictated their texts to professional scribes who were also responsible for the copying of the manuscripts.[30] One may imagine that the editors of rabbinic works had scribes at hand who would first write down the many oral traditions during the process of collecting material and later write the *sugyot* and tractates according to the editors' instructions. Since no copyright existed in antiquity, with each re-copying certain changes would have been introduced to the text.[31] This process can account for the differences between the manuscripts without the assumption of copyist-editors who form part of Becker's and Schäfer's development theory. The composition of texts was differentiated from mere copying in antiquity, and the composers (authors or editors) had a much higher social status than the writers who were mere secretaries. Even if the latter made certain changes to the texts, either by mistake or deliberately, they did not compose entirely new texts or change texts entirely.

Once rabbinic documents existed in writing, the traditions of earlier rabbis would be available to a much larger group of scholars than the oral traditions of individual teachers had been in tannaitic and amoraic times. Now one had access to the views of a large variety of rabbis without having to contact them directly. Once the views were put in writing, conflicting views would be recognized. The later editors of the Babylonian Talmud already tended to harmonize contradictions, whereas the *Yerushalmi* editors often left disputes undecided. It was now up to the students of the written texts to make sense of the halakhic views of earlier times and to apply them to the new situations and questions of their own time. The newly written "Oral Tradition" was studied in an oral context and reinterpreted over and over again. At the same time commentaries were composed and transmitted in written form alongside the now classical rabbinic documents. Reading, oral discussion, and written interpretation were closely interwoven and have remained so until today.

---

[30] On scribes see Hezser, *Jewish Literacy*, 118–26; Meir Bar-Ilan, "Writing in Ancient Israel and Early Judaism, Part Two: Scribes and Books in the Late Second Commonwealth and Rabbinic Period," *Mikra: Text, Translation, Reading and Interpretation of the Hebrew Bible in Ancient Judaism and Early Christianity* (ed. M. J. Mulder; Corpus Rerum Iudaicarum ad Novum Testamentum II. 1; Assen and Philadelphia: Van Gorcum, 1988), 21–38; E. Randolph Richards, *The Secretary in the Letters of Paul* (WUNT 2. 42; Tübingen: Mohr Siebeck, 1991).

[31] See also C. Hezser, "The Mishnah and Ancient Book Production," in *The Mishnah in Contemporary Perspective* (ed. J. Neusner; Leiden: Brill, 2002), 167–92.

Mark: News as Tradition

Antoinette Clark Wire

When we hear that a piece is composed in performance we understand that it takes shape as it is played or told. It could be improvised on the spot if someone is telling the latest news. Or it could be a traditional story in the family or a song in the region being used in a new setting and so recomposed in performance. But could news that is still in process be a tradition? If tradition is what Gregory Nagy calls "a cumulative process, entailing countless instances of composition/performance,"[1] there is flexibility enough for news to stay fresh and substance enough for its traditional patterns to keep their shape. The shifts that take place may be imperceptible even to the performer, in line with Albert Lord's observation that sounds within a certain range are perceived as the same even when they differ.[2] Traditional meaning can hold when expressions change, or we might say that sounds change in a changing world in order for meaning to hold.

When we read Homer as oral tradition with the help of Lord, we can almost imagine the great epics being composed by singers performing over generations the feats of their ancestors. But that seems out of place when we turn to the New Testament gospels. They purport to be news about recent events, and in a sect of Judaism whose Scriptures were written. In addition, the gospels are prose, not the poetry that would seem able to sustain the telling of long narratives. Why would anyone call the early narrative about Jesus in Mark a tradition composed in performance?[3]

Most obvious is the apparent origin of the stories in rural Palestine where people farm and fish, not read and write. Catherine Hezser in *Jewish Literacy in Roman Palestine* concedes Bar-Ilan's low estimation of Jewish literacy at about 3% on the grounds that the population was always largely rural.[4] And because we

---

[1] G. Nagy, *The Best of the Achaeans: Concepts of the Hero in Archaic Greek Poetry* (Baltimore: Johns Hopkins University Press, 1979), 8.

[2] A. B. Lord, "The Merging of Two Worlds: Oral and Written Poetry as Carriers of Ancient Values," in *Oral Tradition in Literature: Interpretation in Context* (ed. J. M. Foley; Colombia: University of Missouri Press, 1986), 19–20; idem, *The Singer of Tales* (Cambridge: Harvard University Press, 1960; repr. New York: Atheneum, 1978), 120.

[3] I use "Mark" to name the narrative, not an author.

[4] C. Hezser, *Jewish Literacy in Roman Palestine* (Tübingen: Mohr Siebeck, 2001), 496. M. Bar-Ilan, "Illiteracy in the Land of Israel in the First Centuries C. E.," *Essays in the Social*

know that oral stories do not survive if no one is telling them, we surmise these were told as this sect expanded and sustained itself. This provides a viable context for a performance tradition to develop. Yet Mark seems quite different than Homer's epics which Lord identified as oral tradition from their typical formulas, themes and poetic meter. In fact Mark draws heavily in form and diction on Israel's traditions. It is full of formulas or stereotyped phrases such as "John the Baptizer," "the mortal" (Son of Man), and "Amen I say to you," and full of themes or episodes such as healing stories, callings, and controversies.[5] But poetic meter is missing.

Here Mark is more analogous to Native American oral traditions than the Homeric epic. Dell Hymes finds in Chinook coyote tales what he calls "measured verse," a rhythm of things happening in units of threes or fives introduced by key particles.[6] In Mark we find events told in twos or threes with many parallel lines and enclosures,[7] and linked with the phrase "and right away," "and again" or simply "and."[8] Markan language is illuminated by Wallace Chafe's discourse analysis of speech.[9] Chafe made a silent film about a pear tree and discovered that people from many different cultures retold the story in a barrage of short phrases he calls "intonation units," not sentences as used in writing. Egbert Bakker finds just such speech in Homer, short units loosely linked, that have become traditional by being stylized into a rhythmic "special speech" to weight them with significance.[10] The key to memorable tradition, then, is not

---

Scientific Study of Judaism and Jewish Society, vol. 2 (eds. S. Fishbane and S. Schoenfeld with A. Goldschläger; Hoboken: KTAV, 1992), 55–56.

[5] T. P. Haverly, "Oral Traditional Literature and the Composition of Mark's Gospel," (Ph. D. diss., University of Edinburgh, 1983), 141–285; P. J. J. Botha, "Mark's Story as Oral Traditional Literature: Rethinking the Transmission of Some Traditions about Jesus," *Hervormde Teologise Studies* 47/2 (1991): 317–322.

[6] D. Hymes, "Sung Epics and Native American Ethnopoetics," in *Textualization of Oral Epics* (ed. L. Honko; Berlin: Mouton & Gruyter, 2000), 291–342.

[7] F. Neirynck, *Duality in Mark: Contributions to the Study of the Markan Redaction* (Leuven: Leuven University Press, 1988); J. Dewey, *Markan Public Debate: Literary Technique, Concentric Structure and Theology in Mark 2:11–3:6* (Chico: Scholars Press 1980); W. H. Kelber, *The Oral and the Written Gospel: The Hermeneutics of Speaking and Writing in the Synoptic Tradition, Mark, Paul, and Q* (Philadelphia: Fortress Press, 1983), 66–68.

[8] J. Kleist, *The Gospel of Saint Mark Presented in Greek Thought-Units and Lines with a Commentary* (Milwaukee: Bruce Publishing Company, 1936), 152–53, 137–41; M. Reiser, *Syntax und Stil des Markusevangeliums im Licht der hellenistischen Volksliteratur* (Tübingen: Mohr Siebeck 1984), 99–137.

[9] *The Pear Stories: Cognitive, Cultural and Linguistic Aspects of Narrative Production* (ed. W. L. Chafe; Norwood, NJ: Ablex, 1980); W. L. Chafe, *Discourse, Consciousness and Time: The Flow and Displacement of Conscious Experience in Speaking and Writing* (Chicago: University of Chicago Press, 1994).

[10] E. J. Bakker, *Poetry in Speech: Orality and Homeric Discourse* (Ithaca and London: Cornell University Press, 1997), 1–53; idem, *Pointing at the Past: From Formula to Performance in Homeric Poetics* (Washington D. C.: Center for Hellenistic Studies, Trustees for Harvard University, 2005), 38–55.

necessarily archaic stories in metric form but these bursts of speech made special through traditional measured rhythms. Though Mark is an account of recent events rather than ancient battles, its short phrases, weighted language and traditional forms do suggest oral tradition.

1. Markan Genre or Story Pattern

The challenge in hearing Mark as a performance tradition comes less at the level of phrase or episode than at the level of genre – or as Lord called it for oral composition, story pattern. Most careful readers will concede that we have spoken language here, and oral stories that are cast in stereotyped ways, but we assume an author is required to provide the unity that makes them into a coherent statement, or more recently the attentive reader shares the credit. But we do not imagine that favored long-term tellers could be the unifying artists. We thereby cancel out the significance of the storyteller who becomes the slave making and carrying the bricks for a literary Pharaoh to build his mausoleum. But if we find in Mark story patterns that are circulating orally when Mark is written, signs of recomposition over time in new settings, and sustained attention to speaking and hearing news, the possibility of its being a performance composition increases. And this may in turn suggest how news can also be tradition.

Some positive contributions for understanding the oral story pattern of Mark can be gleaned from a century of efforts to determine the literary genre of Mark. The form critics followed Karl Ludwig Schmidt in recognizing that the gospels were not so much literature as folk tradition. Later analogues are stories about monks, saints and *hasidim* of which Schmidt says, "These 'authors' had no choice to restrain themselves (indeed, they more or less *wanted* to restrain themselves), because they were carried along by a tradition."[11] Dibelius, Bultmann and Dodd all took the proclaiming of Jesus' saving death and resurrection to be the heart of the tradition that shaped other memories of Jesus into gospels, making the gospel *sui generis*.[12] They implied that the story came together through various community uses without individual agency, and the improbability of this set off a return to literary theories of gospel origins.

More recent research sees the gospels centered on Jesus' lifetime and reads them as biographies of a teacher or cult founder. If this is not taken narrowly as a

---

[11] K. L. Schmidt, *The Place of the Gospels in the General History of Literature* (trans. B. R. McCane; Colombia, South Carolina: University of South Carolina Press, 2002), 62, n. 60.

[12] M. Dibelius, *From Tradition to Gospel* (New York: Charles Scribner's Sons, 1935; German, 1919) 1–8; R. Bultmann, *The History of the Synoptic Tradition* (rev. ed. with supplement; New York: Harper & Row, 1968; German, 1931), 368–74; C. H. Dodd, *The Apostolic Preaching and its Developments* (New York: Harper and Row, 1937 and repr. 1964).

literary form, but broadly as a popular practice of telling lives and deaths of prophets, it could contribute directly to a performance approach.[13]

Most recently Adela Yarbro Collins has argued that the genre of Mark is history in the style of the Deuteronomist who incorporates the Elijah-Elisha stories in a wider framework of Mosaic and Davidic traditions.[14] She concludes that Mark is "an eschatological historical monograph," centered, not on Jesus' lifetime nor on his past death and resurrection, but on an open ending toward what is anticipated and not yet fulfilled. Yet she compares Mark with apocalyptic histories focused on the sequence of the end-time rather than with popular expectations of an impending deliverance. Lawrence Wills proposes in response that the incipient genre of the tradition behind Mark and John is both apocalyptic and biographical, combining the themes of the Jewish prophet provoking his expiatory death with the Hellenistic folk hero's exploits.[15]

Studies of oral tradition also contribute toward understanding Mark's story pattern. Motif indexes feature many kinds of concrete stories but not how they are integrated.[16] Folklore study would distinguish the genre of Mark as legend rather than myth or tale because it purports to tell extraordinary actual events, but this does not specify a story pattern.[17] Structuralists who study folklore do consider the coherence of extended narratives. To oversimplify, the French school following Claude Levi-Strauss analyzed stories paradigmatically, that is, looking for patterns of tension and resolution sustained across whole narratives, such as between the natural and the cultivated, or life-giving and death-dealing.[18] The Russian formalists often analyzed syntagmatically in terms of narrative sequence. Vladimir Propp found up to thirty one functions in consistent order in Russian folk tales, for example: the donor tests, the hero acts, the donor rewards.[19] Also using a sequential approach, Albert Lord identified the return story within the wider rescue story in the Slavic and Homeric materials.[20]

---

[13] K. Baltzer, *Die Biographie der Propheten* (Neukirchen: Neukirchener Verlag, 1975), 185–89. Such accounts may be reflected in "The Lives of the Prophets," *The Old Testament Pseudepigraphia*, vol 2 (ed. J. H. Charlesworth; trans. D. R. A. Hare; Garden City, New York: Doubleday, 1985) 395–99.

[14] A. Yarbro Collins, *Mark: A Commentary* (Minneapolis: Fortress, 2007), 38–44.

[15] L. M. Wills, *The Quest of the Historical Gospels: Mark, John and the Origins of the Gospel Genre* (London: Routledge, 1997), 8–18, 157–71.

[16] S. Thompson, *The Motif-Index of Folk-Literature* (6 vols.; Bloomington: Indiana University Press, 1955–58).

[17] A. Jolles, *Einfache Formen: Legende, Sage, Mythe, Rätsel, Spruch, Kasus, Memorabile, Märchen, Witz* (Halle: Niemeyer, 1929; repr. Tübingen: M. Niemeyer, 1982); W. Bascom, "The Forms of Folklore," *Journal of American Folklore* 78 (1965): 3–20.

[18] C. Lévi-Strauss, *The Raw and the Cooked* (vol. 1 of *Introduction to a Science of Mythology*; New York: Harper & Row, 1969; French, 1964).

[19] V. Propp, *Morphology of the Folktale* (2nd ed.; Austin: University of Texas Press, 1968), 25–65.

[20] Lord, *Singer*, 120–24.

A key challenge in identifying any oral story pattern is that traditional stories are not fixed. Tomorrow's telling of the story will have shifted here and inverted there, and the Mark we read can be only one instance of its tradition. Is the story pattern to be sought as the lowest common denominator of all known instances of a tradition, its bare skeleton that tellers variously elaborate? But variations may also be traditional. Better that we recognize that a tradition in some way incorporates all its instances. Lauri and Anneli Honko report that a South Indian performer of the Siri epic spoke of "knots," "joints" or "halting places" in his telling the story, suggesting that the tradition is a network of roads with landmarks where choices must be made before continuing on one path or another.[21] John Miles Foley presses this further when he says that the full complexity exists in the tradition, all the pathways that might be taken, whereas the story being told represents the whole only in part.[22] Yet it can metonymically, part for whole, evoke the full depth and breath of the people's cultural memory, the "story hoard" that holds together the connections between all the piecemeal meanings. I suggest that because a tradition is such an unbounded maze of pathways fading off at the edges of human sight, the story once told becomes the whole story in its actual and available sense. Even though there will have been different tellings of Mark, the one instance we read is our best chance of seeing the story pattern in the Markan tradition.

Those who have tried to delineate an oral story pattern for Mark can be distinguished by the two different paths mentioned in recent structural analysis, one clocking the sequence of events moving toward a transforming climax, the other tracing across the whole story its dynamic polarities. Joanna Dewey has her eye on sequence when she speaks of a process of one performance building on another to create "a continuous, more-or-less coherent narrative" based on the framework of Jesus' ministry, death and resurrection.[23] She nonetheless hears a narrative rich in repeating, encircling and echoing patterns that knit stories together. Others see the sequence dominated by its culmination in Jesus' death and resurrection. George Nickelsburg identified in Mark's passion story most of the twenty-one components of what he called a Jewish persecution and vindication story pattern, among them provocation, accusation, ordeal and vindication.[24] Though he was looking for a literary genre for Mark in conjunction with

[21] L. Honko and A. Honko, "Multiforms in Epic Composition," *The Epic Oral and Written* (eds. L. Honko, J. Handoo and J..M. Foley; Mysore, India: Central Institute of Indian Languages, 1998), 69–71.

[22] J. M. Foley, *Immanent Art: From Structure to Meaning in Traditional Oral Epic* (Bloomington: Indiana University Press, 1991); idem, *How to Read an Oral Poem* (Urbana and Chicago: University of Illinois Press, 2002), 109–24

[23] J. Dewey, "The Survival of Mark's Gospel: A Good Story?" *JBL* 123 (2004): 503, 495–96. See also her "Oral Methods of Structuring Narrative in Mark," *Int.* 43 (1989): 32–44.

[24] G. W. E. Nickelsburg, "The Genre and Function of the Markan Passion Narrative," *HTR* 73 (1980): 153–84, especially 155–63.

the themes of Messiah and Temple, he had to concede that the persecution-vin-
dication pattern reflects "a generic type of narrative that was a conventional
medium for telling stories about persecuted righteous persons." Thomas Haverly builds his case for Mark as performance tradition on its formulas and
themes, but he suggests in response to Nickelsburg that Jesus provokes threats to
destroy him already in chapter three, so the story pattern from provocation to
vindication could integrate the entire gospel performance.[25]

A second approach has followed the French rather than the Russian structuralist bent and looked for dynamic polarities that indicate the story pattern.
David Watson, drawing from Bruce Malina and others, sees the Jesus of Mark
reversing the honor-shame values of his culture and cultivating a new family
among the culturally shamed through acts of humility and compassion.[26] Richard Horsley sees a struggle of the rulers and the ruled underlying the story at each
key point.[27] The tradition was never loose fragments, he thinks, but was focused
on Jesus – seen through stories about Moses the liberator and Elijah the renewer
– as God's instrument in the people's resistance to the Jerusalem elite, the Herods and Rome. Fernando Belo brings the French structuralist and political
approaches together in a sweeping analysis of Mark in terms of the tensions
between pollution and cleansing, debt and gift, passion and resurrection.[28] In
Ched Myers' reading of the gospel through the parable of the strong man's
house, Jesus is the stronger one who binds the strong man and plunders his
goods.[29] Pieter Botha stresses that the Markan Jesus enters a world that is understood to be possessed by Satan and announces God's kingdom as the reversal of
all existing power relations, a reversal that will take place through people with
faith in God for whom all things are possible.[30]

This too-brief sketch shows that significant work has been done toward the
oral story pattern of Mark, and that many interpreters deal in some way with
both the story's tensions and sequence.[31] I will consider first the tensions that

---

[25] Haverly, "Oral Traditional Literature," 313–16.

[26] D. F. Watson, "The 'Messianic Secret:' Demythologizing a Non-Existent Markan
Theme," *JT* (2006): 33–44.

[27] R. A. Horsley, "A Prophet like Moses and Elijah: Popular Memory and Cultural Patterns
in Mark," in *Performing the Gospel: Orality, Memory and Mark. Essays Dedicated to Werner Kelber*
(Minneapolis: Fortress, 2006), 178–83, 188–92; idem, *Hearing the Whole Story: The Politics of
Plot in Mark's Gospel* (Louisville: Westminster John Knox, 2001).

[28] F. Belo, *A Materialist Reading of the Gospel of Mark* (Maryknoll, New York: Orbis Books,
1981), 98–232.

[29] C. Myers, *Binding the Strong Man: A Political Reading of Mark's Story of Jesus* (Maryknoll,
New York: Orbis, 1988).

[30] P. J. J. Botha, "Mark's Story of Jesus and the Search for Virtue," in *The Rhetorical Analysis
of Scripture: Essays from the 1995 London Conference* (eds. S. E. Porter and T. H. Olbricht;
Sheffield: Sheffield Academic Press, 1997), 156–84; idem, "Mark's Story as Oral Traditional
Literature," 304–31; idem, *"οὐκ ἔστιν ὧδε* ... Mark's Stories of Jesus' Tomb and History,"
Neot 23 (1989): 195–218.

[31] For example, Joanna Dewey identifies key tensions in "The Gospel of Mark as Oral

characterize the story pattern, then the sequence that it takes, and finally how
the two are integrated and where the scribe fits in.

2. Story Pattern as Conflict

One key tension in Mark occurs between Jesus and the legal authorities, often
called the scribes and/or Pharisees. Both Jesus and they are attributed authority,
explain what God requires, and interpret the meaning of Scripture, but each
questions the other's conduct and considers the other to be misleading the
people. The scribes accuse Jesus of expelling demons by the power of the ruler
of demons, and Jesus accuses Pharisees and scribes of nullifying God's commands with their traditions (3:22; 7:8, 13). The scribes and Pharisees are depicted as well established and defending their practices as traditions of the elders,
whereas Jesus is shown speaking from a heavenly calling and defending his
authority in the prophetic tradition of John the Baptist (9:7; 11:27–33). The
conflict is dramatized in concrete stories about fasting, eating, divorce or cleansing rather than as general principles, though we hear an occasional concluding
summary: "the Sabbath is for people, not people for the Sabbath," or "declaring
all foods clean" (2:27; 7:19).

On the cosmic level the tension is suspended between God and Satan. After a
kind of title the story begins with the first person speech of God attributed to
Isaiah announcing, "I will send my messenger ahead of you," and again, when
the Spirit comes down on Jesus, "You are my beloved son. I delight in you!"
(1:2, 11). This divine initiative continues as the Spirit drives Jesus out into the
desert to face Satan, and Jesus returns to announce God's rule in Galilee. This
rule is not presented as an established condition but as something coming into a
hostile environment. Jesus' first act of power is to silence and cast out an unclean
spirit who exposes him as God's holy one (1:23–27). When accused of casting
out demons by Beelzebul, he identifies their accusations as blasphemy against
God's Spirit (3:22–30). Three other times Jesus expels life-threatening spirits,
from the fishers on the sea, the man living among the graves, and the boy with
seizures (4:35–41; 5:1–20; 9:14–27). The graveyard story clearly implicates
Rome in the unclean spirit's name, Legion, in its not wanting to be sent out of
the country, and arguably in the herd of swine (5:1–20). Because such exorcism
stories are marginalized in Matthew and Luke and disappear in John, this aspect?
of Mark is only now being recognized for its significance.[32] In a world that is

Hermeneutic," *Jesus the Voice and the Text: Beyond the Oral and the Written Gospel* (ed. T. Thatcher; Waco-Texas: Baylor University Press, 2008), 74–75.
    [32] Myers, *Binding*, 190–94; Botha, "Mark's Story of Jesus," 170–84; Horsley, *Hearing*,
121–48.

Satan's, held captive to the one who looks out from the tribute coinage, God is seen arriving to reclaim the people made in God's image and created for partnership and love of God and neighbor (12:13–17, 27; 10:2–9; 12:28–34).

The third level of tension takes place in the people. Faced with the challenge of God's Spirit to Satan's rule, they are torn between trust and fear. Four fishers and eight others, "many tax collectors" and "many women" follow Jesus (1:16–20; 3:16–19; 2:14–15; 15:41), yet their trust is mercurial and their conduct is increasingly ruled by fear of hunger or shame or death. It is those from the crowd, people in the most desperate straits, who become the models of trust, whether by Jesus' challenge to them – "Don't be afraid. Just keep trusting." "All things are possible for the one who trusts!" – or by their own initiative – "I trust! Help my distrust!" "Your trust has made you well." (5:36; 9:23; 5:34; 9:24; 10:52).

It is evident in these conflicts that the storyteller does not take a neutral position. The whole weight of the story banks on the coming of God's rule which is described in process of expelling destroying spirits, exposing empty authorities, and displacing fear with trust. This is the news it is telling. At the same time there is a heavy counter-weight of reality, seen from the start in the Spirit's driving Jesus out to be tested by Satan. Satan possesses (or Rome occupies?) the present time and the story's space, the legal authorities keep the pressure on Jesus, and the disciples' fear is the order of the day. This realism is the default setting, never in doubt, though it is challenged frontally by the announcement of God's overriding power that gives Jesus "authority...not like the scribes" (1:22) and elicits the trust that heals and saves. The storytellers who make this challenge take on the powers of the world and rejoice in each thrust and parry in the struggle against established structures.

This story pattern could be called the *agōn* or contest in the most basic, even mythic sense, whether it is told in the idiom of the oppressor as a destruction and counter-destruction, or in the subversive or comic vein to expose the weakness of those who are so sure they rule.[33] Each episode tells the whole story – the threat dispelled, the hunger gone – and any scene well told can stand for them all. It is indicative of this that I can remember only one episode of many Appalachian stories told me about the landlord and the Bryan boys. This time they lure his sheep down to the creek and take one each spring for the Bryan table while he complains about how his herd does not grow under their care. Similarly, but in urban California, Mrs. Irvine had stories about her sons and the San Anselmo police. In the one I remember each son is pulled over for speeding on Bolinas Avenue until the last one lets on that the speed limit sign was washed away in the winter flood and the cops have to tear up all the tickets. One story embodies the entire repertoire or can trigger another until they build into a

---

[33] Cf. Wills' translation and interpretation of the *Life of Aesop* in *The Quest*, 35–50, 181–215.

crescendo. Each storyteller highlights the contrast between the contending parties, develops suspense through rhythmic patterns, and above all flouts established authority and celebrates the local heroes. The Markan stories can be more complex, even circling on several axes, but the dynamic holds.

Mark raises some questions that do not immediately fit this agonistic pattern. Who is Jesus? Why does he restrict news about himself? And does the good news of God's rule ever get told? A voice from heaven calls Jesus my son and delight, and warns the disciples to hear him (1:11; 9:7), signifying that this local man is intimate with God. This parallels the case of another first century Galilean miracle-working rabbi: "A voice from heaven goes out and says, 'All the whole world is fed on account of Hanina ben Dosa, and Hanina, my son, satisfies himself with a pan of carob pods from a Sabbath evening to a Sabbath evening!'"[34] It is those opposing Jesus who give him titles of honor: unclean spirits call him Holy One of God and Son of the Highest God, Herod names him John the Baptist resurrected, the disciple he rebukes as Satan calls him the Messiah, the High Priest calls him Messiah the Son of the Blessed, Pilate calls him King of the Jews, several High Priests call him Christ the King of Israel, and the crucifying centurion calls him a Son of God (1:24; 5:7; 6:14–16; 8:29; 14:61; 15:2, 9, 12; 15:32; 15:39).[35] These names, whether ironic or concessions of his strength, are hardly reliable in a narrative where Jesus responds by calling himself the mortal or otherwise cutting them off (1:25; 5:8; 8:30–33; 14:62; 15:2). Those who follow him are open-mouthed, astounded, stumped: "So who is this that the wind and the sea obey him?" (4:41).

At the same time Jesus restricts news about himself. Only hints suggest the aim:

1. Strategic: Jesus claims time to proclaim God's rule before suppression (1:38; 9:9).
2. Ethical: Jesus refuses honor, having come not to be served but to serve (10:45).
3. Esoteric: Jesus limits knowledge of his work to a chosen group (4:10–13).
4. Theological: Jesus won't let his fame compete with God's (1:37–38; 5:19; 10:18).
5. Dramatic: the restrictions show how quickly the news spreads (1:45; 7:36).
6. Apologetic: the restrictions show why the early stories are not confessional (8:30).

Is there a tension between Jesus' theological, ethical and perhaps strategic aims and early tellers' delight in the dramatic news and their own special role in it? Or

---

[34] *b Ta'anit* 24b; my translation from A. Wire, *Holy Lives, Holy Deaths: A Close Hearing of Early Jewish Storytellers* (Atlanta: Society of Biblical Literature, 2002), 113.

[35] One sympathetic character calls him Son of David, but Jesus later undermines that (10:47–48; 12:35–37).

are all these explanations efforts of tellers to deal with the traditional conundrum of a prophet's reticence? In any case there is narrative tension between Jesus proclaiming God's rule and others proclaiming Jesus.

And there is discord between the opening and closing of Mark. What starts "The beginning of the gospel of Jesus Christ"[36] ends "They said nothing to anyone, for they were afraid." The word "gospel" or "good news" is best understood in terms of its use throughout Mark, usually with the verb "to announce," "to proclaim." The gospel is a public proclamation to all hearers (1:14–15) that must be proclaimed to all nations before the end (13:10) and proclaimed so as to include the anointing woman's story (14:9), while later manuscripts of Mark require that it be proclaimed to every creature (16:15). The two other uses of the word "gospel" are promises to those who proclaim the gospel: whoever loses his or her life for Jesus' sake and for the gospel will save it (8:35), and no one who leaves home for his sake and the gospel will lose a reward (10:29–30). With so much riding on this proclaiming, how can the story end untold?

Some speculate that the "proper ending" was interrupted or lost, or choose one of several endings that were added from other gospels in early centuries (or two such endings with modern editions). Better that we consider how the contradiction arose. All references to the word "gospel" other than Jesus' initial announcement fit only loosely into their contexts, either doubling something otherwise said (1:15; 8:35; 10:29), breaking the verbal tense or person (13:10; 16:15) or falling outside the narrative line (1:1; 14:9). Could a teller be making explicit that the gospel is for all nations, and naming Jesus Christ as the one proclaimed? Yet the ending still seems to take it all away, or at least take gospel transmission from a recognized circle of disciples and root it among women who told about not having told.

We must recognize that in spite of the strong story pattern in which God is expelling Satan, Jesus is exposing the legal authorities, and trust is breaking through fear, stated powers are still assumed to be in control, Jesus' reticence is flouted, and fear has the last word. In this context who Jesus is remains a question rather than an answer, and whether the good news of God's rule will get out to all people remains to be seen.

---

[36] In line with the original Sinaiticus, I take the following phrase "Son of God" to be secondary. For an analysis of this variant see A. Yarbro Collins, "Establishing the Text: Mark 1:1," *Texts and Contexts: The Function of Biblical Texts in Their Textual and Situative Contexts* (eds. T. Fornberg and D. Hellholm; Oslo: Scandinavian University Press, 1995), 111–27.

3. Story Pattern as Sequence

The pattern of the Markan story can also be described as a sequence. The introductory scene in Mark tells the arrival of a prophet in a time of crisis. John appears according to a prophecy attributed to Isaiah. He announces the sign of baptism for those who repent in order to escape, we later learn, from some sign of destruction he has announced against their ruler Herod Antipas for taking his brother's wife (6:17). Crowds come from everywhere to be baptized, including Jesus after John predicts a stronger one will baptize with God's Spirit. The end of John's story comes when Herod serves his head on a platter, but only after John has been vindicated by Herod's double declaration that Jesus is John raised from the dead (6:14, 16).[37]

The five elements in this telling of John's story – appearance in crisis, giving of a sign, the following of crowds, official suppression, and vindication – are reflected in multiple Jewish stories from this period about prophets who give a sign of destruction and/or deliverance.[38] Their oral provenance is indicated not only by their widespread survival in literature but also by their basic function to announce the signs that were gathering crowds and, after suppression, to celebrate the vindication that fueled further hopes. Many of these popular stories are preserved in Josephus where they are heavily colored by his view that these prophets are frauds.

At this time [of bandits and imposters] a certain man arrived in Jerusalem from Egypt saying he was a prophet and commanding the populace to go with him to the hill named Mount of Olives which lies opposite [the city] half a mile away. For he said he wanted to show them from there how when he gave the command the walls of Jerusalem would fall down, through which he also promised to provide them entrance. But Felix, when he learned these things, commanded his soldiers to take up arms, and, having set out from Jerusalem with many mounted men and foot-soldiers, he struck those with the Egyptian and killed four hundred of them, and took two hundred alive. But the Egyptian himself ran away from the battle and vanished.[39]

Here the story pattern is clear: the Egyptian's appearance in a crisis, his sign of the falling walls, the crowds, suppression by Felix, and vindication in his escape. The question is whether this sequence can provide the story pattern for the Markan account of Jesus. Jesus appears in Galilee within miles of Herod's capital city of Tiberius just after Herod Antipas arrests John the Baptist. Jesus announces

---

[37] Cf. Josephus, *Ant.* 18. 109–119 for an apparently more widespread account of John's vindication through the defeat of Herod's army by his own wife's father.

[38] See twenty four stories about prophets living from 150 BCE to 150 CE who give such signs and sixteen new stories from this period about signs given by Hebrew Bible prophets in my *Holy Lives,* 183–277.

[39] Josephus, *Ant.* 20. 169–172, my translation from *Holy Lives,* 263, cf. 242 for Josephus, *J. W.* 2. 261–263.

the sign of God's impending rule. Like the Egyptian's falling walls and Theudas' split river, this sign revives a traditional hope that represents deliverance to those who welcome it but destruction to those who do not. Each prophet is suppressed before the sign is fulfilled. Yet in each case hope for it goes on in continued telling of the story, as can be seen when Paul arrives in Jerusalem and is mistaken for the Egyptian still expected to return (Acts 21:38).

Objections could be raised to taking Mark as the story of a prophet's sign on the grounds that Jesus in Mark refuses to give the Pharisees a sign (8:11–12) and he warns his disciples about false prophets "who give signs and wonders to mislead the elect" (13:22). But this concern about Jesus being identified with sign-giving prophets makes sense precisely because his story is close to theirs. So he will not work signs to impress the authorities, he does not claim to be a prophet or the son of a prophet (except as rejected 6:4), and he knows that most prophets are false – all, of course, qualities of a true prophet.

The end of the Markan story of Jesus that tells his suppression and vindication also follows the pattern found in the stories of prophets' signs. Jesus is persistent to the death, neither evading the pilgrimage city at the time of Passover nor compromising with authorities there. His vindication in Mark comes in the words to the women at the tomb, brief as they are, announcing that he is alive and has gone ahead to Galilee. Like the Egyptian he is at large and will soon be seen.

But between the prophet's opening appearance when the sign is announced and the closing suppression and vindication, the story pattern about the prophet's sign has only one intermediate element, the gathering of the crowds. Can this single factor adequately explain the long and complex narrative of Mark? Though interpreters have favored readings of Mark that stress Jesus' role, the stories are in fact at least as much about how he is received. People follow the prophet in great numbers, and this very following mobilizes the authorities to destroy him. After a few days the town squares are too small for his crowds, and soon after the religious and political authorities are plotting to eliminate him (1:45; 3:6). This would seem to be enough about this prophet to show his touch with the crowds and bring on his suppression. But the story continues six times this long with more elaborate accounts, stronger accusations and crowds of thousands. This extension of the story (doubtless also with contractions) is not a unified literary achievement but an aggregation of accounts of Jesus' growing following, reflecting what could be the interests of successive tellers and their hearers in how the healed trust, how the disciples fear, and how Jesus fails to control news about himself while teaching the ways of God's kingdom. Finally what stands out is not any interpretive thread but the concrete events snowballing toward a climax of popular acclamation and official suppression. Meanwhile Jesus provokes the legal authorities, starts to heal Gentiles, and at Passover heads to Jerusalem predicting he will be killed.

In Jerusalem there may be a second beginning of the prophet's sign story. He appears as if for the first time, mounted and hailed by crowds, and he gives a very different sign by throwing those who are buying and selling out of the temple. Such a critique of worship practices was not strange for prophets, but here after days of debate he is betrayed by a disciple, tried by local and imperial courts, and crucified the following morning. Three days later his tomb is found empty. This time the five elements of the story have happened quickly: appearance, sign, crowds, suppression, vindication. At least after the temple's burning in 70 CE, Markan storytellers took Jesus' action there as a sign of its destruction, framing it with the story of a fig tree cursed for not bearing fruit (11:12–23).[40] The fulfillment of this second sign reasserts the credibility of Jesus' initial sign of God's coming rule which remains outstanding but empty after the hope of delivery from Rome is dashed. If the destruction foreseen by sign has taken place, can the deliverance foreseen by sign be far behind?

Though Mark is a gospel of action rather than interpretation, Jesus twice sits down to teach, and in each case he reinterprets a sign. First, God's coming rule is interpreted in parable as a sure and full harvest in spite of multiple bad soils, no productive work, and the smallest of seeds (4:1–34). This shifts the wartime focus on God's kingdom as Rome's defeat toward a broader vision of God's possibility at the point of human impossibility through the speaking and hearing of such news. Second, Jesus' sign of overturning the tables of power is interpreted to point beyond Jerusalem and its temple toward a glorious reversal at the arrival of the mortal one "after this tribulation" (13:3–37). In Mark the harvest and the transformation of power are yet to come. This means that the sequence of events from the prophet's arrival, the sign and the crowds through suppression to vindication is still happening, not only in its conclusion but from beginning to end. The prophet's task continues and is passed down to Jesus' followers because God's judgment and deliverance are not over. This is particularly evident in the second half of the gospel. Each prediction of Jesus' passion introduces a passion teaching to his disciples (8:31–9:1; 9:31–37; 10:32–45). Not only are John the Baptist and Jesus "delivered over," but so will be his followers (1:14; 9:31; 10:33; 14:18–21; 41–43; 13:9–13). Jesus' repeated instruction to them is "watch out," "stay alert" (13:33–37; 14:34–38).

4. Integration of Story Patterns

When the story pattern of Mark is seen in two ways, paradigmatically as *agōn* or conflict story and syntagmatically as story of a prophet's sign, there should be

---

[40] For further stories of prophets' signs of destruction from this period, see Wire, *Holy Lives*, 183–223.

greater clarity and depth of vision than either approach can provide alone. The conflict stories need not be relegated to a subordinate role as mere crowd-gatherers between the sign's announcement and its suppression. Since oral stories survive only when told, we can assume they must have been told continually from their beginnings, each functioning as the whole story about Jesus in the synchronic sense of the challenge met or the plight overcome. But once people were telling news of this prophet's sign, his death and his preceding them to Galilee, tellers would be favored who could bring multiple stories of God's controversy, Jesus' feats, and the disciples' struggles into the account of the sign they were watching for. This in turn intensified the conflict stories within a sequenced plot. And the listeners who favored one teller over others became the guardians of the tradition by cheering a fine account and curbing any telling that played loose with the stories they knew and the news they were spreading.

What both approaches to Mark's story pattern show in different ways, and intensify when taken together, is the unfinished nature of Mark's story, its character as news of something in process. Each account of God facing down Satan, Jesus taking on the authorities and human trust overcoming fear assumes the domination of the powers that be. At the same time, each telling of the prophet's sign is a claim that the suppressed and vindicated prophet was right and the sign of God's rule will yet be fulfilled. What is prefigured in the conflict stories and anticipated by the prophet's outstanding sign is that a new order is coming. The focus is not, however, on a future time but on the present process of telling the story that makes trust out of fear and mobilizes people toward the new reality. In this process it is not evident that the tellers or hearers sensed any contradiction between accounts of the feats that gathered the crowds and the suppression that followed, knowing as they did how empires handle such threats, and relying as they did on the women's news that the story was not over. This news had become their sustaining tradition while it continued to unfold in their telling.

Both the story patterns of repeated conflict and of successive signs reach their climax in the Jerusalem scenes. The harsh reality is that in spite of Jesus' repeated efforts to prepare his disciples for what would happen, he is betrayed, denied and deserted by them, turned against by the crowds, condemned by the Sanhedrin, delivered up by Pilate, reviled by those crucified with him and, in his own words, abandoned by God as he dies. This leaves the gospel as good news hanging on the thread of a rumor among women that a young man at the tomb said Jesus was raised and went ahead of them to Galilee.[41] How this can be enough to reverse the bitter outcome of this story is not apparent, but it seems to

---

[41] Galilee is alternately thought to represent the place of Jesus' ministry and their following (1:14–9:50) or the land of the Gentiles (cf. Matt 4:15). In addition it could be the place where they find themselves as war survivors in the 70s.

be so understood. Does the very fact that the gospel is being told show that some went and found him, so the speaker is confident that others can as well? But there is no story of someone finding Jesus, which may signal that God's kingdom has not yet come in power and remains hostage to human fear. But a way ahead has been pointed, not by Jesus' own trust which gave way to despair on the cross, but by God's act of raising and sending him ahead. This suggests that Jesus is to be seen by a follower the way God was seen by Moses from the cleft in the rock – not face to face as in the appearance stories, but from behind as the one being followed, as a mortal moving in God's way and leading others into trust, a trust rich enough to make them the good soil that produces a full harvest.

The risk here is extreme, as these storytellers make plain. If one death was not enough, how many will be enough? Who can demonstrate that Jesus was not deluded up until the end when he discovered that God would not rescue him? Is this the sacrifice of Isaac without the ram? In reaction some will reject any vision of the world as God's struggle with evil, choosing to see nature as neutral and humans able to live within it in life and in death. But the experience of those who tell the Markan story may not allow this. Their country is occupied by an imperial system geared for maximum exploitation, their chief leaders are corrupt, their people are possessed by fear. They must confront the reality they know. And they do it, to their credit, not with simplistic formulas of comfort, but with the account of a man who trusted God and died for it, and with the story of people who, to quote Mark on the disciples headed to Jerusalem, "were [...] shocked and afraid," and, nonetheless, "following" (10:32).

5. News as Tradition in Writing

It appears that news can be tradition as people pass on the story that orients them to what can yet happen because of what has just happened and what is now happening. But why might such tradition be written? How would this occur and what happens to the news at this point? Three possible triggers for writing Mark could be community conflict, social crisis, and the story's shift into a literate setting. The Lutheran tradition saw Mark's writer subordinating the miracle stories and their theology of glory to the passion story's theology of the cross. But the cross was hardly introduced by the writer. Kelber's *Oral and Written Gospel* takes Jesus' critique of the disciples, his family, and the prophets in Mark as the writer's opposition to their oral persuasion.[42] Yet it is not clear that criticism of these groups is focused on the oral medium itself, nor that it begins only with writing.[43]

---

[42] Kelber, *The Oral and the Written Gospel*, 96–105.

[43] See Joanna Dewey's response to Kelber's thesis and his rejoinder in Thatcher, *Jesus, the Voice, and the Text* (73–78, 249–52).

Social crises have been suggested as other possible reasons that the Markan tradition was written, whether in Palestine or in Rome. But persecution, war, or slavery is no time to arrange a handwriting project or to carry a codex. In contrast, the story told was consummately portable and persuasive, and did, in fact, spread when people scattered. The crisis of a great teller's death might trigger a transcription of the story, but there are no hints of this in Mark of the kind we find at the end of the fourth gospel (John 21:20–24). More likely the story arrived in a literate setting where a gospel codex could complement an Isaiah scroll or could be presented to a patron, not replacing the storytelling but affecting it over time.

To move from scribal motivations to methods, how traditions become written is suggested in A. N. Doane's four options: transcription during a performance, a performer's autograph, an imitation of traditional speech, and scribal re-performance.[44] Albert Lord observed that before electronic media transcription could not happen during performance without breaks intolerable for the speaker and hearers, and he found that the literate teller did not transcribe songs well from silent memory.[45] Third, an author imitating oral speech without very close attention to the story people knew would not find his work accepted in this setting.

The fourth option of scribal re-performance is the mode of writing that would most naturally follow a composition in performance. Here the scribe – who is a part of the traditional audience if not a performer himself, or else why would he transcribe? – takes on the responsibility to tell Mark in writing, that is, to engage his audience with its familiar tradition in a shifted setting. This means he works under the same conditions as previous tellers. Alan Kirk following Michael Fishbane speaks of scribal writing in Israel as "the continuation of the tradent dynamics that brought the work into existence."[46] The restrictions are set by the community whose tradition the scribe transmits because it will not accept a rendition that is not the story it remembers, yet he must make the story memorable. In this setting neither an exact-to-the-syllable transcription nor a free imitation would be thinkable. A second scribe who copies the first text will work within the same boundaries as long as he is functioning in the tradition's community. A text that moves outside the community will probably lose its value and disappear. But the community could begin to value the written text's letters, syllables and words more than its sentences, episodes and structures of

[44] A. N. Doane, "Oral Texts, Intertexts and Intratexts: Editing Old English," *Influence and Intertextuality in Literary History* (eds. J. Clayton and E. Rothstein; Madison: University of Wisconsin Press, 1991), 80–81.

[45] Lord, *Singer of Tales*, 126–29.

[46] A. Kirk, "Manuscript Tradition as a *Tertium Quid*: Orality and Memory in Scribal Practices," *Jesus, the Voice, and the Text*, 222–25; M. Fishbane, *Biblical Interpretation in Ancient Israel* (Oxford: Clarendon, 1985), 86–88, 412–13.

meaning.[47] Here the tenacity of the performer overpowers his creativity and he preserves what is old at the expense of engaging the new. The time when this happens may be located by the point when interpretation appears in addition to the tradition because the tradition is no longer able to interpret itself.[48]

To meet Markan scribes I decided to go back to single manuscripts rather than reading our Nestle-Aland composite text, hoping to see the flexibility among manuscripts that Kirk has recently called manuscript *mouvance*.[49] To my shock I found that there is no early manuscript of Mark. The only surviving Greek papyrus manuscript more than a few verses in length is Chester Beatty I (P45) of the third century which includes a good deal of Chapters 6 through 9 and shreds of four other chapters, but no line and no page is complete.[50] To get anything near a full text I had to settle for the great Greek manuscripts of the fourth century which present almost the whole Bible, and I adjusted my Nestle text to the original hand of the Sinaiticus by about three changes per page. Some Sinaiticus texts may be very old copies of copies, but do we know this for Mark? The early scribe I wanted to meet did not show his face, and I learned that I am dependent on a text that I cannot in good conscience call a scribal re-performance at all – collected, edited, and beautifully copied as it is, probably on imperial commission. We are that far from the telling of Mark, oral or scribal.

Now I concede what John Foley said that once offended me, that we cannot "assume without fear of jeopardizing the viability of the entire [oral tradition] enterprise, that the work as it survives represents what was without doubt an oral performance."[51] What we can say in the case of Mark is that the probability of composition and re-composition by favored tellers in community-monitored performance – oral and then for a time scribal – far outweighs the probability of one writer composing this Gospel alone from stories scattered for forty years. This means that our attention can now shift to those who were telling and then inscribing this story in its first century, and to how and why they told it.

In this connection we do not recognize how strongly we have been programmed by Luke's projection in Acts of the church expanding in and from

[47] E. C. Colwell, "Method of Evaluating Scribal Habits: A Study of P45, P66, P75," *Studies in Methodology in Textual Criticism of the New Testament* (Grand Rapids, MI: Eerdmans, 1969)106–24.

[48] J. Assmann, "Cultural Texts Suspended between Writing and Speech," *Religion and Cultural Memory: Ten Studies* (Stanford: Stanford University Press, 2006; German 2000), 101–21.

[49] A. Kirk, "Manuscript Tradition," 225–34, who attributes this usage to John Dagenais' adaptation for manuscripts of Paul Zumthor's term for oral tradition.

[50] *The Chester Beatty Biblical Papyri Descriptions and Texts of Twelve Manuscripts on Papyrus of the Greek Bible, Vol. 2: Fasciculus II, The Gospels and Acts* (ed. F. G. Kenyon; London: Emery Walker Limited, Text 1933, Plates 1934). Yet on this scribe see Colwell, *Studies*, 116–17

[51] J. M. Foley, "The Rhetorical Persistence of Traditional Forms," in *The Singer of Tales in Performance* (Bloomington, Indiana: Indiana University Press, 1995), 81.

Jerusalem through the apostles' public preaching. Yet even Luke portrays only Peter and John in this role, concedes broader influence to the seven Hellenists, and soon shifts his focus onto Paul whom he does not consider an apostle. Other scenarios need to be proposed and tested, including the two below projected from a Mark composed in performance. One depends heavily on early Christian traditions, the other on internal Markan evidence.

In the first scenario the second-century title of this gospel is taken as an indication that its scribe was named Mark, since this name added no special authority. The name in turn suggests a possible origin of the narrative in the Jerusalem church of Mary the mother of the John Mark featured in Acts 12–15. Supporting evidence that Mark presents a tradition distinct from Paul's gospel is the split between Paul and Barnabas who is associated with Mark, a dispute Luke attributes to Paul's intransigence while Paul claims he alone acted with integrity (Acts 15: 36–41; Gal 2:13; Col 4:10). Peter, on the other hand, seems to be depicted living in the home of Mary of Jerusalem when Luke says he returned there after escaping from jail and then left quickly, slipping out of Jerusalem soon after (Acts 12:6–19). Though no longer attested in Jerusalem by mid-century, Peter's name is linked to Mark in 1 Peter 5:13 and in Papias according to Eusebius (*Hist. eccl.* 3. 39. 15). When the Jerusalem church flees in wartime and/or when Mary dies, Mark could be drawn back from mission in some Greek-speaking city (Phlm 24; Col 4:10; 1 Pet 5:13; 2 Tim 4:11) to transcribe the gospel she has told.

A different scenario takes its clue from this gospel's orientation to Galilee. In Mark Jesus is depicted living strictly in Galilee, except for forays north with his followers to escape the crowds, until his only and final visit to Jerusalem. This suggests Galilee as the provenance for this tradition. Here the stories could have continued circulating in an area where some Jewish towns survived through the turmoil of the first and second centuries and became a base for later rabbis. The gospel ends with an instruction, first to the disciples and then to the women, to follow Jesus back to Galilee where they will see him (14:28; 16:7). The women's vision at the tomb, like that of the disciples on the mountain, is too bright for them and they are afraid, "telling nothing to anyone" (16:5–8; 9:2–6). But their account later surfaces, suggesting a sustained experience of Jesus among Galilean women that became a composition site for this gospel. Though Luke/ Acts adheres to a strictly Jerusalem resurrection and church birth story, Matthew and John integrate Jerusalem and Galilee resurrection stories and each tells of Jesus himself appearing to Galilean women/an (Matt 28:8–10; John 20:11–18). Only Paul omits all mention of women in his resurrection account (1 Cor 15:5–8), and he tells no event from Jesus' life in Galilee, indicating how separately these traditions were developing in the early years when he met with Peter and James (Gal 1:18–19). We lack the name of a favored teller of the Galilean tradition. John focuses on Mary of Magdala at the tomb, while the other gospels take pains to give the names of several witnesses (Matt 28:1; Mark 16:1; Luke 24:10), suggesting that this story of Jesus could have been told by a number of women. Someone named Mark transcribes the story when it is known in Greek-speaking cities.

The History of the Closure of Biblical Texts

Werner Kelber

1. Prologue

In an essay entitled "Technology Outside Us and Inside Us" Walter Ong[1] developed basic principles of a media-sensitive hermeneutics that have informed my work over the years and that provide a theoretical underpinning for this paper. Writing and print, as well as electronic devices, according to Ong's thesis, are technologies that produce something in the sensible world outside us but also affect the way our minds work. Handwriting slowly undermined and partially replaced the predominantly oral lifeworld, print drastically altered major aspects of Western civilization, and the electronic medium is about to usher in a transformation of global dimensions. External changes have always been plainly in evidence, especially at epochal threshold events such as the alphabetic revolution in ancient Greece around 700 B. C. E.,[2] or the fifteenth century shift from script to print[3] – events which scarcely left a single sphere of human activities untouched. But, and this is Ong's point, we have not been sufficiently aware of the depths to which media technologies have penetrated the human psyche:[4]

> Writing, print, and electronic devices of various sorts
> are all devised to deal, directly or indirectly, with
> the word and with thought itself. Of all technologies,
> they affect man's interior most. Indeed, in a curious
> way they enter into man's interior itself, directly
> affecting the way in which his consciousness and
> unconsciousness manage knowledge, the management
> of his thought processes, and even his personal
> self awareness.

---

[1] W. Ong, "Technology Outside Us and Inside Us," *Faith and Contexts,* vol. 1 (eds. Th. J. Farrell and P. A. Soukup; Atlanta: Scholars Press, 1992), 189–208.

[2] E. A. Havelock, *The Literate Revolution in Greece and Its Cultural Consequences* (Princeton: Princeton University Press, 1982).

[3] E. L. Eisenstein, *The Printing Press as an Agent of Change,* 2 vols. (Cambridge: Cambridge University Press., 1979)

[4] Ong, "Technology Outside Us," 194.

Chirography, typography, and electronics are, for Ong, an "interiorized phenomenon, something registering inside humans,"[5] affecting cognitive faculties,
patterning thought processes, altering modes of discourse and research, reinforcing, complexifying and even deconstructing reasoning processes.

For some time now my own work in biblical studies has examined ways in
which our ritualized print habits of reading and writing, editing and authoring
have – until recently – stylized our perceptions of ancient and medieval modes
of communications. All along, a concern of mine has been to highlight the
magnitude of what I have termed the typographical captivity which has shaped
our methodological tools, sharpened our critical methods, and swayed our assumptions about ancient texts. In terms of media sensibilities it is no exaggeration to claim that print was the medium in which modern biblical scholarship
was born and raised, and from which it has acquired its formative methodological habits, its intellectual tools and, last not least, its historical theories. For all
practical purposes, it was not handwritten manuscripts but the print Bible, the
first mechanically constructed major book of print technology, that has served,
and continues to serve, as the centerpiece of modern biblical scholarship.

Mindful of the power of media, in the ancient and medieval past, in modernity and in current biblical scholarship, this paper attempts an overview of the
history of the biblical texts from their oral and papyrological beginnings all the
way to their triumphant apotheosis in print culture. In macro-historical perspectives, a trajectory is observable that runs from scribal multiformity, verbal
polyvalency, and oral, memorial sensibilities toward an increasing chirographic
control over the material surface of biblical texts, culminating in the autosemantic print authority of the Bible.

2. The Mouvance of Tradition

A few years ago David Carr published an exceedingly ambitious book which
discusses ways in which people in ancient Near Eastern civilizations produced,
worked, and lived with texts, or, more specifically, ways in which writing and
literature functioned orally, scribally, and memorially in predominantly educational contexts. In *Writing on the Tablet of the Heart* Carr[6] has constructed a
paradigm of the ancient verbal arts which will serve as a useful starting point for
my deliberations.

Writing, texts, and literacy, Carr suggested, have to be understood as core
constituents of educational processes. From Mesopotamia to Egypt, and from

---

[5] Ong, "Technology Outside Us," 191.
[6] D. M. Carr, *Writing on the Tablet of the Heart: Origins of Scripture and Literature* (Oxford:
Oxford University Press, 2005).

Israel to Greece and into the Hellenistic period, literacy and education were closely interconnected phenomena. Indeed, literacy and education were virtually synonymous as long as it is understood that neither concept conveys what it has come to mean in the print culture of European and North American modernity. Concepts derived from the contemporary experience of literacy in the West are too narrowly focused on the technical ability of reading and writing. In the ancient Near Eastern cultures what mattered most was the kind of literacy that went beyond alphabetic competence to include training in and mastery of the tradition. A literate person was not necessarily an alphabetically skilled individual but one knowledgeable in the tradition. Education likewise entailed more, and often something other, than training in the rudiments of writing and reading. The principal aim of education was the internalization of texts on people's minds and hearts for the purpose of generating and/or reinforcing what today we might call the cultural identity of a people. Skilled scribes were expected to possess or acquire mastery of their core writings by way of memorization and recitation. Scrolls, therefore, functioned less as reference systems or text books and more as memory devices or, to use Carr's preferred term, as instruments of "enculturation."

Carr's "enculturation" model has no counterpart in today's Western world of communications and it is, I should like to claim, unlike many conventional concepts of textual composition and transmission currently in use in the scholarly study of ancient Near Eastern, classical and biblical literature. Recitation and memorization, essential features for Carr's reconstruction, are predominantly unacknowledged in the historical, critical paradigm, and the oral, performative dimension is still regularly bypassed. Biblical criticism, with rare exceptions, tends to view the tradition predominantly as a literary one, imagining a tight nexus of textual interfacing, implying that oral performance was a mere variant of writing. Disposed to put the emphasis on writing and texts, the historical paradigm tends to predicate a textual world that is both constituted and constrained by literary predecessors and datable sources.[7]

Carr's "enculturation" paradigm seeks to capture the behavior of the ancient manuscript tradition, biblical texts included, from a new angle. A whole edifice of historical conceptual tools is at stake. Ideas formed around editing, copying, revision, and recension are all subject to rethinking and may be used only with reservation. Notions about authorship, tradition, composition and originality or authenticity, all deeply entrenched in the historical paradigm, require reconsideration. One of the corollaries of Carr's model is that the materiality of communication as it manifests itself in the technology of writing and in the physical

---

[7] U. Eco in *The Name of the Rose* has memorialized the premise of intertextuality: "Until then I thought each book spoke of the things, human and divine, that lie outside books. Now I realized that not infrequently books speak of books: it is as if they spoke among themselves." U. Eco, *The Name of the Rose* (San Diego: Harcourt Brace Jovanovich, 1983), 286.

format and layout of writing surfaces is taken into serious account. For example, one needs to devote more critical thought to the fact that the scroll was virtually useless for strictly literary information retrieval, source critical extrapolations, reference checks and cross referencing. It was useful mainly to people who knew more or less what to look for, to people, in other words, who had already stored the content in their minds and hearts. In short, Carr's "enculturation" paradigm summons us to construct a new theory of the verbal arts in the ancient communications world.

There can be no question, texts were in fact subject to a high degree of literal copying; many were stored and consulted for reference purposes. And yet, the notion that scribes exclusively copied extant texts in literal fashion, or juggled multiple texts that were physically present to them, is in many instances not a fitting model for the communications dynamics in the ancient world. The core traditions in particular, namely those texts that mattered most educationally, were not consistently carried forward by way of literal copying. Rather, scribes who were literate in the core curriculum carried texts as mental templates. They had ingested the tradition consisting of one or more than one text and were thus able to write or rewrite the tradition without any need for a physical text. Importantly, rewriting – namely the reactivation of texts – was a hallmark of the ancient enculturation process. Thus when the historical paradigm discovers textual stratification, postulating literary sources, stages, or layers, one will in many, though not all, instances more aptly speak of compositional phases characteristic of the process of rewriting culturally significant traditions.

It is difficult to arrive at a historically valid terminology that captures the dynamics of what appears to have been a generally fluid, oral-scribal and memorial transmission. Biblical studies in particular still lack the language to define appropriately the ancient media paradigm of the interfacing of orality and scribality with memory. I have found the designation of *mouvance*[8] helpful in describing the nature of the Jewish and Christian biblical traditions, especially in their respective initial stages. The term was initially coined by the medievalist Paul Zumthor who applied it to the manuscript tradition of French medieval poetry. Observing a high level of textual variation involving not only modifications of dialect and wording but also more substantial rewritings and the loss, replacement, or rearrangement of whole sections of a piece, he introduced *mouvance* to characterize this textual mobility.[9] Authorial anonymity and textual mobility

---

[8] To my knowledge, Alan Kirk was the first to apply the term to Second Temple Judaism, to early Christianity, and to the early rabbinic tradition. A. Kirk, "Manuscript Tradition as *Tertium Quid*: Orality and Memory in Scribal Practices," *Jesus, the Voice, and the Text* (ed. Tom Thatcher; Waco: Baylor University Press, 2008), 215–34.

[9] As Zumthor described it, the medieval poetic material spread both temporally and geographically "not merely by virtue of the text's physical movements as it circulates in manuscripts or in the mouths of reciters and is handed down to posterity, but also as a result of an

were, in his view, connected features. Anonymity suggested that a text was not regarded as the intellectual property of a single, individual author but was subject to recurring rewritings. By analogy, large parts of the ancient Near Eastern and Mediterranean textual tradition, including the early manuscript traditions of both the Hebrew Bible and the New Testament, may be understood as *mouvance*, e. g., as a (living) tradition in process of persistent regeneration. From the perspective of the stability of later critical editions, we shall see, the early masoretic and Jesus traditions can appropriately be described as *mouvance*, e. g., as living tradition subject to reactivation and revisions.

3. Jewish and Christian Textual Pluriformity

Re-thinking the Jewish and Christian biblical tradition from the perspective of *mouvance*, I commence with a reflection on the genesis of the masoretic Textus Receptus, the normative text of the Hebrew Bible. When we study the Hebrew Bible we are handed the Masoretic Text, and when we learn elementary Hebrew, we are confronted with Tiberian Hebrew, the linguistic system of the masoretic scholars who produced the text between the seventh and tenth century C. E. All biblical scholars, Jews and Christians alike, grow up on the masoretic Textus Receptus, a text, moreover that was reproduced numerous times in carefully, handwritten copies. We are all familiar with the conventional picture, prevalent in many Introductions to the Bible, of a Jewish scribe bent over his manuscript while copying the Torah in meticulous fashion. This picture of the scribal expert, reinforced by its reproduction in countless print text books, continues to affect the conventional understanding of Judaism as a religion of the book. Sensibility to oral-scribal dynamics may modify and certainly complicate this picture.

It is well known that prior to the discovery of the Dead Sea Scrolls no single manuscript of the Hebrew Bible/Old Testament existed that was older than the ninth century C. E. With the availability of the Dead Sea Scrolls we have been unexpectedly projected back to an early state in the making of what came to be the Hebrew Bible. Written roughly between the first century B. C. E. and the first century C. E., these Scrolls are a millennium removed from what used to be the oldest available copy of the Masoretic Text. A past hidden from us for centuries has been lifted into historical consciousness and it has facilitated a new approach to the compositional history of the Masoretic Text.

Scholarship had some difficulty facing up to the new textual realties that were provided by the Scrolls. How deeply it was beholden to conventional patterns of

---

essential instability in medieval texts themselves." P. Zumthor, *Oral Poetry: An Introduction* (Minneapolis: University of Minnesota Press, 1990), 45–46.

thought may be demonstrated on the example of the famous Isaiah scroll, one of the best preserved among the Dead Sea manuscripts. Millar Burrows, eminent representative of the first generation of Qumran experts, observed a remarkable agreement between the ancient Isaiah scroll and its Masoretic Textual version. In some cases, where the Isaiah scroll differed from the Textus Receptus (in terms of orthography, morphology and lexical items), he postulated copying mistakes that pointed to an inferior textual quality of the ancient scroll. In other cases, he judged variants of the ancient scroll to be superior and adopted them as a means of amending and improving the masoretic standard. In either case, therefore, he was inclined to evaluate the ancient Isaiah scroll not as an entity in its own right, but rather from the perspective of the established norm of the Textus Receptus, eager to assert that the text of the Isaiah scroll "confirms the antiquity and authenticity of the Masoretic Text."[10] In short, the centrality of the masoretic Textus Receptus was the criterion for scholarly judgments.

Burrows' eminent textual scholarship, one recognizes in retrospect, operated under distinct text critical and theological premises. As far as text criticism was concerned, he held that its primary objective was "to detect and eliminate errors in the text as it has come down to us, and so to restore, as nearly as possible, what was originally written by the authors of the books."[11] In different words, text criticism, in his view, was designed to recover the original text. It is a premise ill-suited, we shall see, to comprehend and appreciate the copious nature of the manuscript evidence. Theologically, he insisted, that in spite of the fact that the transmission of scriptural texts has "not come down to us through the centuries unchanged," the "essential truth and the will of God revealed in the Bible, however, have been preserved unchanged through all the vicissitudes in the transmission of the text."[12] This, too, represents a position that is not well suited to face up to the nature of tradition as it appeared in light of the Dead Sea Scrolls. Burrows' premises generated an optical illusion that made us see the new textual evidence for something other than it really was.

As more and more variables of biblical texts were identified at Qumran, the notion of a Masoretic Text existing in the period roughly of the first century B. C. E. was increasingly called into question. A sense of *mouvance*, and active transcription of tradition is ever more difficult for us to overlook. Textual pluriformity had to be accounted for as a phenomenon *sui generis*. Few experts have taken it more seriously than Eugene Ulrich, the chief editor of the Qumran scrolls. Far from disregarding, explaining away or rationalizing textual variability, he, along with others, has moved it to center stage: "The question dominating the discussion of the history of the biblical text is how to explain the plu-

---

[10] M. Burrows, *The Dead Sea Scrolls* (New York: Viking Press, 1955), 314.

[11] Burrows, *The Dead Sea Scrolls*, 301.

[12] Burrows, *The Dead Sea Scrolls*, 320

riformity observable in the biblical manuscripts from Qumran, the MT, and the versions."[13] Textual pluriformity is now a dominant issue.

The scholarly assimilation of the new textual evidence is still very much in progress. As a result of some fifty years of intense academic labors, however, a number of points seem certain. One, the textual condition of the Dead Sea Scrolls is not specific to that community but appears to be typical of Judaism in general at that period in history. By and large, the fuller textual evidence with regard to scriptural texts – the Dead Sea Scrolls, the Samaritan Pentateuch, the Septuagint, the New Testament, and Josephus in his dealings with scriptural materials – "demonstrate[s] bountifully that there were variable literary editions of the books of Scripture in the Second Temple period."[14] As far as the ancient scriptural traditions are concerned, variability does not represent an exceptional behavior. Two, one needs to exercise caution in stigmatizing the variants as secondary, aberrant, deficient, wild, or non-biblical. All too often, these are judgments based on the criterion of later standards of normativity. Textual pluriformity was an acceptable way of textual life at that time. Three, the textual situation at Qumran does not reveal text critical efforts in the sense of comparing and selecting variants for the purpose of arriving at a norm. The community appears to have lived in textual pluriformity. Four, there is no evidence for the masoretic Textus Receptus having achieved the status of normativity in the Second Temple period. Textual pluriformity was a way of life at a time when both Christianity and rabbinic Judaism were in their formative stages. Five, the text critical search for "the original text" is not only fraught with technical, philological difficulties but, more importantly, contrary to the dynamics of the textual realities on the ground.[15] Six, just as many of us have come to question the notion of "normative Judaism" prior to the Second Revolt, 132–135 C. E., so will we now have to be skeptical about the concept of a single "normative biblical text" in that period. Seven, the consequences of Roman imperialism were devastating: destruction of Qumran in 68 C. E., destruction of the Jerusalem temple in 70 C. E., destruction of Masada in 74 C. E. The political realities at the time were anything but conducive to sustained scholarly labors aimed at accomplishing a standard text. Eight, scribes were not merely copyists loyal to the letter of the text, but creative traditionists as well. This is the point where the picture of scribes meticulously copying the Torah needs to be modified. Nine,

---

[13] E. Ulrich, *The Dead Sea Scrolls and the Origins of the Bible* (Grand Rapids: Eerdmans, 1999), 80.

[14] Ulrich, *Dead Sea Scrolls*, 9–10.

[15] Ulrich, *Dead Sea Scrolls*, 15 has raised a crucial question for the reconceptualization of the project of text criticism: "should not the object of the text criticism of the Hebrew Bible be, not the single (and textually arbitrary?) collection of Masoretic texts of the individual books, but the organic, developing, pluriform Hebrew text – different for each book – such as the evidence indicates?"

clearly there is in Second Temple Judaism broad reference to the Law, and the Law and the Prophets, but we should not think of them as "biblical" authorities as if "the Bible" in its canonized sense had already been in existence. In the words of James Barr, "the time of the Bible was a time when the Bible was not yet there."[16] Not only was "the Bible" not in existence, but at Qumran, Enochic literature was no less important than Deuteronomy, and Jubilees just as vital as Isaiah. Ten, we can be certain that in the Second Temple period two or three textual editions of the Pentateuch were in circulation. But when we accord them canonical, or semi-canonical status we are probably making retrospective judgments reconfiguring history according to later developments and categories.

Perhaps the Qumran evidence may be assimilated into a new historical paradigm as far as the relations between the masoretic norm and scriptural (rather than biblical) traditions were concerned. Instead of imagining a densely intertextual web with the Masoretic Text at center stage and biblical manuscripts gravitating toward it, we might envision multiple scriptural versions, including what came to be the masoretic norm, finding their hermeneutical rationale in recitation, oral explication and memorization, with some textual bodies such as the Pentateuch and prophetic literature assuming authoritative significance.

It is in the context of this scribal, scriptural environment of textual *mouvance* that we will have to grasp the early Jesus tradition as an insistently pluriform phenomenon.

In terms that are sensitive to media realities, one might say Jesus of Nazareth presented himself as a vocal, rhetorical authority. Viewing him as an aphoristic, parabolic teacher, historical critical scholarship has made great efforts in retrieving the *ipsissima verba*, his so-called original sayings. Let us see how the search for the original sayings looks from the perspective of genuinely oral sensibilities. When Jesus, the aphoristic, parabolic teacher, recited a story or saying at one place, and then journeyed to another place, to recite, with audience adjustments, that same story or saying to a different audience, this second performance cannot be understood as a secondary version, or copy, of the original rendition. Rather, the second rendition is as much an authentic performance as the first one. This suggests that the notion of the one original word makes no sense in oral performance. Likewise, the concept of "variants" is problematic as far as oral performers in the ancient world are concerned because there is no one "original" from which variants could deviate. In the predominantly oral culture in which Jesus operated each oral rendition of a story or saying was an original, indeed the original. While historical critics are inclined to sift through the textual tradition in search for the one original, oral culture operates with a plurality of originals. More is involved here than a mere change from singular to

---

[16] J. Barr, *Holy Scripture: Canon, Authority, Criticism* (Philadelphia: Westminster, 1983), 1.

plural. The coexistence of multiple original renditions suggests equiprimordiality, a principle that reflects cultural sensibilities that are quite different from and contrary to the notion of the one, original speech. One of the first Western scholars to fully conceptualize the notion that in oral tradition there was no such thing as an original rendition and variants thereof was Albert Lord.[17]

The early chirographic rendition of the Jesus tradition, no less than the scribal tradition preceding the Masoretic text, is characterized by a remarkable pluriformity. In both instances, fixation on an assumed textual normativity or originality has blinded us to grasp and appreciate the existent scribal tradition in its own right and on its own terms. As far as the early papyrological evidence of Jesus sayings is concerned, it, too, appears to be characterized by fluidity rather than by foundational stability. The text critic David Parker has stated the case provocatively: "The further back we go, the greater seems to be the degree of variation."[18] Parker adds that this situation is "not an unfortunate aberration" but rather "part of the way in which they [the Christian scribes] copied their codices."[19] While his is not the only way to explain the phenomenon of scribal fluidity, Parker's observation nonetheless appears at variance with historical critical premises about tradition. While historical and textual criticism by and large operates on the assumption of a foundational text at the beginning, the actual scribal evidence on the ground suggests pluriformity at the outset and something akin to a foundational text at a later, secondary stage in the tradition. The analogy to the early history of the textual tradition of the Hebrew Bible is striking.

If, by way of an example cited by Parker,[20] one sifts through the papyrological evidence of Jesus' sayings on marriage and divorce one recognizes that the problem is not simply one of explaining the differences among Mark 10, Matthew 5 and 19, and Luke 16, an issue well known to biblical scholars. Assessment of the full scribal evidence confronts us with both an amount and degree of variability that goes far beyond Markan, Matthean, and Lukan adaptations and is not readily explicable by a single textual genealogical tree that would take us back to the one root saying. The recovery of the original rendition would seem to be an unattainable goal. In Parker's words, "a single authoritative pronouncement [by Jesus on marriage and divorce] is irrecoverable."[21] Perhaps one should add that the project of retrieving the single original saying is contrary to the intentions of the tradition. We have no excuse for reducing the tradition to

---

[17] A. Lord, *The Singer of Tales* (Harvard Studies in Comparative Literature 24; Cambridge: Harvard University Press, 1960, repr. 2000), 101.

[18] D. C. Parker, *The Living Text of the Gospels* (Cambridge: Cambridge University Press, 1997), 188.

[19] Parker, *The Living Text of the Gospels,* 188.

[20] Parker, *The Living Text of the Gospels,* 75–94.

[21] Parker, *The Living Text of the Gospels,* 183.

simplicity where there is complexity, and for claiming single originality where there are multiple originalities.

It is worth noting that the reason for the *mouvance* of the Jesus tradition is not that these sayings were considered unimportant. To the contrary, as Parker rightly observed, the "basic reason for the complexity in the passages [on marriage and divorce] [...] and in many others of Jesus' sayings is precisely the importance accorded them."[22] Issues pertaining to marriage, divorce and remarriage have been pressing ethical concerns in the past as much as they are urgent matters for our modern churches. But it is precisely the great importance attributed to these matters that accounts for the variability in the rendition of the sayings tradition. In Carr's terms, texts that mattered most in terms of educational knowledge and cultural identity were most likely to be subject to frequent rewritings. It was precisely because of the ever-present relevance of sayings on marriage, divorce and remarriage that a verbatim transmission was not the most desirable mode of securing the tradition. To transmit Jesus' word(s) faithfully meant to keep them in balance with social life, needs and expectations. In paraphrasing a statement by Ong (in response to a student's question why Jesus did not resort to writing) one might say that his (Jesus') sayings were considered far too important to be frozen into scribal still life.

It is easier to explain, Parker observed, what the early Jesus tradition is not, and "harder to find a suitable language to describe what it is."[23] If we say that this tradition eschewed stability we have characterized it negatively from the point of view of later developments. If one describes it, with Parker, as a "free" and "living" tradition,[24] one has arrived at an appropriately positive definition but still lacks explanation for the phenomenon. In a footnote, Parker himself adduces Ong's observation that manuscripts "were in dialogue with the world outside their own borders. They remained closer to the give-and-take of oral expression."[25] The validity of Ong's remark manifests itself with particular force in the case of the early scriptural traditions of both the Hebrew Bible and the Jesus tradition. When viewing the early scribal tradition of Jesus sayings from the perspective of oral-scribal dynamics, it appears to be operative at the intersection with speech, or more precisely perhaps, it has every indication of being enmeshed with and empowered by oral dynamics. In four ways at least, this early scribal tradition functioned in keeping with the oral, performative sensibilities: like oral performance, the early scribal tradition was made up of variables and multiforms; it was, secondly, constituted by plural originals not by singular originality; thirdly, it sought, despite its chirographic materiality, to stay with the

---

[22] Parker, *The Living Text of the Gospels*, 75.

[23] Parker, *The Living Text of the Gospels*, 200.

[24] Parker, *The Living Text of the Gospels*, 188.

[25] W. Ong, *Orality and Literacy. The Technologizing of the Word.* (London: Methuen, 1982; repr. 1988), 132.

flux of temporality; and fourthly, it enacted tradition that was not transmission per se, but composition in tradition. Both in terms of compositional intent and audience adjustment, the early scribal tradition of Jesus sayings still operated according to basically oral dynamics.

One should take note here that the model of Second Temple scribalism in so far as it is characterized by pluriformity and oral dynamism, has been observed in the rabbinic tradition as well. Taking advantage of the developing field of orality-scribality studies, recent books by Martin Jaffee and Elizabeth Shanks Alexander have genuinely advanced our understanding of the scribal production and transmission, recitation, and reception of the rabbinic texts.[26] At Qumran and in the post–70 C. E. rabbinic tradition, Jaffee explained, the scrolls functioned in an oral-traditional environment, where they were publicly recited and in a secondary discourse explicated. Rabbinic scribes and teachers drew on the oral-performative tradition for textual compositions which in turn were subject to re-oralization. In Jaffee's view, we should imagine the rabbinic tradition as "a continuous loop of manuscript and performance,"[27] which never yielded a ground zero on the basis of which the original instruction or the one authentic text was recoverable. In keeping with Jaffee's approach, Alexander used the oral conceptual lens to focus not, or not exclusively, on the transmissional and interpretive processes of the Mishnah, the foundational document of rabbinic Judaism, but primarily on its "performative effect", trying "to imagine what would *result* from performing its materials."[28] Developing a concept of the ancient transmitters of the early rabbinic materials as active shapers rather than passive tradents of the tradition, she concluded that the pedagogical benefit of the mishnaic performances lay not merely in the transmission of content but in "imparting a method of legal analysis"[29] that trained the students to practice modes of legal analysis on their own.

When set against the background of the ancient Near Eastern and Mediterranean culture of communication, the performative-chirographic dynamics of the early scriptural materials of the Hebrew Bible, the Jesus sayings, and the rabbinic tradition make good sense: by and large they were embedded in an oral biosphere where scribal-oral-scribal interfaces were the rule. It was the operative logic of these traditions to reactivate (not repeat!) themselves rather than to

---

[26] M. S. Jaffee, *Torah in the Mouth: Writing and Oral Tradition in Palestinian Judaism, 200 BCE – 400 CE* (Oxford: Oxford University Press, 2001). E. Shanks Alexander, *Transmitting Mishnah: The Shaping Influence of Oral Tradition* (Cambridge: Cambridge University Press, 2006). An early driving force in approaching rabbinics from hermeneutical and oral-scribal perspectives was S. D. Fraade, *From Tradition to Commentary. Torah and Its Interpretation in the Midrash Sifre to Deuteronomy* (Albany: State University of New York Press, 1991).

[27] Jaffee, *Torah in the Mouth*, 124.

[28] Alexander, *Transmitting Mishnah*, 169.

[29] Alexander, *Transmitting Mishnah*, 171.

reach for closure. To comprehend their operations, especially in their early stages, we should think of recurrent performativity rather than intertextuality.

4. Codex and Canon

Undoubtedly, the well-documented early use of the codex in the Christian tradition provided a technological innovation that was to be instrumental in ushering in wide-ranging cultural changes. Many of these changes were slow in coming and not immediately effective. On the macro-level the codex paved the way for the media transfer from the chirographic to the typographic identity of the book, unwittingly mediating the Bible's eventual apotheosis in print culture. On the micro-level it served as a convenient storage place for depositing numerous texts in a single book, and provided a more efficient access than the scroll. No doubt, in so far as the codex supplied the base for multiple and miscellaneous textual items in a single volume it created the material condition for the biblical canon. However, the causal connection between codex and canon must not be pressed too far. Illustrious fourth century codices such as Sinaiticus, Alexandrinus, Vaticanus and the fifth century Ephraemi Rescriptus, for example – frequently invoked as illustrations of unified Bibles – tend to blind us into assuming that volumes containing the whole Bible were common practice. Yet, not only were these codices "[...] not produced as one *volume* in our sense of the word,"[30] but books carrying the whole Bible were the exception rather than the rule in ancient and medieval history. Even complete Greek New Testaments were relatively rare. The full canonical implications of the codex were only slowly realized and in the end it was print technology that finalized the canonical authority of the Bible.

But the format of the codex had a more subtle, less widely acknowledged, impact on the verbal art and on human consciousness. Compared with the scroll, it provided a more stable material surface which in turn encouraged experimentation with the newly acquired writing space. Below we shall have occasion to observe how techniques for formatting and arranging materials were developed which, combined with the convenient page-turning practice, were ideally suited to focus the mind on comparative readings and cross-referencing, and to encourage habits which in turn affected the perception of texts and textually perceived traditions. Thus, in taking advantage of the book format and exploring its writing space, the codex created opportunities for textuality coming into its own. In terms of the principles enunciated in Ong's essay on "Technology Outside Us and Inside Us," cited at the outset, one could say that the codex helped interiorize textuality in ways not previously experienced.

---

[30] Parker, *The Living Text of the Gospels*, 195.

Canonicity is a topic that has for a long time commanded wide-ranging interests in biblical studies, history of religion, and more recently in literary criticism.[31] It seems agreed that the canonization of both the Jewish and the Christian Bible was a process that extended over centuries. The Jewish canon came into existence roughly between 200 B. C. E. and 200 C. E., a period that is partially synchronous with Second Temple Judaism. The Christian canon reached a semblance of agreed uniformity in the fourth century, but a dogmatic articulation of canon and canonical authority did not occur until the Council of Trent (1546 C. E.).

In the case of the Christian canon, something of a modern scholarly consensus about the criteria and rationale for canonicity appears to have been reached. Among the criteria, apostolicity, orthodoxy, and customary usage of texts are cited by many. The reasons for canon formation are usually seen in a defense against Marcionism, gnosticism, and Montanism. One notes that the overall argument falls along the lines of orthodoxy versus heresiology, categories that are no longer quite fashionable in current historical scholarship.

From a broadly cultural perspective one might suggest that the canon formation, both in Judaism and in Christianity, has to be understood against the background of the ideational and textual pluralism that was characteristic of Second Temple Judaism. Jan Assmann[32] has seen this quite clearly. The need for canonicity, he reasoned, arises out of the experience of an excessive textual pluralism and lack of ideational uniformity which undermine the *raison d'etre* of the tradition. In that situation, the canon responds to the "Bedürfnis, zu verhindern, dass 'anything goes', eine Angst vor Sinnverlust durch Entropie."[33] The selective privileging of texts, therefore, manifests a will to curtail entropy, that tendency, lodged in the tradition, toward diffusion and exhaustion of energy. To define this particular canonical function, Assmann has coined the phrase of the "Bändigung der Varianz,"[34] a taming of the phenomenon of variance. From this perspective, one may view the canon as a means of safeguarding tradition by controlling and defining it, and thereby (re)asserting the cultural identity of a people. Canonicity thus understood signified an approach to the pluriform scribal tradition via selectivity and exclusivity. It secured cultural identity, but it did so, and this is a crucial argument of this essay, at the price of

---

[31] Th. von Zahn, *Geschichte des Neutestamentlichen Kanons*, 2 vols. (Erlangen and Leipzig, 1888–92). J. Leipoldt, *Geschichte des Neutestamentlichen Kanons*, 2 vols. (Leipzig, 1907–8); W. G. Kümmel, *Introduction to the New Testament* (14th ed.; trans. A. J. Mattill; Nashville: Abingdon Press, 1965), 334–58. H. Y. Gamble, *The New Testament Canon: Its Making and Meaning* (Philadelphia: Fortress Press, 1985); *Canons* (ed. R. von Hallberg; Chicago: University of Chicago Press, 1983).

[32] J. Assmann, *Das kulturelle Gedächtnis: Schrift, Erinnerung und politische Identität in frühen Hochkulturen* (Munich: Beck, 1992), 103–29.

[33] Assmann, *Das kulturelle Gedächtnis*, 123.

[34] Assmann, *Das kulturelle Gedächtnis*, 123.

closing the textual borders. Viewed against the *mouvance* of the Jewish and Christian textual tradition, the creation of the canon marks a principally authoritative and unmistakably reductive move.

In highlighting early triumphs of textual rationality, we are turning to Origen's *Hexapla* and Eusebius' *Canon Tables*. In the words of Anthony Grafton and Megan Williams, Origen's *Hexapla* "was one of the greatest single monuments of Roman scholarship, and the first serious product of the application to Christian culture of the tools of Greek philology and criticism."[35] In the perspectives we have been developing, the *Hexapla* is a prime example of a sophisticated utilization of the potentials of the codex by way of experimenting with format and layout and implementing new forms of textual arrangements. It is, in the words of Grafton and Williams, a "milestone in the history of the book," even though "its form, its contents, and above all its purpose remains unclear."[36]

As the titular designation implies, the *Hexapla* was a codex, or rather a series of almost forty codices, which arranged different versions of the text of the Jewish Bible in six parallel, vertical columns: the Hebrew version, the Greek transliteration of the Hebrew rendition, the Greek versions of Aquila (a proselyte to Judaism), Symmachus (an Ebionite), the Septuagint (LXX), and Theodotion (a Hellenistic Jew), in that order. There is now broad agreement that what prompted the massive project of the *Hexapla* was the conundrum of textual pluriformity that Origen encountered. "The reason for the Hexapla," states Ulrich, "was that the multiplicity of texts and text traditions proved problematic for one espousing the principle that, because the text was inspired, there must be a single text of the Bible."[37] Grafton and Williams express themselves more cautiously: "Only in its original context of almost unlimited textual and translational variety can we fully appreciate the nature and function of the Hexapla."[38]

Yet, granted textual pluriformity and variability, precisely how is one to understand and appreciate the rationale for constructing the *Hexapla*? What did Origen intend to accomplish by undertaking a textual enterprise of such colossal proportions? From our perspective, we recognize that he was himself not as well informed about the pluriformity of textual versions and traditions as we are today. He assumed, for example, that the Hebrew text type was identical with that from which the LXX had been translated, whereas current scholarship

---

[35] A. Grafton and M. Williams, *Christianity and the Transformation of the Book: Origen, Eusebius, and the Library of Caesarea* (Cambridge: Belknap Press of Harvard University, 2006), 131. Informed sensitivity to the media dimensions of scroll and codex places the work by Grafton and Williams on *Christianity and the Transformation of the Book* far above the conventional philological and theological approaches to patristics.

[36] Grafton and Williams, *Christianity and the Transformation of the Book,* 87.

[37] Ulrich, *Dead Sea Scrolls,* 225.

[38] Grafton and Williams, *Christianity and the Transformation of the Book,* 130.

suggests that neither the LXX nor the Masoretic Text are homogeneous, and that the textual character in both traditions changes from book to book. But Origen was sufficiently aware of textual pluriformity of biblical texts to embark upon the intellectually demanding, economically expensive, and physically grueling work of selecting, reproducing and collating six versions of the Bible. Indeed, "[t]he complex *mise-en-page* of the Hexaplaric columns must have presented significant logistical challenges to the scribes who created and reproduced them."[39] Scholars generally share the view that Origen's principal purpose was a sound text that could serve as reliable basis both for Christians themselves and for their disputes with the Jews. While this may well have been Origen's ultimate goal, it is not directly evident from the *Hexaplaric* arrangement. As a matter of fact, constructing a single text is precisely what he did not do. Rather than composing a standard text, he exposed his readers to a textual pluriformity, albeit on a drastically reduced scale. Could one perhaps interpret Origen's masterpiece the way Eusebius appears to have read it: as a concession that in fact no single authoritative text could be reconstructed,[40] or that it was up to readers to sort things out for themselves?

Be that as it may, in juxtaposing texts, one next to the other, and in inviting comparative reading, one text with the other, Origen constructed a textual universe that constituted a virtual counter model to the *mouvance* of the performative tradition.

Origen's innovative use of parallel columns in his *Hexapla* appears to have provided Eusebius with a model for his *Canon Tables*.[41] In principle, Eusebius' tables constituted something of a numerical grid that captured all four gospels. He had divided the gospel texts into small sections and then supplied each section with a number as well as a reference to its location in the tables. The tables themselves consisted of ten columns each carrying the section numbers marked on the margin of the gospel texts. In this way, table one numbered the sections common to all four gospels; table two to four those sections common to three gospels, table five to nine those common to two gospels; and table ten listed section numbers with no apparent parallels. Something else altogether was in play here than the rewriting of texts, namely the mathematization of texts. By virtue of the numerical logic, an entirely new approach to reading and understanding the four gospels was introduced. Comparative thinking across the gospel narratives was now a possibility. But it was accomplished at the price of imposing a numerical logic which enclosed the gospels into a tight system, or better perhaps, into the illusion of a closed system. What Eusebius and his staff of

---

[39] Grafton and Williams, *Christianity and the Transformation of the Book,* 105.

[40] Grafton and Williams, *Christianity and the Transformation of the Book,* 170: "Eusebius read the Hexapla as Origen had meant it to be read: as a treasury of exegetical materials, some of them perplexing, rather than an effort to provide a stable, perfect text of the Bible."

[41] C. Nordenfalk, *Die Spätantiken Kanontafeln,* 2 vols. (Göteborg: O. Isacson, 1938).

secretaries and notaries had constructed was a strictly documentary environment of such logical persuasion and on such perfect a scale that the mind has to remove itself from the project to discern its artificiality. The *Canon Tables* had no basis in the real life of the gospels nor did they leave any room for social engagement, for participation in the oral-scribal-oral loop, or for compositional involvement in memorial processes. No wonder Grafton and Williams entertained the view that Eusebius was anticipating aspects of the modern library system. His experimentation with systems of information storage, they wrote, "represented as brilliant, and as radical, a set of new methods for the organization and retrieval of information as the nineteenth-century card catalogue and filing systems would in their turn."[42]

5. Memory and Manuscript

From later perspectives, it is evident that codex and canon, *Hexapla* and *Canon Tables* were harbingers of things to come. At the time, however, the cultural potential of the new formatting techniques provided by the codex was far from being fully explored. It was a matter of centuries for the scribal medium to optimize its material resources, and for human consciousness to interiorize scribal technology. The immense textual compilations accomplished by Origen and Eusebius were peak performances standing out in a culture that by and large remained heavily beholden to oral, scribal, and memorial *modi operandi.*

As suggested above, codex and canon did not immediately translate into an universally acknowledged authority of the Bible as a single, unified book. To the extent that textual uniformity was an essential ingredient of the authoritative Bible, medieval manuscript culture, even though it had advanced beyond the scribal technology of the Second Temple period, was by its very nature not qualified to produce identical copies because it was "of the essence of a manuscript culture that every copy is different, both unique and imperfect."[43]

Moreover, throughout patristic and medieval times the Bible was operational more often in plural form than as solitary authority. Collections of the Minor Prophets, for example, or a clustering of the Psalms into the Psalter, and of the gospels into gospel books enjoyed broad usage. Missals, breviaries, and lectionaries, widely used as service books in the medieval church, tended to disperse biblical texts into *lectiones*. There was a sense, therefore, in which the biblical tradition in the Middle Ages was experienced more as a collection of many books and a plurality of auditions than as a single text between two covers.

---

[42] Grafton and Williams, *Christianity and the Transformation of the Book*, 230.

[43] Parker, *The Living Text of the Gospels*, 188.

One will further have to remember that for the longest part of its existence the Bible was largely present in the lives of the people as an oral authority: proclaimed, homiletically interpreted, listened to, and internalized. Nor did the oral proclamation always emanate from the Bible itself. The *Book of Hours*, for example, composed of psalms and biblical quotations, was often a household's sole book, known from memory by millions and recited aloud at each of the eight traditional monastic hours of the day. Duffy's claim is thus very much to the point: "If we are to understand the point of contact between people and the written word [of the Bible] in the late Middle Ages, there is no more fundamental text than the *Book of Hours*."[44] While the chirographic Bible was rare in the hands of lay people, some of its contents existed via the *Book of Hours* in the hearts of millions.

Last but not least, the Bible's authority coexisted on equal footing with that of the councils and the oral and written tradition. On theological grounds, the medieval church operated with a plurality of authorities. For a millennium and a half, therefore, there was no such thing as the sole authority of the Bible in Western Christendom. It was only with print technology, and accompanying theological developments, that a standardized text and duplication of that text was a feasible proposition. *Sola scriptura*, we may safely claim, was a concept technically unworkable and theologically unthinkable prior to the invention of printing.

The oral authority of the Bible brings us to the phenomenon of memory. Regarded since ancient times as the well-spring of civilized life, it was a continuing force in the Middle Ages, a period in Western history that was in fundamental ways a memorial more than a documentary culture.[45] It was by no means uncommon for people to have instant recall of biblical texts, whether they had memorized them from start to finish, or whether they were in command of a selection of passages, or merely knew a series of aphorisms and stories. Augustine stands for many theologians who were entirely comfortable in combining the rigors of the manuscript culture with the demands of memory. Peter Brown has vividly described his bookish environment: "on the shelves, in the little cupboards that were the book-cases of Late Roman men, there lay ninety-three of his own works, made up of two hundred and thirty-two little books,

---

[44] E. Duffy, *Marking the Hours: English People and their Prayers, 1240–1570* (New Haven: Yale University Press, 2006), 42.

[45] F. A. Yates, *The Art of Memory* (Chicago: University of Chicago Press, 1966). M. J. Carruthers, *The Book of Memory: A Study of Memory in Medieval Culture* (Cambridge: Cambridge University Press, 1990). Credit for the modern rediscovery of the force of memory in Western civilization, from antiquity to the rise of the sciences, goes to Frances Yates' *The Art of Memory*. Mary J. Carruthers has almost singlehandedly reconceptualized medieval studies from the perspective of memory in her classic work *The Book of Memory*. Both books have exerted deep influence on the humanities and to a degree on the social sciences.

sheafs of his letters, and, perhaps covers crammed with anthologies of his ser-
mons, taken down by the stenographers of his admirers."[46] But the man who
surrounded himself with books, many of which he had composed himself, was
persuaded that the quality of his intellect was intricately linked to the powers of
memory. Writes Brown: "His memory, trained on classical texts, was phenom-
enally active. In one sermon, he could move through the whole Bible, from
Paul to Genesis and back again, via the Psalms, piling half-verse on half-
verse."[47] Augustine's competence in and cultivation of memory was not only
essential for his retention of knowledge and mental compositioning, but, in the
end, for the quality of his thought. Memory and manuscript interacted in ways
we can hardly imagine today.

For more than a millennium, roughly from the time of the sack of Rome (410
C. E.) to the invention of printing (ca. 1455 C. E.), a general shift from oral,
rhetorical sensibilities to a developing chirographic control over the organization and growth of knowledge is observable. Manuscripts increasingly became
important tools of civilized life, and from the eleventh century onward an
ever-growing scribal culture shaped the processes of learning. Brian Stock has
meticulously documented the world of communications and cultural transformations in the high Middle Ages. It is a complex story. Oral-scribal-memorial
interfacing dynamics constituted "not one but rather many models, all moving
at different velocities and in different orbits."[48] There was the high culture of the
papacy and monasticism, of the chanceries and diplomacy, of jurisdiction and
above all of scholasticism. Undoubtedly, those were orbits that excelled in
thinking and formulating complex philosophical, theological, legal, and linguistic ideas often with signal keenness of intellect. Theirs was a culture of written
records that both benefited from and contributed to the developing chirographic communication. But one must guard against facile premises concerning links
between a developing medieval documentary life and a restructuring of consciousness. The processes entailed in the interiorization of medieval scribalism
are intricate, raising deep questions regarding the interfacing of the materiality
of language and knowledge with mind and memory. In the most general terms,
however, it seems fair to say that relentless scribal labors enhanced the textual
base of knowledge; that knowledge, in so far as it was managed by a working
relationship with manuscripts, was apt to become detached from the oral, traditional biosphere; that in the minds of the literate elite, "oral tradition became
identified with illiteracy";[49] and that knowledge processed scribally would foster

---

[46] P. Brown, *Augustine of Hippo: A Biography* (Berkeley: University of California, 1967),
428.

[47] Brown, *Augustine,* 254.

[48] B. Stock, *The Implications of Literacy: Written Language and Models of Interpretation in the
Eleventh and Twelfth Centuries* (Princeton: Princeton University Press, 1983), 34.

[49] Stock, *The Implications of Literacy,* 12.

comparative and critical thought. But it needs to be restated that this mutual interpenetration of scribal technology and human thought is observable predominantly among the chirographic elite.

Thus while professional scribality began to exercise effects on mind and consciousness, and the Bible became the most studied book in the West whose language and contents permeated medieval language, literacy still remained the privilege of few, and reading and writing did not instantaneously result in literate intellectualism. And this is the other part of the complex medieval communications world: the chirographic technology was, and continued to be, a tedious, backbreaking business.[50] By typographical standards, writing one letter after the next, and word after word, was exceedingly slow work, and the time spent on completing a manuscript of average length was inordinate. And so was the price of a manuscript. The copying of existing manuscripts aside, the manufacture of new texts usually was the result of a division of labor. There was the *dictator* or intellectual initiator of a text who was frequently unable to write himself/herself. There was secondly the *scriptor* who in taking dictation may or may not have had an intellectual grasp of what (s)he was writing. Moreover, medieval Bibles for the most part did not have chapter and verse divisions. It was only around 1200 C. E. that the first chapter divisions were introduced into biblical manuscripts, and around 1500 C. E. that biblical texts began to be atomized into individually numbered sections or even verses. Neither the rabbis nor Augustine, neither Maimonides nor Thomas Aquinas ever cited "the Bible" the way typographic folks do.

Nor did medieval intellectuals read the Bible quite the way we do. Reading was still widely, although not exclusively practiced as an oral activity. To be sure, some aids to the visual apperception of biblical texts were in usage. Punctuation symbols and the beginnings of word and chapter division, initially introduced in support of oral recitation, in fact imposed a visual code that was to facilitate silent reading habits. Still, far into the high Middle Ages, reading was regarded as something of a physical activity, requiring good health and robust energy. In short, reading was associated with dictation and recitation more than with private reflection.[51]

Standing in a complex communications web of chirographic technology, memory, oral recitation, and homiletic exposition, the Bible was anything but a closed book with a single sense. Augustine's hermeneutics, for example, could

---

[50] D. A. Troll, "The Illiterate Mode of Written Communication: The Work of the Medieval Scribe," *Oral and Written Communication: Historical Approaches* (ed. R. L. Enos; Newbury Park: Sage Publications, 1990).

[51] P. Saenger, "Silent reading: Its Impact on Late medieval Script and Society," *Viator* 13 (1982): 367–414. P. Achtemeier, "*Omne verbum sonat*: The New Testament and the Oral Environment of Late Western Antiquity," *JBL* 109 (1990): 3–27. F. D. Gilliard, "More Silent Reading in Antiquity: *non omne verbum sonat*," *JBL* 112 (1993): 689–94.

strictly hold to the theory of a divinely inspired and unified book of the Bible, while at the same time keeping entirely aloof from literalism. He had no patience with those who thought the Word of God was plain and obvious for all to grasp. What a misunderstanding of the Bible it was! How could one incarcerate the immense mysteries of the Book into the prison house of the single sense? Veiled in mystery as the Bible was, it served to inspire hearers and readers to reach out for newer and deeper senses hidden beneath, between, or above the literal sense. Impressively articulated in his classic *De Doctrina Christiana* (Augustine ca. 426), the seven steps of hermeneutics were less a matter of exegetical discernment and more of spiritual exercises that would take hearers from the fear of God, to piety, the love of God and love of neighbor, to justice, mercy, the vision of God, and all the way to a state of peace and tranquility."[52]

Augustine's conviction of the plural senses of the Bible was widely shared in the Middle Ages. The classic theory of interpretation which dominated large segments of Western Christendom espoused the fourfold sense of biblical texts: the literal or plain sense, the oblique or allegorical sense, the homiletical and often ethical sense, and the spiritual sense which gestured toward deeper or higher realities.[53] Whether one acknowledged this fourfold sense, or merely practiced a twofold sense, or inclined toward a threefold interpretation, the spiritual sense was in all instances accorded the position of priority. That the biblical text was open to plural senses was entirely taken for granted. Such was the nature of truth that it comprised multiple senses. It was as if the experience of textual pluralism had been projected into hermeneutics. Allen Orr's conclusion that biblical literalism appeared late in the history of Christianity, and in connection with the Reformation and the so-called Counter-Reformation has much to commend it.[54] And both the Reformation and the so-called Counter-Reformation, as we shall see, marked a period that was closely tied in with the print medium.

6. *The Word Made Print*

There were intellectual forces at work in medieval culture that directed the focus toward texts and developed a textually grounded (theo)logic to unprecedented heights. Around the turn of the thirteenth to the fourteenth century William of Ockham (1285–1349?), a Franciscan monk from Surrey County in

---

[52] Aurelius Augustinus, *On Christian Doctrine* (trans. D. W. Robertson; New York: Macmillan/London: Collier, 1958), 38–40.

[53] H. de Lubac, *Exégèse Médiévale: Les Quatres Sens de l'Écriture,* 4 vols (Paris: Aubier, 1959–64).

[54] H. A. Orr, review of Philip Kitcher, *Living with Darwin: Evolution, Design, and the Future of Faith* (Oxford: Oxford University Press) in *New York Review of Books* 16 (2007): 33–35.

England, whose skepticism toward philosophical realism moved the particular, the experiential, and the contingent to the center of inquiry, exploring the notion of distinctiveness, including the distinctive nature of texts.[55] Scripture, indeed all texts, he reasoned, were operating according to something akin to an intrinsic, linguistic economy, and the operations of the mind – everybody's mind – were such that they could access the internal textual logic via the *cognitio intuitiva*. From the perspective of media sensibilities, we observe an intellectualism that is fully at home in the prevailing chirographic culture and thoroughly exploiting its inner resources.[56] In nominalism, of which Ockham was a prominent representative, the notion began to assert itself that the full potential of biblical texts was to be found less in their oral proclamation and auditory reception than in their very own textual economy. With Ockham, the closure of the biblical text was about to receive a hermeneutical, indeed theological justification. That premise of the closed text was soon to receive powerful technological support through the print medium.

Between 1452 and 1455 Johannes Gutenberg produced the first print Bible, henceforth universally known as the 42–line Bible. It is not immediately obvious why he selected a book as monumental in scope as the Bible to implement a technology that was very much in its infancy. At first glance, print's technical effects of duplication appear to point to the propagation of faith as his principal objective. But many arguments speak against it. The casting of close to 300 different characters was labor-intensive and hiked up the price of the print Bible.[57] Moreover, Latin, the language of the Vulgate, was no longer marketable; few people could actually read the Latin print Bible. Last but not least, Gutenberg's undertaking was not a commissioned project and for this reason required vast capital investments. Analogous to developments we observe at the launching of the electronic medium, the print medium effected the entrée of entrepreneurship into the communications world. Capitalism took hold of the new medium with a vengeance. A new technological and economic culture was emerging that was not infrequently predicated on substantial financial risk-taking. In Gutenberg's case, the print Bible brought its master no economic profit

---

[55] M. McCord Adams, *William of Ockham*, 2 vols. (Notre Dame: University of Notre Dame Press, 1987; repr. 1989). G. Leff, *William of Ockham: The Metamorphosis of Scholastic Discourse* (Manchester: Manchester University Press, 1975).

[56] Carruthers, *The Book of Memory* (158) observed that Ockham's "whole scholarly life until 1330 was spent in the greatest of European universities, his circle the most 'bookish' of the time." When, following the papal interdiction in 1330, Ockham lived isolated in Munich, he repeatedly complained that he had been deprived of access to all the books he needed to consult, although he appears to have composed writings in exile and managed to circulate them out of Munich.

[57] A. Ruppel, *Johannes Gutenberg: sein Leben und sein Werk* (Berlin: Gebr. Mann, 1939; repr. 1947). A. Kapr, *Johannes Gutenberg: the Man and his Invention* (trans. Douglas Martin; Brookfield: Scolar Press, 1996).

whatsoever. As is well known, he died a poor man, enmeshed in lawsuits and unable to pay his debts.

To the viewers and readers of the first major machine-made book in Western civilization, the most striking feature was sameness and proportionality. Prior to the invention of printing, sameness in this sense of complete identity had never been experienced. No one jar was like the other, and no two manuscripts were quite alike. The copies of Gutenberg's two-volume Vulgate represented models of stunning sameness, setting the highest standards of calligraphic virtuosity. By virtue of their unprecedented spatial formatting and finality of precision they expressed a sense of unearthly beauty. Giesecke[58] who, aside from Eisenstein,[59] has written the most comprehensive, modern work on the technology and cultural implications of print technology, has suggested that aesthetics, in particular the Renaissance ideal of beauty in the sense of complete proportionality, must have been uppermost on the mind of Gutenberg.

Owing to the duplicating effects of typography, textual pluriformity was now being effectively challenged by the ideal of uniformity. Theology and biblical scholarship were increasingly operating in a media environment that was losing touch with Jewish and Christian textual pluriformity. One either viewed the *mouvance* of tradition as something that had to be remedied text critically, or one was beginning to lose sight of it altogether. In short, the notion of *mouvance* was supplanted by what was to become the icon of textual stability. Moreover, the Bible's complete standardization, combined with its breathtaking beauty, projected a never before visualized model of authority. Indeed, it was in part at least a result of the technically facilitated uniformity that contributed to the Bible's unprecedented authority. But again, it was an authority that was accomplished at the price of isolating the Bible from its biosphere. The printed pages, in all their perfectly proportioned beauty, created the impression that sacred Scripture was closed off in a world of its own, uniformly spatialized, consummately linearized, and perfectly marginalized, a world, that is, where in the words of Leo Battista Alberti any alteration of any kind would only distort the harmony. Now, but only now, was it possible to visualize the premise of *sola scriptura*, not merely to conceptualize it theologically.

It is often pointed out that the Protestant Reformers still exhibited profoundly oral sensibilities with respect to Scripture. *Sola scriptura* notwithstanding,

---

[58] M. Giesecke, *Der Buchdruck in der frühen Neuzeit. Eine historische Fallstudie über die Durchsetzung neuer Informations- und Kommunikationstechnologien* (Frankfurt/Main: Suhrkamp, 1991). Giesecke (141–43) cites a programmatic statement concerning the Renaissance ideal of beauty by the Italian architect and art historian L. Battista Alberti (1404–1472) in *De re edificatoris* (Florence 1485): "Beauty is a harmony of all component parts, in whichever medium they are represented, juxtaposed with such a sense of proportionality and connectivity that nothing could be added or altered that would not distort it" (Giesecke's trans.).

[59] Eisenstein, *The Printing Press*, 1979.

Scripture remained a living presence for all of them. Martin Luther, Martin Bucer, John Calvin, Thomas Cranmer, William Tyndale and others spoke and wrote a scripturally saturated language because they were at home in Scripture and Scripture in them. Their respective theological positions remained fully cognizant of and sympathetic toward the power of oral proclamation. Luther never viewed his vernacular translation simply as a linguistic feat, but rather as a Pentecostal reenactment of the bestowal of the Spirit.[60] The presence of scriptural orality in the theology of the Reformers cannot be in doubt.

Equally significant, however, was the influence of the print medium. The typographic apotheosis of the Bible deeply affected the Reformers' theological thinking on scriptural authority, tradition, memory, interpretation and numerous other features. Seven hermeneutical and theological developments, all of them in varying degrees bound up with the new medium, were instrumental in bringing about tension and conflict with the oral, scribal, memorial world of verbalization. One, the rejection of the fourfold sense of the Bible[61] aided and abetted the rationale for the closure of biblical texts. Two, the increasingly high regard for the *sensus literalis* jeopardized the hermeneutical pluralism cultivated by the medieval church. Three, the repudiation of allegory – the very figure that generates worlds of correspondences – was a contributing factor toward reducing biblical interpretation to intra-textual literalism. Four, the unprecedented elevation of the Bible to *sola scriptura* conjured up the notion of the Bible as a free-standing monolithic artifact detached from tradition. Five, Luther's premise of *scriptura sui ipsius interpres* had the effect of closing the Bible in unto its own interior textual landscape. Six, the steady marginalization of memory effected a shifting of the interpretation of the Bible toward a fully textualized, documentary model. Seven, perhaps most ominously, the rejection of tradition, this larger-than-textual life of communal memory, disconnected biblical texts both from their vital sustenance and their performance arena. To be sure, some of these features had been anticipated, implicitly or explicitly, in the manuscript culture of ancient and medieval theology, and especially in nominalism's *via moderna* of the fourteenth and fifteenth centuries. One cannot make print the sole determinant of these developments. But the Word made print, namely the inauguration of the medium which "is comfortable only with finality"[62] heavily contributed toward viewing the Bible as a closed book, or, better perhaps, toward fantasizing it as a closed book. Typography was a major, although not the only, factor that effectively reified the biblical texts and generated a high degree of plausibility for thinking of the Bible as an authority that was standing on its own.

---

[60] J. O. Newman, "The Word Made Print: Luther's 1522 New Testament in an Age of mechanical Reproduction," *Representations* 11 (1985): 95–133, especially 117–23.

[61] Lubac, *Exégèse Mèdièvale* (1959–64).

[62] Ong, *Orality and Literacy*, 132.

No doubt, these are extraordinary developments not only with respect to the status and interpretation of the Bible, but for Western intellectual history in general. In their aggregate, they amounted to an unprecedented elevation of scriptural authority seeking to hold Scripture firmly to its chirographic space and thereby depriving it of the oxygen of tradition. It is not entirely surprising that links between the severe reductionism instituted by the sixteenth century Reformers and nineteenth and twentieth century fundamentalism have been drawn. In a recent study, James Simpson[63] developed the thesis that the Reformers were the protagonists not (merely) of modern liberalism, but rather of modern fundamentalism. He is convinced that the rise of what he calls the sixteenth century fundamentalism was intrinsically linked with the power of the high tech of the fifteenth century. Simpson is not the first one to offer observations of this kind. In the past, Eisenstein has advised us to project not merely the single trajectory of Humanism, Renaissance and Reformation toward Enlightenment and modernity, but to acknowledge other trajectories as well. Fundamentalism in the sense of literal interpretation and inerrancy of the Bible, Eisenstein observed, while strictly speaking a late nineteenth and twentieth century Protestant, North American phenomenon, was in the age of Erasmus, "just beginning to assume its modern form."[64] Unless we recognize this development, she stated, "the appearance of fundamentalism in the age of Darwin or the holding of the Scopes trial in the age of Ford become almost completely inexplicable."[65] Needless to say, for Eisenstein, the genesis of sixteenth century fundamentalism is closely allied with the printing press and its impact on the formatting, reading, and interpreting of the Bible. On the whole, however, Eisenstein exercised a careful balance in recognizing print's consequences for better and for worse: "The impact of printing on the Western scriptural faith thus pointed in two quite opposite directions – toward 'Erasmian' trends and ultimately higher criticism and modernism, and toward more rigid orthodoxy culminating in literal fundamentalism and Bible Belts."[66]

Luther, it is well known, was fully conscious of the unprecedented potential of the print medium: "Typography is the final and at the same time the greatest gift, for through it God wanted to make known to the whole earth the mandate of the true religion at the end of the world and to pour it out in all languages. It surely is the last, inextinguishable flame of the world."[67] We know that he was in

---

[63] J. Simpson, *Burning to Read: English Fundamentalism and Its Reformation Opponents* (Cambridge: Belknap Press/Harvard University, 2007).

[64] Eisenstein, *The Printing Press*, 366.

[65] Eisenstein, *The Printing Press*, 440.

[66] Eisenstein, *The Printing Press*, 366–67.

[67] The citation is from Luther's *Tischreden* written down by Nikolau Medler (1532) and cited by Giesecke, *Der Buchdruck*, 163 and 727, n. 167: "*Typographia postremum est donum et idem maximum, per eam enim Deus toti terrarum orbi voluit negotium verae religionis in fine mundi innotescere ac in omnes linguas transfundi. Ultima sana flamma mundi inextinguibilis.*"

possession of print copies of Johann Reuchlin's *De Rudimentis Hebraicis,* of a Hebrew Bible (first published by the North Italian Jewish Soncino press in 1488) and of Erasmus' Greek New Testament. To a large extent, therefore, his work of Bible translation was carried out with the assistance and on the basis of print materials. About Luther's translation of the New Testament while sequestered at the Wartburg Castle (1521–1522), Eisenstein writes: "Clearly he was better equipped by printers than he would have been by scribes during his interval of enforced isolation."[68] Additionally, he utilized printed copies of the Bible and the New Testament as tools for proclamation, propaganda, and polemic. But he could not have anticipated the full impact the print Bible would have on the religious, social and political landscape of Europe. No medium escapes the law of unintended consequences, and the print medium was no exception.

The print Bible was by no means the unmixed blessing that its inventor and many of its promoters had envisioned. It effected historical developments *ad bonam et ad malam partem.* On one level, the rapid dissemination of the vernacular print Bible raised literacy to a level never before seen in Europe; it created a steadily growing readership and encouraged further vernacular translations. Moreover, general accessibility to the Bible posed a challenge to authoritarian control over the Bible, and fostered democratic instincts about ownership and content of the Bible. On a different level, however, "the infallibility of the printed word as opposed to the 'instability of script' was recognized even by contemporaries as a fiction."[69] The serious malaise that was affecting the print business, Newman observed, was of a twofold kind: "First: printers were hasty and negligent in the practice of their trade. Second: they were concerned above all with the pursuit of profits"[70]. Luther himself was increasingly disturbed that "his" printed Bible had been pirated to the point where ever more printed texts of ever poorer quality were in circulation: "I do not recognize my own books [...] here there is something left out, there something set incorrectly, there forged, there not proofread."[71] In other words, the very medium that was capable of standardizing the text, had set into motion a process of accelerated reproduction that resulted in textual inaccuracies. But in the mechanical medium, textual errors were likely to be multiplied a hundredfold and a thousandfold. One is bound to ask: did the new medium recapitulate, perhaps even aggravate, textual pluriformity, the very condition it had set out to overcome?

The globalizing tendencies inherent in typography were making themselves felt not only in the rapid dissemination of textual variants but in conflicting interpretations of the Bible as well. Notwithstanding its typographical orderli-

---

[68] Eisenstein, *The Printing Press,* 367 –68, n. 225.
[69] Newman, "The Word Made Print," 101.
[70] Newman, "The Word Made Print," 102.
[71] Newman, "The Word Made Print," 110.

ness, the ever more widely publicized content of the Bible became a bone of fierce contention. Among a steadily growing readership, the biblical texts were exposed to unprecedented scrutiny. Inevitably, scriptural discrepancies came to light. But whereas in chirographic culture, theological controversies stayed confined to a small circle of theological experts, in print culture, disputes were publicized across regional and national boundaries. In this way, the new medium marketed dissension and deepened disagreements.

Last but not least, vernacular Bibles became the rallying points for national aspirations, demarcating linguistic and ethnic boundaries, and contributing toward the rise of nation states. "It is no accident that nationalism and mass literacy have developed together."[72] While the new medium thus gave momentum to national languages and identities, it also helped draw new lines of religious and national division, and strongly exacerbated Catholic-Protestant polemics. Eisenstein articulated the provocative theory of typography's unintended implication in the dissolution of Latin Christianity and the fragmentation of Europe, asserting that "Gutenberg's invention probably contributed more to destroying Christian concord and inflaming religious warfare than any of the so-called arts of war ever did."[73]

7. *Afterthought*

The preceding reflections oblige us to extend, however sketchily, our survey of the history of the closure of biblical texts into modernity and early postmodernism. Closed-model thinking asserted itself in a variety of seemingly unrelated phenomena, many of them of significant consequence in the intellectual history and biblical scholarship of the West. Affinities with the print medium are not directly transparent, but always present at least as a subliminal influence. No doubt, closed model thinking was effectively countered by quantum theory, relativity theory, evolutionary thinking, a revival in rhetoric and receptionist theory and lately by the electronic medium. But the point here is to trace connections between print and closed-model thinking.

"Perhaps the most tight-fisted pre-Cartesian proponent of the closed system [...] was the French philosopher and educational reformer Pierre de la Ramée or Petrus Ramus," writes Ong.[74] Thanks to Ong's historically and philosophically masterful study of the thought of Pierre de la Ramée, we are now well informed about changes in the sixteenth and seventeenth century educational

---

[72] Eisenstein, *The Printing Press*, 363.

[73] Eisenstein, *The Printing Press*, 319.

[74] W. J. Ong, "Voice and the Opening of Closed Systems," *Interfaces of the Word. Studies in the Evolution of Consciousness and Culture* (Ithaca and London: Cornell University Press, 1977), 330–31.

system in France and across Europe.[75] Ramus' intellectual bent approached knowledge by way of definitions and divisions, leading to still further definitions and more divisions, until every last particle of information was dissected, categorized and located in a closed system. Ong has dramatically described Ramism as "a quantification system which is almost certainly the most reckless applied one that the world has ever seen."[76] Ramus' quantified epistemology, soon to be adopted by thousands of his followers across Europe, drove him to view all intellectual activities in spatial clusters and corpuscular units, in dichotomized charts and binary tables. "Insofar as a strong stress on closed system thinking marks the beginning of the modern era," states Ong, "Ramus, rather than Descartes, stands at the beginning."[77] To some degree, this quantifying drive and binary logic grew out of certain aspects of medieval logic, especially nominalism, but there also exists a relationship, however subliminal, between the rapidly growing technology of letterpress printing and the relentless spatialization and diagrammatization of knowledge. Ong has seen this clearly: "The diagrammatic tidiness which printing was imparting to the realm of ideas was part of a large-scale operation freeing the book from the world of discourse and making it over into an object, a box with surface and 'content' like an Agricolan locus or a Ramist argument or a Cartesian or Lockean idea."[78] For whereas in oral communication words are without borders, and in the ancient scribal, oral, memorial culture boundaries are only beginning to be drawn, it was, again, the printed page that created the illusion that knowledge was an autosemantic world within firmly drawn borders, fully captured on visual surfaces, spatialized, linearized, hence subject to spatial, diagrammatic scrutiny.

Ramism, interacting with Humanism and Protestantism,[79] and fed by the forces of typography, provided the cultural matrix for the rise of modernity's historical, critical scholarship of the Bible. It was a generally post-Gutenberg and specifically humanistic, Ramist, and Protestant intellectualism that laid the groundwork for the philological and historical examination of the Bible, namely the print Bible.

Among key features that typify the rising philological paradigm of biblical scholarship, the following four may be cited. One, print was the medium from

---

[75] W.J. Ong, Ramus, *Method and the Decay of Dialogue: From the Art of Discourse to the Art of Reason* (Cambridge: Harvard University Press, 1958; repr. 1974, 1983, 2004).

[76] Ong, *Ramus, Method and the Decay*, 203,

[77] Ong, "Voice and the Opening of Closed Systems," 331.

[78] Ong, *Ramus, Method and the Decay*, 311,

[79] Pierre de la Ramée (1515–1572 C.E.), a Huguenot convert from Catholicism, was murdered in the St. Bartholomew's Day Massacre. Joseph Julius Scalinger (1540–1609), eminent French classical scholar, text critic and philologist, and one of the founding figures of the historical, critical paradigm, likewise converted to Protestantism. On Scaliger, see A. Grafton, *Joseph Scaliger: A Study in the History of Classical Scholarship*, 2 vol. (Oxford – Warburg studies; Oxford: Clarendon Press/New York: Oxford University Press, 1983–1993).

which the text critical, philological approach to the Bible received formative methodological habits and intellectual tools. Owing to the duplicating powers of the print medium, humanistic scholars were awash in print materials – a situation that was conducive to imagining tradition on the logic strictly of textual dynamics. By and large, intertextuality was now considered a root condition of all biblical texts. Two, biblical interpretation increasingly privileged the *sensus literalis sive historicus*, freezing the meaning of texts in their assumed historical matrix. Rather than finding the texts' rationale in their oral explication, memorization, and reception, scholars tied interpretation to the historical locus behind the texts. Three, the use of the stemmatic method locked textual versions in a tight, genealogically conceived textual diagram. Performativity was now replaced by stemmatics. Four, humanistic editors faced textual pluriformity by seeking to secure the "original" text, even though the reconstructed archetype as a rule was more often than not a virtual text that did not correspond to any historically attested textual form. It is worth speculating that the fidelity to the putative stability of the textual archetype was driven by the desire to transcend the hazards of temporality that were endemic to textual pluriformity.

These essential components of the historical, philological paradigm came to influence, indeed define modern biblical scholarship. It is in this paradigm that most of us in academia – Jews and Catholics and Protestants alike – have been raised and educated, a paradigm, moreover, that has largely kept us uninformed about the life of biblical texts in the ancient, orally-scribally and memorially empowered tradition.

Turning to more recent developments, what comes to mind is the narrative criticism of biblical stories that got under way in the late 1960s and has flourished ever since.[80] For many of us who had a hand in it, the exploration of the narrative nature of biblical stories was an exhilarating experience. We experienced the application of narrative criticism to the Bible as liberation from a long history of ideational and historical referentiality. The old dichotomies of faith versus history, theology versus narrative, history versus fiction, kerygma versus myth, we realized (slowly but surely) were inadequate and indeed outdated as a result of the discovery of narrative logic and narrative causalities.

However, in shifting the interpretive model from meaning-as-reference to meaning-as-narrative, biblical interpreters were inclined to adopt features of the so-called *New Criticism*, the very method which had prevailed roughly from the 1930s to the 1950s in Anglo-American literary criticism. In one of the best

---

[80] W. H. Kelber, *Mark's Story of Jesus* (Philadelphia: Fortress Press, 1979); R. Polzin, *Moses and the Deuteronomist: A Literary Study of the Deuteronomic History* (New York: Seabury Press, 1980); R. Polzin, *David and the Deuteronomist: 2 Samuel* (Bloomington: Indiana University Press, 1993). D. Rhoads, Joanna Dewey, and D. Michie, *Mark as Story: An Introduction to the Narrative of a Gospel* (2nd ed.: Minneapolis: Fortress Press, 1999).

books on the literary criticism of the gospels, Stephen Moore[81] correctly observed *New Critical* undercurrents in the narrative criticism of the Bible, pointing out the irony that biblical critics had embraced the creed of the holistic nature of story at a time when literary critics generally had long abandoned it.

In some quarters, the tendency of narrative criticism to view biblical narratives as stable, self-referential worlds came to be regarded as a self-absorbed bourgeois mentality."[82] Historically more to the point is the attempt to trace the *New Criticism* back to Coleridge and Kantian aesthetics. But there is a media dimension to this twentieth century phenomenon as well. Ong has observed that the closed-model thinking characteristic of (one form of) narrative criticism was flourishing at a time in Western cultural history when the technologizing, objectivizing impact of printing had reached its peak. "Nothing shows more strikingly the close, mostly unconscious, alliance between the Romantic movement and technology."[83] Centuries of the interiorization of print had made it artistically desirable and academically acceptable to view texts, including narrative texts, as autonomous object-worlds.

---

[81] S. D. Moore, *Literary Criticism of the Gospels: The Theoretical Challenge* (New Haven: Yale University Press, 1980), 3–68.

[82] T. Hawkes, *Structuralism and Semiotics* (Berkeley: University of California Press, 1977), 154–55.

[83] Ong, *Orality and Literacy*, 161.

Part II: Speaking in the Shaping of New Genres

Plenitude and Diversity:
Interactions between Orality and Writing

John Miles Foley

Overview

The present contribution is divided into six parts. First, I consider the trajectory of theory in oral tradition studies from the groundbreaking research of Milman Parry and Albert Lord to the present, with attention to the complexity of the field as it has emerged over the past two decades. To emphasize the inherent diversity of the subject, the second and third parts are devoted, respectively, to a model for rationalizing that diversity and to briefly explaining various approaches to oral tradition. Fourth, with a realistic sense of complexity and heterogeneity in hand, I then turn to a short discussion of unity within diversity, that is, of shared issues across the spectrum of oral traditions. The fifth section presents several invented proverbs intended to recall crucial aspects of oral traditional morphology and dynamics in a memorable, easily apprehensible way. Finally, toward the end of the article I describe and illustrate the striking (if also counter-intuitive) homology between oral tradition (OT) and Internet/digital technology (IT), both of which function by navigating through networks of potentials. Despite their superficial differences, these two thought-technologies derive their expressive power not from the fixity associated with texts but from the rule-governed variation that stems from navigating through webs of potentials.

1. The trajectory of theory

The so-called Oral-Formulaic Theory, pioneered by Parry and Lord through textual analysis of Homer and on-site fieldwork among oral epic singers in the Former Yugoslavia, portrayed oral tradition as, effectively, "un-literature."[1] In

---

[1] On the history of Oral-Formulaic Theory, see J. M. Foley, *The Theory of Oral Composition: History and Methodology* (Bloomington: Indiana University Press, 1988; repr. 1992). For bibliography on the application of this method to more than 100 traditions, see J. M. Foley, *Oral-Formulaic Theory and Research: An Introduction and Annotated Bibliography* (New York: Garland, 1985). Updates to the latter resource are available in L. E. Tyler, "Annotated Bibli-

other words, they and their followers envisioned a medium that did not depend in any way on "letters" (as distinct from "literature," a term that derives from Latin *littera* and more immediately from medieval Latin *litteratus*, a lettered person). Crucially, they also assumed that oral tradition represented a single, unified phenomenon across all cultures, eras, languages, and social contexts. The result was a binary model that restricted verbal art to one or the other of two mutually exclusive categories, and which created the so-called Great Divide concept of orality versus literacy.[2] Less obviously, this either-or categorization also limited the social function of oral tradition to the literary dynamic of entertainment and instruction.

To understand how the theory developed with its unique strengths and weaknesses, it is necessary to consider its origins and early deployment. Parry's initial analyses of Homer were, of course, entirely textual: he sought to prove composition in oral performance by demonstrating the patterned, traditional nature of epic phraseology.[3] The next step, undertaken with Lord and their native assistant Nikola Vujnović (himself an epic singer or *guslar*), dramatically expanded the inquiry by collecting and analyzing performances of unambiguously oral epic in the Former Yugoslavia in the 1930s. And when the on-site field investigation seemed to confirm hypotheses derived via textual analysis, the Oral-Formulaic Theory was considered "proven" and quickly extended to dozens of other traditions from the ancient and medieval eras as well as to contemporary oral traditions.[4] A whole new world of verbal art was opening up, and the

---

ography to 1985," *Oral Tradition* 3 (1988): 191–228, available online at http://journal. oral-tradition. org/files/articles/3i–ii/9_annotated_bibliography. pdf; and C. S. Quick, "Annotated Bibliography 1986–1990," *Oral Tradition* 12 (1997): 366–84, available online at http://journal. oraltradition. org/files/articles/12ii/7_annotated_biblio. pdf. By the early 1990s this approach had coalesced with other approaches, such as Performance Theory, Ethnopoetics, and Immanent Art, described below.

[2] An early critic of that universalism was Ruth Finnegan, in her study *Oral Poetry: Its Nature, Significance, and Social Context* (Cambridge: Cambridge University Press, 1977; repr. Bloomington: Indiana University Press, 1992). See now her study, *The Oral and Beyond: Doing Things with Words in Africa* (Chicago: University of Chicago Press, 2007), an extremely wide-ranging and well-informed survey.

[3] See esp. M. Parry, *The Making of Homeric Verse: The Collected Papers of Milman Parry* (Oxford: Clarendon Press, 1971, repr. 1987), 1–190, 191–239.

[4] On the fieldwork undertaken in the Former Yugoslavia, see A. B. Lord, "General Introduction," *Serbocroatian Heroic Songs* (*Srpskohrvatske junačke pjesme*), vol. 1 (Cambridge, Mass. and Belgrade: Harvard University Press and the Serbian Academy of Sciences, 1954), 3–20; and St. Mitchell and G. Nagy, "Introduction to the Second Edition," *The Singer of Tales* (by A. B. Lord; 2nd ed.; Cambridge, Mass.: Harvard University Press, 2000), vii–xxix. Original transcriptions and translations of South Slavic epics collected by Parry, Lord, and Vujnović are available in the series *Serbocroatian Heroic Songs*, with vols. 1–2, 3–4, 6, and 14 published to date. See also J. M. Foley, ed. and trans., *The Wedding of Mustajbey's Son Bećirbey as Performed by Halil Bajgorić* (Folklore Fellows Communications, vol. 283; Helsinki: Academia Scientiarum Fennica, 2004), with an open-access hypertext edition available at http://oraltradition. org/zbm.

Parry-Lord theory seemed to offer a perspective that fundamentally rationalized its complex "otherness."

This revolutionary comparative method was based on a very narrow analogy between Homeric epic and South Slavic Moslem epic, which happened to agree quite closely in genre, phraseology, and narrative patterning,[5] but that restriction was not at first given due consideration. Soon, however, two objections would arise. First, reports from fieldwork revealed a great deal more variety among oral traditions than the Theory predicted – variety in structure, medium, culture, genre, and performer and audience.[6] Not all traditions depend on phraseology that uses the *formula* as defined by Parry and Lord, and oral traditions that wholly lack contact with written traditions prove rare. Each culture prescribes a set of performance arenas that are to some extent *sui generis*, and the genres that exist and morph within their ecologies of oral traditions are likewise comparable only to a degree. Performers may ply their trade alone or in groups, with or without musical accompaniment, and as a result of formal training or not, while audiences may consist of from one to several thousand listeners and may be highly restricted (by age, gender, or some other parameter) or open to all interested parties.

Second, and particularly in Homeric studies, scholars asked how such an apparently mechanical concept of composition could support the universally acknowledged aesthetic excellence of the *Iliad* and *Odyssey*. If oral tradition was primarily an exercise in the fluent manipulation of prefabricated diction and narrative sequence, then how do we understand Homer's art? Does "swift-footed Achilles" mean anything beyond "Achilles"? Is it merely a metrical filler? Does it have any relationship to the particular contexts in which it occurs? (It seems not to speak to individual moments or situations, in fact, and that "non-fit" confounds many literary critics.) Do the typical scenes of Feasting or Lament have any meaning beyond the structure they provide, or are we condemned to reading them merely as mnemonic support? To be fair, some of these concerns stem from a deeply textual concept of verbal art, and that bias would need to be exposed before much progress could be made in understanding how oral traditions mean. But both of these objections – from fieldwork and from aesthetics – were real and telling, and they have received a great deal of attention in the wake of the initial enthusiasm over the Oral-Formulaic Theory.

Overall, then, we can prescribe a three-stage evolution in the theoretical understanding of oral traditions. The first growth consisted of a groundbreaking

---

[5] On the analogy between South Slavic Moslem epic and the Homeric poems, see J. M. Foley, *Homer's Traditional Art* (University Park: Pennsylvania State University, 1999), esp. 37–111.

[6] On the tremendous diversity of oral traditions worldwide and from ancient times to the present day, see the journal *Oral Tradition*, all 24 years of which are now available online as a searchable, downloadable, and free-of-charge resource at http://journal.oraltradition.org.

demonstration of the oral traditional roots of the Homeric texts that have survived to us, arising from the textual analysis of the *Iliad* and *Odyssey* and from the
detailed and persuasive analogy with the directly observable phenomenon of
South Slavic oral epic. The second growth was marked by extension of these
findings to more than 100 other traditions, initially to Old English, Old French,
and Byzantine Greek, but soon afterward to Biblical studies and to manuscript-
based and living traditions from six of the seven continents. Although from the
perspective of later developments it is easy to fault the Great Divide concept that
informed these original discoveries and their later applications, it is important to
recognize that the binary model cleared thinking space to consider multiple
species of verbal art that did not fall into the category of literature. If the first and
second stages of the trajectory seem in retrospect too coarse-grained, we should
remember that it was their initial approximations that created a new field of
inquiry and made later, more fine-grained investigations possible. One has to
proceed from broad generalizations toward an appreciation of complexity and
diversity, not vice versa.

With the third growth, some crucial perspectives started to emerge. Most
centrally, scholars began to realize that the thesis of universal, archetypal, and
entirely separate categories of orality and literacy amounts to a crude oversimplification. In fact, as becomes more and more apparent almost daily, there are
and were multiple oralities and multiple literacies across different cultural en-
vironments and within the same culture. Likewise, abundant evidence has ac-
cumulated to show that these two (supposedly) mutually exclusive verbal technologies can and do exist within the very same person. A given individual can
master and use a panoply of different *registers*, or socially shaped expressive
channels, deploying the appropriate register for each communicative act.[7] Expert and celebrated performers of oral traditions can – like professor and oral
poet Paolo Zedda of Cagliari, Sardinia[8] – live and thrive within both oral and
textual milieus.

---

[7] Dell Hymes defines registers as "major speech styles associated with recurrent types of
situations" ["Ways of Speaking," *Explorations in the Ethnography of Speaking* (eds. R. Bauman
and J. Sherzer; 2nd ed.; Cambridge: Cambridge University Press, 1989), 440]. See further
Foley, *The Singer of Tales in Performance*, 49–53; idem, *Homer's Traditional Art*, 65–88, and idem,
How to Read an Oral Poem (Urbana: University of Illinois Press, 2002), 113–22.

[8] See P. Zedda, "The Southern Sardinian Tradition of the *Mutetu Longu*: A Functional
Analysis," *Oral Tradition* 24 (2009): 3–40; available online at http://journal. oraltradition. org/
files/ articles/24i/02_24. 1.pdf.

2. A model for oral traditions

With maturation of the theory a critical challenge has presented itself: just how do we approach the plenitude and diversity that is oral tradition? The sobering reality is that oral traditions dwarf literature in number, variety, and social functions. As numerous and as various as world literatures from the ancient period to the present indisputably are, oral traditions are vastly more widespread and heterogeneous.[9] And then there is the underappreciated criterion of social dynamics; whereas literatures entertain and instruct in characteristic ways, oral traditions chronicle history, heal the body, memorialize religious events and individuals, convey behavior models, provide "curricula vitae" published on oral networks, map territories, and in general serve myriad non-literary purposes. How do we grasp all of this remarkable diversity without falling victim to the trap of descriptive reductionism? Is there any coherent pattern that rationalizes such extraordinary variety in language, genre, dynamics, and social embedding?

One approach to answering the challenge is to focus on *composition, performance,* and *reception* to examine a spectrum of forms that serve their constituencies in many different ways. In other words, instead of naming certain traditions or genres or speech-acts "oral" or not, with whatever qualifications we deem necessary to the explanation, we can explore how traditions are maintained, shared, and experienced by those who actually use them. By following this path, we will avoid excluding oral traditions that do not exactly square with whatever example or analogy we choose to summon, and we will not automatically disqualify traditions that interact with texts. Our inquiry will pursue the underlying technology of communication rather than the external features of this or that form or genre. Our notion of oral tradition will thus be systematic rather than descriptive, and thus far more diagnostic of expressive dynamics.

For this purpose I have proposed a four-part system of flexible, overlapping categories: Oral performance, Voiced texts, Voices from the past, and Written oral traditions.[10] Note, incidentally, that these four types emphatically do not constitute an evolutionary sequence from oral to written. All four may well exist in the same culture, and a given form may belong to one category without ever having had a prior existence in any other. Here is a table explaining their relationships and differences, with an example for each one:

---

[9] As recognized very early by W. Ong, who put the number of true literatures that have ever existed at about 100, as opposed to the tens of thousands of languages invented and used by *Homo sapiens* – all, presumably, supporting oral traditions at one time or another (*Orality and Literacy: The Technologizing of the Word* [London: Methuen, 1982], p. 7).

[10] For a full discussion of this model, see Foley, *How to Read an Oral Poem,* 38–52.

A Spectrum of Oral Traditions

Category	Composition	performance	Reception	Example
Oral performance	Oral	Oral	Aural	Central Asian epic
Voiced texts	Written	Oral	Aural	Slam poetry
Voices from the past	O/W	O/W	O/W	Homeric epic
Written oral traditions	Written	Written	Written	Bishop Njegoš

In the first category, *Oral performance*,[11] an epic bard from any of the Turkic nationalities in Central Asia, for example, composes and performs orally for an audience that receives the epic aurally.[12] Although the oral poet may be exposed to a written source, every aspect of his involvement in maintaining and sharing the epic is textless. As a general rule across genres and cultures, the literacy of any performer often proves an irrelevant measure of the "orality" of a tradition, since individuals can master and control a menu of both oral and written registers for different communicative tasks. *Voiced texts*,[13] on the other hand, are composed in writing, whether pen-in-hand or using a word processor. The crucial determining factor, however, is that they are intended solely for oral performance; publication as texts is not normally even considered as an outlet. This category houses slam poetry, for instance, a genre in which highly literate poets write out poems that they then memorize before discarding the manuscript. Such poems exist in memory and "appear" only in active, live performance; as a result, they morph over time in ways that textually fixed (print-published) artifacts cannot.[14]

Voices from the past[15] are oral traditions that because of the accidents of time and place reach today's prospective audience only in textual form. Whether through explicit witness to their oral provenience or because writing and texts were simply not available until late in their history, we can establish that such traditions are clearly oral-derived. That much is unambiguous. But we must be judicious, since it is dangerous, unnecessary, and misleading to proceed beyond the limits of our available knowledge – to base research on hypothetical scenarios of origin and transmission that cannot be proven. Thus this category of Voices from the past speaks to oral-derived texts that have employed both oral and textual technology at some point in their history, but whose exact history

---

[11] Foley, *How to Read an Oral Poem*, 40–43.

[12] On Central Asian epic, see K. Reichl, *Turkic Oral Epic Poetry: Traditions, Forms, Poetic Structures* (New York, Garland, 1992); idem, *Singing the Past: Turkic and Medieval Heroic Poetry* (Ithaca: Cornell University Press, 2000); and idem, *Edige: A Karakalpak Oral Epic as Performed by Jumabay Bazarov* (Folklore Fellows Communications, 293; Helsinki: Academia Scientiarum Fennica, 2007).

[13] Foley, *How to Read an Oral Poem*, 43–45.

[14] See esp. M. Eleveld, *The Spoken Word Revolution Redux* (Bel Air, Cal.: Sourcebooks Mediafusion, 2007); Foley, *How to Read an Oral Poem*, 97–102, 156–65.

[15] Foley, *How to Read an Oral Poem*, 45–50.

and identity cannot be unearthed. Since modern fieldwork has shown that textuality and oral traditions not only co-exist but interact, and since the chief criterion of how verbal art works is the language or register within which it morphs and through which it communicates, the role of textuality is certainly no reason to deny oral traditional roots. Better to remain agnostic about scenarios for which we have no primary, irrefutable evidence, and at the same time to take full account of the oral traditional structure and expressivity of such works. We will find no more celebrated example of this kind of oral-derived text than Homer's *Odyssey*, which reveals phraseological and narrative patterning associated with oral tradition even though it reaches us only after a long, poorly understood manuscript history. If we deny Homer his oral traditional language, we will inevitably misread his (and his tradition's) poem.[16]

Our fourth category, *Written oral traditions*,[17] may seem a contradiction in terms, but only if we cling to the long-superseded binary model of orality versus literacy. In fact, this type of oral tradition – which is composed and performed in writing and intended solely for textual consumption by silent readers – places the emphasis where it belongs: on the register of language as the determining factor. Take the example of the nineteenth-century Montenegrin archbishop Petar II Petrović Njegoš,[18] who learned the South Slavic oral epic tradition as a young boy in his native village. Later, long after he became a highly educated cleric and accomplished intellectual, he wanted to write poetry, and had a choice of two very different kinds of media. Familiar with the poems of the European literary elite, he could have selected any one of the currently fashionable forms in Italian, French, German, and so forth. But instead he chose to compose poems that treated a variety of topics, including contemporary political concerns, in the decasyllabic poetic diction of his youth. Because he was fluent in this oral traditional register, he could use it to write poetry for print publication; he could in effect "sing on the page." And since the medium he chose was a specialized, highly idiomatic language, it is best understood by an audience fluent in the same register. That Njegoš wrote for readers is beyond doubt; that, as another dimension of the same process, he was also composing oral poetry is likewise indisputable.

---

[16] On traditional structure in Homer, see J. M. Foley, *Traditional Oral Epic: The Odyssey, Beowulf, and the Serbo-Croatian Return Song* (Berkeley and Los Angeles, 1990; repr. 1993), 121–57 (phraseology) and 240–77 (typical scenes). On the idiomatic implications of structure, see Foley, *Homer's Traditional Art*, 201–37 (phraseology), 169–99 (typical scenes), and 115–67 (story-pattern).

[17] Foley, *How to Read an Oral Poem*, 50–52.

[18] Foley, *How to Read an Oral Poem*, 50–51, 64.

3. Viable approaches

In the much-discussed area of approaches to oral tradition, the first principle is to avoid the parochialism of a single, exclusive method and to consider multiple viable options. The reason for this commitment to pluralism is not far to seek. If literature (rightly) demands a broad spectrum of approaches to interpretation, then how much more important is methodological pluralism for oral traditions, which as we noted above dwarf literary works in number, variety, and social functions? Essentially, the idea is to assemble multiple tools – or rather a tool-kit – for multiple interpretive jobs, rather than to restrict ourselves to a single, clumsily adjustable tool.

Over the years many approaches to oral tradition have arisen and enjoyed various degrees of acceptance and application, among them structural analysis, comparative studies, rhetorical studies, psychoanalysis, myth-ritual studies, the historical-geographical method, feminist inquiries, and numerous others.[19] Many of these methods are still practiced and could bear mention here. For our purposes, however, I will focus on three approaches that have gained currency over the past 15 years, and have been successfully applied to a wide variety of oral traditions from the ancient world to the present day: performance theory, Ethnopoetics, and Immanent art.[20]

performance theory simply asks the question "What difference does performance make?" And in answering that question this approach insists on the special meaning generated idiomatically by "keys to performance," that is, by certain features of composition, performance, and reception that signal the audience to understand the proceedings in some non-literal, more-than-textual way.[21] Thus a recurrent phrase or a particular kind of musical accompaniment or even an individual's costume may serve to place the performance within a recognizable frame of reference, a "place" in which the audience knows what kind of discourse to expect. In this regard it is easy to understand how reduction of a performance to a text robs an oral tradition of so much of its meaning-bearing potential. Some signals (such as recurrent diction, for example) can survive the transition to textuality – as long as the new, readerly audience is fluent in the register and can recognize the telltale keys – but many other signals will necessarily perish.

[19] See R. Lévy Zumwalt, "A Historical Glossary of Critical Approaches," *Teaching Oral Traditions* (ed. J. M. Foley; New York: Modern Language Association, 1998), 75–94.

[20] For more on these three approaches and their interrelationships, see Foley, *The Singer of Tales in Performance*, esp. 1–59; and *How to Read an Oral Poem*, 79–94, 95–108, and 109–24.

[21] For more on Performance theory, see R. Bauman, *Verbal Art as Performance* (Prospect Heights, Ill.: Waveland Press, 1977); idem, *Story, Performance, and Event: Contextual Studies of Oral Narrative* (Cambridge: Cambridge University Press, 1986); and, with D. Braid, "The Ethnography of Performance in the Study of Oral Traditions," *Teaching Oral Traditions* (ed. J. M. Foley; New York: Modern Language Association, 1998), 106–22.

Ethnopoetics, etymologically the poetics of the group, seeks to interpret oral traditions on their own terms, whatever those terms may be. In a sense this approach is anti-colonialist, in that it opposes the imposition of a foreign frame of reference in favor of searching out the native structure and expressivity of the given oral tradition.[22] For instance, it was an ethnopoetic perspective that put the lie to the assertion that Native American oral traditions were not composed in poetry by pointing out that these narratives had their own kind of metrical organization – the breath-group and the pause.[23] But whatever the particular features one encounters in a given oral tradition, ethnopoetics advocates an interpretation on its own terms followed by a transcription that reflects those features and a re-performance by the reader who then embodies that transcription. For Dennis Tedlock this means restoring the variations in loudness and intonation, the real-time linear definition, and especially the silence to performance of Zuni stories. For Dell Hymes it entails rediscovering the natural structural demarcations of verse, line, stanza, scene, and act in order to bring tales from Northwest Coast peoples back into true focus.[24]

Our third approach, *Immanent art*, starts by recasting the "repetition" identified by Parry-Lord Oral-Formulaic Theory as "recurrence." Moving from structure to meaning, this method looks at formulas, typical scenes, and story-patterns as idiomatic signals rather than merely tectonic strategies. From this vantage point, the specialized language or register of an oral tradition is a socially situated instrument that because of its immanent associations can support extremely economical communication.[25] If Homer's phrase *chlôron deos* ("green fear") is understood with its poetic value of "supernatural fear" (notwithstanding the fact that neither constituent has any literal link to the gods), then the audience/reader's experience is richer. If Andromache's speech pleading with

[22] Ethnopoetics has taken two main forms – structural and performative. On the structural approach, see D. Hymes, *"In Vain I Tried to Tell You": Essays in Native American Ethnopoetics* (Philadelphia: University of Pennsylvania Press, 1981); idem, "Ethnopoetics, Oral-Formulaic Theory, and Editing Texts," *Oral Tradition* 9 (1994): 330–70, available online at http://journal.oraltradition.org/files/articles/9ii/9_hymes.pdf; and *"Now I Know Only So Far": Essays in Ethnopoetics* (Lincoln: University of Nebraska Press, 2003). On the performative approach, see D. Tedlock, *The Spoken Word and the Work of Interpretation* (Philadelphia: University of Pennsylvania Press, 1983); and *Finding the Center: The Art of the Zuni Storyteller*, (ed. idem; rev. ed.; Lincoln: University of Nebraska Press, 1999).

[23] On the breath-group as a metrical determinant, see D. Hymes, "Discovering Oral Performance and Measured Verse in American Indian Narrative," *New Literary History* 7 (1977): 431–57; repr. in rev. form in Hymes, *"In Vain I Tried to Tell You"*, 79–141. On recognizing pause as a signal for lineation, see Tedlock, *Finding the Center*, esp. xii ff.

[24] See note 22 above.

[25] For more on this approach and in particular on the concept of *traditional referentiality*, see esp. J. M. Foley, *Immanent Art: From Structure to Meaning in Traditional Oral Epic* (Bloomington: Indiana University Press, 1991); idem, *The Singer of Tales in Performance*, 29–98; idem, *Homer's Traditional Art*, 13–34; and idem, *How to Read an Oral Poem*, 109–24.

Hektor not to return to the battlefield is also recognized as the typical scene of Lament, then we realize she is already mourning her husband – destined for death even as he stands there before her. And if we recognize Homer's *Odyssey* as a species of the widespread Indo-European Return Song, then we will be able to solve three longstanding cruces: (a) why the story follows a non-chronological sequence (the idiomatic order for this tale-type); (b) why Penelope steadfastly refuses to recognize Odysseus for so long (the idiomatic role for the woman who is the focal character in this tale-type); and (c) why the story culminates as it does (the woman, not the man, is the central hero in this kind of story, and the couple's rapprochement in Book 23 is the actual climax).[26]

In offering these three approaches (and favoring none above the others), let me reaffirm that diversity of perspectives is the goal. The notion of a "complete" or "final" interpretation is a textual and logocentric illusion in any case, since any hermeneutics worth the name remains an open-ended process with multiple, revisable possibilities built into the inquiry. But in the present case the reality is yet more stark: the tremendous variety of subjects and experiences, across such expanses of time and space, simply precludes using a single, exclusive tool for addressing the panoply of oral traditions. For such a plurality of traditions we need nothing less than a plurality of approaches.

4. Shared issues across a diverse spectrum

In seeking unity within such diversity, let us start not by compiling a list of shared cross-cultural features (unavoidably a Pyrrhic exercise), but rather by highlighting some significant points of common emphasis. By framing these points as questions, I mean to emphasize that the correspondences are heuristic, in other words that we can project important comparisons and contrasts by posing these queries. It is not so much in the answers, then, but in the process of inquiry that we can begin to appreciate similarities and differences among oral traditions. Here are the five queries:

1. How does a given oral tradition communicate?
2. What kind(s) of audience does it support or engage?
3. What assumptions are implicit in its structure and idiom?
4. What social function does each oral tradition serve?
5. What group or individual identity/identities does it foster?

Such questions have been addressed to a broad variety of oral traditions that show diversity in ethnic origins, languages (and linguistic possibilities), performers, audiences, genres, social functions, and orality-literacy interactions, and

---

[26] See note 16 above.

here we can examine only a very small sample. For instance, Fatos Tarifa has described the longstanding institution of Albanian oral law,[27] known as the *kanun* of Lekë Dukagjini, an Albanian prince and compatriot of George Kastriot Skanderberg (1405–68). Committed to writing only in the early twentieth century, this body of law existed and functioned as a wholly oral resource for about five hundred years. As a secular code, it governed birth practices, marriage ceremonies, generational and gender roles, mortuary customs and inheritance rules, criminal and civil matters, and a great deal more. A much different kind of oral tradition, slam poetry,[28] serves as a vehicle for social commentary in large and medium-sized cities throughout the United States, and is rapidly spreading in Europe and Central America as well. In this case the performance venues are clubs, coffeehouses, and (for national competitions) theatres and auditoriums, and performances are rated numerically to determine winners in both individual and team competitions. Although the poems presented in such situations start their lives as texts, they reach their vocal, highly participatory audiences only via live performance, thus falling into our category of Voiced texts.

Homeric oral epic reaches us only as a manuscript-prisoned tradition, a Voice from the past, but in recent years questions like those listed above have opened up new windows on this ancient oral tradition. We are beginning to grasp the near-certainty that "Homer" is a code-name, an anthropomorphization, for the tradition itself, and that if such a person ever existed his real-world identity has been overlain by centuries of legend.[29] Thus if the contemporary lives of Homer do not agree about his era, his parentage, his native region, or his repertoire, those contradictions are simply a measure of the legend's morphology and ubiquity. We are also starting to plumb the idiomatic depths of Homeric poetry, delving beyond literal, lexicon-based signification to the traditional connotations that the epic register supports.[30] Additionally, it has become more apparent that the *Iliad* and *Odyssey*, though supremely important, existed within a wider ecology of oral poetic forms, including the works of Hesiod, the Homeric Hymns, the (mostly lost) Epic Cycle, and lyric poetry. Understanding the great epics as stemming from an oral tradition has also shed light on their Panhellenic nature, their Indo-European heritage, and even the ways in which we need to

---

[27] F. Tarifa, "Of Time, Honor, and Memory: Oral Law in Albania," *Oral Tradition* 23 (2008): 3–14; available online at http://journal.oraltradition.org/files/articles/23i/02_23.1tarifa.pdf.

[28] See Eleveld, *The Spoken Word Revolution Redux*; Foley, *How to Read an Oral Poem*, 97–102, 156–65.

[29] See Foley, "Individual Poet and Epic Tradition: The Legendary Singer," *Arethusa* 31 (1998): 149–78; and idem, *Homer's Traditional Art*, 49–63; also B. Graziosi, *Inventing Homer: The Early Reception of Epic* (Cambridge: Cambridge University Press, 2007).

[30] See Foley, *Traditional Oral Epic*, 121–57 (phraseology); 240–77 (typical scenes). On the idiomatic implications of structure, see Foley, *Homer's Traditional Art*, 201–37, 169–99, and 115–67.

understand their variants in order to assemble faithful editions. Similar investigations have been made of Old English oral-derived poetry such as the epic
Beowulf, another Voice from the past, with similar results.[31]

Sardinian *mutetu* offers us another competitive oral tradition,[32] but unlike
slam poetry this improvisatory art belongs to the category of Oral performance.
Observing a welter of compositional rules involving meter, music, stanzaic
form, and word-order mirroring, three to five *cantadori* respond to an assigned
topic and to each other, continuously and serially dueling among themselves to
create the most apt response. Group performances customarily last from two to
three hours, and are attended by rapt, knowledgeable audiences on feast-days of
patron saints, with front-row enthusiasts regularly making audio recordings of
the events. This poetic genre finds a counterpart in the Basque tradition of
bertsolaritza,[33] where once again a small cadre of singers (*bertsolari*) compose and
duel within a tightly rule-governed medium. At events in the Basque Country it
is quite common to hear the audience singing along with the poet during the
final couplet of an oral poem that has never existed before the moment of its
utterance. This remarkable phenomenon is no mystery, however: because metrical, musical, rhyming, and other guidelines help to determine which paths
performers can take, by the end of the stanza all fluent participants – *bertsolari* and
audience alike – realize the inevitability of the last few steps.

As a final example, consider the cultural cross-section of oral traditions encountered by our research team in rural Serbia.[34] Alongside the well-collected
and well-studied epic, numerous other oral traditional species populate the
village ecology: lyric or women's songs, healing charms, genealogies, funeral
laments, folktales, recipes, and what might be called "folk speech." Some of
these are performed by women in octosyllabic lines and others by men in
decasyllabic format, but each genre does service by supporting a social function
for the community. Epics subtend group identity and furnish behavior models
(not seldom by narrating what *not* to do), lyrics figure prominently in a broad
range of ritual and interpersonal events, healing charms treat physical and psychological afflictions, genealogies recall the 13–15 generations that lead to contemporary extended families, funeral laments mourn the deceased and help to
heal family and friends, folktales amuse and divert (and not seldom offer an
encoded lesson), and recipes take the place of a box of index cards or an online
data-base for food preparation. Over time these traditions have adapted to

---

[31] See Foley, *Traditional Oral Epic,* 201–39 and 329–58; idem, *Immanent Art,* 190–242; idem,
The Singer of Tales in Performance, 181–207; idem, *Homer's Traditional Art,* 263–79; idem, *How to
Read an Oral Poem,* 102–7.

[32] See Zedda, "The Southern Sardinian Tradition of the *Mutetu Longu,*" 3–40.

[33] See the special issue of *Oral Tradition* devoted to Basque oral traditions (22, ii [2007]),
available online at http://journal. oraltradition. org/issues/22ii.

[34] Foley, *How to Read an Oral Poem,* 188–218.

changes in politics, religion, current events, and other cultural realities; like South African praise-poetry, they are rule-governed enough to persist but malleable enough to accommodate often radical change.[35]

5. Proverbs on oral tradition

Because the Protean, highly idiomatic nature of oral traditions is inherently difficult for we readers of texts to grasp, let me enlist the aid of an oral traditional genre – proverbs – in order to succinctly and (I hope) memorably encapsulate some fundamental features of the medium. To begin, a straightforward admission: these seven proverbs have of course been constructed for the purpose of demonstration, and are in every respect non-genuine. Nonetheless, I hope they can engage some of the explanatory, indexical power of real proverbs, and thus serve as helpful reminders of some core issues in oral tradition studies.

1. *Oral tradition works like language, only more so.* Like language itself, oral traditions are living, evolving entities that do their social work not by remaining static and inflexible but by varying according to implicit rules; that is, they adapt within limits. Characteristically, oral traditions use more highly specialized, more densely coded forms of flexible language than are employed for non-specific, everyday speech.

2. *"Oraltradition" is a very plural noun.* In contrast to the early belief that orality and literacy are mutually exclusive categories, fieldwork and analysis have shown that oral traditions dwarf literature in number, variety, and diversity of social functions.

3. *performance is the enabling event, tradition is the context for that event.* Performance, whether actual or rhetorical (as in oral-derived texts), is an essential part of the meaning; it enables and directs a particular kind of reception. Tradition, understood as the set of idiomatic implications to which any performance institutionally refers, provides the ambient context for faithful reception.

4. *The play's the thing, and not the script.* Oral tradition cannot be contained in the pages of a prompt-book; it lives only in emergent performance, whether actual or rhetorical.

5. *Composition and reception are two sides of the same coin.* As with any language-based transaction, both composer and receiver must be fluent in the particular coded language (or register) they are using to communicate. They must play the game by the same set of rules.

---

[35] See esp. J. Opland, *Xhosa Oral Poetry: Aspects of a Black South African Oral Tradition* (Cambridge: Cambridge University Press, 1983); R. H. Kaschula, *The Bones of the Ancestors Are Shaking: Xhosa Oral Poetry in Context* (Cape Town: Juta Press, 2000) and idem, "Mandela Comes Home: The Poets' Perspective," *Oral Tradition* 10 (1995): 91–110, available online at http://journal. oraltradition. org/files/articles/10i/8_kaschula. pdf.

6. *True diversity demands diversity in frame of reference*. Given the tremendous variety of oral traditions, we must be prepared to engage not one but multiple interpretive approaches. If restricting ourselves to a single perspective fore-shortens our appreciation of literature, how much more reductive will parochi-alism prove in regard to the far broader spectrum of oral traditions? A multi-purpose tool-kit of methods will best suit the task as the field develops.

7. *Without a tradition there is no language, without a speaker there is only silence.* In oral tradition there is no conflict between tradition and the individual, as has sometimes been maintained. Once again, the analogy to language is instructive: to foster communication, one needs a speaker, a shared code, and a receiver.

6. An unexpected homology: Oral Tradition and Internet Technology

One of the severest handicaps to an appreciation of oral tradition on its own terms has been the text-centered mentality with which academic research is burdened. Struggle as we may, it remains extremely hard to escape what amounts to an "ideology of the text,"[36] whereby we automatically construe verbal art as a linear, page-bound, static experience. This attitude, at root a cultural default, has led to such distortions as reducing a multimedia perfor-mance to a silent, lineated text, and in the process ignoring such fundamental (and determinative) features as structure and idiom, intonation, pause, gesture, vocal melody, instrumental accompaniment, performer-audience interaction, and myriad other aspects of many-sided works of more-than-textual verbal art. In forcing oral traditions into a textual format, we rob them of their ability to mean.

Perhaps counter-intuitively, the new media associated with digital and In-ternet communication offer us a way out of this impasse. First, there is the matter of the analogy or homology between oral tradition (OT) and Internet technology (IT).[37] Notwithstanding superficial differences, both of these media operate by presenting networks of potentials that the user – in OT the perfor-mer and audience, in IT the web-designer and -surfer – can navigate through. In place of fixed textual artifacts that offer only a one-way passage through lines, paragraphs, pages, and so forth, OT and IT present opportunities for multiple routes and co-creation, for an experience that is ever-emerging in real time. Surfers in both technologies are always making choices, helping to determine their experiences as they negotiate the pathways of their story-web or world-

---

[36] See Foley, "The Ideology of the Text," in the Pathways Project, online at http://www.pathwaysproject.org/pathways/show/IdeologyOfTheText.

[37] For a full, multimedia discussion of this homology, see J. M. Foley, "Navigating Path-ways: Oral Tradition and the Internet," *Academic Intersections* 2 (2008), online at http://edcom-munity.apple.com/ali/story.php?itemID=13163.

wide web. This is the kind of enabling dynamic Homer had in mind when he described ancient Greek oral epic singers not in terms of their memory or voice or repertoire, but rather by celebrating their Muse-given knowledge of the *oimai* ("pathways").[38]

Second, the OT-IT homology, instructive in itself as a perspective on comparative media, is also an open invitation and challenge to leverage the very latest medium to more faithfully represent humankind's first (and *per capita* still most dominant) medium. At my Center for Studies in Oral Tradition, we have responded by creating a number of electronic prostheses. One of these strategies is the eCompanion, which supplements textual representation with open-access, web-based digests of photos, audio, and video. Such multimedia caches have been deployed in connection with our journal, *Oral Tradition*,[39] itself now available as a searchable and free-of-charge resource on the web, and with my book entitled *How to Read an Oral Poem*.[40] Another IT resource is the eEdition,[41] which melds a dual-language textual presentation of a South Slavic oral epic with a glossary, apparatus, and sound file via hypertext. It too is open-access and requires no fee for usage. Finally, the Pathways Project,[42] which both studies and illustrates the OT-IT homology, consists of both brick-and-mortar and electronic components: (1) a "morphing book," which can be read in multiple ways and sequences; and (2) a website that allows the surfer to fashion a personal version of its interlinked inventory of dozens of small chapters or "nodes." All of these initiatives seek to take advantage of the reality that OT and IT – unlike books – mime the very way we think.

Summary

In short, then, the watchword for the study of oral traditions must be the natural plenitude and diversity of the field, and with recognition of those defining dimensions comes a responsibility to seek a more responsive model and a variety of interpretive approaches. To my mind that model must avoid both the discredited binary of orality versus literacy and parochial descriptions based on a small selection of examples, and must instead highlight the fundamental parameters of composition, performance, and reception. Accordingly, in order to suit the diversity of oral traditions we need not one but multiple approaches.

---

[38] See the description at *Odyssey* 8.479–81:"For among all mortal men the singers have a share in honor and reverence, since to them the Muse has taught the *pathways*, for she loves the singers' tribe."

[39] Visit http://journal.oraltradition.org/.

[40] Visit http://oraltradition.org/hrop/.

[41] Visit http://oraltradition.org/zbm.

[42] Visit http://www.pathwaysproject.org/pathways/show/HomePage.

With such rationalizing ideas in mind, the unity within the remarkable diversity of oral traditions is far easier to grasp. Toward the end of this contribution I offered seven home-made proverbs in an attempt to capture difficult concepts simply, and closed with a brief examination of the homology between oral tradition and digital/Internet media. Overall, it is a very exciting time to be enmeshed in these studies, as the world continues to open up its rich store of oral traditions.

Transmissions from Scripturality to Orality: Hearing the Voice of Jesus in Mark 4:1–34[*]

Kristina Dronsch

Gewiss, ich hörte stets nur meine eigene Stimme, aber meine Stimme war zugleich die Stimme der Toten, insofern es den Toten gelungen war, Textspuren von sich selbst zu hinterlassen, die sich durch die Stimmen der Lebenden zu Gehör bringen.[1]

In her well-known book *Holy Lives, Holy Deaths: A Close Hearing of Early Jewish Storytellers*[2] Antoinette Clark Wire introduces us to the world of storytelling. She writes, "Telling and retelling stories was a structural characteristic of the biblical tradition," which she sees continued in Early Jewish writings (p. 2). Wire describes storytelling as "effective communication" (p. 4). This is precisely the main focus of my interest in the following essay: to inquire into the way in which the Gospel of Mark offers effective communication, to ask what are the strategies used in the writing of the Gospel of Mark which makes it an effective form of communication and what function these strategies have. In continuing with Wire's important insights on "effective communication," we can say that effective communication always has two aspects that can be examined: effective production and effective reception.

While the predominant flow of current biblical studies is more interested in aspects concerning effective production and continues to offer many new and groundbreaking insights for studies of the biblical text (especially of the Gospel of Mark), there are a few studies which focus exclusively on the issue of effective reception of the Gospel of Mark, by which I mean the reading of a story. This is even more astonishing when we keep in mind that "we cannot escape the fact that we are able to gain access to these [oral/aural] dimensions only through the written text."[3] This statement of Holly E. Hearon notes that the singling out

---

[*] I am most grateful to the two editors of this volume, Robert Coote and Annette Weissenrieder, for their help and support correcting the English text.

[1] St. Greenblatt, *Verhandlungen mit Shakespeare: Innenansichten der englischen Renaissance* (Frankfurt am Main: Fischer-Taschenbuch-Verl., 1993), 9.

[2] A. C. Wire, *Holy Lives, Holy Deaths: A Close Hearing of Early Jewish Storytellers* (Atlanta: Society of Biblical Literature, 2002).

[3] H. E. Hearon, "The Implications of Orality for Studies of the Biblical Text," in *Performing the Gospel: Orality, Memory, and Mark: Essays Dedicated to Werner Kelber* (eds. R. A. Horsley, J. A. Draper, and J. M. Foley; Minneapolis: Fortress Press, 2006), 3–20: 8.

of the issue of effective reception is a necessary condition for any understanding of what we might call the "social embeddedness" of any biblical text. Yet in considering the aspect of the reception of effective communication we must also be aware of our own personal social embeddedness – at both an individual and cultural level. Pierre Bourdieu notes:

S'interroger sur les conditions de possibilité de la lecture, c'est s'interroger sur les conditions sociales de possibilité des situations dans lesquelles on lit [...] et aussi sur les conditions sociales des productions des *lectores*. Une des illusions du *lector* est celle qui consiste à oublier ses propres conditions sociales de production, à universaliser inconsciemment les conditions des possibilités de sa lecture.[4]

Here we have a pertinent warning against any temptation to project our own relationship with ancient biblical texts onto their past readers. Thus we face the problem of developing a theoretical approach. A theory is required which takes the cultural differences of those who read biblical texts into consideration. In the work of Umberto Eco a theory is identified which demonstrates an awareness of the warning referred to earlier. Eco's theory is characterized by its fundamental approach to those practices of reception that are culturally determined. Eco's theory attempts to couple the singular acts of the interpretation of meaning with a culturally-determined principle of generating meaning. The latter assumes a correlation between singular acts of interpretation and an abstract system of cultural competence.

Eco explains the readers' interpretative cooperation with reference to the model-reader. This reader needs to keep in mind the cultural codes the text is obliged to adhere to and needs to follow the strategy of the text. In considering the cultural competence of the readers Eco places the act of reading in the center as the crucial activity with respect to establishing the model-reader of Mark 4:1–34. While reader-oriented approaches in biblical studies (for example: reader-response-criticism) do take into account reading as the fundamental activity, they do not, however, consider the cultural skills that differentiate contemporary reading conditions from reading governed by the cultural codes of antiquity. By ignoring the cultural codes of reading reader-oriented approaches are subject to the temptation of developing an "ethnocentrism of reading" because these approaches ignore the fact that ancient texts – such as biblical texts – in no way imply the existence of a solitary and silent reader in search for meaning.

---

[4] P. Bourdieu, "Lecture, lecteurs, lettrés, litérature," *Choses dites* (ed. P. Bourdieu; Paris: Editions de Minuit, 1987), 132–143. Inquiring into the conditions of the possibility of reading means inquiring into the social conditions which make possible the situations in which one reads ... and inquiring also into the social conditions of the production of *lectores*. One of the illusions of the *lector* [from the point of view of the reader] is that which consists in forgetting one's own social conditions of production, and unconsciously universalising the conditions of the possibility of one's own reading. P. Bourdieu, *In Other Words: Essays Towards a Reflexive Sociology* (trans. M. Adamson; Stanford, CA: Stanford University Press, 1990), 94–105, 95.

Due to this fact of cultural difference it is necessary to break with the concept of maintaining an uncritical attitude, which assumes that all texts have been read and received according to the criteria that characterize our own relationship to the written word. In the context of Greco-Roman antiquity reading is to be understood as reading aloud. As Paul Achtemeier has convincingly shown, reading written text aloud was the common practice in Greco-Roman antiquity.[5] Passages from Plato's Phaedo[6] and Theaetetus[7] are impressive evidence for this fact, but also passages from Theon[8] or on hearing in the letters by Pliny the Younger[9]. The same is true for the biblical texts. Acts 8:26–40 is proof of this practice: Philip hears the Ethiopian read; that is only possible when this man reads aloud. In the Apocalypse of John (1:3) we are also faced with the practice of reading aloud:

Μακάριος ὁ ἀναγινώσκων καὶ οἱ ἀκούοντες τοὺς λόγους τῆς προφητείας.

For the vast majority of our contemporaries today, reading a musical score is the appropriate analogy to reading a text in Greco-Roman times, since texts conveyed meaning only as they sounded and were heard.[10] This is even more important to remember within the context of *scriptio continua:* Uncial manuscripts are not divided into paragraphs or lines, no punctuation is found in the text (or if punctuation is found, it has no function for the surface structure of the written text; rather it is just for prosodic effects).[11] Finally, there are no spaces between words. The text is simply presented as letter after letter. In contemporary times, however, the way in which a text is laid out forms an important part of a reading aid. All aspects of layout are absent in ancient texts. Therefore, texts

---

[5] P.J. Achtemeier, "Omne Verbum Sonat: The New Testament and the Oral Environment of Late Western Antiquity," *JBL* 109 (1990): 17–19. Achtemeier's conclusion has been modified by Frank D. Gilliard, "More Silent Reading in Antiquity: Non Omne Verbum Sonabat," *JBL* 112 (1993): 689–694.

[6] See for example: Plato, *Phaed.* 97β: ἀκούσας μέν ποτε βιβλίου.

[7] See for example: Plato, *Theaet.* 143b. c.

[8] See for example: Theon, *Progymnasmata* 61.

[9] See for example: Pliny, *Ep.* IX, 36.

[10] I am grateful to Prof. Dr. James Noel of San Francisco Theological Seminary for his very helpful comment that the sounded text is not only found in Greco-Roman times but can be seen as a multicultural phenomenon. In the slave-biography of O. Equiano, *The Life of Olaudah Equiano or Gustavus Vassa, the African* (Toronto: Dover, 1999), the following passage is found. "I had often seen my master and Dick employed in reading; and I had a great curiosity to talk to the books, as I thought they did; and so to learn how all things had a beginning. For that purpose I have often taken up a book, and talked to it, and then put my ears to it, when alone, in hopes it would answer me; and I have been very much concerned when I found it remained silent" (p. 42).

[11] See J. Penny Small, *Wax Tablets of the Mind: Cognitive Studies of Memory and Literacy in Classical Antiquity* (New York: Routledge, 1997). Small reminds us, "In antiquity prosody was emphasized, while the syntactical uses of punctuation did not appear until the Middle Ages" (p. 20).

written in *scriptio continua* make no distinction between visual and aural aspects, a distinction which today enables us to differentiate between printed and oral media. On account of this fact a text in antiquity is not revealed through sight but through sound for its effectiveness.[12]

What does that mean with respect to Mark 4? Let us take a look at the parable chapter, which is characterized by a situation where the Markan Jesus speaks. Here we can identify an intense prosody within these verses with many assonances. Listen for example to the verbs used in Mark 4:4–8: ἔπεσεν [...] ἦλθεν [...] κατέφαγεν [...] ἔπεσεν [...] εἶχεν [...] ἐξανέτειλεν [...] ἀνέτειλεν [...] ἔπεσεν [...] ἔδωκεν [...] ἔπεσεν [...] ἔφερεν (Mark 4:4a. b, 5a. b, 6a, 7a. d, 8a). In verse 8 we find a strong stylisation through assonances: ἀναβαίνοντα [...] αὐ-ξανόμενα [...] τριάκοντα [...] ἑξήκοντα. Just the last word ἑκατόν leaves this prosody.

If we look at 4:10–13 the following assonances leave us with a strong impact of a sounded, a hearable text: τοῖς [...] αὐτοῖς [...] ἐκείνοις [...] αὐτοῖς (4:10b, 11a, 11c, 13a), μή [...] μήποτε (4:12b, 12d, 12e). Moreover, we find lots of verbs ending with –ωσιν (especially in 4:12). The assonances continue in 4:14–20, in which many verbs end with –ωσιν und –οσιν and where an increasing number of οι-tones can be identified. The only exception is found in v. 14. In Mark 4:21–22 many η-tones give the text a prosodic structure. If we compare verses 21–22 with verse 12 we can find nearly the same prosodic structure. In 4:24–25 the verbs ending with –θησεται are simplified in order to render the text easier to hear.

In Mark 4:26–29 the η-tones are particularly dominant: ἡ [...] βάλη [...] καθεύδη| [...] αὐτομάτη ἡ γῆ. At the end of theses verses, however, the ος-endings and ον-endings are predominant. The same assonances are found in Mark 4:30–32, so that these verses are closely connected with Mark 4:26–29 from the point of view of prosody. Mark 4:33–34 is sound structured through-out to the αις- and οις-tones. The introductions to the speech situations ("he said") which organize chapter 4 are also important for the prosody of the text and make it easier for the reader to hear a text because the repetitive character enables the reader to discern repeated tonalities.

A text without any layout meets special requirements of the reader. "Because all the letters were run together, the major problem every reader faced was figuring out what was a word."[13] Thus the rhetorical stylisation of the written material gains in importance for the reader to single out what was actually written.

---

[12] Evidence for this understanding is found at Dionysios Thrax, Τέχνη γραμματική, chapter 2 and Quintilian, *Inst* 1,7,30–31: "*ego, nisi quod consuetudo optinuerit, sic scribendum quidque iudico quomodo sonat. Hic enim est usus litterarum, ut custodiant uoces et uelut depositum reddant legentibus.*"

[13] Small, *Wax Tablets*, 24.

The alternative to visual structuring of a manuscript to indicate organization of meaning is to include oral indications of structure within the material. Individual points, for example, can be stressed by repetition, and formal parallelism of the repetition will make its importance even more evident.[14]

In Mark 4:1–34 we can find a strong rhetorical stylisation of the text, mainly through the recurrence of particular words: Mark 4:1–2 starts with a situation that is characterized by the use of the word διδάσκειν. The διδάσκειν-situation is introduced through polyptota and paronymy (διδάσκειν [...] ἐδίδασκεν [...] διδαχῇ). Mark 4:1 and 4:2 are connected by anaphoric links: (v. 1: καὶ πάλιν [...] καὶ συνάγεται [...] καὶ πᾶς [...] v. 2: καὶ ἐδίδασκεν [...] καὶ ἔλεγεν).

In Mark 4:3–9 many word repetitions can be identified; note for example the polyptota ἄλλο (v. 5a) [...] ἄλλο (v. 7a) [...] ἄλλα (v. 8a). In v. 5 we find what could almost be described as a play on words: οὐκ εἶχεν γῆν πολλήν [...] μὴ ἔχειν βάθος γῆς [...] μή. ἔχειν ῥίζαν.

Many polyptota can be found in Mark 4:10–13, but for the majority and most well-known the reader already has heard in Mark 4:1–9: ἐγένετο [...] γίνεται (Mark 4:10a, 11c) is tied to Mark 4:4a. The polyptota παραβολάς (v. 10b) [...] παραβολαῖς (v. 11c) [...] παραβολήν (v. 13b) [...] παραβολαῖς (v. 13c) is tied to παραβολαῖς from Mark 4:2, The words αὐτόν (2 x in v. 10b) [...] αὐτοῖς (v. 11a) [...] αὐτοῖς (vv. 12f.) [...] αὐτοῖς (v. 13a) are connected with 4:2b. The polyptota ἀκούοντες ἀκούωσιν Mark 4:12c) stands in relation to 4:3 and 4:9.

In Mark 4:14–20 the main polyptota is: σπείρεται (v. 15b), ἐσπαρμένον (v. 15e), σπειρόμενοι (v. 16), σπειρόμενοι (v. 18), σπαρέντες (v. 20).

In Mark 4:14–20 many word repetitions are also found: εἴσιν (in Mark 4:15a, 16a, 17b, 18a, 20a), οὗτοι (in Mark 4:15a, 16a, 18b), εὐθύς (Mark 4:15a, 16b, 17c), and ὅταν (in Mark 4:15c, 16b). The already well known repetition of ἕν from Mark 4:8 is also found in 4:20.

Many word repetitions are found in Mark 4:23–25: ἔχει in 4:23a, 25a. c.d; καὶ ἔλεγεν αὐτοῖς in 4:21, 24; ἵνα 4:21c, 22b. d; τεθῇ in 4:21c. d. Anaphoric connections are also found: οὐχ [...] οὐ [...] οὐδέ in 4:21d.22a. c, and the already well known polyptota ἀκούειν ἀκουέτω is found in v. 23b and v. 24b; the polyptota αὐτοῖς (4:21a, 24a) [...] αὐτῷ (v. 25b) [...] αὐτοῦ (v. 25d) beneath λύχνος [...] λυχνίαν in 4:21b. d. Rhetorically introduced with paronymy is φανερωθῇ [...] φανερόν in 4:22b. d and μέτρῳ [...] μετρεῖτε [...] μετρηθήσεται in 4:24.

In Mark 4:26b–29 the following polyptota are present: σπόρον [...] σπόρος in Mark 4:26c, 27c, γῆς [...] γῆ in Mark 4:26c, 28a and στάχυν [...] στάχυϊ in Mark 4:28. As is also an anaphoric stylization with καί (Mark 4:26a, 27a. b.c) and ὡς (Mark 4:26c, 27d) and εἶτα (Mark 4:28).

Also in the last verses the following word repetitions are present: ὅταν in Mark 4:31b, 32a, ἐπὶ τῆς γῆς in 4:31b. c und πάντων in 4:31c.

---

[14] Achtemeier, "Omne verbum sonat," 17f.

A further rhetorical aspect of the text are the *etymologisierenden Stammwieder-holungen*[15] such as σπείρων σπεῖραι (Mark 4:3); ἀκούειν ἀκούετω (Mark 4:9); βλέποντες βλέπωσιν [...] ἀκούοντες ἀκούωσιν (Mark 4:12); μέτρῳ μετρεῖτε μετρηθήσεται (Mark 4:24).

To sum up: Mark 4:1–34 is a strongly rhetorically stylised text within a continuous speech situation that is manifest in the text and emphasized by recurrence. This recurrence appears on the level of the sentence (including anaphorical links) and the words (mostly as polyptota in the same sentence). This prosody and rhetorical stylization has a particular impact on individual units of composition (Mark 4:1–2, 3–9, 10–13, 14–20, 21–25, 26–32, 33–34), while the individual units are linked, at the same time, to all the other sections of Mark 4:1–34 through word repetition. Yet the lexical-prosodic form of Mark 4:1–34 is also characterized by numerous consonances as well as word repetitions and points to a reception of the text aiming to make listening to the text easier. Therefore, the main aim of my thesis is to demonstrate that the purpose of the text Mark 4:1–34 is to trigger a way of speaking which is determined for the ear because the visual format of the ancient manuscript contained virtually no information about the organization and development of the content it intended to convey.

If we now return to our assumption made before, that texts in *scriptio continua* do not distinguish between the visual and aural aspects, which today enable us to differentiate between printed and oral media, we can, therefore, conclude with Small that texts are nothing more than "a variant of oral utterance [...] due to the lack of procedures for transforming writing into text." Reading is no longer only a visually based process "that depends on the recognition of orthographic units"; reading is instead a process "which is based on how the letters reflect the sound of the speech."[16] Reading is therefore oral performance "whenever it occurred and in whatever circumstances."[17] That indicates that "effective communication" (Antoinette Clark Wire) in respect of the aspect of reception requires sound and a reader who can make the "vocal effects"[18] heard.

Therefore according to antiquity's cultural code, hearing also has a function in written communication. It is necessary to make a letter heard in order to understand a text. Thus the issue of hearing gains in importance within the context of the act of reading because it is necessary to make letters audible in order to understand a text. It follows that the appeals to listen in Mark 4:1–34

[15] G. Lüderitz, "Rhetorik, Poetik, Kompositionstechnik im Markusevangelium," *Markus-Philologie. Historisch, literargeschichtliche und stilistische Untersuchungen zum zweiten Evangelium* (ed. H. Cancik; WUNT 33; Tübingen: Mohr Siebeck, 1984), 165–203, 180.

[16] Small, *Wax Tablets*, 24.

[17] Achtemeier, "Omne verbum sonat," 17.

[18] W. Shiner, *Proclaiming the Gospel: First Century Performance of Mark* (Harrisburg, PA: Trinity Press, 2003), 162.

receive their meaning within the written communication. The call to listen (Mark 4:3, 9, 23, 24) is the appeal to the model-reader to hear his or her own voice within the act of reading. As Whitney Shiner has convincingly shown, reading is a matter of voicing the text.[19] Therefore, the concentrated use of the imperatives of ἀκούειν in Mark 4 can be explained in relation to written communication. What is meant here are the physical ears of the listeners and not, as secondary literature often asserts, the inner readiness and ability to accept the teachings of Jesus. If the text does not reach our physical ears it remains mute and devoid of meaning.

This statement seems even truer due to the fact that the Markan text itself is taking no interest in a discussion of the issue of the oral conditions of a specific culture within the medium of writing. As Robbins has convincingly shown with reference to the beginning of the Gospel of Mark (Mark 1:1–8),

[t]here is no break what is written and what is oral in the Markan narration in these verses. The narrator's narration, the narrator's recitation of a blend of Exod 23:20 and Mal 3:1, the narrator's recitation of Is 40:3, the narrator's description of John and how people came to him, and the narrator's recitation of what John preached flow continuously forward into one another.[20]

Particularly in Mark 1:2 we have a situation where the written medium (Scripture) is speaking in the first person: ἰδοὺ ἀποστέλλω. The Scripture speaks as an ego.

What is noticeable about the central figure in Mark is that Jesus is always referring to the written media in a speech situation. Jesus, while speaking, refers to written media (to Scripture: see for example Mark 12:10; 14:21; 11:17; in Mark 10:4: Jesus refers to an βιβλίον ἀποστασίου that is written). Also the act of reading is of importance in the Gospel of Mark. We can find situations where the Markan Jesus – while speaking – refers to reading, while quoting the Scripture; cf. 2:25; 12:10, 26. It is also noticeable that the Gospel explicitly envisions a reading entity (cf. Mark 13:14) – and if we take a closer look at Mark 13:14 we find that ὁ ἀναγινώσκων is used in an oral situation where Jesus talks.

Let us also take a short look at the use of εὐαγγέλιον in the Gospel of Mark. In 8:35 and 10:29[21] we find εὐαγγέλιον used in an oral situation where the Markan

---

[19] See Shiner, *Proclaiming the Gospel*, 77–101.

[20] V. K. Robbins, "Interfaces of Orality and Literature in the Gospel of Mark," in *Performing the Gospel: Orality, Memory, and Mark: Essays Dedicated to Werner Kelber* (eds. R. A. Horsley, J. A. Draper, and J. M. Foley; Fortress Press: Minneapolis, 2006), 125–146, 131.

[21] E. Struthers Malbon, "Disciples/Crowds/Whoever: Markan Characters and Readers" in *In the Company of Jesus: Characters in Mark's Gospel* (Louisville, KY: Westminster John Knox Press, 2000), 70–99: 98–99. Malbon has shown that Jesus' statements of the "whoever" type, with which Mark 8:35 and 10:29 are introduced, are "left open for others to be included [...] – others including, if not especially, whoever hears or reads Mark's 'gospel of Jesus Christ, the Son of God' (1:1)."

Jesus speaks, in which εὐαγγέλιον is differentiated from Jesus. Within the Gospel of Mark we found that the Markan Jesus makes a distinction between him (ἐμοῦ) and εὐαγγέλιον. To distinguish between these two qualities clearly makes sense when εὐαγγέλιον refers to something different from Jesus but connected with him: that is a written medium the written Gospel (and not what Jesus has said and has done). Therefore, in 8:35 and 10:29 we have a situation where the Markan Jesus refers to Scripture. Not only the Scripture known from the Old Testament, but also the Scripture of the Gospel of Mark is included in the expression εὐαγγέλιον.

To sum up: within the Markan Gospel itself there are no indications of a dichotomy between orality and the written text, both are connected throughout the whole Gospel. And, reading is an important aspect of the Gospel of Mark.

Yet in order to make readers lend their voices to the text, the Gospel of Mark employs another strategy which influences readers beneath the prosodic and rhetorical structure of the text. It invites readers to give sound to the voice of Jesus. That is why the appeals to listen in Mark 4:1–34 appear in the sections where the Markan Jesus speaks. The speech in the text is not just a rhetorical fiction, which helps the reader to represent the absent Jesus as a speaking figure in the text; it is rather the voice of Jesus, which can be heard during the act of reading. The speech situation in Mark 4:1–34 serves to empower the scriptural context of the Gospel of Mark as a powerful word of writing – in precisely this combination of letter and word. The formal principle of speech is about the process of communicating the gospel, in which the situation of speech is assigned a function that supports the written word. This means that the speech in the text is not to be taken as a rhetorical figure which serves to hide the fact that there exists no speech in the written medium. The prevalence of orality, not only because the dead are not able to speak, but also because speech and the written medium exclude each other, is understandable because in our culture speech and text are modelled by the pattern life versus death.[22] While speech is connected with life, writing is connected with death. The reason why the Gospel of Mark transformed the words of Jesus into a written context is not because Mark wanted to end a theology of living oral tradition. On the contrary, the orality was used for the benefit of the power of writing.[23] Writing would

---

[22] See B. Menke, *Prosopopoiia. Stimme und Text bei Brentano, Hoffmann, Kleist und Kafka* (Munich: Kaiser, 2000), 11f.: "Als eine fehlende Verlebendigung der Toten (und der toten Texte) ist die Prosopopoiia ein Gegenmodell zur Allegorie: Sie ist maskierende, verhehlend Figur und verhehlte Figuration. Während die Prosopopoiia die Verlebendigung der schriftlichen toten Texte in der Stimme fingiert, ist die Allegorie die Figur der Schriftlichkeit und der toten Bedeutung."

[23] This sketched out interrelationship between orality and writing agrees with the statement of J. M. Foley, *Homer's Traditional Art* (University Park: Pennsylvania State University Press, 1999), 3: "scholarship over the past twenty years has taught us to distrust the false dichotomy of 'oral versus written' and to expect complex inventories and interactions of oral and literate in the same culture and even in the very same individual."

only be an accumulation of mute letters waiting for readers to breathe their spirit into it. Yet by presenting an imagined situation for the words of Jesus in Mark 4, Scripture lends itself a voice that is incorporated within itself. Connecting back to the power of Jesus' own words, this voice now exercises power over the readers of Mark 4:1–34. For this reason, while the Gospel of Mark is – as Joanna Dewey has pointed out – an "oral-aural event," this is not to be understood as being in opposition to writing, but precisely because the medium of writing makes use of elements of orality.[24] Therefore, the meaning of ἀκούειν refers to a particular circumstance that combines the aspects of speech and writing while reading aloud.

Kittel's thesis, expounded in the article "ἀκούω" in *TDNT*, according to which human hearing stands in relation to the revelation of the word of God because the hearing of a person represents correspondence to the revelation of the Word, is in need of revision from the aspect of respecting the codes of Greco-Roman times. The same holds for Hans Weder's thesis that hearing in merely passive terms is the anthropological correlation to the Protestant doctrine of justification.[25] According to these definitions, hearing gains its full meaning when the listener is addressed by a strictly external word. What is heard is the word of God which I cannot fill with sound myself. However, if the understanding rests on those cultural codes of hearing prevalent in antiquity, the meaning of ἀκούειν cannot be limited to sense perception in a speech situation. Rather, the definition must take into account a situation of written communication that is based on reading aloud and in which the one who utters the sounds is, at the same time, also the one who hears it. However, the presence of the person whose words are uttered is not necessary. On the one hand, the German exegesis of parables emphasizes that Jesus himself maintains his communication orally, with the medium of orality warranting the meaning of hearing. On the other hand, this understanding misjudges the codes prevalent in Greco-Roman antiquity, according to which the mediation of knowledge in written form can only take place in the form of an analogy to oral communication. Therefore, the speech situation presented in Mark 4 serves the purpose of establishing a relationship with the readers that follows the rules of human communication. Consequently, the fact that the identity of the addressee in Mark 4:1–34 remains open serves the purpose of establishing a close relation

---

[24] While J. Dewey, "The Gospel of Mark as an Oral-Aural Event: Implications for Interpretation," *The New Literary Criticism and the New Testament* (eds. E. S. Malbon and E. V. McKnight; JSNTSup 109; Sheffield: Sheffield Academic Press, 1994), 145–163: 145, is interested in the oral performance for a live audience, she is not really interested in the written material: "When we recognize how oral and aural the media world of early Christianity was, we also have to recognize the destabilization of the text itself."

[25] See H. Weder, *Neutestamentliche Hermeneutik* (Zürcher Grundrisse zur Bibel; Zürich: Theol. Verlag, 1989), 145–152, 204–230.

Kristina Dronsch

between the readers and what is written. Within the context of oralized reading the readers become the instrument of the afterlife of a (passive) writing. The text, not being able to forgo the voice of the reader, incorporates a voice into itself that, connected to the power of Jesus' own words, now exercises power over the readers. For this reason hearing is also not a receptive act, but an act of perception that is relevant to understanding. Accordingly, the dichotomy between hearing and seeing as presupposed by Kittel and Weder is implausible when faced with the codes of antiquity. The model-reader must instead be so competent as to not construe hearing and seeing as two separate acts of perception.[26]

With the presupposition of reading aloud it is now clear why Mark 4:12 and 4:24 mention hearing and seeing at the same time. Secondary literature often explains Mark 4:24 ("See what you hear") with the remark that the word "how" would be expected instead of "what." France notes, "The difference lies in how they hear them, rather than in what they hear. Mark's sense is clear enough – a call to pay careful attention to what is heard – but the syntax is awkward."[27] If, however, the model-reader reads aloud, lending his or her voice to the visually perceived letters, the "what" denotes the writing, and the readers are instructed to pay attention to what is made audible while reading aloud. Reading aloud, hearing and seeing are not separate acts of perception. While the eye is apprehending the written signs and is "perceiving" the letters, the ears "understand" the letters. After searching the meaning of ἀκούειν in Mark 4 it is possible to say that hearing has a meaning in written communication and that ἀκούειν is not based on a dichotomy between the oral and the written material.

If we now ask for the reason why the narrative world of Mark is presented as a coherent world inhabited by the words of Jesus we can find the answer: Jesus is absent. Through the act of reading the absent Jesus is present. Given the absence of Jesus, the presence of Jesus' λόγος in the scriptural context constitutes the possibility of making this λόγος audible again by reading aloud. I do not agree with Werner Kelber's statement "[…] Mark could ill afford to let the living Lord speak, because he created the form that was designed to silence him."[28] Instead, the written Gospel is the only access to the voice of Jesus in a time when he is absent. The voice of Jesus can be reanimated by the voice of the reader. There-

---

[26] Cf. Quintilian, *Inst.* 1,1,34: "*nam prospicere in detrum, quod omnes praecipiunt, et prouidere non rationis modo sed usus quoque est, quoniam sequential intuenti priora dicenda sunt, et, quod difficillimum est, diuidenda intentio animi, ut aliud uoce, aliud oculis agatur,*" and Cicero, *De or.* 150: "*ut in legendo oculus sic animus in dicendo prospiciet quid sequatur, ne extremorum, verborum cum insequentibus primis concursus aut hiulcas voces efficiat aut asperas.*"

[27] R. T. France, *The Gospel of Mark. A Commentary of the Greek Text* (NIGTC; Grand Rapids: Eerdmans, 2002), 210.

[28] W. H. Kelber, *The Oral and the Written Gospel: The Hermeneutics of Speaking and Writing in the Synoptic Tradition, Mark, Paul, and Q* (Bloomington: Indiana University Press, 1983), 209.

fore, it is required that a reader will be an instrument for the words of Jesus. Let us take a look at section Mark 4:14–20. The section Mark 4:14–20 is characterized by a centering of hearing with regard to the λόγος and underlines four different kinds of hearing, which in their different qualities lead to different receptions of the logos. This central section of the text is a focused narration about processes of perception and reception that are developed with regard to the λόγος. Mark 4:14–20 represents an innovative hermeneutical acroamatic compendium that is guiding the entire process of the reception of the Markan narrative. Mark 4:14–20 in particular (as a metacommunicative-interpretive segment dealing with the reception of the λόγος through hearing) is thus a model for the exemplary use of the written text, whose pragmatic goal consists in the education of the readers, so that they may prove to be those sowed on good soil, having perceived the λόγος in a manner that is fertile because it begins with hearing. Considering the end of the narrative of the Gospel of Mark, Jesus' absence demonstrates the necessity for a written gospel. This holds even more truth when the last aural witnesses refused to play their role in Mark 16:8 (καὶ οὐδενὶ οὐδὲν εἶπαν). The readers are asked to seek for a connection between the narrative world and their world, that is, to act as aural witnesses of the written gospel. For Mark 16:8 makes the point that the time of narrative is over, that there is nothing left to hear.

With the presupposition that the Gospel of Mark remains deficient without the voice of the readers, the relationship between the text and the readers gains fundamental relevance, now that the Gospel of Mark performs its own part as the powerful word of writing. Due to Eco's theory it is not too bold a claim that modern research about the historical Jesus and his parables has followed the textual strategy of the Gospel of Mark in an exemplary way. The modern assumption that in essence the Gospel tradition is in continuity with Jesus precisely reflects the textual strategy of the Gospel of Mark, which performs the scriptural, i. e. written, communication of the gospel as the effective and enduring continuation of Jesus' teaching. Of all texts, the Gospel of Mark offers that kind of decontextualization (concerning the specific purpose of use and the community of origin) that seems to have been necessary in order to achieve transformations in collective maintenance of information.[29]

---

[29] If R. Bauckham, "For Whom Were Gospels Written," in *The Gospels for All Christians: Rethinking the Gospel Audiences* (Grand Rapids: Eerdmans, 1998), 9–48, is right with his assumption that the Gospels were most probably written for wide dissemination throughout the Christian community and not for specific local communities, the decontextualization we can find in the Gospel of Mark is a strategy to gain access to many Christian voices throughout the Christian community.

Memory and Form Criticism:
The Typicality of Memory as a Bridge between Orality and Literality in the Early Christian Remembering Process

Ruben Zimmermann

Early Christian tradition can be described as the process of remembering the life and death of Jesus. Although there may be broad consensus on this basic statement, the details within the process remain unclear. According to Jan and Aleida Assmann and others,[1] memory always needs media and form to be constructed, conserved, and communicated. Various forms, such as diaries, finger rings, photos, or gravestones are used by individuals to remember biographical events. Similarly, collective and even cultural memory[2] is shaped by means of special media, which, according to Aleida Assmann, can be distinguished in a more abstract way in metaphor, writing, images, bodies and locations.[3] Although several forms of collective memory are frequently used by different groups, each group generates special forms which can be regarded as typical for a certain memory and which help to construct the identity of that group.

The following paper deals with the question of the media used in the early Christian communities to remember the life and death of Jesus. I would like to focus on language-based memory, not taking into account the various other forms such as archeological artifacts or rituals.

My main hypothesis is that memory requires the repetition and typification of certain forms in order to gain collective meaning. The process of remembering thus does not only inevitably lead to the development of certain forms and genres; in addition, this development of forms can be viewed as a decisive step from oral to written memory.

---

[1] See *Medien des Gedächtnisses* (eds. A. Assmann, M. Weinberg and M. Windisch; Stuttgart/ Weimar: Metzler, 1998); *Medialität und Gedächtnis. Interdisziplinäre Beiträge zur kulturellen Verarbeitung europäischer Krisen* (eds. V. Borsò, G. Krumeich and B. Witte; Stuttgart/Weimar: Metzler, 2001); *Medien des kollektiven Gedächtnisses. Konstruktivität – Historizität – Kulturspezifität* (eds. A. Erll and A. Nünning; MCM 1; Berlin/New York: de Gruyter, 2004).

[2] J. Assmann, *Das kulturelle Gedächtnis. Schrift, Erinnerung und politische Identität in frühen Hochkulturen* (5th ed.; Munich: C. H. Beck, 2005).

[3] In A. Assmann, *Erinnerungsräume. Formen und Wandlungen des kulturellen Gedächtnisses* (Munich: C. H. Beck, 1999), 2nd part.

1. Memory, Media and Form

The meaning of conventionalized forms in individual memory was demonstrated by Frederic C. Barlett in his study, *Remembering*.[4]

Barlett studied serial memory in particular and was able to show that individual memories are often superimposed with genre schemata. For example, the participants in the study often added the typical first sentence of a fairy tale ("Once upon a time") even if this sentence was missing in the stories they were working with. In doing this, they categorized stories of a different genre into the familiar genre of "fairy tale."

The focus of Barlett's study on individual memory processes is also applicable to cultural memory. Collective memory takes place particularly by means of categorization of individual events into well-known and pre-shaped forms.

In order to preserve the remembered past of a cultural community for future generations, this past must be stabilized. Therefore, we can draw on Assmann to characterize the particular achievement of cultural memory as the assignment of meaning to the distant horizon of cultural communication.[5] Both the direct participants in the communication as well as the subsequent generations should be able to understand certain events and insights.

According to Jan Assmann, this stabilization is reached particularly through "form and conciseness as mnemotechnical processes." As examples, he points to the function of literary forms of expression or linguistic styles: "Rhyme, assonance, parallelism membrum, alliteration, meter, rhythm, and melody are processes of this stabilization that, within the flow of time, grant permanence to that which is fleeting."[6]

Every cultural community possesses a basic inventory of conventionalized forms by means of which the past can take shape and can become an object of cultural memory. "The form is not reinvented over and over again. Instead, it exists within a tradition that requires and adopts it."[7] Modifying one of Jan Assmann's terms, Astrid Erll and Klaudia Seibel have spoken of "forms of re-use" (*Wiedergebrauchs-Formen*) that prefigure cultural memory.[8] Genres can be

---

[4] F. C. Barlett, *Remembering: A Study in Experimental and Social Psychology* (Cambridge: Cambridge University Press, 1967 [1932]), 123, 180ff.

[5] A. Assmann and J. Assmann, "Das kulturelle Gedächtnis." *Erwägen. Wissen. Ethik* 13.2 (2002): 239–247; "Kultur als Lebenswelt und Monument," in *Kultur als Lebenswelt und Monument* (eds. idem and D. Harth; Frankfurt a. M.: Fischer, 1991), 11–25, here 14.

[6] Assmann, "Das kulturelle Gedächtnis," 241.

[7] Assmann, "Das kulturelle Gedächtnis," 239.

[8] See A. Erll and K. Seibel, "Gattungen, Formtraditionen und kulturelles Gedächtnis" in *Erzähltextanalyse und Gender Studies* (eds. V. Nünning and A. Nünning; Weimar: Metzler, 2004), 180–208, 189, 191: "Wiedergebrauchs-Formen sind daher bedeutungsgeladene (sic!) Träger von Ideologien des kulturellen Gedächtnisses, d. h. von Vergangenheitsversionen, Geschichtsbildern, Konzepten kollektiver Identität sowie von Wert- und Normvorstellungen."

defined as such forms of re-use in which a genre can be described as the conventionalized form of a text.[9] In literary genres, such as historiography or historical novel, this act of memory may be immediately understandable. However, as Richard Humphrey states, there is little point in speaking of "genres of
memory"[10] because "memory and remembering [...] form the basis of any
fiction and thus any fictional genre" and that means that "there are only genres
of memory."[11]

The past is primarily communicated by narratives; story is the main form in
remembering history. This basic statement is only of little help if we want to
focus the process of remembering on details. However, it is of much greater
help in directing the way in which we might discover more insights into the
style and development of early Christian tradition. Telling a story can be viewed
not only as a special way of talking; using linguistic theories, stories may be
analyzed with regard to their narrative structure and techniques.

Hayden White pointed out that an understanding of the past is finalized only
if the plot of a narration is analyzed (emplotment). White distinguished the four
basic plots: romance, tragedy, comedy and satire. In other words, White assumes
a form-finding process as an important stage in remembering the past. I would
like to take up this assumption and take it a step further.

Narration or, more generally, language-based treatments of the past cannot
be limited to four general plots. As a consequence, we intend to look at the
individual linguistic forms and genres used in early Christianity in order to
remember the Jesus story. While certain genres have a stronger connection to
written texts, there are marked forms of speech that belong more closely to oral
communication. Nevertheless, they also demonstrate the typicality and connection to form that enable communication. Oral speech is also often characterized by "forms of re-use," primarily when the narrative process is meant to be
conducive to social stabilization.

("Forms of re-use are thus meaningful carriers of the ideologies of a cultural memory. They are
carriers of versions of the past, of historical images, of concepts of collective identity as well as
of concepts of values and norms.") Jan Assmann spoke of "Wiedergebrauchs-Texten, -Bildern
und -Riten" ("re-use texts, images and rituals"), see J. Assmann, "Kollektives Gedächtnis und
kulturelle Identität," in *Kultur und Gedächtnis* (eds. idem and T. Hölscher; Frankfurt a. M.:
Suhrkamp, 1988), 9–19, here 15.
    [9] A. Erll and A. Nünning, "Gedächtniskonzepte der Literaturwissenschaft. Ein Überblick,"
Literatur, Erinnerung, Identität (ed. A. Erll; Trier: WVT, 2003), 2–27, here 10: "The concept of
genres as 'locations' of memory [...] points paradigmatically to the variety and complexity of
literature/memory relations."
    [10] See H. van Gorp and U. Musarra-Schroeder, "Introduction: Literary Genres and Cultur-
al Memory," *Genres as Repositories of Cultural Memory* (ed. idem; Amsterdam/Atlanta, Ga.:
Rodopi, 2000), i–ix, here iii.
    [11] R. Humphrey, "Literarische Gattung und Gedächtnis," in *Gedächtniskonzepte der Litera-
turwissenschaft. Theoretische Grundlegung und Anwendungsperspektiven* (eds. A. Erll and A. Nünning; MCM 2; Berlin/New York: de Gruyter, 2005), 73–96, here 74.

2. Forms and Functions of Memory

The existence of linguistic "forms of re-use" can be described as a memory that establishes itself through intertextual relations. The conventionalization of certain textual characteristics is the result of a remembering process of communication in which repetitions and updates of a certain form reveal continuity. For example, when a past event is told repeatedly in a certain way or in a distinctive style (e. g. with irony, praise etc.), the memory of this event is molded into this special form. Moreover, the memory is made possible only by this form.

Linguistic forms, however, are in no way vehicles of memory without content. As form-giving entities they have a definitive impact on the processes of memory of any culture.[12] In the genre of historiography, Hayden White named this meaning-giving characteristic of form "the content of the form."[13] Taking up the concepts of Russian formalism (Jury Lotman) and of the Prague School (Roman Jacobson), Ansgar Nünning speaks from a literary-critical perspective of a "semanticizing of literary forms."[14] The linguistic portrayal processes and structures act thus as independent bearers of meaning and play a central role in the granting of meaning in memory processes. The form and structure of the language are perceived as the sediments of the content, such that they allow for the meaning potential in the memory process that then grants meaning for the producers, tradents and recipients of the artifacts of memory. One can determine three different functions that fulfill the connection to forms in the process of remembering: a) a tradition-giving function; b) a community-giving function; c) a meaning-giving function.

The tradition-giving function

The memory of events and characters from the past is a process of interpretation that classifies contingent experiences into defined patterns of thought and comprehension. Known patterns must be used in order to interpret unknown and thus incomprehensible events. A particular cultural community has such a set of patterns which allows these processes of recollective interpretation. Thus, the Cinderella fairy tale can be used as a known pattern to explain the contemporary rise of pop stars.

---

[12] Erll and Seibel, "Gattungen, Formtraditionen und kulturelles Gedächtnis," 191: "Collective identities, values, norms and the relationships between the sexes are not stabilized in memory cultures only by means of defined media of memory. Their formal processes such as parable, epos, allegory, tragedy and Bildungsroman contribute to the communication of cultural meaning."

[13] H. White, *The Content of the Form. Narrative Discourse and Historical Representation* (Baltimore, Md./London: John Hopkins University Press, 1987).

[14] A. Nünning, "Semantisierung literarischer Formen," *Metzler Lexikon Literatur- und Kulturtheorie*: 603–604; see also regarding this term W. Schmid, "Die Semantisierung der Form. Zum Inhaltskonzept Jury Lotmans," *Russian Literature* 5 (1977): 61–80.

However, the events are not completely subordinated to these formalized interpretive processes. A current application of the pattern itself forms and changes the pattern. Therefore, against the background of contemporary genre theory, it is not possible to understand the existence of genres as "classification grids." Genres can no longer be regarded as "normative a priori sets" as was the case in the era of "normative *Gattungspoetik*" (genre poetics). However, those, such as Benedetto Croce, who therefore radically deny the existence of genres are equally mistaken. Drawing on Klaus Hempfer (genre theory) and Rüdiger Zymner, I would instead like to speak of a "synthesizing constructivism" that understands genres as a part of a communicative practice.

"We differentiate, thus, between 'genres' as phenomena of the historical, literary or general linguistic communication system, observable because of specific text constituents, and their scientific description."[15] Hempfer speaks of *faits normatifs* that are perceptible for the analyzer as norms of communication in texts but that can also be differentiated from facts such as the birth of Napoleon.[16]

Rüdiger Zymner regards this "understated nominalism" of developing genres as a part of a hermeneutic practice in communication acts. Zymner notes, "The cognitive subject bases itself upon quasi-normative facts, on textual evidence and traditional ways of thinking about the genres so that the construction is in actual fact a reconstruction."[17] Correspondingly, the form in the remembered communication act is simultaneously assumed as well as constituted and extended. Thus, the formalizing memory is central to the process of the construction of tradition.

The community-giving function

Linguistic forms are also a "medium of collective memory." The sociologist Maurice Halbwachs, a pioneer of modern memory research, investigated in particular the role of social groups in the processes of collective memory.[18] Remembering does not take place only in concrete social groups. Common acts of memory also create collective identity. In the same way that literature is a "medium of the portrayal and reflection, the modeling and construction of memory and identity,"[19] language-based communication acts can prefigure this literalization process. In the process of collective and thus also cultural remem-

---

[15] K. W. Hempfer, *Gattungstheorie: Information und Synthese* (UTB 133; Munich: Fink, 1973), 125.

[16] See Hempfer, *Gattungstheorie*, 125.

[17] R. Zymner, *Gattungstheorie. Probleme und Positionen der Literaturwissenschaft* (Paderborn: Mentis, 2003), 59.

[18] See M. Halbwachs, *Das Gedächtnis und seine sozialen Bedingungen* (2nd ed.; Frankfurt a. M.: Suhrkamp, 2006 [1925]); idem, *Das kollektive Gedächtnis* (Frankfurt a. M.: Fischer, 1991).

[19] A. Erll, "Einleitung," in *Literatur, Erinnerung, Identität*, (ed. A. Erll; Trier: WVT, 2003), iii–ix, here: v.

bering, certain forms or media of memory are established that then become carriers of memory. In this process, the conventionalized forms of language, the genres in particular, are able to become the condition for and the medium of expression for cultural memory.[20]

Collective identity can be constructed to a large extent by means of formally conventionalized memory. A community talks about the same events; however, the events are not talked about each time in a different but rather in a recognizable way. This does not require literal continuity but it does require a structural or formal identity. The memory of certain events that deviates and updates itself is recognizable due to the use of a defined form. Thus, the form guarantees the permanence and the stabilization of the memory as well as of the community.

This can be seen, for example, in a community's myths of origin as well as, in extreme cases, in the canonization of certain memory literature. The construction and consolidation of a set of form-giving elements can be described as a type of canonization process that presages the path from oral to literary memory.

The meaning-giving function

The memory culture that is guaranteed by conventionalized forms links the collective dimension to the individual dimension of memory. In this process, genres become the meaning-giving models for the codification of life experiences. Mimesis thus describes not only a simple reflection of realities but rather a *poiesis*, or in modern terms, a construction of collective as well as individual reality by means of the medium of language.[21] Narrative genres in particular become lendable models for the narration and interpretation of personal life experiences, as recently demonstrated primarily by William L. Randall[22] or Paul Ricœur.[23] Drawing on Aristotle's literary mimesis theory, Ricœur has described the understanding of a narration as a threefold mimetic process:[24] The concrete construction as well as the understanding of a documented text (*configuration*)

---

[20] See first Van Gorp and Musarra-Schroeder, *Introduction*, i–ix.

[21] Vittoria Borsò also emphasizes the "constitutional mediality of memory:" "storage techniques are not devices external to memory for the reproduction of pre-existing knowledge stored in the functional memory. Instead knowledge of the past is first produced through the relationship of medium and form," V. Borsò, "Gedächtnis und Medialität: Die Herausforderung der Alterität. Eine medienphilosophische und medienhistorische Perspektivierung des Gedächtnis-Begriffs," *Medialität und Gedächtnis* (eds. idem, G. Krumeich and B. Witte), 23–54, here 36.

[22] See W. L. Randall, *The Stories We Are: An Essay in Self-Creation* (Toronto: University of Toronto Press, 1995).

[23] See P. Ricœur, *Zeit und Erzählung. vol. 1: Zeit und historische Erzählung; vol. 2: Zeit und literarische Erzählung; vol. 3: Die erzählte Zeit* (Übergänge 18/1–3; Munich: Fink, 1988/1989/1991; orig. *Temps et récit*, Paris: Éditions du Seuil, 1983/1984/1985).

[24] See the overview in Ricœur, *Zeit und Erzählung*, Vol. 1, 87–135, as well as the entire structure of the three volume work.

always requires pre-understanding and pre-development (*préfiguration* = mimesis I) to which the text can be related. Genres are such pre-existing memory concepts that prefigure the memory process because both producers and recipients of literary works must refer to them. Understanding, however, occurs only in the refiguration and reconstruction of the temporal and life-world existence of the reader (*refiguration* = mimesis III). In this way, working productively with texts in their specific form leads to "narrative identity" through the process of prefiguration, configuration and refiguration.[25] Memory genres thus become the recollective and interpretive space of one's own life history.

3. Early Christianity as a remembering community

Let us now look specifically at early Christianity. Jesus of Nazareth, his words and his deeds as well as his fate on the cross are central subjects of early Christian memory. In recent Jesus studies there have been several attempts to look at Jesus by drawing on various considerations of memory theory[26] and to speak of "Jesus remembered."[27] Memory theory is also being increasingly employed to help explain the origins of Christianity and particularly the transmission of early Christian texts.[28]

---

[25] See particularly Ricœur, *Zeit und Erzählung*, Vol. 3, 392–400, here 395: "The delicate offspring that originates from the union of history and fiction is the assignment of a specific identity to an individual or a community that one can call its *narrative identity*." The term narrative identity is expressed most precisely in the work *Soi-même comme un autre* (german: Paul Ricœur, *Das Selbst als ein anderer*, Munich: Fink, 1996; first published in 1990).

[26] See *Kultur und Gedächtnis* (eds. J. Assmann and T. Hölscher; Frankfurt a. M.: Suhrkamp, 1988); *Mnemosyne. Formen und Funktionen der kulturellen Erinnerung* (eds. A. Assmann and D. Harth; Frankfurt a. M.: Fischer, 1991); *Gedächtnis und Erinnerung* (ed. E. P. Fischer; München: Piper, 1998); *The Oxford Handbook of Memory* (eds. E. Tuving and F. I. M. Craig; Oxford: Oxford University Press, 2005).

[27] J. D. G. Dunn, *Christianity in the Making I: Jesus Remembered* (Grand Rapids, Mich.: Eerdmans, 2003). See also J. Schröter, *Erinnerung an Jesu Worte. Studien zur Rezeption der Logienüberlieferung in Markus, Q und Thomas* (WMANT 76; Neukirchen-Vluyn: Neukirchener, 1997); idem, *Jesus und die Anfänge der Christologie. Methodologische und exegetische Studien zu den Ursprüngen des christlichen Glaubens* (BThSt 47; Neukirchen-Vluyn: Neukirchener, 2001); idem, *Von Jesus zum Neuen Testament. Studien zur urchristlichen Theologiegeschichte und zur Entstehung des neutestamentlichen Kanons* (WUNT 204; Tübingen: Mohr Siebeck, 2007).

[28] See the instructive collection of *Memory, Tradition, and Text. Uses of the Past in Early Christianity* (eds. A. Kirk and T. Thatcher; Semeia Studies 52; Atlanta, Ga.: SBL Press, 2005), also the research review idem, "Jesus Tradition as Social Memory," in *Memory, Tradition, and Text*, 25–42; *Performing the Gospel: Orality, Memory, and Mark. Essays Dedicated to W. Kelber* (eds. R. A. Horsley et al.; Minneapolis, Minn: Fortress Press, 2006); O. Schwankl, "Recordati sunt. 'Erinnerungsarbeit' in den Evangelien," in *"Für alle Zeiten zur Erinnerung." Beiträge zu einer biblischen Gedächtniskultur* (eds. M. Theobald and R. Hoppe; SBS 209; Stuttgart: Katholisches Bibelwerk, 2006), 53–94; Th. Söding, *Ereignis und Erinnerung. Die Geschichte Jesu im Spiegel der Evangelien* (NRW-Akademie der Wissenschaften, Vorträge G 411; Paderborn:

I would like to continue along this path. In addition to the fundamental conviction that the retrospective of remembering and not the idealization of the beginnings is definitive, further studies are necessary to look particularly at the details of the process of remembering. How does remembering manifest itself? How can the details, such as the transition from oral narrative tradition to written text tradition, be better understood?

The development of certain linguistic forms into media of memory plays a central role. Schröter recognized that certain forms in which the Jesus tradition existed and was passed on were discovered before the development of written narratives such as the gospels as a macro genre.[29] This argument adopts some of the correct insights of early form criticism, which pointed out that memory always takes place medially, not only connected to language but also connected to a form.[30] M. Dibelius, for instance, recognized that collective memories are not completely free. Instead, in Dibelius' words, they take place in a fixed form according to a certain "style:" "Because the unknowns that create this style work according to super-individual laws. Therefore, the style characterizes the genre."[31] Classic form criticism used sociological considerations to anchor form construction in typical transmission situations, or in more modern terms, in "memory situations," and came up with the term *Sitz im Leben* (setting in life, sociological setting) to describe this aspect. This describes not a coincidental or historically unique situation but a typical situation of the passing on of tradition. Correspondingly, memory research assumes a typicality of the recollective situation. Collective memory requires concrete locations in which a particular community can form and carry out its common recollection. The *Sitz im Leben*[32] is thus a mnemotope, a memory location that can be described ideal-typi-

---

Schöningh, 2007); *Jesus, the Voice, and the Text: Beyond the Oral and the Written Gospel* (ed. T. Thatcher; Waco, Tex.: Baylor University Press, 2008), R. Rodriguez, *Structuring Early Christian Memory: Jesus in Tradition, Performance, and Text* (LNTS; London: T.&T. Clark, 2009); more critically G. Häfner, "Das Ende der Kriterien? Jesusforschung angesichts der geschichtstheoretischen Diskussion," *Historiographie und fiktionales Erzählen. Zur Konstruktivität in Geschichtstheorie und Exegese* (eds. idem and K. Backhaus; BThSt 86; Neukirchen-Vluyn: Neukirchener, 2007), 97–130, 103: "Looking at it as a whole, I have not been able to convince myself that the category of memory is an appropriate hermeneutical model for Jesus research."

[29] Schröter, *Anfänge*, 42.

[30] See on this my remarks in R. Zimmermann, "Formen und Gattungen als Medien der Jesus-Erinnerung. Zur Rückgewinnung der Diachronie in der Formgeschichte des Neuen Testaments," *Die Macht der Erinnerung* (eds. O. Fuchs and B. Janowski; JBTh 22/2007; Neukirchen-Vluyn: Neukirchener, 2008), 131–167; also with focus on parables idem, "Gleichnisse als Medien der Jesuserinnerung. Die Historizität der Jesusparabeln im Horizont der Gedächtnisforschung," *Hermeneutik der Gleichnisse Jesu. Methodische Neuansätze zum Verstehen urchristlicher Parabeltexte* (ed. idem; WUNT 231; Tübingen: Mohr Siebeck, 2008), 87–121.

[31] M. Dibelius, *Die Formgeschichte des Evangeliums* (7th ed.; Tübingen: Mohr Siebeck, 1961), 7.

[32] S. Byrskog, "A Century with the 'Sitz im Leben'," *ZNW* 98 (2007): 1–27.

cally as a part of the formalized memory and is a component of the stabilization of cultural memory. It is the production and reception of a specific, common linguistic tradition that definitively promoted the construction of Christian group identity by adopting and demarcating the forms and traditions of the environment.

Drawing on earlier form criticism, I am convinced that linguistic forms for the preservation of early Christian memory were not first discovered through the literary efforts of the Evangelists. Instead, much earlier, short forms acted as the media of a primarily oral memory culture. We can describe such typified short forms as genres which can still be recognized within the macro writings of the Gospels. Parables, for instance, may be seen as such a form in which the collective memory of early Christianity became the definitive and identity-giving media of memory.[33]

4. Parables – as a case study

Triggered by more recent research on the oral culture of memory,[34] the efforts to definitively substantiate continuity from the oral to the written Jesus tradition has, for the first time, demonstrated the importance of linguistic form for the memory capability of a community.[35] Along with poetically-formed texts (e. g. in the *parallelism membrum*), figurative narrative texts or parables (Birger Gerhardsson speaks of "narrative Meshalim") in particular have played a central role in the collective memory of the early Christians.[36] Figurative texts can be more easily memorized than abstract texts and thus they in particular were able to become the material for a narrative community. Even the ancient rhetoricians were familiar with the importance of images in support of memory, an example of this being the famous method of loci.[37] More recently, Armin D. Baum

---

[33] S. Byrskog, "Memory and Identity in the Gospels: A New Perspective," in *Exploring Early Christian Identity* (ed. B. Holmberg; WUNT 226, Tübingen: Mohr Siebeck, 2008), 33–57.

[34] See the overview in D. C. Rubins, *Memory in Oral Traditions. The Cognitive Psychology of Epic, Ballads, and Counting-out-Rhymes* (Oxford: Oxford University Press, 1995); also J. M. Foley, "Memory in Oral Tradition," in *Performing the Gospel: Orality, Memory, and Mark* (eds. idem, R. A. Horsley and J. A. Draper; Minneapolis, Minn: Fortress, 2006).

[35] See in particular B. Gerhardsson, *Memory and Manuscript. Oral Tradition and Written Transmission in Rabbinic Judaism and Early Christianity* (Uppsala: Uppsala University Press, 1961); also R. Riesner, *Jesus als Lehrer. Eine Untersuchung zum Ursprung der Evangelien-Überlieferung* (3rd ed.; WUNT II/7; Tübingen: Mohr Siebeck, 1988), especially 392–404: "protective transmission."

[36] See B. Gerhardsson, "Illuminating the Kingdom. Narrative Meshalim in the Synoptic Gospels", *Jesus and the Gospel Tradition* (ed. H. Wansbrough; JSNT. S 64; Sheffield: Sheffield Academic Press, 1991), 266–309.

[37] See Quint. *Inst.* XI 2,39; Plat. *Phaedr.* 267a, see H. Blum, *Die Antike Mnemotechnik*, (Hildesheim: Georg Olms Verlag, 1969), here particularly 12–32: "the mnemotic images."

pointed out in an interesting article the great importance of imagery for the powers of memory.[38] He reflects on the psychological research on memory that has empirically proven that language-based images are much easier to memorize than abstract facts.[39] "The more figurative a piece of information is, the more the verbal codification system is assisted by the imaginal system."[40] Thus one can conclude that figurative narrative texts or, in our definition, parables[41] have a constitutive role in oral memory cultures. At the same time they offer the opportunity to create a bridge in the transition from orality to literality in early Christianity.[42]

Furthermore, we can single out the community-giving dimension of figurative texts and particularly of parables in early Christianity. The disciples of Jesus told parables and thus called an oral community of memory to life that did not end with the writing of the Gospels. The remarkably large number of parables in document Q or the Sayings Source preserves an early stage of this memory culture in the transition from orality to literality. Drawing on Richard A. Horsley and Jonathan Draper, we can understand Q as "oral derived text," which means that even though Q is accessible to us today only as an intertext from written sources, it has preserved a form of oral narrative culture that bonded together the group of early Christians.[43] And, like Werner H. Kelber, even when

---

[38] See A. D. Baum, "Bildhaftigkeit als Gedächtnishilfe in der synoptischen Tradition," *ThBeitr* 35 (2004): 4–16.

[39] The "dual-coding-theory" of Paivio is definitive. He proved that memory functions through a combination of verbal and imaginal encoding; see A. Paivio, *Mental Representations: A Dual Coding Approach* (Oxford/New York: Oxford University Press, 1986); idem, *Images in Mind: The Evolution of a Theory* (New York: Harvester Wheatsheaf, 1991).

[40] Baum, "Bildhaftigkeit," 8.

[41] See R. Zimmermann, "How to Understand the Parables of Jesus: A Paradigm Shift in Parable Exegesis," *Acta Theologica* (2009/1): 157–182, here: 170: "A parable is a short narrative (1) fictional (2) text that is related in the narrated world to known reality (3) but, by way of implicit or explicit transfer signals, makes it understood that the meaning of the narration must be differentiated from the literal words of the text (4). In its appeal structure (5) it challenges the reader to carry out a metaphoric transfer of meaning that is steered by co-text and context information (6)."

[42] In this regard, the radical difference assumed by W. H. Kelber between orality and literality must be contradicted, see W. H. Kelber, *The Oral and the Written Gospel: The Hermeneutics of Speaking and Writing in the Synoptic Tradition, Paul, Mark, and Q* (Philadelphia, Pa.: Fortress, 1983; repr., Bloomington/Indianapolis, Ind.: Indiana University Press, 1997), here: 210: "Both in form and content the written gospel constitutes a radical alternative to the oral gospel." For critical discussion see Schröter, *Erinnerung*, 27–30, 40–65; further idem, "It's not easy to take a fresh approach." Reflections on "The oral and the written gospel" (An interview with Werner Kelber), in *Jesus, the Voice, and the Text*, 27–43.

[43] See *Whoever Hears You Hears Me: Prophets, Performance, and Tradition in Q* (eds. R. A. Horsley and J. A. Draper; Harrisburg, Pa.: Trinity Press, 1999). In their definition of an "oral derived text, Horsley und Draper refer to Foley: "works that reveal oral traditional features but have reached us only in written form", see J. M. Foley, *Immanent Art: From Structure to Meaning in Traditional Oral Epic* (Bloomington, Ind.: Indiana University Press, 1991), 15.

one recognizes a quantum leap in the tradition in the Gospel of Mark, it would
be a mistake to believe that oral forms of communication did not exist alongside
and subsequent to the written sources.[44] The written texts were simultaneously
aural texts that did not finalize a memory culture so much as set it in motion.
Partial texts such as the relatively cohesive parables played a decisive role in this
process.

Let us look more closely at the parables of the Q document. Although the Q
document comprises a remarkable number of parables, they have hardly been
considered as a specific linguistic form within research on Q. Most analyses of
individual parables are found in the commentaries[45] or as a marginal treatment in
the context of larger works on other subjects.[46] Alongside sporadic publications[47] on the explicit topic parables in Q have been categorized according to
one of the fundamental questions of Q research, that is whether Q should be
placed into the prophetic or wisdom tradition (John. S. Kloppenborg, Chris-
toph Heil). Furthermore, the path of transmission of individual parables has
been traced from the document Q through the Synoptics up to the Gospel of
Thomas (Jacobus Liebenberg). The parables in Q have also been considered in
their ethical dimension, which, as recipient-oriented texts, make models of
action available to the reader (Michael Labahn).

---

[44] See also W. Kelber, "Orality and Biblical Studies. A Review Essay," *RBL* 12 (2007): "In
ancient Israel, scribal activity worked hand in glove with an intense oral, communal life [...]
For the most part, scriptural knowledge was acquired by listening to oral recitations in the
absence of textual aids because scriptural traditions were essential part of the oral, communal
repertoire." (p. 19)

[45] H. T. Fleddermann, *Q: A Reconstruction and Commentary* (Biblical tools and studies 1;
Leuven: Peeters, 2005); R. Valantasis, *The New Q: A Fresh Translation with Commentary* (New
York: T.&T. Clark, 2005); the only German commentary up to now is presented by D. Zeller,
Kommentar zur Logienquelle (3rd ed.; SKK. NT 21; Stuttgart: Katholisches Bibelwerk, 1993).

[46] R. Uro, "Apocalyptic Symbolism and Social Identity in Q," in *Symbols and Strata: Essays
on the Sayings Gospel Q* (ed. idem; Göttingen: Vandenhoeck & Ruprecht, 1996), 67–118;
M. Ebner, *Jesus – ein Weisheitslehrer? Synoptische Weisheitslogien im Traditionsprozess* (HBS 15;
Freiburg i. Br.: Herder, 1998); J. Liebenberg, *The Language of the Kingdom and Jesus: Parable,
Aphorism, and Metaphor in the Sayings Material Common to the Synoptic Tradition and the Gospel of
Thomas* (BZNW 102; Berlin/New York: de Gruyter, 2001); P. Rondez, *Alltägliche Weisheit?
Untersuchung zum Erfahrungsbezug von Weisheitslogien in der Q-Tradition* (AThANT 87; Zürich:
Theologischer Verlag, 2006).

[47] J. G. William, "Parable and Chreia. From Q to Narrative Gospel," *Semeia* 43 (1988):
85–114; J. S. Kloppenborg, "Jesus and the Parables of Jesus in Q," in *The Gospel behind the
Gospels. Current Studies on Q* (ed. R. A. Piper; NT. S 75; Leiden: Brill, 1995), 275–319; Chr.
Heil, "Beobachtungen zur theologischen Dimension der Gleichnisrede Jesu in Q," in *The
Sayings Source Q and the Historical Jesus* (ed. A. Lindemann; BEThL 158; Leuven: Peeters, 2001),
649–659; G. Kern, "Parabeln in der Logienquelle Q. Einleitung," in *Kompendium der Gleich-
nisse Jesu* (eds. R. Zimmermann et al.; Gütersloh: Gütersloher, 2007), 47–60; M. Labahn, "Das
Reich Gottes und seine performativen Abbildungen. Gleichnisse, Parabeln und Bilder als
Handlungsmodelle im Dokument Q," in *Hermeneutik der Gleichnisse Jesu*, 259–282.

This deficit is particularly noteworthy because it is generally recognized that parables play a definitive role in Q. Harry T. Fleddermann summarizes: "Parables play a prominent role in Q. [...] It is tempting to list the parables with speeches and dialogues as one of the longer forms of Q."[48]

However, the choice of texts that form the basis of such studies varies according to the definition of parable. This large spectrum ranges from a reduction to ten texts limited to "long parables"[49] up to a selection of twenty-eight texts in "*Das Kompendium der Gleichnisse Jesu.*" The literary and theological function of the parables is also defined differently according to the focus and method. The *Kompendium der Gleichnisse Jesu*[50] published in 2007 offers a first overall interpretation of the parable texts in Q reconstructed on the basis of the "Critical Edition."

Along with the memorizability of individual parables, the speculation arises that parables can become links in the preservation and transmission of larger units of narration. Fleddermann states that parables are consciously placed at "strategic points."[51] By tracing the composition of the document Q according to the Critical Edition, one can see that parables often occur at exposed places, for example at the beginning or end of a section, leading Kloppenborg to speak of "initial stories" or "concluding witness."[52] Thus, five of the seven sections end with parables.[53]

The proximity to oral narrative culture is also revealed in the parables of Q through the return to experienced life worlds. They preserve the life world of the Galilean farmer by telling about harvesting work (Q 6:43–45; 10:2; 13:18f.) or life in a smaller household (Q 6:47–49; 11:14–20; 13:20f.).[54] Nevertheless it

---

[48] Fleddermann, *Q. A Reconstruction and Commentary*, 93f.

[49] Kloppenborg, "Jesus and the Parables of Jesus in Q," 285–287, which integrates texts particular to Luke ("the Rich Farmer," Luke 12:16–20; "the Lost Drachma," Luke 15:8–10); Fleddermann also speaks of 10 parables because although he excludes the parable from the texts particular to Luke, he at the same time summarizes each of two parables into "double parables" ("The Householder and the Servant Left in Charge," Q 12:39–46*; "The Mustard Seed and the Leaven," Q 13:18–21), see Fleddermann, *Q: A Reconstruction and Commentary*, 94.

[50] We have identified a total of 28 texts in the Kompendium as parable texts. The supporting role in the composition of Q as a whole is demonstrated by the structure table in G. Kern, "Parabeln," 54f.

[51] See Fleddermann, *Q: A Reconstruction and Commentary*, 95: "The author often sets parables at strategic points."

[52] See Kloppenburg, "Jesus and the Parables in Q," 318.

[53] See on the closing parables at the end of the sections A: Q 3:2–7:35 (parable = Q 7:31–35); B: Q 9:57–11:13 (parable = Q 11:9–13); C: Q 11:14–52; D: Q 12:2–13:21 (parable = Q 13:20f.); E: Q 13:24–14:23 (parable = Q 14:16–23*); F: Q 14:26–17:21 (parable = Q 15:4–7*); G: Q 17:23–22:30.

[54] See a systematic overview of the concrete figurative domains in Zimmermann, *Kompendium der Gleichnisse Jesu*, 36–39. Further on the sociological-geographical localization, for example R. L. Rohrbaugh, "A Peasant Reading of the Parable of the Talents/Pounds: A Text of Terror?," *BTB* 23 (1993): 32–39; W. R. Herzog II, *Parables as Subversive Speech. Jesus as*

would be inappropriate for two reasons to narrow our view of the parables in a backward-turning socio-historical way. On the one hand, these life styles are recollected in contemporary communication contexts so that a conscious mixing of the social relationships occurs with pedagogical intention. The individual tradents, narrators and listeners are meant to reflect on their own social relationships in the remembering process. Thus space is created for a variety of social points of view that has historically been disregarded, such as in the domain of finance or justice.[55] Because the realistic dealings of the parable characters can become an ethical (contra)model for one's own shared life, the social community constitutes itself through the parables in various narrative situations.[56]

As much as the parables in Q have to a certain extent been fixed in their structure, perceptible in their repetition in Matthew and Luke, the spectrum of variation particularly in the parable of the feast (Matt 22:1–14 versus Luke 14:16–23) shows that one certainly can not assume a linguistically completely fixed – or even literary – form. This leads to several concluding thoughts.

5. Memory and Form Criticism – Some Final Statements

In order to be able to reflect on and to communicate memories, it is necessary to do more than simply put them in order. They also require medial linguistic mediation, which, however, does not have to be reinvented every time. Forms that are well-known and recognized in a communication community – in literature called "forms of re-use" – are employed in order to shape the memory in a certain way.

Even if "narrations" hold a prominent position in the remembering process,[57] it is nevertheless necessary to differentiate between different narrative genres; otherwise the memory can be not limited to the form of the narration. Shorter linguistic forms such as parables can also become linguistic media for remembering Jesus.

We do not adopt a genre model that regards genres as given, established entities in the sense of earlier normative *Gattungspoetik* (genre poetics). Instead,

---

Pedagogue of the Oppressed (Louisville, Ky.: John Knox Press, 1994); W. Bösen, "Die Figurenwelt der Gleichnisse," *WUB* 24 (2002): 60–66; *The Lost Coin: Parables of Women, Work, and Wisdom* (ed. M. A. Beavis; London: Sheffield Academic Press, 2002).

[55] For example see the parable of the entrusted money (Q 19:12–26) or the parable of the defendant going to trial or punishment (Q 12:58f.).

[56] "(The parables are seen as) a codification designed to stimulate social analysis and to expose the contradiction between the actual situation of its hearers and the Torah of God's justice." See Herzog II, *Parables as Subversive Speech*, 28; again Labahn, "Das Reich Gottes und seine performativen Abbildungen."

[57] See H. E. Hearon, "Storytelling in Oral and Written Media Contexts of the Ancient Mediterranean World," *Jesus, the Voice, and the Text*, 89–110.

genres are dynamic forms with distinctive features that enable recognition through typification but at the same time remain open.

Thus, in the memory process of early Christians, well-known linguistic forms such as wisdom sayings, chreia or Meshalim were not only used, they were also reshaped and reinvented in the collective memory process. For example, the Meshalim/parables experienced an unprecedented boom.

In this, a process of interaction takes place. Certain forms shape memory. Additionally, memory is shaped by these forms within this very process. Finally, we detect the beginning of a "semantization of the form." To give an example: The fact that one remembered the narrative teller in parables also shaped the process of Christological interpretation so that Jesus himself was able to be regarded as a parable or as "the image of God." Genres can be characterized as typified, recognizable linguistic forms of communication. They are, however, not limited to literal communication. Oral communication also requires typified linguistic patterns that enable comprehension.

When collective memory occurs, it requires such typification and repetition notably in order to bring the past to mind in a community-giving way.

In the same way that early form criticism recognized that linguistic forms themselves are subject to a history of origination and modification and are tied to certain situations (*Sitz im Leben*), I am convinced that genres play a central role in the tradition process of early Christianity. There were, however, no pure and fixed forms at the beginning, as was believed by early form criticism. Instead forms are shaped, modified and reinforced only in the process of transmission. A genre thus proved and established itself during transmission.

From a dynamic viewpoint, a decisive step in the fixation and literalization of memory can be seen in the linkage to genre. The form-bound memory is no longer completely free. Its wording may not be defined; however, the prominent characteristics and structures that place it into a genre are set. Thus we perceive a relative fixation of the linguistic form located between a freer oral memory and a memory set down literally in text.

The Gospel of Mark in the Interface of Orality and Writing

Richard A. Horsley

In our conversations over the past twenty years or so about orality and writing the focus and emphasis have shifted gradually from their opposition to their interface. While there is growing interest in considering the Gospel of Mark, for example, in oral performance, our consideration takes carefully into account the kinds and functions of writing. With the field of biblical studies so heavily embedded in and committed to the assumptions and procedures of print-culture, those of us interested in oral performance and the relation of orality and writing have struggled to learn from scholars in other fields. Comparative research and the interdisciplinary reflections of theorists have proven particularly stimulating and helpful.[1] Such research and theoretical reflection have reinforced my own interest in the social-political context of written texts and particularly of oral performance. Meanwhile recent research in text-criticism of biblical and related books and on scribal practice in Judea and the ancient Near East have resulted in significant implications for our consideration of the interface of orality and writing. With a more precise sense of the how the interface of orality and writing differed for scribal culture and popular culture, we may be able to reach a greater appreciation of the composition and oral performance of Mark's Gospel by focusing on the importance of traditional cultural patterns in the plotting of the Gospel story.

1. The Interface of Orality and Writing

It has been evident for some time that reading and writing were as limited in Roman Palestine as in the rest of the Roman Empire.[2] Especially when we are working in a field in which it has been a standard operating assumption that in ancient "Judaism" literacy was widespread and books readily available, however, it is important to have wider documentation that literacy was limited largely to scribal circles and administration, and was often used as an instrument

---

[1] Especially suggestive and helpful is the work of John Miles Foley, e. g., in *The Singer of Tales in Performance* (Bloomington: Indiana University Press, 1995).

[2] See esp. W. V. Harris, *Ancient Literacy* (Cambridge: Harvard University Press, 1989).

of power by the wealthy and powerful.[3] Scrolls, on which some texts were inscribed, were not only expensive and cumbersome and not readily accessible, but virtually impossible to read unless one already knew the text. Insofar as literacy (writing and reading) was limited to scribal circles and administrators in Roman Palestine, the interface of orality and writing was significantly different for the cultural elite (scribal circles), on the one hand, and the non-literate ordinary people, on the other. We can now sketch a more precise if also more complicated picture of the differential interface of orality and writing on the basis of recent text-critical research on copies of books later included in the Hebrew Bible and other texts among the Dead Sea Scrolls, and from recent studies of ancient scribal training and practice in Judea and the ancient Near East.

Research on the Dead Sea Scrolls is significantly challenging some of the basic assumptions of biblical studies. Close analysis of the manuscripts of the books that were later included in the Hebrew Bible have led to two fundamental conclusions.[4] (1) Many of the books of the Pentateuch and the Prophets later included in the Hebrew Bible existed in multiple textual traditions or versions; and (2) all of those versions were still undergoing development into late second-temple times. The scriptures that were later recognized as biblical were still developing. Moreover, judging from the number of copies of given texts found in the caves at Qumran, it seems clear that other books (e. g., *Jubilees*, sections of *1 Enoch*) also held considerable authority, at least for scribal circles, perhaps rivaling the authority of the books of the Pentateuch and Prophets that were included in the Hebrew Bible in late antiquity.[5] The books later included in the Bible thus had only relative authority in Second Temple times. Also authoritative, at least for the Qumran community, were the Community Rule and the Damascus Rule, in which rules for the community are not derived exegetically from books of torah. Also sharing or rivaling the authority of books of torah were the regulations promulgated by the Pharisees, their "traditions of the ancestors" not written in the books of Moses, that were also at times included in the state law of the temple state, according to Josephus' account (Josephus, *Ant.* 13. 296–98, 408–409).

If there was such fluidity in and among authoritative books and traditions in scribal circles such as the Qumranites and Pharisees, and if literacy was limited largely to scribal circles, then what did the ordinary people know of authoritative books and through what channels? The Qumranites were off in their desert community, and the scribes and Pharisees were retainers in service of the temple-state and high priesthood based in Jerusalem.

---

[3] Extensive documentation in C. Hezser, *Jewish Literacy in Roman Palestine* (Tübingen: Mohr Siebeck, 2001).

[4] E. Ulrich, *The Dead Sea Scrolls and the Origin of the Bible* (Grand Rapids, MI: Eerdmans, 1999).

[5] R. A. Horsley, *Scribes, Visionaries, and the Politics of Second Temple Judea* (Louisville: Westminster John Knox, 2007), chap 6, and references there.

Recent studies of scribal training and scribal practice have made clear that even though writing was limited largely to scribal circles, the division between scribal and popular does not correspond to a division between written and oral. The relatively wide use of writing by the literate minority in the ancient Near East and Greco-Roman antiquity did not bring a sudden shift from a previously oral culture to a written culture. Scribes were the well-trained and cultured officers or staff who served in the courts or administrations of ancient Near Eastern monarchies and temple-states, such as in Judea. Their disciplined education and learning was what qualified them to serve. As the Jerusalem scribe Jesus ben Sira explains, learned Judean scribes devoted themselves to learning and cultivating all segments of the Judean cultural repertoire, the torah of the Most High and prophecies as well as various kinds of wisdom, so that they could serve among the rulers (Sirach 38:24–39:11).

Recent studies of scribal culture have shown that scribal cultivation of texts was oral as well as written, or oral-written.[6] Scribes learned to read and write. But besides copying texts from one scroll onto another, they learned texts (along with the broader contents of the traditional cultural repertoire) by oral recitation, so that the texts were "written on the tablet of their heart" as well as on the scrolls. Having thus "mastered" the texts, they could then recite them from memory as appropriate to the situation. Biblical scholars have tended to project their own practices onto ancient Judean scribes, such as Ben Sira and leaders of the Qumran community, imagining that they were engaged in studying and interpreting written texts. As Martin Jaffee pointed out, the key passage in the Community Rule about the regular evening gatherings of the community, usually taken as referring to "studying" a (written) text, should be more precisely translated:[7]

And the many shall watch together for a third of every night of the year, to recite the book (*liqro' hasseper*), to search law/justice (*lidrosh mispat*), and to bless together (*lebarek beyahad*). (1QS 6:5–8)

That is, the scribal-priestly community at Qumran was holding nightly *oral recitations* of a book, presumably of torah (Deuteronomy?), the text of which was inscribed in their memories as well as on the scrolls they kept, along with recitations of rulings (those listed in the Community Rule?) and communal blessings. Biblical scholars commonly represent Ben Sira and the Qumranites as engaged in interpreting the law. But Ben Sira does not cite torah passages and interpret them. And while the Qumranites produced interpretations (*pesharim*) of prophetic books, they rarely cite torah passages and interpret them. Both Ben

[6] See especially D. M. Carr, *Writing on the Tablet of the Heart: Origins of Scripture and Literature* (Oxford: Oxford University Press, 2005); and Horsley, *Scribes*, chaps 4–5.

[7] M. S. Jaffee, *Torah in the Mouth: Writing and Oral Tradition in Palestinian Judaism, 200 BCE – 400 CE* (New York: Oxford University Press, 2000), chap 1. Translation mine.

Sira and the Qumranites emphasize rather a personal adherence to the covenant and obedience of its laws. Learned Judean scribes were engaged primarily in appropriating important texts by memorization and recitation, on the basis of which they could then again recite or recall statements and phrases as appropriate to certain situations.

Texts composed by Qumranites provide an indication of more general scribal relation to authoritative written texts (scriptures), which is basically oral-memorial. I focus purposely on the Damascus Document (CD) because it is notable for having more "quotations" than other Qumran texts (i. e., other than testimonia, etc.). Several significant points can be observed. (1) The text as a whole takes the form of a renewal of the Mosaic covenant. (2) The language or discourse of the text generally is rife with the language registers familiar to us as to them from Judean scriptures (some proto-biblical). (3) Sometimes a phrase here or a clause there is cited (evidently from memory) that we recognize as probably having existed in a scriptural text that the composers and performers of the Damascus Document must have known memorially. Modern translators-editors place many phrases and clauses in italics as if they were quotations. But no such indication is even hinted at in the text itself. (4) Sometimes, but relatively rarely (6X), a phrase or clause is introduced with the formula "it is written," but without attribution to any particular book (1:15; 4:20; 5:1–2; 9:5–6; 11:18, 20). But why is this explicit indicator given in such a small minority of cases where scripture is cited (evidently from memory)? Presumably this formula signals that an authoritative basis is being given for the ruling or admonition to which it attaches a phrase or clause that stands written in a sacred writing (scripture). But only once is the citation attributed to a particular book ("written among the words of the prophet Isaiah," 7:11–12). (5) More often a citation is introduced by "Moses (or the rule of the Torah) says/said" (4X – 5:9; 7:7–8; 8:14; B2:15–16) or "God says/said" (10X – 6:13–14; 7:14; 8:8–9; 16:14–15; 9:9; 10:16; 13:23–24; with variations in 3:7–8; 3:20–21; 4:13–14). Most striking is that most of the so-called "quotations of scripture" (sacred writing) are references to *speech* by God or Moses or "the rule of the (oral?) teaching." What modern scholars think of as written on scrolls in the Qumran community were apparently (also) inscribed in scribes' memory and understood as oral commands or prophecies.

Josephus offers an example of how the authority of legal tradition worked in practice in the Jerusalem temple-state. In the summer of 66 C. E. priests led by the temple-captain had cut off any further sacrifices on behalf of the emperor and Rome, in reaction against the brutal repressive actions by the Roman governor Florus. The nobles, chief priests, and most notable Pharisees, however, did not quote from a written scroll of torah. They rather brought in "priestly experts on the ancestral laws" who claimed that the ancestors had accepted sacrifices of/for foreigners (*J. W.* 2. 411, 417). Sacred scrolls of torah had been *e+* laid up in the Temple. But what was authoritative for the conduct of the temple-state was memorial knowledge of ancestral regulations orally recited.

Some of the recent research on scribal practice particularly oriented to scribal educational curriculum, however, has not paid sufficient attention to the writing side of scribes' service of the temple-state, particularly the different kinds of writing discussed by Susan Niditch.[8] Particularly in societies where writing is relatively rare, not an everyday reality, writing has a strong "magical" (numinous) quality. Some ancient writings accomplished by scribes were not intended for regular consultation. Some were laid up in temples or palace store-rooms as specially inscribed texts. Some of those were also "constitutional" in function. The obvious illustration from second-temple times may be the great ceremony of reverential recitation – with translation for the Aramaic-speaking people who could not understand the Hebrew text that Ezra was reciting – of "the book of teaching of Moses" that legitimated Ezra's reform of the early temple-state in Jerusalem (Nehemiah 8). While the texts stood written on scrolls laid up in the Temple, scribes thought of their contents as something spoken by Moses or by God through a prophet, and they had the texts written on their hearts, to be accessed memorially.

While oral-memorial learning and recitation of texts, mainly in (archaic) Hebrew, played a prominent role in the oral-written culture of scribal circles, oral communication was dominant among the non-literate ordinary people who spoke Aramaic. With regard to ordinary Judeans' and Galileans' interface with written texts, moreover, it is difficult to find any evidence that they had much if any direct contact with the scriptures of the Judean temple-state, either in oral or written form. Ordinary people would presumably have known of the existence of authoritative written texts laid up in the Temple. But it is not clear how, if at all, they would have become familiar with the contents of those texts. Scribes and Pharisees were based in Jerusalem. There is little or no evidence of their activity in the villages of Judea where the vast majority of ordinary Judeans lived. Galilee did not come under the control of the temple-state in Jerusalem until 104 B. C. E., when the Hasmonean high priesthood forced the Galileans to live under "the laws of the Judeans" (Josephus, *Ant.* 13.318). But there was considerable turmoil until the reign of Herod (37–4 B. C. E.). And other than the controversy stories in Mark that are deemed to have little value as historical reports and Josephus' accounts of his own and his opponents actions in Galilee in 66–67 C. E., there are no references to Pharisees (or other scribes) being active in Galilee. Archaeologists are clear that the synagogue buildings excavated mainly in Galilee (with their "Torah-shrines" where scrolls were evidently laid *✓* up) date from the fourth and fifth centuries and afterwards.[9] Hence it is unclear

---

[8] S. Niditch, *Oral World and Written Word* (Louisville: Westminster John Knox, 1996).

[9] References and further discussion in R. A. Horsley, *Archaeology, History, and Society in Galilee* (Harrisburg: Trinity Press International, 1996), 131–145.

how the first century Galileans who comprised the first followers of Jesus would note
have known the contents of the Judean scriptures.

The people, however, were hardly ignorant of the traditions of Israel. Victory
songs such as the Song of Miriam (of the Sea), the Song of Deborah, and the
Song of Hanna were sung by Israelite villagers long before being taken up into
official historical narratives composed by scribes in service of monarchs.[10] Ancestral legends were told long before being shaped into an official narrative that
climaxed in the Davidic-Solomonic kingship. The Mosaic Covenant was renewed regularly and the people recited the Ten Commandments and inscribed
paradigmatic covenantal summaries on their doorposts independent of the collection and development of law-codes by scribes in service of the monarchy and
their inclusion in the books of Exodus, Leviticus, and Deuteronomy. All such
Israelite traditions continued to be cultivated in village communities, presumably for centuries. In study of agrarian and other societies anthropologists have
long since worked with the concept of the "little tradition" parallel to the "great
tradition" to explain the differences in the way ordinary people cultivate and
draw upon their cultural tradition (social memory) in comparison and often in
contrast with the way the educated (scribal) elite shape and cultivate their cultural tradition to support the prevailing power-relations.[11]

Outside of the Gospels, the most accessible evidence for the operation of
Israelite popular tradition in Judea and/or Galilee comes from Josephus' historical accounts. First, the very social forms taken by the popular messianic
movements in 4 B.C.E. and again in 67–70 C.E. (*Ant.* 17.271–285; *J. W.*
2:55–65) and the popular prophetic movements in Judea just after the mission of
Jesus (*J. W.* 2.259–263; *Ant.* 18.85–87; 20:97–98, 169–171) were informed,
respectively, by the tradition (social memory) of the popularly acclaimed ("messiahed") king David and by the tradition of Moses and Joshua leading the exodus
and entry into the land.[12] Second, the actions of the Galileans in several incidents
of the revolt in 66–67 recounted by Josephus were rooted in their commitment
to the covenantal commandments.[13] Scholars still working with the older syn-

---

[10] See R.B. and M.P. Coote, *Power, Politics, and the Making of the Bible* (Minneapolis: Fortress, 1990).

[11] J.C. Scott, "Profanation and Protest: Agrarian Revolt and the Little Tradition." *Theory and Society* 4 (1977): 38, 211–46, is particularly helpful in application to the Gospels and Jesus' movements; for the latter, see R.A. Horsley, "Israelite traditions in Q," in *Whoever Hears You Hears Me: Prophets, Performance, and Tradition in Q* (eds. R.A. Horsley and J.A. Draper; Harrisville: Trinity Press International, 1999), chap 5; and R.A. Horsley, *Jesus in Context: Powers, People, and Performance* (Minneapolis: Fortress, 2008), 68–71, 151–156, 207–210, in which I prefer the terms "popular tradition" and "official" or "elite tradition."

[12] See the discussion in R.A. Horsley. "Popular Messianic Movements around the Time of Jesus," *Catholic Biblical Quarterly* 46 (1984): 471–93; and "'Like One of the Prophets of Old': Two Types of Popular Prophets at the Time of Jesus," *Catholic Biblical Quarterly* 47 (1985): 435–63.

[13] See R.A. Horsley, *Galilee: History, Politics, People* (Valley Forge, PA: Trinity Press International, 1995), chap 6.

thetic construct of "Judaism" have claimed these as evidence of the Galileans knowledge of "the Torah" (i. e., the written text of the Pentateuch, which was only later defined as part of the Hebrew Bible). The ten commandments of the Mosaic covenant, however, were widespread common knowledge among the Galilean as well as the Judean villagers. As evident in these examples, Galilean and Judean villagers actively cultivated Israelite tradition in their village communities. But we should not imagine that in order to do this they had to be acquainted with the contents of texts that existed in writing and in the memories of the scribes. They knew very well that there were such written texts. But it is difficult to discern how they would have become familiar with much of their contents except through such contacts as they had with ordinary priests when attending pilgrimage festivals in Jerusalem. And of course we also have little or no evidence for how much of the contents of authoritative Judean texts (other than the customary ritual practices they carried out) were known by ordinary priests, many or most of whom were neither scribes nor literate.

2. The Gospel of Mark's Relation to Written Texts

To consider the Gospel of Mark in the interface of orality and writing, we can focus on three questions in particular.

(1) How does the Gospel compare with Judean (scribal) texts that already existed in writing?

One of the suggestive questions my mentor Krister Stendahl asked of his students was why the Jewish "sect" that developed into early "Christianity" did not simply produce a fourth division of the Jewish scriptures. On the standard assumption that the early Christians were literate, some of them being "authors" who "wrote" Gospels (that is, in the Judean context, were trained scribes), the issue must be sharpened. Given the remarkable level of continuity with Israelite tradition that the Gospels presuppose and articulate, then we would have expected the (supposedly) literate Christian "authors" to produce new texts patterned after one or another of the kinds of texts already revered and authoritative. That the issue Stendahl posed (as reformulated) is a serious one is illustrated by the previously unknown texts found among the Dead Sea Scrolls. At least one community of Judeans contemporary with the Jesus movements continued to produce and cultivate new texts of torah and new prophetic books similar in form and content to the already authoritative ones.[14] Stendahl's question also leads into the *genres* part of the theme of this conference.

---

[14] Discussed in Horsley, *Scribes*, chap 6.

It is tempting to use some of the currently fashionable constructions of the historical Jesus as foils. If Jesus was a sage and his teachings predominantly sapiential sayings, as American Q scholars and leading members of the Jesus Seminar have it, then why do we not simply have in the Bible a book of "The Wisdom of Jesus ben Joseph" patterned somewhat after the "Wisdom of Jesus ben Sira" (Ecclesiasticus)? If Jesus was an apocalyptic visionary focused on a scenario of the last judgment and end-time, as more conservative neo-Schweitzerian interpreters have it, then why do we not have in the Bible a book of revelation to Jesus similar to Daniel 7 or the Animal Apocalypse in *1 Enoch* 85–90? Or if Jesus was a prophet leading a renewal of Israel, why do we not have in the Bible a book that combines stories and oracles of a prophet patterned after Isaiah or Jeremiah? Maybe it is because no learned scribes like Jesus ben Sira or the scribes who produced the books included in *1 Enoch* had stepped into "Jesus movements" to shape and cultivate Jesus traditions similar to the way previous Judean scribes composed on the basis of previous scribal cultivation of Judean texts.

What we have in the Gospel of Mark, and evidently in the other Gospels as well, is a story that is not only about but has emerged from among ordinary people in the village communities of Galilee and nearby regions and a story oriented to the interests of ordinary people. If we attend to the dominant plot of the overall story, Mark focuses on Jesus spearheading a renewal of Israel as the new Moses and Elijah over against the rulers of Israel and their scribal representatives.[15] Mark has Jesus repeatedly criticize and condemn the scribes and Pharisees, who scheme against Jesus, for their efforts to exploit the people. The other Gospels present more or less the same basic story of Jesus leading a renewal of Israel over against the rulers of Israel. Matthew and Luke also include the same large blocks of Jesus' speeches, including blunt condemnation of the scribes and Pharisees. Mark and the other Gospels are popular, not scribal texts.

(2) What was the Gospel's relation to the Judean "scriptural" texts?

It has been standard in biblical studies to represent Mark and other Gospels as quoting from the written texts of scripture. That is, working on the assumptions of modern print culture and not ordinarily making distinctions between villagers and the literate elite, Gospel scholars have conceived of the "authors" of the Gospels in more or less scribal terms, working from readily available written scrolls. This standard conception, however, requires reexamination on the more precise sense of the interface of orality and writing now emerging from the recent research sketched above.

---

[15] Laid out in R. A. Horsley, *Hearing the Whole Story: The Politics of Plot in Mark's Gospel* (Louisville, KY: Westminster John Knox, 2001), chap 5.

The Gospel of Mark introduces "quotes" and other references with the formula "(as) it is written" (*gegraptai*; 1:2; 7:6; etc.).[16] We can presumably conclude from this formula at least that the existence of written texts was known to Mark (and generally known). A study of the frequent use of the same formula in the *Didache* concluded that it is an appeal to the scripture as authority, while the words quoted may be from memory rather than from direct consultation of a scroll.[17] That a prophecy or a law was "written" on a scroll, especially if it were a revered prophecy of great antiquity, gave it an added aura of authority, for ordinary people as much as for the literate elite. Virtually all of the instances where the Gospel of Mark uses the formula are references to a prophecy now being fulfilled. That it stands "written" lends authority to the prophecy and its fulfillment in John or Jesus (Mark 1:2–3; 9:12–13; 14:21, 27) or to Jesus' application of the prophecy to the Pharisees or the high priests (7:6–7; 11:17). In several of those same cases "it is written" is just a general appeal to authority, with no particular "quotation" given (9:12–13; 14:21).

In the few cases in Mark where particular words or phrases are quoted, they do not appear to have involved consultation of a written text. In two cases the "quotes" are composites from two different prophets. Mark 1:2–3, ostensibly quoting "the prophet Isaiah," begins with lines similar to what we read in our written texts of Mal 3:1 and Isa 40:3. The anonymous "quotation" in Mark 11:17 includes lines similar to what we know in our written texts of Isaiah (56:7) and Jeremiah (7:11). We recognize that the anonymous "quotation" in Mark 7:6–7 derives from Isaiah (although the citation is not very close to written texts of Isa 29:13; similarly Isa 6:9–10 in Mark 4:12). And in Mark 14:27 the short line supposedly quoted from Zech 13:7 looks like a proverb that may have been well-known, even before the composition of the book of Zechariah. The best explanation for all of these cases, particularly the ones of composite "quotations" and the proverb, would seem to be that Mark's knowledge of this material is oral-memorial, and not from examination of written texts. But it is oral-memorial knowledge that does not appear close to what we would expect of scribes whose knowledge would presumably have been closer to one or another of the written textual traditions (examples of which were found among the Dead Sea Scrolls).

The other supposed quotations of scripture in Mark are of three sorts. (a) In two episodes of the Gospel, Jesus recites "the commandments (of God)" as commonly known oral tradition. The citations are directed, respectively, against the scribes and Pharisees from Jerusalem who have voided God's word and the man who has by implication violated the commandments in accruing great

---

[16] The following discussion builds on but goes beyond my previous discussions in *Whoever Hears You Hears Me*, 140–144; and *Hearing the Whole Story*, 57–61.

[17] I. Henderson, "Didache and Orality in Synoptic Comparison," *JBL* 111 (1992): 292.

wealth (7:9–13; 10:17–22). Jesus' followers' spontaneous singing of a well-known psalm and Jesus' reference to the ecstatic David's declaration in the words of another well-known psalm are similarly derived from oral tradition. (b) At three different points Mark's Jesus challenges the Pharisees, high priests and scribes, and Sadducees, respectively, with the phrase "have you never/not read," claiming that their written text supports his action or position against theirs (Mark 2:25; 12:10; 12:26). In all three cases the historical incident or statement by God or a psalm would almost certainly have been common knowledge in oral tradition. Especially in the incident about David and the bread from the altar, "Jesus'" version is strikingly different from what the Pharisees would have "read" in any of the variant written versions. (c) In the only places where Mark refers to Moses as having "written," it was for the Pharisees or the Sadducees (10:3–5; 12:19), and by implication not for ordinary people (who would not have been able to read what was written).

Mark's relation to Judean scriptures can thus be summarized in three key points. First, the Gospel and its audience knew of the existence of written texts, indeed viewed the written texts as authoritative, finding their fulfillment in Jesus' mission. Second, Mark appealed to scriptures as supporting its (Jesus') position against that of the scribes and Pharisees, who should have known them well because they could read. Third, the Gospel's citations of lines ostensibly "written" in scripture show significant discrepancies with written versions of the texts, greater than would be expected from scribal (-like) cultivation (some contact with the written text). It is thus much easier to explain Mark's knowledge of the contents of the scriptures as derived from (Galilean) popular tradition in interaction with the official scribal tradition based in Jerusalem than as coming from a scribal-like cultivation of oral-written texts, which would presumably have resulted in closer acquaintance with one or more of the written versions of lines cited.[18]

A key and important difference between Qumran texts such as the Damascus Document and the Gospel of Mark, which both stand in and continue Israelite tradition, is that the former are in the *language registers* of previous scribal texts (some of which later became biblical) while the Gospel narrates new events with references and allusions to figures and events known from Israelite tradition, but not in the language register of scribal texts of torah. The situation is different with regard to prophetic forms, which were popular forms that were taken up secondarily into the scribal collections of prophetic oracles. But prophetic activity, including the delivery of oracles, continued in the popular tradition, as exemplified in John the Baptist and Jesus ben Hananiah as well as Jesus ben Joseph.[19]

---

[18] H. Hearon, "Mapping Written and Spoken Word in the Gospel of Mark" in this volume makes the further point that what Mark refers to as "it is written" is encountered as spoken word.

[19] Horsley, "'Like One of the Prophets of Old'."

To ward off the possible impression that Mark might be an anomaly, an exception among the Gospels that otherwise fit a scribal mold, we can note the somewhat similar relation to "scripture" displayed by Matthew, which interpreters have characterized as scribal on the basis of the saying included at Matt 13:52, "every scribe trained for the kingdom of heaven." The Gospel of Matthew, however, seems to have little interest in "the writing(s)" (scriptures) or in what "is written." Matthew refers to "the scripture(s)" (3–4x) only when following Mark (following the Two-Document hypothesis). Similarly, except for one instance, Matthew's references to "it is written" (9x) come when Matthew is following Mark or in Jesus' responses to the testing by the devil and the reference to John the Baptist, which come to Matthew from pre-Matthean material paralleled in Luke, often included in Q. Moreover, Matthew omits some of the references to "it is written" or to Moses writing in episodes derived from (parallel to) Mark. So the reputation of Matthew as thoroughly acquainted with the scriptures must depend almost completely on his famous "formula quotations," as Krister Stendahl pointed out.[20]

Once we are focusing on the interface of orality and writing, however, we may want to listen carefully to the formula that introduces those "quotations": "this was (done) to fulfill what was *spoken* (by the Lord) through the prophet" (*hina plerothe to hrethen (hupo kyriou) dia ton propheton*). Twice Isaiah is mentioned, once Jeremiah, and only once does Matthew have "for thus it was *written* through the prophet" (2:5). Little attention has been paid to the oral medium indicated in *to hrethen*, perhaps because of the print-cultural assumptions about scripture in biblical studies. It has been assumed that the specific "passages" or "lines" that were "quoted" stood in and were quoted from written texts. Matthew does seem to have a bit more knowledge of the content of Isaiah and other prophetic books than does Mark. But the words are presented as *spoken* by God through the prophets or by the prophets.

Considering the fluid state of the scriptural books according to recent text-critical studies, it seems all the more difficult to determine if "Matthew" was consulting a written text of Isaiah or other books. Stendahl's enduring contribution is his painstaking examination of the words and phrases in Matthew compared with various written versions of the scriptural passages quoted. He concluded that (the school of) "Matthew" was sometimes following (or closest to) the Masoretic textual tradition, sometimes the Septuagint, and sometimes other textual traditions. That is, given "quotations" in the Gospel of Matthew are not all that close to a particular written version. I double-checked this conclusion for many of these "quotations," comparing the contents with the LXX and/or the Hebrew in the standard critical edition. My judgment that they

---

[20] K. Stendahl, *The School of St. Matthew: And its Use of the Old Testament* (2nd ed.; Philadelphia: Fortress, 1968).

are not all that close, either in lines or wording (except for the very brief references), is quite provisional. In any case, the Matthean "formula quotations" need to be more carefully reexamined in comparison with the results of Eugene Ulrich's and other text-critics' research.

Among the provisional conclusions that could be drawn from the Matthean recitations of what the Lord spoke through the prophets are three. First, Mat- *1* thew's knowledge of the contents of the scriptures is oral-memorial. Second, *2* Matthew was less concerned than the Qumranites to attribute the authority of writing to what he was quoting. Third, however "scribal" "Matthew" is judged *3* to be by modern scholars, its knowledge of "what was spoken" by a prophet was not the result of oral-written cultivation (learning and recitation) of scriptural texts but of popular knowledge that involved some interaction with "scribes and Pharisees" whom the Gospel criticizes so sharply.

(3) When and to what extent did the Gospel itself exist in writing?

Another important question in the consideration of the emergence of the Gospel of Mark in the interface of orality and writing is when and to what extent the Gospels existed in written form. The "default" position in the field of biblical studies has been *writing* expressed in such terms as "authors" who "wrote" texts which our colleagues in text-criticism can "establish," and that such written texts were widely distributed and were widely read and known in written form. In the last decade or so, however, text-critics such as Eldon Epp and David Parker in New Testament are saying that the fragmentary manuscripts from the second and third centuries are so diverse that they cannot even establish that there were a finite number of textual traditions, much less establish an "original" or "early(iest)" written text.[21] Some text critics are now open to discussions about how oral performance might help explain the multiformity of Gospel texts. Also text-critics are finding that the making of new copies of a revered text such as a Gospel was *ad hoc* (someone asked to have a copy of a copy made before sending it back to the sender), in a situation where the text was being recited aloud in communities of believers. As Whitney Shiner has explained, "readers" could learn the Gospel from hearing previous oral performances. In the mid-second century, in Justin Martyr's report, "the memoirs of the apostles and the writings of the prophets were read (recited) for as long as time permits."[22] Over two centuries later, Augustine mentions that many people learned to recite large portions of the Gospels from hearing them recited in community assem-

---

[21] See E. J. Epp, "The Multivalence of the Term 'Original Text' in New Testament Textual Criticism," *Harvard Theological Review* 92 (1999) 245–81; and David Parker, *The Living Text of the Gospels* (Cambridge: Cambridge University Press, 1997).

[22] W. T. Shiner, *Proclaiming the Gospel: First Century Performance of Mark* (Harrisburg, PA: Trinity Press International, 2003), 26.

blies.[23] Written copies were not made in any quantity until the establishment of Christianity under Constantine.[24] Before then (and perhaps afterwards as well), however, written copies of texts were evidently of secondary, ancillary importance in the communication of the Gospels, but surely helped enhance their authority.[25]

note

As a result of this recent research, it seems we should question the standard default position in biblical studies that Mark and other Gospels were necessarily composed in writing by individual authors, widely distributed, and widely read from somewhat standardized written copies. Surely it enhanced the authority of the Gospel that it was written down. But the Gospel was known primarily from hearing it performed in community assemblies and could be quoted or recited from memory, including by lectors in the community gatherings.

From what we are learning of the interface of orality and writing, therefore, it appears that Mark was not a Judean scribal composition, but a story about ordinary people in Galilee that originated from a community or movement of ordinary people. Mark and the people among whom it originated and was performed knew of the existence of written texts that had authority, the Judean scriptures, and even appealed to their authority. But its/their knowledge of (some of) the contents of those books was not scribal-like, that is from scribal oral-written cultivation of the scriptures, but rather from popular oral tradition in some interaction with scribal-priestly elite. Mark existed in writing, in various versions, in the second and third centuries. But it was cultivated primarily by oral performance, learned by hearing and recited memorially.

3. *The Plotting / Composition of the Gospel midst the interface of orality and writing*

Part and parcel of appreciating (that) Mark (was communicated) in oral performance has been the recognition of the Gospel as a sustained story. Partly by borrowing from modern literary criticism, many biblical scholars have moved well beyond the view of Mark as a container of separate little stories or 'a string of beads loosely strung together' to a recognition that the Gospel is a plotted narrative in a sequence of episodes. It has been difficult, however, for biblical scholars trained in a field built on the assumptions of written culture to imagine

Past View

---

[23] Shiner, *Proclaiming*, 34, 107.

[24] K. Haines-Eitzen, *Guardians of Letters: Literacy, Power, and the Transmitters of Early Christian Literature* (Oxford: Oxford University Press, 2000).

[25] Given the numinous quality of writing in a predominantly oral communication environment, this may be the implication of the statement at the end of John's Gospel (20:31): "These [signs] are written so that you may come to trust that Jesus is the Messiah [...], and through trusting you may have life in his name."

how performance of the overall story could have been accomplished without writing (without written composition and/or reading from a written text). Several pioneers in investigation of oral communication and oral performance, building on work in other fields, have opened up important aspects of oral performance. Werner Kelber discerned the oral narrative patterns and devices in the different kinds of pre-Markan stories (which I recently attempted to discern also in the overall Markan narrative).[26] Pieter Botha has taught us to look not for the formulas that Parry and Lord found in the Iliad and Odyssey but for the formulas and cues in Mark's narrative that correspond to those in "Homer's" epics.[27] In a series of articles, Joanna Dewey taught us to listen for oral devices for "structuring" narrative, for the interwoven tapestry in the story, and to think of the implications of Mark as an "oral/aural event."[28] And, apropos of the integral relation of story and performance, we are learning from the work of Parry and Lord and others that while particular features and episodes change from performance to performance, the overall story remains consistent. Hence the importance of "hearing the whole story," in contrast with the standard agenda in biblical studies of ascertaining the precise meaning of a particular term or other text-fragments that are components in that larger story and of reducing the narrative to its implicit theology.[29]

All of these important steps have further illuminated Mark as an orally performed story, yet we are still struggling to appreciate the plotting of the overall narrative. What remains difficult even for those who recognize Mark as a sustained story, I think, and perhaps also for those of us who also recognize the interface of orality and writing, is to imagine the formation, the composition, of the whole (Gospel) story. Perhaps because we are so habituated to composition in/as writing we have particular difficulty imagining how a text of the length and complexity of Mark could have been composed other than in writing – even though many epics that are orally performed (and composed) are much longer and more complex in plotting than Mark and the other Gospels.

---

[26] W. Kelber, *The Oral and Written Gospel: The Hermeneutics of Speaking and Writing in the Synoptic Tradition, Mark, Paul, and Q.* (Philadelphia: Fortress, 1983); R. A. Horsley, "Oral Performance and Mark: Some Implications of *The Oral and Written Gospel*, Twenty-Five Years Later," *Jesus, the Voice, and the Text: Beyond the Oral and Written Gospel* (ed. T. Thatcher; Waco: Baylor University Press, 2008), 45–70.

[27] P. J. J. Botha, "Mark's Story as Oral-Traditional Literature: Rethinking the Transmission of Some Traditions about Jesus," *Hervormde Teologiese Studies* 47 (1991): 304–31.

[28] See especially J. Dewey, "The Gospel of Mark as an Oral-Aural Event: Implications for Interpretation," *The New Literary Criticism and the New Testament* (ed. E. S. Malbon and E. V. McKnight; Sheffield: Sheffield Academic Press, 1994), 248–257; and eadem, "Mark – A Really Good Story: Is That Why the Gospel of Mark Survived?" *JBL* 123 (2004): 495–507.

[29] Which I sought to emphasize in analysis of Mark as oral performance in Horsley, *Hearing the Whole Story*. In the course of the last few decades, in conferences such as this, the discussion has moved well past any dichotomy between orality and writing and well beyond any simple opposition or alternatives of oral vs. written composition.

Many interpreters are thus still yearning for that ephemeral definition of a genre that will explain what kind of text they are reading in Mark. We cannot quite discern "the whole story" because we are not sure what we are listening for. Hence the continuing appeal to many readers of the hypothesis that the new genre of the Gospel was an adaptation of the Hellenistic "life" of a hero, as in the biographies woven from the scenes and speech fragments of Hellenistic heroes to be honored and emulated. But the Hellenistic "biography" cannot account for the narrative coherence of Mark. Moreover, this hypothesis runs counter to the Gospel's continuity with Israelite tradition, gives little or no attention to historical social context, and leaves us unable to explain and appreciate how the story references the cultural tradition in which performer, text, and audience are embedded.

Attempting to counter our biblical studies training to focus on isolated verses and pericopes, I have recently attempted to discern and consider the broader traditional cultural patterns that may be evident in the Second-Temple Judean and "early Christian" texts we interpret. Most obvious seems to be the Mosaic covenant pattern followed by and evident in such texts as the Community Rule and Damascus Document from Qumran and the covenant renewal speeches in Luke 6:20–49 and Matthew 5–7. But there are other patterns as yet less obvious to our discernment. Insofar as we are still thinking of Mark's story in terms of a sequence of episodes, we are looking for the ancient cultural form that will "explain" the arrangement of episodes in their Markan sequence. The sequence of episodes, however, may not be the same thing as the plotting of the story (in this case main plot and subplots, dominant conflict and subordinate conflicts). I have been hoping that fuller awareness of some of the broader traditional patterns in (popular) Israelite culture might help us appreciate the inclusion/selection (not the sequence) of episodes (themes, motifs) and the dominant plot/conflict, leaving the sequence of episodes for later consideration, perhaps along the lines pioneered by Dewey.

With regard to fuller appreciation of the plotting of Mark's story Anne Wire's extensive work on early Jewish stories has some important implications.[30] The multiple examples of various types of stories she has assembled and analyzed are surely expressions (and evidence) of some of the broader cultural patterns operative in Judean society at the time of Jesus. Wire groups scores of early Jewish stories according to four distinctive foci: stories of prophecies at birth, of wondrous provisions, of prophets' signs of destruction or deliverance, and of martyrdom and vindication. These four kinds of stories account for much of the contents of Matthew and Luke as well as some of the main themes of Mark and John. In a concluding section on "Early Jewish Stories

---

[30] A. Clark Wire, *Holy Lives, Holy Deaths: A Close Hearing Early Jewish Storytellers* (Leiden: Brill, 2002).

and Gospel Formation," Wire outlines key implications for the composition of Mark.[31]

Of greatest significance for further exploration of Mark as oral performance/narrative is Wire's fundamental approach, starting from deeply rooted patterns in Israelite culture as evident in the culture in which Jesus operated and the Gospel story emerged. She suggests that "the seed" of the composition (and continuing performance) of the Gospel was provided by one type of story (of "the prophet's sign") into which was incorporated other material, including other types of stories ("wondrous provision" and "martyrdom and vindication").

Wire's hypothesis can be strengthened by closer attention to the stories of prophets near contemporary with Jesus and the nascent Gospel story. That prophets announced or performed signs crops up only in the stories in the *Lives of the Prophets* and the general references or summaries in Josephus' histories (*J. W.* 2.259 and the parallel in *Ant.* 20.168–169; *J. W.* 6.285–86, in reference to "the false prophet" and "many prophets" in Jerusalem during the Roman siege).[32] Not only is "the sign itself [...] not named," but in most of the stories, the prophets are not represented as announcing or performing a sign (of destruction or deliverance). The accounts of prophets near contemporary with Jesus, however, do appear to attest a broad cultural pattern deeply rooted in Israelite tradition.

Most of the stories and accounts of prophets/prophecies in late Second-Temple times, and not taken from the *Lives of the Prophets*, refer to one or another of two kinds of prophets patterned after the prominent prophets in Israelite history and tradition. Prophets such as Jesus ben Hananiah pronounced God's judgment on rulers and/or the ruling city/house of Jerusalem, that (attempted to) kill(ed) them. Prophets such as the Samaritan, Theudas, and the "Egyptian" led their followers out to the wilderness or to the Mount of Olives to participate in new acts of deliverance patterned after the key formative deliverance events of the exodus and the taking of land led by Moses and Joshua; again the rulers killed them (or attempted to) and suppressed their movements. Prophets who preached repentance under the threat of judgment, such as John the Baptist, should probably be grouped with the latter, since they were clearly leading movements of renewal, particularly of the renewal of the Mosaic covenant. Both types of prophets were directed against and were a threat to the rulers, who took action to eliminate the prophets and suppress their movements. Both kinds of prophets were deeply rooted in and patterned after the corresponding type of prophets in Israelite history and tradition, Moses, Joshua,

---

[31] Wire, *Holy Lives*, 389–393.

[32] This is one of the principal reasons that the prophets denigrated by Josephus should not be labeled "sign-prophets," *vs.* P. W. Barnett, "The Jewish Sign-Prophets: Their Intentions and Origins," *NTS* 27 (1980–81): 679–697.

Ahijah, and Elijah-Elisha, as prophetic leaders of movements of deliverance and renewal, on the one hand, and Micaiah ben Imlah, Amos, Micah, Jeremiah, as prophets pronouncing oracles and engaging in symbolic actions, on the other. And the prophet-leading-a movement of resistance and renewal could easily include oracular prophecy in condemnation of rulers, as in the paradigm of Elijah.

The prominence of this pattern among Judeans (and Galileans) in late Second-Temple times, under Roman rule, may well be attested in some of the stories that Wire identifies from the *Lives of the Prophets,* that reimagined earlier oracular prophets as leaders of movements of repentance, renewal, and resistance. Ezekiel, for example, who gives signs of both destruction of rulers and renewal of Israel, is transformed into a new Moses leading a new exodus in a story addressed to Judeans under Roman rule (and preaching repentance and judgment against Jerusalem and unfaithful Judeans in exile).[33]

The deeply ingrained cultural pattern of a prophet like Moses, Joshua, and/or Elijah leading a movement of renewal of Israel in resistance to oppressive/foreign rulers was thus also broad and inclusive. Not only in the book of Exodus, but in many of the summaries of the exodus and wilderness wandering (e. g., in various psalms and covenant renewal prayers), Moses was a prophet through whom wondrous provision was made (for manna and water from the rock). Elijah offered a paradigm of a prophetic healer as well as wondrous provider during the drought under Ahab's despotic rule. And Moses was the mediator of the covenant, followed by Elijah as its renewer among the twelve tribes. This broad cultural pattern of the prophetic renewer of Israel appears to provide a narrative paradigm that would even have suggested as well as included the summoning of protégés (Elijah-Elisha; perhaps already Moses-Joshua) and appointment of the Twelve, sea crossings, healings, wilderness feedings (Mark 3:35–8:22), and covenant renewal dialogues (Mark 3:31–35; 10:2–12, 17–31), and covenant renewal meal (14:22–25) for the prophet Jesus engaged in the general program of renewal of Israel.

In exploring the effective operation of this broad and inclusive pattern of a prophet like Moses (Joshua–Elijah) leading a renewal of Israel against the rulers of Israel we must press behind the moment(s) of composition and performance to the earlier cultivation and effects of the pattern in the society. As Wire explains in her reflections on procedure, "the synchronic study of the text's formal features as they function in its community needs to be fit back into the diachronic study of its longstanding traditions." If anything, a great deal more weight should be given to the plotting of contemporary popular prophetic movements according to the "scripts" implicit in the social memory of ancient liberation movements such as the exodus and prophet-led renewal movements

---

[33] Wire, *Holy Lives,* 191–195.

such as the one led by Elijah and other *bene-nebi'im*. In the case of historical figures and movements, whether those led by Theudas and the Egyptian or those led by John the Baptist and Jesus bar Marya, the effects of the cultivation of cultural tradition/memory did not suddenly emerge with a given performance, but had been operative in the interaction of prophet and followers that resulted in popular movements and in the emergence of new social memory (e. g., "Jesus-traditions") focused on them. Indeed it was out of the cultivation of that new social/cultural memory – the "synoptic (gospel) tradition" – that the Gospel story of Mark developed, following and adapting the "script" of the prophet leading a renewal of Israel in resistance to the rulers.

This complex traditional cultural "script" of a prophet like Moses and Elijah leading a renewal of Israel over against the rulers can thus be seen to underlie and to "explain" the plotting of Mark's Gospel story, both in its broadest sequence of events and in the inclusion of particular themes and episodes.

In a welcome step that is unusual among biblical scholars, Wire includes in her inquiry the political perspective inherent in the prophetic stories, which we can then see is also the political perspective inherent in the cultural pattern that they attest as well as express. In Josephus' accounts of the renewal and resistance movements led by Theudas and the Egyptian and the Samaritan prophet, the sequence of events in the narrative is determined to a considerable degree by the political-economic-religious structure of the historical situation of Judeans and Samaritans under Roman rule, which is fundamentally similar to that assumed in stories of earlier prophets. In crisis situations in which domestic rulers based in Jerusalem and/or imperial rulers are oppressing the Israelite people, agrarian producers living in village communities, prophets announcing God's imminent new acts of deliverance generate a following (and/or pronounce God's judgment) that poses a threat to the rulers' domination and economic base. The domestic and/or imperial rulers take action to eliminate the prophet and suppress the movement which, even if ostensibly successful, may create popular martyrs and leave simmering resentment, along with new social memories of popular prophets and their resistance movements.

Broadly speaking, this is also the plot of the much more complex story of Mark's Gospel. Launching a renewal of Israel in Moses- and Elijah-like acts that generate a wide following in the villages of Galilee, Jesus finally enters Jerusalem, where he boldly condemns the Temple and high priestly aristocracy (the face of Roman rule).[34] Anticipated by the Pharisees' and Herodians' plotting

---

[34] It may be the unhistorical and (in origin) theological habit in biblical studies of imposing modern synthetic constructs such as "Judaism," of which Jerusalem and its Temple were supposedly the sacred center, that leads to the assumption that a restoration of Jerusalem and even the Temple would be at the center of a renewed Israel. Some oracles of the later prophets, particularly those who advocated the establishment of the Jerusalem temple-state, do focus on a restored Temple or Zion. But images of a rebuilt Temple at the center of a restored Israel is

against him and prefigured by Antipas' execution of John, the chief priests finally arrest him and hand him over to the Roman governor for crucifixion as a rebel leader, which makes him a martyr who inspires the continuation of the movement. This broad sequence of events in Mark, like the similar sequence in accounts of the other prophets, is determined by the basic political-economic structure of the historical situation, as can be determined from other sources, such as Josephus' broader histories of Second-Temple times, the instructional speeches of Ben Sira, and the woes against the rulers in the Epistle of Enoch (*1 Enoch* 94–102).

In addition to the broad sequence of events determined by the structure of the historical situation, the cultural pattern of prophetic leaders was complex in its inclusion of themes and motifs. And the richness of the themes and motifs of the renewal of Israel it included can be can be seen in several episodes included in the Markan story and in "Jesus traditions" that developed parallel to the episodes included in Mark. For example, the operation of the traditional pattern of a prophet like Moses and/or Elijah engaged in the renewal of Israel is already evident thematically in organization (even in the sequence) of some of the material incorporated into Mark's more complex story. It has long been striking to readers of Mark that there are two sets of "acts of power" that come in the same sequence in Mark 3:35 to 8:26: sea-crossing, exorcism, healing, healing, wilderness feeding. That the second set in Mark has the second healing after the wilderness feeding is attributable to Mark's framing the ensuing step in the narrative with two healings of blind people (8:22–26 and 10:46–52). It thus appears that prior to the composition of Mark's whole story, there existed "chains" of Jesus' "acts of power" arranged in a sequence that presents Jesus as a combination of new-Moses (sea-crossing and wilderness feeding) and new Elijah (healing people representative of Israel) engaged in a renewal of Israel. Jesus was already understood and represented as the prophet engaged in renewal of Israel. Mark's story is a complex elaboration of the same traditional pattern and incorporated other representations of Jesus such as prophet.

Another example: parallel to the multiple episodes in which Mark represents Jesus prophesying destruction of the Temple as well as performing a prophetic action symbolizing God's condemnation of the Temple are traditions of Jesus'

---

rare in later second-temple texts (references and discussion in R. A. Horsley, *Jesus and the Spiral of Violence: Popular Jewish Resistance in Roman Palestine* [San Francisco: Harper & Row, 1987], 286–292). Even scribal circles were critical of the Temple and particularly of the incumbent priestly rulers (discussion of key texts in R. A. Horsley, *The Revolt of the Scribes: The Origins of Apocalyptic Literature* [Minneapolis: Fortress, 2009], esp. chaps 4, 7, and 10). The popular prophets and their movements around the time of Jesus, like the popular messianic movements before and after, were directed against the Jerusalem rulers and ruling institutions, which were the face of (indirect) Roman rule in Judea and Galilee. Opposition to Jerusalem rulers is strong in all of the canonical Gospels, as well as in the Jesus-traditions they incorporated.

prophetic condemnation of the Temple in other Gospels (e. g., John 2; *Gospel of Thomas* 71; Luke/Q 13:34–35a). The representation of Jesus as a prophet pronouncing/performing God's judgment on the Temple and its incumbent priestly rulers must have been operative in earliest Jesus tradition. As articulated explicitly in Mark's episode of Jesus' demonstration against the Temple, Jesus' prophetic condemnation of the Temple was an adaptation of the long-standing prophetic tradition of prophetic pronouncement as attested in Jeremiah's famous prophetic indictment of the Temple (Jeremiah 7; 26). That the tradition of prophetic pronouncement against the Jerusalem ruling house/the Temple continued into the first century is dramatically illustrated by Jesus bar Hananiah's persistent lament of the imminent destruction of the city and its Temple in the 50s and 60s C. E., recounted by Josephus (*J. W.* 6.300–309). The prominent prophetic traditional pattern of prophet leading movement of renewal and resistance may already have included condemnation of the Temple (e. g., as implied in Josephus' accounts of the Egyptian). But if not, it would have been easily incorporated in the pattern, in which resistance to the rulers was already integral.

In yet another example of other features of prophetic tradition, Wire includes in her study several (popular) cultural memories of how earlier Israelite prophets (Isaiah, Ezekiel, Zechariah) were killed, usually by the rulers. That this had become a standard image of some of the most revered prophets is evident, for example, in the sketches in the *Lives of the Prophets*. Jesus was remembered as yet another prophet, both in his role of indicting oppressive rulers and in the very form of his speech. In at least two prophecies in material usually included in Q from which Matthew and Luke expanded the Markan story Jesus refers to prophets having been killed for prophesying against the rulers (Luke/Q 11:49–51; 13:34–35). It is thus clear from other (i. e., non-Markan) early traditions of Jesus' prophetic statements that Jesus, who spoke boldly of earlier prophets murdered, and John the Baptist were understood as the latest in the long line of prophets persecuted and killed for prophesying against the rulers, who now stood under God's judgment for murdering the divine messengers.

There are thus several indications in Jesus-traditions themselves, as well as in earlier Israelite culture, that the deeply rooted Israelite cultural pattern of a prophet (like Moses-Joshua-Elijah) leading a movement of renewal of Israel in resistance to Israel's rulers was inclusive of a number of motifs of the liberation of Israel from unjust and/or foreign rulers. The pattern included renewal of the Mosaic covenant as well as new exodus and taking of land. It could easily assimilate, or perhaps already included, prophetic pronouncements against rulers. If Elijah-Elisha were included in the operative cultural memory as well as Moses, the pattern included both prophetic disciples and representatives of the twelve tribes. Even acts of wondrous provision were included in the many exodus-wilderness summaries and in the Song of Moses (Deut 32) and stories of Elijah's acts of power. The killing of the prophet by the rulers was already part of the overall pattern. The only major step in the overall story of Mark's Gospel that was not already included or easily included in the prophet of renewal pattern was the vindication of the prophet. And, as Wire argues, this was easily attached to the prophetic story by adapting another type of stories that expressed another cultural pattern deeply rooted in Judean culture, that of martyrdom and vindication.[35] In Mark Jesus' martyrdom and vindication is closely linked, almost fused with the prophet leading the new exodus deliverance and the renewal of the Mosaic covenant, as Jesus transforms the Passover meal celebrating the exodus into a covenant renewal meal in anticipation and commemoration of his martyr death (14:22–25). With the device of the abrupt and "open" ending, with the empty tomb and both Jesus' and the white-clad figure's directions that the followers should meet Jesus in "Galilee" (14:28; 16:5–8), Mark's Gospel story sees the vindication of Jesus in the continuation and spread of his movement of renewal to which the hearers are called in repeated performances of the story.

Given the complex plotting of the Gospel story, however, there are subplots and other themes woven into the narrative that complicate the basic traditional story or "script" of the prophet leading a movement of renewal. For example, as Jesus catalyzes the movement of renewal that includes the twelve disciples as representative figures of Israel, the disciples, led by "Rock," increasingly misunderstand his agenda, protest at the direction he is taking, and deny, desert, and disappear when he is arrested. In contrast with the increasing misunderstanding and denial of the disciples, moreover, is the emergence of women in the story, as representative figures of Israel undergoing renewal (the hemorrhaging woman and the twelve-year old women) and as witnesses of the crucifixion and empty tomb and paradigms of faithful adherence. More difficult to assimilate into the basic "script" of the prophet leading a movement of renewal, and perhaps in some tension with it, is the theme or subplot of whether and/or in what way Jesus is also a popular messiah leading a movement of resistance to the rulers (Mark 8:27–33; 11:1–10; 12:35–37; 14:61–62; 15:1–5, 16–20, 31–32).[36] Like the story of the prophet leading a movement, the story of a popular messiah leading a movement of resistance was deeply ingrained in Israelite tradition, primarily in the social memory of the young David "messiahed" by the early Israelites (2 Sam 2:1–4; 5:1–4), and actively operative in Judean and Galilean society at the time of Jesus and the development of the Gospel story.[37] Such

---

[35] For their "prologues," before launching into their main narrative of Jesus' renewal of Israel (including covenant renewal) over against Israel's rulers, Matthew and Luke then drew upon yet another type of early Jewish stories, those of prophecy at birth, on which see Wire, *Holy Lives*, Part I.

[36] See further the provisional explorations of these and other sub-plots in my *Hearing the Whole Story*, esp. chaps 4, 9, and 10.

[37] See further the discussion, with references, in Horsley, "Popular Messianic Movements."

subplots, however, are complications of and subsidiary to the dominant plotting of the popular prophet leading a movement of renewal in Mark.

It may be that fuller attention to the fundamental traditional Israelite cultural pattern of a prophet leading a movement of renewal over against the rulers, which already included a number of themes and motifs evident in Mark, will enable us to appreciate how the Gospel story could have developed, with its overall plot and its inclusion of themes and episodes. This would entail fuller exploration of the stories included in the Israelite cultural repertoire, including the popular tradition (insofar as that is accessible), and investigation of corresponding storytelling in which those stories were performed in the interface of orality and writing, as Antoinette Clark Wire has pioneered.

Performance Events in Early Christianity:
New Testament Writings in an Oral Context

David Rhoads

The purpose of this essay is to propose a template to explore how the writings now in the New Testament might have been presented orally to early Christian communities. I will refer to these presentations as "performance events." The following features may be considered key elements of a performance event: the act of performing; the composition-as-performance; the performer; the audience; the location; the cultural context; the socio-historical context; and the rhetorical impact on audiences. I will reflect briefly on these elements as prolegomena for developing performance scenarios that might serve as a context for interpreting specific New Testament documents in a largely oral culture. The key point is that each of these elements of the performance event contributes to the meaning and impact of a performance – and therefore also to our interpretation of the meaning and impact of a New Testament writing. The purpose of this sketch of elements is not to identify a particular event for a particular writing but to provide a template to explore the repertoire of diverse possibilities.

I became interested in performance over three decades ago after hearing that the British actor Alec McGown was performing the Gospel of Mark in major theaters to rave reviews. Since then, as an integral part of my teaching and research, I have given memorized performances of the Gospel of Mark, Galatians, Philemon, I Peter, James, and the Book of Revelation, the Sermon on the Mount, and scenes from John. Only in recent years have I begun to grasp fully the centrality and importance of performance in early Christianity. I am delighted to present this essay in honor of Anne Wire as a tribute to her pioneering work in the field of orality and literacy studies.

The premise of this essay is that context is critical for interpretation. There is no meaning that is not affected by context. If the New Testament writings were originally performed orally to early Christian communities, then we need to be as specific as we can about the contexts in which performances occurred. Such performances were always situated. It is my purpose to explore the general dynamics of those performance events as a basis for interpreting New Testament writings.[1]

Performance events have gotten little attention in New Testament studies.[2] In fact, a curious lacuna in New Testament studies is the exploration of those

---

[1] For ancient and modern resources on biblical performances, see www. biblicalperformancecriticism. org.

[2] Exceptions include W. Shiner, *Proclaiming the Gospel: First Century Performance of Mark* (New York: Trinity Press international, 2003) and R. Richards, *Paul and First-Century Letter Writing: Secretaries, Composition, and Collection* (Downers Grove, Ill.: InterVarsity Press, 2004).

specific occasions in which a writing that is now in the New Testament was orally presented to a first century Christian community. Everyone agrees that ancient Mediterranean societies were heavily oral cultures in which close to ninety-five percent of the people were not literate.[3] Even the small number of people who could read and/or write – mostly elite males along with some of their slaves and retainers – were steeped in orality.[4] Everyone agrees that the writings would have been heard rather than read silently.[5] However, only recently has work begun on the oral features of the texts, the nature of their performances, and their oral impact on audiences.

We scholars have traditionally worked out of a model for print medium that is based on the way we experience the biblical writings in the modern world. A print model looks like this:

Writer ———— text —————— individual silent reader

In this model of first century writings, the author composed in the act of writing. The writing was fixed in a text. People either read the text silently or aloud. Or the text was read to an audience. We have imagined that such an oral presentation to an ancient community was simply a straightforward reading of what was written and therefore faithful to the text as a text. We have assumed that writing was the dominant component while the oral presentation was peripheral and added little. The contemporary scholar engages the text as a silent reader and interprets its meaning and its impact as a written text. Given these assumptions, we already know all that we need to know for interpreting the written text. We do not need to study the performance event. It would make little difference. The written text predominated.

---

[3] On orality in general see W. Ong, *Orality and Literacy: The Technologizing of the Word* (London: Routledge, 1982); J. Goody, *The Interface Between the Written and the Oral* (Cambridge: Cambridge University Press, 1987); and R. Finnegan, *Literacy and Orality: Studies in the Technology of Communication* (New York: Blackwell, 1988). For antiquity, see especially R. Thomas, *Literacy and Orality in Ancient Greece* (Cambridge: Cambridge University Press, 1992) and S. Niditch, *Oral World and Written Word* (Louisville: Westminster John Knox, 1996). On early Christianity, see W. Kelber, *The Oral and the Written Gospel: The Hermeneutics of Speaking and Writing in the Synoptic Tradition, Mark, Paul, and Q* (Bloomington: Indiana University Press, 1987) and P. J. J. Botha, "Greco-Roman Literacy as Setting for New Testament Writings," *Neotestamentica* 26 (1992): 195–215.

[4] For literacy rates, see especially W. Harris, *Ancient Literacy* (Cambridge: Harvard University Press, 1989) and C. Hezser, *Jewish Literacy in Roman Palestine* (Tübingen: Mohr Siebeck, 2001). Estimates range from a high of fifteen percent in urban areas to as little as two to three percent literacy in some other (more rural) places in the empire. Definitions may include a minimal capacity to sign one's name. Some could read and not write, and vice-versa. See L. B. Yaghjian, "Ancient Reading," *The Social Sciences and New Testament Interpretation* (ed. R. Rohrbaugh; Peabody: Hendrickson, 1996).

[5] See, for example, P. Achtemeier, "*Omni Verbum Sonat*: The New Testament and the Environment of Late Western Antiquity," *Journal of Biblical Literature* 109 (1990): 3–27 and H. Gamble, *Books and Readers in the Early Church: A History of Early Christian Texts* (New Haven: Yale University Press, 1995).

However, this scenario is not what happened in the oral medium of the cultures of the first century. In such oral cultures, an oral/aural medium predominated, and written documents (handwritten scrolls) were peripheral. Memory arts were more important than the technology of writing. Composing was not done with pen in hand in the act of writing. Rather, speeches and stories were composed in memory by ear and performed orally, often without recourse to anything written at all. It is likely that the early Christian tradition, even with lengthy compositions like gospels and letters, often went from oral performance to oral performance. Oral dictation was the primary means to get something transcribed into writing. The alphabetic markings on the scrolls were basically signs that recorded speech, a repository of sounds to be recycled back into speech. Virtually all reading was done aloud, even private reading. Performers, if they themselves could read, may have used the scrolls to practice memory work for performances, but even then they would have pronounced the sounds aloud or had someone read the sounds to them. When writing occurred, it served the needs of performance. The oral predominated.

Here is what an oral model of communication might look like:

Oral composer — oral performance ——— communal audience.

In this model, the "author" composed orally and may (in the case of the gospels) have been the performer of the initial oral versions. The oral composition was not fixed but fluid, and each performer (including the composer who performed) would have done at least some re-composing in performance. Each performance would be distinctive and in some sense an original. The composition-as-performance would manifest features typical of ancient oral arts as well as arts of performance. The receptor audience would be communal. There would be oral interaction with the audience during the performance. In some few instances, there may have been a written "transcription" of the oral composition, but it would have been peripheral – used as an aid to memory in preparation for a performance, possibly used for reading aloud to an audience, but perhaps held closed in performance as a symbol of authority/authenticity, or not used at all in the performance itself. A written transcription may also have served as a helpful (but perhaps not necessary) means to bear the oral composition from one geographical location to another.

Changing the model of communication from print to orality has enormous significance for the way we as scholars study the writings now in the New Testament; and it has great implications for our interpretations of these writings. The change of medium is nothing less than a fundamental paradigm shift in the field of biblical studies.[6]

---

[6] T. Boomershine, "Biblical Megatrends: Towards the Paradigm for the Interpretation of the Bible in the Electronic Age," *SBL Seminar Papers* (ed. K. Richards; Atlanta: Scholars Press,

Simply put, the writings we have in the New Testament are examples of "performance literature," that is, literature that was meant for performance – like music or theater or ancient poetry. It is difficult to imagine musicologists studying scores of music without ever hearing a performance. Nor can we imagine theater scholars studying scripts of ancient drama without having seen performances of the plays or without trying to determine how they may have been performed and experienced in ancient times. Yet we biblical scholars have studied the literature of the New Testament for centuries without ever hearing them performed as stories or speeches or epistolary orations, without trying to determine how they may have been performed in the early church, and without constructing ancient performance scenarios as a basis for interpretation.

In the 1980's, Hans Frei lamented the "eclipse of biblical narrative," the loss of the power of biblical story in favor of a fragmentation of the text into sources and redactions for historical reconstruction or in favor of abstractions into doctrinal formulations and ethical lessons.[7] Biblical scholarship has addressed this loss of story, and it has gone a long way toward recovering the narrative dynamics and the rhetorical force of the biblical stories. In fact, there is much less fragmentation of the text now into sources and redactions; most scholarly work takes for granted the surface meaning and impact of the text as we have it, either as written narrative or as epistolary rhetoric.

Now we are addressing another threshold; we are becoming aware of the related "eclipse of biblical performance" – the centuries-long loss of the immediacy and power of the gospels and letters performed orally, as they were first experienced in the early church. Studies are now emerging to redress this loss. We are at the beginning of this process; yet already the various efforts seem to be coalescing into a discipline that we refer to as "performance criticism."[8] As the process continues, much scholarship on the New Testament may eventually be done with a new framework for analysis.

1989), 144–157 and J. A. Loubser, *Oral & Manuscript Culture in the Bible: Studies in the Media Texture of the New Testament* (Stellenbosch: Sun Press, 2007). On paradigm shifts, see T. Kuhn, *The Structure of Scientific Revolutions*. Third edition (Chicago: University of Chicago Press, 1996). On the implications of such a paradigm shift for Biblical Studies, see the documentary video by E. Botha, "Orality, Print Culture, and Biblical Interpretation" (eugenebotha@co. za).

[7] H. Frei, *The Eclipse of Biblical Narrative: A Study in Eighteenth and Nineteenth Century Hermeneutics* (New Haven: Yale University Press, 1984).

[8] D. Rhoads, "Performance Criticism: An Emerging Methodology in Second Testament Studies, Part I," *Biblical Theology Bulletin* 36 (2006): 1–16 and idem, "Performance Criticism: An Emerging Methodology in Second Testament Studies, Part II," *Biblical Theology Bulletin* 36 (2006): 164–184. Compare also W. Doan and T. Giles, *Prophets, Performance, and Power: Performance Criticism of the Hebrew Bible* (New York: T&T Clark, 2005); T. Giles and W. Doan, *Twice Used Songs: Performance Criticism of the Songs of Ancient Israel* (Peabody: Hendrickson, 2009); and *Performing the Gospel: Orality, Memory, and Mark* (eds. R. Horsley, J. Draper, and J. M. Foley; Minneapolis: Fortress Press, 2006).

The purpose of this essay is to identify elements of performance events in the early church as a basis for re-thinking our methods of study and our interpretations of the New Testament writings in their original context. The obstacles to this effort are considerable, and much of this study will be based on speculation – as much of New Testament scholarship has always been. There are very few and very limited descriptions of such events and no accounts of the immediate communal outcomes of performances. We have enough difficulties constructing *any* event in the ancient world, let alone something as ephemeral as an oral performance. The difficulties are complicated by the cultural and temporal divide between us and them, between now and then. How could we ever replicate a performance? Emotions are expressed with differing facial expressions and postures in different cultures. Gestures mean different things and accompany different acts. Volume of voice conveys different meanings. Various inflections and intonations bear diverse associations. Ancient cultural assumptions and traditions of storytelling are far from us. We can perform these texts ourselves in ways that seem comfortable and natural to us, but that does not mean it will be like what they did in the first century.

However, a cultural divide like this has not heretofore kept us from trying. We have so many different (re)constructions of the historical Jesus that it makes our heads spin. But the effort is illuminating and informative. Nothing is lost in our efforts to understand the New Testament writings or the events that lie behind them. This is what performance criticism seeks to do. In this essay, however, I am not giving a reconstructed record of a particular performance event. Rather, I am interested in providing an overall template of factors that would have been part of a performance event.

To reconstruct performance events, there are methods that are helpful and illuminating.[9] More specific to this study, we can scour the literature of the ancient world for descriptions of performances. We can consult ancient rhetorical handbooks that give directions for oration. We can study sculpture and paintings that depict orations and gestures related to speeches. We can learn about oral performers in the ancient world – storytellers, actors, rhapsodes, and orators. We can investigate the venues in which these traditions were performed. We can look for descriptions of performance events. We can infer many things from the texts themselves about how performances may have been carried out. We can notice the features of oral speech and performance in the writings. We can listen to the sounds in the composition and seek to understand the role that sound plays in the structure and rhetoric.[10] We can study the repertoire of images and associations evoked by the performer. We can discern

---

[9] See, for example, Shiner, *Proclaiming*, passim.
[10] M. Lee and B. B. Scott, *Sound Mapping the New Testament* (Salem, Oreg.: Polebridge Press, 2009).

clues to likely actions and gestures by a performer. We can learn from comparable performers and performance events in living oral cultures. And we ourselves can offer performances and be an audience for performances of these writings in living languages – as means to experience vicariously an analogue of what ancient performances may have been like. From these and other sources, we can begin to piece together what various early Christian performance events may have been like.

The following features may be considered key elements of a performance event: 1) the embodied nature of performance; 2) the composition-as-performance; 3) the performer; 4) communities of reception; 5) the setting of place and time; 6) the cultural ethos; 7) the socio-historical context; and 8) the rhetorical impact on audiences. This essay is prolegomena then to efforts to depict specific ancient performance events for specific New Testament writings. It is meant to open a conversation – raise issues, suggest possibilities, and give examples. This work is based on several presuppositions. I am assuming that compositions now in the New Testament were originally performed and experienced as stories or letters or apocalypse and *not as scripture*. Also, I am assuming that in the first century these compositions were performed in their entirely. Furthermore, I assume that they were most often presented from memory rather than read from a text. Finally, I am imagining these events as occasions when the compositions were initially performed for first audiences, with some consideration given to repeat performances for the same audiences (but never really the same) or secondary performances to different audiences.

In light of these assumptions, I will reflect on various aspects of each of these elements, with the recognition that the features overlap and interrelate and are often ways of depicting the same thing from different aspects.

1. The Embodied Nature of a performance

To understand performance, we cannot be satisfied with the simple contrast between the written and the oral – because performance involves so much more than sound.

performance is more than oral. A performance involves a shift from written to oral, a change of medium that has a much different impact than silent reading. Sound alone is capable of bearing meaning and emotion in ways not possible by the silent script of a text. The oral performance includes all the dynamics of voice quality and inflection: volume, pitch, pace, pronunciation, pauses, and so on. Yet a performance is much more than just "oral." The performance expresses not only sound but physicality and presence. The performer is expressing composition in action: the movements, the gestures, the pace, the facial expressions, the postures, the movement of the mouth in forming speech, the spatial

relationships of the imagined characters, and the temporal development of the
story in progressive events displayed as on a stage. Nor can we discount the sheer
force of the bodily presence of the performer to evoke emotions and commitments. A performance is an event; and people do not just hear it, they experience it.[11]

   performance is "seeing in imagination." The performer's voice and body generate
"seeing." As such, the act of hearing by the audience is in a sense also "visual,"
because speaking/ moving/ acting stimulates the "imaginative seeing" in a vig-
orous way that is not replicated by silent reading or by sound alone. As the
storyteller displays the characters in action, the audience experiences the scene
being portrayed in imagination. Words and gestures and movement on the part
of the performer help the audience "picture" the people and actions being
portrayed. We need to account for the stimulation of the imagination as an
integral part of the persuasive power of a composition. Consider how the author
of *Revelation* wrote down what he "saw" so that the audience too would "envision" it and thereby participate in it.

   The Whole Event. Many factors comprise and shape the whole performance
event. The social locations of the audience shape the experience of the performance event. Add to this the ways in which the physical setting – such as a house
or an assembly hall or an open market place – shapes the nature of the performance and the reception of it. As we shall see, cultural ethos and socio-historical
events also impact the experience. And, in so far as the audience makes active
contributions to a performance, the communal experience of audience participation becomes an integral dimension of the performance. To account for all
this, we need to talk about the holistic experience of a performance in interaction with an audience in a certain location at a particular time in the life of a
particular culture – and not just the oral sound of the speaking. More than a text
or a performance, it is an event. The whole context is part of the embodiment.
More than a seeing or a hearing, it is an experience. The imagined experience of
this performance event is a critical basis for interpretation.

2. Composition-as-performance

The composer prepares not just words but a performance. And composition
takes place in performance. Hence, the composition-as-performance is not a
written text but a living word, with a life of its own as distinct from its written

---

[11] On contemporary performance arts, see for example, R. Pelias, *Performance Studies: The
Interpretation of Aesthetic Texts* (New York: St. Martin's Press, 1992). For an aesthetic of pres-
ence, see A. R. Bozarth, *The Word's Body: An Incarnational Aesthetic of Interpretation* (Lanham:
University Press of America, 1997).

form. The story is not on the page. It is in the mind and body of the performer. The sound is out in public space. In ancient texts, therefore, the composition was not the words alone but the embodied performance. In addition, composers no doubt composed and recomposed over many performances. And other performers of the "same" story re-composed as they performed. Consequently, there is no "original composition" as such, but many versions of the same basic story. There were a series of composers. While this may not be as true of letters, it would very likely have been true of Gospels.

How important was memory? The first century was a memory culture more than it was a manuscript culture.[12] Collective memory was crucial in the predominantly oral cultures of the first century. And performance was the main means to generate and shape the collective memory. Memory feats were praised and celebrated in antiquity. Memory was in some sense valued by and cultivated for everyone. Memory training was prominent in the educational system for elites. The ancient rhetoricians developed artificial memory techniques. And they composed with oral patterns of speaking that served both to facilitate recall by a performer and to make the performance memorable for the audience.

In her study of memory, Mary Carruthers has argued that medieval culture [and by extension ancient culture] was fundamentally a "memorial culture."[13] Her investigation changed some of her most fundamental views. "Many things," she writes, "that I had believed could not be done, such as composing difficult works at length, had to be entertained as possibilities – even as expected and much admired behavior."[14] Jocelyn Small has shown how memory predominated over writing and was crucial to every aspect of orality and literacy. Therefore, understanding how memory worked in an oral culture is critical for a construction of performances.

How did composition work in ancient oral cultures?[15] In terms of the composition of gospels and letters, there are three factors in the equation: orality, memory, and

---

[12] On memory, see M. Carruthers, *The Book of Memory: A Study of Memory in Medieval Culture,* Second edition (Cambridge: Cambridge University Press, 2008); F. Yates, *The Art of Memory* (Chicago: University of Chicago Press, 1996); J. P. Small, *Wax Tablets of the Mind: Cognitive Studies of Memory and Literacy in Classical Antiquity* (London: Routledge, 1997); M. Jaffee, *Torah in the Mouth: Writing and Oral Tradition in Palestinian Judaism: 200 BCE–44 CE* (New York: Oxford University Press, 2001); D. Carr, *Writing on the Tablet of the Heart: Origins of Scripture and Literature* (Oxford: Oxford University Press, 2006); and P. J. J. Botha, "New Testament Texts and Reading Practices of the Roman Period: The Role of Memory and Performance," *Scriptura* 90 (2005): 621–640.

[13] Carruthers, *Book,* 9.

[14] M. Carruthers, *The Book of Memory: A Study of Memory in Medieval Culture* (1st ed., Cambridge: Cambridge University Press, 1990): 260. Quoted in Botha, "New Testament Texts," 636.

[15] On composing in antiquity, see Small, *Wax Tablets,* 177–201 and J. M. Foley, *The Theory of Oral Composition: History and Methodology* (Bloomington: Indiana University Press, 1988) and idem, *The Singer of Tales in Performance* (Bloomington: Indiana University Press, 1995).

(potentially) literacy. In an oral culture, composing is almost exclusively done orally, not as an act of writing. In addition, every performance was, in some sense, an act of re-composition. Here are several possibilities for imagining the act of composing and re-composing.

a) A gospel may have been composed orally in memory before any performance or in the course of a number of performances that gave the composer a chance to develop and hone the composition. This option does not require literacy.

b) Other performers may have heard and retold the story. Here the performer is someone other than the composer of the first version(s). This involves significant gifts of memory based on hearing and retelling. Here performances involved re-composing. At some point, this oral composition may have been written down based on a performance or the memory of a performance. This option also does not require literacy.

c) A gospel or a letter may have been dictated previous to a performance. The composition would have been composed mentally in memory and dictated to a scribe, perhaps in sections. The gospels may have been initially composed this way and then performed by the composer or someone else. In the case of letters, the performer was surely someone other than the composer. A letter was composed, dictated, and scribed in one location and performed by someone else in another location.

d) The performer may have used the written text as a means to learn and practice the gospel or letter. The performer may not have used the text in the act of performance. In such a case, the performer would have learned the composition in memory by reading it aloud or by listening to someone else read it aloud. Here, the performance as an act of re-composition may have been somewhat circumscribed by the text of the scroll. Or the performer may have shaped the story anew in the context of the performance. In this case, the performance as an act of re-composition would have been more fluid.

e) The handwritten scroll may have been used by a performer in the act of performing. The performer would basically have read the composition. Here the performance as an act of re-composition would have, to an even greater extent, been circumscribed by the written text.

The point is that under any and all circumstances the performance is in some sense an act of composition. Composing and re-composing was done in performance. Even if the performer has read a scroll or has given a close recounting of a previous performance or of a manuscript and even if the performance involved a performer who had performed the same composition previously, the performance would be unique. Because each telling is in some sense an original, the performance of a text is not just an interpretation of the writing; rather, it is a composition in its own right. As we have argued, a performance is more than the words spoken. It is the voice inflection, the facial expressions, the gestures, and the movement, along with audience participation. This will change with each performance.

Furthermore, it is improbable that a performance was done by rote memorization from a previous performance or a manuscript – especially in the case of storytellers. First, every effort at memory involves mistakes. Second, storytellers were expected to repeat a story with their individual style. Such improvisation was highly valued in many circles. Third, there were only a few who even aimed for "memorization" in antiquity, limited perhaps to actors, some rapsodes, poets, some tradents of the rabbinic traditions, and the rhetorician Quintilian – all of whom were among the very small percentage of literate elites.[16] Fourth, even when there were efforts to do word-for-word memorization, the ancients did not even think of words as discrete entities as we do; instead they considered a "word" to be a speech utterance, which could refer to a phrase or a clause or a sentence (a "saying") or even to what we would call a paragraph. Fifth, ancients did not think of "being true" to a story or to a piece of wisdom as an accurate word-for-word repetition but as a faithful grasping of the gist of it. Sixth, performers shaped their stories in light of the location in which they were performing. Finally, performers shaped their stories in light of the make-up, circumstances, and values/beliefs of their audiences.

In addition, as we shall see, there may have been "interruptions" that affected the composition-as-performance. A performer of 1 Corinthians might stop and explain what Paul meant by his advice. Performers customarily would shorten or lengthen a performance depending on audience interest. Hostile audiences, such as the performer of Paul's letter may have encountered in Galatia, might interrupt performers, leading them to defend their position. Or the performer may have engaged in conversation or debate after the entire composition was completed. All these may have contributed to the composition on any given occasion.

Every performance was in some sense an "original." The tradition was fluid, with some traditions being more fluid than others. Mark and Q may have been quite fluid, likely growing and changing in the course of many performances. In the case of Matthew, with its rabbinic origins, there may have been an effort to be faithful to the wording of the composition. Perhaps those who presented letters also had an obligation to the sender to be faithful to what the sender-composer had written. A performer of Revelation was probably eager to stay fairly close to the written scroll, especially in light of the composer's interdiction against anyone who would add anything or take anything away from the composition. However, in general, fluidity of the composition-as-performance would be most typical.

---

[16] See, for example, Small, *Wax Tablets*, 6–8.

Compositions were presented as a whole. It is likely that compositions were presented in their entirety, especially in the first century.[17] The length of time to present a gospel or letter was not prohibitive for audiences. Most New Testament writings take thirty minutes or less to perform. The gospels range from an hour and a half (Mark) to four hours (Luke). They may have been even longer, given a performer's interaction with the audience. Such performance lengths were not unusual in the ancient world. Actually, it is not unusual for us, when we consider the length of films or theater productions or sports events. Furthermore, the internal logic and plot development of each gospel suggest that much would be missed *and* much would be misunderstood if audiences heard only part of it. It is hard to imagine that communities receiving a letter would hear only part of it. Because all of these compositions were not yet considered to be scripture and were performed in a variety of venues, the idea that they early on broke the larger compositions into shorter segments is quite unlikely.

The experience of a composition as a whole is a significant feature of the performance event. For this reason, modern interpreters will benefit from having experiences of listening to each New Testament writing in its entirely as a basis for interpretation.[18]

Genres of composition affect the styles of performance The genre of a composition-as-performance shapes the nature of a performance. In my own performing of New Testament compositions as a whole, I am led to perform differing genres in differing styles of performance. Narrative genres with characters make demands on performers that are different from letters performed as speeches of rhetoric. Performing the fast-paced narrative of Mark keeps one animated and moving and engages the performer in all the lively skills of storytelling. However, when the genre changes within Mark and teaching occurs, the style of performing also changes. For example, there is a stage direction for the performer to sit when the script say that "Jesus sat out on a boat" and addressed (presumably loudly) a huge crowd on shore (Mark 4). This style reinforces Jesus' address to outsiders. Later the performer is led to sit and speak intimately when Jesus "sat down" to prophesy (quietly, even "secretly") about the future with four disciples in his inner circle (Mark 13). This style reinforces Jesus' address to insiders. Later, in the temple, where Jesus is not one of the official authorities, he is standing up to

---

[17] On brief oral traditions, see H. Hearon, *The Mary Magdalene Tradition: Witness and Counter-Witness in Early Christian Communities* (Collegeville: Liturgical Press, 2004).

[18] There are now two CDs available for listening to the entire New Testament in Greek: M. Phemister, *Audio Greek New Testament: Westcott and Hort Greek New Testament* (Grand Rapids: Christian Classics Ethereal Library, 2003) and J. Simon, *Greek-Latin New Testament Audio Reading Series* (Austin, TX: greeklatinaudio. com, 1999). There is a similar movement in studies of Homer, in which scholars are encouraged to *listen* to Homer. See M. Edwards, *Sound, Sense, and Rhythm: Listening to Greek and Latin Poetry* (Princeton: Princeton University Press, 2002), 61.

teach. The ebb and flow of Matthew is also related to alternating segments of teaching and action when, for example, Jesus "sits down" to deliver the "sermon on the mount" (Matt 5:1–7:27). By contrast, it seems appropriate to stand when pronouncing woes on the Pharisees (Matt 23:1–39). Long narrative scenes in John are very much like theater and may lend themselves to a dialogue between several performers.

Letters suggest another style, because the performer addresses the audience as though they were the recipients of the letter. The rhetorical genre of Paul's angry and passionate letter to the Galatians makes different demands on a performer than the reflective letter to the Philippians. The performance of James evokes the image of meditations by a sage who is slowly and carefully examining gems of wisdom. 1 Peter invites an occasional tone of dissimulation as it seeks both to honor and to subvert human figures of authority. The apocalyptic genre of Revelation expresses intensely almost every emotion in the human repertoire as it excites the vivid imagination of the audience in warnings and with visions of horror and hope. Extreme physical expressions and emotional outbursts seem most appropriate for portions of Revelation as rhetorical means to bring audiences through a catharsis to reject their attachments to the Roman Empire and to embrace an allegiance to the New Jerusalem.

As I have suggested, brief forms within the larger genres evoke different performance styles. I enunciate the specific parts of Mark's parables slowly and emphatically to emphasize the allegorical and obscure nature of their function as riddles. I tell Luke's parables so as to bring them to a climactic punch line. The stories of conflict between Jesus and demons are loud and violent. The healing stories move from concern to hopefulness to astonishment. Jesus pronounces blessings in Matthew, and Paul curses the opponents in Galatia. These require emphatic announcement. In Galatians, I use gestures to help the audience track the timeline from Abraham to the giving of the Law to the appearance of Jesus. Admonition to a community, such as we get in various passages in 1 Corinthians, calls for one kind of tone, whereas general ethical instruction such as we have at the end of 1 Thessalonians calls for another tone. Virtually every passage becomes an opportunity for interpretation as the performer seeks performative ways to be faithful to the composition and to bring it alive to an audience.

Can we make some correlations between the forms/genres and certain styles of performance in antiquity? It seems as if we can do this to some extent in relation to story, teaching, oration, letter, and perhaps apocalypse. If so, it may help us to imagine better various performance scenarios of a composition and its potential impacts on audiences.

3. The Performer

The early Christian communities had no un-embodied experience of the stories and the letters. Their experiences of the gospels and the epistles and their responses to them were therefore highly contingent on the role of the performer. The performer was the medium that bore the potential meanings and impacts of the story/letter upon the audience in a particular context. Every aspect of the performer's identity, familiarity, trustworthiness, appearance, movements, and expressions were part of the experience. In the performance of a narrative, the performer was acting out each character and event of the story. In the performance of a letter, the performer was personifying the sender in presenting the dynamics of the argument. The performer needed to be engaging and forceful. Unless the performer could captivate an audience and hold its attention, the performance and its intended effect would be lost to them.

The Performer. Who might have performed the gospel narratives? It is amazing how little we know about this and can only infer from general practices. Storytelling in general was probably most common among non-elites (which may be why we have so little information about storytellers in antiquity). Men and women engaged often in regaling people with stories. Literacy was not required for storytelling. It is reasonable to imagine that non-literate storytellers could have composed and performed stories the length of our gospels, especially Mark and John.

For those who were literate, reading aloud or listening to a manuscript being read to them may have helped with memory practice and recall. Because reading before a gathered group was less engaging and because absolute recall was not expected of the performer, storytellers gifted in memory would have been able to manage performing a whole gospel. If Matthew was written in a scribal community, it is possible that the scribes themselves were performers and learned well what they had written – since the act of writing itself could enhance memory. Luke seems to have had a patron, Theophilus. Is it possible that the patron, at least initially, also provided a professional performer for the Gospel of Luke and for Acts? After all, the patron was eager not mainly to produce a script but to publish the composition in performances.

What about the letters, say those of Paul? Would a person from the recipient community read the letter when it was received from Paul? People capable of performing a letter by reading or by memory probably would have been a very small percentage of the community, just as it was a small percentage of the society. The issue would have been to find someone the community trusted who could read with meaning and facility. The early Christian movement was likely comprised predominantly of peasants and the urban poor; however, there is reason to think that some elites and their retainers may have been in communities, perhaps as leaders and patrons. Elites themselves may not have been able to read, at least not with facility. Nevertheless, elites often had their slaves read to them; and so a slave of one of the elite members could have performed such a duty for the assembly. If the early communities included slaves, even ones whose masters were not part of the community, these slaves may have been trained to write and/or to read. This scenario would be especially interesting if one of the themes of the letter was slavery/freedom. It would have been very awkward, for example, if a (another) slave of Philemon had read Paul's letter to Philemon regarding the freeing of Onesimus!

It would also be interesting to consider whether a community would hire a professional reader for the letters and whether they could even afford that. However, it is not likely that the community would have trusted someone not a member of the community with a letter that bore great importance to them. Besides, in order to make sense of the letter orally, the performer would need to know Paul, as well as the community – its culture and beliefs, its situation and needs. There was probably at least one person in each of Paul's churches able to read his letter. However, even if the person able to read was a member, that person may not have been entrusted with the task, especially if such a person was the only one in the assembly who could decipher the scroll. Given that so much of the meaning and impact of a manuscript depended on the oral interpretation in performance, the audience would not have given credence to the performance of the letter if they did not trust the performer.

Most likely, however, the person presenting a letter would be the emissary who brought the letter to the community from Paul.[19] Both Paul and the community would have trusted such a person. If such were the case, the person would have been with Paul in formulating the letter, witnessed him dictating the letter, and knew well what Paul's concerns were. Paul would probably have given instructions on how to present the letter. This familiarity with the origin of the letter would enable the performer to answer questions or explain things in the letter for the recipient community. Besides, the trip would also allow the performer time to study and learn the letter well on the journey.

It may be that letter carriers in antiquity were not the same person who read/performed the letters they carried. However, given the important nature of the matters in Paul's letters and their address to a community rather than to an individual, it may have been important to have the letter carrier perform it. Besides, it is likely that the letter carrier was more than an epistolary functionary. Paul did not just send a letter. He sent a person, an emissary, with a letter. Or it may be that a member of the community read the letter while the carrier was responsible to bring news of Paul and explain the letter to the community on behalf of Paul. In this case, the reader from the recipient community probably

---

[19] On Paul's letter carriers, see Richards, *Paul*, 188–209.

180 *David Rhoads*

needed time to become acquainted with the letter and practice it before it was presented to the community.

Keep also in mind that the emissary-performer would be a "commissioned-agent" of Paul. Such an agent would have re-presented Paul. There are many arguments that the letter was a substitute for Paul and bore his authority. Based on our understanding of commissioned agents in antiquity, we can imagine that the agent *becomes* that person. "Whoever receives me receives not me but the one who sent me" (Mark 9:37). In a sense, the letter bore the "apostolic presence."[20] However, it is not the letter on a handwritten scroll that people experienced, but the embodied letter – the performer being Paul in the official act of presenting the letter. So it was the *letter-performer* who bore the apostolic presence. And the selection of the person to represent him would have been an important matter for Paul. The familiarity with Paul on the part of the emissary may even have enabled that person to mimic Paul's mannerisms of speaking style in the course of the performance as a means to reinforce Paul's "presence."

It is not clear how other letters in the New Testament and Revelation circulated and were performed. Some of these letters were designed for circulation. Can we assume that an emissary went from place to place in Asia Minor with 1 Peter or Revelation and performed in different assemblies? It may have been important to the originator of the letter to have someone bring it who could also perform it and explain it – or even to adapt it to different contexts

The Social Location of the Performer. The social location of the performer would have been important to the authenticity of a gospel or a letter. Consider any performance by someone whose social location is radically contrary to the content of the composition or different from the social location of the audience. I have difficulty imagining a gentile performing Matthew. Imagine how incongruous it would have been for a wealthy person to perform James. Perhaps Paul's choice of Phoebe as a female to perform Romans was a brilliant move that avoided taking sides (despite her ethnicity) in an agonistic struggle between male Judeans and male Gentiles that might have been exacerbated by a performer who was either a Judean male or a Gentile male.

The respect for the performer on the part of the audience would be important. For a gospel or letter, the performer needed to embody the values, beliefs, and actions enjoined by the story/text being performed, because the performer was seeking to have the values and beliefs of the story embodied in turn in the actions and dynamics of the communal life of the audience. In general, an audience did not separate the story or the letter from a particular performer or from the social location of that performer. That may be one reason why there

---

[20] R. Funk, "The Apostolic Parousia: Form and Significance," *Christian History and Interpretation* (eds. W. R. Farmer, et. al.; Cambridge: Cambridge University Press, 1967), 249–269 and R. Ward, "Pauline Voice and Presence as Strategic Communicator," *Semeia* 65 (1995): 95–135.

was a suspicion of writing in antiquity – because you could not really understand what the words meant or whether the advice was to be trusted, apart from knowing the person telling them.[21] So unless the performer had integrity in relation to that which was being urged upon the audience, the audience would not have received the story nor would they have acted upon the letter being presented.[22] Note, for example, how Paul would prefer that Timothy deliver (and therefore perform?) his letter to the Philippians (although he had to settle for Epaphroditus), because Timothy was the only one who knew how to "look to the interests of others" instead of his own interests – which is the main theme of Philippians (2:19–30).

What difference did it make if the performer read aloud or performed from memory? I am persuaded that performing from memory was more common than reading, even in the case of letters. The problem with reading is that it was not easy to do. The script was continuous; that is, there were not spaces between words, sentences, or what we would call paragraphs. The script was small and often irregular. There was only one upper-case letter after another – with no punctuation marks of any kind. As such, a handwritten scroll functioned basically as a repository for sounds, similar to the way a musical score gives notes to represent sounds. All the rest – inflection, volume, pauses, transitions, and so on – was provided orally by the reader or performer. Reading the sounds (aloud of course) could be slow and tedious for a gathered community. In addition, the scroll was not easy to manage, and there were not yet reading desks or podia. Even if one could read with facility, the scroll required the use of both hands, the right one to hold the scroll and the left one to scroll it for the next column of writing. Often it was held on the lap for reading.

The point is that reading did not lend itself to an engaging performance of a story or letter.[23] The performer could not look at the audience and would be limited to the use of the voice as a means to performance. Other performance arts such as gestures, bodily expression, and movement would not be in play. This would make the performance less meaningful and less engaging. Nevertheless, at least in terms of the use of the voice, I would argue that even so-called "readings" would have been more of a performance than a reading.

It may be the case that even to read with facility, the reader needed to know the manuscript practically by heart anyhow. Besides, someone trained in reading

---

[21] P. J. J. Botha, "Living Word and Lifeless Letters: Reserve Towards Writing in the Greco-Roman World," *Hervormde Teologiese Studies* 49 (1993): 742–759.

[22] Hence, the importance of the motif of imitation in relation to the performance of Paul's letters. Consider the line of imitation in Paul: Jesus to Paul to the leaders to the community. Paul may have thought of the performer-agent as relevant to that chain.

[23] Compare Isocrates, "When someone reads it aloud without persuasiveness and without putting any feeling into it, but as though he were reciting a table of figures, it is natural, I think, that it would make an indifferent impression upon its hearers." *Orations* 5. 25–27 translated by G. Norlin, Loeb Classical Library (Cambridge: Harvard University Press, 1928).

was also trained in memory. It would have been difficult to go back and forth between memory and reading, because it was so difficult to find one's place in a scroll. There is some evidence that, in general, letters were read. However, given the nature of most New Testament letters – addressed to a public assembly and bearing the marks of rhetorical orations – it seems likely that they were performed from memory.

Knowing a gospel or letter in memory would have greatly enhanced the meaningfulness and power of the presentation. This is what storytellers and orators in that culture would do. More than all else they had to hold their audience. It was what audiences expected. Audiences may not otherwise have tolerated it. This would be no less true for Christian assemblies than other gatherings. Nevertheless, this is certainly an open matter and there are good arguments on both sides.

The Presence of Scrolls. First-century Christians would have thought of the gospels and letters not as scrolls but as performances they had experienced. Nevertheless, a scroll may occasionally have been present when the gospel stories were told and more likely when letters were presented.[24] Scrolls may have been present to authenticate the composer of a letter. Some sculptures show orators with a closed scroll held with the left arm, leaving the right arm and hand for gesturing. Of course the scrolls would have been indecipherable to the audience.

Overall Styles of performing in Antiquity. The style of performance may have differed greatly from performer to performer, from audience to audience, from setting to setting, from circumstance to circumstance. I have already suggested that different genres engendered differing styles of performance. In his pro-claiming, Paul may have had a different style of performance in Galatia (graphic presentation of the death of Jesus), in Thessalonica (where he may have sounded too much like street philosophers), or in Philippi (where he may have evoked strong Roman opposition). So, too, each of his letters may have called for a different style or tone or pace.

We have every reason to think that performances were very lively and ani-mated across the board in the Greco-Roman world – for rhetoricians, story-tellers, rhapsodes, actors, imperial criers, and Rabbinic tradents. Cicero said that narrative examples should be presented in such a way that "they seem to be placed before the eyes as vividly as if they were taking place in our actual presence."[25] Elites tended to look down on popular storytellers and actors

---

[24] On reading practices, see, for example, W. D. Shiell, *Reading Acts: The Lector and the Early Christian Audience* (Leiden: Brill, 2004) and A. Millard, *Reading and Writing in the Time of Jesus* (Sheffield: Sheffield Academic Press, 2000).

[25] Cicero, *On the Making of an Orator*, 5. 53. 202, quoted in Quintilian, *The Education of the Orator* 9. 1. 27 translated by H. Butler, Loeb Classical Library (Cambridge: Harvard University Press, 1920). Cited by W. Shiner, "Oral Performance in the New Testament World," *The Bible*

among the peasant classes for having a bombastic style of emoting meant to draw the audiences into dramatic participation.[26] Such a style may have been necessary in part due to the size of an audience or for a performance that was in noisy public space. Other popular storytellers may have been much less dramatic, especially for small and more intimate audiences. Some rhetoricians urged performers to tell stories in a realistic way "so that we seem" as one ancient rhetorician put it, "to recount everything just as it took place."[27]

There was a common view in the rhetorical handbooks that emotion was a key means of moving and changing an audience. Aristotle has an extensive discussion of emotions to be evoked by the performer, because the orator persuades hearers "when they are roused to emotion by his speech."[28] And the performers were themselves to express the emotions that they wished to evoke from the audience. The expression of emotions would have been many and complex. Emotions would have followed the nature of the subject matter and the context: angry in Galatians, sarcastic in 2 Corinthians, somber in the depictions of Jesus' death, frightened or hopeful in the narration of Revelation, and so on.

Of course we cannot recover any of these myriad live performances among early Christians. Nevertheless, we have the "scripts" to analyze. In this regard, the contents of the New Testament scrolls contain "stage directions" for performers. There are two kinds of clues in the texts that help us to infer the some features of performances. One is *oral arts* of communication embedded in the texts that convey various storytelling patterns and memorable language and sound effects and rhetorical sequences, all of which give us some clues as to the style of the performance.[29] Many of these same features served to facilitate memory on the part of the performer as well as the audience. Second, we also have clues as to what we might call the *performance arts*.[30] The written compo-

---

in *Ancient and Modern Media: Story and Performance* (eds. H. Hearon and P. Ruge-Jones; Eugene: Wipf and Stock, 2009), 54.

[26] See, for example, *The Education of the Orator*, Quintilian 2.12.9–10 and 3.8.59–60 translated by H.E. Butler, Loeb Classical Library (Cambridge: Harvard University Press, 1920).

[27] *Rhetorica ad Herennium*, 3.14.24 translated by H. Kaplan, Loeb Classical Library (Cambridge: Harvard University Press, 1954).

[28] *The Art of Rhetoric*, 1.2.5 translated by J.H. Freeze, Loeb Classical Library (Cambridge: Harvard University Press, 1926).

[29] As examples of oral art in letters, see C. Davis, *Oral Biblical Criticism: The Influence of the Principles of Orality on the Literary Structures of Paul's Letter to the Philippians* (Sheffield: Sheffield Academic Press, 1999; J. Harvey, *Listening to the Text: Oral Patterning in Paul's Letters* (Grand Rapids: Baker Books, 1998); and E. Wendland, *Finding and Translating the Oral-Aural Elements in Written Language: The Case of the New Testament Epistles* (Lewiston: Edwin Mellen Press, 2008). On narrative, see J. Dewey, "The Gospel of Mark as an Oral-Aural Event," *The New Literary Criticism and the New Testament* (eds. E. Malbon and E. McKnight; Sheffield: Sheffield Academic Press, 1994), 145–161.

[30] On performance arts in oral cultures, see R. Baumann, *Story, Performance, and Event: Contextual Studies of Oral Narrative* (Cambridge: Cambridge University Press, 1978) and

sitions themselves give many explicit expressions reflecting and guiding the oral performance – such as volume ("screamed"), movement ("entered"), gestures ("touched"), facial expressions ("wept"), body movement ("looked up"), sound effects ("they beat their breast"), and so on. These narrative descriptors told the story and *also* served as stage directions for performance. They are prevalent throughout most New Testament texts. Hence, in analyzing the New Testament writings for their orality, we can identify a number of features that give witness to the dynamics and styles of ancient performers.

4. Communities of Reception

It is critical to remember that the audience is a communal group gathered in a specific venue experiencing the performance. The term audience may be somewhat misleading. Today we think of an audience as any gathered group, whether they know each other or not. It is possible in antiquity that the performance of a gospel was done in a public place so as to gather such an audience. However, in ancient performance events of early Christianity we are more than likely speaking about the audience as a "community of reception."

The audience as community. The collective nature of the audience shapes how it responds. In the contemporary world, we have an almost completely individualistic experience of biblical writings, because we read or study them in private. Even when do we hear them in a group, for example as readings in worship, we tend to process them as individuals. This is partly due to the fact that as audiences in theaters or films we have come with one or two others and do not know anyone else. This is partly true also in church, although there common values are shared and we seldom talk about the experience together afterward. We scholars and students would do well to have some communal experiences of these writings as performances in order to imagine the dynamics of "group responses" (and even interruptions) to a performance.

Gathering. It is not clear how communities or audiences gathered for a performance. The performance may have occurred at the regular gathering for meals or worship. Given the length of time to do a gospel, the occasion probably would have been announced to the community ahead of time, especially if the performer was visiting the community. In an oral culture, word of such an important event would spread quickly. Perhaps a visiting gospel-bearer may have been in a village for awhile so that people would get to know that person.

R. Finnegan, *Oral Poetry: Its Nature and Significance* (Bloomington: Indiana University Press, 1992). For performance in antiquity, see *Oral Performance and Its Context* (ed. C. J. Mackie; Leiden: Brill, 2004) and T. Olbricht, "Delivery and Memory," in *Handbook of Classical Rhetoric in the Hellenistic Period–330 B. C. to 400 A. D.* (ed. S. Porter; Leiden: Brill, 2001). Shiner, *Proclaiming*, passim, has a discussion of ancient rhetorical sources on performance.

When an emissary arrived in a city with a letter of Paul, presumably a time and place for assembly was passed by word of mouth among community members.

The makeup of the audience. The make-up of the audience was significant, because performance is shaped in part by the social location and personality of the audience.[31] In this regard, the performance will have different meanings for different audiences. This has been illustrated for me often in my own performances. I was amazed how the women prisoners of a local jail grasped the warning in James against the poison of the tongue. When I performed Mark to a medium security prison for men, the warning against what comes out from the heart – illegal sexual acts, thefts, murders, expressions of greed, and so on (7:21–23) – took on new significance! Responses to the violence in Revelation against oppressors have differed radically depending on whether the makeup of the audience is an oppressor group or an oppressed group. Luke sounds very different to the poor than it does to the rich. The importance of social location to meaning and response was as true of ancient audiences – a gentile audience compared to a Judean one or an audience in Asia Minor compared to one in Palestine or Rome or an urban audience in contrast to a rural audience or a male audience as opposed to a female audience. Storytellers likely would have adapted their performances to the presence of elites, in terms either of praise or condemnation.

A single audience may also have been comprised of people from diverse social locations. The thrust toward diversity in the early churches, such as the church at Corinth, assured this. So when we interpret a text as an oral composition, we are not necessarily dealing with an ideal audience or a homogeneous audience but with diverse hearers in a communal audience. We see instances in the New Testament where some members of an audience leave (such as we find in John 6:60–71 and 8:59) or fall asleep (Acts 20:7–12) or threaten to kill (Luke 4:28–30; John 8:59) and where the composition reminds hearers to "Stay awake!" (Mark 13 and Rev. 16:15). Consider how Paul's Letter to Philemon might have affected in different ways Philemon, Onesimus, and other members of the house assembly – women, slaves (male and female), freedmen, other patrons – as they each experienced this letter together in a gathered community.

The makeup of an audience shapes the content and performance of a letter. If there were Judaizers anticipated in the assemblies at Galatia, Paul may have composed the letter to generate an action that would subsequently exclude them from the community (Gal. 1:6–9). However, the communities at Galatia may not have accepted Paul's arguments. The complex composition of the community in Corinth – rich and poor, strong and weak, gentiles and Judeans, and people with diverse theological/ethical perspectives – must have been a night-

---

[31] On social location and related bibliography, see D. Rhoads, *From Every People and Nation: The Book of Revelation in Intercultural Perspective* (Minneapolis: Fortress, 2005), 1–27.

mare for Paul (and for the performer) as Paul tried to generate unity and also to set boundaries. It did not necessarily work. Recall how Antoinette Wire re-constructed the suppressed voices of women prophets in Corinth who resisted Paul's message, because, not able to break free of his own male/elite-retainer origins, Paul did not apply the gospel appropriately to their differing social location (1990).[32] *Galatians* was addressed to several assemblies, perhaps of diverse make-up. Paul's letters were sooner or later circulated. The Catholic Epistles went from assembly to assembly, being read or performed from memory, often over a wide area. Revelation circulated across seven or more cities. No doubt there were different communities in the same city, such as we might imagine to be the case in Ephesus. Surely the composer and the performer were aware of these complexities and anticipated them.

As means to expand our interpretive methods today, we might imagine diverse audiences for performances of each writing now in the New Testament as a heuristic device to imagine how they were experienced and understood. An illuminating exercise would be to project how peasants and elites, slaves and masters, women and men, Judeans and Romans, as well as others in an audience, might have experienced, say 1 Peter – as a way to understand its potential for meaning and its complex rhetoric. Imagine, for example, Mark being delivered to an all peasant audience in contrast to one in which both peasants and elites were present. What would jump out at us in new ways? Peter Oakes at Manchester University, England, has reported to me that he does an exercise on a New Testament letter in which he assigns a different social location to each student, asks them to study the letter in question, gives them an oral experience of the writing, and then discusses with them their reactions from the perspective of their chosen social location. The multi-valence of a text and its rich potential for multiple valid meanings and rhetorical impacts become quite obvious when we consider complex and diverse audiences.[33]

The audience actively participated in the performance. A failure to respond to a performance in progress was noteworthy: Pliny expresses shock when two friends insulted a performer because they "sat quietly throughout, never opening their lips, stirring their hands, or rising to their feet" (Pliny, *Letters*, 6. 17. 1–3). A Greek rhapsode is quoted by Plato as saying that he knows he will not receive the prize in a competition if he does not see "his audience weeping, casting terror glances, and stricken with amazement" (Plato, *Ion.* 535e.)(quoted in Shiner).

Whitney Shiner has an extensive discussion of audience participation. He argues that audiences of gospels and letters might have done such things as

---

[32] A. Wire, *The Corinthian Women Prophets* (Minneapolis: Fortress Press, 1990).

[33] D. Rhoads, *From Every People*, 1–27 and *The Meanings We Choose: Hermeneutical Ethics, Indeterminacy, and the Conflict of Interpretations* (ed. C. Cosgrove, London: T. & T. Clark, 2004).

cheered, jeered, clapped, hooted, stood, stamped their feet, laughed, wept, gasped, shouted, heckled, given various verbal responses of acclamation, and other forms of interruption.[34] He argues that one can identify "applause lines" (in Mark) that were designed to evoke positive acclamations.[35] Consider what is in the gospels: miraculous healings, exorcisms, calming of storms, mortal conflicts with opponents, attack on the temple, entrance to Jerusalem, whippings, and a crucifixion. Mark is recounting dramatic events. We would be foolish to imagine that people were not emotional and responsive when they heard them. Composers and performers surely anticipated audience responses; and, in turn, audiences were quite capable of shaping a performance as it went along.

In antiquity, there were predictable and unpredictable interactions between performer and audience. The performer would clearly be trying to create and shape a community; at the same time, an active community of reception would in turn shape and influence the performance. It is difficult to know how to assess and imagine this dynamic with oral performances of gospels and letters. We need to recall that these stories and speeches were not yet treated as scripture. And there would have been different audience responses to storytelling than to the directness of letters or orations. I can imagine peasant audiences howling with delight when the Markan Jesus outwits the authorities. I can see the wealthy protesting the woes against the rich in Luke or peasants cheering the prediction of the demise of the rich in James. Imagine, for example, how the diatribes in Romans would have worked to anticipate and counter any resistance by an audience. Choose any writing in the New Testament and begin to imagine the interaction between performer and audience. It changes the way we think about these so-called "writings."

Meaning and Impact are negotiated between performer and audience. The audience is therefore crucial to the meaning/impact of a performance. Meaning is negotiated between the performer and the audience. We cannot separate audience from performer. They are in an interwoven, symbiotic relationship. A performance is an interactive event. In this sense, a performance event is the "site of interpretation." A performance does not work until the audience works it out – irony, humor, riddles, catharsis, force of an argument, and so on. My own experience with performing confirms this. When the audience laughs early on, I change the way I say later lines in order to evoke this response again.

---

[34] Shiner, *Proclaiming*, 143–152.
[35] Shiner, *Proclaiming*, 153–170.

5. Setting of Time and Place

The physical location of a performance is also important, because the "place" itself makes a difference in the performance event.

Many possible locations. We can posit many different locations for early Christian gatherings in the ancient world – a village market place, an assembly hall, a reception hall, a synagogue, a theater, the house of a poor person, the house of an elite person, an urban tenement building, or out in an open space between villages. The occasion may have been a gathering for teaching or worship or for a community meal or just for a performance by itself. Sometimes the location was ready-made with a set of expectations. At other times, the performance created the arena by the event itself.

Location influences a performance. How might the location of a performance have contributed to its style, its meaning, and its reception? The issues are complex. The actual physical configuration offers certain possibilities and limits others. The physical size of the location affects the number of people who can be present. Would people sit (on what?) or stand? This in turn may signify formality or a sense of intimacy. The location may be in the open where anyone can join the audience, and where people come and go. Or it might be private. Did the venue reflect wealth or poverty? What other activities took place in this location? What other groups may have used this venue? What set-up for a performance was likely (such as a *triclinium* or in a market place) and how would that affect the style and manner of performance? How would the context of worship shape a performance? Or the context of a meal?

The time of a performance can be significant. A performance could occur in the morning as women gathered at the well or by the community ovens. Here we can add late afternoon, which might connect the venue with a time after men have come back from labor in the fields. The darkness of evening around a fire or in a room with dimly lit lamps would be a time when families might gather. The time of day will have resonances with the time and mood of the story being told. It will affect who might be present.

Settings raise expectations and limit possibilities. Like genres, contexts raise expectations, in this case expectations of what *does* or *does not* happen in a particular place; as such, different places foster or inhibit certain audience responses. In my own experience of performing, it makes a difference in the audience response if I am performing in a church or a university or a theater or a prison or a lounge or an open place. For example, people respond to humor more freely in secular settings compared to religious settings. In performing the passion narrative of Mark successively to different groups of inmates in a jail, I found myself orally re-translating the story with language they would best connect with their context – such as "bound over" for "handed over" and "take into custody" for "seize" and "perjury" for "false witness."

No doubt in antiquity, houses, public assembly buildings, and other places raised and limited particular expectations that shaped the performance event. For example, quotations from the Judean Scriptures would be heard differently in a synagogue than in a Greek market place. Kinship language would have distinct resonances in a house or in a place where burial associations met. If we imagine Philippians being performed in a place where soldiers may have given allegiance to Caesar, this would profoundly affect how people heard the claim that "at the name of Jesus every knee will bow." It would be counterintuitive but interesting to imagine James being performed in the house of a wealthy patron. With its overt support and covert critique of the hierarchical system of Roman society, 1 Peter will sound different in a private as compared with a public setting.

Obviously, we cannot know precisely where a letter or reading may have occurred. I am encouraging us to imagine various likely venues and then ask how each one may fit with the text and/or illuminate it. This is no different than imagining a certain social situation and then seeing how the writing fits. Of course, each composition would likely have been performed in several different venues. So how would it have been heard in these different places?

6. Cultural Ethos

Cultural ethos is the life-world in which the performance event occurs. Cultural ethos refers to the whole complex of language, traditions, practices, and customs in which performer and audience are immersed in a society as a basis for shared communication and understanding. This includes the language – its social level, its range and complexity, and its status as means of communication. Ethos includes the scope of worldviews, traditions, shared history, social memory, and images vital to the identity and life of the community, including inter-oral and textual associations. It also includes the repertoire of oral arts and performance arts that function to enable mutual understanding and influence. And it includes the customs of behavior and the scripts of interaction that characterize the daily life and relationships in the society. There may be overlapping and conflicting layers to this ethos – the Christian community, a rural or urban setting, the context of empire.

When interpreting a composition in performance, we need to be alert to the aspects of the cultural ethos that the composition draws upon: language register, traditions, verbal arts, and cultural patterns. Our knowledge of the context will be indispensible for understanding so many facets of a composition in performance: performance arts, storytelling practices, epistolary and rhetorical conventions, as well as the images that evoke shared cultural memories. Clues to these include the word fields evident in a composition. For examples, Philippians has much language about friendship and politics and military procedures. These will assist us in connecting with the same language in the layers of ethos in Philippi.

Cultural ethos is not static. The performance itself, if successful in influencing its audience, may be instrumental in bringing innovation and transformation in many aspects of the cultural ethos. Images may be transformed: the messiah suffers; the death on the cross is a victory; people are strongest when they are weak. Cultural assumptions may be challenged: the last shall be first; those who save their lives will lose them; blessed are the poor. Concrete realities may be given metaphorical meaning: Christians are brothers and sisters; the community is part of a new "nation;" the Holy Spirit generates a "new creation." Traditions can be in conflict: the little traditions and the great traditions; the law versus grace; idolatry versus fidelity to the true God. performances are encounters with ways of seeing and of being in the world. As such, they can affirm existing realities or be a strong force in subverting and transforming them. Openness to this phenomenon and understanding how it works are an important part of the analysis of a performance event and its potential outcomes.

7. Socio-Historical context

In understanding meaning and rhetoric in biblical performances in antiquity, we need to imagine differing audiences under divergent circumstances – persecution, conflict, oppression, war, social unrest, poverty, prosperity, and so on – in specific locations hearing each composition in performance. It is true that for a long time we scholars have been saying the same thing about the crucial importance of context for interpreting the New Testament as written documents. However, when we talk about the oral power of a composition in performance to communal audiences in particular contexts, we are now speaking in fresh ways about echoes and associations, about an enlivened imagination, about a richer meaning potential of a text, and about a greater intensity and immediacy of experience. To do so is to speak in fresh ways about a "politics of performance" (Ward 1995).

Historical context shapes meaning. The socio-historical circumstances make a difference in what the performance means and how it works to generate a particular impact. Imagining specific socio-historical circumstances for a performance event intensifies our understanding of "reception." For example, what danger might the Roman prisoner Paul have been inviting for the Philippians when he wrote a contra- imperial letter to a Christian community in this Roman military colony? How could performance criticism help us to imagine concrete scenarios for the audience reception of this letter in performance in the Philippian community? When I performed the Sermon on the Mount in a

Latvian pulpit before the break-up of the Soviet Union (with KGB in the congregation), every word (such as "blessed are the meek" and "love your enemy") took on new meanings. Likewise, imagining an actual performance and audience of Mark's Gospel in a specific location (such as Galilee) in the immediate aftermath of the Roman Judean War of 66 to 70 C. E. opens up new possibilities for interpreting the echoes of that war throughout the whole Gospel. When I performed the Book of Revelation after the 9/11 attack on the world trade center, the narration of merchants and sailors watching and grieving the burning of Rome (Rev 18:9–18) took on fresh meaning and power. Similarly, first century Judean refugees of the Roman Judean War now in Asia Minor may have had the recent burning of Jerusalem in 70 C. E. by the Roman Empire in mind when they were invited by the performer of Revelation to imagine the burning of Rome (Rev 18:9–18). What responses might audiences have had to such a scene?

8. Rhetorical impact on the audience

The final factor in the dynamics of the performance event is the potential rhetorical effect/impact upon an "ideal" audience. By rhetoric, I mean the impact of the entire composition-as-performance and the dynamics surrounding the whole event. In performance, there is no separating composition and context, form and function, content and rhetoric, story and discourse, meaning and impact. The whole experience of performance represents the content as embodied in the presentation and received by the audience. In general, meaning has to do with ideas, beliefs and values; however, in performance, meaning is to be interpreted in terms of relationships – the performer seeking to transform an audience with a story or a speech, to evoke emotional commitments, and/or to impel them to action.

Expanding the possibilities of rhetorical impact. We are referring not simply to talking tradents passing on a tradition, certainly not in some neutral way, because, given the nature of the New Testament compositions, the rhetoric of a performance seeks to change the world, shape communities, generate new relationships, bear/evoke the power of the Spirit. The transformation that may take place in the community, in some sense, itself constitutes an interpretation! As such, with performance, we ask in fresh ways not primarily what a composition *means* but what it *does* in performance What is the total impact of a performance – subversion of cultural values, transformation of worldview, impulse to action, change of behavior, emotional effect, ethical commitment, intellectual insight, political perspective, re-formation of community, the creation of a new world?

What does the-composition-in-performance ideally lead the audience to become and how does it do it? Put another way, what does a story or a letter seek to lead an audience to become – such that they may be different people in the course of and as a result of experiencing the performance? Also, as an oral composition-in-performance, *how* does it have such an impact? I am thinking quite specifically here about the performance event: In 1 Corinthians, what does Paul want people to do in response to his advice about the practices around the Lord's supper and speaking in tongues, and how does his verbal art lead them to do it? What does Paul want the community of Galatians to do about the Judaizers, and how does the oral rhetoric persuade them to do it? Given the ending of Mark, what does Mark want the hearers to do at the conclusion of hearing the gospel, and how has he led them to that point to be empowered to do it? What actions and decisions does James urge upon people who have experienced his wisdom, and how does the letter engender that? What might the different communities of the seven cities do upon hearing *Revelation*, and how has the letter "persuaded" them to do it?

What might happen actually in the community immediately after the performance? Of course, we can also ask what the community might actually have done. Exploring the various options of response is salutary. We do not have a record of responses. We tend to assume that if the writing has been preserved, then the community or communities must have reacted favorably and conformed to the rhetoric of the letter. But we do not know that. We might even assume that reactions were mixed, particularly in relation to diverse social locations of people in the audience-community. Communities may have been divided over the responses to a letter or a gospel or the apocalypse. My point is that we need to imagine the range of possible responses – in actions, attitudes, commitments, beliefs, values, relationships to insiders and outsiders, resistance to the empire, and so on. We know from 2 Corinthians that Paul's communities, for example, did not in fact respond positively to a visit or a letter. I am convinced that we could benefit greatly by pushing the rhetorical envelope and imagining concretely what a community might have done in response to a performance – indeed while still gathered. Such specific uses of our imagination may sharpen our understanding of the meaning and rhetoric of a composition-in-performance and the issues involved in it.

Dispersal. It is interesting to ask how a community may have dispersed. Did the performer engage in conversation and then dismiss them? Was there a liturgical benediction that signaled dispersal? Did people just wander off during and after the performance? And how did the performance have an impact upon people after they left the communal gathering? Can we imagine the difference the performance might have made in the daily lives of the community as they dispersed to their homes or labor?

In this regard, we need to imagine that the rhetorical impact takes place not only in the immediate responses of the audience during and just after the performance, but also in the attitudinal, behavioral, and relational changes that may have taken place subsequently in the community as a result of the performance. Was the expectation that outsiders would be converted or born again and become insiders? What would that mean in their daily lives? Were people expected to change as a result of the performance in the social relations or in their family configurations or in their resistance to Caesar? What would slaves, and masters, wives and husbands, young and old do when they left the community gathering after hearing 1 Peter? What did Luke want people to do about their possessions? What did Matthew want people to do about their relationship with Roman soldiers? Again, the enlivening of the imagination about specific possible outcomes of a performance event as it played out in daily life can sharpen our grasp of the meaning and rhetoric of the New Testament writings as compositions-in-performance.

Power. In all these factors, we may be able to think afresh about the power dynamics involved in a performance event – not only in terms of the physical, cultural, and historical contexts, but particularly in the face-to-face relationships between the performer and the audience as well as between different factions within the community of reception. We could apply our knowledge of relationships in ancient collectivist cultures to the immediacy of a performance scenario – such as patron-client relationships, colleague-colleague relationships of challenge and riposte, various familial relationships, master-slave relationships, insider-outsider relationships, and relationships with different authority figures. Constructing performance scenarios and imagining how they might play out in a community with people of particular social locations – and their implied relationships with each other – may sharpen our understanding of the meaning of a New Testament writing and its potential impacts.

Conclusion

There is obviously much more to be done in exploring the range of possibilities to depict the features of a performance event. However, an obvious next step is to use these elements to develop various "performance scenarios" for specific New Testament writings as a means to interpret them. That is to say, from all these elements of the performance event, we can imagine a concrete performance context for a gospel or a letter or the apocalypse as a basis for interpretation. The question for performance criticism is this: How can we find rigorous ways to analyze all these elements of the performance event together so as to provide viable scenarios to interpret specific written texts as performance literature and thereby transform the ways we understand the New Testament?

Performance Criticism as an Exegetical Method:
A Story, Three Insights, and Two Jokes

David Trobisch

1. A Story

Once upon a time, seven blind men lost their way in the woods. After wandering for a while they arrived at a clearing and heard a voice say, "I am a green Helifant." The seven blind men were terrified. They had not heard of a green Helifant before.

But after a while their curiosity grew stronger than their fear, and the first blind man approached the strange creature. He touched its toes and said: "A green Helifant is very small." The second man climbed on the creature's back and shouted: "A green Helifant is very tall." The third one touched one tusk and said, "It is like a spear. It will kill us!" The fourth one touched the tail. "It is like a snake. It will bite us!" The fifth one smelled its breath and said, "It stinks like a garbage can." The sixth blind man was a very thoughtful man. He touched the toes, climbed on the back, inspected the tusk and the tail, and smelled the creature's breath, but because he was very thoughtful and did not want to jump to any conclusions, he did not say anything to anyone.

But the seventh blind man was like most exegetes. He was a coward. He said, "I will not go near the thing. I will analyze what it said. And it said that it is green. The *Rana clamitans melanota*, the Green Frog, is green. This creature is like a frog."

"Ha, ha, ha," the green Helifant shouted. "All of you are right," and laughing it disappeared into the forest.

The seven blind men finally found the way back to their village. But when they talked to their neighbors, nobody would believe them. None of them had ever heard of a green Helifant. "What should that be?" they said, "A creature that is tall and small at the same time, that is like a spear, like a snake, that stinks like garbage and looks like a frog? Never have we seen anything like that. – Ha, ha, ha!" the neighbors laughed and went back to their homes.

But the seven blind men knew that what they had experienced was true. They quarreled with each other by day and by night and if they have not died, they are listening to this story.

2. Three Insights

What does an elusive green Helifant have to do with the scholarly exploration of texts from antiquity? Three things: Scholars are blind, scholars learn through comparison, and scholars create consensus by communicating with each other.

Scholars are blind. We cannot experience past events directly, we have to do so indirectly. Even when we examine evidence, we cannot always see the significance. For example, we do not understand ancient calendars and ancient currency the way we understand our own. We are like blind men and women stumbling through a forest.

Scholars learn by comparing the unknown with the known. Because we cannot find answers to our questions by looking directly at our object of interest, we compare the new evidence with evidence that we have already placed in a context. We understand by relating the unknown to what we know. The better we paint the overall picture, the easier it is for us to place a new piece of evidence.

Scholars create consensus by communicating with each other. We strive for objectivity by verifying and accepting the experiences of our colleagues as if these experiences were our own. In this regard the seven blind men in our story fail. They do not acknowledge each other's observations and therefore are stuck in eternal discussions. Only the sixth blind man has a comprehensive experience. He touches the toes, climbs on the back, inspects the tail, and smells the creature's breath, but he does not communicate his experience to the others. If an experience is not shared, it is irrelevant to the scholarly discourse. This is why publishing is an essential part of scholarship and science. The German language does not differentiate between scholarship and science: both are called *Wissenschaft*. The word references a methodological approach to observations and theory: *ein Vorgang, der Wissen schafft*.

Scholarship constructs theories from verified text observations by controlling the process through documented *exegetical methods*. Exegetical methods describe paths through the jungle of evidence, promising that if you follow the proposed methodological guidelines, the seemingly random appearances will find structure and a consistent image will emerge.

The Greek word *theoria* is put together from *thea* and *horaō*. *Thea* can carry three meanings: the act of watching, the spectacle that is being watched, or the point from where something is watched. The basic meaning of *horaō* is: to see. In Greek literature, the word *theoria* describes the experience of a spectator at a sports game or at the theater, or in more general terms, the activity of observing and contemplating from a distance.

The connection between θέα (the view) and θεά (the Goddess) is intriguing. The words are spelled the same way but pronounced slightly differently. One of the characteristics generally attributed to the Divine is omnipresence, the ability to be everywhere at once. When scholars develop a theory they strive to put seemingly disparate observations in a context that transcends time and place. If a theory works, it should be applicable to past and future events.

The word *methodos* is put together from *hodos*, the path, and the preposition *meta*, suggesting a way around something, or a way to follow in pursuit of knowledge. In narratives the word often translates as "trick" or "ruse."

In this sense an exegetical method is a way around. It is a trick, a ruse to look at a text from a distance and study it in context in order to extract an interpretation that was not apparent at first glance.

To give an example: The last sentence of Luke's gospel reads, "And they worshiped him, and returned to Jerusalem with great joy; and they were continually in the temple blessing God" (Luke 24:52–53).[1]

The Greek word for "they were blessing" in some handwritten copies is *eulogountes*. But another manuscript tradition uses *ainountes*. There is no significant difference in meaning between these two words. Most surviving manuscripts, however, present both readings connected with "and" *ainountes kai eulogountes*, which the translators of the King James Version rendered as: they were "praising and blessing God."

On first sight these text observations may not make sense. The first edition of Luke certainly had only one of these three documented variants, didn't it? Why say the same thing twice? Why change a perfectly good word for another good word? And why combine two synonyms?

The Gospel According to Luke is not the only writing, the New Testament is not the only collection of writings, and the Christian Bible is not the only book transmitted by hand for hundreds of years. There is a wealth of evidence available outside of the Bible. By stepping back and looking at the evidence in the larger context of book production in antiquity, a theory can be developed about why these changes were made and who typically made them. After such a contextual theory is established, it can be applied to specific passages like Luke 25:53.

Studying cases where both the master manuscript and copies of this master manuscript are extant, scholars recognized a pattern. It seems that scribes who encountered two different readings in two different copies of the same text, tended to combine both by adding a conjunction.[2] This theory satisfies the observations made in Luke 24:53; only the conjunction *kai*, "and," is added between the two synonyms. The technical term for such readings is *conflation*, the flowing together of two or more traditions. The guiding principle suggested by this theory is that interpreters of conflate readings should assume that con-

---

[1] English quotations from the Bible present the NRSV. *The Holy Bible: Containing the Old and New Testaments with the Apocryphal/Deuterocanonical Books: New Revised Standard Version* (New York: Oxford University Press, 1989).

[2] *The New Testament in the Original Greek: Introduction, Appendix* (eds. B. F. Westcott and F. J. Anthony Hort; London: Macmillan, 1896), 49–52.

flation is younger and each one of the shorter readings is older than their combination.

A theory makes assumptions based on probability. It interprets the individual event within the context of the probable, not the possible. Probability is calculated by dividing the number of actual events with the number of possible events. The function of an exegetical method is to make an assessment of probability by studying actual events, discerning a pattern, and placing text observations within the context of this pattern.

performance criticism as an exegetical method encourages the interpreter to place text evidence within the context of what we know about actual performances of text in antiquity.

Performance Criticism and Form Criticism

The reading experience in antiquity differs considerably from a modern reading experience. Whereas reading is mostly a silent, solitary activity today, the manuscripts of antiquity were designed by authors, editors, and publishers to record sound; published literature was intended to serve as a script to be interpreted to an audience by a performer.[3] Form-critical approaches stress the importance of understanding the situation of communication in which a text functions, and performance criticism can provide the necessary contextual information.

"Sitz im Leben"

The Pope received a phone call from Jesus Christ. "The good news is that I have returned," Jesus said. "And the bad news?" the Pope asked. "I am calling from Salt Lake City."

Much will depend on who tells this joke and to whom. It makes a difference if a Mormon, a Catholic, a Protestant, or a Jewish person tells it. And it will make a difference who listens. The joke may mock Catholics (if a Mormon tells it to a Mormon), it may express an uneasiness with organized religion (if a Protestant tells it to a Protestant), or it may be an expression of poor taste (if a Jew tells it to a Catholic). In the context of this article the joke simply explains the form-critical term *Sitz im Leben* and the importance of assessing the situation of communication. Its historical value would be mostly sociological, documenting attitudes of a segment of the population. To the question of whether the Pope even answers phone calls, the joke contributes little.

---

[3] D. Trobisch, "Structural Markers in New Testament Manuscripts with Special Attention to Observations in Codex Boernerianus (G 012) and Papyrus 46 of the Letters of Paul," *Pericope: Scripture as Written and Read in Antiquity, vol. 5: Layout Markers in Biblical Manuscripts and Ugaritic Tablets,* (eds. M. C. A. Korpel and J. M. Oesch; Assen: Koninklijke van Gorcum, 2005), 177–190.

Performance criticism and form criticism are closely related.[4] Form criticism tries to describe how a specific text was communicated by answering questions like: Who talks to whom, where, when, and why?

The Christian Bible is put together from texts that belong to a wide number of genres reflecting diverse communication settings. An Aramaic saying of Jesus may have changed its genre as it was translated into Greek and became part of a canonical gospel, and the genre may have changed again as it was used by Christians in their worship services. When we read Paul's letter to Rome today, we do not read the letter that was actually carried by a trusted messenger. We read Romans, as we call it, as part of a carefully arranged and edited collection of letters. The letter has ceased to be a private communication between two parties, protected from the preying eyes of outsiders. It is now directed to the public – it has become literature.[5]

Because traditional texts tend to shift their genre as they are passed on, many German Biblical scholars prefer to talk about *Formgeschichte*, the history of form, rather than *Formkritik*, form criticism.[6] Keeping in mind that the function of a text may change as the historical genre of the same text shifts, performance criticism concentrates on the moment a text is published, when it stops being a private communication between specific persons and becomes a communication between an author and an undefined public. performance criticism describes the impact of the Christian Bible as literature.

Jesus Tells a Bathroom Joke

In Matthew's gospel Jesus talks about hypocrites who stand at busy intersections and pray so others will see them. Jesus rebukes such practices and says, "But whenever you pray, go into your room and shut the door and pray to your

---

[4] Connections to other exegetical methods in addition to form criticism are explored by David Rhoads, "Performance Criticism: An Emerging Methodology in Second Testament Studies – Part II" *Biblical Theology Bulletin* 36 (2006): 164–184. In this essay, Rhoads, who was one of the first New Testament scholars to promote performance of Biblical texts as an exegetical approach, compares performance criticism to form and genre criticisms; narrative, reader-response, and rhetorical criticisms; textual, oral, and social-science criticisms; speech act theory, linguistic criticism, and translation studies; ideological criticism, theater, and oral interpretation studies. The author concludes that performance criticism should be seen as a discrete exegetical approach in its own right.

[5] D. Trobisch, "Das Neue Testament im Lichte des zweiten Jahrhunderts, "*Herkunft und Zukunft der neutestamentlichen Wissenschaft* (ed. O. Wischmeyer; *Neutestamentliche Entwürfe zur Theologie* 6; Tübingen, Basel: Francke, 2003, 119–129).

[6] M. Dibelius, *Die Formgeschichte des Evangeliums* (Tübingen: Mohr Siebeck, 1919); K. Koch, *Was ist Formgeschichte?: Methoden der Bibelexegese: Mit einem Nachwort, Linguistik und Formgeschichte.* (Neukirchen-Vluyn: Neukirchener Verlag, 1974); G. Theißen. *Urchristliche Wundergeschichten. Ein Beitrag zur formgeschichtlichen Erforschung der synoptischen Evangelien,* (Studien zum Neuen Testament 8, Gütersloh: Mohn, 1974); K. Berger. *Formgeschichte des Neuen Testaments* (Heidelberg: Quelle & Meyer, 1984).

Father who is in secret; and your Father who sees in secret will reward you" (Matthew 6:6). Like our homes today, houses in antiquity had at least one room that could be locked: the bathroom. Jesus was trying to be funny; his original audience was expected to laugh.

Once an interpreter accepts the form-critical assessment that this saying of Jesus may be based on a joke he made in public, the irony of the other statements in the context becomes apparent. How likely is it that a pious person would stand at a street corner and pray in order to be seen? Or that he or she would have someone "sound the trumpet" when they went to give alms "in the synagogues and in the streets" (Matt 6:2)? Don't we know from our own standup comedians that exaggeration is part of a strategy to make us laugh at ourselves? If Jesus was joking, then the criticism of the "hypocrites" might just be a criticism from within, a call for renewal, an attempt to communicate through humor. Jesus, a pious Jew, is asking other pious Jews to return to their own ideals, to remember God's commandments and promises.

The text continues, "Your Father knows what you need before you ask him. Pray then in this way: Our Father in heaven, hallowed be your name [...]" (Matt 6:8–9). The editor of the Sermon on the Mount, who used the saying of Jesus to introduce the Lord's Prayer, may have already missed the irony. The genre shifted from a joke to an exhortation. And in the tradition of Christian preaching, Jesus' caricature of a Pharisee has often been interpreted as disparaging Jews; it was easily turned into political propaganda. Considering the medieval pogroms and the mass murder of Jews in the 20th century, committed by professed Christians, this misinterpretation is no laughing matter.

Experimental

In 1947 the Norwegian anthropologist Thor Heyerdahl and five other daring seafarers launched a balsa wood raft outside the port of Callào in Peru. They sailed more than 4000 miles across the Pacific Ocean and landed on the Raroia Atoll in the Tuamotu Archipelago 101 days later.[7] The voyage demonstrated that it was possible for a primitive raft to sail the Pacific and that Polynesia was well within the range of prehistoric South American seafarers. Based on linguistic, physical, and genetic evidence, however, many anthropologists remain convinced that Polynesia was settled from the Asian mainland in the west and not from South America. But some apparent American influences like the sweet potato as part of the Polynesian diet find a satisfactory explanation in Thor Heyerdahl's theory.

In very much the same way performance criticism of the New Testament can demonstrate possibilities and create plausibility for new understandings that

---

[7] Th. Heyerdahl, *The Kon-Tiki Expedition: By Raft Across the South Seas* (London: Allen & Unwin, 1950).

otherwise seem far-fetched. Like experimental archeology, which recreates tools, events, and settings of the period studied, performance criticism recreates the situation of a performance of literature for which the New Testament originally had been designed. And like experimental archaeology, performance criticism can be used to test methods and theories.[8]

Experiential

By performing the text, the word becomes flesh. Interpreters explore possible authorial intentions, the basic structure of the argument, reactions from the audience, and subtexts of underlying humor and irony, some or all of which might have escaped their attention had they only studied the text sitting at a desk and reading it quietly to themselves.

During a performance, text is simply experienced; the analysis takes place afterwards, when an emotional distance from the performance has been established. A debriefing session after the performance, preferably the following day, will typically help students reach a high level of exegetical and theological reflection.

After engaging text through performance, one often finds that a specific text can be understood in more than one valid way. Like other forms of art, performance of literature will only present one of several possible interpretations, not necessarily the most authoritative one, or a scholastically viable reading. Especially in those rare cases when the setting allows for repeat performances before the same audience, and the interpreter performs the same text in several different ways, the multi-faceted nature of human communication through art becomes evident. Developing a variety of possible interpretations is a crucial step of scholarly discourse; the performance of texts before an audience helps to achieve this goal.

Historical Criticism

Like other literary critical assessments, performance criticism may be perceived as opposing the historical critical approach prevalent in Biblical Studies since the Enlightenment. This is not accurate. Whereas more traditional methods like source criticism and tradition criticism concentrate on the early stages of texts, i.e. the written sources and oral traditions that were used to weave a text together, performance criticism as a historical approach concentrates on the moment the finished literary product is presented to the public for the first time. Obviously, the authorial intention at the time of publication is limited to the

---

[8] J. M. Coles, *Experimental Archaeology* (London: Academic Press, 1979). *Experimental Archeology* (eds. D. W. Ingersoll, J. E. Yellen, and William Macdonald; New York: Columbia University Press, 1977).

implied author's intention as promoted by the publisher, and does not necessarily represent the original message of the historical author.

For example, in the New Testament, Acts is presented as the account of Luke (Acts 1:1–2 references the third gospel), the account of Paul's travel companion (we-passages in Acts, cf. Acts 28:11ff.) and the account of the physician (Col 4:14), who finishes his narrative while Paul is still alive (Acts 28:30–31). Each of these statements is contested on historical grounds. But at the same time, if the implied author and the implied literary setting are dismissed, the text will not function anymore as it was designed when published.[9]

Furthermore, historical-critical approaches tend to concentrate their efforts on genuine material only. They are interested in the historical author and audience. One of the strengths of any literary approach, including performance criticism, is to give spurious material the voice it deserves. Spurious writings are an attempt, sometimes a desperate attempt, to contextualize a cherished tradition, to reinterpret it, to make it meaningful for an audience at a time and place quite different from the original setting of the writing.

Summary

Performance Criticism takes the character of New Testament texts as Hellenistic literature seriously. As a historical method it recreates the situation for which these texts were designed, and encourages the interpreting performer to experiment and explore multiple possibilities of authorial intention, structure, argument, and audience reactions through the act of performing the text before an audience. As a literary approach it encourages the student to appreciate the beauty of the New Testament as literature.

---

[9] D. Trobisch, "Die narrative Welt der Apostelgeschichte," ZNT 18 (2006): 9–14.

Part III: Seeing in the Shaping
of New Genres

A Theory of the Message for New Testament Writings or Communicating the Words of Jesus:

From Angelos to Euangelion

Kristina Dronsch / Annette Weissenrieder

1. Introduction

Within biblical studies Werner Kelber has developed a rigorous media theory in terms other than a chronological development. This theory has enjoyed wide reception and can now be regarded as a paradigmatic contribution to New Testament exegesis.[1]

A brief statement of his theory should form the starting point for its implementation in this paper. According to Kelber, three different media within an Early-Christian traditional process are to be distinguished: "orality, the sayings genre, and the narrative gospel. [...] Orality, saying gospel, and narrative gospel are meant to be viewed as characteristic components in the tradition, not as sequential stages in an orderly process."[2] "Orality" is marked by a situation of entirely oral communication, "saying genres" – like Q or the gospel of Thomas – by a situation of written communication. Nevertheless, this is undebted to aspects of orality, because only words of Jesus stand without narrative framing in the foreground, in order "to retain the living voice of Jesus and to extend it to the communal present."[3] And here a media "decay history" already becomes visible which is typical for Kelber's media theory:[4] "yet all of this was accomplished through writing, and writing is deconstructive to the vital concerns of orality."[5] This continues then in "nar-

---

[1] See the recently published book that argues exclusively on the basis of Kelber's media theory: *Jesus, the Voice, and the Text. Beyond the Oral and the Written Gospel* (ed. T. Thatcher, Baylor University Press: Waco, Texas, 2008). Thatcher speaks of Werner Kelber's "Media History of Christian Origins" (p. 1).

[2] W. Kelber, "Narrative as Interpretation and Interpretation of Narrative: Hermeneutical Reflections on the Gospels," *Orality, Aurality, and Biblical Narrative* (ed. L. H. Silberman; Semeia 39. Altanta: Scholars Press, 1987), 107–133, 116.

[3] Kelber, "Narrative as Interpretation," 118.

[4] In his more recent work, including in this volume, Kelber has turned to aspects of written texts in antiquity which – consistent with his concept of "mouvance" – acknowledge the performative character of ancient written processes. Here interestingly a media adjustment of the written text to the voice takes place by which Kelber characterizes the early scribal tradition of Jesus sayings, in line with the close communication to be unfolded further below.

[5] Kelber, "Narrative as Interpretation," 118.

rative gospels." "While the second order (= the saying genre, D/W) was (*inter alia*) committed to the two authentic speech acts, the narrative gospel in turn deprived aphorisms and parables of their oral status by subordinating them, together with a good deal of additional materials, to the literary ordering of narrative. [...] Orality, the voice of the living Jesus, the ground and life of the tradition [...] were overruled by the more complex ordering of narrative textuality."[6]

For Kelber writing differs from orality in three main aspects: a) Orality is shaped by the dialogical interaction between speaker and audience, while written communication is marked by a communication situation that is not present. Kelber maintains that oral words are bound "to the authority of the speaker and unseparable from auditors, they are inevitably enmeshed in the human lifeworld. [...] Oral utterance cannot exist in transauthorial objectivity."[7] b) While a verbal communication situation totally receives its meaning from this unique performance situation, this cannot just be assumed for a written communication situation. "Spoken words breathe life, drawing their strength from sound. They carry a sense of presence, intensity, and instantaneousness that writing fails to convey."[8] Therefore he concludes: "In orality, we saw, words have no existence apart from speaker and hearers. The tendency is for words to actualize their meaning in the performance of oral delivery. [...] With the written gospel the cooperation between speaker and hearers is abolished. [...] The writer works in a state of separation from audiences, and hearers or readers are excluded from the process of composition. [...] From the perspective of synoptic orality, therefore, the gospel's text marks the breakdown of the authentic act of live communication."[9] c) The written communication is laid out by its fixation of the words and sentences and is to be geared totally to stability. In contrast, a verbal communication situation is to be understood as a vital, living performance, so that according to Kelber parables and aphorisms count as a verbal communication situation: "The oral transaction of aphorisms and parables consists in multiple recitals, tailored to specific circumstances, without the auditors ever hearing them as departures from binding texts. [...] One knows no way of testing speech against fixed models."[10] That's why the verbal communication according to Kelber is to be understood as an event which lives on in the immediate physical presence of its listeners at the moment of oral performance. The speaker and audience achieve what Kelber calls a "*homeostatic balance*" or "*oral synthesis*" due to the fact of "a continuous process of adjustment of language to communal expectations, of social to linguistic realities."[11] Written words exist independently of the people who use them. When speech is written down, words lose their oral character, because "Distanz, Entfremdung und eine Aufschiebung des Signifikationsprozesses [sind] unauflöslich mit der Verschriftlichung mündlicher Traditionen verbunden."[12]

---

[6] Kelber, "Narrative as Interpretation," 118.

[7] Kelber, "Narrative as Interpretation," 122.

[8] W. Kelber, *The Oral and the Written Gospel. The Hermeneutics of Speaking and Writing in the Synoptic Tradition, Mark, Paul and Q* (Philadelphia: Fortress Press, 1983), 18–19.

[9] Kelber, *The Oral and the Written Word*, 91–92.

[10] Kelber, "Narrative as Interpretation," 117.

[11] Kelber, *The Oral and the Written Gospel*, 19, 92.

[12] W. Kelber, "Die Fleischwerdung des Wortes in der Körperlichkeit des Textes," in *Materialität der Kommunikation* (eds. H. U. Gumbrecht and K. L. Pfeiffer; Frankfurt: Suhrkamp, 1988), 36–37, 40.

The works of Kelber have thus decisively refuted the traditional understanding inherent in classical genre criticism, which holds that every tradition takes its leave of simplicity and progresses by stages to ever greater complexity. On the contrary, Kelber argues, every performance of the oral word was unique, original, and in discontinuity with every other oral performance.

Kelber develops not a genealogical concept of the passing on of the Jesus' tradition, from simplicity to complexity, but instead a counter-genealogical concept which turns the genealogical concept upside down: the complexity and diversity of the verbal communication is confronted with the stability of the written communication. Therefore, Kelber does not speak of passive Evangelists, who are interested merely in saving the tradition, as e. g. Bultmann argued; rather Kelber holds "that the written gospel cannot be properly perceived as the logical outcome of oral proclivities and forces inherent in orality."[13] Instead the written text of the gospels has to be viewed "as a counterform to oral speech and not as an evolutionary progression of it."[14] Due to this fact, the Evangelists were not seeking to preserve the voices of oral performers, but rather to silence them,[15] in order to reshape the past in view of present needs.

The question of orality, writing and communication in biblical studies is – as the rapid success of Kelber's proposed theory has shown – not only a deeply hermeneutical question, but also a perhaps even stronger media-theoretical one: Behind Kelber's concept stands the conviction that the way both we and the people of New Testament times use language depends on which of the three media is involved. If one asks him- or herself what inheres a valid and effective meaning of the relationship of the transformation of the oral to the written gospel in the Kelber's concept, then it seems to be clear that they are both of importance regarding to media of the use of language: the oral gospel is ascribed to a living, unique, dialogue-oriented use of language, and the written word to a use of language geared toward fixation, stability, and non-reciprocity. Despite these qualitative differences, both media belong to the use of language and thus equally to the field of the discursive, and are assigned to "speaking" or "telling" and not to "pointing out" or "showing." Within the field of the discursive, Kelber is able to raise the oral gospel's standing, because here dialogue-oriented communication is the standard. Kelber's media theory appreciates the value of reciprocal communication as "successful" language use. In contrast, non-reciprocal communication, as in the *written* gospels, is prone to be evaluated negatively, as media decay.

The following applications of Kelber's theory represent an invitation to a change of perspective regarding the relative value of the oral and the written word. This change of perspective does not share two linguistic premises Kelber's, namely (1) to focus the nucleus of the Jesus' tradition(s) in dialogical language use and (2) to focus the written and the oral gospels as linguistic media only in the field of the discursive. Therefore we attempt to formulate for understanding the oral and written gospel the consequences of not reducing this

---

[13] Kelber, *The Oral and the Written Gospel*, 90.

[14] Kelber, *The Oral and the Written Gospel*, 91.

[15] See Kelber, *The Oral and the Written Gospel*, 91. "Mark's writing project is an act of daring and rife with consequences. To the extent that the gospel draws on oral voices, it has rendered them voiceless. The voiceprints of once-spoken has rendered them voiceless. [...] For the moment, language has fallen silent."

communication to linguistic media and with that to the modalities of the discursive. For this purpose, we will concentrate on the written word. Through the dimension of showing in the written word, we argue for a rehabilitation of scripture as written gospel.

It must be said that the change of perspective represented in our approach has been influenced decisively by the works of the media ethicist and theorist Raffael Capurro, the work of philosopher Sybille Krämer as well as the work of communication scientist John Durham Peters.

As we have seen, in the debate on orality and literacy – which thanks to Kelber is also a debate in biblical studies – one assumption is the supposed *difference* between written and spoken word. Within this debate – and also with Kelber – language itself remains "von den variablen Medien ihrer phonischen oder graphischen Aktualisierung – zumindest dem Begriffe nach – abgesetzt."[16] Thus it is typical that within the concept of orality a heterogeneity is entailed which results from the performative character of the oral gospel. Along with Krämer we assume that such heterogeneity is not limited to orality and speech but that in "der Sprache selbst, und nicht erst in ihren medialen Realisierungen, [...] sich das Spannungsverhältnis von Sagen und Zeigen angelegt [findet]. Die Sprache, eben weil sie immer nur als verkörperter Sprache gegeben ist, ist von fundamentaler Heterogenität."[17]

For Kelber, dialogue is the unqualified guarantor of successful communication and intersubjective connection. The dialogue flows in "oral synthesis" between the dialogue partners.[18] Hence the media theory of Kelber is based on a model of successful dialogical *face-to-face-communication* (*Nahkommunikation*). With Peters we want to suggest a change of perspective, namely that dialogue based on "a continuous process of adjustment of language to communal expectations, of social to linguistic realities"[19] forms rather the exception than the rule. This is obvious in the gospel of Mark, if we take into consideration the words, speeches and activities of Jesus, which not only document the lack of understanding of the members of the synagogues [Mark 1:27], the Jewish scribes, Pharisees, and Saducees [Mark 2:1–3:6; 9:11ff.; 12:28ff.; 12:35ff.; Mark 7:9–13], but also the crowd [Mark 5:39; 14:34] and even Jesus' disciples [Mark 8:14–21; 8:31–33; 9:9–10]. This is also true for the relatives of Jesus and residents of his hometown: His mother, brothers and sisters come to Jesus to bring him back because they have the impression he is crazy [Mark 3:20f., 31–35]. This failure of face-to-face-communica-

---

[16] S. Krämer, "Die Heterogenität der Stimme. Oder: Was folgt aus Friedrich Nietzsches Idee, dass die Lautsprache aus der Verschwisterung von Bild und Musik hervorgeht?," in *Stimme und Schrift. Zur Geschichte und Systematik sekundärer Oralität* (eds. W. Wiethölter, H.-G. Pott and A. Messerli; Munich: Wilhelm Fink Verlag, 2008), 57–73, 63.

[17] Krämer, "Heterogenität," 63: with regard to the idea of the "embodied language" a misunderstanding is to be avoided. Embodiment means not only the body restraint of the speech as well as a body-based interaction of the communicators, but this concept also includes the embodiment of language, for example, in the texture of the writing.

[18] Kelber, *The Oral and the Written Gospel*, 19.

[19] Kelber, *The Oral and the Written Gospel*, 92.

tion can be shown in an instructive way in Mark 6:1–6. This story reflects above all one thing: the failing of a dialogue communication situation between Jesus and his listeners in his father's city. Not understanding Jesus' speech, his listeners ask themselves, where does Jesus' knowledge come from and what is the wisdom that has been given to him. Jesus' answer is typical: "A prophet is not dishonored, except in his hometown and among relatives and in his own household." With this answer Jesus destroys the idea of a successful face-to-face-communication (*Nahkommunikation*) because it seems not possible to depend on the arguments and assumptions of others, especially in close social relations. The relationship of cousinhood and household (*oikos*) can not be seen as a guarantor of successful communication. What is so remarkable in the statement of Jesus is his acknowledgement that he understands (prophetic) communication as distance event. To perceive, however, in the failure of successful reciprocal dialogue only a single devastating result is to recognize only one half of the statement from Mark 6:4: "the first part of the saying has a double negative, and the saying as a whole has a double statement involving first a negative statement and then a positive one (in this case a negative followed by an exception)."[20] Precisely in this exception lies a productive result of the communication envisaged here. While the idea of a successful dialogical face-to-face-communication (*Nahkommunikation*) indeed fails, a non-dialogical, non-reciprocal communication succeeds: the prophetic word works if it is sent out. The prophet is not *dishonoured* (Mark 6:4a) but acquires fame, when the reciprocity of the speech is suspended and Jesus' words subsequently become public, broadcast to unknown, anonymous, and various listeners.

We summarize: In the gospel of Mark narrated reactions to Jesus' word or speeches give reason to accept that with personal opponents to Jesus personal encounters take place which lead to little or no "oral synthesis." Rather there occurs a communication situation which makes clear that hearing remain inaccessible; already the verbal communication situation introduced aims not, as one might think, at "oral synthesis," but posits a difference between the listeners in the narrative and those who are in fact related to each other in the dialogue. These conclusions speak in favor of rehabilitating the non-dialogue communication situation as suggested by Peters.[21] The ideal of a communication on the basis of a dialogical speech in living presence will – as the examples have shown – not be attained always in the dialogue itself. In light of this assumption, Kelber's statement that "[o]ral utterance cannot exist in transauthorial objectivity"[22] cannot be maintained. It is not the speaker Jesus who controls the effects of his speech; control lies instead completely with the receivers or listeners.

One may not, then, assume for the oral gospel a heterogeneity that eventuates automatically in oral synthesis, since a communication concept based on the directness of a dialogical immediacy is no longer valid. What is required instead

---

[20] A. Yarbro Collins, *Mark. A Commentary* (Hermeneia, Minneapolis MA: Fortress Press, 2007), 292.

[21] J. Durham Peters, *Speaking into the Air. A History of the Idea of Communication* (Chicago, London: University Press, 1999), 30.

[22] Kelber, "Narrative as Interpretation," 122.

is a communication concept[23] that takes seriously non-reciprocity as "ein Strukturmerkmal der Kommunikation unter den Bedingungen von Differenz".[24]
This gives us our point of departure for considering an alternative theory of the
message within the New Testament writings.

Therefore precisely this difference should provide the necessary access to the media
understanding of the written gospel, because the difference "zwischen denen, die auf-
einander Bezug nehmen wollen, welche qualitativ als Verschiedenheit untereinander
oder quantitativ als Entfernung voneinander aufzufassen ist,"[25] has to be seen as our point
of departure for understanding the written gospel. After Jesus the fact is: οὐχ ἔστιν ὧδε –
he is not here any more (Mark 16:6b; cf. Luke 24:6; Matt. 28:6; John 20:2). Jesus is
absent – in the communication events between Jesus and the hearing audience a quantitative difference emerges due to distance. With it the obvious problem has to be considered: "wie […] die an Christus Glaubenden in der von Christus verlassenen Welt"[26]
can continue their existence as a community based on communication of Jesus' word.
Specifically the absence experienced as a difference between the believers and Jesus
Christ stood therefore in the center of the reality of early Christianity. This experience of
absence is the basic starting point from which the verbal media of the early church are to
be unfolded. Therefore the media involve a level of description and an interpretative
perspective to bring communicative processes to validity beyond "dialogue." Such an
approach to communication poses the question of how the mediation between the one
who is absent and the one who is present can occur. Nevertheless, the prominent role of
the application is a religious one: "To take ancient texts of religious experience seriously
as writing we must take the medium of writing seriously. […] In a sense we have not yet
taken the media character […] seriously enough, especially if we treat it only as a semantic
channel for transportation."[27] In this sense we want to concentrate our attention on
narrative gospels as an embodiment to be understood as a non-reciprocal communication
situation, obviously in the perspective of a messenger[28] who serves then "als Archetypus

---

[23] See Peters, *Speaking*, 7 for his instructive definition of communication: "'Communication' is a word with a rich history. From the Latin *communicare*, meaning to impart, share, or
make common, it entered the English language in the fourteenth and fifteenth centuries. The
key root is mun- (not uni-), related to such words as "munificent", "community", "meaning",
and *Gemeinschaft*. The Latin *munus* has to do with gifts or duties offered publicly – including
gladiatorial shows, tributes, and rites to honor the dead. The Latin *communicatio* did not signify
the general arts of human connections via symbols, nor did it suggest the hope for some kind of
mutual recognition. Its sense was not in the least mentalistic: *communicatio* generally involved
tangibles. In classical rhetorical theory *communicatio* was also a technical term for stylistic device
in which an orator assumes the hypothetical voice of the adversary or audience; *communicatio*
was less authentic dialogue than the simulation of dialogue by a single speaker". Here we see
that the dominant branch of meaning in communication has to do with imparting, and has less
to do with a dialogic process.

[24] S. Krämer, *Medium, Bote, Übertragung. Kleine Metaphysik der Medialität* (Frankfurt: Suhrkamp, 2008), 104.

[25] Krämer, *Bote*, 103.

[26] C. Dietzfelbinger, "Die größeren Werke (Joh 14,12f.)," *NTS* 35 (1989): 27–47, 34.

[27] St. M. Wasserstrom, "The Medium of the Divine," *Experentia Vol 1. Inquiry into Religious
Experience in early Judaism and Early Christianity* (eds. F. Flannery, C. Shantz, and R. A. Werline;
SBL. SS 40, Atlanta: SBL, 2008), 75–82, here 77–79.

[28] Already in 1913 W. Riepl mentioned in his book *Das Nachrichtenwesen des Altertums. Mit
besonderer Berücksichtigung auf die Römer* (Leipzig/Berlin: Teubner, 1913), 123, that "für die

der Fernkommunikation."[29] With it we try to set up a "postal paradigm."[30] In this perspective it is to be considered that a large part of the communication is not dialogue centered but a communication situation which is simply without reciprocity. At the same time this perspective of the messenger we are postulating is to be understood, as regards the writings of the New Testament, as a critical challenge to attempts to make media autonomous and or to regard them as sovereign agents. Jan Assmann has likewise reminded us that every media-sensitivity runs the risk of reducing complex operations of meaning construction monocausally to what he calls "Mediendeterminismus."[31] This danger does not exist with our notion of the messenger. The entity the messenger conveys is not his person but the message he transmits. "Im Boten, der mit 'fremder Stimme' spricht, kommt ein für das Mediengeschehen typisches Verfahren zur Geltung, bei dem das übertragende Medium sich gegenüber dem zu übertragenden Gehalt zurücknimmt und neutralisiert."[32] It follows that the written gospels are not to be viewed as instruments, but as means or mediator.

The mediality concept suggested here is to be understood at the same time as a contribution discovering the performance character of the New Testament *texts*. The written gospels are in no way to be understood as the end product of a process of articulation, but are the beginning of a communication that takes place without the immediate in-person interaction between the parties communicating, not least given that the basic situation of the entire New Testament is the absence of Jesus Christ.

Also amidst these preliminaries the observation of David Parker and Eldon Epp is significant. They point to the remarkable scribal fluidity of Jesus materials, a point comparable to that made by Peters on disseminational aspects of communication that lie outside direct and intended interaction.[33] As Parker has stated, the written tradition of Jesus sayings demonstrated a higher degree of variation in the early period, being "at its most fluid in the first century of its existence."[34] Thus we must dispense with a model of

---

mündliche und schriftliche Nachrichtenbeförderung des Altertums, namentlich bei den Römern, [...] als Universalorgan der Bote in seinen verschiedenen Gestalten" was the only remaining possibility for a postal paradigm.

[29] R. Capurro, "Theorie der Botschaft," (http://www. capurro.de/botschaft.htm 18).

[30] Capurro, "Theorie der Botschaft," 5. Therefore Capurro asks for an "Angeletik", a term which refers to R. Capurro, *Leben im Informationszeitalter*, (Berlin: Akademie-Verlag, 1995), 97–114.

[31] J. Assmann, *Das kulturelle Gedächtnis: Schrift, Erinnerung und politische Identität in frühen Hochkulturen*, (Munich: C. H. Beck, 1992), 25: "Die mediengeschichtliche Deutung läuft Gefahr, die Prozesse monokausal auf einen reinen Mediendeterminismus zu verkürzen, während die geistesgeschichtliche Deutung für die zweifellos zentrale Bedeutung der Schrift und ihrer wachsenden Einbeziehung in kulturelle Traditionen und gesellschaftliche Institutionen in erstaunlicher Weise blind geblieben ist."

[32] Krämer, *Bote*, 39.

[33] Peters, *Speaking Into the Air*, 62: "Dialogue still reigns supreme in the imagination of many as to what good communication might be, but dissemination presents the saner choice for our fundamental term. [...] Open scatter is more fundamental than coupled sharing [...]".

[34] D. C. Parker, *The Living Text of the Gospels* (Cambridge: Cambridge University Press, 1997), 200.

foundational stability followed by dispersion and variability, and instead think with Parker of "initial fluidity followed by stability."[35] This fluidity within the materiality of the New Testament manuscript tradition clearly indicates that the New Testament texts are the beginning of a communication in which writing serves not as end but as medium. It acts as a mediator between the absent Jesus and those who read and hear his words.

Therefore we have to show that in antiquity the figure of the messenger is relevant within the scope of communication processes in order to enhance the postal paradigm, and we have to show how the messenger functions within a communicative process. Moreover we want to include artifacts, in which we not only encounter the concrete course of transmission of information in antiquity, but also recognize clearly the performative act within the relevant relations of transference.[36]

2. Graphical material: Dimensions of messengers in visual media in antiquity

Already in antiquity the transmission of news had central meaning, and also in antiquity one had different possibilities of transmission. For the transmission of messages Herodotus spoke of the day runner ἡμεροδρόμοι or express courier δρομοκήρυκες (Hdt. 6,105; Ain. *Takt.* 22.3), who could cover great distances on foot. Private messengers came from the households of city councils, or they were travellers whose official journey led to particular places. They were often familiar with the sender, as Cicero describes in detail.[37] Besides the private or state messenger, animal messengers are familiar to us, as for example, dogs (Ain. *Takt.* 31.32) and birds such as pigeons or swallows (Plin. *HN.* 10.34). Besides the private or state messenger, we also see animal messengers, for example dogs (Ain. *Takt.* 31.32) and birds such as pigeons or swallows (Plin. *HN.* 10.34). Nonetheless, these were more often used as heralds to announce the arrival of the travelling messenger. However, the unfamiliar express couriers are seldom the object of visual art; animal messengers are more common.

However, in the textual and visual images of antiquity messengers are more than just transmitters of news. This is evident from the fact that numerous images have come down to us showing messengers no matter how small the space. Why? If the news alone was the main point, one could easily have represented the progress of the story along with perhaps an animal messenger to indicate mediation. But instead the ancient painters devoted themselves in detail to the messenger. The messengers were central.

---

[35] Parker, *Living Text*, 70.
[36] Although the messenger is well known from Ancient Near East, we concentrate on the Greco-Roman context: S. A. Meier, *The Messenger in the Ancient Semitic World* (Harvard Semitic Monographs 45. Atlanta: Scholars Press, 1989); J. T. Greene, *The Role of the Messenger and Message in the Ancient Near East* (BJSt 169, Atlanta: Scholars Press, 1989).
[37] Cic. *Fam.* 4,9,1; 4,10,1; *Att.* 5,20,8.

We come across visual images of the Greek messenger Hermes as well as the Roman Mercurius or female Iris. They are shown as messengers who can conquer long distances as well as cross between the worlds of gods and people. Often they are illustrated in the so-called knee position, which shows them in a hurrying or running posture.

Although Hermes, Mercurius and Iris act as messengers, they are seldom illustrated on coins. In antiquity coins were often used to spread political news or news concerning the cult. The connection of coins with messengers might seem obvious to us today, but it did not apply in antiquity. Instead the gods' messengers appear on vase paintings, amphoras, as well as wine craters and as images on walls, especially in Pompeii. In most cases, the pictures retell visually stories that were in circulation orally and in writing. This is especially significant for images on vases and wine craters, because these play a decisive role in the transition from orality to written texts.

Already in the Odyssey we learn of travelling poets who did not reproduce narrative poems exactly but inevitably as variations. Shorter or longer word groups (formulas) were used to express recurring ideas, but always in varying arrangements. Only with the increasingly prevalent rhapsodes did a standardised form of the Homeric poems begin to appear. The relatively complicated structure of lyric and epic poems allowed less space for improvisation. Those who were not able to memorize texts by heart – but were still interested in the intricacies of mythical stories – were forced to rely on the public recitation of epic poems, which sometimes also took place in large rhapsodic competitions. This perception is valid as long as we take the context of public and professional performance into consideration.

However, let's put ourselves in the situation of the audience: The Iliad comprises approximately 15,000 verses. The audience will be completely unable to reproduce many of these verses independently. The listeners remain dependent solely on their memory. Therefore, behind the recollection of the main thread of the story, a simple version of the myth remains. Now this simple pattern offers the starting point for the work of reminiscence, or remembering, which is further strengthened by talk among the listeners. Accordingly such recollection does not proceed passively, but in an act of independent reproduction.[38]

If we analyze the vase images from this perspective, we see that these are always similarly reduced to the narrative core. The correspondence with the text is limited to the general outline. Indeed one might also say that the vase images do not revert at all to a text, as it were, but to what has remains of recollection in memory and interchange among hearers. The iconography of the vases is stamped in its basic structure, therefore, by a culture of hearing and remembrance.[39] If we recognize here the postal principle, we find ourselves likewise immediately in the hearing process and therefore in the process of close communication and the messengers who escort us into the world of the gods. Therefore, the messengers also serve on our behalf. They help us in the work of reminiscence. In this enclosed world of myth as message, the amphoras and craters include us.

---

[38] See the nuanced analysis from L. Giuliani, *Bilder nach Homer. Vom Nutzen und Nachteil der Lektüre für die Malerei* (Quellen der Kunst; Freiburg im Breisgau: Rombach, 1998).

[39] Cf. Cic *De Oratore* 2,357: *acerrimum autem ex omnibus nostris sensibus esse sensum videndi; quare facillime animo teneri posse ea, quae perciperentur airbus aut cogitatione, si etiam oculorum commendatione animis traderentur* – "Man kann etwas am leichtesten behalten, wenn das, was man durch das Gehör oder durch Überlegung aufnimmt, auch noch durch die Empfehlung der Augen in das Bewusstsein dringt."

In what follows, we want to develop in detail the picture of the messenger available to us from ancient iconography.

In iconographical representation, the figures of both Hermes, Mercurius,[40] and Iris are all alike: As a general rule they are shown with a messenger's stick (originally probably the shepherd's staff: *kērykeion, caduceus*) which idéntifies them as a messenger διάκτορος of Zeus and/or Hera, a feature that distinguishes the messenger from a mere companion, and that is especially prevalent in iconographical representation.[41] By such representation not only is the postal function aimed at the sending of news, but also the messenger takes over, by order, protective and rescue functions. In this sense the transmission is more than, and expanded by, news.

That Hermes/Mercurius and Iris have the ability to cover large distances appears in several attributes: Both messengers are recognized by their wings, and Hermes (and sometimes also Iris) is shown also with winged shoes, all of which means that long distances can be bridged, even the distance between the worlds of the gods, people, and the underworld. Hermes is also often shown in a long travel garment which covers the body almost completely, and also at times a kind of fur cape, the so-called Petasos, which covers only the shoulders. Iris is distinguished by her multicolored dress – the rainbow – *induitur velamina mille colorum iris et arcuato caelum curvamine signans* (Ov. *Met.* 11,5989–590), and by the fact that she can render her messenger services also in other figure.[42] In addition Iris can be equipped with a writing board, a wreath of honor, or part of a sacrificial animal. Also Hermes's or Mercurius's attributes refer to the fact that they communicate between the worlds: Thus in numerous pictures we find a cock swaggering to the feet of Hermes/Mercurius, referring to a competition, or an *aries*, or ram, referring to a sacrifice by people honoring Hermes or Mercurius. Moreover Hermes is often escorted by a sheep or *aries*, which he sometimes carries also on his shoulders, a reference to his rural background but also to sacrifices in his honor.

The images of Hermes/Mercurius and Iris indicate different facets of the re-spect between messengers on one hand and message on the other: the messenger refers (1) to the distance to be overcome within a communication situation and its heteronomy, (2) to the category of the "third," (3) to the question whether a message was transmitted, in antiquity under assumed neutrality, and (4) to the question of "embodiment."

2. 1 Distance und Heteronomy[43]

The pictures which show Hermes or Iris in their function as messengers come to us from the sixth century B. C. E. and later. Representations on vases and wine craters were

---

[40] Hermes is son of Zeus and Maia: Homer, *Il.* XXIV 331f. and *Od.* XIV 435ff. His sphere with respect to Zeus extends from the god's messenger, to the person who is makes sacrifices, to his role in Mount Olympus as one of the youngest of the gods. Hermes also plays a role in, for example, the spheres of Aphrodite, Dionysus, and Apollo. Iris, daughter of Thaumas and Electra [Hes. *Theog.* 266], however, is shown in the majority of her images as a messenger of Hera.

[41] Homer *Il. XXIV* 389. 445.

[42] She is going to Hypnos as his mother Nyx (Nonn. *Dion.* 31,106–198) and to Dionysos as Hermes (Nonn. *Dion.* 20,261–291).

[43] With the phrase "abständige Kommunikation" we allude to Krämer, *Bote*, 110f.

especially popular, everyday objects that one encountered in multiple ways.[44] The amphoras convey stories that are well known from ancient myths,[45] and seldom manifest independence by telling new stories.[46] If we describe the communication assigned to messengers in the visual images of antiquity, it is clear that a spatial distance must be overcome. This distance can nevertheless be represented spatially through a very narrow space, because the amphoras and craters mostly tell a story of which the errand is only one aspect: the amphora has much to illustrate besides the always considerable distance between parties in the errand.

At first it is striking, with regard to such images, that communication is not determined by a spatial distance between the transmitter on the one hand and the messengers and receiver on the other hand. More noteworthy is the wide variety of communication that makes itself visually understood through the various gestures:

In iconography Iris resembles Nike, because both are winged and both carry a *kērykeion*, so that they were hardly to be distinguished and often could be mistaken for each other. And they have comparable functions: They are messengers during war and they are shown being served with sacrificial scenes. Therefore in pictorial representation they are also hardly to be distinguished. Iris is illustrated in this way not only in Greco-Roman but also Jewish antiquity.

---

[44] We have already mentioned that the Hermes's figure is also extant in statue form. It is noteworthy that Hermes statues come down to us in materials that point to use by simple folk, because they are carved of wood – mostly to the robust cedar. In Roman art, this wood was used also later, especially in Pompeii. There we find Hermes in numerous pictures and statues.

[45] Hermes as an *aries*'s bearer, as he is described, for example, in Pausanias V 27. 8, is found illustrated on numerous amphoras [Simon, *Die Götter der Griechen* (Munich: Hirmer, 1969), table 288; Zanker, *Wandel der Hermesgestalt in der attischen Vasenmalerei* (Bonn: Habelt, 1965), 15; E. Pfuhl, *Tausend Jahre griechische Malerei* (Munich: Bruckmann, 1940), table 418], e. g. for example on a red-figured Stamnos in Louvre G 185 (Corpus Vasorum Antiquorum III i c table 20,2. 3); similarly also on a relief from Lokroi Epizephorioi in the museum of Reggio, where Hermes carries the Aries on his shoulder and the hind legs of the Aries rest on his breast, the forelegs on his back. Besides the images with an Aries, Hermes is more often shown engaged in cattle robbery, which he carries out at the behest of his mother Maia: Corpus Vasorum Antiquorum Pologne I. III table 2, 3b. Hermes as a son of Zeus is shown numerous times, mostly as a messenger or companion. As a son of Zeus and Maia he finds a place in the sculpture group on the Parthenon: he is last and youngest of the gods.

[46] So, for example, Hermes as a child: Corpus Vasorum Antiquorum Munich 5 table 227 [Zanker, *Wandel der Hermesgestalt,* 62f.]; in connection with the acts of Hercules, who defeats the lion with Hermes' help: black figured amphora in Boston: Corpus Vasorum Antiquorum Boston 1 table 44,3; and two black-figured amphoras in Munich Corpus Antiquorum Vasorum 8 table 392,1 and 395,2; catching of the Cretan bull: black-figured amphora in Munich 1779 – Corpus Vasorum Antiquorum Munich 12 table 43,1; Hermes who helped Heracles gain admission to Mount Olympus [Zanker, *Wandel der Hermesgestalt,* 14ff.] see also Corpus Vasorum Antiquorum 8 table 385,1.

J. Paul Getty Museum, Villa Collection, Malibu, CA. Attributed to Class of Neck Amphorae with Shoulder Pictures, 530–520 B.C.

It is noteworthy that the focus of the messenger's run by Iris, Hermes or Mercurius is not on the transmitter of the message, but on the sender. Thus on this vase Iris is fixed on Hera, who does not appear in the picture at all. Therefore mediation and separation are intimately juxtaposed. Iris' glance backward shows this. As messenger she is on the move in the space between the heterogeneous worlds between which she (and Hermes/ Mercurius) mediates, between gods or between God and a human being. Mediation as illustrated here is the germ cell of the visual media theory of antiquity. However, how is this mediation shown?

The scene shown is widespread in antiquity: Hermes, here as a messenger of Zeus, helps the robed Pandora find her way from the underworld. He is dressed as a youth shown in *chiton* and *chlamys*, and marked by his winged hat, winged shoes and the *kērykeion*. On the right Pandora is to be seen ascending; beside her stands Epimetheus, the brother of Prometheus.[47] Above both floats Eros. However, though Hermes was sent, actually, as a messenger to Pandora, his message and his look do not apply to the ascending Pandora. His communication rests with Zeus, on whom his entire attention is concentrated. Therefore his upper body, and especially his face and right hand, are directed not upon the goal of his message, but upon the message-giver, Zeus. Only Hermes' legs seem directed toward the underworld. Only his legs indicate that he was generally involved in the events of Pandora's ascent. The command of Zeus, and the news of the ascent and their escort, therefore assume a division or even splitting of the messenger; on the level of the image, this expresses itself through the absence of the messenger during the events of the ascent. The messenger Hermes bridges therefore the distance between the world of the gods and the underworld, but he does not remove this distance. He marks rather the starting point of the events. Again the result seems to dispense with him and to be foreign to him.

This scene of the consideration of Hermes as divine messenger to his order-giver Zeus is found especially in the work of a mannerist, called by some the "Affekter," who paints the respect between messenger and transmitter of the news in the way same over and over

---

[47] All four figures are in particular marked by inscriptions on the scroll crater.

Red figured Krater: Oxford 525 CVA III table 21,1-2
© Corpus Vasorum Munich

again, epitomizing the picture of the messenger in vase painting. In the middle of his vase pictures sits Zeus, enthroned on an admirably decorated armchair, or he stands; before him is Hermes, who does not run without looking back to him, as the two salute each other with upraised right hands.[48]

Iris, Hermes and Mercurius belong to the vertical mediators, or the mediators of the sacred. A comparable scenario presents itself when one turns to the poets or rhapsodes, who also act as mediators of the gods and do not speak from their own knowledge. In Plato's phrase, they are the "unknowing mediators;"[49] they become the "unreal talking." And just this function matches the representations on the amphoras and wine craters of antiquity: these too act as the unreal talking, while they take up visually the message of the rhapsodes and continue the mediating contact of divine inspiration.

2. 2 Relationality: The category of the "third"

The obvious question is: why do the vase painters fall back on the figure of Iris, Hermes or Mercurius, if this is not found in a written presentation? In other words, why do the artists not help themselves with an easy symbol or representation of a means of conveyance to represent the process of communication? With such a symbol, however, the communication would be limited to transmitter – news – receiver and thus be an example of dyadic communication which tapers to a point inter-subjectively within a constellation of simply self and "other." This is the basis of alternative significant communication theories, like for example the view of Luhmann and Parsons, who speak of a two-sided contact, between ego and alter ego, or of Buber, who speaks of reciprocal events between "I and you."

---

[48] H. Mommsen, *Der Affekter* (Mainz: Philipp von Zabern, 1975), table 4. 30, 41, 44, 69, 86, 88; cf. also J. Boardman, *Schwarzfigurige Vasen aus Athen* (Mainz: Philipp von Zabern, 1974), table 155.
[49] Plato, Ion 530f.; see also Krämer, *Bote*, 113.

In the visual images we are considering, this dyadic model with the messenger is disrupted; or, as Serres puts it, "[E]s gibt einen Dritten vor dem anderen. [...] Es gibt stets ein Medium, eine Mitte, ein Vermittelndes. Er [der Dritte KD/AW] ist das Wesen der Relation, er geht ihr voraus und diese geht auch ihm voraus."[50] Joachim Fischer discovers in the messenger a "figuration of the third," as he calls it, which places the "social potential of the medium" of the messenger in the foreground.[51] The category of the *third* is a social category in that it does not arise from multiplicity or plurality, but creates a new understanding of the figure constellation as an additional "other." At first, the *third* is simply the mediator between parties who are not in contact with each other. Whoever mediates and transmits a message simultaneously connects the parties and creates distance, all at the same time; in the case of Hermes or Iris, he or she creates the identity of the superior – usually Zeus or Hera, an identity that leaves no space for the voice of the other, because Hermes or Iris clearly does not turn his face that way. The messenger creates a relation that can nevertheless not be called neutral. The posture of Hermes on representational images of everyday objects provides, therefore, one level: a relation between sender and addressee of news that expresses a tension.

The iconographical material linked with symposia can further deepen these associations with regard to the relation of sender to addressees, as they incorporate the one who views the pictures on the drinking vessels in the communication.[52] A series of 6th century B. C. E. Greek ceramics used as drinking vessels with symposia portray frontal positions of an illustrated person, which is infrequent in ancient crater representations. The drinking vessels which show a winged woman surrounded by a pair of eyes and two Satyrs are particularly interesting for us. E. Simon has shown that later representations further clarify this scene: The messenger is accosted by the Satyrs and is pursued. The fact that it probably concerns the messenger Iris of interest to us clarifies an addendum of a name on one of the ocular bowls. E. Simon shows that Iris plays the role of the messenger of Hera: Iris is sent by Hera to intercept the victims consecrated to Dionysos. Therefore Iris is urged to rob the meat sacrifice from the altar, which the Satyrs, by order of Dionysos, try to prevent. Simon infers this not from literary reports, of which there are none, but from satyr's plays referring to "Iris", of which there are only a few fragments.[53]

Between two eyes facing forward the winged messenger Iris is seen here on or in place of a nose, partly in light relief. What is noteworthy, however, is that we see the messenger at the moment of danger, as she is about to enter her messenger service: Beside each eye is a satyr, sometimes as an armed warrior, in profile. These two satyrs are bound together in

---

[50] M. Serres, *Hermes I – Kommunikation* (Berlin: Merve, 1991; frz. *Hermes I – La Communication*, Paris: Éditions de Minuit), 97.

[51] J. Fischer, "Figuren und Funktionen der Tertiarität, zur Sozialtheorie der Medien," *Massenmedien und Alterität* (eds. J. Michael and M. K. Schäffauer, Frankfurt: Vervuert, 2004), 78–86, 82.

[52] F. Frontisi-Ducroux, "La mort en face," *Metis* I,2 (1986): 197–215.

[53] Cf. the so-called *Brygosschale*. E. Simon, "Opfernde Götter," *The Eye of Greece*: Studies in the Art of Athens (Cambridge: University, 1982), 125–129. Cf. also Aristoph. *Aves* 1202–1259.

Cleveland Museum of Art. 26.514 – ABV 630,3 © Museum of Art, Cleveland

direct view of each other. They represent a world they share that does not incorporate the viewer.

The viewer is captured completely by the world of the eyes, which confront the viewer, a participant in the numerous social and sociable ceremonies of that time, including symposia banquets. What does such a confrontation by the crater mean? The interruption caused by such severe fronting of the eyes entails that it is the viewer who drinks from the crater who is now informed by Iris and her message. The fact that Iris turns her gaze to the side and back does not at all indicate that she is averting her gaze from the banqueter. Rather it indicates, as we have seen, the regard that she bestows on the one who has ordered her sent, namely Hera or Zeus, from whom she has received the message. Who is the receiver of the message? And into which world is the message directed, the world of the satyrs or of the banqueter? Does Iris receive the message to supervise the sacrificial victims? And are the viewers then those who offer their victims?

And nota bene: What looks back directly at the participants in the banquet, as their eyes catch sight of the side of the wine crater, is their own death, illustrated inside of the crater. Or at least their potential death, which threatens the banqueters if they do not heed the message. Such a confrontation is part of the symposium. Death is present as a challenge. In the visible world, banqueters are confronted by the visibility of other, potentially death dealing individuals.

2. 3 Self-neutralization?

We have shown that when messengers are depicted in the visual contexts of antiquity, central messages are conveyed that change the entire constellation of figures. Something is in motion. The messenger brings luck or misfortune. However, how does the messenger behave compared with his message?

It has been often pointed out that the messenger neutralizes himself, as it were, as when Peter Sloterdijk says, "Der Botschafter muss gewissermassen zu einem Neutrum werden, als wäre er nur ein reiner Kanal."[54] This also means that the messenger takes no sides, but is "an embodiment of a foreign voice," of the voice representing the middle without having to stand in the middle. Sibylle Krämer speaks in this connection also of the "indifference as a self-neutralization."[55] And extraordinarily the messenger can more strongly embody the

---

[54] P. Sloterdijk, *Sphaeren II – Globen* (Frankfurt: Suhrkamp, 1999), 676.
[55] Krämer, *Bote*, 118f.

Tyrrenian Amphora. Berlin F 1704 © Antikenmuseum, Berlin

stranger than someone communicating by letter. We encounter this "external visualization" – *Fremdvergegenwärtigung* – by the neuter representation of the messenger in numerous pictures.

Hermes appears often as a messenger of Zeus. As an example, the volute crater from Oxford shown above can serve us again: On the left in the picture one sees Zeus standing, identified by an inscription. He thus stands out as a superior. On his right one sees Hermes with *chiton, chlamys,* winged hat, winged shoes, and *kērykeion* hastening away, but without letting his eyes off Zeus. His movement distinguishes him as a messenger. The fact that he operates in the sequential scene on the right as a neutral messenger shows that he is not called specially by name. The messenger is the megaphone of the Zeus, lending to Zeus a voice and carrying out his orders as the one who accompanies gods and human beings. Hermes, who in other contexts is quite able to stand as his own self in the foreground, here conspicuously recedes. He is portrayed, but not as a person in the center. This is the neutrality that Hermes normally assumes as a messenger of the Zeus.

   We have no wish to conceal the pictures at odds with the neutrality of the Hermes, in which Hermes stands in the center as himself. Here too he is on the move as a messenger. In the picture below, for example, Hermes is next to his birthplace, a cave in the mountains of Kyllene, as emphasized in the addendum: "I am Hermes the Kyllenier." Hermes is shown here as a stately bearded man with screen hat, *kērykeion,* and winged shoes. Here too he conveys a message. However, he is not just the neutral mediator of the Zeus, but refers to his own identity.

2. 4 Embodiment

We have seen that it is the task of the messenger to correspond, while she or he materializes distances between *significant* and *significat.* This happens not only in visual images, but also in ancient verses by a physiognomic texture which consolidates linguistic statements through the sensuousness of the body, its capacity to affect the senses. Therefore, the message materialises itself, as seen especially intrinsically in the famous bowl of the Nikosthenes painter.

   In the center stands a recovering warrior, at the intersection of death and life, because Thanathos on the left and Hypnos on the right both try to retrieve him, while his mother

Iris; left side © BM E 12 – ARV 126,24.

on the far right rushes toward him. She is either Eos or Europe – the warrior accordingly Memnon or Sarpedon. However, besides Thanatos, Hypnos, and the mother, yet a fourth person intervenes, probably the messenger Iris, shown here completely without wings but with the *kērykeion*. It is noteworthy that the upper part of Iris' body is not turned toward a superior or order-giver. Therefore one thing is clear: If we assume that the bowl is meant as a memory aid in recounting a story, then the key to a better understanding must lie beyond what is depicted. The solution lies in the figure of the messenger Iris, who here embodies Zeus: the latter has carried out a wager of fate between Achilles and Memnon. The fact that the fate of death fell on Memnon is recorded in writing. While Iris turns to Thanatos as a messenger, the painter enlists only the body memory of the messenger to tell the story. She protects and certifies the message, and in this sense she is an embodiment of Zeus, the one who gives the orders.

Therefore, from the iconography of the messenger in antiquity four important attributes are revealed for a theory of ancient media, which we posit for application to New Testament texts: (1) the messenger connects worlds, communicates over a distance, but is always dependent on the one who gives him his orders. (2) The category of the third embodies the messenger between *significant* and *significat*. (3) The messenger neutralizes himself but nevertheless does not give up his own identity. (4) The sense of the message materializes itself in the messenger's physical existence; he or she embodies not only the superior, but also materializes the text as a reminiscent sign and hermeneutical key.

3. The messenger in the Gospels Mark, Luke and John

In this part we want to analyse the concepts of message transmission in the New Testament writings, particularly the Gospels of Mark, Luke and John. Any process of message transmission presupposes a situation in which sender and

~ some common basis of understanding. We have used iconograph-
...erial as material artifact as a basis for getting at such a common understanding. From this material we can emphasize: without messengers, no distant communication (*Fernkommunikation*). But, as we have seen, messengers are not only
a link in an information chain, they also have to be understood as a medium of
communication. Messengers do not just bear messages; they are also media of
transmission. Therefore, we have to assume an understanding of media whereby
"Medien im Akt der Übertragung dasjenige, was sie übertragen, zugleich mit-
bedingen und prägen."[56]

From a messenger perspective, we must first accept, with respect to Jesus, that
the relevant communicating processes in the early Christianity movement are
not of face-to-face-communication, and therefore we must assume that the
postal paradigm is what is found in the New Testament writings. In light of the
absence of Jesus, a premise of all the written Gospels, we propose to analyze,
using the figure of the messenger explained above, how distant communication
(*Fernkommunikation*) functions in Mark, Luke, and John. Our goal is to elucidate
how from a narrative point of view the gospels reflect this messenger perspective and how within this perspective the written gospel acts as mediator between
the absent Jesus and the present reader.

3. 1. The Gospel of Mark:

"The beginning of the gospel (εὐαγγέλιον) of Jesus Christ, the Son of God[57]as it has been
written in Isaiah the Prophet: Look, I am sending my messenger before your face, who
will set your way in order. The voice of someone shouting in the wilderness: 'Prepare the
way of the Lord; make his paths straight!'"

The Gospel of Mark begins with an opening phrase whose meaning is the
subject of controversy among modern commentators. We want the disputed
aspects of the three opening verses of the gospel of Mark to be considered in
such a way that their interpretation reflects the media concept in our messenger
perspective. We would like to make it plausible through our reading of Mark
1:1–3 that the εὐαγγέλιον is to be understood as a messenger and therefore as the
medium of the absent Jesus Christ.

---

[56] Krämer, *Bote*, 84.
[57] The presence or absence of "Son of God" in the original version of Mark 1:1 presents a
difficult textual problem. While the majority of manuscripts have "Son of God", there are at
the same time important manuscripts, e. g. Codex Sinaiticus, which lack this phrase. The usual
text-critical argument holds that in doubtful cases the shorter reading is the stronger (lectio
brevior potior) and that therefore here the shorter reading, without the genitive "Son of God,"
is to be preferred. However, there are also text-critical reasons for arguing that the phrase "Son
of God" dropped out. Since nomina sacra were often abbreviated, the loss of the phrase
through homoioteleuton is plausible. Moreover one must bear in mind that in principle the
retention of "Son of God" in v. 1 cannot be excluded on grounds of Mark's narrative style.

A first evidence for our interpretation can be given by an etymological understanding: The word εὐαγγέλιον is known from literary evidence from as early as the eighth century B. C.[58] From its etymology the substantive εὐαγγέλιον means "good news" or the reward given to the bearer of good news. This double meaning is rooted in the adjective εὐάγγελος, because εὐαγγέλιον "bedeutet das, was zu einem εὐάγγελος gehört. [...] Für den, zu dem ein εὐάγγελος kommt, ist das, was zu einem εὐάγγελος gehört, eine frohe Botschaft, für den εὐάγγελος selbst ist εὐαγγέλιον Botenlohn."[59] The etymology of εὐαγγέλιον indicates that it functions as a medium. The εὐαγγέλιον is the medium which is transferred in the act of performance. The εὐαγγέλιον mediates as a *tertium quid*, the expected third entity between the εὐάγγελος and the one to whom the εὐάγγελος is directed. Therefore the εὐαγγέλιον is exactly what is required in a situation involving distance: The εὐάγγελος brings from far away the εὐαγγέλιον for the addressee. Concerning the materiality of the εὐαγγέλιον, we can discover a double coding: on the one hand it possesses a materiality as news, and on the other it possesses a materiality as reward, which with respect to the senses makes possible the manifestation of the magnitude of the good news in the size of the messenger's fee.

If we take a closer look at the use of εὐαγγέλιον in Greek literature, we can see that "gospel" for the ancient world "was something of a 'media' term, connoting the announcement of a message that was news to its hearers."[60] The same can be said if we look at the use of εὐαγγέλιον by Jewish authors like Josephus and Philo. Here "the 'gospel-language' connotes the announcement of any significant or joyous news [...]."[61] It is therefore appropriate to interpret the beginning of the gospel of Mark in a media-perspective by pointing out that the word εὐαγγέλιον in the gospel of Mark can be understood as a messenger.

It has been often noted that the word εὐαγγέλιον in the gospel of Mark – as compared with the other gospels – is used quite often.[62] While the verb εὐαγγελίζεσθαι is absent from Mark, we find the noun seven times.[63] And evidence suggests that in Mark the noun is used for a time when Jesus is absent. In Mark 13:9 Jesus warns his followers that they will be summoned to appear before governors and rulers 'on my account' (13:9). Verse 10 explains that this will happen as 'the gospel is proclaimed to all nations': thus a time when Jesus is absent is envisaged. One could, with minimal alteration to the sense of verse 10, replace 'the gospel' by 'Jesus Christ' and in verse 9 'on my account' by 'on account of the gospel'. In Mark 14:9 we find again a setting where Jesus is absent: wherever the gospel is proclaimed "in the whole world", the woman's spontaneous act to Jesus in the house of Simon the leper at Bethany will be told in remembrance of her. But do we have to imagine a time when Jesus is absent in Mark 1:1, where the word εὐαγγέλιον is mentioned for the first time? And furthermore: how should we understand the notion that εὐαγγέλιον in Mark 1:1 has a beginning (ἀρχή) and is therefore something to be continued?

---

[58] The earliest attestation is found in Homer, *Od.* 14,152. 166 with the meaning "payment for a favorable report".

[59] Friedrich, *ThWNT*: 719.

[60] J. P. Dickson, "Gospel as News: euangel- from Aristophanes to the Apostle Paul," *NTS* 51 (2003): 212–230, 213.

[61] Dickson, "Gospel," 215.

[62] Evidence for this is given when we note that the noun euangelion is not found in Luke's or in John's Gospels and is deepened when we discover that Matthew omits three of Mark's uses of to euangelion on the lips of Jesus (Mark 1:15; 8:35; 10:29)

[63] We find it two times in a genitive connection (Mark 1:1, 14) and five times absolute in the words of Jesus (Mark 1:15; 8:35; 10,29; 13:10, 14:9).

Mark 1:1 as an independent sentence, without a predicate, introduces the "beginning of the gospel". Most modern commentators believe that ἀρχή is only the heading of the prologue and closely connected to the account of John the Baptist (Mark 1:4–8). In this interpretation, the gospel of Jesus Christ starts with the account of John the Baptist. But if v. 1 is already linked to John the Baptist, the same has to be true for vv. 2–3. However, the καθώς which begins v. 2 indicates that v. 1 should not be regarded as syntactically free-standing, since καθώς does not normally introduce a new sentence, but links what follows to what precedes. And therefore, vv. 2–3 are "a scriptural comment on v. 1 rather than the beginning of a new section introducing John the Baptist."[64] This observation is even truer for καθώς γέγραπται, which has a kataphoric function: "its function is to act as a bridge between a previously mentioned factor or event and the Old Testament citation."[65] Therefore from a syntactical viewpoint we have to set aside any interpretation that supposes that Mark 1:1–3 refers only to the account of John the Baptist.[66]

The juxtaposition of vv. 1 and 2 suggests that the "beginning of the gospel" is related to *scripture*, since the formula "as it is written" is regularly used in Jewish cultural contexts for the citation of scripture; "more particularly, it suggests that this 'beginning' is related to the book of Isaiah."[67] The formula "it is written" in Mark 1:2 is the most complete and explicit citation of scripture in the Gospel of Mark and Mark 1:2 is also unique insofar as it is the only scriptural citation not made by characters in the narrative. The Greek perfect tense of καθώς γέγραπται implies a past action with permanent results, so that the written book of Isaiah is not viewed as a dead letter but in the act of reading as a living voice. The fact that the whole quotation is attributed to the book of Isaiah has been explained in various ways.[68] That Mark has attributed the whole catena to Isaiah should not to be understood as a mistake; rather it functions as an interpretative link for relating the εὐαγγέλιον with a concept of message and gospel in the book of Isaiah in an intertextual way.

Let us start with Mark 1:2. What we find in Mark 1:2 is an ego-centric speech-act of scripture. The scripture speaks as an "I" who is sending a messenger. This is an important point for understanding: Scripture can speak as an "I"

---

[64] R. T. France, *The Gospel of Mark. A Commentary on the Greek Text* (NIGTC, Grand Rapids, Mich: Eerdmans 2002), 50.

[65] Marcus, *Way*, 17. Cf. G. Arnold, "Markus 1,1 und Eröffnungswendungen in griechischen und lateinischen Schriften," *ZNW* 68 (1977): 123: "Alle so (sc. with καθώς γέγραπται – D./W.) eingeleiteten Zitate beziehen sich auf den unmittelbar vorhergehenden Kontext."

[66] An asyndetic start of a narrative with "it happened" as in Mark 1:4 is not foreign to biblical narrative style (cf. in LXX Gen 6:1; 12:11; 14:1; 17:1; 21:22, also John 1:6).

[67] See Collins, *Mark*, 134.

[68] This ascription to the book of Isaiah is technically incorrect, since only 1:3 is actually from Isaiah, while Mark 1:2 is a mixture of Exod 23:20 and Mal 3:1.

because it functions as a medium, a medium which *shows* the words of God. The ego-centric speech-act has to be understood as "uneigentliche Rede," because the scripture speaks with a foreign voice, the voice of God. Here we find *in nuce* a media concept that will be in the same way important for the written gospel.

If we take a closer look at the book of Isaiah, we find in Isa 40–65 the language of gospel. Especially Isaiah 40:1–11 appears to have been regarded by various traditions within Judaism as a *locus classicus* for Isaianic salvation and it connotes – particularly the "announcement of hitherto unknown news of great eschatological import."[69] Of further interest from our media perspective is that the gospel language in Isaiah 40–65 functions in a specific way. The gospel in Isaiah presents a mode of distribution of news which can be characterized by its disseminational quality and suspension of reciprocity. The dispenser of the good news is invariant and explicitly insensitive to individual differences; he addresses himself to an anonymous mass (see Isa 40:9; 41:27; 60:6; 61:1). This news proclaimed by scripture in the Gospel of Mark includes a first part about a messenger coming to set in order the way of an addressed "you", and a second part in which a voice in the wilderness shouts to prepare the way of the Lord. Since Mark has nicely paralleled 'you' with the Lord in Mark 1:3, we have to follow that interpretative link and identify that 'you' with Jesus Christ, the only figure mentioned so far.[70] That is the beginning of the gospel to be found in the Markan narrative. So we can conclude that one of the organizing principles of the Markan composition seems to be the demonstration that the beginning of the good news happened "as it has been written in Isaiah the prophet" (1:2).[71] Therefore, the beginning is not limited to the context of John's baptism (Mark 1:4–8) and for sure εὐαγγέλιον was not a title for a literary genre when Mark was written. The ἀρχή – defined by the following εὐαγγέλιου– sets the beginning in the context of the announcement of the disseminated news of salvation written in the book of Isaiah and is – at the same time – the beginning of the Markan narrative in written form in a time when Jesus is absent.[72] Thus the concept of ἀρχή has a complex function in Mark 1:1, since what follows immediately is both a quotation from scripture and the beginning of a written narrative. This is

---

[69] Dickson, "Gospel as News," 220.

[70] The addition "Son of God" by some of the manuscripts might function as clarification that the addressed "you" is Jesus the son of God who is in close relation to the Lord, because in a scriptural context lord can only mean God.

[71] See J. Marcus, *Mark 1–8. A New Translation with Introduction and Commentary* (Anchor Bible 27, New York/London: Doubleday, 1999), 139.

[72] Cf. J. Schröter, "Konstruktion von Geschichte und die Anfänge des Christentums," in: J. Schröter, *Von Jesus zum Neuen Testament. Studien zur urchristlichen Theologiegeschichte und zur Entstehung des neutestamentlichen Kanons* (WUNT 204; Tübingen: Mohr Siebeck, 2007), 37–54: 46: "Durch diese Verwendung des Begriffes εὐαγγέλιον werden das Wirken Jesu sowie dessen Fortsetzung in der Zeit seiner Abwesenheit zur Grundlage einer Erzählung, die Vergangenheit, Gegenwart und Zukunft innerhalb eines Gesamtentwurfs integriert [...]."

So 3 beginings ἀρχή ?
1. Isiah 2. Jesus 3. John the Baptist
4. Written Narrative

noteworthy, since in the case of Mark the written narrative as a whole is open-ended, and important predictions and premises remain unfulfilled (like the proclamation of the gospel to all the nations [Mark 13:9f.; 14:9] and Mark 16:6–8) when the story comes to an end.[73]

Since we have to understand the quotations of vv. 2–3 as syntactically linked with v. 1, "it is through this fulfilment of these scriptural passages that the good news finds its beginning".[74] And the good news is about a messenger who will set the way of the absent Jesus Christ in order. While most commentators identify this messenger with John the Baptist, who is mentioned for the first time in v. 4, we have to set aside this interpretation not just for the syntactical reasons mentioned, but also for the reason that the only "actors" mentioned by Mark 1:2 are εὐαγγέλιον and Jesus Christ. M. A. Tolbert has argued that the messenger refers to Jesus, who prepares the way for God, as Jesus is the only figure mentioned so far, but this is problematic because of the "you" of v. 2, which we have identified as Jesus. In Tolbert's analysis the only possible referents of the "you" are the readers.[75] This conclusion seems implausible because the beginning is about the gospel *of* Jesus Christ. Therefore, the scripture of Isaiah announces to Jesus that a messenger will be sent before him to set his way in order. But who then is the messenger, if he is not John the Baptist and Jesus? The only possible answer is: the messenger is the εὐαγγέλιον. The εὐαγγέλιον is the messenger to set the way of Jesus Christ in order. Within this understanding εὐαγγέλιον functions as a medium – as a third – connecting the absent Jesus with the Christian community. The news announced in the written book of Isaiah already introduced us with the disseminational quality of gospel language, and this is exactly what is envisaged in Mark 1:3. "The voice of someone shouting in the wilderness: 'Prepare the way of the Lord; make his paths straight!'" As Shiner has pointed out: "The voice in the wilderness […] gives us something to do. 'You all! Prepare the way of the Lord! You all! Make his paths straight!'" […] God's herald cries in the wilderness to anyone there, 'Prepare the way of the Lord!' I can also hear the command as addressed to myself […]."[76] The gospel is a message to be provided by those who are the ones to pave the way of the Lord. The gospel is leaving the crucial matter of paving the way to the listener, not the master.

But is it plausible that a written communication situation is envisaged? It is noteworthy that Isaiah 40:4 is also cited in the Community Rule discovered at Qumran: "And when

---

[73] Cf. on this point, though with a different exegetical interest, E. M. Becker, *Das Markus-Evangelium im Rahmen antiker Historiographie* (WUNT 194; Tübingen: Mohr Siebeck, 2006), 238–252.

[74] France, *Gospel of Mark*, 61.

[75] M. A. Tolbert, *Sowing the Gospel: Mark's World in Literary-Historical Perspective* (Minneapolis: Fortress, 1989), 239–248.

[76] W. Shiner, *Proclaiming the Gospel. First-Century Performance of Mark* (Harrisburg: Trinity Press International, 2003), 185.

these become members of the Community in Israel according to all these rules, they shall separate from the habitation of unjust men and shall go into the wilderness to prepare the way of Him, as it is written, *prepare in the wilderness the way of [...], make straight in the desert a path for our God* (Isa 40: 3). This is the study of the law which He commands by the hand of Moses, that they may do according to all that has been revealed from age to age, and as the Prophets have revealed His Holy Spirit" (1QS 9:17–20).[77] Here we find a specific interpretation of Isa 40:3: the preparation of the way of the Lord motivated the community to live in conformity to the written Law! Therefore, the preparation of the way of the Lord – as living in conformity with the written Law – is now the work of the community members.

This lends support to our interpretation of Mark 1:3 as a link to prepare the way of the absent Jesus Christ through the medium of written gospel which has to be heard by its readers. So the written gospel engages in a purely one-way act, because the quotation from scripture takes the form of a direct address to each and every listener to the gospel. Furthermore, we have seen that the gospel is leaving the crucial matter of paving the way to the listener, not the master. In this narrative perspective we must therefore understand John the Baptist as the first one who is preparing the way of the Lord, but his preparation does not succeed, as Mark 1:14 and Mark 6:14–29 inform us. Thus is paving the way left to the readers and hearers of the written gospel.

In this media perspective it is important that the genitive "the gospel of Jesus Christ" (Mark 1:1) is more likely to be understood as a subjective genitive – but not so as to suggest that Jesus is the herald of the gospel rather than the gospel is the herald of the absent Jesus. The gospel of Mark is the good news that the absent Jesus himself proclaims through the written "book" of Mark, and at the same time the gospel is the representation of the voice of Jesus.[78] In this way the written gospel is the extension of the body of Jesus, giving the words of Jesus a voice in written form. Therefore, there is a line of continuity concerning "gospel", but not a straight line that can be traced from Jesus to the post-Easter church, but a line of continuity from the absent Jesus Christ to the written gospel.

The gospel functions as a messenger in a situation of distant communication between the absent Jesus and the believers. The written gospel gives the absent Jesus a body and a voice in the sense of a *repraesentatio soni*, and therefore has to be understood as bringing the absent Jesus to presence.[79] This medial extension of

---

[77] Translation from G. Vermes, *The Dead Sea Scrolls in English* (4th ed. London: Penguin, 1995), 109. It is noteworthy that the text of Mark connects the phrase "in the wilderness" with "the voice of one calling out" in its reading of Isa 40:3; whereas the reading reflected in the Community Rule links "in the wilderness" with "prepare the way of the Lord" (see Marcus, *Way*, 13,15).

[78] Therefore, it has also an objective nuance.

[79] Representation does not mean replacing someone absent but bringing absent ones to presence. That is how the story of the Gerasene man in Mark 5 functions: as a *repraesentatio soni* for the "many ghosts." The phrase "we are many" shows that the man cannot speak with his own voice, but with a foreign one.

the absent Jesus in the body of the gospel implies the powerlessness of the written gospel as container of a foreign voice. That is why in the gospel of Mark the gospel and Jesus are paralleled (cf. Mark 8:35; 10:29). Due to this powerlessness the authority of Jesus (cf. e. g. 1:22 and further more) and the call to the recipients to pave the way of the Lord by proclaiming the gospel to all the nations (cf. Mark 13:9f; 14:9) is emphasized.

3. 2 The Gospel of Luke

We have seen that the choice of the messenger is central in the ancient myths. But not only in the myths. Even the Roman state had its messengers, who were officially employed. The credibility of the messengers was of central interest.

The messenger plays an important role behind the transference of information. That is, the reliability of the messenger has a prominent role in successful communication. Among the criteria for a good choice of the messengers, it is frequently said that they must be suitable (*idoneus*), reliable and faithful (*fidelis*), but also must have access to the addressee and his reliability (*cedatarius*). The qualities demanded here like dependability and credibility were transferred to the messenger to fulfill the purposes of the absent transmitter; nevertheless, this is to be understood not in a sense of fidelity to the letter of the message, but the fidelity to the sense intended by the sender. It is not about preserving, but about passing on directly. Therefore, the protection of the message aims as Horst Wenzel has explained, not at the authentic preservation of the message, but at the dependability of the messenger.[80]

We have shown that in Mark εὐαγγέλιον acts even as a messenger. How does the situation present itself in the gospel of Luke? Here we have a triple messenger's model. At first we have the prologue: Here we encounter vocabulary which we also meet in tragedies on the one hand, Homer on the other hand, but especially also scientific literature in antiquity. We want to show that Luke stylizes himself as messenger and steps therefore into the role of the rhapsode, as the interpreter of the gods, as we have already shown for amphoras and vases. For Luke it has to do with reliability of communication. But there is also a second aspect. It is certainly not by chance that the gospel of Luke is the gospel in which ἄγγελοι play a central role. As already Julius Schniedewind demonstrated, an ἄγγελος is a person who delivers a message.[81] At this point we return to Homer: Here Hermes[82] and above all Iris[83] are called ἄγγελοι of the gods. Both stand under the protection of the gods. Therefore *angeloi* are, just like the author, mediators or

---

[80] H. Wenzel, *Hören und Sehen. Schrift und Bild. Kultur und Gedächtnis im Mittelalter* (Munich: Beck, 1995), 262.

[81] J. Schniewind, *Euangelion II*, 218ff. and idem, ἀγγελία, *ThWNT* 1 (1953): 56–71.

[82] Platon *Crat.* 407 e ἔοικε περὶ λόγος τι εἶναι ὁ Ἑρμῆς, καὶ τὸ ἑρμηνέα εἶναι καὶ τὸ ἄγγελον; Hom. *Od.* 5,29 σὺ γὰρ αὖτ ετά τ' ἄλλα περ ἄγγελός ἐσσι Hom. *Hymn.* Cer 407 ἐριούνιος ἄγγελος ὠκύς; *Hymn. Merc.* 3 ἄγγελος ἀθανάτων ἐριούνιος.

[83] So e. g. Homer *Ill.* 2,786; 3,121.

interpreters of vertical reality. However this arises not from religious language, but from the language of public life. Nevertheless, the angels fulfill a further purpose in Luke: Not only do they speak in someone else's name, but also they have a part in the performativity of the divine word: Thus the announcement by the angel and the conception of Elizabeth and then Mary collapse together, and the suffering of Christ on the cross is anticipated in the conversation with the angel in Gethsemane.

For reasons of space we concentrate only upon the prologue, because here the concept διήγησις is found: At first it is striking that the prologue consists of a single sentence. This begins in the protasis with a causal subordinate clause, of which an infinitive suggesting close regulation forms the basis; again a subordinate clause follows, which contains an important explanation of the subject. Then the apodosis commences with a main clause which allows the writer to emerge boldly as an author, ἔδοξε κἀμοί, however at the same time to withdraw his person. The prologue ends in a final clause. The prologue shows, in style and choice of terms, numerous resemblances to historical and scientific prologues in antiquity, but it differs in one point from all the others: it is striking that the author says nothing about his name or person. With ἔδοξε κἀμοί he makes a momentary appearance, but then withdraws again to neutral space[84].

Briefly, in a few verses, Luke outlines two different concepts: First, he differentiates himself using concepts that connote concise instruction and clear order, invoking these with a historiographical intention of putting the theological frame of meaning in the foreground. Secondly, however, the author expresses a very different and distinctive concept, by imposing on himself, just as within the messenger perspective, a certain neutrality, owing not just to his historiographic concept, but to his understanding as messenger. This means, in terms of our theory of messengers, that the author of the gospel becomes the messenger. With his message he not only conveys communication, but with it he also protects a space of power (*Herrschaftsraum*). In this respect Luke undertakes a kind of "telecommunications" of power.

The use if the term διήγησις is significant, instead of the more Semitic ῥῆμα.[85] When this is used in antiquity as a noun, it refers less to a narrative or story than to a limited communication of facts with the purpose of concise instruction; the term is delivered to us impressively in the Hippocratic Epidemics.[86] In the same way, the wide use of this concept in rational medicine in

---

[84] See CH *Prorrhet.* 2,2; Galen, *Plac. Hipp. Plat.* 8,2,1; Galen, *Cur. Rat. Ven. Sect.* XI, 312,11 (Kühn).

[85] L. Alexander, *The preface to Luke's Gospel. Literary convention and social context in Luke 1. 1–4 and Acts 1. 1* (Cambridge: Cambridge University Press, 1993), 113. See also T. Callan, "The Preface of Luke-Acts and Historiography," *NTS* 31 (1985), 576–581; different: C. K. Rothschild, *Luke-Acts and the Rhetoric of History: An Investigation of Early Christian Historiography* (WUNT 2. 175; Tübingen: Mohr Siebeck, 2004).

[86] It is mentioned in the scholarly debate that the term also could refer to a historiographical

antiquity shows that it is less about history. The use of the concept in this area points rather to the condition of the story as a narrative sequence which must be followed. This connotation is confirmed by ἀνατάσσομαι which means "put in a row," which is not really synonymous with "reproducing a story," the meaning often suggested by exegetes, but rather connotes an "inflexibility."[87]

In contrast Luke uses the term πράγματα, which in LXX is sometimes used for רבד, although this means word.[88] It is noteworthy that this concept in contrast to διήγησις has in view the content of the message, rather than merely a particular event. With this concept the author of Luke stresses just not the unfolding of a history, but much more the statement of a theology, because these events also unfold in heaven (cf. Aristoph. *Nu.* 228). Also in Herodotus historical exposition is taken into consideration, however always from a human perspective. In a similar way, the term ἀπ' ἀρχῆς is a neutral or "derogatory" reference to authenticate a tradition. Galen uses it in saying "things which I have learned / heard" referring to the Hippocratic and Platonic tradition (Kühn IV, 767).

The term αὐτόπται further substantiates this interpretation, because the term refers to a person who has a personal experience, a person who has facts at first hand. This is further confirmed by the fact that in this context a concept is used which is often used also for the god's messengers or the god's servants Hermes or Iris, ὑπηρέτης. This concept often characterizes someone performing a service; in relation to Hermes, the mediator's position is called messenger with it.[89] The term κατηχήθης is noteworthy also. The term comes up for the first time in the first cent. C. E.: "when you meet me, I will inform you myself by word of mouth of much that is not generally known."[90] It is striking that the verb appears to denote "to gather information" in official or forensic contexts. In the New Testament the term is used often when exact instructions are made, as in Gal. 6:6; Rom 2:18; 1 Cor 14:19.

We note once again the emphasis on "I/me", in apposition with the verb παρακολου-θέω. If the verb occurs in context with πράγματα and ἀρχή, it means "attend minutely" or "follow closely."

This short overview of the use of terms in the prologue shows that the author was especially concerned to emphasize two aspects: A message, it is stressed, is first accepted personally, and then becomes a concise, neutral mediation of the message. In contrast to Mark's gospel, the message has not an imperative connotation, but an indicative. The gospel of Luke intends to persuade receivers (personified as Theophilus) by facts, not to request that they follow the message only by imperative.

---

event. As one representative we can mention W. C. van Unnik, "Once More St. Luke's Prologue," *Neotestamentica* 7 (1973): 7–26, here 12–15.

[87] Liddell/Scott, *Greek-English Lexicon*, 122 cite Plut. *Mar.* 6 und Phld. *Lib.* 29.

[88] See Psalm 63:4; Prov 13:13.

[89] Aeschylus *Pr.* 954; cf. also 983.

[90] Agrippa, *Vita* 366 (translation: Thackeray LCL).

3. 3 The Gospel of John

The Johannine gospel is well known for its distinctive language. In the follow-ing, we want to investigate the figure of the Johannine Paraclete from the perspective of the messenger. While we have seen in the gospel of Mark that the word εὐαγγέλιον is used in a prominent way and can be understood as a mes-senger for the absent Jesus, we note that in the gospel of John we find neither the substantive εὐαγγέλιον nor the verb εὐαγγελίζεσθαι. But if we follow the in-tertextual link provided by Clement of Alexandria, who says that the gospel of John is a "spiritual" gospel (πνευματικόν εὐαγγέλιον)[91] we might – bracketing any "Gattungsfragen" – get a clue for connecting our media perspective of written gospel with the pneumatic character of the gospel of John. Clement's early attempt to determine the particular understanding and character of the Fourth gospel gives us reason to search for special words in the Fourth gospel with a "spiritual" connotation. And in this perspective an examination of the Johannine figure of the Paraclete-Spirit will be especially instructive for under-standing what could be meant by a "spiritual" gospel in a media-sensitive way. And if we also take into consideration "that the Fourth gospel was written, not for a Johannine community isolated from the rest of the early Christian move-ment, but for general circulation among the churches in which Mark's gospel was already being read,"[92] we have to understand his way of creating a πνευ-ματικόν εὐαγγέλιον as a specific contribution to communicative processes in written form in the face of the absence of Jesus Christ in the early Christian movement.[93]

It is noteworthy that the gospel of John reflects on the problematic nature of the absence of Jesus in a very intensive way. This happens in the farewell discourse[94] (John 13:31–16:33). In this farewell discourse the announcement of Jesus' departure is given in a paradoxical understanding of time. The reader of the gospel of John gets informed about Jesus departing at a time when Jesus is already absent, so that we find in the text of the farewell discourse the an-nouncement of something that is both soon to happen and has already happened "als prospektive Verhältnisgabe Jesu erzählte retrospektive Verhältnisnah-

---

[91] Cited by Euseb, *h. e.* VI 14,7.

[92] R. Bauckham, "John for Readers of Mark," *The Gospels for all Christians* (ed. R. Bauck-ham, Grand Rapids and Cambridge: Eerdmans, 1998), 147–171, here 171.

[93] F. Porsch, *Pneuma und Wort: Ein exegetischer Beitrag zur Pneumatologie des Johannesevange-liums* (Frankfurter theologische Studien 16, Frankfurt: J. Knecht, 1974), 406 has emphasized the close connection between the absent Jesus and the Paraclete and sees especially in the figure of the Paraclete a "hermeneutical key" to the understanding of this 'pneumatic gospel' but without any media-sensitivity.

[94] Cf. A. Dettwiler, *Die Gegenwart des Erhöhten. Eine exegetische Studie zu den johanneischen Abschiedsreden (Joh 13,31–16,33)* (FRLANT 169, Göttingen: Vandenhoeck & Ruprecht, 1995), 299: The main concern of the farewell discourse is "die nach der *Abwesenheit Jesu*".

me."[95] And within this paradoxical understanding of time the farewell discourse is focused on the promise "I will not leave you orphaned" (John 14:18), which implies a permanent presence of Jesus, and on the promise of the Paraclete to come when Jesus is absent (cf. John 14:16; 14:26; 15:26; 16:7b–11; 16:16f.).[96]

Etymologically παράκλητος is a passive verbal adjective from παρακαλεῖσθαι with the meaning, "einen als Beistand oder Zeugen *zur Hilfe Herbeigerufenen*."[97] Because παράκλητος acquired in time an active meaning of one who spoke on behalf of someone, some exegetes favor a forensic sense to the term παράκλητος, defining it as a legal assistant in court. Most scholars who accept the sense "advocate" highlight the forensic and legal aspects of the παράκλητος. But this *terminus technicus* narrows the meaning of παράκλητος in an incorrect way because it is found in a much broader sense in the Gospel of John. Therefore we have to agree with Dettwiler, who understands the Paraclete in its multifunctionality within the narrative of the gospel: "die innerjoh[anneische] Funktionsvielfalt des Begriffs als auch die hierbei aufblitzende Innovativität des joh[anneische] Sprachgebrauchs gegenüber seinen religions- und traditionsgeschichtlichen Vorgeprägtheiten [ist] zu respektieren."[98] The uniqueness of the word παράκλητος and its various functions in the gospel of John can be best understood in a media perspective, where the παράκλητος functions as messenger and is best described as "mediator" to Jesus[99]. This is because the παράκλητος stands in a functional unity with the absent Jesus, and the continuity between Jesus and the Paraclete is the dominant feature of the Paraclete passages in the gospel of John.[100]

When we look at the Paraclete sayings within this farewell discourse, we are offered an understanding of the figure of the Paraclete as a "gift" of the absent Jesus for the ones remaining once Jesus has departed. The Paraclete, of which is said that he will not come as long as Jesus is present (cf. John 16:7), takes up his work once Jesus departs. He is the "gift" which will be given when Jesus is absent (cf. John 14:16). Here is a situation we have

---

[95] J. Rahner, "Vergegenwärtigende Erinnerung. Die Abschiedsreden, der Geist-Paraklet und die Retrospektive des Johannesevangeliums," *ZNW* 91 (2000): 72–90.

[96] Just once more, in 1 John 2:1, is the Paraclete mentioned.

[97] H. Thyen, "Der Heilige Geist als παράκλητος," *Studien zum Corpus Iohanneum* (ed. idem; WUNT 214, Mohr Siebeck: Tübingen, 2007), 663–688, 664.

[98] Cf. Dettwiler, *Gegenwart*, 181f.; see also J. P. Louw, E. A Nida, *Greek-English Lexicon of the New Testament Based on Semantic Domains*, vol. I (New York, 1989), 142: "A rendering based upon the concept of legal advocate seems in most instances to be too restrictive."

[99] T. Gates Brown, *Spirit in the Writings of John. Johannine Pneumatology in Social-scientific Perspective* (JSNTS 253, London/New York: T&T Clark, 2003), prefers – but with another interest – also the translation of παράκλητος as mediator. Her main interest is to show that the Paraclete functions as "a subordinate broker" because "he facilitates Jesus' work as broker in that the Paraclete makes Jesus available to a vast number of clients after Jesus has departed and become separated from them in time and space." (196)

[100] For these compelling parallels between Jesus and the Paraclete see G. M. Burge, *The Anointed Community: the Holy Spirit in the Johannine Tradition* (Grand Rapids, Mi: Eerdmans, 1987), 140–143. C. Bennema, *The Power of Saving Wisdom: An Investigation of Spirit and Wisdom in Relation to the Soteriology of the Forth Gospel* (WUNT 2. 148, Tübingen: Mohr Siebeck, 2002), 219 has pointed out: "[…] John's understanding of the Paraclete […] and the uniqueness of the Paraclete concept must be sought in John's own description of the Paraclete, in which the relationship of the Paraclete to Jesus is dominant."

described as prominent in our message perspective: Due to Jesus' departure we have the situation, now well known to us, of those who want to stay in relation with each other but have become separated from each other in time and space, in a quantitative way. The role of the Paraclete is closely connected to this experience of difference. Therefore, the figure of the Paraclete gives us an answer to the question how the words of Jesus can be transmitted between those who are separated from each other in space and time (Jesus and his followers). That is to say, the Paraclete is "the presence of Jesus when Jesus is absent"[101] – not in an essential way but in a mediated way.

The relevance of the Paraclete is obviously due to the fact of communicative processes. Most of the verbs describing the work of the Paraclete relate to communication: the Paraclete is speaking, witnessing, announcing, teaching. But at the same time within this situation of communication the Paraclete does not communicate in an autonomous way, but is charged to transmit what has been given to him. The Paraclete is sent by Jesus (15:26; 16:7; 14:16) and offers what Jesus has (John 16:14) and what Jesus has said (John 14:26). For this reason we have to understand the Paraclete as not acting in an autonomous way. He rather has to be understood as a medium, because he is characterized by its heteronomy: "He will speak only what he hears [...] for he will take what is mine and declare it to you." (John 16:13–14) Therefore, the Paraclete who is sent represents Jesus in a genuine way. He not replacing Jesus when Jesus is absent but rather he mediates his presence. The Paraclete can be seen as a type of mediator for the absent Jesus because the work and words of the παράκλητος never belong to him but represent the continuation of the absent Jesus. The Paraclete functions as a third and stands in relation to the believers and the absent Jesus and is therefore, as Bennema has rightly pointed out, a "mode of communication."[102]

In John 15:26 we read that the Paraclete will "witness" on behalf of Jesus. The act of witnessing is one of the main aspects of the messenger. The role of the witness is to transform a perception into a verbal expression. To give something heard or seen a verbal face means to "translate" a "private" experience into a "public" experience. Especially in situations of uncertainty and innocence a witness brings truth of events due to his credibility. That is why the witness of the Paraclete is said to be true. The relationship between the witness and the hearer can be described as asymmetric in a double sense, because someone who is witnessing does this witness not on his own account but rather on account of the impressions he has seen or heard, in order to give important information to those who have not been where the witness has been. Due to this fact, "one of the prominent qualities required of a successful messenger was that he has to be faithful and true."[103] And that is why the Paraclete is called the Spirit of truth (John 14:7; 15:26 16:13), because this is the quality of the Paraclete as messenger. This Spirit of truth will guide the believers into all truth (John 16:13). It is noteworthy that we also find the motif of "way" here, as in the Mark 1:2–3. So the characterization of the Paraclete as witness shows once more that he has to be understood in a messenger perspective.

We cannot say "that the Paraclete makes Jesus continually present to the disciples."[104] Instead we have to say that the Paraclete represents Jesus because the Paraclete

---

[101] R. E. Brown, *The Gospel According to John*, vol. 2 (AB, New York: Doubleday, 1970), 1139.

[102] Bennema, *Power of Saving Wisdom*, 220.

[103] Meire, *Messenger*, 168.

[104] Different: Brown, *Spirit*, 210.

functions as a medium of the absent Jesus. He creates a relationship between Jesus and his followers in which the Paraclete is a third. In this media perspective sayings to the effect that Jesus' followers will "see" Jesus after his departure (John 14:19; 16:16) can be understood easily and we do not need explanations like the one by the commentators Malina and Rohrbaugh, who interpret the seeing sayings as indications of experiences of an altered state of consciousness in which the followers actually "see" Jesus.[105] The Paraclete functions as mediator who makes Jesus visible.

But how are we to understand this visibility if the Paraclete is also witnessing to the presence of an absent one? The only possibility for this seeing in a mediated way to be possible is that the written gospel of John itself "übernimmt die Funktion des Parakleten."[106] The embodiment of the absent Jesus mediated through the written gospel means the renunciation of the written gospel to appear as something autonomous. It belongs to the heteronomy of the messenger that his mediating functions can be replaced through "non-personal" entities and this is what we found here. But in the narration of John this non-personal entity of the written gospel is accentuated as a personal entity, the Paraclete – he has to be viewed as the *repraesentatio soni* of the absent Jesus in a personal manner. The believers are not left as orphans, because Jesus has sent the Paraclete, who mediates between the believers and the absent Jesus. The phrase in John 14:17 that the believers know the Paraclete gives us evidence that this figure is a present reality and this reality is the written gospel.

Therefore, we can conclude that the Paraclete is the mediator in which the absent Jesus comes to presence in written form. That is why the Paraclete is "in" the disciples (John 14:17) in the same way like Jesus is in the disciples (John 14:23–24), because in every act of reading aloud the voice of Jesus mediated through the Paraclete rules over the reader of the gospel. The believers are instruments who in the act of reading lend their body for the voice of Jesus mediated through the Paraclete.

McLuhan said "that it is too typical that the 'content' of any medium blinds us to the character of the medium."[107] On one hand this paper has tried to focus on the character of the medium in a postal paradigm which we have worked out to be significant for the early Christian movement. Therefore we have focused on the gospels of Mark, Luke, and John in order to understand them as media. We have analyzed the medium of the written gospel using a theory of the messenger. Within this perspective of the messenger the written gospels cannot be viewed as "the breakdown of the authentic act of live communication."[108]

---

[105] Cf. *Social-Science Commentary on the Gospel of John* (eds. B. Malina, R. Rohrbaugh; Philadelphia: Fortress Press, 1992), 231–232, 282–285.

[106] S. Alkier, *Die Realität der Auferweckung in, nach und mit den Schriften des Neuen Testaments* (Neutestamentliche Entwürfe zur Theologie 12, Tübingen: Francke Verlag, 2009), 168.

[107] Marshall McLuhan, *Understanding Media: The Extensions of Man* (New York: Mentor, 1964), 24.

[108] Kelber, "The Oral and the Written Word," 92.

Instead we have seen that they enable live communication in a mediated way under the conditions of distance, separation and non-reciprocity. The work of the messenger is to reconcile the distance, not to eliminate the difference. The words of Jesus found in the written gospels are in no way a marker of a dialogical face-to-face-communication (*Nahkommunikation*), but they do count under the condition of a quantitative distance in our messenger perspective as *repraesentatio soni* of the absent Jesus.[109] The words of Jesus in the written gospels represent the absent Jesus.

While on one hand we have analyzed the character of the written gospel as medium, as *repraesentatio soni* of the absent Jesus, we have on the other hand also focused on the content of the written gospel. Our main thesis has been that the content of the written gospel gives us a clue for understanding its mediality. Here we have seen that in our messenger perspective the medium "writing" neutralizes itself. The written gospel represents Jesus' words by stepping back from its media presence in written form. In the written gospel Jesus' words and actions appear in an immediate way. That means that writing in early Christian communication processes could not be understood as an insufficient and inadequate substitute for a dialogic face-to-face-communication act, but rather functions as a mediator. Therefore McLuhan's dictum, "The medium ist the message" should be modified in a specific way: "Das Medium ist nicht einfach die Botschaft; vielmehr bewahrt sich an der Botschaft die Spur des Mediums."[110] By leaving the content up to the conditions of written media, the gospels of Mark, Luke and John show indirectly and in three specific ways what they are and how they function. In the gospel of Mark the εὐαγγέλιον functions as medium; it is the *repraesentatio soni* of Jesus. In the gospel of Luke we found the "I" of the Evangelist working as a messenger responsible for the correct *diegesis* of what has happened and to what the readers do not otherwise have access to. And in the gospel of John it is the prominent figure of the Paraclete who guarantees within the medium of writing the *repraesentatio soni* of the absent Jesus. Within the gospels of Mark, Luke and John, these are the traces of the medium writing. Their function is to represent the absent Jesus in an adequate und immediate way – and therefore, to give the impression that they are independent of written media. *but they are not.*

---

[109] See S. Krämer, "Erfüllen Medien eine Konstitutionsleistung? Thesen über die Rolle medientheoretischer Erwägungen beim Philosophieren," *Medienphilosophie: Beiträge zur Klärung eines Begriffs*, (eds. S. Münker, A. Roesler, M. Sandbothe, Frankfurt a. M.: Suhrkamp, 2003), 78–90; 78: "Entscheidend ist [...] die für den antiken griechischen Denkraum so einzigartige Inszenierung dialogisch-agonaler Mündlichkeit im Medium der Textualität."

[110] Krämer, *Bote*, 81.

Women Prophets/Maenads Visually Represented in Two Roman Colonies: Pompeii and Corinth

David L. Balch

Corinthian Christian women prophets experienced "enthusiastic" speech, as did Dionysian female maenads. This article examines Roman domestic art as a means of inquiring into similar phenomena among Dionysian and early Christian women. Frescoes on Pompeian domestic walls visually represent maenads killing king Penthus of Thebes as well as Dirce, queen of Thebes and a maenad, being killed. H. G. Beyen, an art historian, describes these two frescoes as amphitheater art. Since both Pompeii and Corinth were Roman colonies founded in the first century BCE and both had amphitheaters, I argue that such Dionysian amphitheater art would have been painted on the domestic walls of Corinthian domus. This leads to an investigation of the myths, rituals, and visual representations of the cult of the Roman Dionysus compared and contrasted with the myths, rituals, and verbal representations of Pauline Corinthian Christians.

1. Roman domestic art in Pompeii and Corinth: Dionysus and death

The question addressed in this paper is whether Roman domestic art can contribute to our understanding of women prophets in Corinth.[1] To some degree, Pompeii is typical of first century BCE and first century CE Roman domestic art.[2] Among the many visual images in Pompeii, two are crowded with female prophets, that is, with Dionysian maenads: 1) the maenads killing Penthus, king of Thebes, and 2) Dirce, queen of Thebes and herself a maenad, being executed. The question and its apparent answer raise another question: why is death so prominent when we view women prophets in a Roman colony?[3]

---

[1] See A. C. Wire, *The Corinthian Women Prophets: A Reconstruction through Paul's Rhetoric* (Minneapolis: Augsburg Fortress, 1990) and J. Økland, *Women in Their Place: Paul and the Corinthian Discourse of Gender and Sanctuary Space* (New York: T&T Clark, 2004).

[2] D. L. Balch, *Roman Domestic Art and Early House Churches* (WUNT 228; Tübingen: Mohr Siebeck, 2008) 28–29.

[3] For background see E. W. Leach, *The Social Life of Painting in Ancient Rome and on the Bay of Naples* (Cambridge: Cambridge University, 2004), 132 and Balch, *Roman Domestic Art*, 22–23, 132–36, 204–05.

The answer to the second question is simple, although startling: the art historian Beyen[4] classifies both frescoes as "amphitheater art." Explicit amphitheater art became popular in the reign of Nero; the Pompeian amphitheater itself was built in the second quarter of the first century BCE,[5] so was a century old by Paul's time. Pompeii had become a Roman colony when defeated by Sulla in the Social War (80 BCE). Corinth, also a Roman colony, was founded by Julius Caesar about the same time (44 BCE).

1. 1 Two Roman colonies, Pompeii and Corinth: two amphitheaters

Like Pompeii, Corinth had an amphitheater. Archaeologists debate its date, but Welch[6] suggests that the closest formal parallels to the architecture place it in the late first century BCE. Spawforth discusses a related letter, still extant among the letters of the emperor Julian; he reconstructs the letter's historical background as follows:

In 54 [CE], to mark the accession of the emperor Nero, a cult of the emperors was instituted at Corinth by the member cities of the Achaean League, its focus an annual imperial festival, which included *venationes* (and, no doubt, gladiatorial shows).[7]

In this letter, dated between 80 and 120 CE (Spawforth 224),[8] the city of Argos objects to contributing finances to these Corinthian spectacles (Spawforth 227–28). Two brief quotations from the letter:

For it is not to furnish gymnasts or musical contexts that the Corinthians need so much money, but they buy bears and panthers for the hunting shows which they often exhibit in their theaters (409A, trans. Wright, *Julian* [LCL], vol. III, #28).

But the Argives are not so well off for money, and compelled as they are to slave for a foreign spectacle held in the country of others, will they not be suffering unjust and illegal treatment […]? (409B)

Animals for these Corinthian spectacles included expensive lions, leopards, cheetahs, and also bulls (Spawforth 217, 228). Three writers whom Welch cites all relate Dionysus to gladiatorial games in Athens, and all three refer to the Corinthians' enthusiasm for the slaughter of animals and human beings.

---

[4] H. G. Beyen, "The Workshops of the 'Fourth Style' at Pompeii and in its Neighbourhood," *Studia Archaeologica Gerardo van Hoorn Oblata* (Leiden: E. J. Brill, 1951): 43–65 (55).

[5] L. Richardson, Jr., *Pompeii. An Architectural History* (Baltimore: Johns Hopkins University, 1988), 134.

[6] K. Welch, "Negotiating Roman Spectacle Architecture in the Greek World: Athens and Corinth," in *The Art of Ancient Spectacle,* (eds. B. Bergmann and C. Kondolen; New Haven: Yale University, 1999), 124–45 (137).

[7] A. J. S. Spawforth, "Corinth, Argos, and the Imperial Cult: Pseudo-Julian, *Letters* 198," *Hesperia* 63/2 (1994): 211–32 (226).

[8] Compare M. E. Hoskins Walbank, "Evidence for the Imperial Cult in Julio-Claudian Corinth," *Subject and Ruler: The Cult of the Ruling Power in Classical Antiquity* (ed. A. Small; JRA Supp 17; Ann Arbor, 1996), 201–13 who (212) dates Pseudo-Julian earlier than Spawforth does, in the first century CE "not long after the institution of the imperial contests."

In regard to the gladiatorial shows the Athenians have so zealously emulated the Corinthians, or rather have so surpassed both them and all others in their mad infatuation, that whereas the Corinthians watch these combats outside the city …, the Athenians look on at this fine spectacle in their theatre under the very walls of the Acropolis, in the place where they bring their Dionysus into the orchestra and stand him up, so that often a fighter is slaughtered among the very seats in which the Hierophant and the other priests must sit." (Dio Chrysostom, *Or.* 31. 121, trans. Cohoon and Crosby in LCL)[9]

When the Athenians, out of rivalry with the Corinthians, were thinking of holding a gladiatorial show, he [Demonax] came before them and said: "Don't pass this resolution, men of Athens, without first pulling down the altar of Mercy." (Lucian, *Demonax* 57, trans. Harmon in LCL; compare Philostratus, *Apollonius* 4. 22)

The Roman colonies of Pompeii and Corinth both had amphitheaters, and their residents earned reputations for eagerly enjoying the bloody spectacles.

This suggests that the amphitheater art of the Roman colony Pompeii might also be found in Roman Corinth, and just as certainly in Corinth's neighboring cities, Athens and Sicyon. Rife recently published frescoes from graves in Corinth's port of Kenchreai, concluding that "the decorative program of tomb 4 closely resembles the Campanian tradition and, more generally, western Roman painting."[10] Discussing Corinth's fountain of Peirene, famous as the site where the Corinthian hero Bellerophon tames Pegasos with Athena's help, Robinson[11] also draws parallels to frescos in Pompeii. Unlike Pompeii, Corinth has few remaining frescos, but those few frescoes show specific similarities with Pompeian, western Roman art. The two Roman colonies' enthusiasm for viewing the bloody deaths of other humans suggests that the domestic art common in Pompeii visually representing such deaths would also have been shared.

1. 2 Methodology: Roman domestic art and texts, the latter only if they support the art

Art is not text; archaeologists typically distrust the latter. Bookidis[12] is quite cautious with the evidence of textual sources. In her survey of Corinthian

---

[9] Dio, *Or.* 31 is dated between CE 70 and 81, within 10 to 20 years of Paul's death (*Dio Chrysostom* [trans. J. W. Cohoon and H. L. Crosby; LCL, 1979], III, 4). Dio assumes that his audience in Rhodes knows the reputation of the Corinthians. For statues of Dionysus and the Athenian theater of Dionysus visually represented on coins, see F. W. Imhoof-Blumer, P. Gardner, and A. Oikonomides, *Ancient Coins Illustrating Lost Masterpieces of Greek Art: A Numismatic Commentary on Pausanias* (Chicago: Argonaut, 1964 [orig. 1885]), plates BB xx and CC vii; CC ix–x; CC x–ix. A coin of Domitian (CE 81–96) visually represents a statue of Dionysus in Sicyon, Corinth's neighboring polis (Imhoof-Blumer et al., *Ancient Coins,* 29).

[10] J. L. Rife, et al., "Life and Death at a Port in Roman Greece: The Kenchreai Cemetery Project, 2002–2006," *Hesperia* 76/1 (January–March 2007): 143–81 (165).

[11] B. A. Robinson, "Fountains and the Formation of Cultural Identity at Roman Corinth," in *Urban Religion in Roman Corinth: Interdisciplinary Approaches* (ed. D. N. Schowalter and S. J. Friesen; Cambridge: Harvard University, 2005), 111–40 (119, 126).

[12] N. Bookidis, "Religion in Corinth: 146 B. C. E. to 100 C. E.," in Schowalter and Friesen, *Urban Religion in Roman Corinth,* 141–64 (164).

religion Bookidis rarely mentions Dionysus, the god whose two statues stood in the Corinthian market place according to Pausanias' text. My paper is based primarily on questions growing out of Roman art; nevertheless, I will also employ written texts to make suggestions about the sacred visual world of the Corinthians, supported by numismatic evidence of Corinthian temples and cult statues. I will never draw a conclusion based merely on texts.

The most important texts relating amphitheater spectacles to Corinth in Paul's decades are by Dio Chrysostom, and Pseudo-Julian, close to the time of Paul. Pausanias traveled through Corinth and its neighboring cities a century after Paul, in the 170s CE.[13] Reading Pausanias, *Description of Greece*, Book 2: *Corinth*, I find considerable overlap between the statues and paintings that he records having seen in Corinth and its neighboring cities, and the visual representations published in the Italian encyclopedia PPM.[14]

Pausanias records civic monuments, not domestic spaces, but Romans characteristically transferred statues and paintings, which Greeks had commissioned for their temples, into Roman domestic spaces. For example, key images of Isis and Io that were in the Temple of Isis in Pompeii are also found in a prominent location in the market (*macellum*), as well as in several Pompeian *domus*,[15] just as the Madonna and Child are found today both in Italian churches and in their homes. Discussing the frescoes in one particular house in Pompeii, Bergmann draws a general conclusion: "In the Roman world, tragic myth pervaded the very heart of family life, the domus."[16] When Paul preached in a Corinthian *domus* or *insula*, he and his auditors would have been viewing some of the statues and frescoes that Pausanias records having seen in public temples, but I will suggest this only when there is an earlier, primary source in Campanian domestic art.

---

[13] Pausanias, [trans. W. H. S. Jones; LCL], I, ix–x. For evaluation see C. Habicht, *Pausanias' Guide to Ancient Greece* (Berkeley: University of California, 1985). Speaking in Corinth's port city in 156 CE, Aelius Aristides, "The Isthmian Oration" observes, "So numerous are the treasures of paintings all about it [wisdom], wherever one would simply look, throughout the streets themselves and the porticoes" (*Or.* 46.28, in *The Complete Works by Aelius Aristides* [trans. C. A. Behr; Leiden: Brill, 1981], II. 274). Referring to the myth of the birth of Dionysus, Aristides refers to "those terrifying and impious paintings" (*Or.* 46.41, trans. Behr II. 277, with nn. 62, 80). D. C. Spitzer, "Roman Relief Bowls from Corinth," *Hesperia* 11 (1942): 162–92 discusses second century CE terracotta relief bowls with scenes of Dionysiac rites. I thank Cavan Concannon for the references to Aristides and Spitzer.

[14] PPM: *Pompei: pitture e mosaici*, ed. Ida Baldassarre (Istituto della Enciclopedia Italiana; Rome: Arti Grafici Pizzi, 1990–2003), 10 vols., plus a supplement, *La documentazione nell'opera di disegnatori e pittori dei secoli XVII e XIX* (1995). Pliny *NH* 35.15 notes, "some say painting was discovered at Sicyon, others in Corinth" (trans. Rackham. See also *NH* 35.16, 24, 58, 75–77, 123–127, 134.)

[15] Balch, *Roman Domestic Art*, chap. II.

[16] B. Bergmann, "The Roman House as Memory Theater: The House of the Tragic Poet in Pompeii," *The Art Bulletin* 76/2 (1994): 225–56 (249).

2. Dionysian myth, ritual, and visual representations in Corinth, Athens, and Sicyon

Seaford[17] notes "evidence in the historical period for a growing demand for the Dionysiac mysteries among men, which found expression partly in the initiation of men into the female *thiasoi* [...]." Male participation might form the basis of accusations, a possibility also faced by male, Christian, charismatics in Corinth. The Athenian Demosthenes polemicized against Aeschines, including describing Dionysian ritual, in 330 BCE as follows:

On arriving at manhood you assisted your mother in her initiations, reading the service-book while she performed the ritual, and helping generally with the paraphernalia. At night it was your duty to mix the libations, to clothe the catechumens in fawn-skins, to wash their bodies, to scour them with the loam and the bran, and when their lustration was duly performed, to set them on their legs, and give out the hymn: "Here I leave my sins behind, Here the better way I find." And it was your pride that no one ever emitted that holy ululation so powerfully as yourself.... In day-time you marshaled your gallant throng of bacchanals through the public streets, their heads garlanded with fennel and white popular; and as you went, you squeezed the fat-cheeked snakes, or brandished them above your head, now shouting your *Euoi Saboi!* Now footing it to the measure of *Hyes Attes! Attes Hyes!* – saluted by all the old women with such proud titles as Master of Ceremonies, Fugleman, Ivy-bearer, Fan-carrier; and at last receiving your recompense of tipsy-cakes, and cracknels, and currant-buns. (Demosthenes, *De Corona* 259–60, trans. Vince in LCL)

2. 1 Visual representations of the deaths of Dionysus and Penthus in Roman colonies

Corinth is no longer inhabited by any of the old Corinthians, but by colonists sent out by the Romans. This change is due to the Achaean League. The Corinthians, being members of it, joined in the war against the Romans [...]. When the Romans won the war, they carried out a general disarmament of the Greeks and dismantled the walls of such cities as were fortified. Corinth was laid waste by Mummius, who at that time commanded the Romans in the field, and it is said that it was afterwards refounded by Caesar [...].(Pausanias 2. 1. 2: *Corinth*, trans. Jones)

Roman colonization provides a crucial political, social, economic, religious, and aesthetic context for both Pompeii and Corinth.

On the market-place, where most of the sanctuaries are, stand Artemis surnamed Ephesian and wooden images of Dionysus, which are covered with gold with the exception of their faces; these are ornamented with red paint. They are called *Lysius* and *Baccheüs*,[18] and I too give the story told about them. They say that Pentheus treated Dionysus despitefully

---

[17] R. Seaford, "Dionysiac Drama and the Dionysiac Mysteries," *Classical Quarterly* 31/2 (1981): 252–75 (265).

[18] Near the theater, Athens also has "two temples and two statues of Dionysus" (Pausanias, I. 20. 3). Corinth's neighboring polis, Sicyon, also has two statues (Pausanias, II. 7.5–6), a text assuming knowledge of Antiope and Dirce (see below).

(*hubrizonta*), his crowning outrage being that he went to Cithaeron, to spy upon the women, and climbing up a tree beheld what was done. When the women detected Pentheus, they immediately dragged him down, and joined in tearing him, living as he was, limb from limb. (Pausanias II. 2.6–7)

Pausanias' report of Dionysus in Corinth is supported by numismatic evidence. An early coin (42–41 BCE, only two years after Caesar refounded Corinth) images Dionysus holding a cantharos and thyrsus.[19] Touring Athens, Pausanias (I. 2.5) mentions the cult statue of Dionysus by Alcamenes (fifth century BCE), represented on numerous coins (Imhoof-Bloomer et al., *Ancient Coins*, plate CC i–v).

The two statues, named Dionysus Deliverer (*Lysius*[20]) and Dionysus Frenzied (*Baccheüs*), had their faces painted red. Versnel[21] is certain that it refers to an annual ritual drama in which Dionysus dies. Earlier Harrison had interpreted Dionysus as "Eniautos Daimon" (year god),[22] an expression of the universal yearly cycle of decay, death, and renewal, which occurs both in the natural world and in initiation, the most famous Greek vegetation deity.

Some authors do narrate Dionysus' death. Diodorus of Sicily[23] narrates myths about Dionysus (I. 23, III. 62–74 and IV. 1.5–5. 5) and Orpheus (IV. 25). Diodorus has a description of the myths and rituals, which includes an Orphic version of his death, which includes a new birth (*neon gennethenai*; III. 62. 6 and 8; compare Strabo, *Geography* 10. 3. 1)[24]

Diodorus then narrates the myths of three different persons named Dionysus, because the stories of Dionysus were difficult for "historians" like Ephorus to

---

[19] *Roman Provincial Coinage I: From the Death of Caesar to the Death of Vitellius (44 BC–AD 69)* (eds. A. M. Burnett, M. Amandry, and P. R. Ripollès; London: British Museum, 1992), I/I, 250, #1122, from the time of Antony.
[20] F. Graf, "Dionysian and Orphic Eschatology: New Texts and Old Questions," *Masks of Dionysus* (eds. T. H. Carpenter and C. A. Faraone; Ithaca: Cornell University, 1993), 239–58 (242–43): "*lusis*, the freedom procured by Bakkhios [...] The term *lusis* cannot just mean death as the freeing of the soul from the body [...] It has to be more, namely, release from punishment after death that would otherwise be in store for humankind." For this title R. Seaford, *Dionysos* (New York: Routledge, 2006), 55, 70–71 cites Plato, *Republic* 364be and a Pelinna gold leaf from the fourth century BCE. For other epithets of Dionysus, see Diodorus IV. 5.1–2.
[21] H. S. Versnel, "Dionysus, the King and the New Year Festival in Hellas," *Triumphus: An Inquiry into the Origin, Development and Meaning of the Roman Triumph* (Leiden: E. J. Brill, 1970), 235–54, (244, n. 8).
[22] P. McGinty, *Interpretation and Dionysus: Method in the Study of a God* (New York: Mouton, 1978), 120, with nn. 53–54, discusses Nilsson's late realization that the child Dionysus is awakened only every other year, so can hardly be a mythical representation of the yearly birth of vegetation. See Diodorus Siculus III. 65. 8; IV. 3.2.
[23] Diodorus, trans. Oldfather (LCL), 1, pp. ix–x: Diodorus wrote 56–36 BCE, a century before Paul.
[24] On the date, ritual, and ideas of Orphism, W. Burkert, "Orphism and Bacchic Mysteries: New Evidence and Old Problems of Interpretation," in *Kleine Schriften III: Mystica, Orphica, Pythagorica*, (ed. F. Graf; Göttingen: Vandenhoeck & Ruprecht, 2006), 37–46.

Plates 1-4) Casa di D. Octavius Quartio (II 2,2; PPM III 100–05), outdoor biclinium

Plate 1) east wall behind the biclinium: Thisbe grieving and bloodied Pyramus dying, after being attacked by a lion.

Plate 2) on the north wall to the diners' right, an amphitheater scene, a lion pursuing deer (Balch CD 229). For a similar fresco painted in the amphitheater itself, see PPM. *La documentazione nell'opera di disegnatori e pittori dei secoli XVII e XIX* (1995), 105–11, #52.

Plates 3–4) directly in front of the biclinium (west), the goddess Diana, angry at being viewed nude, metamorphosizes Actaeon into a deer, who is devoured by his own
dogs (Balch CD 230–231); note: plastic sheets protect these two frescoes and produce
poor photographs. Not shown by a plate: visible to the left (south) from the biclinium
and just out the back gate of the garden, the amphitheater (II 6). The garden (south)
offers a statuette of Hercules strangling snakes (see Balch 180, n. 44 and 156, n. 73).
*Death is either visually represented or actually available for viewing entertainment on all four
sides of this dining area.*

date (III. 74. 6; IV. 1–2)! The first battles Titans in Egypt (III. 68–73), exchanges mortality for immortality (*athanasia*), and becomes king of the entire world (III. 73. 8). The second was born of Zeus and Io; the third – Greek – Dionysus was born of Zeus and Semele, so from Zeus' thigh (III. 74. 1, a double birth narrated in III. 62. 10, 64. 3–7, and IV. 2.1–4, a "second epiphany," III. 62. 10). The "most ancient" Dionysus was an Indian with a long beard (III. 63. 3), while the third was a young, effeminate boy of unusual beauty (III. 64. 6; IV. 4.2, 5; 5. 2). Diodorus associates the various Dionysi with the vine, including a story told by the Teans that, "even to this day, at fixed times in their city a fountain of wine, of unusually sweet fragrance, flows of its own accord from the earth." (III. 66. 2; compare Plutarch, *Isis and Osiris* [Mor.] 365A)[25]

I conclude that the red color on the faces of the two statues of Dionysus on the market place in Corinth might possibly refer to an Orphic version of the death of Dionysus, and might have done so as early as Paul's visit to the city. However, even though Dionysus often appears in Pompeian art, Dionysus himself is never visually represented dying. The basic source for this attempt at reconstructing Corinthian domestic art is Pompeian/Campanian art, correlated with textual sources, but textual sources alone, in this case ones narrating Dionysius' death, are not sufficient.

Since the primary source of this paper is not literature, Pausanias' observation of Dionysus' red faces raises a question about Roman domestic art. In the visual world, where does one see red blood? The answer is, in amphitheater frescoes and mosaics (see Balch CD 117, 212, 228b [see plates 1–4], 282a); blood flows from both animals and humans as they die. The bloody death to which Pausanias himself (II. 2.7) refers when he mentions Dionysus' red face is that of Penthus, narrating that the women "dragged him down, and joined in tearing him, living as he was, limb from limb," a story narrated centuries earlier by Euripides, *Bacchae* 708–68, 1063–1152. Euripides does not narrate Dionysus' own death, but that of Penthus. In Pompeii Penthus[26] (plate 5) is visually represented surrounded by maenads just before his mother Agave kills him, which Økland (112) says is "the foundation myth of the cult of Dionysos in the area [Corinth]". Penthus, a Dionysian character, is visually represented in a Pompeian fresco that Beyen labels "amphitheater art" (n. 4), and the actual visual representations in Pompeii with red blood flowing are also amphitheater art.

---

[25] Commenting on Temple B in fifth-century BCE Corinth, C. Bonner, "A Dionysiac Miracle at Corinth," *AJA* 33 (1929): 368–75, writes (373), "I think that the peculiar apparatus of the little temple at Corinth is best explained by the assumption that its purpose was to produce a flow of wine from the temple on certain great occasions." Bonner cites Euripides, *Bacchae* 704–11; Pausanias VI. 26. 2; Pliny, *Nat. Hist.* 2. 231; 31. 16; and Athenaeus, 5. 198c and f, who cites Kallixeinos of Rhodes (third century BCE).

[26] Balch, *Roman Domestic Art*, 129, plate 7 and CD 209, 209a, from the Casa dei Vettii, Pompeii (VI 15,1; PPM V 526, 529–30), triclinium n, east wall. R. Merkelbach, *Die Hirten des Dionysos: die Dionysos-Mysterien der römischen Kaiserzeit und der bukolische Roman des Longus* (Stuttgart: B. G. Teubner, 1988) does not include this scene in his plates (compare n. 39 on Dirce).

Plate 5) Casa dei Vettii, Pompeii (VI 15,1; PPM V 526, 529–30), triclinium n, east wall: Agave and maenads surround Penthus, king of Thebes, just before his mother kills him (in situ).

2. 1. 1 The Roman Dionysus, god of wine harvest, no longer of tragedy?

This fresco of Penthus moments before his murder is in the Casa dei Vettii in Pompeii, owned by two freedmen brothers.[27] Spawforth[28] has shown that the Corinthian elite were Greek freedmen from prominent Roman families and Italian *negotiatores*. One might explore connections between the art of freedmen in Pompeii and Corinth.[29]

---

[27] J. R. Clarke, *The Houses of Roman Italy 100 B. C.–A. D. 250: Ritual, Space, and Decoration* (Berkeley: University of California, 1991), 208.

[28] A. J. S. Spawforth, "Roman Corinth: the Formation of a Colonial Elite," *Roman Onomastics in the Greek East: Social and Political Aspects* (ed. A. D. Rizakis Meletemata 21; Paris: Boccard, 1996), 167–82. Benjamin Millis, "The Social and Ethnic Origins of the Colonists in Early Roman Corinth," *Corinth in Context: Comparative Studies on Religion and Society* (eds. Steven J. Friesen, Daniel N. Schowalter, and James Walters; Leiden: E. J. Brill and Atlanta: SBL, forthcoming summer, 2010).

[29] On the "participation of the freedman in Roman cultural identity," figures which "multiply through small or medium-sized towns like Pompeii and Herculaneum," see the programmatic book by A. Wallace-Hadrill, *Rome's Cultural Revolution* (Cambridge: Cambridge University, 2008), 454.

I pause to express surprise. Merkelbach (2) observes that after the fourth century, tragedies were no longer performed in Athens. Dionysus remained the god of vegetation and wine. Romans became masters of all Greek-speaking countries; from this time there are hundreds of inscriptions and thousands of images, not of the dynamic god of the Athenians, but the older god of nature (3). In the Imperial period, the cult of Dionysus became a religion of the beautiful (4). The friendlier side of the god remained; violent sufferings were forgotten. Dionysus was no longer the god of tragedy, but now only a god of the wine harvest (4).

Similarly, a current exhibition at the National Gallery of Art[30] focuses on the beauty of Roman domestic art. On the National Gallery website, Paul Zanker emphasizes the beauty, especially the heterosexual, beautiful, naked pairs of lovers visually represented in frescoes and mosaics in Pompeii. The two main characters in this art are Dionysus and Aphrodite/Venus. For example, in the Villa dei Misteri just outside Pompeii, Dionysus reclines on Ariadne's/Aphrodite's lap (plate 6).[31] Zanker says the myth is beside the point: the real subject is the union of lovers, personal fulfillment, the shared consumption of wine, not a fairytale world, but a mythological world that people could enter. Few frescoes focus on disaster or war: not Troy, but Helen of Troy is visually represented.[32] House owners wanted to banish the unpleasant from their houses. This is not merely escape; rather living with such fantasies is the intensification of daily life.

Both Merkelbach and Zanker neglect what Beyen (55) calls "amphitheater art." For example, Zanker mentions the many frescoes of Actaeon and Diana, represented indeed with beautiful, naked bodies, but in her anger Diana has turned Actaeon into a deer, so that he is being eaten alive by his own dogs, as were Christians in Nero's gardens (Tacitus, *Annals* 15. 44)! Some historians of Roman domestic art write as if there were no amphitheater in Pompeii, assuming that the art is simply decorative, without this social context, misrepresenting Pompeian/Roman aesthetic values that visually represent both sex and the death of animals and of humans as entertainment. Some of those with beautiful, naked bodies in Dionysian settings, for example, Penthus and Dirce, are being *murdered*![33]

---

[30] The National Gallery of Art website, under "Videos and Podcasts," offers a lecture by P. Zanker, "To Live with Myths in Pompeii and Beyond." Contrast Zanker's oral remarks with B. Bergmann in the exhibit catalogue, "Staging the Supernatural: Interior Gardens of Pompeian Houses," in *Pompeii and the Roman Villa: Art and Culture Around the Bay of Naples* (ed. C. C. Mattusch; Washington: National Gallery of Art, 2008), 53–69 (62–64, with nn. 25–34).

[31] Balch, *Roman Domestic Art* CD 85, 88; Merkelbach, *Die Hirten*, plates 2–3.

[32] This overemphasizes Helen: the Trojan war is visually represented, for example, in the Casa del Criptoportico (I 6,2) and the Casa di D. Octavius Quartio (II 2,2). See Balch, *Roman Domestic Art*, 96, 177, 182, 184.

[33] See M. T. Andreae, "Tiermegalographien in pompejanischen Gärten. Die sogennanten Paradeisos Darstellungen," *Rivisti di Studi Pompeiani* 4 (1990): 45–124. Also K. M. Coleman, "Fatal Charades: Roman Executions Staged as Mythological Enactments," *JRS* 80 (1990): 44–73 with plates II–III, and Coleman, "Ptolemy Philadelphus and the Roman Amphithea-

Plate 6) Villa dei Misteri (just outside Pompeii), room 5, central (eastern) wall: Dionysus lying on Ariadne's/Aphrodite's lap (in situ)

2. 1. 2 "Resistance" to worship of Dionysus in Roman Athens and Corinth

The oldest sanctuary of Dionysus [in Athens] is near the theatre. Within the precincts are two temples and two statues of Dionysus, the Eleuthereus (Deliverer) and the one Alcamenes made of ivory and gold. There are paintings here – Dionysus bringing Hephaestus up to heaven.... Besides this picture there are also represented Pentheus and Lycurgus paying the penalty of their insolence to Dionysus. (Pausanias I. 20. 3, 4, trans. Oldfather in LCL)

When commenting on the two statues of Dionysus on the market in Corinth and here commenting on the two temples and two statues of Dionysus near the theatre in Athens (II. 2.6 and I. 20. 3), Pausanias recalls the story of Penthus, here adding Lycurgus,[34] "paying the penalty of their insolence (*hubrisan*) to Dionysus." Diodorus narrates the stories:

... the whole populace everywhere thronged to meet him [Dionysus] and welcomed him with great joy. There were a few, however, who, out of disdain and impiety (*huperephanian kai asebeian*), looked down upon him and kept saying that he was leading the Bacchantes about with him because of his incontinence and was introducing the rites and the mysteries that he might thereby seduce the wives of other men, but such persons were punished by him right speedily. For in some cases he made use of the superior power which attended his divine nature and punished the impious, either striking them with madness or causing them while still living to be torn limb from limb by the hands of the women; in other cases he destroyed such as opposed him by a military device which took them by surprise. For he distributed to the women, instead of the thyrsi, lances whose tips of iron were covered with ivy leaves; consequently, when the kings in their ignorance disdained them because they were women (*hos an gunaikon*) and for this reason were unprepared, he attacked them when they did not expect it and slew them with the spears. Among those who were punished by him, the most renowned, they say, were Pentheus among the Greeks, Myrrhanus the king of the Indians, and Lycurgus among the Thracians. Now the myth relates..., but Dionysus, bringing his forces over, conquered the Thracians in a battle, and taking Lycurgus alive put out his eyes and inflicted upon him every kind of outrage, and then crucified (*anastaurosai*) him.... (Diodorus III. 65. 2–5; compare IV. 3.4)[35]

---

ter," *Roman Theater and Society* (ed. W. J. Slater; Ann Arbor: University of Michigan, 1996), 49–68. On frescoes of Actaeon see Balch, *Roman Domestic Art*, 26–28, 170–71, 179–80, with CD 19, 120, 230–31.

[34] A fresco of Dionysus pursued by Lycurgus was painted in the Casa di M. Gavius Rufus (VII 2,16–17; PPM VI 530–85, at p. 575); also A. Farnoux, "Lykourgos I," *Lexicon Iconographicum Mythologiae Classicae* [LIMC] 6. 1 (1992): 309–19; 6. 2, 157–65.

[35] Aeschylus (525–456 BCE) had already written a satyric play on the Lycurgean trilogy. See H. W. Smyth, trans. *Aeschylus* (LCL, 1926), II, 420; also Apollodorus III. 5, who wrote in the first or second century CE. A scholiast on the Iliad also tells the story (M. L. West, ed. and trans., *Greek Epic Fragments* [LCL, 2003], 244–47). For a graphic, bloody description of the maenads tearing Penthus limb from limb, see Theocritus, "The Bacchanals" (J. M. Edmonds, trans., *The Greek Bucolic Poets* [LCL], 325–29), who wrote in the reign of Ptolemy Philadelphus (270s BCE).

The crucifixion scene does catch my eye. Paul writes, "we proclaim Christ crucified!" (1 Cor 1:23; see 1:17–18.) Burkert observes that the new kings, the Ptolemies of Egypt and the Attalids of Pergamum, "appropriated the patronage of Dionysiac worship."[36] Diodorus' information suggests that this aspect of the Dionysian myth legitimates royal power disposing of opponents, e. g. according to 3 Macc 2:29–30, legitimates Ptolemy Philopator (221–204 BCE), it is said, forcing Jews to submit to Dionysian rites, offering "equal citizenship with the Alexandrians" as a reward.[37]

2. 2 Dirce and the city of Sicyon, a polis near Corinth

As Pausanias writes (II. 5.5–6; 6. 1–6; 10. 1–2, 4), Antiope, whom Zeus raped, was a daughter of the king of Thebes.[38] Euripides and Apollodorus (3.5.5) say she ran away to Epopeus in Sicyon, a city near Corinth. Her father died, after which his brother, Lycos, became king of Thebes. Lycos brought Antiope back to Thebes, where she was kept in confinement and mistreated by the king and his wife, Dirce. But one day her bonds untied themselves, and she found her sons, the sons of Zeus, who recognized her. Dirce had ordered them to tie Antiope to a bull, but in a typical tragic reversal, they tied Dirce herself to the bull. When she was dead, they threw her body into a spring that was then called by her name. One does not offend the sons of God or mistreat their mother, Zeus' beloved, even if one is a maenad.

There is a famous, large sculpture of Zethos and Amphion, Dirce and Antiope, with a bull, the Toro Farnese, now in the National Archaeological Museum in Naples (plate 7; Balch, *Roman Domestic Art* CD 128, 128a), a Roman copy of a statue commissioned by the kings of Pergamon. The sculptor did not represent the bull dragging Dirce, but the previous moment, when the young men are tying her to the bull, showing their strength and resolution, symbolically, the strength and resolution of the kings of Pergamon. Once again, we see the Dionysian ideology of kings who sponsored the cult of Dionysus.

The fresco of Dirce being executed[39] (plates 8–10) is in the same triclinium in Pompeii as the scene of maenads dismembering Penthus. Both the sculpture and

---

[36] W. Burkert, "Bacchic *Teletai* in the Hellenistic Age," in Carpenter and Faraone, *Masks of Dionysus*, 259–75 now in his *Kleine Schriften* III (cited n. 24) 120–36.

[37] Burkert, "Bacchic *Teletai*," 263 [*Kleine Schriften* III, 123], n. 24. Scholars debate the motif of "resistance"; see McGinty's "Index of Subjects" (263) under this rubric for various scholars' opinions. J. S. Tuman, *Communicating Terror: The Rhetorical Dimensions of Terrorism* (Thousand Oaks: Sage, 2003), distinguishes *terror from below* from *terror from above* (state terror), the latter of which Roman sponsors of amphitheater games were perpetrating.

[38] "Antiope," in *Euripides: Selected Fragmentary Plays*, (eds. C. Collard, M. J. Cropp and J. Gilbert; Chippenham: Antony Rowe, 2004), II, 259–329, and Balch, *Roman Domestic Art*, 128–31.

[39] Casa dei Vettii (VI 15,1; PPM V 531–33), triclinium n, south wall; Balch, *Roman Domestic Art*, 129, plate 7, CD 210, 210a. On the freedman owners of the house, see n. 27. Compare

Plate 7) Toro Farnese (3.7 m. high) from Caracalla Thermae, Rome, now in National Archaeological Museum, Naples, inventory 6002: Zethos and Amphion tie Dirce (with her Dionysiac thyrsus lying below her) to a bull, with their mother, Antiope (behind the bull, so not seen in this view), beloved of Zeus, standing nearby observing.

the fresco represent Dirce, herself a maenad, a follower of Dionysus, being killed. Not only those who resist Dionysus (Lycurgus and Penthus), but even his followers (Dirce) who offend the deity die. The scene is popular in Pompeii, being visually represented at least nine times.[40]

Dirce is also mentioned in 1 Clem 6. 1–2. Following the story of the martyrdom of Peter and Paul (chap. 5), the author continues:

> To these men who have conducted themselves in such a holy way there has been added a great multitude of the elect, who have set a superb example among us by the numerous torments and tortures they suffered because of jealousy. Women were persecuted as Danaids and *Dircae* and suffered terrifying and profane torments because of jealousy. But they confidently completed the race of faith, and though weak in body, they received a noble reward. (trans. Ehrman in LCL, my emphasis)

The scene was popular on the walls of Pompeii, and surely also in Rome, Corinth, and Sicyon (a city named in the myth), because the owners of those houses had seen "Dirce" dragged to death in the amphitheater.[41]

3. Comparison of Dionysian and Corinthian Christian enthusiasm

I comment first on the similarities between Bacchic frenzy and Christian charismatic experience, and in conclusion, on the differences. The Dionysian maenads' frenzy is not only visually represented in Pompeian frescoes, for example, in the frescoes of Penthus and Dirce being killed, but their ecstasy is also presented in significant texts. Strabo, who wrote under Augustus, has a digression (*Geography* 10. 3. 7–23) on the history and "theology" of Bacchic frenzy, "the Dionysiac and Orphic arts" (10. 3. 23), related especially to Cretan and Phrygian tradition (10. 3. 7), even though, he writes, "I am not in the least fond of myths" (10. 3. 22).[42]

---

three frescoes in F. Heger, LIMC 3. 2 (1986): 504–05. Merkelbach, *Die Hirten,* has a plate neither of the sculpture nor of any one of the nine frescoes of this subject in Pompeii and Herculaneum, which misrepresents the Roman Dionysus (compare n. 26 on Penthus). L. B. Joyce, "Dirce Disrobed," *Classical Antiquity* 20/2 (2001): 221–38.

[40] E. W. Leach, "The Punishment of Dirce: A Newly Discovered Painting in the Casa di Giulio Polibio and its Significance within the Visual Tradition," Mitteilungen des deutschen archäologischen Institutes, Römische Abteilung = Römische Mitteilungen 93 (1986): 157–82, plates 49–59, color plates 1–2, at p. 159, n. 7 lists examples. Recent excavators have discovered a ninth fresco: U. Pappalardo, "Nuove ricerche nella 'Villa Imperiale' a Pompei," 329–38 in *Nuove Ricerche Archeologiche a Pompei ed Ercolano* (eds. P. G. Guzzo and M. P. Guidobaldi; Studi della soprintendenza archeologica di Pompei 10; Naples: Electa, 2005) 337, plate 11.

[41] As argued by Coleman, "Fatal Charades," 72–73.

[42] There was a scholarly consensus that Dionysus was foreign, until his name was discovered in Linear B tablets (Later Minoan II). See McGinty, *Interpretation,* 225, n. 25 and Seaford,

Plate 8 above) Casa dei Vettii
(VI 15,1; PPM V 531–33),
triclinium n, south wall: Dirce,
wife of the king of Thebes,
being tied to a bull by Amphion
and Zethus, sons of Zeus, with
a Dionysiac thyrsus lying on the
ground below Dirce, as in the
Toro Farnese (in situ)

Plate 9 left) Casa di C. Iulius
Polybius (IX 13,1–3; PPM
X 257, 259), triclinium (EE),
continuous narrative of Dirce
among maenads, captured by
Amphion and Zethus; on the
right (not shown) an archaic
statue of Dionysus (in situ).
Further to the viewer's right
in the same fresco, the visual
representation in plate 10

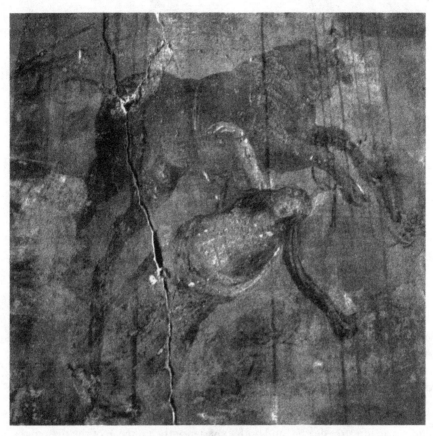

Plate 10) Casa di C. Iulius Polybius (IX 13,1–3, PPM X 261), bull dragging Dirce after she was captured by Amphion and Zethus; on the left (not shown) an archaic statue of Dionysus (in situ). This amphitheater scene is in Polybius' dining room.

Now this is common both to the Greeks and to the barbarians, to perform their sacred rites in connection with the relaxation of a festival, these rites being performed some-times with religious frenzy (*enthousiasmo*), sometimes without it; sometimes with music, sometimes not; and sometimes in secret (*mustikos*), sometimes openly (*phanero*) [...] In the first place, the relaxation draws the mind away from human occupations (*apo ton an-thropikon*) and turns the real mind (*ontos noun*) towards that which is divine; and secondly, the religious frenzy seems to afford a kind of divine inspiration (*epipneusin tina theian*) and to be very like that of the soothsayer [...]. For although it has been well said that human beings then act most like the gods when they are doing good to others, yet one might better say, when they are happy [...]. (10.3.9, trans. Jones in LCL)

Now most of the Greeks assigned to Dionysus, Apollo, Hecate, the Muses, and above all to Demeter, everything of an orgiastic (*to orgiastikon*) or Bacchic (*to bakchikon*) or choral nature, as well as the mystic element in initiations (*to peri tas teletas mustikon*); and they give the name "Iacchus" not only to Dionysus but also to the leader-in-chief of the mysteries (*ton archegeten ton musterion*), who is the genius of Demeter. And branch-bearing, choral dancing, and initiations (*teletai*) are common element in the worship of these gods. (10.3.10)[43]

Reading Strabo, the Corinthian Christians' "gifts" (*charismata*, 1 Cor 1:7; 7:7; 12:4, 9, 28, 30, 31; 2 Cor 1:11) or "spiritual persons" (*pneumatikoi*, e.g. 1 Cor 2:10–15; 3:1, 16; 12:1, 3–4, 7–11, 13; 14:1, 12, 14–16, 32) seem common, even typical, in Greek or "barbarian" worship. Both Strabo and Paul write of being in-breathed with spirit (Strabo 10.3.9; and Paul, e.g. 1 Cor 2:4, 10–15; 3:1, 16; 6:17, 19; 10:3–4; 12:1–4, 7–13; 14:1–2, 12–16; Rom 5:5; 8:9, 11, 16, 23, 26, etc.). Strabo mentions a "real mind" that turns toward the divine, while Paul contrasts pneumatic experience with the mind (Strabo 10.3.9; 1 Cor 14:14). Both comment on the relation of being possessed by the spirit to ethics, doing good to others (Strabo 10.3.9; 1 Cor 6:9–11, 17–18; 7:5; 8:7–13, etc.). Both anticipate life after death,[44] and both experience the presence of the divine, the vision of God, in the present. Clement of Alexandria plays on this common expectation and experience:

Then thou shalt have the vision of my God (*katopteuseis ton theon*; plate 11),[45] and shalt be initiated (*telesthese*) in those holy mysteries, and shalt taste the joys that are hidden away in heaven, preserved for me,

---

Dionysos, 15–16. Strabo does call them "foreign" (*xeninkon*), and says the Athenians were ridiculed by comic writers for being "hospitable to things foreign" (*philoxenountes*; Strabo 10.3.18).

[43] For other texts describing Dionysian rituals, see Herodotus, *History* IV.78–79; Pausanias, *Description* VIII.15 (the Eleusinian mysteries, including the priest "beating with rods the Folk Underground"); Plutarch, *Roman Questions* 112 (on ivy exciting madness; *Mor.* 291AB); Plutarch, *The Face on the Moon* (initiates' expectation mingled with confusion; *Mor.* 943CD); Plutarch, *Frag.* 178 (initiates wandering through darkness, terrorized, then experiencing new freedom; trans. F. H. Sandbach in LCL XV, 316–25).

[44] For example, Isocrates, *Panegyricus* 28–29; Plutarch, *Sayings of Spartans* 2–3 (Mor. 224EF) and *Consolation to his Wife* 10 (Mor. 611DE). C. P. Jones, "Towards a Chronology of Plutarch's Works," JRS (1966): 61–74 (71), dates the *Consolation* between CE 85 and 95.

Plate 11) Casa dei Ceii, Pompeii (I 6,15; PPM I 442–45), triclinium (e),
west wall, central zone, epiphany of Dionysus with a halo of light around his head (in situ)

"which neither ear hath heard nor have they entered into the heart" (1 Cor 2:9) of any
man
"And lo! Methinks I see a pair of suns, And a double Thebes" (Euripides, *Bacchants*
918–19)
said one who was reveling in frenzy through idols, drunk with sheer ignorance [...]
Come, thou frenzy-stricken one, not resting on thy wand, not wreathed with ivy! Cast
off thy headdress; cast off thy fawnskin; return to soberness. I will show thee the Word....
Therein revel no Maenads, sisters of "thunder-smitten" Semele, who are initiated in the
loathsome distribution of raw flesh, but the daughters of God, the beautiful lambs.... The
maidens ... swiftly they pursue the sacred band (*thiason*) [...]. Quit Thebes; fling away thy
prophecy and Bacchic revelry and be led by the hand to the truth [...]. O truly sacred
mysteries! O pure light! In the blaze of the torches I have a vision of heaven and of God
(*tous ouranous kai ton theon epopteusai*). I become holy by initiation. The Lord reveals the
mysteries [...]. (Clement of Alexandria, *Exhortation to the Greeks* 12, trans. G. W. Butter-
worth in LCL, pp. 252–57)[46]

Strabo's "enthusiasts" and Paul's "spiritual" Corinthians have not only the "spirit" in common, but also questions about the relation of the spirit to the mind,
and its relation to ethics; they also share the anticipation of life after death, while

---

[45] An epiphany of Dionysus is visually represented in the Casa dei Ceii (I 6,15; PPM
I 442–45), triclinium (e); Balch 17, plate 6, CD 84b. Compare 1 Cor 9:1; 2 Cor 12:1–9. Also
Diodorus 1. 25. 3, "manifesting her (Isis') very presence [...]."
[46] Clement is cited by Seaford, *Dionysos*, 260, who comments: "Clement had, of course,
profound knowledge of the pagan mysteries, and it is difficult to believe that he had not been
initiated into the mysteries of Dionysus."

hoping for a vision of God in the present. A further commonality is that ecstatic
religion typically expresses social/religious protest:

> The cult of Dionysus seems to have exercised a similar appeal not only for women but
> also for men of low social status. [...] He was essentially a god of the people, offering
> freedom and joy to all, including slaves as well as freemen excluded from the old lineage
> cults [...]. It seems that we have another of these peripheral cults involving spirits of
> foreign (here supposedly Thracian) origin which inflicted 'illness' on downtrodden men
> and women, and at the same time offered a means of escape and cure in the associated
> cathartic rituals.[47]

Some Greek city-states sanctioned maenadic activities, but still regarded such
feminine activity with suspicion, worship that might involve *hubris*. Paul too
writes, "not many of you were wise by human standards, not many were powerful, not many were of noble birth" (1 Cor 1:26). He recognized the similarity:
"You know that when you were pagans, you were enticed (*egesthe*) and led astray
(*apagomenoi*) to idols that could not speak." (1 Cor 12:2 [NRSV])

Here I turn to Otto's reading of Dionysus, assisted by McGinty's exposition.[48]

> At the most general level Otto interpreted Dionysos as the religious expression of the
> world in its primordial aspect [...], the universe in its most passionate and furious state,
> seen as it created and destroyed. Other deities presented other 'faces' of reality to man –
> loving, playful, ordering, etc. – but Dionysos expressed the beauty and horror inextri-
> cably tied to the process of Becoming. (McGinty 165)
>
> In this original unity all dualities – suffering and joy; life and death; etc. – were held
> together in a stormy chaos which preceded and underlay the emergence of discrete
> individuated forms [...] The world of Dionysos was the world of the primordial Femi-
> nine, nourishing and fostering, enraptured in the wonder of all life.... Yet, though
> motherly, it was also a world of madness, since the security of the routine world was
> abolished and everything was transformed [...] Reflecting this duality in his relation to
> men, Dionysos brought both joy and suffering. Many of his epithets expressed this
> contradiction, so that it was clear that the Greeks thought of him as both the most fearful
> and the most delightful of the gods [...] To a large extent Otto's analysis was an attempted
> vindication of Nietzsche's insights in *The Birth of Tragedy* [...] Nietzsche had emphasized
> the contradictory nature of Dionysos as both a cruel, brutal demon and a mild, gentle
> ruler. (McGinty, *Interpretation*, 166–68)[49]

---

[47] I. M. Lewis, "Strategies of Mystical Attack: Protest and its Containment," *Ecstatic Religion*
(New York: Routledge, 1989, 2nd ed.) 91. Compare Seaford, *Dionysos*, chap. 8: "psychology
and philosophy."

[48] McGinty, *Interpretation*, chap. 5, interpreting W. F. Otto, *Dionysus: Myth and Cult* (trans.
R. B. Palmer; Bloomington: Indiana University, 1965).

[49] For an evaluation and critique of Nietzsche, see McGinty, *Interpretation*; also H. Cancik,
"Die Geburt der Tragödie," *Nietzsches Antike: Vorlesungen* (Stuttgart: J. B. Metzler, 1995),
50–63 and H. Cancik and H. Cancik-Lindemaier, "Nietzsches 'Mysterienlehre'," *Philolog und
Kultfigur: Friedrich Nietzsche und seine Antike in Deutschland* (Stuttgart: J. B. Metzler, 1999),
35–49.

Plate 12) Casa di M. Lucretius Fronto (V 4,a; PPM III 1010−13), tablinum (7), south wall, central zone, triumphal procession of Dionysus (with wine cup) and Ariadne (in situ)

A final similarity is that both enjoy wine while celebrating life and joy. Pompeii has many visual representations of friends enjoying symposia/convivia with wine (plate 12),[50] also central in early Pauline house churches (1 Cor 10:3−4, 16; 11:21; compare John 2:1−11; 6:53−56).[51] Dionysus brought joy and suffering, life and death. The Roman Dionysus has been interpreted to emphasize exclusively life and beauty, but as this paper has shown, the Roman Dionysus was present at both poles of human experience, life and death.

---

[50] Dionysus' epiphany occurs in a *dining room* in the Casa dei Ceii (see plate 7). Compare Balch, *Roman Domestic Art*, 202−03, n. 58, 212, 223−24, 233, with CD 84b, 88, 252−252b, 300−01.

[51] Compare Rev 18. 3; 19:9, 17−18, and esp. 14:17−20, a reference to the "wine press of the wrath of God, [...] and blood flowed from the wine press, as high as a horse's bridle, for a distance of about two hundred miles." Here Christian apocalyptic too becomes bloodthirsty.

4. Summary and conclusions: comparisons and contrasts

The primary goal of this essay has been to play at reconstructing the Corinthians' sacred visual, domestic world, therefore, to argue that certain visual representations in Pompeii, a Roman colony whose domestic visual representations are still extant, would also have been seen in Corinth, another Roman colony founded about the same time, in the mid- to late-first century BCE. Both colonies also enjoyed amphitheater games from the first century BCE onwards.

The primary subject of this essay and the basis of comparison is Roman domestic art, assuming some similarity in the aesthetic of Italian and Greek colonies of Rome. Supporting this comparison are both literary texts, e. g. Dio Chrysostom, Pseudo-Julian, Diodorus, Strabo, Aristides, and Pausanias, and to a limited extent, the contemporary archaeology of Corinth. Dio's remarks and Pseudo-Julian's letter, both near Paul's time, show that fascination with bloody spectacles was common to both colonies. Pausanias mentions statues and frescoes in Corinth that are also important in Pompeii; contemporary archaeologists, when they find Roman art in Corinth, typically draw parallels to Pompeii and Ostia.

Roman domestic art reflects and interprets Dionysian myths, as many ancient authors narrated them. The mythical stories of Dionysus punishing those who "resist" him, Lycurgos and Penthus, are visually represented in Pompeian domestic art, as is the punishment of Dirce, one of his maenads, who mistreats Zeus' beloved, Antiope. Beyen describes these frescoes as "amphitheater art," and other Pompeian amphitheater art visually represents red blood flowing from animals and humans. Merkelbach is incorrect that Dionysus became simply a cult of the beautiful in the Roman world. Zanker similarly misinterprets Pompeii by characterizing the houses as spaces where occupants entered into myths primarily by viewing beautiful, nude, heterosexual gods and goddesses, especially Dionysus and Aphrodite, myths which intensified everyday life and banished unpleasantness.

Freud knew that human life is characterized by both sex and death, both of which are popularly visualized in Pompeian art. Nietzsche and Otto interpret Dionysus as a god of both life and death, and centuries after Euripides, both are still visually represented in Dionysian settings on Roman/Pompeian walls. These narratives of "resistance" and its consequences would have been seen on domestic walls in Corinth, Athens, and Sicyon, where death was also a popular spectacle.

Many similarities between Dionysian and Corinthian Christian enthusiasm are detailed above. The primary contrasts lie in the core stories, the myths, and therefore, the rituals of the two gods. Those who resist Dionysus are torn limb from limb, or crucified, or dragged to death by a bull. Bloody rituals embodying these stories are acted out on human bodies in amphitheaters. In contrast, Jesus willingly gives himself to be crucified (1 Cor 2:2; 11:23–25; 2 Cor 4:10, 11; 13:4), ritually embodied in a meal: "so then, my brothers and sisters, when you come together to eat, wait for one another. " (1 Cor 11:33 [NRSV])

Contrasts are evident not only between the myths and rituals of Dionysus and Pauline Corinthians, but also in their respective anthropologies. Those who owned domus and commissioned domestic visual representations of Penthus and Dirce in Corinth, as argued in the paper above, purchased other humans in order to enjoy the spectacle of their deaths in the theater:

The Athenians ran in crowds to the theatre beneath the Acropolis to witness human slaughter, and the passion for such sports was stronger there than it is in Corinth today; for they would buy for large sums adulterers and fornicators and burglars and cut-purses and kidnappers and such-like rabble (*ethne*), and then they took them and armed them and set them to fight with one another […] And thou, O Dionysus, dost thou after such blood-shed frequent their theatre (*theatron*)? (Philostratus, *Life of Apollonius* 4. 22, trans. Cony-beare in LCL)

Paul, however, verbally visualized himself as one of those sentenced to death as a spectacle, and he attempted to persuade the Corinthian believers that God values humans who are low and despised, those who are nothing:

For I think that God has exhibited (*epideixen*) us apostles as last of all, as though sentenced to death (*epithanatous*), because we have become a spectacle (*theatron*) to the world, to angels and to mortals (1 Cor 4: 9 [NRSV]).

Consider your own call, brothers and sisters: not many of you were wise by human standards, not many were powerful, not many were of noble birth. But God chose what is foolish in the world to shame the wise; God chose what is weak in the world to shame the strong; God chose what is low and despised (*exouthenemena*) in the world, things that are not (*ta me onta*), to reduce to nothing things that are, so that no one might boast in the presence of God (1 Cor 1: 26–29).

The Didactics of Images:
The Fig Tree in Mark 11:12–14 and 20–21[1]

Annette Weissenrieder

In ancient times, objects of art have a peculiar liveliness of their own, especially those artifacts which evoke an act of speech through the inscriptions provided with them. The philosopher and art historian Horst Bredekamp has recently presented an interpretation of this quality: the inscription has made the viewer move his lips, and lend his voice to the object. Image and speech act are connected with each other.[2] Thus one who sees the inscription "Roma" on ancient coins understands and voices its message: this object is affiliated to Rome. Visual images combined with written texts require that we interpret them as a comprehensive phenomenon. This interplay between image and speech act will be examined here in the image of the fig tree as represented in the gospel of Mark.

The fig tree occurs two times in the middle of Mark 11. In Mark 11:14, Jesus says to the fig tree that bore no fruit: "May no one ever eat fruit from you again." He then finds it dried up in Mark 11:20. It is interesting that Jesus and his disciples encounter the fig tree on their way to and from the Great Temple where he knocks down the tables of the moneychangers which did business in order to change money for the taxpayers and whose coins were spilled on the ground.

At the temple in Jerusalem the tax levied on Jews was probably a half shekel. These coins were the only money accepted by the temple but probably were not in everyday commerce. The silver shekel and half-shekel of "Tyre" have been minted from around 126 B.C.E. until 57 C.E. The coinage of "Tyre" was debased under Roman control. It is interesting that the coins during the time of Herod's the Great reign maintained the silver purity the temple tax required but were of cruder fabric and style. These shekels most probably were not blank but have on the obverse a head e.g. of Melgarth with a knotted wreath around his neck, on the reverse often the inscription ΤΥΡΟΥ ΙΕΡΑΣ ΚΑΙ ΑΣΥΛΟΥ (of Tyre

---

[1] My heartfelt gratitude goes to my colleagues at the Graduate Theological Union, Annette Schellenberg and Rossitza Schroeder [Director of the Centre of Art and Religion] for the opportunity of critically discussing the essay.
[2] H. Bredekamp, "Theorie des Bildaktes," unpubl. paper; Gadamer-Professur at the University of Heidelberg 2005.

Silver shekel, RPC I 4664, obverse laureate head of Melqarth right;
reverse ΤΥΡΟΥ ΙΕΡΑΣ ΚΑΙ ΑΣΥΛΟΥ, eagle left, palm frond behind, ΡΞ
(year 160 = 34/35 C.E.) and club left, P monogram right © E. Lang.

the holy and inviolable) and the letters **KP** or **KAP** to the right next to an eagle
which might be the abbreviation for ΚΑΙΣΑΡ, *Caesar*.

Coins are one of the oldest modes of communication. In antiquity they are
one of the few media through which all subjects could be reached by the
potentate.[3] When we consider that only perhaps 10% of the female and male
citizens in the Roman Empire could read,[4] we can appreciate the significance of
coins as media for distributing genuine, concerted propaganda.[5]

Therefore, we are confronted in the gospel of Mark with a complicated
image program. The fig tree is the hermeneutical key to the understanding of
this image program, because it acts as a connector between the different scenes.

---

[3] It is uncertain whether the emperor conveys praise of himself, or if other people simply
express this about him. One thing is for certain: in Rome until the reign of Augustus, the
Tresviri had been responsible for the origin of the coins. In this sense, they had a direct
influence on the issuancing of coinage. With the reign of Augustus, the right of coinage lay in
the hands of the emperor, or rather with the staff of his mint. It is perhaps possible to draw some
general conclusions regarding propaganda: while the imperial mint praises the emperor, the
general public is also expected to do this analogously. It is possible that the public is therefore
simply demonstrating a psychological reflex to honour the emperor that has as its origin the
propaganda of the imperial mint. The minting of coinage can thus be seen directly to reflect
imperial political programs. Cf. M. Bergmann, *Die Strahlen der Herrscher: Theomorphes Herr-
scherbild und politische Symbolik im Hellenismus und in der römischen Kaiserzeit* (Mainz: Verlag
Philipp von Zabern, 1998), 91ff.

[4] W. V. Harris, *Ancient Literacy* (Cambridge MA: Harvard University Press,1989), 158f.
Catherine Heszer in this volume mentions that only perhaps 3% of the female and male citizens
in the Roman Empire could read.

[5] Cf. A. H. M. Jones, *Essays in Roman Coinage, presented to H. Mattingly* (Oxford: Oxford
University Press 1965), 13ff. The term 'propaganda" regarding coins is not without contro-
versy. Cf. A. Burnett, "The Iconography of Roman Coin Types in the Third Century B. C.,"
NC 146 (1986): 75; A. Wallace-Hadrill, "Image and Authority in the Coinage of Augustus,"
JRS 76 (1986): 66–87 and B. Levick, "Propaganda and the Imperial coinage," *Antichthon* 16
(1982): 105–107.

Rhetorically, it is presupposed by the author of the gospel of Mark that his contemporary audience would have immediately understood the meaning of the images of the fig tree. For us today the images are strange. They are no longer embedded in our sphere of knowledge. Generally interpretation of the image takes one of two approaches: The fig tree is either understood *literally*, in which case the image reflects the actual landscape of Palestine, or it is understood *symbolically* (or *intertextually*), so that we must determine its meaning from the stock of images in the traditions available at that time.

In principle the *literal interpretation* is possible. Along with olive trees there were fig trees in the countryside of Palestine and Syria. Thus the didactics of the images of the fig tree in Mark 11, as numerous scholars since Jülicher suggest, are oriented toward the *obvious* and *simple rural world of images* drawn from the realities of the land.[6]

Thus, some scholars presume that the tree in question was a winter fig that does not ripen until spring.[7] In this way they attempt to deal with the problem that otherwise it would have been completely senseless for Jesus to have looked for figs to be in season. Why is he looking for figs out of season? A second

---

[6] A. Jülicher, *Die Gleichnisreden Jesu I*, (Tübingen: Mohr Siebeck, 1920; repr. Darmstadt: WBG 1969), 118. See also *Die Gleichnisreden Jesu 1899–1999: Beiträge zum Dialog mit Adolf Jülicher* (ed. U. Mell; Beih. ZNW 103; Berlin/New York: de Gruyter, 1999). D. Flusser, who interprets in his book *Die rabbinischen Gleichnisse und der Gleichniserzähler Jesus. 1. Teil: Das Wesen der Gleichnisse* (Bern/Frankfurt a. M.: Peter Lang, 1981), the image side of the parables as "pseudorealistisch" (p. 35): They only pretend to be grounded in every day life but they imply a traditional allegorical meaning. The parables are in this sense literary genres as artifical genres. David Stern carries Flusser's approach on; cf. D. Stern, "Jesus' Parables from the Perspective of Rabbinic Literature: The Example of the Wicked Husbandmen," *Parable and Story in Judaism and Christianity* (eds. C. Thoma and M. Wyschogrod; New York/Mahawah: Paulist Press 1989), 42–80; idem, "Rhetoric and Midrash: The Case of the Mashal," *Prooftexts* 1 (1981): 261–291; idem, *Parables in Midrash. Narrative and Exegesis in Rabbinic Literature* (Cambridge MA: Harvard University Press, 1991); idem, "Imitatio Hominis: Anthropomorphism and the Character(s) of God in Rabbinic Literature," *Prooftexts* 12 (1992): 151–174. Stern stresses that Jewish parables become established from a story with implied message and *nimshal* – the allegorical application. The rabbis reshape the midrash against the background of the realia. In this sense the *meshalim* are fictive and at the same time real stories. L. Schottroff, *The Parables of Jesus* (Minneapolis: Fortress Press, 2006) takes up the attempts of rabbinical exegesis and deepens this social-historically. See also the instructive articles by R. Zimmermann, "Formen und Gattungen als Medien der Jesus-Erinnerung. Zur Rückgewinnung der Diachronie in der Formgeschichte des Neuen Testaments," *Die Macht der Erinnerung* (eds. O. Fuchs and B. Janowski; JBTh 22/2007; Neukirchen-Vluyn: Neukirchener, 2008), 131–167; idem, "Gleichnisse als Medien der Jesuserinnerung. Die Historizität der Jesusparabeln im Horizont der Gedächtnisforschung," *Hermeneutik der Gleichnisse Jesu. Methodische Neuansätze zum Verstehen urchristlicher Parabeltexte* (ed. idem; WUNT 231; Tübingen: Mohr Siebeck, 2008), 87–121 and see also his essay in this volume.

[7] On this see for example E. Hirsch, *Die Frühgeschichte des Evangeliums I* (2nd ed.; Tübingen: Mohr Siebeck. 1951), 124f.; H. L. Strack and P. Billerbeck, *Kommentar zum Neuen Testament aus Talmud und Midrasch, vol. I* (Munich: C. H. Beck, 1922), 857.

interpretation links this analysis with the feast of booths, a time when one could indeed expect figs. This would point toward an interest in the temple as well as the relationship to the Gentiles. In the context of the feast of booths one interpreter sees the following symbolism: In Jesus the king comes into the city and the Lord comes into his temple.[8]

In my opinion both interpretations are unsatisfactory. In view of the comment, "For it was not time/season for figs," it is unlikely that the appearance of the "(withered) fig tree" had to do exclusively with the realities of the Palestinian environment. This comment makes Jesus' expectation appear unreasonable. The problem is that this simple rural world of images may not be oriented toward Judea and Syria but is oriented to our world today. Thus we have, for example, broad knowledge about the realities in Palestine: we hear plausible statements about vegetation in the Synoptic Gospels as information about the realities of the land, because we think we can transfer these into our own sphere of knowledge. The result is a failure to appreciate the force of metaphors for Mark 11. The question remains open, not least, why Jesus noticed the fig tree on the way to the temple, or to say this in another way: Why does the fig tree in Mark 11 occupy such a central role whereas it remains unmentioned or at least not so central in this context in the other Gospels. Are we dealing here with local color that was known only to the author of Mark's Gospel?

Hence again and again interpreters have searched for traditions which would offer a *intertextual or symbolic interpretation* of the withered fig tree. The most obvious possibility is the Old Testament background. The fig tree symbolizes Israel, which did not produce fruit and therefore lost all privileges as God's people. In contrast, faith in God is central. According to A. de Q. Robin the motif of the fig tree refers to Micah 7:1–6; following rabbinic usage the author of Mark could refer to an entire passage in scripture by citing only the introductory words: "Woe is me! For I have become like one who, after the summer fruit has been gathered, after the vintage has been gleaned, finds no cluster to eat; there is no first-ripe fig for which I hunger."[9] The early church then supposedly applied the story of the fig tree to faith, as Mark 11:22ff. describes. In this Robin sees a clue, that "from the very early period the full significance of our Lord's action was not appreciated."[10] This argument, however, is too hypothetical to be persuasive.

The majority of scholars draw on Jeremiah 7 and 8. Thus, J. W. Doeve draws a connection between the cleansing of the temple and the motif of the fig tree. According to him, the account of the fig tree simply is to be interpreted as the fulfillment of God's word in Jer 7:20, where it says, "My anger and my wrath

---

[8] Especially C. W. Smith, "No Time for Figs," *JBL* 79 (1960): 315–327, esp. 327.

[9] A. de Q. Robin, "The Cursing of the Fig Tree in Mark XI: A Hypothesis," *NTS* 8 (1961/62): 276–281, here 280.

[10] Robin, "Cursing of the Fig Tree," 280.

shall be poured out on this place, on human beings and animals, on the trees of the field and the fruit of the ground; it will burn and not be quenched."[11] Doeve sees a two-fold substantiation of his thesis: On one hand, the wrath of God against Jerusalem has already broken out, turning the curse into an eschatological fact. On the other, it is clear from the circumstances of the case (that it was not the time of figs) that the image is dealing with an eschatological curse. It is doubtful, however, whether Jer 7:20 was also interpreted eschatologically in Judaism.

Other scholars such as G. Münderlein[12] or H. Giesen[13] attempt to make the motif of the fig tree understandable on the basis of a series of Old Testament passages, in particular Jer 8:13ff. This passage is located in the context of Jeremiah's laments over the temple: "When I would gather them, says the Lord, there are no grapes on the vine, nor figs (σῦκα LXX) on the fig tree (pl. ἐν ταῖς συκαῖς LXX); even the leaves are withered."[14] The combination of motifs – the search in vain for figs and the withered fig tree together with explicit connection with the temple – strongly suggests an association with Jeremiah. Giesen even dared to take another step when he connected also the motif of hunger for figs with Jeremiah.[15]

But the linguistic agreements are less impressive than these scholars would have us believe. Thus in Mark 11:13 καὶ ἰδὼν συκῆν refers to ὁ ἰδὼν αὐτό, but the withering of the root of the tree, which in the Septuagint is described with κατερρύηκεν, is depicted by the verb ξηραίνω. This substitution is certainly not insignificant for interpretation, since it comes up in a special context.[16] I will return once more to this later.

So far we have seen that in the Jewish tradition or more precisely, the Old Testament tradition, the withered fig tree can be an image for God's judging action, which especially concerns the people of Jerusalem as a people and can be

---

[11] J. E. Doeve, "Purification du Temple et Desséchement du Figuier: Sur la Structure du 21eme Chapître de Matthieu et Paralléles (Marc XI. 1–XII. 12; Luc XIX. 28–XX. 19)," *NTS* 1 (1954/55): 297–308, esp. 303–304, 306.

[12] G. Münderlein, "Die Verfluchung des Feigenbaums," *NTS* 10 (1963/64): 89–104.

[13] H. Giesen, "Der verdorrte Feigenbaum – Eine symbolische Aussage? Zu Mk 11,12–14. 20f.," *Biblische Zeitschrift* 20 (1976): 95–111.

[14] According to W. R. Telford, *The Barren Temple and the Withered Tree: A Redaction-Critical Analysis of the Cursing of the Fig-Tree Pericope in Mark's Gospel and Its Relation to the Cleansing of the Temple Tradition* (JSNT Suppl. Ser. 1; Sheffield, England: JSOT Press, 1980) refers to B. Meg. 31b and B. Ta'an. 29a–30b where a day of fasting is described, which the destruction of the first temple is mourned. C. H. Dodd refers to the trove of sayings in Jeremiah, which is picked up in the destruction of Jerusalem in the New Testament, but especially in Mark (C. H. Dodd, *According to the Scriptures: The Sub-structure of New Testament Theology* [London: Nisbet, 1952], 86–87).

[15] Giesen, "Der verdorrte Feigenbaum," 104.

[16] One may argue that this substitution is insignificant if we take the conditions of oral tradition into consideration: Specific words would not be that important.

associated with the temple. Accordingly, should the "withered fig tree" be understood as an image of judgment which Mark 11 simply updated? If so, the following interpretation suggests itself: The disciples would thereby emerge as partly responsible for the catastrophe indicated by the symbolic withering of the fig tree. This is hardly conceivable since Mark explicitly emphasizes their hearing – ἀκούειν.

In what follows I will attempt to reconcile the "literal interpretation" with an "intertextual or symbolic interpretation" by utilizing an emblematic interpretation (*emblematische Interpretation*). Examination of material artifacts bearing images and texts will demonstrate that in Roman antiquity the fig tree is encountered in relation to foundation myths. Stemming from legends about Aeneas and about Romulus and Remus[17], these foundation myths were in a special way again taken up in the rule of Augustus. The association of the fig tree image with the founders of Rome is especially striking on coins, which are documented in the first century B. C. E. and the first century C. E. represent a particularly well defined tradition and which are documented as late as the time of Alexander Severus.

The fig tree can appear in combination with the founding fathers to stand for Rome, but can also by itself refer as a symbol to the foundation sagas. Thus fig trees became an emblem which appeared as the so-called "holy tree" in the Roman Forum at four locations. We can see the meaning of the fig tree for the 1st. century C. E. in a specific locale, as well as the background of the story in the legends about Rome's founding fathers. From this, the story of the withered fig tree might have been located in Rome rather than in Palestine and refer as a symbol to the founding fathers standing for Rome rather than to the Holy Temple of Jerusalem.

I. The didactics of visual images:
The fig tree as an emblem for the founding of Rome and its founding fathers

Lobed leaves like those of the fig leaf appealed to the Greek sense of beauty and later also to that of the Romans and from time immemorial were a favorite motif in pottery paintings and in small artifacts.

Romans had special appreciation for the fig tree[18]. One aspect of this connection is its convergence with persons and divinities of the time whose essential

---

[17] For the following I was inspired by J. G. Frazer, *The Golden Bough. A Study in Magic and Religion, vol. II* (London: McMullen 1910), 10, 318.

[18] T. P. Wiseman, *The Myths of Rome* (Exeter: University of Exeter Press, 2004), 52 points to the ten Sibyls, "Bronze statues of Sibyl and of Attus Navius stood at the Comitium. Close by was a sacred enclosure where the stone and razor were buried, and 'Navius' fig tree', evidence of another of his miracles, was carefully preserved as a guarantee of the freedom of the Roman People."

Fig Leaf, Kameiros, Rhodes, ca. 500 B.C. © A. Weissenrieder

characteristics were associated with the fig tree. First, the fig tree teams up with Romulus and Remus as suckling infants in relation to the founding of the city and with Roma, the goddess of the city Rome.[19] It also teams up, however, with the adult Romulus, who entered into the history of the Roman Empire as a war hero. The fig tree became the "holy tree" representing the founding father of Rome, namely, Romulus, who was later updated in the person of Augustus. In addition, the fig tree was also an (important) feature of the second founding story of Rome, the Aeneas myth. The fig tree together with the twins was portrayed on coins, cameos, in paintings, and reliefs and played a fundamental role at four central locations in the *Forum Romanum*.

1. 1 The Prototype: The Portrayal of the Fig tree and the Foundation of the City of Rome

It may be a trivial observation that since the second century B. C. E. the entire Mediterranean world was part of the history of an empire ruled from Rome, the extent of which was considerably extended by Pompey, Caesar, Augustus, and finally Trajan. And by the middle of the first century C. E. the city of Rome has become the political and social center of the empire. So it is no wonder that anyone even partially involved in domestic political situations, situations which culminated both in excesses like civil wars and in simultaneous successes in external politics, reflected on the supposed founding figures of the city. The city did not lack founders. No less than five individual founding personalities are known to us. The most important founding figure is Romulus.[20] His images was

---

[19] D. C. Lopez, *Apostle to the Conquered: Reimagining Paul's Mission* (Minneapolis: Fortress, 2008) tries to relate the topic of "nation"–*gens* with the myth of Romulus and Remus; see also the article of H. O. Maier, "Barbarians, Scythians and Imperial Iconography in the Epistle to the Colossians," *Picturing the New Testament: Studies in Ancient Visual Images* (eds. A. Weissenrieder, F. Wendt and P. v. Gemünden; Tübingen: Mohr Siebeck, 2005), 385–407.

[20] Livius 1. 3. 10–4. 3: "To Numitor, the elder, Procas bequested the ancient kingship of the Silvian nation. Yet, violence proved more potent than a father's wishes or respect for seniority. Amulius beat his brother and ruled. Adding crime to crime: he killed his brother's male

especially vigorously utilized in the political propaganda of Augustus and his immediate successors.

So from the middle of the fourth century or the beginning of the third century B. C. E. in writing and images we encounter the twins Romulus and Remus under the fig tree, the *ficus ruminalis*, sitting as they are suckled by the mother wolf Roma.[21] This constellation of motifs is especially frequently documented for us on coins.[22]

---

offspring, and Rhea Silvia, his brother's daughter, he appointed a Vestal under pretense of honoring her, and by consigning her to perpetual virginity, deprived her of the hope of children. But the fates were resolved, as I suppose, upon the founding of this great city, and the beginning of the mightiest of empires, second to that of gods. The Vestal was forced, and having given birth to twin sons, named Mars as the father of her doubtful offspring, whether actually so believing, or because it seemed less wrong if a god were the author of her fault." We hear the story differently from Dionysius 1.77. 1f.: "In the fourth year after this, Ilia, upon going into a temple grove for Mars to get some pure water that might be used for sacrifices, was forced by someone in the temple precinct. Some have the opinion that one of the suitors of the girl came, loving the slave girl; others that it was Amulius himself, and that, since his purpose was to destroy her as much as to sate his desire, he had arrayed himself in as much armor as would render him most terrible to see and that he also kept his features disguised as safely as possible. But most writers relate a fabulous story to the effect that it was an image of the god, whose place it was, many others even add that the suffering was accompanied by divine works, including the sudden disappearance of the sun and a darkness spread over the sky, and that the appearance of the image was more wondrous than that of men according to stature and beauty. They say that the violator, comforting the pain, out of which it became clear that he was a god, said to the girl to never mourn for her suffering, for the communication of marriage made her toward the divinity who entered the place, and would be born to her out of the violation two infant boys far excelling men in virtue and the arts of war. And having said these things he was enveloped in a cloud and, being lifted away from earth, went up though air."

[21] Theodor Mommsen [*Gesammelte Schriften* V, Berlin: Weidmannsche Buchhandlung, 1908] writes on the she-wolf: "Die Wölfin vom Capitol ist als Wahrzeichen Roms mit einer solchen Bedeutungsintensität ausgestattet, wie man dies von keinem anderen Wahrzeichen der Stadt sagen kann. Weder die attische Eule noch der Berliner Bär sind im Bewußtsein der Menschen so sehr das Symbol dieser Städte, wie die Bronzestatue im Konservatorenpalast es für Rom geworden ist. Die Bedingung hierfür ist zunächst die hohe schöpferische Qualität der Bronzeplastik. [...] Als entscheidendes Element kam aber die Wirkung des Mythos hinzu, der sich um das Bildwerk rankt." See also *Social Struggles in Archaic Rome* (ed. K. A. Raaflaub; Oxford: Blackwell, 2005); idem, "Born to be Wolves? Origins of Roman Imperialism," in *Transitions to Empire* (eds. R. W. Wallace and E. M. Harris; Norman, Okla.: University of Oklahoma Press, 1996), 273–314; idem, "Epic and History," *The Blackwell Companion to Ancient Epic* (ed. J. M. Foley; Oxford: Blackwell Publishing, 2005), 55–70; J. Vansina, *Oral Tradition as History* (Madison: University of Wisconsin Press, 1985); J. von Ungern-Sternberg, "Romulus Bilder: Die Begründung der Republik im Mythos," *Mythen in mythenloser Gesellschaft, Das Paradigma Roms* (ed. J. Graf; Stuttgart/ Leipzig: Teubner, 1993), 88–127; *Vergangenheit in mündlicher Überlieferung* (eds. idem and H. J. Reinau; Colloquium Rauricum; Stuttgart: Teubner, 1988), and T. P. Wiseman, *Remus* (Cambridge: Cambridge University Press, 1995).

[22] See e. g. H. C. Grueber, *Coins of the Roman Republic in the British Museum*, 3 vols. (London: British Museum, 1910; repr. London: British Museum, 1970), vol. 1,145,1; 284, 562; 514–517; 926–927; 3208–3209; 4018; 4023; H. Mattingly and R. A. G. Carson, *Coins of the*

Denarius of Sestio Pompeio Festulo, 135–126 B.C.; RRC 235/1; ©ANS[23] 1999.13.1

Also the prevalence of statues or bas reliefs of the mother wolf with the children positioned under a fig tree gives us a notion of the familiarity with this story. The combination of the nursing mother wolf, rescued twins, and the fig tree is so prominent that all subsequent combinations of these images evoke the same idea. This holds to a special degree also for the fig tree, which in the first century B. C. E. had impacted the *Forum Romanum* and its surroundings.

The nourishing aspect stands at the center of this imagistic tradition and is represented visually by the mother wolf and the fig tree. The naming of the fig tree as *ficus Ruminalis* is etymologically connected with *Ruminalis* or *rumis*, which stands for the female breast,[24] or with the toponymic connection with the

---

Roman Empire in the British Museum, 6 vols. (London: British Museum, 1932–1962; repr. London: British Museum, 1962), II, 223–224; III, LXXIV, 9; E. A. Sydenham, *The Coinage of the Roman Republic* (New York: American Numismatic Society, 1976), 95, table 14; 297, b–d; 530; 781a table 22; 965; M. H. Crawford, *Roman Republican Coinage,* 2 vols. (Cambridge: Cambridge University Press, 1974), 20,1; 21,2; 183,1; 183,3–4; 235, table XXXVI,1; 388,1a,1b table XLIX,10 e11; 472,2; H. Mattingly, E. A. Sydenham, C. H. V. Sutherland, R. A. G. Carson, *The Roman Imperial Coinage,* 10 vols. (London: British Museum, 1923–1994), II, 193, table XIII, 249; II, 194 table I,12; III, 649; III, 734; IV, 15 table 6,9; VII, Tessalonica 187,229; VII, Cizico, 71; VII, Roma 354; R. A. G. Carson, *Coins of the Roman Empire* (London and New York: Routledge, 1990), table 41, 607; L. Breglia, *La prima fase della coniazione romana dell'argento* (Roma: P&P Santamaria, 1952); R. Thompsen, *Early Roman Coinage: A Study of Chronology,* 3 vols. (Copenhagen: Nationalmuseets Skrifter, 1957–1961; repr. vol. 1 1974), 50,4, p. 51, fig. 7, p. 101.

[23] See e.g. Eu. La Rocca, "La memoria delle origini: le immagini della lupa con I gemilli in età romana," *La Lupa Capitolina di Claudio Parisi Presicce* (eds. Eu. La Rocca and A. Mura Sommella et al.; Roma and Milano: Elemond Editiori Associati, 2000), 21–33.

[24] At this point is to be expelled to the goddess "Rumina" who is often connected with the fig tree and the tradition around Romulus and Remus. Cf. also Ph. C. Robert, "Art. Rumina," *DNP online,* Brill, 2009.

Denarius of Nero; Roma with a Victory in her hand; On the bottom:
Romulus and Remus and a Fig-Leaf © ANS 1819.24.1

Etruscan *Rum*, that is, the goddess Roma.[25] Thus in the veneration of the fig tree
the story of the saving of the twins and the story of the goddess Roma are put
together. The connection between the city of Rome and its legendary founder
is made apparent on coins on which a leaf of the fig tree is represented on the
reverse together with the she-wolf, Romulus and Remus and Roma.

Especially typical is of course the inscription on the verso of the coin: RO-
MA. With this title, accordingly, both the goddess as well as those in the engraved group with the fig tree are designated. Although a nourishing function is
attributed to the fig tree, it is striking that nowhere in the visual images are the
fruits of the tree also displayed.

Moreover, it is noteworthy that the cultic veneration of Roman might ex-
ternally relied more readily on Roma, whereas the veneration of the foundation
of Roman might internally was molded by Romulus and the fig tree.

Thus, numerous cults and monuments in honor of Rome which are dedicated to the goddess Roma are found in Greece. But also in Palestine, Syria, and
Caesarea coins were minted the Roman goddess adorning the obverse.

So far we have taken our bearings from images that point to Romulus the
child as the foundation figure. However, alongside of these, numerous images
are found depicting the adult Romulus, who like Mars, acts bellicose, erects the
holy walls around the city, and consequently strengthens the security of its
inhabitants and potently extends Roman imperial territory, until finally he was
deified by Mars as he was carried away and entered into the heaven of the gods as
Quirinius.

Caesar had already set himself the task of rehabilitating the myth of Romulus.
Of his successor Dio Cassius reports that the senators "wished to call him by
some distinctive title, and men were proposing one title and another and urging

---

[25] Cf. Ph. C. Robert, "Art. Rumina," *DNP online*.

Belvedere Altar, Vatican Museum: apotheosis © DAIR 75.1289

its selection, [Octavian] was exceedingly desirous of being called Romulus [...]".[26] Moreover, Suetonius calls him the second founder of the city of Rome and of the Roman Empire.[27]

1. 2 The Fig tree as a Cultural Commemoration of Rome's Founding Fathers

Besides images of the fig tree, numerous ancient textual sources are to be found with partially perplexing descriptions of multiple fig trees. Four different fig trees, which were positioned almost exclusively in central locations in the *Forum Romanum* and which played a central role in the cultic observances of the inhabitants are mentioned.

We know from Pliny that one fig tree was located at first in front of the temple of Saturn, but then was transplanted, since the meaning of the fig tree was brought into question by proximity to the statue of Silvanus and vice versa.[28] Pliny lists a second fig tree together with an olive tree and a grape vine near the so-called *lacus Curtius*. The tree stood before the temple of the god

---

[26] Dio Cass. 53. 16. 7–8 (LCL E. Cary).
[27] Suet. Aug. 7; see also Florus 2. 34.
[28] Plinius *HN* 15. 20. 77.

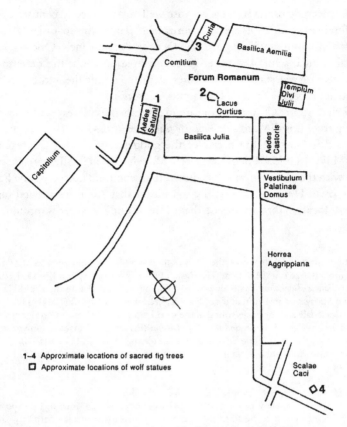

Map of the Forum show the four possible places, where sacred fig trees stood

Quirinus which represents the raptured Romulus. This tree was called *ficus Curtia*. [29] Finally, according to statements by Venius Flaccus, Pliny, and Tacitus[30] all concurring with one another, the third tree stood in the *Comitium*. Disagreement prevails in the sources (and not only at this place), whether this fig tree is the particular one that was to be revered for the rescue of the twins, the *ficus ruminalis*.[31] It is certain, however, that visual sources give us information

---

[29] Fest. 172.25ff.

[30] Tacitus Ann. 13.58.

[31] See e.g. Tacitus. Cf. F. Nichols, *The Roman Forum* (London: Longmans, 1877), 170f.; and also J. Small, *Cacus and Marsyas* (Princeton: Princeton University Press, 1982), 80; M. Hammond, "A Statue of Trajan Represented on the 'Anaglypha Traiani,'" *MAAR 21*: 137; G. De Sanctis, "La leggenda della lupa e dei gemelli," *RivFC* 38 (1910): 82. Flaccus knows the tree *Ficus navia* according to the augur Attus Navius, which is also mentioned in Cicero (*De div.* 1.17), Livius (1.36) and Dionysus (*Ant. Rom.* 3.71) although with their own connotations.

about the meaning of the fig tree, because well into the second century C. E. we find references to it.[32] Of special interest is certainly the so-called *Anaglypha Traiani*,[33] a monument which portrays a sacrifice in two panels. One displays the sacrificial animal, while the other gives information about the ceremony. In both panels a fig tree stands in the center, depicted beside the statue of Marsyas, who also appears on a coin of L. Marcius Censonius.[34]

All ancient sources known to me are in agreement with respect to the fourth sacred fig tree. It is the *ficus ruminalis* or *ficus Romularis* (Livy and Ovid), which was named for *rumis* – the breast of the goddess Rumina or the teat of the animal.[35] Livy,[36] Ovid,[37] Pliny,[38] Plutarch,[39] Servius,[40] and finally Varro[41] connect the tree with the place where the twins were rescued and nursed on the Palatine near Lupercal. Hence it is certainly significant that Augustus moved his residence to a location directly beside that of the founding father Romulus.

---

[32] It still remains unclear where the *Ficus curtia* was and the commentaries are discussing different models. See e. g. M. Grant, *The Roman Forum* (London: Spring Books, 1970), 113; P. Zanker, *Forum Augustum: das Bildprogramm* (Tübingen: Ernst Wasmuth, 1968), 25. A. Piganiol, "Le Marsyas de Paestum et le roi Faunus," *RA n. s.* 6, 1921/22 (1944): 118.

[33] The exact date and the background of the sacrifice are still unclear and a point of scholarly debate. M. Boatwright, *Hadrian and the City of Rome* (Princeton: Princeton University Press, 1987), 182–190; J. Carter, "The So-Called Balustrades of Trajan," *AJA* 14 (1910): 310–317; W. Seston, "Les 'Anaglypha Traiani' du Forum Romain et la politique d'Hadrian en 118," *MEFRA* 44 (1927): 154–183.

[34] RRC 363.

[35] Ch. Hünemörder, Art. "Feige," *NP*, Brill 2009 online.

[36] Livius 1. 4. 5: "So they made shift to discharge the king's command, by exposing the babes at the nearest point of the overflow, where the fig-tree Ruminalis – formerly, they say, called Romularis – now stands. – *ita, velut defuncti regis imperio, in proxima alluvie ubi nunc ficus Ruminalis est – Romularem vocatam ferunt – pueros exponunt.*"

[37] Ovid *Fast.* 2. 411ff.

[38] Plinius HN 15. 20. 77: "*Colitur ficus arbor in foro ipso ac comitio Romae nata sacra [...] ob memoriam eius qua nutrix Romuli ac Remi conditores imperii in Lupercali prima protexit, ruminalis appellate quoniam sub ea inventa est lupa infantibus praebens rumin (ita vocabant mammam) – miraculo ex aere iuxta dicato, tamquam comitum sponte transisset Atto Navio augurante.*"

[39] *Rom.* 4. 1 "Now there was a wild fig tree hard by, which they called Ruminalis, either from Romulus, as is generally thought, or because cud-chewing, or ruminating, animals spent the noon-tide there for the sake of the shade, or best of all, from the suckling of the babes there; for the ancient Romans called the teat "ruma," and a certain goddess, who is thought to preside over the rearing of young children, is still called Rumilia, in sacrificing to whom no wine is used, and libations of milk are poured over her victims"; *De fort. Rom.* 320 C–E.

[40] Servius *Ad Aen.* 8. 90: "*rumore secundo hoc est bona fama, cum neminem laederent: aut certe dicit eos ante venisse, quam fama nuntiaret venturos. aut 'rumore' pro 'Rumone' posuit; nam, ut supra diximus, Rumon dictus est: unde et ficus ruminalis, ad quam eiecti sunt Remus et Romulus. quae fuit ubi nunc est lupercal in circo: hac enim labebatur Tiberis, antequam Vertumno factis sacrificiis averteretur. quamvis ficum ruminalem alii a Romulo velint dictam, quasi Romularem, alii a lacte infantibus dato: nam pars gutturis ruma dicitur. ergo si fuerit 'Rumone secundo' favente fluvio intellegimus.*"

[41] Varro *L. L.* 5. 54.

1. 3 The founder of the city as the personification of the "Golden Age"

Romulus and Remus around the fig tree was, however, not the only one of the programmatic images in the *Forum Romanum*. It also appeared in connection with other representations as one of the programmatic images that could stand for the golden age. The trees designate the *societas festae pacis* (the common, fortunate peace, Pliny) or the *pax Romana*. These are the accomplishments of civilization that ultimately the Roman emperor had to guarantee. Internally, peaceful conditions are safeguarded by the assurance of income, the adoption of a Roman lifestyle, and the promotion of the general welfare, as Gnaeus Iulius Agricola is able to report.[42] At the same time, the external military expansion and success of the Roman Empire are the basis for the internal stability of the Empire.[43]

Architecturally, the group in the statuette is the center of the representational complex of the altar in the *campus martius*, the so-called *Ara Pacis*.

A small frieze portraying a festival procession is carved around the entire altar, likely depicting the entry of the emperor after his victories in the East; further reliefs of various personifications are found on it. At the left of the entrance steps on the west side Mars appears with Romulus and Remus and on the right stands Aeneas with the sacrifice. Both reliefs are connected with the fig tree. On the side toward the exit a representation of Roma is found as an allegory of bellicose Rome, whose shield once again displays the mother wolf with the twins and the allegory of peace in the image of a woman – symbolizing the earth goddess Telus and Venus combined in equal measure.

Thus one can assert: "The new divinities no longer embody mythical forms, but rather values and powers, which can only be described with attributes."[44] Consequently an attribute or an attitude evokes a complete agenda of images, like the numerous coins minted under Augustus that present the fig tree with the mother wolf and the twins.[45]

One could object that a fig tree simply represents a humble plant, too insignificant for the choice of this motif to bear such weight, and that it is particularly questionable whether the motif of the fig tree in the framework of foundation saga of Rome would have been familiar in Palestine. So it is essential to note that we can verify numerous finds of Roman coins bearing this complex of images in Palestine. Among them are coins with the twins under the fig tree being nursed by the mother wolf and some which portray the *Ara Pacis* as a symbol of peace

---

[42] Fest. 172. 25ff.

[43] Cf. Tac. *Agricola* 21.

[44] Zanker, *Augustus*, 178.

[45] J. B. Giard, *Bibliothèque Nationale: Catalogue des Monnaies de l'Empire Romain I* (Paris: Bibliotheque Nationale, 1976), number 920 = W. Niggeler, *Münzen und Medaillen Auktion* (Basel: Bank Leu, 1966), 2nd part number 1028.

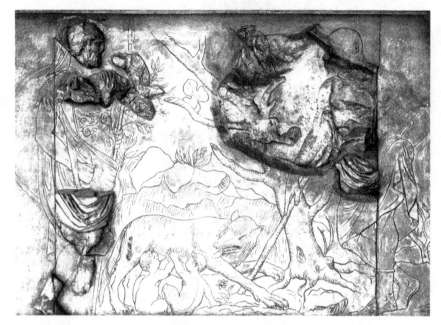

Ara Pacis © DAI Cologne

encompassing the world. In addition, the goddess Roma sitting on the throne or the representation of her bust appears on numerous coins. All of these have an inscription in common: Roma.

II. The historical classification of the withered fig tree

What does the motif of the fig tree associated with the suckling twins Romulus and Remus and with the goddess Roma on the coins and on the *Ara Pacis*, have to do with the withered fig tree in Mark 11? The connection would be provided if Jesus' saying about the fig tree, which produces no fruit and for that reason withers, alluded to Rome's foundation saga, in particular and Augustus's new version of the saga and its intensification by Claudius and Nero. Jesus' word on the cursing of the fig tree thus would point to a historical event.[46]

---

[46] See the collection of essays of *Jesus, the Voice, and the Text: Beyond the Oral and the Written Gospel* (ed. T. Thatcher; Waco/Texas: Baylor University Press, 2008): R. Rodriguez, *Structuring Early Christian Memory: Jesus in Tradition, Performance, and Text* (LNTS; London: T.&T. Clark, 2009); cf. also the collection of *Memory, Tradition, and Text. Uses of the Past in Early Christianity* (eds. A. Kirk and T. Thatcher; Semeia Studies 52; Atlanta, Ga.: SBL Press, 2005), *Performing the Gospel: Orality, Memory, and Mark. Essays Dedicated to W. Kelber* (eds.

The fig tree together with the portrayal of the twins Romulus and Remus could be associated with the emperor and the procurators, because, in material images, in the place where otherwise the bust of a potentate would appear, the metaphor of the tree and the twins now stands as an emblem of Rome, its political world power and its revival of the *aurea aetas* of the founding fathers.[47] As already indicated, with Augustus the iconographic expression also changes. The iconography now concentrates less on the mythological stories and much more on the attributive representation of values, which were inculcated in the population through directive messages. The legends on the coins referring to the potentates must have intensified this association. The founding of Rome by the founding father Romulus, symbolized by the holy fig tree, is strengthened and intensified by the new founding father Augustus.

Can we presume that the common people like the readers of the Gospel of Mark would have associated the emblems on the obverse and verso of the coins with the princes and potentates? In my opinion there can be no doubt about it.

There are four reasons for this: For one, it is noteworthy that as a rule there is no indication of the monetary value on the coins. The motifs on coins, therefore, communicated in such a way that one could do without the values! This then suggests further that the motifs became so familiar through being used over a long period of time. Coins admittedly were originally currency in the sense of bearing value and served as a means of exchange, or commodity, although they were not at first the primary mode of monetary interchange. However, from the beginning on – provided with inscription and image by the state – they served also for intentional transmission of news. For this reason coins are readily called "the newspaper of the little people" or also "*biblia pauperum*" in numismatic academic literature.[48] "In short the coin is consequently the state's metal money with the subsidiary function of an instrument for news and communication."[49] Moreover, the agenda of images on coins, as we have seen, is reinforced

---

R. A. Horsley et al.; Minneapolis, Minn: Fortress Press, 2006); O. Schwankl, "Recordati sunt. 'Erinnerungsarbeit' in den Evangelien," *"Für alle Zeiten zur Erinnerung"*. *Beiträge zu einer biblischen Gedächtniskultur* (eds. M. Theobald and Rudolf Hoppe; SBS 209; Stuttgart: Katholisches Bibelwerk, 2006), 53–94; an interesting critical contribution is prepared by G. Häfner, "Das Ende der Kriterien? Jesusforschung angesichts der geschichtstheoretischen Diskussion," in *Historiographie und fiktionales Erzählen. Zur Konstruktivität in Geschichtstheorie und Exegese* (eds. idem and K. Backhaus; BThSt 86; Neukirchen-Vluyn: Neukirchener, 2007), 97–130.

[47] An excellent contribution regarding the historical situation is prepared by J. J. Collins, "The Jewish World and the Coming of Rome," in *Symbiosis, Symbolism, and the Power of the Past: Canaan, Ancient Israel, and their Neighbours from the Late Bronze Age through Roman Palestine: Proceedings of the Centennial Symposium* (eds. W. G. Dever and S. Gitin; W. F. Albright Institute of Archaeological Research and American Schools of Oriental Research: Jerusalem, May 29/31, 2000, 2003), 352–361.

[48] R. Göbl, *Antike Numismatik. Bd. 1: Einführung Münzkunde, Münzgeschichte, Geldgeschichte, Methodenlehre. Praktischer Teil* (Munich: Battenberg Verlag, 1978), 23 (in italics).

[49] Göbl, *Antike Numismatik*, 29 (in italics).

by means of reliefs, cameos, altars but also by means of the *ficus Ruminalis* in the *Forum Romanum*. According to Zanker[50] these reliefs do not allow any doubt that they also could be read by the average viewer. They were an image for the world power Rome and the founding of this world power by the potent founding father Romulus, who was carried away to become the god Quirinius. They not only point back to the past but also to the present in that they show Augustus as the second Romulus who stabilized the land with respect to external politics and consolidated the golden age internally.

That this message about the identification of the fig tree with Rome could be understood by everyone is demonstrated especially by the fact that historians like Tacitus find it worth mentioning that even this holy *ficus Ruminalis* suddenly lost its leaves in the year 58 and so was cut down. Tacitus says: "In the same year, the tree in the Comitium, known as the Ruminalis, which eight hundred and thirty years earlier had sheltered the infancy of Remus and Romulus, through the death of its boughs and the withering of its stem, reached a stage of decrepitude which was regarded as a portent [...]. *Eodem anno ruminalem arborem in comitio, uae octingentos et triginta ante annos Remi Romulique infantiam texerat, mortuis ramalibus et, arescente trunco deminutam prodigii loco habitum est* [...]."[51] This was evidently perceived as a worrisome sign not only by the simple folk. Subsequently the fig tree in the Forum, the so-called *ficus Curtia* became the object of reverence and in this move then also received a change in name. Only in this way, in my opinion, is it possible to explain the confusion in the ancient sources about the identification of the true fig tree.

So it is finally not coincidental that, using a model that was already in circulation under Caligula, Nero had a new coin minted that emphasizes the special position of the fig tree as an emblem for Rome.

The Caligula Coin

The coin that Caligula had minted shows a team of four horses on the apex of the temple roof, in the middle stands Victoria, who holds a wreath in each hand, on her right we find Aeneas (also connected with a fig tree), Anchises, and Julius, and on her left Romulus as an adult holding a *spolia opima* and the twig of

---

[50] Zanker, *Augustus*, 179f.

[51] Tac. *Ann.* 13. 58 (LCL V). Pliny NH 15.77 "*Colitur ficus arbor in foro ipso ac comitio Romae nata, sacra fulguribus ibi conditis magisque ob memoriam eius quae, nutrix Romuli ac Remi, conditores imperii in Lupercali prima protexit, ruminalis appellata, quoniam sub ea inventa est lupa infantibus praebens rumim, (ita vocabant mammam), miraculo ex aere iuxta dicato, tamquam in comitium sponte transisset Atto Navio augurante. nec sine praesagio aliquo arescit rursusque cura sacerdotum seritur. fuit et ante Saturni aedem, urbis anno [. . .] sublata sacro a Vestalibus facto, cum Silvani simulacrum subverteret.*" Cf. also W. R. Telford, "More Fruit from the Withered Tree: Temple and Fig-Tree in Mark from a Graeco-Roman Perspective," *Templum Amicitiae. Essays on the Second Temple presented to Ernst Bammel. Horbury*, (Sheffield: JSOT, 1991), 264–304.

Caligula © ANS 1944.100.39338

a fig tree. The emphasis on Aeneas and Romulus can be seen in Forum statues in Carthage and Pompeii.[52] While Aeneas is shown as *pius* Aeneas, Romulus was the warrior-king and he is shown as Romulus *triumphans*. The propaganda embodied in Romulus as the Romulus *triumphans* highlighted Augustus', Caligula's, and later also Nero's own role with their triumphs.

The pediment of the Temple of Quirinus and the Nero Coin

Caligula's numismatic message is picked up by Nero and sharpened. A relief of a pediment of the Temple of Quirinus is very interesting: In the middle Augustus stands with Roma and Fortuna. Among the figures adorning the ornamental gable area, in the middle is seen Romulus with the fig tree and Mars Ultor, who was Romulus' adopted father. Now Nero draws the parallel between Augustus and the founder of the city Romulus. Here the role of the second founder of the city and of the deified human being falls to Augustus. In this context a coin from the year 58 is remarkable: Nero's head is pictured on the obverse. On the reverse a representation of Roma is found as an allegory of bellicose Rome and the allegory of peace and triumph in the image of a woman.

However, inasmuch as Nero associates this with the representation of his bust on the obverse, he makes one thing clear: the Roman Empire interprets representing the fig tree not as a bad omen, but relates it to the long positive tradition.

---

[52] P. Riis, "An Aeneas in the Ny Carlsberg Glyptotek?," *In Memoriam Otto J. Brendel* (ed. L. Bonfante, Mainz: von Zabern, 1976), 167; similar M. Grant, *The Six Main 'Aes' Coinages of Augustus* (Edinburgh: Edinburgh University Press, 1953), 104.

Obverse: NERO KLAV KAIS SEBA GER AVTO; Head Nero laur. r.;
reverse: Roma std. l. holding Victory, legend: ROME © ANS 1974.26.2116

The Jewish version of the fig tree and the she-wolf suckling Romulus and Remus

A noteworthy development can also be noted in Galilee, where evidence of the
Roman motif of the sacred fig tree and the suckling she-wolf has shown up not
only on coinage but also recently on another archaeological find. Two researchers, Richard A. Freund and Rami Arav, leaders of the Bethsaida Excavation
Project, have discovered the motif of the nursing she-wolf on a small basalt
originally in a first century C. E., Roman imperial cult temple built by Herod
Philip in honor of Livia Julia in Bethsaida across the Jordan from Chorazin,
where it is now in the gable of the synagogue.[53]

One could argue that the motif of the nursing animal does not correspond
precisely with the representations known to us; both the second suckling child
and the fig tree are missing in Freund and Arav's find. However, we know of
numerous images, among them a bronze fitting metal from the Roman-Ger-
manic Museum in Cologne, which represent the child in a manner consistent
with the image of the suckling in this gable. Besides, it is not at all unusual in the
funeral art (*Sepulkralkunst*) to depict only one nursing child, as for example the
grave gable which is to be seen in the Viennese Art-Historical museum, the
grave urn in the archaeological museum in Florence or also a lamp [Kestner-
museum, Hannover, Germany]. It is also common for the fig tree or aspects of

---

[53] Cf. E. R. Goodenough's work, *Jewish Symbols in the Greco–Roman Period*, vol. 1 (New
York: Pantheon Books, 1953), 194–195, it is Figure 492, from the Chorazin synagogue. He
did not think to associate it with Romulus and Remus. It is obviously a hybrid version made to
look like the classical view but with slight differences. He simply says: "Fig. 492 shows an
animal suckling her young."

Decorative piece with the suckling she-wolf and Romulus and framed
from decoration of a fig-leaf; © Richard A. Freund

the tree to be used as a decorative framework for the main motif of the nursing
she-wolf. The comparable images suggest that the nursing she-wolf on the
basalt refers to the story of Romulus and Remus as an image for Rome.

Almost all the decorative pieces that would fit in this Roman imperial cult
temple have been taken away, but among those that remain some parts of the
frieze have a design similar to the basalt. Freund and Arav have a scattered series
of such decorative pieces, and they can show that the rest were simply hauled
away for use in buildings in other places, such as the main synagogue gable of the
synagogue at Chorazin in the fourth century C.E. where this decorative piece
appears with the frame of figs and the fig leaf. This common practice, called
"spoilia," allowed for the instant production of decorations for a new building.

The two threads of motifs, the withering of the fig tree together with the
renaming of the *ficus Curtia* to *ficus Ruminalis* as it is documented for us by some
authors and the minting of the coin of Nero intersect in the year 58 C.E. This
dating offers us a concrete clue to the historical context of the passage about the
fig tree. The tradition of the fig tree in Rome can, therefore, just like the Old
Testament passages, convey the punishing action of God, but it has the advantage also of explaining the proximity of the fig tree to the temple in Mark.
Through it we can see the meaning of the fig tree for the 1st century C.E. in a
specific locale, as well as the background of the story in the legends about
Rome's founding fathers. From this, the story of the withered fig tree might
have been located in Rome rather than in Palestine.

III. Rome – The withered Fig tree?

We have seen that the fig tree appears on coins as well as in reliefs as an allegory
for the founding of Rome and for the founding figures of Romulus and Augus-

tus. But is it also obvious from the gospel of Mark that the fig tree refers to Rome and the founding fathers, and what repercussions do these political dimensions then have in connection with the miracle of the fig tree? Did the visual images on coins, and state reliefs have an effect on the Gospel text?

It is interesting to examine Mark's terminology for withering: ἐξηραμμένην ἐκ ῥιζῶν v. 20. Especially striking is the participle ἐξηραμμένην, because the Septuagint and also numerous ancient sources use rather the verb κατερρύηκεν for the withering of a plant. Now it is surely notable that except for the reference to this passage in the writings of the church fathers Gregory of Nyssa and Clement and the continuing historical explanations of the Christian historian Oribasius, the concept of withering is drawn mostly from medical sources. It is especially abundant in writings that investigate the way nourishment affects the human body, e. g. the Pseudohippocratic text *De Victu*[54] or Galen's *Locis affectis* or *De simplicium medicamentorum temperamentis ac facultatibus*.[55] There are also numerous references in the *Epitomae medicae libri septem* of Paul of Aegina.[56] Interestingly, these passages speak not of drying up leading to the death of the whole body, but rather of an occasional loss of liquid from a single organ or body limb. Thus *De mulieribus* cites the drying up of the milk in the breast of a breastfeeding mother and *De Victu I* mentions the "driest water [in the body], [...] because the fire has the moisture from the water, and the water the dryness from the fire"[57] and in the Epidemics we find the commentary "may the body dry up in the sickbed [...]."[58] According to these references the concept ξηραίνω marks not the complete decease of a body part, but a temporary state of the body which can be changed absolutely back. The New Testament also has reports of drying up in the body, namely with the healing of the "withered hand" on the Sabbath and the healing of the woman with the flow of blood. Therefore, the use of the concept ξηραίνω could point to the fact that Jesus appeals here to the tree as a human body and personifies it.

Nevertheless, this makes sense only if the fig tree is a personification also in connection with the entry into the temple in the 1ˢᵗ century C. E.

This suggestion is strengthened even more if we factor in verses 13 and 14 of Mark 11. After Jesus first ascertains that, contrary to his expectation, the fig tree bears nothing but leaves, he addresses the fig tree personally with the pronoun αὐτῇ, which is further reinforced by ἐκ σοῦ ("from you").

---

[54] CH *Vict* 21,7.
[55] Galen *Loc. Aff.* VIII,172 (K.); *Meth. Med.* X,410 (K.); *Simpl. Med. Temp. Ac Fac.* XII, 146. 147. 294 (K.); *Thrasyb. Med.* V,852 (K.); *usu part.* III, 471 (K.).
[56] Paulus *Epit.* VII. 3.1; VII. 3.8; VII. 3.12; VII. 3.16; VII. 3.20.
[57] CH *Vict. I* 35.
[58] CH *Epid.* VII, 222.

Could it be that the fig tree in Mark 11 does not refer to Jerusalem but rather to Rome personifying the city's founders and refounders – Romulus, Augustus, Caligula and most recently Nero?

First: As we have seen above, the argument of those who endeavor to make Israel the key to the understanding of the Markan passage, attempts to make the motif of the fig tree understandable from several Old Testament texts, chiefly from Jeremiah. As a central text, however, Jer 8:13ff. is referred to most, which is located in the context of Jeremiah's laments over the temple, so that a connection from there is already suggested: "When I would gather them, says the Lord, there are no grapes on the vine, nor figs (σῦκα LXX) on the fig tree (pl. ἐν ταῖς συκαῖς LXX); even the leaves are withered."[59] The combination of motifs – the search in vain for figs and the withered fig tree – actually suggests an association with Jeremiah. Giesen even dared to take another step when he connected the motif of hunger for figs with Jeremiah.

But the linguistic parallels, such as v. 13 καὶ ἰδὼν συκῆν referring to ὁ ἰδὼν αὐτό in Jeremiah, are weakened by Mark's use of the verb ξηραίνω for the withering of the root of the tree, where the Septuagint would use κατερρύηκεν. This contrast is certainly not insignificant for interpretation, as we have seen.

Second, it is noteworthy that in the gospel of Mark the insignia of the ruler are transferred to Jesus, in order to disqualify him as king of the Jews. These insignia – the scepter, the red robe, and the conqueror's garland – were transferred from the founding father Romulus to the Roman emperors following Caesar and Augustus. And it is finally also significant that these insignia are known to us only by means of visual images, rather than handed down by means of texts.[60] If, therefore, these insignia are referred to in the gospel of Mark, why then should there not also be a reference to Rome's founding father?

Third, it is certainly significant that church fathers such as Irenaeus name the place of origin for Mark's gospel as Rome. They might have had knowledge about the local color of the text that is accessible to us only with difficulty.

I come to the following conclusion: From my perspective we have to take other media – written and visual material into consideration in order get a better understanding of our written oral text. I tried to disclose here with the help of the fig tree three components of a didactics of images: The politization of a single image act, the embodiment of the image act found in nature like the fig tree at the Forum Romanum and the speech act of the story. I wanted to show

---

[59] Cf. Telford, *The Barren Temple and the Withered Tree* refers to B. Meg. 31b and B. Ta'an. 29a–30b. Dodd, *According to the Scriptures*, 86–87.

[60] Cf. A. Weissenrieder, "The Crown of Thorns: Iconographic Approaches and the New Testament," *Iconography and Biblical Studies. Proceedings of the Iconography Sessions at the Joint EABS/SBL Conference, 22–26 July 2007* (eds. I. de Hulster and R. Schmitt; Münster: Ugarit Verlag, 2010).

that a didactics of the visual image does not negate the language but provokes it
and vice versa: rather that the didactics of the textual images can be extended by
the medium of the visual image.

Part IV: Writing in the Shaping of New Genres

A "lying pen of the scribes" (Jer 8:8)?
Orality and Writing in the Formation of Prophetic Books

Annette Schellenberg

Asked about orality and writing in the Old Testament, scholars often quote Jer 8:8–9: "How can you say, 'We are wise, and the Torah of YHWH is with us,' when, in fact, the lying pen of the scribes has made it into a lie? The wise shall be put to shame, they shall be dismayed and taken; since they have rejected the word of the LORD, what wisdom is in them?" These verses are commonly understood to reflect criticism of the/a Torah in written form as opposed to the oral word of YHWH,[1] or, even more generally, a "protest against the authority of the written texts that were understood as subverting oral tradition and the authority of the prophet."[2] How, however, does such an interpretation of Jer 8:8–9 fit in with the many recent studies that maintain that there was no dichotomy between the oral and the written in ancient Israel?[3] And how is these

---

[1] Cf. R. P. Carroll, "Inscribing the Covenant: Writing and the Written in Jeremiah," *Understanding Poets and Prophets: Essays in Honour of George Wishart Anderson* (ed. A. G. Auld; JSOTSup 152; Sheffield: Sheffield Academic Press, 1993), 61–76; B. Duhm, *Das Buch Jeremia* (Kurzer Hand-Commentar zum Alten Testament 11; Tübingen/Leipzig: Mohr Siebeck, 1901), 88–90; M. A. Klopfenstein, *Die Lüge nach dem Alten Testament: Ihr Begriff, ihre Bedeutung und ihre Beurteilung* (Zürich/Frankfurt a. M.: Gotthelf-Verlag, 1964), 132–137; Ch. Maier, *Jeremia als Lehrer der Tora: Soziale Gebote des Deuteronomiums in Fortschreibungen des Jeremiabuches* (FRLANT 196; Vandenhoeck & Ruprecht: Göttingen, 2002), 302; K. Schmid, *Buchgestalten des Jeremiabuches: Untersuchungen zur Redaktions- und Rezeptionsgeschichte von Jer 30–33 im Kontext des Buches* (WMANT 72; Neukirchen-Vlyn: Neukirchener Verlag, 1996), 67f.; K. van der Toorn, "From the Mouth of the Prophet: The Literary Fixation of Jeremiah's Prophecies in the Context of the Ancient Near East," *Inspired Speech: Prophecy in the Ancient Near East*; Essays in Honor of H. B. Huffmon (eds. J. Kaltner and L. Stulman; Edinburgh: T&T Clark, 2004), 191–202, 199.

[2] W. M. Schniedewind, *How the Bible Became a Book: The Textualization of Ancient Israel* (Cambridge/New York: Cambridge University Press, 2004), 117.

[3] Cf. D. M. Carr, *Writing on the Tablet of the Heart: Origins of Scripture and Literature* (Oxford: University Press, 2005); S. Niditch, *Oral World and Written Word: Ancient Israelite Literature* (Library of Ancient Israel; Louisville: Westminster John Knox, 1996); Schniedewind, *How the Bible*; K. van der Toorn, *Scribal Culture and the Making of the Hebrew Bible* (Cambridge/London: Harvard University Press, 2007); *Die Textualisierung der Religion* (ed. J. Schaper; FAT 62; Tübingen: Mohr Siebeck, 2009); S. Talmon, "Oral Tradition and Written Transmission, or the Heard and the Seen Word in Judaism of the Second Temple Period," in *Jesus and the Oral Gospel Tradition* (ed. H. Wansbrough; JSOTSup 64; Sheffield: Sheffield Academic Press, 1991),

studies' catchword, the notion of "interplay" between orality and writing, relevant with respect to the relationship between (original) prophets and those "scribes" (prophetic editors)[4] responsible for the formation of the prophetic books?[5]

The fleeting nature of oral performances makes the question about orality in the past difficult. In the case of the OT, it is most likely that much of the narrative, legal, prophetic, cultic and wisdom material originated as oral traditions. However, all these traditions grew over a long period of time, so that attempts to reconstruct oral pre-stages of given texts are so hypothetical that most scholars do not pursue them anymore. Rather, OT scholars ask about "oral elements" in OT writings[6] or about the general role orality and writing played in the formation and use of OT texts. This last question is the one addressed in this article. While still very hypothetical, it is worth asking, not least because of its close relation with the question about the *Sitz im Leben* (setting in life) of given texts (genres).

Based on a comparison between ANE (Ancient Near Eastern) and OT prophetic texts and close observations mainly of the book of Jeremiah,[7] in the following I will argue that until late in the postexilic time, OT prophetic com-

---

121–158. See also the reviews by W. M. Schniedewind, "Orality and Literacy in Ancient Israel," *RelSRev* 26 (2000): 327–332; J. van Seters, "The Origins of the Hebrew Bible: Some New Answers to Old Questions," *JANER* 7/1 (2007): 87–108; 7/2 (2008): 219–237.

[4] In the following, the terms "original prophets" and "prophetic editors" are used to distinguish between the prophets who stood at the beginning of a prophetic book and their later editors, while at the same time indicating that the word "prophet" should not automatically be reserved for the former.

[5] On this question, cf. *Writings and Speech in Israelite and Ancient Near Eastern Prophecy* (eds. E. Ben Zvi and M. H. Floyd; SBL Symposium Series 10; Atlanta: SBL, 2000); E. W. Conrad, "Heard but not Seen: The Representation of 'Books' in the Old Testament," *JSOT* 54 (1992): 45–59; M. H. Floyd, "Prophecy and Writing in Habakkuk 2,1–5," *ZAW* 105 (1993): 462–481; R. Lessing, "Orality in the Prophets," *Concordia Journal* 29 (2003): 152–165; M. Nissinen, "How Prophecy became Literature," *SJOT* 19 (2005): 153–172; J. Schaper, "Exilic and Postexilic Prophecy and the Orality/Literacy Problem," *VT* 55 (2005): 324–342.

[6] Cf. R. C. Culley, "Orality and Writtenness in the Prophetic Texts," in *Writings and Speech*, 45–64; Niditch, *Oral World*, 8–24; for a critical evaluation of the endeavor to distinguish between oral and written style, cf. J. van Seters, "Prophetic Orality in the Context of the Ancient Near East: A Response to Culley, Crenshaw, and Davies," in *Writings and Speech*, 83–88.

[7] The book of Jeremiah provides a good starting point for the question of orality and writing at the different stages in the formation of prophetic books. It provides more references to the written than any other prophetic book and even contains a description of how it came into being and was used (Jer 36). Moreover, with the Hebrew and Greek text there are two written editions of the book preserved, which not only shows that the editing processes of prophetic books went on until a late time but also that the people behind these processes did not necessarily constitute a homogenous group (see below with n. 53). Finally, the Greek version of Lamentations and Baruch illustrate how the traditions about Jeremiah and Baruch continued to grow even in much later times.

positions were not officially linked to an institutional setting, but were in the hands of unofficial "followers". From this thesis and observations on the OT prophetic texts, one can hypothesize that those responsible for the formation of prophetic compositions were driven by a "prophetic impetus" themselves. They were involved in the composition of prophetic texts because they wanted the "word of YHWH" to be proclaimed to and understood by their contemporaries.

1. The two ends of the story: oral prophets and written prophetic books

Let us start with the original prophets. The OT clearly depicts them as "oral prophets": as men (and women) who raised their voices also in a literal sense in that they went out to the public and proclaimed their words orally. In the call narrative of Jeremiah, for example, one learns that Jeremiah is called by YHWH to "speak" (דבר pi.) everything he commands (cf. Jer 1:7), and it is Jeremiah's "mouth" (פי) in which God puts his words (cf. 1:9). The prophet is asked by God to "speak" (אמר) to the people and to "proclaim in the hearing of Jerusalem" (קרא + באזני ירושלם; cf. 2:2; similarly 11:6; 17:19f; 19:2; 26:2). Through the voice of Jeremiah the words of God are delivered orally, as are additional words from the prophet himself. Accordingly, these words are often introduced with a call to "hear". While the verb "to hear/listen" (שמע) often is synonymous with "to pay attention" and "to obey" in the book of Jeremiah and other OT writings, its basic meaning still reflects the understanding that words of God and humans were received through *hearing*, i. e. orally.

To be sure, the OT depiction of ancient Israelite prophets cannot simply be taken at face value. First, the memories and traditions about the prophets who later became "classical" were enriched massively over the course of time. Jeremiah's call narrative (Jer 1), for example, shows striking similarities with the call narrative of Moses (Exod 3–4) where the question of whether Moses is eloquent enough for his commission is an important element (cf. Exod 4:10). While there are good reasons to question the historicity of both these reports, these doubts do not diminish their informative value with regard to the general understanding of prophets mirrored in them: prophets are commissioned by God to proclaim God's words, and this proclamation normally takes place orally. A second *caveat* to be considered is that the classical OT prophets became classical only later. In their own times they were not classical but belonged to a minority among the prophets. From short remarks in the OT, for example, the frequent critical reference to "priests" and "prophets" together (see for example Isa 28:7; Jer 14:18; 23:11; Lam 2:20), and from comparisons with ANE data we know that the OT downplays more institutional prophets who were part of the court or temple personnel. According to their status, they would have proclaimed their words not on the streets but at the court and the sanctuaries. Moreover, passages like 1 Sam 19:18–24 indicate that there might have been prophets who primarily prophesied in nonverbal forms.

The qualifications of the OT picture of prophets, however, do not impair the general insight that, ordinarily, (original) prophets were involved with oral and not with written words. This is no surprise, given that ancient Israel was an "oral world". While "writing is not confined to just scribes per se [...] in the poetic and narrative worlds of the Hebrew Bible,"[8] and beginning with the 8th and 7th century BCE there was "a shift toward a broader literacy,"[9] the fact remains that the large majority of the population in ancient Israel was illiterate.[10] Hence, it was nothing more than normal that the prophets communicated orally as long as this was possible.[11]

The oral character of prophetic proclamation is the reason why only a fraction of ancient prophetic words withstood the test of time. The OT, for example, mentions many prophets, with or without name, from whom no or almost no words are remembered. Alongside them, however, there is a distinct group of ancient Israelite prophets whose destiny was different. Not only were their words (and actions)[12] remembered and written down, but also they were further cultivated and expanded by later generations. We know about this process mainly through its final result: written prophetic books, some of which are of impressive length. Evidently, prophecy had become a written phenomenon.[13] With the finalization and canonization of the Old Testament, prophetic books became sacred texts – texts for which it is crucial even today that they are proclaimed *orally*, both in Jewish and in Christian religious contexts.

---

[8] Carr, *Writing*, 118; for an overview on biblical references to writing and reading, cf. ibid., 116–122; Niditch, *Oral World*, 78–98.

[9] Schniedewind, "Orality," 331. Cf. D. W. Jamieson-Drake, *Scribes and Schools in Monarchic Judah: A Socio-Archaeological Approach* (JSOTSup 109; Sheffield: Sheffield Academic Press, 1991), passim; chart ibid., 216.

[10] Cf. Ben Zvi, "Introduction," in *Writings and Speech*, 1–29, 5; Carr, *Writing*, 122; van der Toorn, *Scribal Culture*, 10–11.

[11] The ANE texts that mention prophets confirm that prophets primarily communicated orally – even though these texts constitute a one-sided selection in that most of them concern prophets who did not have direct access to the addressees of the prophetic oracles.

[12] With the focus on orality and writing one must not forget that this category does not capture the whole range of prophetic activities. Rather, the communication process from God through the prophet to the people also included nonverbal forms (visions, symbolic actions).

[13] The change is reflected in Dan 9:2 (Daniel studies the *book* of Jeremiah), and Sir 38:34–39:3 (Ben Sira describes the wise as one who studies the Torah, the Prophets, and Wisdom). See also the changed characterization of prophets in Chronicles.

2. Ancient Near Eastern prophecy and history of research

Between the first utterances of prophets and the canonization of the (Latter) Prophets lies a long phase in which prophetic words were interpreted over and over again: in oral recollections and written versions of single oracles, in shorter and longer collections of several of these oracles with suitable introductions, in new editions with notable additions, and in interconnections with other prophetic compositions. This development of OT prophetic texts is unique in the world of the ANE.[14] From the entire ANE, so far only one other prophetic "book" was discovered: the "book" (ספר) of the seer Balaam, which survived in form of a plaster inscription in Deir 'Alla (Jordan). In all the other regions less close to ancient Israel nothing comparable was found. The Egyptian texts sometimes labeled as "prophecy"[15] differ from the OT ones in character (political propaganda; entertainment) and in that they cannot be traced back to oral prophets at all but were literary compositions from the very beginning.[16] The prophetic texts from ancient Mesopotamia[17] differ from the OT ones in that they remain close to the oral prophets and the situations that triggered a recording of their messages. With the exception of some Assyrian oracles that were copied together with other oracles on larger tablets (→tuppu), these texts remained untouched after having been written down originally.

The comparison of the prophetic texts from the OT with those from Mesopotamia shows that both the phenomenon of oral proclamations of prophetic words and the written record of some of these words was normal in the ANE. What is unusual and demands explanation is that the words of some of the ancient Israelite prophets were transmitted and interpreted over generations and in this process were transformed into longer prophetic compositions, recorded in writing.

---

[14] But cf. A. Lange, "Literary Prophecy and Oracle Collection: A Comparison between Judah and Greece in Persian Times," in Prophets, Prophecy, and Prophetic Texts in Second Temple Judaism (eds. M. H. Floyd and R. D. Haak; New York/London: T&T Clark, 2006), 248–275, 261–275, who points to Greek oracle collections as a parallel to the ancient Israelite phenomenon.

[15] Cf. N. Shupak, "Egyptian 'Prophecy' and Biblical Prophecy: Did the Phenomenon of Prophecy, in the Biblical sense, exist in Ancient Egypt?," Jaarbericht Ex Oriente Lux 31 (1989–1990): 5–40.

[16] On its own, this second argument is not decisive. With the changed understanding of OT prophecy and the recognition that many OT prophetic texts do not derive from original prophets but still are "prophetic" in character (see below, 6), the relationship of the Egyptian "prophetic" texts to OT prophecy needs further consideration.

[17] For the prophetic texts of ancient Mesopotamia cf. Prophets and Prophecy in the Ancient Near East (ed. M. Nissinen; SBLWAW 12; Atlanta: SBL, 2003); with a focus on the question of orality and writing, cf. K. van der Toorn, "From the Oral to the Written: The Case of Old Babylonian Prophecy," in Writings and Speech, 219–234; M. Nissinen, "Spoken, Written, Quoted, and Invented: Orality and Writtenness in Ancient Near Eastern Prophecy," in Writings and Speech, 235–271.

Based on the basic observation that the prophets themselves were not scribes but proclaimed their words orally, critical scholarship has been interested in the formation of prophetic books from the very beginning. With time, different aspects of the question were prioritized.[18] In a first phase, the focus was on the oral words of the prophets. Evaluating these words as more "authentic" and valuable than the later additions, scholars sought to identify them by the method of Form Criticism. In a second phase, the focus turned to the later additions, investigated as a literary phenomenon with the method of Redaction Criticism. The change in focus was combined with a change in the appraisal of those who "added" words. Originally they were seen as "students," praised for recording the authentic (oral) prophetic words but also disdained for the lesser quality of their own (written) additions. Later on, however, the same people were recognized as "editors" (*Redaktoren*), praised for comprehending the metahistorical character of prophetic words and disclosing the relevance of older words with learned and creative exegetical interpretations.[19] Especially in Europe the redaction-historical studies became more and more sophisticated, both regarding the number of redactional layers distinguished in single prophetic books and regarding the interconnections detected between different prophetic books.

What often got forgotten with such sophistication, however, were questions about the concrete circumstances in which the growth from oral prophetic words to written prophetic books took place. Who was responsible for the first collections and compositions of prophetic words? Who were those who carried on the process over many generations? What was their profession and place in society? How did they know about a prophet's words and the respective prophetic compositions? What were the processes that led to their new editions? And for whom were these new editions meant, how were they used? Bringing these and similar questions to the fore, recent studies about orality and writing in ancient Israel ushered in a new phase in the study of the formation of prophetic books.

Questions about orality and writing and the milieu in which the prophetic books were produced and used are much more than just technical. Rather, they are closely related with the question about the genre of prophetic compositions, their *Sitz im Leben* and purpose.[20] Were the first collections of prophetic oracles

---

[18] Cf. K. Schmid, "Klassische und nachklassische Deutungen der alttestamentlichen Prophetie," *ZNThG/JHMTh* 3 (1996): 225–250.

[19] Cf. O. H. Steck, *Die Prophetenbücher und ihr theologisches Zeugnis: Wege der Nachfrage und Fährten zur Antwort* (Tübingen: Mohr Siebeck, 1996).

[20] Cf. Ben Zvi, "Introduction," 9–12; E. Ben Zvi, "The Prophetic Book: A Key Form of Prophetic Literature," *The Changing Face of Form Criticism for the Twenty-First Century* (eds. M. A. Sweeney and idem; Grand Rapids, Mich./Cambridge: Eerdmans, 2003), 276–297; M. H. Floyd, "Basic Trends in the Form-Critical Study of Prophetic Texts," in *The Changing Face*, 298–311.

produced by the prophets themselves,[21] or by their followers as a reaction to the marginalization and rejection of the prophet? Were they the product of archivists, who more or less randomly copied together different oracles of one prophet?[22] Were prophetic books composed at the royal court, as support for the king's authority? Were they developed at schools, used as "course materials" for students? Were they written by priests, who saw themselves in line with the prophets from the past and idealized themselves accordingly? Or were they composed by scribes, who hid behind prophets from the past to express their criticisms?[23] Alternatives like these, all of which disputed among scholars, make clear that it is the very character of the OT Prophets that is in question.

There are several reasons for the multiplicity of theories produced in the scholarship. *First* and foremost, the data are sparse and much remains hypothetical. *Second*, most prophetic books grew over a long period of time, in which different phases need to be distinguished. *Third*, the character of ancient Israelite prophecy changed over the course of time. Preexilic prophecy is not the same as exilic and postexilic prophecy. In particular, in the context of the question about the setting in life of prophetic compositions we should note the phenomenon of later prophetic texts that echo and interpret not just older passages within the same composition – a practice that started early on in ancient Israel – but other writings, most often older prophetic compositions and also the Pentateuch and others. Apparently, in the postexilic time "prophecy" became more and more the domain of professional scribes (*Schriftgelehrte*) who studied not only the Torah but also older prophetic writings.[24] *Fourth*, in prior periods, in contrast to this last period before the canon of the *nebi'im* was closed, there are no indications that the *whole* prophetic corpus was studied in the *same* milieu. Most of the 15 Latter Prophets clearly constitute independent compositions with their own peculiar characteristics – another reason for the above mentioned proliferation of scholarly theses about the *Sitz im Leben* of prophetic literature.

---

[21] Cf. R. E. Clements, "The Prophet as an Author: The Case of the Isaiah Memoir," in *Writings and Speech*, 89–101; Lessing, "Orality," 164.

[22] Cf. the idea of Davies, "Pen or iron," 74–75.

[23] Cf. P. R. Davies, "The Audiences of Prophetic Scrolls: Some Suggestions," *Prophets and Paradigms: Essays in Honor of Gene M. Tucker* (ed. S. B. Reid; JSOTSup 229; Sheffield: Sheffield Academic Press, 1996), 48–62, 58.

[24] Later on, scribes from the very same circles promoted the Latter Prophets together with the Former Prophets as a second part of the canon. The bracket around the *nebi'im* (cf. Josh 1:7, 13; Mal 3:22) indicates that they understood the Prophets as interpreters of the Torah.

3. (Orality and) Writing in the world of prophets

Already at the level of the original prophets it is evident that the question of
orality and writing is related to the question about the *Sitz im Leben* of given
genres and the social location of the people behind respective texts. Above (2.)
we have seen that in the world of the ANE, prophets primarily proclaimed their
words orally, either to the public or to individuals like the king. At the same
time, however, we know from ANE as well as OT texts that it was not unusual
for prophets also to come into contact with writing. In the case of the ANE
prophecies, this has to do with the close ties between prophets and the royal
court. The king and his administration were interested in the (supportive) utterances of the prophets. Hence, some of these utterances were written down to
bridge a distance in space (i. e. to bring a prophetic message to a different
place),[25] and in rare cases to bridge a distance in time (i. e. to record a prophetic
message for the future).[26] Some documents from Mari, which mention that it
was the prophet himself who asked for a scribe in order to convey his message to
the king,[27] show how much the prophets were part of this institutional world.

That prophets could make use of writing is also documented in two ostraca
from Lachish that mention prophetic letters.[28] Writing is also referred to in all
three Major and some of the Minor Prophets from the OT. Here, the connection between writing and the *Sitz im Leben* of the respective compositions is less
obvious. Let us therefore start with an example, the book of Jeremiah, and a
careful inventory of all the references to writing found in it.[29]

The references to writing in Jeremiah can be grouped into four types: *(1)
Prophetic letters.* According to Jer 29, Jeremiah himself wrote such a letter. The
report about the circumstances and the copy of the letter itself, whether real or
invented, indicate when and how prophets utilized writing. In the case of
Jeremiah, it is the situation that requires a written form of communication.
Jeremiah wants to deliver a message from God to the Judeans in the Babylonian
exile but he cannot do so in person because he is far away in Jerusalem. Hence he
sends a "letter" (ספר) through Elasah and Gemariah, two kinsmen of his who

---

[25] So the prophetic letters from Mari and the single oracles on small tablets from Nineveh. It
is to be assumed that many such tablets with prophetic oracles did not come down to us,
because they were discarded after they had served their purpose (reached the addressee); cf.
Nissinen, *Prophets*, 98.

[26] So the oracles on the collection tablets from Nineveh. Cf. van der Toorn, "From the
Mouth," 191–194.

[27] Cf. Nissinen, *Prophets*, 45 (ARM 26 210); 74 (ARM 26 414).

[28] Cf. Nissinen, *Prophets*, 215 (Ostraca 3), 216–217 with n. b (Ostraca 6), 217–218 (Ostraca
16).

[29] Cf. Carr, *Writing*, 145–149; Carroll, "Inscribing," 61–76; Niditch, *Oral World*, 104–105;
P. J. Scalise, "Scrolling through Jeremiah: Written Documents as a Reader's Guide to the book
of Jeremiah," *RevExp* 101 (2004): 201–225; van der Toorn, "From the Mouth," 194–200.

went to Babylon on official political mission. The phenomenon of writing is not presented as something special in Jer 29. The chapter does not give details about who actually wrote the letter and how it was delivered to the people in Babylon. The letter itself reads exactly like oral proclamations of Jeremiah (and the written reports about them, respectively): Jeremiah "quotes" God verbally, i. e. delivers the message as words spoken by God in the first person. That God speaks is further stressed by the messenger's formula, which is employed several times to set smaller units apart (cf. 29:4, 8, 10, 16, 17, 21). The Judeans are addressed directly, i. e. in the second person, and are asked to "listen" (שמע) to the word of YHWH (cf. 29:20). With its "oral" style the letter shows how easy it is to imitate an oral communication in writing.[30] While oral and written communication each have their own characteristic features, elements of both these sets of features can be used both orally and in writing.[31] In Jer 29:24–32 another letter of a prophet is mentioned, this time not from Jeremiah to Babylon, but from the otherwise unknown prophet Shemaiah from Babylon.

(2) Scrolls with collections of Jeremiah's oracles. There are several other passages in Jeremiah that refer to written documents containing the prophetic words of Jeremiah (cf. 25:13; 30:2; 36:2, 28, 32; 45:1; 51:60). Some of these passages mention Baruch, son of Neriah, as the one who wrote down these words at Jeremiah's dictation (cf. Jer 36; 45:1). We will come back to these passages later (see below, 6.).

(3) Legal documents. Twice the book of Jeremiah mentions legal documents, namely a "decree of divorce" in 3:8 and a "deed of purchase" in 32:10–16 (cf. 32:44). Again, in neither of these passages is writing presented as something special. This is no surprise: legal processes required written documents early on and constituted one of the areas where ordinary people, including prophets, came into contact with the written. Not unlike today, the words written in such documents were effective whether or not the people involved could read and understand them. Writing was used in legal processes because it was associated with stability and permanence.

(4) Writing metaphors. The same notion of permanence is mirrored in four other passages in Jeremiah where writing is mentioned metaphorically – interestingly all four times in speeches of YHWH. In 17:1 God states that the sin of Israel is "written" (כתב) with an iron pen, "engraved" (חרש) with a diamond point on the tablet of the hearts. The reference to the sturdiness of the pen implies a deep imprint of the written (i. e. sin) and perhaps a hardness of the writing material (i. e. a stubborn heart,[32] or heart of stone[33]). Conversely, in

---

[30] Cf. Niditch, *Oral World*, 125–127.

[31] Helpful in this context is J. M. Foley's distinction between (1) oral performances, (2) voiced texts, (3) voices from the past, (4) written oral poems; cf. Foley's article in this volume.

[32] Cf. Jer 3:17; 5:23; 7:24; 9:13; 11:8; 13:10; 16:12; 18:12; 23:17; see also 4:4, 14; 17:1.

[33] Cf. Ezek 11:19; 36:26.

17:13 the instability of the writing material (i. e. ארץ, "ground") implies that that which is written on it (i. e. the Israelites) will not endure either. In 22:30 God commands to "write" (כתב) Coniah (Jehoiachin) down as one who will not have successors on his throne. Once written down, the decision cannot be reversed anymore. Most famous, finally, is 31:33, where YHWH announces a command to "inscribe" (כתב) his Torah on the Israelites' hearts. We will come back to this passage at the end (7.). For now it is important to recognize that while the writing metaphor is used only in 31:33 to convey a positive message, the metaphor itself has positive connotations in all four instances.

Similar references to writing can be found in the book of Isaiah (cf. 4:3; 8:1; 10:1, 19; 29:11–12, 18; 30:8; 37:14; 39:1; 44:5; 50:1; 65:6), Ezekiel (cf. 2:8–3:3; 13:9; 24:2; 37:16, 20; 43:11), and some of the Minor Prophets (cf. Hos 8:12; Hab 2:2; Zech 5:1; Mal 3:16).[34] The analysis of these references is difficult as there is always the question of how much they mirror the world of the original prophets and how much they mirror the world of their editors. One has to reckon with the possibility that the latter depicted the former "in their own image,"[35] to adopt the phrase of Ben Zvi. However, difficult as it is to decide to what extent the "pen of the scribes" was "lying" or, better, "self-mirroring", it is still noteworthy that according to the picture given in the OT most of the original prophets were well educated and had close ties to the political and religious establishment.[36] Within this picture, which is closer to the reality of the original prophets than the romantic idea of charismatic prophets, some interaction with the world of writing is only to be expected.[37] In the case of the ANE prophets, such interactions of prophets with writing were enabled by an official

---

[34] On the references to writing in the Lachish letters and the OT Prophets in general, cf. van der Toorn, *Scribal Culture*, 178–188; on the role of writing in Ezekiel cf. E. F. Davis, *Swallowing the Scroll: Textuality and Dynamics of Discourse in Ezekiel's Prophecy* (Bible and Literature Series 21; Sheffield: Sheffield Press, 1989); J. Schaper, "The Death of the Prophet: The Transition from the Spoken to the Written Word of God in the Book of Ezekiel," *Prophets, Prophecy, and Prophetic Texts*, 63–79; B. Seidel, "Ezechiel und die zu vermutenden Anfänge der Schriftreligion im Umkreis der unmittelbaren Vorexilszeit. Oder: Die Bitternis der Schriftrolle," *ZAW* 107 (1995): 51–64; with a focus on Habakkuk, cf. Floyd, "Habakkuk," 470–481.

[35] Ben Zvi, "Introduction," 25. Cf. E. Ben Zvi, "Observations on Prophetic Characters, Prophetic Texts, Priests of Old, Persian Period Priests and Literati," *The Priests in the Prophets: The Portrayal of Priests, Prophets and Other Religious Specialists in the Latter Prophets* (eds. L. L. Grabbe and A. O. Bellis; London/New York: T&T Clark, 2004), 19–30.

[36] Cf. Isaiah's encounters with Ahaz and Hezekiah; Jeremiah's connection with the family of Shaphan (Jer 26:24; 29:3; 36:10–19) and relatives among the officials (Jer 29:3); Ezekiel and Jeremiah being from priestly families. In this context, cf. R. B. Coote, "Proximity to the Central Davidic Citadel and the Greater and Lesser Prophets," in *"Every City shall be Forsaken": Urbanism and Prophecy in Ancient Israel and the Near East* (eds. L. L. Grabbe and R. D. Haak; JSOTSup 330; Sheffield: Sheffield Academic Press, 2001), 62–70, who suggests that the difference between long and short prophetic books has to do with the reputed proximity of Isaiah, Jeremiah, and Ezekiel to the center of power.

[37] Cf. Floyd, "Habakkuk," 462–481, esp. 477–481.

institution, namely the royal court. In the OT, however, one rather gets the impression that the prophets interacted with official institutions from *outside*.

4. Questioning theories of an institutional setting as Sitz im Leben of prophetic compositions

The fact that most of the OT prophets are depicted as "oppositional prophets" makes the emergence of prophetic compositions that bear their name even more remarkable.[38] Who were the people who remembered, collected, and studied older prophetic words and handed them down with their own inter-pretations – a process that over the centuries lead to these long prophetic com-positions so different than all the other ANE prophetic texts found so far?

Recognizing that every theory about the circumstances of the formation of prophetic books is highly hypothetical, in the following I will argue that the genre "prophetic composition" was not developed within an official setting as its *Sitz im Leben* – neither the royal court, nor the temple or schools.[39] To be sure, the last phases of the textual growth of the prophetic corpus took place within a professional scribal milieu (see above, 2.), in which this corpus finally was can-onized with 3 Major and 12 Minor Prophets. Furthermore, one can assume that already earlier official circles were involved in the formation of *some* of the prophetic compositions. Mainly with Habakkuk and Haggai it is likely that there were connections with the priesthood in Jerusalem. However, all this does not justify generalizations. Not least the above (2.) mentioned heterogeneity of the OT prophetic books speaks against the assumption of *one* institutional setting as the place where the formation of all or most of these books took place.

---

[38] On the connection between "oppositional prophets" and the writing down of first oracles, cf. Ch. Hardmeier, "Verkündigung und Schrift bei Jesaia: Zur Entstehung der Schrift-prophetie als Oppositionsliteratur im alten Israel," *TGl* 73 (1983): 119–134, who argues (on the basis mainly of Isaiah) that the first prophetic writings were oppositional literature, trig-gered by the failed effect of the prophetic word on the audience; cf. Lange, "Literary Proph-ecy," 257, 261. Focusing not on the pre- but on the postexilic time, cf. differently E. Ben Zvi, "'The Prophets': References to Generic Prophets and their Role in the Construction of the Image of the 'Prophets of Old' within the Postmonarchic Readership/s of the Book of Kings," *ZAW* 116 (2004): 555–567, who observes that in the book of Kings the generic group of "the prophets" are depicted as marginalized. He interprets this depiction as a reflection of the self understanding of "the literati" in postexilic times, who "saw themselves and construed their community also as powerless minority" (ibid., 565).

[39] On these three areas as places of literacy, cf. L. G. Perdue, *Wisdom Literature: A Theological History* (Louisville/London: Westminster John Knox: 2007), 327–329. Van der Toorn, *Scribal Culture*, 82–108, only distinguishes between royal scribes and temple scribes, and locates the schools at the temple (cf. ibid., 97). Yet another but compatible classification is offered by P. R. Davies, *Scribes and Schools: The Canonization of the Hebrew Scriptures* (Library of Ancient Israel; Louisville: Westminster John Knox, 1998), 74–88; and Niditch, *Oral World*, 60–77, who distinguish between archives, libraries, and schools/education.

More fundamentally, the assumption of an institutional setting as the place where prophetic works were composed and promoted is problematic to uphold in view of the sharp criticism expressed in most of the OT Prophets.[40] The shortcomings of the theory are most obvious in the case of arguments that the formation of prophetic books took place under the auspices of the *royal court*.[41] Obviously, this theory has its chronological limitations, in that in the early postexilic time the Davidic monarchy and even earlier the royal court[42] had ceased to exist, whereas the production of prophetic literature continued to flourish. Concentrating on the pre-exilic and exilic time, those who argue that as in the ANE also in ancient Israel the royal court was in charge of prophetic literature point to the "Deuteronomisms", found mainly in Jeremiah but with some good will also in books like Amos and Hosea.[43] Already the "Deuteronomistic History" itself, however, shows that "Deuteronomists" are not "Deuteronomists," not least when it comes to an assessment of the Davidic monarchy.[44] The silence of the Second book of Kings about Jeremiah (and most of the other classical prophets), as well as Jeremiah's silence about Josiah's reform indicate that the relationship between those who edited the "Deuteronomistic History" on the one hand and Jeremiah (and other prophets) and his (their) editors on the other hand was complicated, even if among the latter there were "Deuteronomists" as well. Without a clear "Deuteronomistic" argument, however, there is not much left that connects the OT Prophets with the royal court. On the contrary, criticism of the king and his politics constitutes an essential element in several of the OT Prophets. The book of Jeremiah, for example, comprises many critical passages against the kings of Judah (esp. in Jer 21–24), including an oracle predicting that none of Jehoiachin's "offspring shall succeed

---

[40] For critical elements in ANE prophecies, cf. M. Nissinen, "Das kritische Potential in der altorientalischen Prophetie," in *Propheten in Mari, Assyrien und Israel* (ed. M. Köckert and M. Nissinen; FRLANT 201; Göttingen: Vandenhoeck & Ruprecht, 2003), 1–32, where he concludes that "die prophetische Kritik in der Bibel im Vergleich mit außerbiblischen Quellen nicht nur wesentlich umfangreicher ist, sondern auch inhaltlich ein schärferes und radikaleres Profil hat […]" (ibid., 31).

[41] Cf. R. B. Coote and M. P. Coote, *Power, Politics, and the Making of the Bible: An Introduction* (Minneapolis: Fortress, 1990), 51, 56–57, 65–66 (different editions of Amos, Hosea, Micah, and Isaiah: court in Jerusalem), 65–66 (Zephaniah, Nahum, and early edition of Jeremiah: Josiah's administration); Schniedewind, *How the Bible*, 84–90 (Amos, Hosea, Micah, and Isaiah: court of Hezekiah in Jerusalem), 149–157 (Jeremiah and Ezekiel: court of Jehoiachin in Babylon); 158–164 (Isa 40–65 and Haggai: Judean royal family).

[42] For a critical discussion about the likelihood of literary production at the "royal court" of the imprisoned Jehoiachin in the Babylonian exile, cf. van Seters, "Origins," 105–106.

[43] Cf. J. Blenkinsopp, *A History of Prophecy in Israel* (rev. ed.; Louisville/London: Westminster John Knox, 1996), 161–165.

[44] For an overview of scholarly theses about and nuances within the "Deuteronomistic History", cf. T. Römer, *The So-called Deuteronomistic History: A Sociological, Historical and Literary Introduction* (London/New York: T&T Clark, 2005).

in sitting on the throne of David, and ruling again in Judah" (Jer 22:30; cf. 36:30). Moreover, two of the prophetic books even refer to foreign kings as the ones chosen by YHWH (cf. Isa 44:28; 45:1; Jer 25:9; 27:6; 43:10). It is more than unlikely that someone from the Davidic dynasty would have commissioned or even tolerated the production of such works.[45]

Similar observations speak against the theory that (all or most of) the ancient Israelite prophetic texts were composed and promoted at the *temple* in Jerusalem.[46] No question, in the ANE prophecy was connected with the cult, and some of the classical prophets had close connections with the priesthood – besides Jeremiah and Ezekiel, who came from priestly families (cf. Jer 1:1; Ezek 1:3), mainly Haggai and Zechariah, who are mentioned in the book of Ezra (cf. 5:1–2; 6:14–15) as driving forces behind the reconstruction of the temple (cf. Hag 1; for the interest in the temple, cf. Ezek 40–48). These and other indications leave no doubt that also in ancient Israel there were connections between prophetic and priestly circles. On the other hand, however, there are many passages in the Prophets that criticize not only nuisances in the cult (cf. Ezek 8) and among the priests (cf. Mal 1), but also question the general relevance of sacrifices (cf. Isa 1; Mic 6) and even the temple (cf. Jer 7; Isa 66).[47] Although one can hardly exclude the possibility that such texts were transmitted and/or composed by priests (or anybody else), it is clear that they do not represent the official viewpoint of the temple. With this, the argument for "the temple" as *Sitz im Leben* of prophetic compositions loses its force. One should rest content with the observation that the likelihood that priests were involved in the composition of some of the prophetic texts is high – not only because some OT texts point in this direction, but primarily for statistical reasons, i. e. the well-founded assumption that among the few who were literate in ancient Israel there was a high percentage of priests.[48]

---

[45] To be sure, the same prophetic books also contain passages with a positive view of the Judean king, especially in predictions about a future restoration of the Davidic dynasty (cf. Jer 23:5–6). However, while such passages *could* have originated under royal auspices, this conclusion is not inevitable. Everybody could hope for a just and righteous king: people critical of the king(s) of their time as well as such from much later times, in which there was no king anymore at all (cf. the late passage Jer 33:14–18).

[46] Cf. (all in view of the postexilic time) Ben Zvi, "Observations," 19–30; Blenkinsopp, *History*, 222–226; Coote/Coote, *Power*, 81–84; Schniedewind, *How the Bible*, 165–194, esp. 166; van der Toorn, *Scribal Culture*, 87–89 (with temple *schools* in mind, see n. 49; for the early phases, van der Toorn suggests followers, see n. 55); in this direction also Schaper, "Death," 63–79. Pointing to the close connections between the temple and the royal court and/or schools, most of these scholars understand the priestly involvement in the editing of prophetic book as a continuation of the work done at the court and/or schools in pre-exilic times.

[47] Ben Zvi, "Observations," 20–22, tries to explain these passages away with the observation that in the Prophets the prophets are depicted in opposition to everyone, even to Israel and "the prophets". While the latter is true, in my view, it does not solve the problem of how such critical texts would have been fostered at the temple.

[48] Cf. Ezra, who is labeled both "priest" and "scribe" (together in Ezra 7:11 and Neh 12:26).

General considerations about the social locations of literate people in antiquity led to a third suggestion about the setting in life of prophetic compositions:
the notion that they were studied and expanded at *schools*.[49] While there are
almost no concrete data about schools in ancient Israel,[50] it is clear that there
must have been places where the next generations of the intellectual elite were
trained – places where literacy was fostered as a matter of principle.[51] However,
it would be an oversimplification to conclude that all writings in ancient Israel
originated and/or were fostered at schools. Not least with the prophetic compositions it is rather unlikely that they should have been part of a "curriculum".[52] Most of these compositions are so critical towards the ruling elite and
even fundamental Israelite traditions (Zion theology, royal ideology, Exodus
tradition etc.) that it is hard to imagine that they were used to educate the young
and prepare the future elite for their roles. Again, it cannot be excluded and even
is likely that teachers and advanced students were aware of the prophetic traditions and that some of them were involved in some of the prophetic books'
formation. However, the likelihood of such an awareness and involvement has
nothing to do with the institution of schools as such; it is given by the mere fact
that teachers and advanced students belonged to the small group of ancient
Israelites who were literate.

5. "Followers" as editors

If ancient Israel's prophetic compositions did not originate in an official setting,
as argued above, how then should one imagine their formation? By whom,
how, and with what purpose were prophetic works composed and handed
down over generations?

These questions are as interesting as they are difficult to answer. The only data
available are the prophetic books themselves. Most of them exhibit traces of a

---

[49] Cf. Carr, *Writing*, 143–151; Davies, "Audiences," 58–62; Floyd, "Habakkuk,"
477–481; A. Lemaire, *Les écoles et la formation de la Bible dans l'ancient Israël* (OBO 39; Fribourg/
Göttingen: Éditions universitaires/Vandenhoeck & Ruprecht, 1981), 72–83; Schmid, *Buchgestalten*, 40–43; van der Toorn, *Scribal Culture*, 101 (with *temple* schools in mind, see n. 46).

[50] For an overview, cf. Davies, *Scribes*, 74–85.

[51] Both writing and writings played an important role at schools and it is more than likely
that older compositions were not only copied, memorized, and interpreted, but over the time
also expanded. Moreover, as "intellectuals" teachers and students probably were well aware of
the different traditions in ancient Israel, including the prophetic.

[52] It is telling that Carr, *Writing*, 143, speaks about a "(Counter)Education in the Prophets"
and even concedes that "we cannot know the development of use of these texts nor the circles
that used them" (ibid., 150). Despite his awareness, however, that in the ANE, prophetic texts
were not used in educational contexts, he insists that the Israelite "prophetic words eventually
became part of a stream of educational-enculturational oral-written literature used in the
formation of (elite) Israelites" (ibid., 150).

longer formation process, in which later additions reflect the intentions of the editors. Most often, however, these traces are vague and scholars do not agree on which of the texts in a prophetic book are redactional, let alone on the extent and date of different redactions. Furthermore, not all of the redactional passages are simply interpretations of older words in a new situation; some of them are rather "corrections", based on different ideologies/theologies. Apparently, those involved in the formation of a given prophetic book did not always constitute a homogenous "school"[53] – the question about these people's identity and intentions becomes more complex. More fundamentally, studies of the prophetic books show that most of them are unique productions. Not least, their different lengths and the variety of their formation processes – some straightforward, others long and complex – speak against the idea of one single model.[54]

No doubt, there were changes over the course of time. For the early phases, the old idea of "students", in the sense of "disciples" and "followers", is the most likely scenario.[55] The book of Kings knows about "sons of the prophets" (בני הנביאם ; cf. 1 King 20:35; 2 King 2:3, 5, 7, 15; 4:1, 38; 5:22; 6:1; 9:1) and the book of Isaiah mentions "students" (לְמֻּדִים; cf. Isa 8:16; 50:4). In the book of Jeremiah, Baruch gives an idea of the closeness of these "students" or "followers" to a prophet and their involvement in the first collections of this prophet's words.[56]

That those who recollected the words of a prophet and turned them into the first prophetic compositions were people who had a personal and not a professional relationship with this prophet is further indicated by the interest that some of the OT Prophets show in the lives of the prophets.[57] Comparison with the

---

[53] The cases of books with major text-critical variants (cf. JerMT/JerLXX) point into the same direction.

[54] Cf. P. R. Davies, "'Pen of iron, point of diamond' (Jer 17:1): Prophecy as Writing," in *Writings and Speech*, 65–81, 78; idem, *Scribes*, 115, 122–125; M. H. Floyd, "'Write the revelation!' (Hab 2:2): Re-imagination the Cultural History of Prophecy," in *Writings and Speech*, 103–143, 126–130; Van Seters, "Prophetic Orality," 87–88.

[55] Cf. J. L. Crenshaw, "Transmitting Prophecy across Generations," in *Writings and Speech*, 31–44, 35–40; Lange, "Literary Prophecy," 256; N. Lohfink, "Gab es eine deuteronomistische Bewegung?" in *Jeremiah und die "deuteronomistische Bewegung"* (ed. W. Groß; BBB 98; Weinheim: Athenäum 1995), 313–382, 340–341 (with the assumption that prophetic texts later "in Bibliotheks- oder Schulzusammenhang gerieten", ibid., 346–347); Niditch, *Oral World*, 119; van der Torn, *Scribal Culture*, 182–188.

[56] Baruch plays an important role in the book of Jeremiah, not only as Jeremiah's scribe (cf. 36; 45:1) but also as his close ally (Jer 32; 43:3; 45 after 44 → Baruch with Jeremiah in exile?). Early on he became a figure of interest in his own right and a focal point for new traditions (cf. Jer 45; the book of Baruch). This latter phenomenon makes it difficult to distinguish between historical information and later tradition.

[57] Cf. van der Toorn, *Scribal Culture*, 184; differently Davies, *Scribes*, 117–118, who focuses on the Minor Prophets, which indeed contain less historical/biographical information. This observation is Davies' main argument for dismissing the idea of followers, even though he

note

prophetic texts from Mesopotamia makes this interest more evident. Written down by royal officials, they contain almost no information about the prophets as persons. The interest is focused entirely on the prophetic oracles, as is obvious in the collection tablets from Assyria, where the principle of arrangement was not personal but topical.[58] The prophetic texts from ancient Israel are quite different: All of them are transmitted under the name of a specific prophet and most grew around the words of such an original prophet. Furthermore, Isaiah, Jeremiah, Ezekiel, and some of the Minor Prophets contain not only prophetic words but also details about the situations in which these words were spoken, as well as reports about incidents in the prophets' lives. With the "confessions" the book of Jeremiah (seemingly) even gives insights into the prophet's emotions. While this is an exception, the interest in a prophet's life constitutes a characteristic element in other prophetic books as well.

Again the situation is complex in that reports about aspects of a prophet's biography are more than memories, but sooner or later become part of a message. As such they also could be invented from scratch and thus do not reflect historical but pedagogical interests in a prophet's biography. A clear example of such prophetic fiction is the book of Jonah. Other prophetic books certainly include fictional biographical elements as well – not least the "confessions" of Jeremiah are to be understood as such. But with the exception of Jonah there is no reason to doubt the historicity of the biographical elements in the OT Prophets altogether. Rather, one gets the impression that there were real memories at the beginning, which later were enhanced with more fictional ones. In most cases the line between reality and fiction is blurred – as is characteristic of memories in general.

a.

b

While the idea of prophetic "followers" cannot be specified in more detail,[59] it explains (a) that some of the ancient Israelite prophets' words were collected and interpreted over generations, even though they were so critical that no official institution could have had an interest in such a process, and (b) that the respective compositions include memories about the prophets' lives.

---

admits that the OT Prophets are diverse (cf. ibid., 115, 122) and cannot easily be connected with an institution (cf. ibid., 122–125).

[58] I. e. the collection tablets do not contain series of oracles from the same prophet but series of oracles on the same topic.

[59] How many followers were involved? What were the steps that led to prophetic compositions? How early were such compositions written down? Who did the actual writing and what was the followers' relationship to the literate elite? What was the followers' primary motivation to collect and interpret prophetic oracles? How did they use the respective compositions and how hand them down? While these questions cannot be answered in general, it is to assume that the situations were different from case to case. Hence, it is important to pay attention to peculiarities in the different prophetic books. Interesting in the case of Jeremiah, for example, are the doublets, which might be an indication of oral transmission among different supporters.

For the followers the trustworthiness of the prophets lay not only in their words but in their behavior/life as well (cf. Isa 28:7–8; Jer 23:14) – even more so in cases like Jeremiah where the prophet's "office" influenced his entire existence (cf. Jer 20:7–9; 26:8–9).

It is safe to assume that many prophets had such followers, i. e. people who were convinced that the divine spoke through them and closely followed what they said and did. With most of these prophets, however, the interest was fleeting and ceased sooner or later – as we can conclude from the lack of more prophetic books. Besides the death of the prophets and the first generation of followers, this process was determined by the decline of the respective states. One of the essential tasks of ANE prophets was to prophesy about affairs of the state, and most fulfilled this task in a "friendly" way by endorsing the king and his policies. While this certainly was a good tactic for the moment, it later could backfire on the prophets when major national catastrophes cost them their reliability. For those prophets, on the other hand, who prophesied critically, such events were a moment of verification. It is no coincidence that from all the pre-exilic prophets from ancient Israel and Judah we mainly have books from those who prophesied critically against their own nation. The fulfillment of prophecies certainly was not the only factor in keeping the formation process of a prophetic book going;[60] but it was crucial.[61] Those already involved in keeping the memory about a certain prophet alive gained additional incentive for going on with their work. As the authority of a prophet grew, new people became interested and the process of interpreting and handing down this prophet's words gained momentum.[62]

Whether or not these later generations of people involved in the formation of prophetic books should be labeled "followers" as well depends on how one understands the term. It makes sense in that it implies that the respective people

---

[60] We may assume that there were other prophets of doom for which the fulfillment of their prophecies was not strong enough an impulse.

[61] For a different explanation of the relation between the message of doom and writtenness of the OT Prophets, cf. R. G. Kratz, "Das Neue in der Prophetie des Alten Testaments," in *Prophetie in Israel: Beiträge des Symposiums "Das Alte Testament und die Kultur der Moderne" anlässlich des 100. Geburtstags Gerhard von Rads (1901–1971), Heidelberg, 28.–21. Oktober 2001* (eds. I. Fischer et al.; Altes Testament und Moderne 11; Münster/Hamburg/London 2003), 1–22. According to Kratz, the OT Prophets contained messages of doom only after 722 (and 587) BCE; i. e. he assumes that the original prophets were not that radical, but their words were radicalized and reinterpreted after 722 and 587 BCE, the two national catastrophes, which the prophetic editors interpreted as YHWH's work. Such processes of reinterpretations of older prophetic words in light of 722 and 587 are more than likely. However, in my opinion, these later developments are more plausible if already the original prophets had a critical potential – a fact that can be dismissed only with radical redaction-historical hypotheses.

[62] With a growing interest in a prophet's words, those who handed down these words also had to explain why the prophet's warnings were not heard and why parts of his words did *not* turn true, or rather: how one has to interpret them to understand how they turned true.

were involved with the prophetic texts not through belonging to an institution but through a personal interest in the prophet and his message.[63] To be sure, the very fact that the formation processes involved writing and even more that the contents of the prophetic compositions reflect a profound understanding of political situations and theological traditions leaves no doubt that these followers were not ordinary people but belonged to the intellectual elite of ancient Israel.[64] Hence it is most likely that many of them had connections with the political and religious institutions in postexilic Judah.[65] However, the institutional connections of the people behind prophetic compositions must not be confused with an institutional connection of these compositions themselves.[66] *Yes*

6. Orality (and writing) in the world of prophetic editors

What does all this mean for the question of orality and writing? If the genre of prophetic compositions indeed was not linked with an institutional setting, there are no data other than the prophetic books themselves to reconstruct the concrete circumstances of these books' formation. As mentioned above, such data are rare in the Prophets and much remains hypothetical. However, some directions for scholarly hypotheses are suggested not only by the argument presented above that the people behind prophetic compositions were involved

---

[63] Cf. Crenshaw, "Transmitting," 40.

[64] In the secondary literature, the term "literati" became popular to refer to the people behind prophetic and other compositions. See for example E. Ben Zvi, "What is New in Yehud? Some Considerations," in *Yahwism after the Exile: Perspectives on Israelite Religion in the Persian Era* (eds. R. Albertz and B. Becking; STAR 5; Assen: Van Gorcum, 2003), 32–48, 45: "In Yehud, prophetic and other written texts were composed, redacted, studied, stored, and reread by the literati of the period as YHWH's word and teaching." No doubt, this statement is true. However, we do not know more about these "literati" than the obvious: that they must have been literate. Furthermore, from the diversity of all these writings we must conclude that they were not one homogenous group. While Ben Zvi, "Prophetic Book," 293–297, speaks about a "same small social group of literati" in postexilic Judah, he acknowledges this last point, in view especially of all the other books produced by this same group but also the differences within the prophetic books. Differently Floyd, "Basic Trends," 309, who thinks that "this diversity [within the OT prophetic books] can no longer be attributed to various different circles of literati engaged in theological debates and partisan conflicts", but assumes that by "cultivating such diversity in theological discourse, they [the same small scribal group] demonstrated all the more convincingly their continuity with preexilic traditions."

[65] Cf. the different possibilities envisioned by Ben Zvi, "Introduction," 10–12.

[66] Cf. van Seters, "Prophetic Orality," 88, who correctly observes that there is not "any reason to suppose that among such supporters there was not a trained scribe who could record the oracles." Cf. Floyd, "Write," 135: "Schools, archives and libraries were undoubtedly centers of scribal activity in the ancient Near East. It is questionable, however, whether we should think of culturally significant scribal activity as something necessarily or exclusively focused in such an institutional setting."

with them not in an official capacity, but also by some hints in the prophetic texts themselves.

Most important in this regard is the book of Jeremiah. Beyond the normal traces of editing processes, it offers references to earlier versions of itself (cf. Jer 25:13; 29:1; 30:2; 36:2, 28, 32; 45:1; 51:60). Most of these references to "scrolls" containing written words of Jeremiah prompt questions and none of them can be taken simply at face value. While some of them might be reminiscences of historical events involving Jeremiah, others clearly belong to later phases in the formation of the book(s). Their "un-historicity" makes these references not less informative, though. On the contrary: besides general ideas about the process of writing down prophetic words they reflect more specific notions of those who actually were responsible for this process.

Jer 30:1ff., a passage that reflects the wish to preserve prophetic words for the future is interesting in this regard. As in Jer 36:2, in 30:2 YHWH commands Jeremiah to write down in a "scroll" (ספר) all the words he (previously?) had spoken; in contrast to Jer 36, however, nothing is said about having these words read to anyone. Rather, 30:3 refers to "coming days" (ימים באים), when YHWH will restore the fortunes of his people. Thus it is implied that the scroll was written to transfer God's words not in space but in time. Interestingly, nothing is said about when and how the people of Israel will hear the words. The primary focus of the passage is that the words were written down for the future.[67]

The notion of an audience is also absent in Jer 51:59–64. The "scroll" (ספר) mentioned in this passage is described as containing "all the disasters that would come on Babylon, all these words that are written concerning Babylon." Perhaps, these words are those from Jer 50f. and the "scroll" is imagined to be a copy of an already written text. The interest of the passage is not in these questions, but in the purpose for which the scroll was produced. According to 51:61, Jeremiah commissioned Baruch's brother Seraiah to carry the scroll to Babylon and to "read/proclaim" (קרא) "all these words" (כל־הדברים האלה) there. No human audience is mentioned. Rather, Jeremiah asks Seraiah to speak to YHWH and to remind him that he had announced his intent to destroy Babylon (cf. 51:62). Afterwards, he is to sink the scroll in the Euphrates and to announce that Babylon will "sink" (שׁקע) likewise (cf. 51:63–64).

Clearly, the last passage discussed reflects a firm belief in the efficacy of YHWH's words and the need to create occasions for these words to be proclaimed. Similarly, there are other indications in the prophetic corpus that those involved in the respective compositions were driven by a "prophetic impetus".[68] The following observations point to a desire of these "prophetic"

---

[67] Cf. Isa 30:8, where the intention of writing down prophetic words for the future is expressed explicitly (עד־עולם).

[68] Cf. Ben Zvi, "Introduction," 14 ("quasi-prophetic status"), 25 ("quasi prophets"); Floyd, "Write," 142–143 ("prophetic desire/concerns"); M. H. Floyd, "The Production of Prophet-

editors to make the prophetic words heard and understood by a broader public.[69]

(1) Many of the prophetic oracles, whether they go back to original prophets
or to editors, are addressed to the (leaders of the) people of Israel. They as well as
others formulated in the third person reflect the intention of conveying a message – be it to warn the addressees about consequences of their behavior, to give
them hope in a difficult situation, or to explain to them a certain position in a
controversial theological/political question. While it cannot be excluded that
such an intention was imitated to give a text a more "prophetic" tone, the
conclusion that the texts indeed were meant to convince a broader audience is
more plausible.

(2) With the prophets setting an example of public proclamation of their
words, it is likely that their followers continued in this tradition. As "students"
they made sure that their master's words were proclaimed to a broader public
after his death, too. Set in the lifetime of the prophet, Jer 36 illustrates the
connection between the production of prophetic compositions and their public
readings. According to 36:2, God asked Jeremiah to write down all the words he
had spoken to him in the past. The text implies that the words written on the
"scroll" (ספר) were words proclaimed by Jeremiah at earlier times. The scroll is a
re-collection and com-position of these words. With the wish that the Judeans
might "turn from their evil ways", 36:3 implies that the scroll was produced to
be read publicly. Apparently, this point was so clear that it did not even need to
be mentioned specifically. Only in 36:5–6 the public reading of the words
becomes an issue. With not very convincing reasons the text explains that Jeremiah could not fulfill this task in person but had to send Baruch, who read the
scroll to the people (cf. 36:10). There are several indications that the text is not a
record of a historical event, but goes back to later editors. In explaining that their
Jeremiah-scroll contained authentic words of Jeremiah, they also mentioned the
practice of reading such scrolls in public.[70]

---

ic Books in the Early Second Temple Period," in *Prophets, Prophecy, and Prophetic Texts*,
276–297, 289; Steck, *Prophetenbücher*, 127ff., esp. 166–177 ("Prophetische Prophetenausle-
gung", "Tradentenprophetie").

[69] For oral performances of prophetic compositions, cf. Ben Zvi, "Introduction," 16–18;
Ben Zvi, "Prophetic Book," 294–295; Conrad, "Heard," 45–59; W. Doan and T. Giles,
Prophets, Performance, and Power: Performance Criticism of the Hebrew Bible (New York: T&T
Clark, 2005); Floyd, "Production," 290–292; Lessing, "Orality," 161–165; Niditch, *Oral
World*, 119–120. With claiming that "literary prophecy became the main form of prophecy
[…], while aural prophecy was more and more marginalized", Lange, "Literary Prophecy,"
259, misses the important point that written texts can both be read/studied and heard/pro-
claimed. Vehemently against the idea of public readings of prophetic texts, cf. Davies, "Audiences," 60–62.

[70] Similarly, Hab 2:2 attests (public) readings (קרא) of prophetic writings.

(3) Reflecting not the pole of the senders but the receivers, Jer 26:17–19 provides another hint that prophetic words were made known to the public even many centuries after the original prophets had died. According to this passage, some of the "elders of the land" recollected a word by Micah of Moresheth (cf. Mi 3:12), as an argument that older prophets prophesied critically and still were not put to death. Whether or not the episode is historical, it shows that it was considered as likely that later generations knew about the words of older prophets. Many prophetic books echo words of other prophets. Normally, scholars explain these echoes with the assumption that the editors of one prophetic book had access to the written version of other prophetic books. Another possibility was that they knew about the words of these other prophetic compositions orally, through public proclamations organized by those involved in the formation of the respective books.

(4) That the editors had an interest in making their work known beyond their own circles is further reflected in the fact that they inserted their interpretations into their compositions. Most probably, these interpretations were developed by a few who, given the contents and techniques of their additions, must have been people trained in studying older traditions and arguing theologically. Either alone or in small groups they studied the older prophetic words and reflected on their meaning for their own time. While this interpretation process was important for *them*, writing down the interpretations was important in view of *others* who were not part of their oral discussions.

(5) A last point to be considered is the custom of intermixing later interpretations with older material. At least in the written versions, the editors did not set any markers to distinguish between the words deriving from the original prophets and those they added. The later additions are introduced together with the original words as the words of the original prophet. An example of this technique is Jer 30:1–3(ff.), the verses already mentioned above. The text implies that the words written down by Jeremiah are the ones that follow after v. 4, the so called "book of consolation" – which is, according to a broad scholarly consensus, an addition from postexilic times. As words of hope spoken in a situation of distress, with Israel and Judah often addressed directly, the "book of consolation" fits into the introductory scenario only partially.[71] Moreover, 30:1–3 does not explain why the words could not already have been proclaimed in the past. Apparently, those who formulated the introduction to the "book of consolation" were not concerned with these questions. Their intention was otherwise: to prove that the "book of consolation" traces back to Jeremiah and to explain why it was not known previously. With this, they reinforce both the

---

[71] Jer 30:1–3 implies that the following words are written down for a time when the fortune of YHWH's people will be restored. Jer 30:4ff., however, is addressed to people whose fortune has not yet been turned.

authority of the prophet (as one who could predict a change in the far future) and the words of the "book of consolation" (as words of Jeremiah). Again, the intention mirrored in the text is most easily understood if the text was not meant for insiders only but was made known to others as well.[72] As often with pseud-epigraphy, it would be a misunderstanding to assume fraudulent intents on the part of those who circulated their own words under the name of a prophet. Interesting in this regard is the short remark in Jer 36:32 that in the second scroll produced by Baruch "many similar words" (דברים רבים כהמה) "were added" (יסף ni.). In the same context that aims at proving that a scroll with words of Jeremiah contains the authentic words of the prophet (cf. 36:4, 6, 17, 18, 27, 32), it is acknowledged that more words were added later, without naming those who added them.

The names of the prophetic editors were not important. Those who were involved in the formation of prophetic books understood themselves to be standing in the tradition of their prophet.[73] Like him they listened to the "word of YHWH" and felt commissioned to make it accessible for others. The difference, of course, is that the prophet heard the "word of YHWH" directly, whereas those later interpreters primarily heard it in studying the prophet's words. Whether or not they had prophetic experiences of their own lies beyond our knowledge – not unlike the case of the original prophets themselves.

7. The "lying pen of the scribes" and the Torah "written on the hearts" (Jer 8:8–9; 31:31–34)

It is time to come back to Jer 8:8–9, the passage quoted in the beginning. How does its reference to the "lying pen of the scribes" fit in with everything considered so far? Unfortunately, the formulations of the two verses are brief and many questions remain open. What is meant by the "Torah" (v. 8), whether or not it is a synonym or an antonym to the "word of YHWH" (v. 9),[74] and what the scribes do with it – all these questions are intensively debated in scholarship. What is clear is that the two verses express a criticism of those who pretend to be wise and feel sure they have YHWH's Torah. In v. 9, these (or other?) "wise"

---

[72] When such composite texts were read, the "I" of YHWH, the "I" of the original prophet, the "I" of the prophetic editors and the "I" of the reader all merged into one; cf. Ben Zvi, "Introduction," 14.

[73] Cf. Steck, *Prophetenbücher*, 170–177.

[74] Some scholars understand the opposition in Jer 8:8–9 as the one between the "Torah" and the prophetic "word of YHWH"; others see it as the opposition between a "Torah" that is identical with the "word of YHWH" and one that is not. In view of the use of the two terms elsewhere in Jeremiah (see in particular Jer 6:19, where both terms are used in parallel), the second explanation is more likely.

(חכמים) people are blamed for having "rejected" (מאס) YHWH's word. In v. 8, they are associated with "scribes" (ספרים) who either are blamed for turning "it"[75], namely the Torah, with the "lying pen of the scribes" (עט שקד ספרים) into a "lie" (שקר), or for being turned themselves by their lying pen into a lie.[76] However the passage is to be understood syntactically, it implies that the (true) Torah of YHWH is not with the wise and blames (all or some?) scribes[77] as liars. Hence, it not only confirms that the relationship between the editors of the book of Jeremiah and "the Deuteronomists" has to be considered carefully, but more generally it fits in very nicely with the above formulated argument that the people involved in the formation of prophetic books did so not in an official capacity. Though literate and erudite, in their prophetic critique they did not count themselves among "the scribes" and "the wise".

However, as much as 8:8–9 criticizes "scribes" and "wise", it is not about the opposition of the *written* Torah (of the scribes) as opposed to the *oral* word of YHWH (proclaimed by the prophets). Such an interpretation, common among scholars, is not only unlikely in view of the positive assessment of writing mirrored in the rest of the book of Jeremiah (see above, 3.), it is also difficult to maintain given the keywords "lie" (שקר) and "reject" (מאס) and their use in other passages in Jeremiah. These other passages indicate that the problem criticized in 8:8f is not *writing* as such but *false* writing.[78] Only in the next verse, 8:10, is it stated that from prophet to priest everybody is involved in lying/fraud (שקר). Allegations that someone lies are frequent in the book of Jeremiah – notably, most often with regard to oral and in particular prophetic words (cf. 5:31; 14:14; 20:6; 23:25–32; 27:10, 14–16; 28:15; 29:9, 21, 23, 31). Especially the leaders are accused of confusing the people with such "words of lie" (cf. 7:4, 8). As result, the people do not "know" (ידע) YHWH (cf. 2:8; 4:22; 5:4f.; 8:7; 9:2, 5) and reject (מאס) his Torah (cf. 6:19; 9:12; 16:11; cf. 26:4; 32:23; 44:10, 23). The question of orality and writing is not important at this point. Lies can be spread with all different means of communication, besides orally (see the passages just quoted) and in writing (cf. 8:8; 29:24–32) also in symbolic actions (cf. 28:10–11).[79]

---

[75] Cf. the suggestion of the BHS to read עָשָׂה as עָשָׂה.

[76] Cf. Maier, *Jeremia*, 298, 300. Other translations are offered by the Zürcher Bibel (2007): "Wahrlich, seht, das hat der Griffel zur Lüge gemacht, zur Lüge der Schreiber", and JPS (1985): "Assuredly, for naught has the pen labored, for naught the scribes!"

[77] The identity and function of these "scribes" is disputed among scholars; cf. Klopfenstein, *Lüge*, 136–137; Maier, *Jeremia*, 301.

[78] Cf. G. Fischer, *Jeremia 1–25* (Herders Theologischer Kommentar zum Alten Testament; Freiburg/Basel/Wien: Herder, 2005), 335–336; J. R. Lundbom, *Jeremiah 1–20* (AB 21A; New York: Doubleday, 1999), 515.

[79] The problem of lying is not a distinctive interest of Jeremiah but concerns prophecy as such. All communication processes are susceptible to distortion and corruption, and this problem is intensified with prophetic communication processes. With God being the sender of

There is another passage in the book of Jeremiah that deals with the Torah, writing, and humans' inclination to deviate from what is good for them: Jer 31:31–34, the famous verses about YHWH's promise of a new covenant with his people. While the passage probably is later than 8:8–9, it is related to the two verses through YHWH's announcement that he will "write" (כתב) his Torah on the hearts of the Judeans and Israelites. Many scholars acknowledge a connection between the two passages, including those who understand Jer 8 as a protest against writing in general or the written Torah in particular. According to some, 31:33 confirms the critical position of 8:8–9 in that it contrasts the scribes with YHWH as the only one entitled to write down his Torah.[80] Others stress the difference between real writing and metaphorical writing: Only 8:8 is about a Torah that actually exists in written form; the point of the Torah of 31:33, however, is that it is internalized.[81] As much as this last point is true, the conclusion that 31:33 is in line with 8:8 in being critical against writing is more than just unlikely – not least because it most probably belongs to the later additions produced by people who were heavily involved in writing down if not the Torah at least some form of the "word of YHWH."

Like 8:8, 31:33 is not about an opposition between the oral and the written. The difference between the two was crucial neither for the prophets nor their editors. 31:34 shows that the promise for the future aims at people "knowing" (ידע) YHWH (cf. Jer 24:7) without needing instructions from others. From 8:8 and other passages in Jeremiah it is clear why such instructions are not seen positively but as a problem:[82] They can be deceitful, whether oral or written. Both (original) prophets and (prophetic) editors most probably were convinced that the "word of YHWH" they proclaimed was the true "word". From others, however, who contradicted them and proclaimed another "truth" they knew that a so called "word of YHWH" could also be false. Furthermore, even with true words there is always the danger that the recipients would either turn them into lies or ignore them totally. Against this background, 31:31–34 plays with the difference between the Torah set "before them" (לפניהם; cf. 9:12; 26:4; 44:10) and the Torah put "within them" (בקרבם; cf. 31:33). Those who wrote this passage saw themselves in line with the original prophets and were com-

---

prophetic messages, the first and most important step of the communication is not traceable for ordinary people (including scholars). In Mari it was usual to double-check prophetic messages with other means of divination (cf. Nissinen, *Prophets*, 16). In Israel prophetic word stood against prophetic word and one had to wait to see which of them came true (cf. Deut 18:22). The contradictory messages of opposing prophets brought uncertainty and weakened the trustworthiness of all prophets. Also those who later were remembered for having been right in their messages could be accused of lying, (cf. Jer 26; 43:2).

[80] Cf. Carroll, "Inscribing," 64–72.

[81] Cf. Schmid, *Buchgestalten*, 66–69.

[82] For the tension between the critical evaluation of teaching in Jer 31 and the positive evaluation of teaching in the book of Deuteronomy, cf. Schmid, *Buchgestalten*, 68–69.

mitted not only to study the "word of YHWH" for themselves but to explain and proclaim it to others, too. While they most probably were convinced of the value of their action, they apparently also knew their limitations. Be it orally or in writing, they could only put the "word of YHWH" *before the people*. Whether or not their audience internalized the divine word was beyond their control – or, theologically speaking, in the hand of God alone.[83]

---

[83] See also the connection of Jer 31:31–34 with Jer 17:1 and other passages about the stubbornness of the Israelites' hearts, which also conveys that only YHWH can change humans' condition.

Writing Songs, Singing Songs:
The Oral and the Written in the Commission of the Levitical Singers (1 Chr 25:1–6)

Roger S. Nam

1. Introduction

The book of Chronicles presents a unique perspective on the spirited debate regarding the placement of ancient Israel along any putative oral-scribal continuum. The reliance on the written traditions in Samuel/Kings places Chronicles at the far end of the literacy side. But whereas this assessment is undisputed, participants in the orality-literacy discussion deal with Chronicles in different ways to support their observations on the level of scribal culture behind the textualization of the HB. Scholars who interpret biblical text arising from a highly scribal tradition parade Chronicles as a definitive example of the literate culture in the Second Temple period.[1] On the opposing spectrum, scholars defending a significant level of oral culture concede that Chronicles falls on the literate extreme of biblical texts, but contend that even Chronicles contains, "nuances of orality, a reminder of the oral context that frames the use of writing."[2] In totality, much of this debate serves to identify the complexity of this question of orality versus literacy beyond a mere dualistic categorization. Although Susan Niditch utilizes the language of an oral-written continuum, she explicitly states the shortcomings of any binary model between orality and literacy.[3] Similarly, Michael Floyd contends that the orality – literacy discussion

---

[1] "There can be no doubt, however, that the Chronicler did in fact use written sources for his work. Both by the actual mode of production and by the self-conscious parading of scholarship, Chronicles is evidently a product from scribal workmanship," K. van der Toorn, *Scribal Culture and the Making of the Hebrew Bible* (Cambridge: Harvard University Press, 2007), 117.

[2] S. Niditch, *Oral World and Written Word* (Louisville, Ky: Westminster John Knox, 1996), 98.

[3] "The process of biblical composition was so complex and the interplay between oral and written so complicated that any reconstruction based on upon the four models offered above (oral to written, oral to written and written to oral, literary imitation, written sources for written composition) risks as much imprecision as the work of the theorists I have criticized in this chapter," Niditch, *Oral World*, 129.

has explanatory power only when it can describe the intricate interface of these
two components of ancient Israel's social world.[4] In a study of orality/literacy in
Second Temple prophecy, Joachim Schaper concludes that "There was, and is,
no simple dichotomy between orality and literacy."[5] From this viewpoint, the
book of Chronicles, as the most literate tradition in the HB, serves as a valuable
resource for probing the intricate relationship of the oral and the written cultures in post-exilic Israel. The complexity of the book of Chronicles matches
this complex interface of the oral and literate culture during the Persian period.

This paper examines 1 Chr 25:1–6 and the description of Levitical singers as a
paradigmatic example of the complex matrix of orality and literacy in biblical
texts of the Second Temple period. Specifically, the commission of the Levitical
singers in 1 Chr 25:1–6, unique to the Chronicler's material, provides an outstanding representative example of such an interface. The passage is unmistakably a product of scribal culture, as its verses demonstrate all of the characteristics
of a deep scribal tradition and multiple layers of literary redaction. By declaring
the genealogical lines of the Levitical singers to the status of prophet, the passage
bestows authority to a scribal act of the composition, editing and collection of
liturgical psalms during the Persian period. The communal psalm inserted after
the successful transport of the ark in 1 Chr 16 illustrates the nature of such scribal
activity of the Levitical singers. At the same time, the careful reworking of this
text serves an additional purpose that embodies the oral elements of ancient
Israel, specifically the legitimization of oral performance in the temple. Rather
than representing the two extremes of a continuum, this passage of the commission of the Levitical singers reveals the multifaceted interworkings between
the cultures of writtenness and orality.

2. The Written Word in the Commission of the Levitical Singers

Both the self-sufficiency of the passage as well as the formal boundary of a
Wiederaufnahme of ויהי מספרם ("And their list was [...]", vv. 1, 7) delineate the
commission in 1 Chr 25:1–6 as a disparate unit.[6] An analysis of the passage

---

[4] "It is practically useless to describe all these possibilities in terms of a binary contrast, as
pertaining to societies with a 'written' culture, and to think of cultural development simply in
terms of a progression from oral to written," M. Floyd, "'Write the Revelation!' (Hab 2:2):
Re-Imagining the Cultural History of Prophecy," *Writing and Speech in Israelite and Ancient
Near Eastern Prophecy* (eds. Ehud Ben Zvi and Michael Floyd; Atlanta: Society of Biblical
Literature, 2000), 122.

[5] J. Schaper, "Exilic and Post-Exilic Prophecy and the Orality/Literacy Problem," *VT* 55
(2005): 337.

[6] The *Wiederaufnahme* (repetitive resumption) serves a deliberate editorial function in setting apart a disparate unit by means of a repeated phrase, W. M. Schniedewind, "Innerbiblical
Exegesis," *Dictionary of the Old Testament Historical Books* (eds. Bill T. Arnold and H. G. M.

discloses both implicit and explicit manifestations of scribal culture. Implicitly, the passage reveals a lengthy diachronic history, congruent with the assessment of the Chronicler as compiler of older written traditions. Explicitly, the text legitimizes the process of scribal composition of psalms for liturgical usage. In analyzing the presumed literacy culture, both of these components warrant examination.

Exegetical study suggests that the genealogical record of 1 Chr 25:1–6 is a scribal product rather than a mechanical textualization from oral lore.[7] In listing the heads of the Levitical singers, the emphasis on Heman and the inclusion of Asaph and Jeduthun point to a specific period within a longstanding textual tradition. Gerhard von Rad argued for a diachronic view of the Levitical singers based of the different patriarchal names throughout Chronicles, but confined the phenomenon to the post-exilic period.[8] Building on Gerhard von Rad, Hartmut Gese suggested four primary stages in the Chronicler's passages concerning the Levitical singers.[9] In stage I, during the start of the post-exilic phase, the sons of Asaph functioned as singers, and they did not carry Levitical authority.[10] In stage II, the sons of Jeduthun combine with the sons of Asaph, and both have Levitical authority.[11] Stage IIIA adds Heman as a third patriarchal line to Asaph and Jeduthun.[12] For Gese, this third stage was the work of the Chronicler himself. In the final stage IIIB, Ethan replaces Jeduthun, Heman gains prominence over Asaph.[13] Because the genealogy of 1 Chr 25 includes Asaph, Jeduthun and Heman, Gese places the composition of vv. 1–6 close to stage IIIA.

Gese followed von Rad in placing this progression of Levitical singer clan names entirely within the post-exilic period. But whereas scholarship has gen-

---

Williamson; Downers Grove, Ill.: Inter-Varsity Press, 2005), 507. Sara Japhet includes v. 7 in the unit, as it concludes the numerical summary, S. Japhet, *1 and 2 Chronicles* (OTL; Louisville, Ky: Westminster/John Knox, 1993), 445. Most commentators, however, see v. 7 as the opening to the expanded list of the genealogical line through the end of the chapter, G. N. Knoppers, *1 Chronicles 10–29* (New York: Doubleday, 2004), 843; W. Rudolph, *Chronikbücher* (Tübingen: Mohr Siebeck, 1955), 167–168; H. G. M. Williamson, *1 and 2 Chronicles* (Grand Rapids, Mich.: Eerdmans, 1982), 168.

[7] Although ethnographic studies show that 1 Chr 25:1–6 may share some features with oral genealogies (limited generational depth, specific social function), the other genealogies in Chronicles strongly suggest that this genealogy is a scribal product, R. R. Wilson, "The Old Testament Genealogies in Recent Research," *JBL* 94 (1975): 169–189.

[8] G. von Rad, *Das Geschichtsbild des Chronistischen Werkes* (Stuttgart: Kohlhammer, 1930), 98–115.

[9] H. Gese, "Zur Geschichte der Kultsänger am Zweiten Tempel," in *Von Sinai zum Zion* (Munich: Kaiser Verlag, 1974), 147–158.

[10] Ezra 2:41; Neh 7:44.

[11] Neh 11:3–19, 1 Chr 9:1–18.

[12] 1 Chr 16:4–7; 1 Chr 16:38–42; 2 Chr 5:12, 29:13–14, 35:15.

[13] 1 Chr 6:31; 15:16–24.

erally accepted Gese's schema of Levitical singers, several have challenged his chronological placements.[14] Most likely, the evidence suggests that the Chronicler used pre-exilic sources in compiling this genealogy of 1 Chr 25:1–6. In studying the psalm superscriptions in relation to the Levitical singers, Nahum Sarna points out that, "If the Levitical clan guilds, Asaph, Korah, Heman, and Ethan, be late inventions, it is strange that Books IV and V of Psalms, which by general consensus are the latest parts of the canonical Psalter, do not ascribe any composition to them."[15] Sarna further identifies major discrepancies between the treatment of the Levitical singer guilds in the psalm superscriptions and the Chronicler, suggesting that they represent two independent traditions. First, the Psalter attributes equal attention to Asaph and Korah, though the latter have very little mention in the Chronicler in any official capacity in public worship.[16] Second, the Psalter ascribes only one Psalm to Heman (Ps 88), though he emerges in the Chronicler as the prime patriarchal line, not just in the genealogical record of 1 Chr 25:1–6, but also in the transport of the ark to Jerusalem (1 Chr 15:17, 19), centrality of worship (1 Chr 6:18, 24, 29), lineage to Samuel and twenty-one generations in comparison to only fourteen for Asaph.[17] These variances suggest that neither the psalm superscriptions, nor the Chronicler directly rely on each other for the Levitical singer genealogies, and both represent genuine pre-exilic sources.

In addition to an independent account of the guild names, a detailed examination of 1 Chr 25:1–6 has several textual difficulties that strongly insinuate a lengthy scribal development. The MT lists the name אשראלה ("Asarelah"), possibly showing a scribal error of parablepsis (v. 2) with the demonstrative אלה. In v. 3, the MT lists only five names, yet describes the individuals as "six under the direction of their father Jeduthun."[18] Interpreters have struggled with the syntactical usage of the rare phrase בדברי האלהים ("by the words of God"), specifically whether it somehow goes with the preceding noun or the following verbal

---

[14] Those who accept Gese's schema include the following: S. J. Devries, *1 and 2 Chronicles* (FOTL 11; Grand Rapids. Mich.: Eerdmans, 1989), 144–145; D. L. Petersen, *Late Israelite Prophecy: Studies in Deutero–Prophetic Literature and in Chronicles*, SBLMS 23 (Missoula, Mont.: Scholars Press, 1977), 61–62. Several scholars offer modifications to the levitical singer chronology of Gese: see Japhet, *1 and 2 Chronicles*, 296; R. Klein, *1 Chronicles* (Minneapolis: Augsburg Fortress, 2006), 348–349; Knoppers, *1 Chronicles 10–29*, 657–658; W. M. Schniedewind, *The Word of God in Transition: From Prophet to Exegete in the Second Temple Period* (JSOTSup 197; Sheffield: Sheffield Academic Press, 1995), 163–164; Williamson, *1 and 2 Chronicles*, 120–121.

[15] N. M. Sarna, "The Psalm Superscriptions and the Guilds," in *Studies in Jewish Religious and Intellectual History Presented to Alexander Altmann on the Occasion of His Seventieth Birthday* (eds. S. Stein and R. Loewe; University, Alabama: University of Alabama Press, 1979), 285.

[16] Sarna, "The Psalm Superscriptions," 285–286.

[17] Sarna, "The Psalm Superscriptions," 286.

[18] The Hebrew text omits the names Shimei, which most translations add on the basis of the LXX, as well as v. 17.

infinitive.[19] The doublet כל־אלה in both the start of vv. 5 and 6 may represent a copying error, or an effort to conflate text.[20] The final listing of "Asaph, Jeduthun and Heman" appears as a curious gloss, explaining the "they" portion of the beginning of the verse. The MT inserts a *samek* to break this name from the preceding words, but the LXX seamlessly integrates these names to the rest of the verse. The order of the guild patriarchs shifts from Asaph, Heman, Jeduthun (v. 1) to Asaph, Jeduthun and Heman (vv. 2–4).[21] Collectively, this unusually high proportion of textual difficulties suggests a lengthy diachronic history beyond the confines of the post-exilic era.

Most significantly, the final seven names under Heman (v. 4) display a universally recognized artificiality:

חנניה חנני אליאתה גדלתי ורממתי עזר ישבשה מלותי הותיר מחזיאות:

("Hananiah, Hanani, Eliathah, Giddalti, Romamti-ezer, Joshbekashah, Mallothi, Hothir, and Mahazioth")[22]

None of these names correspond to any known Semitic onomastic patterns.[23] Four of the names are verbs (הותיר, מלותי, ורממתי, גדלתי), and one of them attaches to a noun (ורממתי עזר). One name is a feminine plural noun (מחויאות), and the remaining two are highly irregular forms (ישבשה, אליאתה). In fact, this list is actually poetic verse, which the Chronicler mistakenly took for a genealogy. Since the nineteenth century, scholars have recognized that a few minor changes in orthography produce the following Psalm:

חנני יה חנני
אליאתה גדלתי ורממתי
עזר ישבקשה מלותי
הותיר מחזי אות

("Be gracious to me, YHWH, be gracious to me;
My God, you, whom I highly exalt
My help when in trouble, I say
Increase my vision and sign").[24]

---

[19] For further discussion, J. W. Kleinig, *The Lord's Song: The Basis, Function and Significance of Choral Music in Chronicles* (JSOTSup 156; Sheffield: Journal for the Study of the Old Testament Press, 1993), 150.

[20] Petersen, *Late Israelite Prophecy*, 66.

[21] Gary Knoppers suggests that the inversion of names deliberately creates an inverted quotation (Zeidel's Law) to highlight the parallel between prophesying and singing. But such a literary artifice does not account for the name order in vv. 2–4, nor the exception of Asaph to this inversion, Knoppers, *1 Chronicles 10–29*, 850–851.

[22] All translations are the author's own.

[23] The list of artificial names was first noticed by H. Ewald, *Ausführliches Lehrbuch der Hebräischen Sprache des Alten Bundes* (Göttingen: Dieterich, 1870), 680. For further discussion see bibliographic references in Williamson, *1 and 2 Chronicles*, 167.

[24] Some commentators explain the non-coherence of this Psalm by suggesting the verse as a composite collection of psalmic sayings, Williamson, *1 and 2 Chronicles*, 167.

Whether the irregularity of names reflects stages of historical development or literary fiction, this list serves as a clear illustration of 1 Chr 25:1–6 as written tradition derived from earlier written sources.[25] The usage of this earliest source must have spanned enough time that the Chronicler mistook its meaning as names, an amount of time beyond the temporal boundaries of the Persian period. The ideology to advance the prominence of Heman partially drives this textual development. By extending to him fourteen sons, the text can now stand at twenty-four individuals, so numerous that the text includes a v. 5 commentary describing the amount of favor God game to Heman. The typological numbers and the repetition of the names, first appearing in general Levitical clans in vv. 2–4, and again in the ordering of the divisions in vv. 9ff, together emphasize the literary polemic nature of this genealogy. In totality, 1 Chr 25:1–6 reveal a heavily literal work, crossing several historical stages.

In addition to the internal clues, the passage explicitly justifies a scribal culture by ascribing their royal origins to David with the attribution "words of David and of Asaph the seer." The passage grants prophetic authority to the heads of the Levitical singers to provide the psalms fit for temple service. The association with David gives authority from a royal basis, but ultimately divine command empowers the clout of the Davidic edict via the phrase בדברי האלהים ("by the words of God"). The passage freely utilizes ideologically charged phraseology to legitimize the greater role of the musician/writers. Verse one describes the Levitical singers as distinctively "set apart" (*hiphil* of בדל√), recalling key priestly passages from the Torah.[26] The heads of Levitical singers are identified with the term נביא ("prophet," vv. 1, 2, 3, 5) and Heman specifically receives the appellation of חזה המלך ("royal seer," v. 5), a title that Chronicler selectively gives to other prophets (1 Chr 21:9; 29:29; 2 Chr 9:29; 12:15; 19:2; 33:18) as well as Asaph (2 Chr 29:30) and Jeduthun (2 Chr 35:15). Their activities are made tantamount to the לעבדת בית האלהים "service of the house of God" (v. 6). This particular phrase appears elsewhere only in Neh 10:33, describing the activities of the elite temple staff. This construction of terms is deliberate and adds a heightened authority to the Levitical singers. Sara Japhet observes that such deliberate language gives the Levitical singers status beyond the orders of officers (1 Chr 26:29ff) and priests (1 Chr 23:13).[27] The singers are not merely

---

[25] J. C. DeMoor cautiously identifies a similar phenomenon in interpreting a list of names as a prayer in an Ugaritic text *R. S.* 24. 246, J. C. DeMoor, "Studies in the New Alphabetic Texts from Ras Shamra," *UF* 2 (1970): 303–327. Wilfred Watson connected this Ugaritic text to the phenomenon in 1 Chr 25:4, W. G. E. Watson, "Archaic Elements in the Language of Chronicles," *Bib* 53 (1972): 206.

[26] The *hiphil* of בדל appears in Lev 20:26, "You shall be holy to Me, for I the LORD am holy, and I have *set you apart* from other peoples to be Mine," as well as five occurrences in Gen 1.

[27] Japhet, *1 and 2 Chronicles*, 437.

musicians, but rather authoritative figures in the center of both the royal court and religious cult.

In fact, the commission in 1 Chr 25:1–6 reveals the term "Levitical singer" to be a misnomer. They were musicians, but in addition, they were clearly composers as well. This authority gave the Levitical singers the authority to write psalms suitable for temple worship. Again, the psalm superscriptions help clarify the written aspect of the prophetic role of Levitical singers. Alongside the superscriptions to David, psalms are associated with Asaph (Pss 50, 73, 74, 75, 76, 77, 78, 79, 80, 81, 82, 83), Heman (Ps 88) and Jeduthun (Pss 39, 62, 77). Although the psalm superscriptions represent a variant tradition from the Chronicler, the presence of these superscriptions supports the cultic singers as psalmists, not necessarily as authorship in the modern sense, but responsible for the scribal activity of compiling psalms suitable for presentation during the burnt offering.

The Chronicler provides an illustration of this scribal activity by compiling a psalm after the successful transfer of the ark to Jerusalem 1 Chr 16. After describing the physical act (1 Chr 16:1–3), which reasonably follows the *Vorlage* of 2 Sam 6:17–19b, the Chronicler adds the call of the Levites, most prominently Asaph, to lead the congregation in prescribed song. The subsequent composition of the musical verse of 1 Chr 16:8–36 is a composite amalgam of several different psalm traditions. The Psalm in 1 Chr 16 begins by borrowing from the thanksgiving Ps 105, which recounts a detailed salvation history from the patriarchs, to Joseph's journey to Egypt, plagues, exodus, wandering in the steppe, conquest and a final call to Torah. But of all of these historical events, the Chronicler only records the portion of Ps 105 that describes the patriarchs. By omitting much of the salvation history of Ps 105 and focusing on the patriarchs, the Chronicler seeks to identify the post-exilic community of the Chronicler as a select few in the midst of a vast world. The Chronicler then borrows from Ps 96, which exalts the people to praise in the midst of other gods and foreign nations. Though most of the Psalm remains intact, the placement in 1 Chr 16 gives it new significance in that God deserves praise in the midst of an uncertain post-exilic context. The poetic song ends with an exhortation (v. 24; cf. Ps 107:1) and the doxology from Book IV of the Psalter (vv. 34–35, cf. Ps 106:47–48). Although not a single verse is original to the Chronicler, this anthology is a unique scribal work that provides expression of thanksgiving (vv. 8–18), lament (vv. 19–22), praise (vv. 23–34) and petition (vv. 35–36) fit for the Second Temple community. Similar to scribal reworking of other psalms (Ps 108, 11QPS^a), the synthesis of earlier source material is not merely a mechanical procedure, but itself a creative scribal act, which revitalizes tradition to a contemporary time. This collection of verses in 1 Chr 16:8–35 illustrate the scribal nature of the Levitical singers in their prophetic call to compile theologically appropriate psalms for the community.

Such an assertion fits with the growing shift of prophecy from proclaimer to writer in the Second Temple period. By examining the prophetic content in Chronicles, William Schniedewind outlines the shift in prophetic function to a scribal culture.[28] In unapologetically citing from the Deuteronomistic History and applying these traditions to the post-exilic context, Chronicles re-invents the prophetic office as "inspired interpreter."[29] 1 Chronicles 25:1–6 characterizes the cultic singers as Second Temple prophets, an office that retains the authority of the monarchial prophets, but places them in the context of the more scribal-oriented world of the Chronicler. Prophets no longer convey verbal messages from the deity as during monarchic times, but rather, their authoritative function manifests in ability to give inspired readings of texts.[30]

Therefore, 1 Chr 25:1–6 embodies aspects of the literate world of the Chronicler. The difficult textual history likely extends to pre-exilic times. In addition, the ideology of the text legitimizes the function of compiling psalms in the hands of the genealogically selected Levitical singers. But ironically, this lengthy scribal work ultimately serves an important place within the oral culture of the Second Temple period.

3. The Spoken Word in the Commission of the Levitical Singers

Despite the unmistakable scribal characteristics of 1 Chr 25:1–6, one must remember that this genealogical passage had to function in an environment with restricted access to literary.[31] In order to advance the ideology of the Chronicler,

---

[28] Schniedewind, *The Word of God in Transition*, 231–241, also W. M. Schniedewind, "The Chronicler as an Interpreter of Scripture," *The Chronicler as Author: Studies in Text and Texture* (eds. M. Patrick Graham and Steven L. McKenzie; JSOTSup 263; Sheffield: Sheffield Academic Press, 1999), 158–180.

[29] Schniedewind, *The Word of God in Transition*, 231–241.

[30] In describing the continuation of the prophetic office in Chronicles, David Petersen asserts, "Just as the Davidic ideal is bound up with the reconstructed temple, so prophecy is, it appears, tied to the work of certain temple personnel, the Levitical singers." Petersen makes this connection based on several elements in the commission of 1 Chr 25:1–6: the prophetic appellatives, the poetic lines and the emphasis on Heman, Petersen, *Late Israelite Prophecy*, 56.

[31] For discussions on the level of literacy, see E. Ben Zvi, "Introduction: Writings, Speeches, and the Prophetic Books – Setting an Agenda," *Writings and Speech in Israelite and Ancient Near Eastern Prophecy* (eds. E. Ben Zvi and M. Floyd; Atlanta: Society of Biblical Literature, 2000), 1–29; D. McLain Carr, *Writing on the Tablet of the Heart: Origins of Scripture and Literature* (New York: Oxford University Press, 2005); R. Hess, "Literacy in Iron Age Israel," *Windows into Old Testament History: Evidence, Argument, and the Crisis Of 'Biblical Israel'* (eds. V. P. Long, D. W. Baker, and G. J. Wenham; Grand Rapids, Mich.: Eerdmans, 2002), 82–102; Niditch, *Oral World*; W. M. Schniedewind, *How the Bible Became a Book: The Textualization of Ancient Israel* (New York: Cambridge University, 2004); van der Toorn, *Scribal Culture and the Making of the Hebrew Bible*; I. M. Young, "Israelite Literacy: Interpreting the Evidence: Part I," *VT* 48 (1998): 239–259; idem, "Israelite Literacy: Interpreting the Evidence: Part II," *VT* 48 (1998): 408–422.

their scribal products had to reach the populace via a non-scribal mode. Consequently, the Levitical singers did not merely compile psalms, but sang them with the people in liturgical contexts. The singing was a crucial aspect of the communal worship.

Such a prominence to the oral components of cultic activity has a long background in the ancient Israel as well as the greater ancient Near East. From the middle of the third millennium B. C., cuneiform evidence shows ritual singers with major roles in the cultic society. Mesopotamian texts most commonly refer to "lamentation-priests" (Sumerian GALA [UŠ. KU]; Akkadian, kalû), whose primary function involves singing during ritual.[32] By the Old Babylonian period (2000–1600 B. C. E.), the cuneiform lexical lists provide nearly 100 terms related to musicians and musicology.[33] These lists associate music with cultic practice, emphasizing the spoken word in temple matters, as several of deities have their own designated singers.[34] The prominence of oral performance in cultic ritual is most pronounced in Ugaritic texts. In the narrative, "Tale of the Goodly Gods," (KTU 1.23) the singers (Ugaritic, šrm), dressed in special garments, are called to invoke the gods in narrative ritual involving food and fire.[35] In several ritual texts, the liturgical order calls on the performance of song with an implied numinous effect in the cult.[36] All of these examples show that musical singing had an integral part of the cultic sphere.

This long-standing tradition of power in musical performance continues into the earliest references to ancient Israel. Interestingly, in the two paradigmatic examples of Archaic Biblical Hebrew (the Song of Miriam and the Song of Deborah), the texts narrate the celebratory performance of singing songs in military victory (Exod 15:20–21, Judg 5:3). The portrayal of musical performance as cultic activity continues in essentially all other genres of the HB. In

---

[32] A. Leo Oppenheim et al., *CAD K, The Assyrian Dictionary of the Oriental Institute of the University of Chicago*, vol. 8 (1971), 91–94.

[33] A. Draffkorn Kilmer, "The Discovery of an Ancient Mesopotamian Theory of Music," *Proceeding of the American Philosophical Society* 115 (1971): 131–149.

[34] Examples include the šr ʿttrt ("singer of Ashtart"); see M. Koitabashi, "Music in the Texts from Ugarit," *UF* 30 (1998): 363–396.

[35] Some have translated this line as "princes" rather than "singers." T. J. Lewis, "The Birth of the Gracious Gods," *Ugaritic Narrative Poetry* (ed. S. B. Parker; Atlanta: Scholars Press, 1997), 209, but other sections of the ritual suggest "singers" as the most appropriate translation. For example, consider the earlier lines, "To be performed seven times with lute accompaniment, with antiphonal response by ministrants," *KTU 1. 23:12*, M. S. Smith, *The Rituals and Myths of the Feast of the Goodly Gods of KTU/CAT 1. 23* (Atlanta: Scholars Press, 2006), 63–64; AO-AT 273 Münster: Ugarit-Verlag, 2000), 258.

[36] In *RS* 24.256:21, a series of songs by "holy ones" (*qdš yšr*) precede the presentation offerings to the deities. In *RS* 24.250+: the singing of songs explicitly occurs several times before the king in the midst of ceremony. These observations are completely congruent with the oral nature of Ugaritic poetic verse with its characteristics of binary pairs and oral type scenes, F. Moore Cross, "Kinship and Covenant in Ancient Israel," *From Epic to Canon: History and Literature in Ancient Israel* (Baltimore: Johns Hopkins University, 1998), 139.

anointing Saul as king, the prophet Samuel associates musical performance with the power to induce the monarch into an ecstatic state (1 Sam 10:5–6). During a military conflict, King Jehoram turns to Elijah, who then asks for a musician to inspire the prophet to perform miracles under divine power (2 Kgs 3:15–16). Other references to music and power occur in the prophetic literature (e. g. Amos 6:5, Isa 5:12), wisdom literature (Song of Songs), and of course, in the Psalter. In all of these cases, the oral performance of song functions to induce a specific state in the hearers.

For the Chronicler, oral performance in the temple reaches an official status with the commission of the Levitical singers in 1 Chr 25:1–6. The passage uses the term נבא ("to prophesy") in vv. 1, 2, 3, rather than a more generic term שיר ("to sing"). Although the precise implication of musical singing as נבא is elusive, as illustrated by the varied LXX translations, the authoritative status of the singing is unmistakable.[37] Specifically, the exhortation to "prophesy with accompaniment of lyres, harps and cymbals" (1 Chr 25:1) equates musical singing to prophetic pronouncement.[38] Verse 3 deliberately reiterates the act of prophecy with the playing of instruments and the actions of ידה ("thanksgiving") and הלל ("praise"). In other words, the legitimization of the Levitical singers to the prophetic office creates an authoritative oral performance act. The text creates imagery of a musical ensemble as mode of hearing the word of YHWH. By associating the prophecy with an entire generation from three distinct patriarchal lines, the passage determines the prophetic singing as much more than a singular phenomena, but rather the creation of an established elite office in the Second Temple cult.

In addition to the specific language of 1 Chr 25:1–6, the Chronicler strategically makes the oral performance of the Levitical singers a crucial event in the order of temple worship. Specifically, Chronicles associates the singing with the burnt offering in several specific places: 1 Chr 16:37–41; 23:30–31; 2 Chr 8:12–14; 2 Chr 23:18. The association of singing with the burnt offering is most specific in 2 Chr 29:21–29 under the portrayal of Hezekiah's temple service. After the blood expiation and the burnt offering "for all Israel," the Chronicler carefully mentions the precise moment of song:

He stationed the Levites in the House of the LORD with cymbals and harps and lyres, according to the ordinance of David and Gad, the king's seer, and Nathan, the prophet, for the ordinance was by the LORD by his prophets. When the Levites were stationed with the instruments of David, and the priests with trumpets, Hezekiah gave the order to offer the burnt offering on the altar. When the burnt offering began, the song of the LORD and the trumpets began also, together with the instruments of King David of Israel (2 Chr 29:25–27).

---

[37] The LXX translates the root נבא as the more generic term ἀποφθέγγομαι in v. 1, the most common Greek equivalent, προφήτης v. 2 and leaves it untranslated in v. 3.
[38] Rudolph, *Chronikbücher*, 170–171.

The specific position of the musical praise in the midst of the burning sacrifice suggests an atonement function with the singing, a connection alluded in the other references to atonement rites in 1 Chr 6:49 and 2 Chr 29:24. The Levitical singing represents the first participatory act of the entire congregation preparing the assembly for sacrifice. Whereas the writing of the liturgical verses restricted the access to the word of YHWH to the few, the public singing empowered the non-literate to access the prophetic proclamation. John Kleinig summarizes the significance of the performance, "It was thus not a peripheral undertaking, conducted, as it were, at the fringes of the sacrificial system, but it was attached to the very centre, around which everything else revolved."[39] Therefore, the prominence to singing within the temple service signals the numinous efficacy of Levitical singing for the entire assembly.

The usage of the psalms in 1 Chr 16 displays similar associations of prophetic power to oral performance. On the momentous occasion of the transfer of the ark to Jerusalem, David appointed certain Levites, notably Asaph to lead liturgical services of song. The Chronicler follows several elements from the Deuteronomistic History, specifically David's blessing on the participants, shared meal. But whereas in 1 Sam 6:17–19, the people get up and leave, in Chronicles the people then participate in worship of thanksgiving as outlined in the Psalm within 1 Chr 16:8–36. Significantly, the Psalm closes with the call to an oral response by "all the people" (v. 36). The oral performance marks a new innovation of the Chronicler and a legitimization of the act in public worship. Unlike the oral narrative poetry of Ugaritic texts, the Psalm of 1 Chr 16:8–36 is clearly a literary poem.[40] But the literary passage was intentionally compiled for oral performance, allowing the post-exilic community to experience the cultic activity.

This scribal development of 1 Chr 25:1–6 served a powerful social function in legitimizing the levitical singers. The performance of song was a featured component of the Chronicler's temple service, and the text had to develop a role for the Levitical singers within the oral culture of the Second Temple period.

4. Synthesis and Conclusions

The literary examination allows us to hypothetically reconstruct both the textual and the socio-historical role of the commission of the Levitical singers

---

[39] Kleinig, *The Lord's Song*, 109.
[40] Frank Moore Cross outlines some of the features of oral poetry. He states, "There can be no doubt, in my opinion, that Ugaritic epic verse was composed orally to music." F. Cross, *From Epic to Canon*, 139.

within the matrix of orality and literacy. Although any biblical reconstruction can appear tenuous, even a heuristic effort can illuminate some of the intricacies of orality and literacy within 1 Chr 25:1–6.

In congruence with ancient Near Eastern cultic practice, pre-exilic Israel likely had specific functions for singers within temple liturgy. The earliest source origins of 1 Chr 25:1–6 likely arise from those roles. In the quest to assign social roles within Second Temple cultic worship, the Chronicler took these traditions and elevated the authority of the Levitical singers by extending the commission to David. The Chronicler both expanded the role of Heman, by mistakenly placing an older psalm into the genealogy and rounded the total number of singers to twenty-four. At the same time, the Chronicler replaces Ethan of earlier Levitical singer tradition and replaced his role as legitimate patriarch with Jeduthun. The genealogy served a social function in making the temple singers with a high prophetic calling associated with King David.

This passage legitimized the role of Levitical singers as both composers of sacred liturgical song, as well as the performers within the temple. By elevating the Levitical singers as prophets, the Chronicler granted them scribal authority to compose and compile psalms such as 1 Chr 16:8–36. But by assigning the performance of these psalms to the burnt offerings, the oral performance of these psalms served as an essential part of the communion with God. Even though prophecy emerges as a more scribal phenomenon for the Chronicler, its association with the post-exilic community finds articulation in oral performance at the temple in the presence of non-literate masses. Ehud Ben Zvi articulates this recurring phenomenon in of orality and literacy in biblical prophecy, "A written text becomes the starting point for oral presentation [...] the communication event here involves not only the written text or a portion thereof, but also how it is read or proclaimed and the interaction between audience and speaker."[41] The written text can only reach the community orally. The oral is powerful because it relies on the authoritative written text.

Therefore, 1 Chr 25:1–6 beautifully illustrates the complexity between orality and literacy in Second Temple culture. Considering post-exilic Yehud as an integrated organism, the sacred traditions manifested themselves in both realms. Can one characterize post-exilic Israel as an oral culture or a scribal culture? An examination of 1 Chr 25:1–6 further unveils the recognition of the question's inadequacy, as one can look at the Levitical singers, who served the community by both writing and singing songs.

---

[41] Ben Zvi, "Introduction: Writings, Speeches, and the Prophetic Books," 16.

"Call on me in the day of trouble …"
From Oral Lament to Lament Psalms

Andreas Schuele

1. Introduction

Ever since the inception of modern form criticism, the lament psalms of the Hebrew Bible have been a key subject of scholarly interest, for seemingly obvious reasons. Despite the variety with regard to both structure and linguistic expression, form critics were able to identify a basic pattern that seemed to be at the heart of this particular genre: lament psalms progress from lament to a confession of trust and expressions of praise.[1] With the sole exception of Ps 88, all of the lament psalms display various combinations of these characteristic elements. A text commonly referred to as a template of a lament psalm is Ps 13[2]:

I. Lament:
"God lament"
(1) How long, O Lord? Will you forget me forever?
How long will you hide your face from me?
"I lament"
(2) How long must I bear pain in my soul, and have sorrow in my heart all day long?
"Enemy lament"
How long shall my enemy be exalted over me?
Petition
(3) Consider and answer me, O Lord my God! Give light to my eyes, or I will sleep the sleep of death, (4) and my enemy will say, "I have prevailed"; my foes will rejoice because I am shaken.

II. Confession of Trust:
(5) But I trusted in your steadfast love; my heart shall rejoice in your salvation.

III. Praise:
(6) I will sing to the Lord, because he has dealt bountifully with me.

---

[1] For an overview of the formal characteristics of a lament psalm see K. Seybold, *Die Psalmen. Eine Einführung* (2nd ed.; Stuttgart: Kohlhammer, 1991), 99.

[2] For a fuller analysis of this psalm see B. Janowski, *Konfliktgespräche mit Gott. Eine Anthropologie der Psalmen* (2nd ed.; Neukirchen–Vluyn: Neukirchener, 2006), 53–58.

Given its brevity, it is significant that all the defining characteristics of a lament psalm are present in Ps 13, which gives reason to assume that this text might have been created almost as a "model" or "structural sample" for this particular genre[3], especially since the content and language of each passage is rather unspecific and un-elaborated.

In addition to the formal outline of a lament psalm, there is also a theological rationale supporting the assumption that the progress from lament to praise is a defining feature of this particular genre. Psalm 50 – a prophetic poem rather than a psalm – culminates in a divine speech, in which God himself instructs his people about true piety and worship:

Hear, O my people, and I will speak, O Israel, I will testify against you. I am God, your God. Not for your sacrifices do I rebuke you; your burnt offerings are continually before me. I will not accept a bull from your house, or goats from your folds. For every wild animal of the forest is mine, the cattle on a thousand hills. I know all the birds of the air, and all that moves in the field is mine. "If I were hungry, I would not tell you, for the world and all that is in it is mine. Do I eat the flesh of bulls, or drink the blood of goats? Offer to God a sacrifice of thanksgiving, and pay your vows to the Most High. Call on me in the day of trouble; I will deliver you, and you shall glorify me." (Ps 50:7–15)

Proper worship, in the perspective of this psalm and that of its neighbor (Ps 51),[4] emerges from a humble spirit and contrite heart (51:17) that submit themselves to the saving powers of God: "Call on me in the day of trouble; I will deliver you, and you shall glorify me" (50:15). In many ways, this line summarizes the theology of lament that one finds over major stretches of the earlier collections of the Psalter, roughly until the completion of the so-called "Messianic Psalter" (Ps 2–89).[5] Bernd Janowski characterizes the dynamic that the lament psalms seek to capture as the movement from "life to death" and from "death to life"[6], building upon the theological conviction that the God of Israel is the one who rescues from death and overcomes the power of chaos and evil. The world, human and other, is made to glorify God, and whatever silences the voices that praise the creator are the enemies that God, for the sake of his own honor and glory, is supposed to blast into oblivion. In a similar venue, Jon D. Levenson has argued that trust in God's rescuing power, which expresses and manifests itself in nature as well as in history, is arguably *the* defining element of Israelite religion.[7]

---

[3] Cf. J. L. Mays, *Psalms* (Louisville Ken: John Knox Press, 1994), 77–80.

[4] On the relationship of Psalms 50 and 51 cf. F.-L. Hossfeld and E. Zenger, *Psalms 2: A Commentary on Psalms 51–100* (Minneapolis: Fortress, 2005), 24: "What the God of the theophany in Ps 50 demands, the person praying in Psalm 51 promises, as is evident especially in vv. 18–19."

[5] For a reconstruction of the transmission history of the Psalter see Hossfeld and Zenger, *Psalms 2*, 1–7.

[6] Janowski, *Konfliktgespräche*, 40.

[7] J. D. Levenson, *Resurrection and the Restoration of Israel: The Ultimate Victory of the God of Life*

In the perspective that Janowski and Levenson have laid out it becomes clear that the lament psalms provided a theological foundation for the religious life of ancient Israel and early Judaism at the various levels of cult, worship, as well as scribal activity. From the Dead Sea scrolls we know that especially psalms from the first third of the Psalter were used for the Sabbath liturgy at Qumran and possibly elsewhere as well. From the many copies that were unearthed one can also infer that the psalms played a significant role in the training of scribes and thus in the educational system of early Judaism. Although this would be a subject in its own right, it seems safe to suggest that the theology of the lament psalms with their characteristic development from lament proper to praise, highlighting the rescuing power of YHWH, permeated and shaped the religious life of Second Temple Judaism in a variety of ways. It is important, however, to realize that this description of their theological character and efficacy focuses on the psalms as *written* texts or "documents." In other words, the perceived movement from lament to praise and, at the content level, from death to life is tied to the literary composition of the psalms. However, a different set of questions and problems presents itself when one shifts the perspective from the "setting in literature" to the "setting in life" (*Sitz im Leben*) of the lament psalms. The founding fathers of form criticism were well aware that the composite form of the lament psalms becomes problematic when one tries to identify specific, real-life contexts that mirror the transition from lament to confession and praise.

2. Setting in Life and Setting in Speech

It has often been noted that the shift from lament to praise as a defining characteristic of lament psalms is the most challenging aspect of their interpretation. What would enable someone who presents herself in a situation of utter distress, vulnerability, and need to switch – literally from one second to the next – to the opposite end of the emotional spectrum? How is this "change in mood" (*Stimmungsumschwung*) explainable if held against the background not just of imagined but real hardships that put the life of an individual at the brink of disaster? Johannes Begrich in particular devoted considerable effort to solving this issue.[8] Since his theory is well known, it may suffice to summarize it here in general terms. Begrich came to the conclusion that the lament psalms as we have

(New Haven/London: Yale University Press, 2006), 209: "Few things are more characteristic of the Israelite idea of the Divine Warrior than the confidence of his beleaguered and oppressed loyalists that their divine patron will not prove impotent in the face of the challenge and allow his justice and his power to be discredited. When at last he manifests his long-acclaimed power, the effects are felt [...] not only in the social realm (with the establishment of justice) but also in the natural realm, in which desiccation and languishing yield to revitalization and health."

[8] J. Begrich, "Das Priesterliche Heilsorakel," *ZAW* 52 (1934): 81–92.

them in written form are actually "incomplete." More precisely, he located the psalms in the cultic life of ancient Israel and interpreted them as part of a ritual process, in which an individual brought her lament before a priest, who would then convey an oracle of salvation.[9] Consequently, the following confession and praise respond to this oracle of salvation, which, however, was not itself included in the composition of a lament psalm.

The most appealing aspect of this theory is that it takes the lament psalms out of the isolation of individual piety and integrates them in the life of the cult and as such in the life of the worshipping community. In this perspective, the "return to life" that Janowski has highlighted is in fact the process in which an individual was restored to the life of the community – a process that was facilitated and validated by the priests. To support his theory, Begrich points to the salvation oracles especially in Deutero-Isaiah and explores the involvement of official cultic personnel, such as prophets and priests, in delivering these oracles to the exilic community.[10]

Put in a different way, the notion is that the lament psalms were the spoken words of an individual in a cultic act, in which he or she received an oracle of salvation. This obviously implies that the situation of that individual had not changed at that point, so that the confession of trust and the language of praise anticipated rather than looked back on God's rescuing and healing actions. While the experience of suffering provides the very real context for lament, trust and praise are meant as expressions of faith in the God who saves from death and restores a person to life.

The most crucial problem with Begrich's view is its speculative nature. We simply do not have any evidence for the lament ritual that Begrich and others see in and behind the lament texts of the Psalter.[11] As a matter of fact, the only text that provides at least partial evidence for the proposed setting in life of a lament psalm also reveals some of the pitfalls of this theory. The birth story of Samuel in 1 Sam 1–2 is arguably the most important biblical narrative that informs our understanding of individual lament. This text tells the story of Hannah, Samuel's mother. She is introduced as one of two wives of Elkanah. While Hannah enjoys the support and love of her husband, she is nonetheless the disadvantaged

---

[9] Begrich, "Heilsorakel," 81: "Wenn ein Einzelner, der im Heiligtum mit seinem Klageliede vor Jahwe getreten ist, sein Klagen und Bitten schöpft hat, so tritt ein Priester auf, der, vielleicht auf Grund eines Opferbescheides, sich an den Beter mit einem Orakel Jahwes wendet und, auf sein Klagen und Bitten bezugnehmend, ihm die Erhörung und Hilfe seines Gottes zusichert. Getröstet durch das göttliche Orakel, spricht der Betende nunmehr die Gewissheit seiner Erhörung aus und schließt mit den Worten des Gelübdes."

[10] Begrich, "Heilsorakel," 85–87.

[11] For a critique of Begrich's position see B. Janowski, "Das verborgene Angesicht Gottes. Psalm 13 als Muster eines Klagelieds des einzelnen," *JBTh* 16 (2001): 43–46 und F. Villanueva, *The 'Uncertainty of Hearing:' A Study of the Sudden Change of Mood in the Psalms of Lament* (VTS 121; Leiden/Boston: Brill, 2008), 2–27.

of the two women because of her barrenness, which earns her the scorn and
contempt of her rival Peninnah. The text also states explicitly that Hannah's
barrenness was no accident but that God had closed her womb and thus kept her
from conceiving a child.

The next scene of the narrative shows Hannah as she walks into the sanctuary
of Shiloh where she prays to God, crying in despair.[12] The text emphasizes that
this is a private and unmediated prayer, which, at this point, neither requires nor
calls for the presence of a priest. Hannah is lamenting and at the same time
bargaining with God to put an end to her infertility. However, it so happens that
the High Priest of Shiloh, Eli, sees her and watches her pray. As the text famously puts it: "As she continued praying before YHWH, Eli observed her
mouth. Hannah was praying silently; only her lips moved, but her voice was not
heard; therefore Eli thought she was drunk" (1 Sam 1:12–13). Hannah's way of
praying is depicted here as unusual and, at least in Eli's perspective, even inappropriate. Thus he misinterprets her facial expression and bodily gestures as
those of a drunk. It is not quite clear, though, what the expected and acceptable
way of prayer would have been: spoken and thus audible words or silent prayer
without any significant body movements. At any rate, Hannah corrects Eli's
perspective and explains how her body language expresses her inner grief and
distress: But Hannah answered, "No, my lord, I am a woman deeply troubled; I
have drunk neither wine nor strong drink, but I have been pouring out my soul
before the LORD. [16] Do not regard your servant as a worthless woman, for I
have been speaking out of my great anxiety and vexation all this time" (1 Sam
1:15–16). The phrase "pouring out one's soul" is a literal translation of the
Hebrew שפך נפש, which is how Hannah characterizes her prayer. It is worth
noticing that she also mentions the "length" of her prayer, apparently another
unusual feature that was likely to meet with the disapproval of authorities like
the High Priest.

The fact that, at first, Eli seems unable to understand what Hannah is doing in
this situation raises the question about the particular character of her prayer.
Only one particular part of this prayer is given in the form of a quote: "She made
this vow: 'O LORD of hosts, if only you will look on the misery of your
servant, and remember me, and not forget your servant, but will give to your
servant a male child, then I will set him before you as a nazirite until the day of
his death. He shall drink neither wine nor intoxicants, and no razor shall touch
his head'" (1 Sam 1:11). The crucial term here is נדר "vow", which is itself part
of a petition: Hannah asks God to turn her fortunes by giving her a male child,
whom she promises to return to God as a nazirite. Vows as part of personal
prayers are mentioned frequently in the psalms, typically in combination with
the verb שלם (pi'el), meaning to "complete" or "pay" one's vows (cf. Ps 50:14;

---

[12] The Hebrew literally speaks of a "bitter soul" (מרת נפש).

56:13; 61:6.9; 65:2).[13] However, as 1 Sam 1:10 suggests, petition and vow follow upon Hannah's prayer, in which she "pours out her soul" to God.[14] While the words are not recorded, the preceding narrative clearly suggests that this part of the prayer includes Hannah's misery as the result of God having closed her womb and of her being humiliated by her rival Peninnah.

If one takes all the elements together that are part of Hannah's prayer, it seems safe to conclude that what we have before us here is the lament part of a "lament psalm of an individual":

"I lament": Hannah's barrenness
"God lament": God as the one closed Hannah's womb
"Enemy lament": Social degradation through Peninnah
"Petition and vow": God asked to change Hannah's fortunes by giving her a son

It is of course interesting that Eli does not seem to be able to "decode" Hannah's gestures and her moving lips as part of her lament prayer – a genre, one would assume, with which he was well acquainted. However, once Eli understands the situation, he resumes his role as priest by conveying to Hannah the divine promise that she will become pregnant and give birth to a son. While the words of Eli in 1 Sam 1:17 are not technically an oracle of salvation, they contain what Begrich sees as the missing piece in the lament psalms, namely a priestly message for the petitioner that his or her request has been heard and will be granted. And in fact, the text does indicate that a change in mood occurs with Hannah: "Then the woman went her way, ate and drank with her husband, and her countenance was sad no longer" (1 Sam 1:18). However, this is also where the report about Hannah's first pilgrimage to the sanctuary in Shiloh ends. While the case can be made that lament prayers had their place in the life of the cult and were (at least typically) followed by an assurance that God would interfere on behalf of the petitioner, there is no mention here of the other characteristic elements of a lament psalm, namely the confession of trust and praise. Hence, there is no evidence that *all* the components of a lament psalm had their setting in life in the *same situation* and would always and necessarily occur together as a unit.

Turning to the next part of the narrative, the reader learns that Hannah did in fact become pregnant and gave birth to her first son – Samuel. Knowing that now it would be for her to fulfill her vow and give Samuel into the care of the priests of Shiloh so that he would be raised as a nazirite, Hannah delays her

---

[13] H. Tita, *Gelübde als Bekenntnis. Eine Studie zu den Gelübden im Alten Testament* (OBO 181; Freiburg (CH)/Göttingen: Vandenhoeck & Ruprecht, 2001); R. Bartelmus, "Tempus als Strukturprinzip. Anmerkungen zur stilistischen und theologischen Relevanz des Tempusgebrauchs im "Lied der Hanna" (1 Sam 2,1–10), " *BZ* 31 (1987): 15–35.

[14] The image of "pouring oneself out" in lament is also present in Ps 102:1. Cf. also Job 7:11; Ps 55:3.

return to the sanctuary until the child was weaned (1 Sam 1:21–24). It is not quite clear how much time passes, but given that in antiquity mothers breast-fed their children for a considerably longer period than in our time, one can assume that at least a couple of years, probably even more, lie between Hannah's first and second visits to the temple in Shiloh. From other biblical traditions one can infer that the presentation of a new-born baby or young child in the temple was part of the religious and cultic life in ancient Israel (cf. Luke 2:22). It is in this context that Hannah speaks her famous prayer of praise. If one looks at this "Song of Hannah" from a form critical perspective, it shows characteristics of a "psalm of praise" as well as of a "hymn" (1 Sam 2:1–10):

Introduction (vv. 1–4):

My heart exults in the LORD; my strength is exalted in my God. My mouth derides my enemies, because I rejoice in my victory. There is no Holy One like the LORD, no one besides you; there is no Rock like our God. ³ Talk no more so very proudly, let not arrogance come from your mouth; for the LORD is a God of knowledge, and by him actions are weighed. ⁴ The bows of the mighty are broken, but the feeble gird on strength.

Narrative part: God's saving actions (vv. 5–8):

Those who were full have hired themselves out for bread, but those who were hungry are fat with spoil. The barren has borne seven, but she who has many children is forlorn. ⁶ The LORD kills and brings to life; he brings down to Sheol and raises up. ⁷ The LORD makes poor and makes rich; he brings low, he also exalts. ⁸ He raises up the poor from the dust; he lifts the needy from the ash heap, to make them sit with princes and inherit a seat of honor. For the pillars of the earth are the LORD's, and on them he has set the world.

Expression of trust in God's power (vv. 9–10)

He will guard the feet of his faithful ones, but the wicked shall be cut off in darkness; for not by might does one prevail. ¹⁰ The LORD! His adversaries shall be shattered; the Most High will thunder in heaven. The LORD will judge the ends of the earth; he will give strength to his king, and exalt the power of his anointed.

This text has been subject of much exegetical discussion. Questions have been raised especially with regard to its form and transmission history. While the song resembles a praise psalm or hymn, the most striking difference is the absence of any reflection on the past suffering of the praying individual and the fortunate turn of events for him or her. Also, the mention of a king (v. 10) does not fit into the immediate narrative context. Thus it has been suggested that Hannah's song was not originally the praise psalm of a mother on the occasion of her child's introduction to the cultic community. Rather, it seems that this text highlights the rescuing and saving power of God and announces the coming of a king in Israel. As such, the song of Hannah sets the stage for one of the main story lines of the books of Samuel. However, even if the song of Hannah may have been inserted in its present context for literary and compositional reasons, it seems safe to assume that the ritual of presenting a child at the temple involved a psalm of thanksgiving or praise.

To summarize our argument so far: While one can certainly agree with Begrich and others that lament, confession of trust, and praise had a cultic *Sitz im Leben*, a text like 1 Sam 1–2 gives reason to believe that, originally, these forms of prayer were associated with different life circumstances of a person and, as a consequence, occurred at different stages and in different contexts of the life of an individual. Thus, one can speak of a *lament process* that could unfold over an extended period of time (several years, in Hannah's case), but there is no evidence for a specific setting in life for the lament psalms as closed literary units as one finds them in the Psalter. Also, drawing out some of the implicit lines in 1 Samuel 1–2, one can conclude that lament and praise were not always and equally involved in a particular situation. Obviously, not all women were barren or in circumstances that called for lament prayers. On the other hand, some women may have done what Hannah did and went to the sanctuary, lamented, and received an oracle of salvation – but without ever being granted what they had requested. No doubt that there were "lament-only" situations that never led to confessions of trust and expressions of praise. 1 Sam 1–2 also suggests that an actual, spoken lament prayer was quite different from what one finds in the biblical texts. The text suggests that Hannah's prayer was more personal and more specific to *her* particular hardship as one finds it in most of the lament psalms. As Claus Westermann noted, in the biblical lament psalms, it usually remains unclear whether a person was physically sick, depressed, marginalized, or persecuted.[15] The metaphors that are used tend to be overwhelmingly thick, expressing the depth of but not necessarily the reason for a person's suffering. Also, lament was not only a matter of well-crafted words and phrases. While we might be inclined to think of lament as a literary art form, the spoken lament that actually occurred when people prayed to "pour out" their souls came with gestures, expressions, and sounds that apparently even cultic officials like Eli did not immediately recognize as proper articulations of lament.

In the final part of this paper, I will turn to examples of lament especially from Greek antiquity that testify to the un-domesticated and sometimes even subversive character of the spoken words of lament. But before this can be done, it seems important to further contemplate the relationship between lament prayer and lament psalm.

---

[15] C. Westermann, *Praise and Lament in the Psalms* (Louisville Ken: Westminster John Knox Press, 1981), 56.

3. From the spoken to the written word of lament

One of the underlying assumptions of form criticism has been that biblical texts, in their present form, are the "fossilized remnants" of the words and practices of ancient Israelite religion. With regard to the psalms, scholars like Gunkel, Begrich, and Mowinckel regarded them as records or transcripts of prayers that were used for a variety of worship purposes.[16] Put differently, these scholars assumed that there were no major differences between the spoken and the written versions of most of the psalm genres. Our analysis has called this basic assumption into question for essentially two reasons: 1. Especially the compositional structure of the lament psalms seems to be the result of careful and intentional theological work and reflection. The transition from lament to praise makes a theological statement about the nature of God and his actions towards the human world. While all the form elements certainly already existed, putting them together in a discrete literary unit seems to have been the work of the various schools and "guilds" that are mentioned in the superscripts of the psalms. Obviously, at some point the psalm texts were used for liturgical and educational purposes, but it seems important to notice that lament and praise in their specific settings in life existed before and continued to exist alongside the written texts. 2. The psalms as we have them explore the language of lament and praise in existential depth rather than with regard to situational relevance. The lament psalms unfold meaning, even if one is neither sick nor persecuted. On the other hand, there is reason to assume that people who came to the temple with a particular need or request used language capable of expressing their particular hardship. It seems that the lament psalms employ the language and images of such particular experiences but mold them into a different genre with a new theological message.

The compositional literary character of lament psalms becomes particularly apparent, if one realizes that the sequence of lament and praise may be the dominant pattern but is certainly not the only way in which these elements can be organized. Federico Villanueva has recently called attention to those lament psalms that show different compositional forms. Villanueva observes that the "change in mood" does not always lead from lament to praise but that, in several instances, the texts show more complicated patterns.[17] There are cases in which praise gives way to lament (Ps 9/10; 27; 40; 89) and there are also examples where the text alternates between the two (Ps 31; 35; 71; 86).[18] Just to pick Ps 86 as an example: after the sequence of appeal, petition, and promise of thanks (vv. 1–13) this psalm ends with lament and petition (vv. 14–17):

---

[16] For a more recent adaptation of this assumption see A. C. Cottrill, *Language, Power, and Identity in the Lament Psalms of the Individual* (New York: T&T Clark, 2008), 9.

[17] Villanueva, *Uncertainty*, 29–41.

[18] Villanueva, *Uncertainty*, 28–29.

O God, the insolent rise up against me; a band of ruffians seeks my life, and they do not set you before them.
But you, O Lord, are a God merciful and gracious, slow to anger and abounding in steadfast love and faithfulness.
Turn to me and be gracious to me;
give your strength to your servant;
save the child of your serving girl.
Show me a sign of your favor, so that those who hate me may see it and be put to shame, because you, LORD, have helped me and comforted me.

Hossfeld and Zenger rightly reject any attempt to "correct" the seemingly awkward structure of this psalm and instead suggest that "the psalm is an artful *relecture* of already existing texts. The creativity of the author of Psalm 86 is shown in the fact that, on the one hand, he has combined conventionalized psalms language in such a way that Psalm 86 as a summary of the "Davidic" psalms [...] and on the other hand, by adopting the Sinai theology of Exodus 33–34, he gives the psalm an overall horizon that then acquires further dimensions of meaning in the context of the Psalter."[19] The key words in this analysis are "artistic relecture," "combine/adopt," and "author." Hossfeld and Zenger, against the traditional form critical school, submit that a text like Ps 86 is the product of literary and theological work and not simply the record of a prayer that individuals prayed in a particular cultic setting. Along similar lines, Villanueva suggests that the different ways of composing lament and praise together express different assumptions about God's presence. Whereas the sequence of lament/praise conveys the certainty about God's willingness to listen to and act on behalf of the petitioner, the opposite movement from praise to lament expresses the *uncertainty* about God's presence.[20] In other words, there is a theological discourse underlying the artful composition of the lament psalms, which reflects on but cannot be reduced to real-life situations in which lament or praise occurred. As Hossfeld and Zenger nicely put it with regard to Ps 86, what one finds here is "theology at prayer."[21]

Another text that seems pertinent with regard to the relationship between oral and written lament is Ps 88. This text is of particular significance because of its unique form: it is the only "pure" lament psalm in the entire Psalter. Instead of a development from lament to confession and praise, the psalm is structured by three invocations, each introducing a new section of lament:[22]

vv. 2–3:   *YHWH, God of my salvation, by day I have cried, and in the night before you; let my petition come before you; incline your ear to my cry. For my soul is full of troubles, and my life draws near to Sheol.*

---

[19] Hossfeld and Zenger, *Psalms 2*, 369.
[20] Villanueva, *Uncertainty*, 256.
[21] Hossfeld and Zenger, *Psalms 2*, 376.
[22] Janowski, *Konfliktgespräche*, 233–234.

vv. 10b–11: *I have called to you, YHWH, every day.* I have stretched out my hands to you.
Can you work a miracle for the dead, or do the shades raise to praise you?

vv. 14–15: *But I, YHWH, am calling to you for help, and in the morning let my petition come*
before you. Why, YHWH, do you reject my soul, why do you hide your face
from me?

Some exegetes have interpreted the structure of this psalm as a peculiar deviation
from the standard form of a lament psalm.[23] However, against the backdrop of
our analysis of 1 Sam 1–2, one reaches a different conclusion: Ps 88 does not
deviate from the "norm," it is a lament text that just never developed into the
more expansive form that also included confessions of trust or expressions of
praise.[24] Whether this means that Ps 88 is closer to the spoken words of lament in
a specific situation of suffering is a debated issue. Several authors have suggested
that Ps 88 is a "psalm in sickness" of someone who feels Sheol closing in on
her.[25] In fact, compared with other lament psalms, Ps 88 is remarkably focused
on the particular experience of someone who faces the reality of dying and
death. However, as other commentators have stated, Ps 88 shows a carefully
developed poetic style that one would not expect from someone fighting for her
life.[26] It seems reasonable to assume that, like all other lament psalms, Ps 88 in its
present form is not the recorded voice of a person in distress; rather, it developed
into a poetic, theological reflection on the reality of dying and death, which
simply did not call for the connection with forms of praise that seem characteristic for the transmission history of other psalms.

4. Lament and Protest

So far, we have examined some of the literary and theological transformations
that lament underwent in the process that eventually led to the lament texts of
the Psalter. This leaves the question, if there any clues about lament as an oral
genre – as spoken rather than written words. For obvious reasons, any hard
evidence is difficult to come by in this case. An additional problem with regard
to ancient Israelite culture is that there is practically no extra-biblical epigraphy
or iconography that could provide evidence of the social or religious context or
the particular expressions of lament.[27]

---

[23] For an overview of the research on Ps 88 see Hossfeld and Zenger, *Psalms 2*, 389–394.

[24] Cf. Mays, *Psalms*, 282.

[25] W. Gross, "Gott als Feind des einzelnen? Psalm 88," *Studien zur Priesterschrift und zu
alttestamentlichen Gottesbildern* (ed. idem; SBAB 30; Stuttgart: Katholisches Bibelwerk, 1999),
160–161.

[26] Janowski, *Konfliktgespräche*, 236; Hossfeld and Zenger, *Psalms 2*, 391.

[27] A particularly helpful volume on lament in Mesopotamia and Ancient Greece is *Lament:
Studies in the Ancient Mediterranean and Beyond* (ed. A. Sutter; Oxford/New York: Oxford
University Press, 2008).

What I wish to do in concluding this essay is to take a look at a lament text from ancient Greece that, in some respects, shows similarities with the lament of Hannah in 1 Sam 1. One of the key texts in Homer's Iliad is the lament of Andromache over the death of her husband Hector. There is consensus that Homer actually modeled Andromache's speech on the oral lament traditions of his time.[28] As far as the literary context goes, Andromache's lament follows the fight in which Achilles kills Hector. This was Hector's self-chosen death that would let him be remembered forever in the legends of future generations. Dying a heroic death is the steep but, in Hector's view, worthy price for entering the immortality of being remembered forever. As is well known, Homer himself was a critic of the heroic ideals of the culture[29] that he depicts in his epic, and he voices this critique by letting Andromache point out what Hector's desire for immortality means for those who belong to him and depend on him.[30] For our purposes it is particularly interesting that Andromache's lament takes a threefold form similar to biblical lament:[31]

You lament	"My husband, you were lost young from life, and have left me a widow in your house, and the boy is only a baby who was born to you and me, the unhappy. I think he will never come of age, for before the head to heel this city will be sacked, for you, its defender, are gone, you who guarded the city."
I lament	"[There are] wives who before long must go away in the hollow shops, and among them I shall also go, and you, my child, follow where I go, the there do much hard work that is unworthy of you … but for me passing all others is left the bitterness and the pain, for you did not die in bed, and stretch your arms to me, nor tell me some last intimate word that I could remember always, all the nights and days of my weeping for you."
Enemy lament"	Or else some Achaian will take you by hand and hurl you from the tower into horrible death, in anger because Hector once killed his brother, or his father, or his son; there were so many Achaians whose teeth bit the vast earth, beaten down by the hands of Hector."

Even from these excerpts the accusational character of Andromache's lament becomes immediately clear. It expresses protest and anger not only about the fact that Hector's striving for heroism means misery and danger for his wife and young child; there is also an emotional component: by not even giving his wife a

---

[28] See G. Holst-Warhaft, *Dangerous Voices: Women's Laments and Greek Literature* (2nd ed.; London: Routledge, 1995), 108–113.

[29] Holst-Warhaft, *Dangerous Voices*, 113–114.

[30] In the larger context of Hector's funeral ceremony it is interesting that none of the women who lament over his death – Andromache, Hecuba, and Helen – praise Hector for his heroic ideals, but portray him as a human being close to his friends and dear to the God's (Holst-Warhaft, *Dangerous Voices*, 112), which seems an indirect way of saying that, by seeking glory on the battlefield, Hector deprived himself and others of profound human relationships.

[31] Translation from C. Perkell, "Reading the Laments of the Iliad," in *Lament*, 97–98.

chance to say good-bye, Hector deprives his wife of the experience of a last embrace to give her comfort in her grief. In this perspective, the threefold form of lament becomes a means of protest against a situation for which the lamenting individual is ultimately not responsible. Lament is a cry out against the experience of powerlessness and imposed suffering.

If one compares Andromache's speech as a sample of lament traditions in pre-classic Greece with the Old Testament, the most striking observation is that, in the psalms, the "you lament" in practically all cases presents itself as "God lament." God is the "you" that is ultimately accused of bringing about suffering or allowing it to unfold. This takes us back to our original example of a lament psalm, Ps 13, with its opening line that puts the responsibility for the misery of the lamenting individual on God: "How long, O Lord? Will you forget me forever? How long will you hide your face from me?"

This gives reason to assume that, in ancient Israel, protest addressed to and expressed against God is not only a literary characteristic of written "psalmic" lament but has its roots in the oral performance of lament. The nature of lament is thus more than silent grief or a way of easing oneself into an unavoidable fate. It is protest against whatever isolates an individual from the "land of the living,"[32] especially when God himself is identified as the one who causes or tolerates suffering and pain. This also affects the public aspects of spoken lament. As we have noted for the case of Hannah, and as one could easily demonstrate with regard to Greek iconography,[33] lament as protest had its place in the public square and, for precisely that reason, was sometimes considered inappropriate or even dangerous and could thus be banned from the public arena.[34]

Coming back to the particular literary character of lament in the psalms, it seems safe so say that, while lament kept its accusatory nature, a shift in emphasis and meaning occurred: one can say that the psalms downplay and at the same time highlight the protest expressed in lament. They downplay it, in as much as lament is typically presented as that which God will overcome and that, consequently, has to give way to confessions of trust and expressions of praise. Put more bluntly, the lament psalms seem to "tame" or "domesticate" the protest of (oral) lament. However, precisely because of the prescribed sequence of lament and praise, the lament psalms hold God himself to the firm expectation of salvation and deliverance. It is simply not an option for God not to interfere and act on behalf of those who are suffering. In this sense, it was a bold and challenging move on the part of the psalmists to let God make an unconditional vow: "Call on me in the day of trouble; and I will deliver you, and you shall glorify me."

---

[32] Cf. Job 28:13; Ps 27:13; 116:9; 142:5.

[33] B. Burke, "Mycenaean Memory and Bronze Age Lament," in Suter, *Lament*, 70–92.

[34] Holst-Warhaft, *Dangerous Voices*, 114–119; K. Stears, "Death Becomes Her: Gender and Athenian Death Ritual," in Suter, *Lament*, 139–155.

"Publishing" a Gospel:
Notes on Historical Constraints to Gospel Criticism

Pieter J. J. Botha

During the third decade of the first century of our era Jesus of Nazareth spoke to his friends, family, followers and foes. He taught and argued and performed various memorable deeds. About a hundredandfifty years later some people in Egypt possessed written texts, on papyrus, reporting some of these sayings and deeds of Jesus. We can safely assume that elsewhere in the Roman Empire others also had such writings in their possession.

This study is a contribution to understanding aspects of the process between those two realities. There is an air of anachronism and idealism to much study done in this regard. Not only do we often answer questions about gospel origins and development in terms of conceptions inappropriate to book history, but even construe many of the questions in a way which presupposes the presence of modern books and modern literacy activities in antiquity. Here I want to explore, rather briefly, possible settings for and conditions in which the gospels *as material artifacts* were produced and utilized.[1]

The proposal is that the historical and cultural constraints of writing and "publishing" in antiquity provide parameters for thinking about the "original contexts" of the canonical gospels.

1. Manuscript Culture

A good place to start one's ethnography of Greco-Roman communication is the characteristics of manuscripts. Considering the manuscript as a functional tool helps to conceptualize Greco-Roman literacy specifically and historically

---

[1] Responding to the lack of consensus in the many answers in the historical questions in New Testament scholarship, Antoinette Wire urges us to address "the more difficult question of who told these stories and what they were asserting, that is, what side of their people's struggle they were on" (A. Clark Wire, "Women's History from Birth-Prophecy Stories," *Christian Origins* [ed. R. A. Horsley; vol. 1 of *A People's History of Christianity*; Minneapolis: Fortress, 2005], 92). This study aims at saying something about *how* these stories were circulating, and how those literacy activities were shaping the struggles of early Christians.

(and not in essentialist terms). In this section I focus on what it meant to read and write in a pre-print society, against the background of Greco-Roman education, as collective and participatory activities without the social and judicial institution of copyright.

Readers, audiences and authors are products of particular historical conditions. By studying the formats of books and their typographical disposition(s) we can learn how they were created, how they were read, and understand something about their possible meanings.[2] In writing and reading materials, technology and human activity interact, and these various specifics must be taken into account when written artifacts are to be understood.[3] Historical investigation requires that textual criticism, the historical study of books and cultural history be interrelated to describe "the variations that differentiate the 'readable space' (the texts in their material and discursive forms) and those which govern the circumstances of their 'actualization' (the readings seen as concrete practices and interpretive procedures)."[4]

When a scribe in the first century took up his writing materials, he started by taking up a blank *roll* of papyrus. Even sheets for codices were cut from rolls. We can assume that the first copies of the Gospels were produced on papyrus rolls.[5]

How should we visualize these book rolls? The standard length for the Herculaneum rolls is 9–10 meters.[6] William Johnson investigated literary rolls from Oxyrynchus and found that rolls were sometimes, and probably often, of a length exceeding 15 meters.[7] What size cylinder do these rolls form? A five

---

[2] Cf. R. Darnton, "History of Reading," in *New Perspectives on Historical Writing* (ed. P. Burke; University Park: University of Pennsylvania Press, 1991), 159; J. L. Machor, "Introduction: Readers/texts/contexts," in *Readers in History: Nineteenth-Century American Literature and the Contexts of Response* (ed. J. L. Machor; Baltimore: Johns Hopkins University Press, 1993), x–xi.

[3] "To reconstruct in its historical dimensions this process of the 'actualization' of texts above all requires us to realize that their meaning depends upon the forms through which they are received and appropriated by their readers (or listeners). Readers, in fact, never confront abstract, idealized texts detached from any materiality. They hold in their hands or perceive objects and forms whose structures and modalities govern their reading or hearing, and consequently the possible comprehension of the text read or heard" (R. Chartier, "Laborers and Voyagers: From the Text to the Reader," *Diacritics* 22 [1992]: 50).

[4] Chartier, "Laborers and Voyagers," 50.

[5] Cf. T. C. Skeat, "The Origin of the Christian Codex," *Zeitschrift für Papyrologie und Epigraphik* 102 (1994): 266. "It is not easy to suppose that a narrative like a Gospel should have first been published in a codex. A Gospel was brief enough to be easily contained in a roll of normal length, and as a narrative it was meant to be read from beginning to end. For this, the codex offered no advantage over the roll." (H. Y. Gamble, *Books and Readers in the Early Church: A History of Early Christian Texts* [New Haven: Yale University Press, 1995], 63).

[6] T. Dorandi, "Herculanean Papyri," *Brill's New Pauly. Encyclopaedia of the Ancient World: Antiquity*, vol. 6 (2005), 186. "Herculaneum rolls" refer to the so-called library of the Villa dei Papiri at Herculaneum.

[7] W. A. Johnson, *Bookrolls and Scribes in Oxyrhynchus* (Toronto: University of Toronto Press, 2004), 143–51.

meter long scroll results in a roll diameter of about five-and-a-half centimeters, and a scroll of fifteen meters rolls up to a diameter of nine centimeters. "The cylinder of a 7.5-meter roll is [...] roughly the same diameter as a can of soda pop; a 10-metre roll roughly the same as a wine bottle; a 20-meter roll slightly smaller than a 2-litre container of Coca-Cola. [...] A diameter as large as 9 or 10 centimeters may, nonetheless, seem daunting."[8]

If we use P45 as a model (i.e., columns of writing of 16×19 cm and inter-columnar space of 2 cm) the gospels set on rolls would entail:

Matthew (49 columns)   49 × 18 = 882 cm.
Mark (32 columns)   32 × 18 = 576 cm.
Luke (48 columns)   48 × 18 = 864 cm.
John (38 columns)   38 × 18 = 684 cm.
Four gospels, single scroll   = 3006 cm.

The size of Matthew's or Luke's gospels as 7 centimeter thick cylinders, or even a 6-metre roll for Mark with a diameter of 6 centimeter reminds us not to think about the gospel production in terms borrowed from modern technology.

A simple juxtapositioning of a modern book and an ancient publication reveals overwhelming differences. The modern book is lightweight, small, easily manageable and all copies of the same publication are exactly alike – something not only *impossible* in antiquity, but probably also unimaginable. Modern books have tables of contents, title pages, indexes, chapter divisions, pages and page numbers: all make for effortless, comfortable use and access to the text itself. The ancient book is a cumbersome, unwieldy scroll, readable while standing up (and when it is not necessary to search for a specific sentence or paragraph), but physically demanding for reference and comparison.[9] Some have proposed that the codex form was preferred (from the second century onwards) for its ease of reference and cross-reference, but that is hard to substantiate, since none of the traces of such reference systems can be found in those earliest manuscripts.

It takes a certain knack to read a scroll, keeping it open at the required place. Unrolling and rolling up are fairly straightforward, but *managing* a scroll either while reading or to locate a reference requires considerable skill and practice.

Once opened a scroll must be anchored, as scrolls will roll themselves up.[10] Working with scrolls is very different from working with codices, a picture mostly left out of accounts of gospel origins. But scroll or codex, working with

---

[8] Johnson, *Bookrolls*, 150.

[9] Discussion and references: P.J.J. Botha, "'I Am Writing This with My Own Hand...': Writing in New Testament Times," *Verbum et Ecclesia* 30 (2009): 1–11, and idem, "The Greco-Roman Book: Contextualising Early Christian Documents," *Acta Patristica et Byzantina* 20 (2009): 1–24.

[10] T. C. Skeat, "Roll Versus Codex – a New Approach?" *Zeitschrift für Papyrologie und Epigraphik* 84 (1990): 297.

ancient manuscripts is not like working with modern printed editions or books. In antiquity, students and scholars did not use study desks, not for writing or for reading. Part of the expertise involved with being a reader at that time was to be dexterous with unwieldy objects.[11]

Unlike our needs and expectations with regard to texts, ancient readers did not imagine their texts to be easily accessible and manageable, nor for them to be diverse sources of information.

Histories of reading identify three "macroscopic oppositions" characterizing modern versus pre-print literacy: an opposition between reading aloud and silent reading; between reading in public and reading in solitude; and between educated and "popular" reading.[12]

1.1 Reading manuscripts

Chartier describes the development of silent, private reading as "undeniably one of the major cultural developments" of modern times.[13] Reading in antiquity was not experienced as a silent scanning, mainly mental activity. It was a performative, vocal, oral-aural event.[14] Reading aloud is an important (not exclusive) feature of ancient literacy: readers usually recited, with vocal and bodily gestures, the texts, which were often memorized beforehand.[15]

Comfortable reading is something *we* are familiar with, but in antiquity reading was a physically demanding activity. Clearly a *different* bodily experience is involved here a physical attitude that demanded considerable technical skill.[16]

---

[11] Greeks and Romans did not use tables for writing or reading, though some made use of reading stands. Sometimes a wooden reading stand was used to hold the scroll; the device could be resting on the lap of a seated reader or placed on a low supporting column. Cf. J. P. Small, *Wax Tablets of the Mind: Cognitive Studies of Memory and Literacy in Classical Antiquity* (London: Routledge, 1997), 160–67.

[12] R. Chartier, "Frenchness and the History of the Book: From the History of Publishing to the History of Reading," *Proceedings of the American Antiquarian Society* 97 (1987): 322–24.

[13] R. Chartier, "The Practical Impact of Writing," *Passions of the Renaissance* (ed. R. Chartier; vol. 3 of *A History of Private Life*; Cambridge (MA): Belknap Press, 1989), 125.

[14] D. M. Schenkeveld, "Prose Usage of AKOYEIN 'to Read'," *Classical Quarterly* 42 (1992): 129–41; W. A. Johnson, "Oral Performance and the Composition of Herodotus' *Histories*," *Greek, Roman and Byzantine Studies* 35 (1994): 229–54; K. Quinn, "The Poet and His Audience in the Augustan Age," *Principat: Sprache und Literatur* (vol. 30.1 of *Aufstieg und Niedergang der Römischen Welt, II*; eds. H. Temporini and W. Haase; Berlin: Walter de Gruyter, 1982), 155–58; J. Svenbro, "Phrasikleia – an Archaic Greek Theory of Writing," in *Literacy and Society* (eds. K. Schousboe and M. T. Larsen; Copenhagen: Akademisk Forlag, 1989), 236.

[15] See P. J. J. Botha, "New Testament Texts in the Context of Reading Practices of the Roman Period: The Role of Memory and Performance," *Scriptura* 90 (2005): 621–40. Of course, silent reading was not only possible but practiced as well. It is self-evident that if one can read one can read silently. Yet modern preferences reflect our times, our technology, our educational practices and our values, and we need to emphasize reading techniques as practiced in antiquity.

[16] R. J. Starr, "Reading Aloud: Lectores and Roman Reading," *Classical Journal* 86 (1991): 337–43.

Vocal articulation is a great help to understanding a text. Discussing the instability of classical Greek writing, Youtie notes that it "might well have created a preference for reading aloud [which] provided, contrary to modern expectation, a quicker route to intelligibility than mere visual inspection."[17]

Punctuation was the responsibility of the *reader*. The use of *scriptio continua* forced the reader to punctuate the text but also aided the reader in memorizing.

The relevant point – in terms of an ethnography of communication – is the recognition of how complex the use of scrolls was, requiring extensive use of vocalization and memory. Today we think of writing as an external store that substitutes memory. Though the connection between writing and memory was apparent to writers and readers of the Roman period, reading was considered more a means of retrieval of what was inside of oneself. The material forms of ancient literacy established a *linear* experience of texts and narratives. The actual articulation of a text, how one thing leads to another, was in itself an important part of the creative process and the linear unfolding of a work bears the traces of that creative process.

We can use the contrast between "intensive and extensive reading" to illustrate a spectrum of reading styles with a slow, repeated, reverent manner on the one end and towards the other end a skimming, discarding style.[18] The typology is useful for historical understanding in order to characterize reading practices. Most of those who read scrolls read "intensively." Typically they had access to only a few books and they read them over and over again, usually aloud and in groups, so that a narrow range of texts became deeply impressed on their consciousness. Today, in contrast, many readers of books read "extensively" and all kinds of material, especially periodicals and newspapers, and read what is at hand only once, then move on to the next item, relying on technology to find and/or to return to information required.

Furthermore, in the context of an orally oriented communication technology, composition and performance of writings are aspects of the same process, and the one cannot be understood without reference to the other. We should not lose sight of the impressive, wide-ranging workings and functions of memory in ancient literacy. We can confidently speak of a culture that fundamentally valued memory skills.[19]

---

[17] H. C. Youtie, *The Textual Criticism of Documentary Papryi: Prolegomena* (2nd ed.; London: Institute of Classical Studies, University of London, 1974), 17 n. 6.

[18] Cf. R. Engelsing, "Die Perioden der Lesergeschichte in der Neuzeit: Das statistische Ausmaß und die soziokulturelle Bedeutung der Lektüre," *Archiv für Geschichte des Buchwesens* 10 (1970): 945–1002, who is interested in demarcating the shift to "modern" reading towards the end of the eighteenth century.

[19] Small, *Wax Tablets*, 81–140; J. Farrell, "The Phenomenology of Memory in Roman Culture," *Classical Journal* 92 (1997): 373–83; B. Bergmann, "The Roman House as Memory Theater: The House of the Tragic Poet in Pompeii," *Art Bulletin* 76 (1994): 225–26.

The written page (column) was understood to be a memory device, and mnemonic techniques affected literary composition. Reading, indeed Greco-Roman literacy, should be understood as the interactive process of familiarizing with others' words *in memory*.[20]

Editing and revision were very much part of the initial stages of book production, the wax tablet stage, or what was known as the author's ὑπομνήμα-τα.[21] This is not to say we must imagine authors plunging forward without ever revising anything, but the logistical problems in substantially editing or revising works of scope (such as, for example, a scroll with 40 columns at 7 meter long) would have been daunting in antiquity.

When we think about literary text production during the Roman period, we need to adjust our expectations. Composing complex works at length with minimal notes (on wax tablets, for example) and extensively relying on memory was very much the norm.

1. 2 Citations, references and manuscripts

Ancient writers and readers do not exhibit a need for precise citation. Clearly they experienced their practices as adequate. Incidentally, this emphasizes once more the role that memorizing and assistants played.[22] The practices of scholarship in the Roman period can be described as "rote familiarity with a finite body of authority, arranged according to rational principles and retained by memory."[23]

When one Greco-Roman writer cites another, he uses the same kind of vague reference as when making references within his own writings. The modern system of citation began in the thirteenth century.[24] A concept of the page simply did not exist in antiquity. Pages could not be cited, not just because works were written on rolls, but because each roll was individually produced by hand and could vary tremendously in the length of text written in any given width and column.[25] The codex was no better, since it too was subject to the same idiosyncrasies of individual, handwritten production.

---

[20] Cf. M. J. Carruthers, *The Book of Memory: A Study of Memory in Medieval Culture* (Cambridge Studies in Medieval Literature 10; Cambridge: Cambridge University Press, 1990), 13.

[21] R. H. Rouse and M. A. Rouse, "Wax Tablets," *Language & Communication* 9 (1989): 177–80; T. Dorandi, "Den Autoren über die Schulter geschaut: Arbeitsweise und Autographie bei den antiken Schriftstellern," *Zeitschrift Für Papyrologie und Epigraphik* 87 (1991): 14–18.

[22] An entertaining example is mentioned by Seneca the Younger: Calvisius Sabinus purchased at great expense slaves to whom he delegated tasks of memorizing the poets, as he himself struggled (*Epistula* 27. 6–7).

[23] R. H. Rouse and M. A. Rouse, *Authentic Witnesses: Approaches to Medieval Texts and Manuscripts* (Notre Dame: University of Notre Dame Press, 1991), 218.

[24] Rouse and Rouse, *Authentic Witnesses*, 221–55.

[25] "The number of lines varies with the height of the column and the size of the writing; but s less than 25 or more than 45 are exceptional. Neither in the roll nor later in the codex, eference was easy, as it could never have been with the roll, was the ancient scribe

All study and research had to be done relying chiefly on memory. Lexica, concordances and indices were not at hand. Awareness of the presence of such aids (and of course, frequent use thereof) affects the attentiveness with which one reads. Ancient researchers knew very well that once read, words would be mostly inaccessible except for what was remembered. There simply was no efficient technology to recover contents of written media.

In his discussion of Plutarch's working methods, Pelling notes

[...] the physical difficulties of working with papyrus rolls. These were hefty and un-manageable things; and indexing, chapter-headings, and even line- and column-num-bering were rudimentary or non-existent. It would be easy to read a roll continuously, at the stage of the preliminary reading; but reading was a two-handed business, and it would be difficult to have more than one roll under one's eyes during composition itself. Even if (for example) a slave held a second roll for an author to compare accounts, or the author himself used a book-rest, combining versions would still be awkward. If two accounts did not deal with events in the same sequence – if, for instance, one narrated chronologically, while the other ordered events thematically-it would be a cumbrous business to roll back and forth to find the parallel account. There were probably no chapter-headings to help. Systematic comparison of two accounts might still be possible; no doubt it was sometimes done. But it would be very inconvenient, and it would not be surprising if authors preferred to rely on their memory.[26]

Greek and Roman historians and biographers frequently claim to have done a wide range of reading (and therefore deserve to be believed), but almost without exception we find them incontrovertibly basing their narrative of individual episodes on a single source.

The curious fidelity to a single source for individual episodes is most easily understood if we make a simple assumption: that, following this initial wide reading, an author would generally choose just one work to have before his eyes when he composed, and this work would provide the basis of his narrative.[27]

1. 3 Books as interactive enterprises

By and large, books in antiquity involved complex collaborative events. Just to author a book typically required multiple roles, such as *dictator, notarius,* and *librarius* – that is, one who composed the words *(dictator),* one who noted them down on the wax tablet *(notarius),* and one who made the fair copy on papyrus *(librarius)* – amongst others.[28]

---

concerned to keep the same number of lines to a column. The number of letters to a line similarly varied" (F. G. Kenyon and C. H. Roberts, "Books, Greek and Latin," *Oxford Classical Dictionary* [2nd ed.; eds. S. Hornblower and A. Spawforth, Oxford: Oxford University Press, 1970]: 173).

[26] C. B. R. Pelling, "Plutarch's Method of Work in the Roman Lives," *Journal of Hellenic Studies* 99 (1979): 92–93.

[27] Pelling, "Plutarch's Method," 92.

[28] T. Dorandi, "Zwischen Autographie und Diktat: Momente der Textualität in der antiken Welt," *Vermittlung und Tradierung von Wissen in der griechischen Kultur* (ScriptOralia 61; eds. W

Ancient authors were deeply reliant on slaves and freedmen, household scholars so to speak. "A scholar was expected to be a walking dictionary, indeed a walking encyclopedia, for quotations and information of all sorts were, as is well known, difficult to check in rolls, even if the right works were available."[29] Indeed, a whole factory of work probably lies behind every ancient writer's production, "and we should not expect a master to 'acknowledge' his servants' help."[30]

Groups of people consisting of individuals with a variety of technical skills and levels of education were involved in the making, publishing and use of a book. We should not imagine a solitary, individual figure arranging index cards and carefully editing a range of textual material in the writing process.

2. Scenarios for Writing a Book

How should we visualize the gospel authors at work? Of course, how they actually went about authoring their texts we cannot know, given current evidence. But we can discern some things about how other people went about creating their texts during the first century.

2.1 The "mad" scientist

An interesting example is a scene in the pseudepigraphical Hippocratic Letters.[31] In this dramatized account the famous doctor investigates the case of the "mad scientist," Democritus, who turns out to be not really mad at all.

And Democritus himself was sitting under a spreading low plane tree, in a coarse shirt, alone, not anointed with oil, on a stone seat, pale and emaciated, with untrimmed beard. Next to him on the right a small stream bubbled down the hill's slope softly. There was a sanctuary on top of that hill, which I conjectured was dedicated to the nymphs, roofed over with wild grapes. He had a papyrus roll on his knees (ἐπὶ τοῖν γονάτοιν βιβλίον) in a very neat manner, and some other book rolls were laid out on both sides. And stacked around were a large number of animals, generally cut up. He sometimes bent and applied himself intensely to writing, sometimes he sat quietly attentive, pondering within himself. Then after a short time of this activity he stood up and walked around and examined the entrails of the animals, set them down and went back and sat down. The Abderites,

---

Kullmann and J Althoff; Tübingen: Gunter Narr Verlag, 1993), 71–83; P. J. J. Botha, "Authorship in Historical Perspective and Its Bearing on New Testament and Early Christian Texts and Contexts," *Scriptura* 102 (2009): 495–508.

[29] E. Rawson, *Intellectual Life in the Late Roman Republic* (London: Duckworth, 1985), 51.

[30] Pelling, "Plutarch's Method," 95.

[31] Which dates from the Roman period, possibly early Empire: Z. Stewart, "Democritus and the Cynics," *Harvard Studies in Classical Philology* 63 (1958): 186; *Hippocrates: Pseudepigraphic Writings* (ed. and trans. W. D. Smith; Leiden: Brill, 1990), 28–29. For the text I consulted Smith, *Hippocrates: Pseudepigraphic Writings.*

standing about me downcast, their eyes not far from tears, said, "You see Democritus' way of life, Hippocrates, how mad he is, how he doesn't know what he wants or what he is doing?" (Hippocrates, *Epistulae* 17. 2).

The pseudepigraphic Letters of Hippocrates, particularly letters 10–17, form a "novella" which depicts a meeting between the famous medical practitioner (ὁ ἰητρός) and the famous philosopher. This fictionalized meeting depicts De-mocritus as a wealthy aristocrat[32] who has adopted Cynicism and is in search of the "nature and location of the gall" (17. 4). In this narrative world, excessive study, like unrestrained laughter, is a sign of mental illness. When a servant (17. 10) appears to handle his books we recognize Democritus as a wealthy, eccentric member of the elite on his country estate – the appropriate setting for a scholar and scholarly pursuits. The underlying values of the narrator are revealed in the 13th letter, where "Hippocrates muses that what Democritus suffers may not be a disease but ἀμετρίη παιδείης, an excess of learning, culture, study, thought to be excess by laymen, but not really so, since excess of virtue is never a bad thing."[33]

This is not a paean to research, but a discourse on the "wretched, unworthy pursuits" (17. 9) that characterize human life. Yet we can note a few aspects relevant to picturing research and authoring.

For instance, one is reminded that writing was done "on the knee."[34] Further-more, reading and literary investigation were activities typically done "outside"; Greeks and Romans did not use rooms as studies. We also note the presence of slave and freedman assistants.

2. 2 The sponsored intellectual

There are a few reports about the work methods of ancient writers but they are often of an indirect nature and surprisingly difficult to interpret.[35] Essentially, there were three stages. (a) The preliminary reading, which could embrace a whole range of sources. (b) The production of the ὑπομνήματα (or ὑπόμνημα). Both stages required readers and secretaries. (c) The writing (dictating to a scribe) of the finished versions. The whole process presupposes the availability, preparation and maintenance of writing materials. For all these activities col-

---

[32] Democritus owns property, his slave (τινι [...] ἐπεδίδου τὰ βιβλία) takes care of his books (17. 2; 17. 10. 7). Hippocrates envies the leisure (ἡσυχίης 17. 3. 11) that Democritus has so that he can engage in scientific endeavors.

[33] Smith, *Hippocrates: Pseudepigraphic Writings*, 24.

[34] B. M. Metzger and B. D. Ehrman, *The Text of the New Testament: Its Transmission, Cor-ruption and Restoration* (4th ed.; Oxford: Oxford University Press, 2005), 27–28; Botha, "'I Am Writing...'," 1–2.

[35] For example: Pliny, *Epistula* 3. 5; Quintilian *Institutio oratoria* 1 *praef.* 7–8; Lucian, *Quo-modo historia conscribendi* 47–48; Marcellinus, *Vita Thucydidis* 47e; Plutarch, *De tranquillitate animi* 464e–465a; Galen, *In Hippocratis epidemiarum I commentarium* 1. 36.

laboration with skilled artisans and slaves or freedmen with education was involved. Add to this the simple fact that writing materials required financial outlay[36] and the rather specific socio-economic stratum of ancient literacy becomes obvious. More specifically, the essential, almost unavoidable role of literary patronage in antiquity becomes visible.

Patronage was a relationship of exchange marked by reciprocity, endurance and asymmetry.[37] Patronage basically entails a transaction of "goods" between two persons of different social status over a period of time, with both persons planning to maintain this relationship. There is little dispute that literary relationships in the Roman Mediterranean world exhibit features of exchanges between author and patron. Both parties occasionally demonstrated frank awareness of these exchanges, even though the terminology of patronage was avoided in describing such exchanges, and the language of "friendship" was preferred by both patron and client.[38] That gave a rhetoric of voluntarism to their interaction, probably to make the necessity of their transactions more palatable. This "friendship" could indicate a wide spectrum of associating, extending to relationships of basically utilitarian, and even exploitative nature, and was many times simply a euphemism for sheer dependency.

Financial considerations played their part, though these were not the only means of support that authors sought from their benefactors. An influential patron could offer prestige to a writer. Such recognition could ensure that audiences at readings were sympathetic and that the author's reputation would spread through the social networks in which both patron and author circulated.

The author, in return, provided the "great friend" with support (in voting rallies, for example), companionship, entertainment and, ideally, acknowledgement in the present and lasting fame in the future. While the powerful and influential patrons of literature came from elite families, the authors could come from all over the social scale, and the assistance they required and their impact on the resources of the patron varied tremendously. Authors could become part of the familiar entourage of the powerful, and take part in the displays of depen-

---

[36] We do not know the cost of papyrus in the Roman provinces, and scholars prefer to avoid the use of "expensive" in this regard. However, the difference between supposedly "not expensive" but "incidentals of a prosperous villager" is patently problematic: T. C. Skeat, "Was Papyrus Regarded as 'Cheap' or 'Expensive' in the Ancient World?" *Aegyptus* 75 (1995): 75–93.

[37] R. P. Saller, *Personal Patronage Under the Early Empire* (Cambridge: Cambridge University Press, 1982), 7–40; A. Wallace-Hadrill, "Patronage in Roman Society: From Republic to Empire," in *Patronage in Ancient Society* (ed. A Wallace-Hadrill; London: Routledge, 1989), 63–87; R. R. Nauta, *Poetry for Patrons: Literary Communication in the Age of Domitian* (Leiden: Brill, 2002), 11–34.

[38] D. Konstan, "Patrons and Friends," *Classical Philology* 90 (1995): 328–42; R. Saller, "Patronage and Friendship in Early Imperial Rome: Drawing the Distinction," *Patronage in Ancient Society* (ed. A Wallace-Hadrill; London: Routledge, 1989), 49–62.

dence of the "lesser friend" (*amicus inferior*), such as the morning *salutatio*. But authors could also become distinguished from other members of the clique by the pursuit of mutual interests with their benefactors, a commonality that might lead to situations of marginalization for the authors.

Patrons and protégés did not form exclusive attachments. In these patronage relationships authors became part of interlocked communities of fellow writers and other potential patrons. The group(s) surrounding patrons celebrated the authors by dinner entertainment.[39] In these wider networks, there were abundant opportunities for reciprocity in the pursuit of reading, writing and critical discussion.

Patrons actively promoting literary pursuits engaged their families, support groups, clientele and other protégés, providing fairly cohesive circles that could result in considerable potential to the expansion of a book's circulation. Patrons provided access to audiences.[40]

performance before an audience physically in attendance was the dominant form of ancient publication.[41] "Publication" was not easy, especially when the public got invited.

[An author] finds himself obliged to run around and beg people to be kind enough to come and form an audience. That too costs him something, for he has to get the loan of a house, to fit up a recitation-hall, to hire chairs, and to distribute notices (*libellos*). And even supposing his reading is a superlative success [...] what he gets out of it is never a friend, never a client, never a lasting gratitude for a service rendered, but only fitful applause, empty compliments, and a satisfaction that is fleeting.[42] *ha*

Patrons arranged and facilitated various opportunities for "publication"; traditionally the author performed to a few friends of the patron, or some kind of contest in which more than one author takes part could be organized. The patron could also provide support for a presentation of the work by trained or dedicated performers (readers), or even sponsor some professional performance in a theatre as some kind of spectacle.

To produce a successful work in the setting of patronage was not without challenges. The author had to be interesting, entertaining and strategic, reassur-

---

[39] Patronage, dinners and gifts were closely connected: W. J. Slater, "Handouts at Dinner," *Phoenix* 54 (2000): 107–22.

[40] L. Alexander, *The Preface to Luke's Gospel* (SNTSMS 78; Cambridge: Cambridge University Press, 2001), 193–200.

[41] The letters of Pliny illuminate this practice: 1.13, 2.19, 3.18, 4.5, 5.12, 7.17; see A. N. Sherwin-White, *The Letters of Pliny: A Historical and Social Commentary* (Oxford: Clarendon Press, 1966), 115. On *recitationes*: Moses Hadas, *Ancilla to Classical Reading* (New York: Columbia University Press, 1954), 60–64; Quinn, "The Poet and His Audience in the Augustan Age," 158–65. On the making public of works by means of oral performance: Gamble, *Books and Readers*, 84; E. Fantham, *Roman Literary Culture: From Cicero to Apuleius* (Baltimore: Johns Hopkins University Press, 1996), 211–21.

[42] Tacitus, *Dialogus de oratoribus* 9.4.

ing his hearers of the intellectual, moral and social respectability of their group and its beliefs and ethos.[43]

2.3 The lecturer's notes

Quintilian has an interesting warning in the preface to his great work.

Two books on the art of rhetoric are presently circulating under my name, although never published by me nor composed for such purpose. One is a two-day lecture which was taken down by the boys who were my audience. The other is made up of notes as my pupils succeeded in taking down from a set of lectures on a somewhat more extensive scale. I appreciate their kindness, but they showed an excess of enthusiasm and a certain lack of discretion of honoring my sayings with publication. Consequently in the present work, although some passages remain the same, you will find many changes and even more additions, while the whole theme will be dealt with greater systematization and with as much perfection as I am capable of.[44]

Oral lectures by Quintilian became texts that circulated widely, but these, interestingly, were not known as his "notes" but as his *books*. They became known well enough to draw comments from the supposed author himself. At least these books were associated with their source. In antiquity, books produced with totally misleading attributions were common. Galen reports many such publications, for instance

[while studying in Smyrna] I wrote three other books to please a fellow-student who was about to travel to his homeland [...] to use them to practice making an anatomical demonstration. But then the young man died and the books came into possession of certain people. It was thought that they belonged to my works, but someone was caught adding a preface of sorts to them and reading them as his own.[45]

Galen's public lectures and demonstrations (and his many books) generated a fairly active distribution of writings associated with his name or his work. The circulation of these writings were mainly initiated and maintained by friends, students and interested intellectuals, but copies of "unauthorized" versions were freely available and in wide circulation. There are two short texts from Galen's own hand that deal with his output.[46] These were written, according to Galen, to help people determine which of the many works circulating under his name were genuine. Remarkably, these lists are not exhaustive: several indisputably genuine texts fail to appear in them.

---

[43] See, for example, F. G. Downing, "Theophilus's First Reading of Luke-Acts," *Luke's Literary Achievement: Collected Essays* (ed. C. M. Tuckett; JSNTSup 116; Sheffield: Sheffield Academic Press, 1995), 91–109.

[44] Quintilian, *Institutia oratoria* 1.pref.7–8.

[45] Galen, *De libris propriis* XIX. 14 [Kühn] = *Scripta minora* 2. 97–101 [Müller].

[46] *De libris propriis (On my own books)*, XIX. 8–48 = *SM* 2.91–14, and *De ordine librorum propriorum (The order of my own books)*, XIX. 49–61 Kühn = *SM* 2.80–90. See P. N. Singer, *Galen: Selected Works* (Oxford: Oxford University Press, 1997), 3–29.

It is clear that "authors" published books by appropriating oral performances and lectures, and many such authors – for whatever reasons – did not acknowledge the origins of those lectures or performances.

Incidentally, these practices remind us forcibly of the fluidity of *all* manuscript traditions in antiquity. What we would call an edition simply did not exist in antiquity; ἔκδοσις (usually translated with "publish") merely indicated the stage at which the author let *a* version out of his own hands. Copying was basically *ad hoc*, determined by innumerable factors and completely outside any formal control. It is impossible to speak of fixed traditions. In the Herculaneum collection (a private library), Philodemus' Περὶ ποιημάτων (*On poems*) was copied by multiple scribes in different ways.[47] In fact, from the scrolls of the collection of the Villa dei Papiri we learn of

a 'coexistence of various and incomplete editions,' which are combined and integrated with each other. These are not just different editions or copies of the same 'book' but textually different ones. This is proved by several cases where we have double or triple copies of the same book […].[48]

When we think about books in Greco-Roman antiquity, we should accept that single, final autographs probably never existed. In reality many participated and contributed to textual traditions endlessly in flux.[49]

Be that as it may, the gist of this description of "reproductive writing" is to point to a fairly prominent setting for the writing of books in antiquity.

2. 4 Networking

During the second half of the second century Philagrus, a Sophist and travelling teacher of rhetoric, was presenting a speech at Athens, professedly an *ex tempore* declamation, when he was interrupted by some among the audience. They recognized that the speech had been given by the orator at his previous location and obtained a written copy thereof. They were reading this aloud, to the speaker's embarrassment and the audience's amusement.[50] To Philostratus, Philagrus of Cilicia is a fraud, but we can see some cultural history here. Speeches were usually learned by heart, and one's notes and even oral speeches could be published – circulated publicly – without one's knowledge.

This incident also shows that there were small but widespread and interconnected groups in the urban areas of the Roman world who had an interest in

---

[47] M. Gigante, *Philodemus in Italy: The Books from Herculaneum* (trans. D Obbink; Ann Arbor: University of Michigan Press, 1995), 29–30.

[48] Gigante, *Philodemus in Italy*, 18.

[49] Appropriately D. C. Parker, *The Living Text of the Gospels* (Cambridge: Cambridge University Press, 1997), 203–13, writes about the NT textual tradition as a "living text." An "original text" is inaccessible to us: Parker, *Living Text*, 204.

[50] Philostratus, *Vitae sophistarum* 579–580.

gaining access to writings and who assisted in the distribution of writings. Their interests were not necessarily limited to "authorized" literary texts, but included notes and drafts. Quintilian writes that he saw Cicero's own notes for some of his speeches (or, at least, what he believes to have been Cicero's authentic notes) more than a century after the author's death. Quintilian thought these notes were collected and copied by Tiro.[51]

We cannot know how common these circles of persons "exchanging notes on how to procure and get copies made of works of scholarship"[52] were, but we know such networks existed. P. Oxy. 2192, a fragment from a letter written about 170 C. E., has two postscripts in different hands:

Make and send me copies of Books 6 and 7 of Hypsicrates' *Komodoumenoi*. For Harpocration says that they are among Polion's books. But it is likely that others have them. He also has prose summaries of Thersagoras' work on the myths of tragedy.

According to Harpocration, Demetrius the bookseller [ὁ βυβλιοπώλης] has them. I have instructed Apollinides to send me certain of my own books which you will hear of in good time from Seleucus himself. Should you find any, apart from those which I possess, make copies and send them to me. Diodorus and his friends also have some which I do not have.[53]

The instructions reflect something of intersecting circles of literate persons interested in books who are also instrumental for the transmission of texts via copying. What is striking is the assumption that books are for sharing. A similar notion can be detected in the prefaces of some of the technical and scientific treatises of the Hellenistic and Roman periods. Lines of communication reliant on written texts and encouraging movement of written text reached over remarkable distances. Not only were copies exchanged for correction, but invitations to share texts characterized these networks.[54]

There were many freedmen and slaves involved in education, and many with skills related to the book trade. It is self-evident that they pursued literary interests unconnected to those of their masters and patrons. A significant number of ancient "publications" must have had not only their origins among such circles of scribes and scholarly assistants, but their dissemination and survival integrally connected to these groups operating next to (or "underneath") the lines of elite communication.

---

[51] Quintilian, *Institutio oratoria* 11. 2.

[52] E. G. Turner, *Greek Papyri: An Introduction* (Oxford: Clarendon, 1968), 87.

[53] C. H. Roberts, "2192. Letter About Books," in *The Oxyrhynchus Papyri, vol. 18* (ed. E Lobel et al.; London: Egypt Exploration Society, 1941), 150–52.

[54] Cf. Alexander, *Preface to Luke*, 47–52.

3. Early Christian Manuscripts

It is not possible to situate the gospels unambiguously in any of the scenarios described, and that is not my intention. At best some parameters for contextualizing the gospel authors at work can be noted. In this sense, it seems that elaborate source-critical theories, and intricate redactional programs intended for select (and individual) readers are inappropriate to the historical settings of the gospel authors at work.

Explorations such as these can also be helpful for scrutinizing our proposals for possible anachronisms. It is interesting, for example, to note how analogies to modern newspapers are used to explain and illustrate the development of the gospel traditions, the origins of the gospel texts, and the characteristics of the different texts[55] – without reflection on the appropriateness of such an analogy and illustration. No one in antiquity had ever seen a newspaper or read one; it would have been impossible for them to visualize their own work as analogous to what newspaper editors do.

We have some material evidence about Christian books from the late second century, and an increasing number from the third century onwards, which can be scrutinized to shed some light on the origins of the New Testament writings. Discussion of these materials usually focuses on the adoption of the codex by early Christianity.[56]

Explanations for this remarkable shift from scrolls to codices in the early church are fairly speculative. Typically the various "advantages" of the codex over the roll are noted. The origins of the new preference, it has been suggested, can be found in the Pauline circle, a group with an eye on functionality.[57] Mark

---

[55] E. g., R. F. Collins, *Introduction to the New Testament* (London: SCM Press, 1983), 158–66, 197–203, 276.

[56] The scroll as medium for publication remained popular until the fifth century, but from the second century Christians began to prefer the codex as their format for publication. Obviously the use of rolls continued. The author of Rv (5. 1) reports a vision of a heavenly roll; Irenaeus' *Against heresies* has come down as a roll (P. Oxy. 405) – which suggests that works of scholarship, distinct from Scripture, were by nature of the scroll, especially in scholastic circles; *Acts of Peter* 20 alludes to Peter rolling up a Gospel book (late 2nd century); the *Acts of the Scillitan Martyrs* 12 refers to books and epistles of Paul in a *capsa*, a container for scrolls. Cf. J. Den Boeft and J. Bremmer, "Notiunculae Martyriologicae IV," *Vigiliae Christianae* 45 (1991): 116–17. Some early Christian art depicts figures with rolls (W. V. Harris, "Why Did the Codex Supplant the Book-Roll?" *Renaissance Society and Culture: Essays in Honor of Eugene F. Rice* [ed. J. Monfasani and R. G. Musto; New York: Italica Press, 1991], 77).

[57] The original function of the codex was basically as an instrument for recording ephemera. Of the considerable number of non-Christian manuscripts of the second century, seventeen are codices. Six of these are "professional manuals" (grammatical, lexical and medical handbooks); eleven are literary texts, of which several clearly are working copies for educational use. These numbers probably indicate an essentially utilitarian attitude toward the codex; it is seen as a practical development of the notebook. "The codex, whether of parchment or

(writing in Rome) has also been nominated as the catalyst for the adoption of the codex.[58] Others also designate "the Christian congregation in Rome" as the first user of the codex.[59]

A number of reasons for selecting the codex have been advanced, such as its portability and ease of use, particularly important to mobile persons,[60] or as an indication of a deliberate break with Judaism,[61] or as an expression of opposition to Roman elite values.[62] There could be some truth in all of these proposals.

It must be emphasized that we do not know the reasons why the codex became important to the church, and many of the reasons enumerated reflect *modern* values (such as costs or ease of reference).

There is more to the early Christian papyri than just their format, and the reasons for reducing the use of scrolls.[63] Some of the characteristics of these early Christian manuscripts have implications for understanding the literary process in earliest Christianity.

One thing that the early Christian papyri from Egypt undoubtedly reveal is the speed with which an early Christian text could disseminate across the Mediterranean world.[64] Such swift distribution of literature was only possible by means of a network of scribes and secretaries, and such networks must have characterized early Christianity basically from the beginning. Interest in and conversion to the Jesus movement by persons with scribal and literary backgrounds must have been part of the Jesus movement and not only within Pauline circles.

We know that the gospels were written in a literary context with literary skills and with literary views of audiences, but they were not published as literature (with the possible exception of the Gospel of Luke and Acts). Despite clear indications of authors engaged in literary composition, the gospels are distinctly not

---

papyrus, would have been familiar to a small businessman like Paul and to the circles in which he moved" (Gamble, *Books and Readers*, 64).

[58] C. H. Roberts, "The Codex," *Proceedings of the British Academy* 40 (1954): 187–89. Roberts has modified his initial proposal; he now argues that "a primitive form of codex" was developed by Christians at Antioch: C. H. Roberts and T. C. Skeat, *The Birth of the Codex* (London: British Academy, 1983), 55–60.

[59] Den Boeft and Bremmer, "Notiunculae Martyriologicae IV," 117.

[60] M. McCormick, "The Birth of the Codex and the Apostolic Life-Style," *Scriptorium* 39 (1985): 150–58.

[61] I. M. Resnick, "The Codex in Early Jewish and Christian Communities," *Journal of Religious History* 17 (1992): 1–17.

[62] G. Cavallo, "Between *Volumen* and Codex: Reading in the Roman World," *A History of Reading in the West* (ed. G. Cavallo and R. Chartier; Oxford: Polity Press, 1999), 87–88.

[63] E. J. Epp, "The New Testament Papyri at Oxyrhynchus in Their Social and Intellectual Context," in *Sayings of Jesus: Canonical and Non-Canonical: Essays in Honour of Tjitze Baarda* (ed. W. L. Petersen et al.; Leiden: Brill, 1997), 47–68; L. W. Hurtado, *The Earliest Christian Artifacts: Manuscripts and Christian Origins* (Grand Rapids: Eerdmans, 2006).

[64] Gamble, *Books and Readers*, 82.

not "high" literature. They were not transmitted (copied) as "proper" literature in the style and format or with the attention to detail that characterize the beautiful literary bookrolls Johnson describes.[65] Most of the early Christian papyri were transcribed not in a "bookhand" but in a "reformed documentary" style.[66]

Their copyists, therefore, appear to have construed the texts in pragmatic rather than aesthetic terms, and intended their reproductions to fulfill practical ends within their communities. Furthermore, the virtual absence of calligraphic skill indicates that these transcriptions were produced by private individuals rather than professionals; alternatively, if they *were* produced by professionals, we must conclude that their labors were personally, not professionally, motivated.[67]

To understand *some* aspects of the origins of the written gospels we should turn to the subservient groups in the shadows of the literary circles, those concealed by the status of patrons and whose names have been obliterated by conventional ideas about authorship.

Cornelius Nepos describes Atticus' "library" staff:

[Atticus] had slaves that were excellent in efficiency, although in personal appearance hardly mediocre, for there were among them servants who were highly educated, some outstanding readers (*anagnostae*) and a great number of scribes (*librarii*); in fact, there was not even a footman who was not expert in both these accomplishments.[68]

Besides depicting the complexities of Roman literacy, the description invites reflection on the fact that sophisticated literacy was not exclusively the domain of the elite. What did those efficient, highly educated readers do when they were on their own, when they had a little time and resources at hand? Where did these people go, and what were their interests and ideals?

In the middle of the first century C. E. one can readily imagine precisely such persons listening to a lecture being delivered by a follower of Jesus, or providing scribal skills to an evangelist requiring notebooks, or participating in the exchange of some Christian lectures written on a μεμβράνα (as mentioned by the author of 2 Tim 4:13).

This participation of scribal networks set in motion a process that would contribute to early Christianity developing as a "textual" religion.[69] Haines-

---

[65] Johnson, *Bookrolls*.

[66] That is, in the style employed for receipts, legal documents, bank accounts and governmental paperwork (B. D. Ehrman, "The Text as Window: New Testament Manuscripts and the Social History of Early Christianity," *The Text of the New Testament in Contemporary Research: Essays on the* Status Quaestionis [eds B. D. Ehrman and M. W. Holmes; Grand Rapids: Eerdmans, 1995], 373 n. 58).

[67] Ehrman, "Text as Window," 373.

[68] Nepos *ad Atticus* 13. 3. Atticus as literary patron: N. Horsfall, *Cornelius Nepos: A Selection, Including the Lives of Cato and Atticus* (Oxford: Clarendon, 1989), 89.

[69] W. V. Harris, *Ancient Literacy* (Cambridge (MA): Harvard University Press, 1989), 220–21, 300–306.

Eitzen investigated the "guardians of letters" in second- and third-century Christianity.[70] She argues that networks of scribes, whose employers, masters, or mistresses sent texts to one another, developed and flourished, and that these networks formed a literary tradition that influenced the content and form of Christian writings. This scribal activity was not merely reduplication but subtle intervention, correction, and adaptation of the tradition.

Such persons and procedures, however, were involved right from the beginning, and the shaping of early Christianity's literary character started there. At least, something like this seems very plausible after some investigation into book production in antiquity, focusing on the information we possess about reading and writing in antiquity.

One of our biggest challenges in this regard is to think about literacy contextually and culturally. Given the distinct materials, tools and activities involved we should probably visualize "Mark," "Matthew," "Luke" and "John" as small groups of "behind-the-scene" literates using their literacy to gain knowledge, explore identity, persuade patrons and audiences, and to facilitate the power and influence of followers of Jesus.

---

[70] K. Haines-Eitzen, *Guardians of Letters: Literacy, Power, and the Transmission of Early Christian Literature* (Oxford: Oxford University Press, 2002).

The Sovereignty of the Son of Man: Reading Mark 2[1]

Daniel Boyarin

Gospel is, as has been noticed before, a fascinatingly new event in the literary world. Variously related by scholars to existing Greco-Roman genres, it has also been characterized, as, in my opinion, it needs to be, as a very early instance of the rabbinic genre which comes to be known as midrash, namely, for the purposes of the present analysis, the building up of new narrative out of complicated partly decontextualized and recombined verses from the Bible. The addressee of the more than well earned honor that constitutes this volume, Prof. Antoinette Wire, has, over decades, worked on the deep connections of the Gospel's Jesus with Jewish traditions of the first century. What I wish to emphasize here is that while the narratives of the Gospels have a kind of simplicity that we associate with folk narrative, the midrashic generation of these stories is by no means naïve; they are the product of complicated relays and hermeneutic activities that underly the narrative sequences, whether birth, passion, or anything that comes in between. I don't believe that we can determine whether these hermeneutic relays were oral or written in material form, but, nonetheless, I would assert their inscriptional character, for sure insofar as they depend on sophisticated and complex interpretative interventions in the reading of written Scripture; perhaps oral, but only, then, in the sense of the term as we find it in "Oral Torah." A case in point, Mark 2.

In her commentary on Mark, Adela Yarbro Collins writes:

> It is preferable to speak of the "interpretation of Jesus" in Mark, rather than the "Christology" of Mark, because systematic, philosophical reflection on the nature of Christ had not yet begun in the movement carried on by the followers of Jesus. In composing his narrative, the author of Mark made use of traditions that already expressed an implicit interpretation of the person and activity of Jesus.[2]

With all due respect (and much is, indeed, due), I will argue almost the precise opposite in this article, claiming that Christology – if not, of course, systematic

---

[1] This paper, written for this volume, is a study for my forthcoming *How The Jews Came to Believe That Jesus was God*. I am grateful to Prof. Richard Hays for his critical input and aid and support.

[2] A. Yarbro Collins, *Mark: A Commentary* (Hermeneia; Minneapolis, MN: Fortress Press, 2007), 44.

philosophical reflection – existed long before Jesus and that Jesus' person, activity, and speech represent an interpretation of Christology and not, as Yarbro Collins and many others would have it, that Christology, or even the Gospel, is an interpretation of Jesus. While I understand well that Yarbro Collins is striving to avoid the anachronisms that result from reading fourth-century categories back into the Gospels, I am much more sanguine about seeing those very fourth-century categories *in nuce* in the Gospel. Another scholar who has articulated a version of the position that Jesus is somehow primary, before Christ, as it were is Joel Marcus, who writes,

> In Mark's Gospel, in other words, a commitment to the 'old, old story' is retained at the same time that story itself is transformed by being read in a new way. Mark has certainly learned much of what he knows about Jesus Christ from the scriptures. He would never have learned it, however, if he had not already known that Jesus Christ is the key to the scriptures.[3]

Again while accepting much (most) of Marcus's interpretative insight, I gently dissent from the final point, suggesting that all of Jesus' self-interpretation and the interpretation in the Gospel comes out of a reading of the "old old story" that had developed prior to its appropriation by this Jew, Jesus of Nazareth: Christ existed before Jesus. Both Yarbro Collins and Marcus engage to some extent in a kind of *ex eventu* reading which partially, in my view, obscures the narrative of Jewish religious history. This narrative only becomes fully clear when the Gospel is understood as entirely a part of the old story and not apart from it. In contrast with both of the above scholars, in my view Jesus was entirely unnecessary for the formation of Mark's Christology, as he is the fulfillment, not the provocation of that Christology. Jesus, in the Gospel of Mark, is the precise fulfillment, I suggest, of well known and ancient pre-Jesus ideas about the Messiah as a divine human (which is not to deny a Markan contribution to the development of such ideas). This article, in its present form, is intended as an answer to the question of "how the 'Son of Man' (ὁ υἱὸς τοῦ ἀνθρώπου) came to appear on Jesus' lips in Mark's Gospel, or for that matter in the tradition as a whole."[4] My simple answer is that the "Son of Man" was on Jesus' lips, because he was a first-century Palestinian Jew, and "Son of Man" was the name that these Jews used for their expected divine-human (Christological!) redeemer.[5]

---

[3] J. Marcus, *The Way of the Lord: Christological Exegesis of the Old Testament in the Gospel of Mark* (Louisville, KY: Westminster/John Knox Press, 1992), 203.

[4] H. L. Chronis, "To Reveal and to Conceal: A Literary-Critical Perspective on 'the Son of Man' in Mark," *New Testament Studies* 51 (2005): 458.

[5] In contrast to Paul who, in my view, occupies another corner of the Jewish traditional world in which different terminology was used. I will elaborate this point further, *Deo volente*, in another essay. To adumbrate a point that must be developed elsewhere, a fundamental error made by Lindars, for example, is to assume that Paul, the Sayings Source, and Revelation can be used as evidence one for the other, such that the absence of the "Son of Man" in one is

The key to Christology is a partial reconsideration of the way that Daniel 7:13–14 works in the Gospel and of Son of Man with respect to other messianic titles, particularly Son of God.[6] I wish to emphasize that the hypothesis entertained here is not a radical revision of Marcus's account but rather, perhaps, a fine-tuning of it or even a taking of it to its ultimate conclusion, a conclusion that Marcus himself backs off from in the end. While there are many other Hebrew-biblical sources that make up the warp and woof of Markan Christology, as Marcus has so elegantly shown in his book, my argument will be that Daniel 7 is the keystone and crucial, dominating figure in the development of Christology.

1. A Read Herring: "The Son of Man" as Periphrasis for "I"

In order, however, to proceed into my own inquiry into the evidence of Mark for the "Son of Man" in early Judaism, I must first show why I do not accept the conclusion of Geza Vermes, who argued that it is just a circumlocution for "I." In a series of articles, culminating in an important essay published as "Appendix E" to the third edition of Matthew Black's *Aramaic Approach*,[7] Vermes attempted to revive a theory that had been advanced and abandoned a century ago to the effect that "The Son of Man" is merely an ordinary Aramaic locution by which someone refers to themselves in the third person, hence "I." I think it can be taken as granted that given Vermes's exhaustive investigation, his study should be considered definitive,[8] and, if it fails, we can consider that suggestion as rejectable.[9] Although an entire array of scholars have already disputed Vermes's conclusion, none have, I think, shown that the interpretations of rabbinic literature adduced by him, do not stand, and that there is, therefore, no evidence whatsoever for the argument that in Aramaic, "son of man" can mean "I" (that it means a human being is, of course, not in doubt at all).[10] I thus accordingly

---

probative for the term being non-titular in the others; B. Lindars, *Jesus, Son of Man: A Fresh Examination of the Son of Man Sayings in the Gospels in the Light of Recent Research* (Grand Rapids, MI: Eerdmans, 1984, c1983), 15.

[6] This latter point will be pursued in a separate paper.

[7] G. Vermes, "Appendix E: The Use of Bar Nash/Bar Nasha in Jewish Aramaic" *An Aramaic Approach to the Gospels and Acts* (ed. M. Black; 3rd ed.; Oxford: Oxford University Press, Clarendon, 1967), 310–28; P. Haupt, "The Son of Man = Hic Homo = Ego," *JBL* 40 (1921).

[8] P. Owen and D. Shepherd, "Speaking up for Qumran, Dalman and the Son of Man: Was *Bar Enasha* a Common Term for 'Man' in the Time of Jesus?" *JSNT* 81 (2001): 84.

[9] And it has been rejected by a host of scholars, from Fitzmyer through Jeremias to Colpe, for all of which references see A. Yarbro Collins, "The Influence of Daniel on the New Testament" in *Daniel: A Commentary on the Book of Daniel* (ed. J.J. Collins; Hermeneia; Minneapolis: Fortress Press, 1993), 94, n. 30.

[10] It should be noted that Norman Perrin, *A Modern Pilgrimage in New Testament Christology* (Philadelphia: Fortress Press, 1974), 70, makes major use of this untenable argument to make

essentially agree with Hans Lietzmann as cited by Vermes to the effect that "His
main findings are that the term is a common one, and that it is used as a kind of
indefinite pronoun (בר נש = *jemand*; לית בר נש *niemand*; בני נש= *Leute*). It is, he
writes, 'die farbloseste und unbestimmteste Bezeichnung des menschlichen In-
dividuums' (p. 38). He then goes on to postulate what seems to him to be the
only logical corollary: as a designation בר נש is by nature inapplicable to any
particular man, let alone to Jesus, the greatest of all men (p. 40)."[11] Lietzmann
put the question brilliantly; his answer, on the other hand, that the Son of Man
must be a Hellenistic *terminus technicus* is a non-sequitur, for even if semantically
and syntactically "Son of Man" in Aramaic means indeed just a person and
nothing else, pragmatically (by which I mean in the case of a particular set of
syntagms), the "Son of Man" *as a citation of Daniel* could certainly have come to
mean the Christ already in Hebrew/Aramaic. An example, just to make this
clear, would be the following: "Rav" simply means "Rabbi," but for the majority of Orthodox Jews in the U. S., "the Rav" means one and only one Rabbi,
Rabbi Joseph Soloveitchik OBM. Let us, then, have a look at Vermes's evidence.

In order to make his case, Vermes must demonstrate the alleged use of בר נש as
a circumlocution meaning "I." Although he gives several examples, in every
one of these, rather than seeing a circumlocution for "I," we can see quite a
different idiom. I shall first discuss an example that Vermes seems to consider
particularly strong.[12] In the first:

Jacob of Kefar Nibburayya gave a ruling in Tyre that fish should be ritually slaughtered.
Hearing this, R. Haggai sent him this order: Come and be scourged! He replied, should
בר נש be scourged who proclaims the word of Scripture? (*Gen. Rabba* vii 2)[13]

Vermes wishes to claim that, "theoretically, of course, *bar nāsh* may be rendered
here as 'one', but the context hardly suggests that at this particular juncture Jacob
intends to voice a general principle. Hurt by his opponent's harsh words, he
clearly seems to be referring to himself and the indirect idiom is no doubt due to
the implied humiliation."[14] Vermes here simply confuses the semantics and the
pragmatics of the sentence. Of course, pragmatically the speaker is referring to
himself, but semantically he is using a general expression. An example from
English will make this clear. In the famous and brilliant lyric from *Guys and
Dolls*, Adelaide sings plaintively: "In other words, just by waiting around for that

---

his case that all Christological use of "The Son of Man" must be post-Easter, an argument that
is, in this respect, repeated by Lindars, *Jesus, Son of Man*.
   [11] Vermes, "The Use," 311.
   [12] Vermes, "The Use," 321–2.
   [13] *Genesis Rabbah* (eds. J. Theodor and H. Albeck; Jerusalem: Wahrmann, 1965), 51. Vermes's translation.
   [14] Vermes, "The Use."

little band of gold [...] a person, could develop a cold!" Of course, pragmatically she is referring to herself; it is her own situation of which she complains, but semantically "a person" in English is an indefinite pronominal form and not a circumlocution for "I."[15] The same is true for this example and, *mutatis mutandis*, all the other ones that Vermes cites. But another should be cited, because, at least, of the *mutatis mutandis*:

When R. Ḥiyya bar Adda died, son of the sister of Bar Kappara, R. Levi received his valuables. This was because his teacher used to say, The disciple of בר נשא is as dear to him as his son. (*Yer Ber.* 5b)

There is not the slightest justification to see a circumlocution for "I" here either. Rabbi Ḥiyya has expressed a general principle that the disciple of a person is as dear to him as his son and the conclusion was drawn on the pragmatic level (in several senses) that he intended his disciple to be his heir.

Another example cited by Vermes turns out to be a counter-example:

Rabbi Shimon Bar Yoḥai said: "If I had been standing on Mt. Sinai at the hour that the Torah was given to Israel, I would have demanded of the Merciful One that that human being would have been created with two mouths, one to be busy with Torah and one to do with it all of his daily needs." Then he changed his mind and said: "If even with only one, the world cannot subsist because of all of the delations, if there were two all the more so!" [Palestinian Talmud *Shabbat* chapter 1, halakhah b, page 3b]

Now it is obvious here, *pace* Vermes, that the Rabbi is not referring to himself as "that man" here, for then he would be, as well, accusing himself of being an informer, which he hardly was and hardly would do.[16] There can be no doubt that here, as well, we must understand "הדין בר נש" here as "One," German "*Mann*" and nothing else. There remains not even one example in which the term Son of Man is a periphrastic usage for "I."

In all of Vermes's examples, then, general principles are stated which are *applied* in the context of the narrative to an individual, usually the speaker.[17] Vermes's argument fails totally because he does not even once observe the

---

[15] Vermes's citation of the answer "You [...]" as confirmation of his thesis hardly needs refuting. Nathan Detroit, of course, would comfort Adelaide by saying: "Ah baby, you'll be married soon." That still doesn't make "a person" = "I" semantically.

[16] This consideration also thoroughly discredits Lindars's reading according to which *bar nesha* here means "anyone [...] who was as deeply conscious of the divine generosity as Simeon himself," Lindars, *Jesus, Son of Man*, 22. Even more sharply than with respect to the interpretation of Vermes, one would ask: Is this the class of people one would suspect of being informers to the Romans and even more so had they two mouths? I think the conclusion is inescapable that here (with or without *haden*=this), the meaning is the human being in general.

[17] See examples cited Vermes, "The Use," 323–7. For similar conclusions reached by slightly different methods, see M. Casey, "Method in Our Madness, and Madness in Their Methods: Some Approaches to the Son of Man Problem in Recent Scholarship," *JSNT* 42 (1991): 18.

difference between semantic (lexical) meaning and pragmatic meaning or between sense and reference. There is, therefore, no evidence, whatsoever for "son of man" being used in Aramaic texts as a circumlocution for "I," as Lietzmann realized.[18]

I conclude, therefore, that Vermes has adduced no convincing evidence that "Son of Man" was ever used as a circumlocution for "I" even in the Palestinian Aramaic of Late Antiquity; still less has he witnesses for the Aramaic of the first century. Vermes's argument thus fails to convince on lexical philological grounds, in spite of its superficial attractiveness for the interpretation of some verses within the Gospels. Given that Vermes's alleged idiomatic usage of "son of man" as periphrasis for "I" proves to be a ghost, another explanation of this genuinely weird usage must be sought. Lietzmann (and a host of others) have sought the explanation in the positing of a "Heavenly Man" or *Anthropos* myth underlying Christology. Rejecting (as have, I think, most interpreters by now) such far-fetched and far-flung explanations, to my mind, the only plausible one that remains is that of the great Jewish theologian and scholar of the last century, Leo Baeck, who wrote: "Whenever in later works 'that Son of Man,' 'this Son of Man, or 'the Son of Man' is mentioned, it is the quotation from Daniel that is speaking."[19] In other words, I fully accept (as I think we must) Vermes's hypothesis of an Aramaic origin (in the oral traditions that lie behind the Gospels) for the phrase, "The Son of Man," but deny his interpretation of that Aramaic

---

[18] For another review of Vermes's evidence, arriving, however, at different conclusions, see Lindars, *Jesus, Son of Man*, 19–24. Lindars accepts only one example as fully relevant and builds his entire case on that, the example being *y Shevi'it* 38d: [Rabbi Shimon] sat at the mouth of the cave [where he was hiding from the Romans] and he saw a hunter catching birds. He spread his net. He heard a voice from heaven [ברת קול] say *dimus* [*Dimissio*], and it was freed. He said [to himself], "a bird does not perish without Heaven, so much more so a human being!" Lindars chooses to translate this as "How much less a man in my position," without any warrant other than the alleged article on *bar nesha*. Given, however, the philological state of the Palestinian Talmud, as well as the centuries later date in any case, to build an entire interpretation of the Son of Man on this one highly doubtful example, seems almost to constitute scholarly legerdemain. There is no reason to imagine that Rabbi Shimon means a man in his position as opposed to any human whatsoever. Once again, a simple generic is being used and applied by the speaker pragmatically to himself: A bird doesn't perish except by the will of Heaven, still less a human being, [so why am I hiding here]? What is most important to recognize is that if this idiom is operative, for instance, at Matthew 8:20: "Foxes have holes, and birds of the air have nests, but *bar enasha* has nowhere to lay his head," it could only mean that foxes have holds and birds have nests but humans have nowhere to lay their heads, which is palpably false (Lindars, *Jesus, Son of Man*, 30), so despite the apparent similarity of this one single exemplum from late-ancient Palestinian Aramaic, we must resist the temptation to treat them as the same linguistic form, *pace* Lindars, *Jesus, Son of Man*, 29–31. Lindars's own solution to this problem involves pure philological fantasy, nothing more or less. In another, longer version of this argument, I will provide further argument against Lindars's position. Insofar as it depends on Vermes's flawed conclusions, it is, in any case, untenable.

[19] L. Baeck, *Judaism and Christianity: Essays* (Philadelphia: Jewish Publication Society of America, 1958), 28–9.

phrase. In what follows in this necessarily brief paper, I shall try to show how the hypothesis of literary allusion to Daniel in this phrase enables stronger readings of a pair of Markan loci.

2. The Dominion (ἐξουσία שׁלטן) of Jesus: Mark 2

In the rest of this paper, I will look at two closely related verses in Mark chapter 2 that, to my mind, evidence that Jesus (the character) understood it as a title for the human one to whom power had been delegated by God, derived from The One Like a Son of Man of Daniel 7 and parallel to the Son of Man of Enoch.

In Mark 2:5–10 we read the following:

> 5 And when Jesus saw their faith, he said to the paralytic, "My son, your sins are forgiven." 6 Now some of the scribes were sitting there, questioning in their hearts, 7 "Why does this man speak thus? It is blasphemy! Who can forgive sins but God alone?" 8 And immediately Jesus, perceiving in his spirit that they thus questioned within themselves, said to them, "Why do you question thus in your hearts? 9 Which is easier, to say to the paralytic, "Your sins are forgiven,' or to say, 'Rise, take up your pallet and walk'? 10 But that you may know that the Son of man has authority on earth to forgive sins" – he said to the paralytic [...].

"But that you may know that the Son of Man has authority on earth to forgive sins." This verse is the crux. Once we have excluded the possibility of "the Son of Man" being simply another way of saying "I," then I think it must be conceded that it is a title here.[20] The Son of Man has authority (obviously delegated by God) to do God's work of the forgiving of sins on earth. From where could such a claim be derived if not from Daniel 7:14, in which we read that the One Like a Son of Man has been given, "authority, glory, kingship;" indeed an "authority that is eternal that will not pass away"? The term that we conventionally translate as "authority" in its New Testament contexts, ἐξουσία, is, of course, exactly the same term which translates Aramaic שׁלטן in the Septuagint, so what Jesus is claiming for the Son of Man is exactly that which has been granted to the (One Like a) Son of Man in Daniel. Given the meaning of the Aramaic *Vorlage* in Daniel, "authority" strikes me as a rather weak rendering; "sovereignty" would be much better. Sovereignty would surely explain why the Son of Man has the power to remit sins on earth. According to this tradition, then, there may be no question; this Jesus claims to be the Son of Man to whom

---

[20] Indeed, even were it possible (which it is not) to entertain Vermes's suggestion on philological grounds, it would be excluded here. If Jesus is not identifying himself by a known title, then his claim to be the one (the only one) who has authority to remit sins would be unrelenting personal arrogance and indeed blasphemy. For this point, see M. Hooker, *The Son of Man in Mark: A Study of the Background of the Term "Son of Man" and Its Use in St Mark's Gospel* (Montreal: McGill University Press, 1967), 84.

divine authority on earth "under the heavens" (Daniel 7:27) has been delegated.[21] In contrast to most interpreters, I would argue, moreover, that this One to
whom authority has been delegated, as a divine figure, is a redeemer king, as the
Daniel passage clearly states, and thus ripe for identification with the Davidic
Messiah, if not always clearly so identified.[22] I thus here directly disagree with
Yarbro Collins's assumption that the title "Son of Man" conceals as much as it
reveals or that we cannot understand that the audience of Mark already understood the epithet.[23] I find much more compelling in this instance the statement
of Joel Marcus:

This conclusion [that the "Son of Man" in the Similitudes is pre-Christian] is supported
by the way in which Jesus, in the Gospels, generally treats the Son of Man as a known
quantity, never bothering to explain the term, and the way in which certain of this
figure's characteristics, such as his identity with the Messiah or his prerogative of judging,
are taken for granted. With apologies to Voltaire, we may say that if the Enochic Son of
Man had not existed, it would have been necessary to invent him to explain the Son of
Man sayings in the Gospels.[24]

I would only shift the terms of the last phrase to indicate that what this means is
that the usage of the Son of Man in the Gospels joins with the evidence of such
usage from the Similitudes to lead us to consider this term used in this way (and
more importantly the concept of a second divinity implied by it) as the common
coin – which I emphasize does not mean universal or uncontested – of Judaism
already before Jesus.

This interpretation of Mark 2:10 as being a close reading of Daniel 7:14
enables us to understand the other puzzling Son of Man statement in Mark 2,
namely:

23 One sabbath he was going through the grainfields; and as they made their way his
disciples began to pluck heads of grain. 24 And the Pharisees said to him, "Look, why are
they doing what is not lawful on the sabbath?" 25 And he said to them, "Have you never
read what David did, when he was in need and was hungry, he and those who were with
him: 26 how he entered the house of God, when Abiathar was high priest, and at the

---

[21] cf. Hooker, *Son of Man in Mark*, 90–1 who seems to take this (in partial contradiction to
her own position earlier) to be significant of a prerogative of "man" in general.

[22] See too, "In claiming this divine prerogative Jesus classes himself as the Son of Man into
the category of the divine, and his superhuman act of healing is the sign for this claim. So
already in 1927 O. Procksch suggested that here 'the Son of Man' stands for the Son of God,"
S. Kim, *"The 'Son of Man'" as the Son of God* (WUNT 30; Tübingen: Mohr Siebeck, 1983), 2.

[23] Collins, *Mark: A Commentary*, 186. See too Hooker, *Son of Man in Mark*, 91 who also
writes that Jesus' hearers, "knew nothing of any authority to forgive sins given to the Son of
man (whatever they might understand Jesus to mean by that term)." Hooker completely
disregards the Danielic context in her own interpretation which takes "Son of Man" here to be
an allusion to Adam.

[24] J. Marcus, *Mark 1–8: A New Translation with Introduction and Commentary* (New York:
Doubleday, 2000), 530. See too Kim, *"The 'Son of Man'*," 90.

bread of the Presence, which it is not lawful for any but the priests to eat, and also gave it to those who were with him?" 27 And he said to them, "The sabbath was made for man, not man for the sabbath; 28 so the Son of man is lord even of the sabbath." ὥστε κύριός ἐστιν ὁ υἱὸς τὸυ ἀνθρώπου καὶ τοῦ σαββάτου

I think that the problems of this sequence of verses are best unraveled if we take seriously its context following the preceding Son of Man verse that I have just treated. If Jesus (the "Markan" Jesus, or the Jesus of these passages) proclaims himself as the Son of Man who has ἐξουσίαν by virtue of Daniel 7:14, then it is entirely plausible that he would claim sovereignty over the Sabbath as well.

Paying attention to the Danielic allusion implicit in every citation of the Son of Man, in accordance with my hypothesis, here, it can be seen that the Markan Jesus is making precisely the same kind of claim on the basis of the authority delegated to the Son of Man in Daniel as he does in 2:10. This enables me to propose a solution to another crux. One objection could be that the Sabbath is not "under the heavens" but in heaven and thus not susceptible to the transfer of authority from the Ancient of Days to the "One Like a Son of Man." I wish to suggest that this objection is entirely answered by the statement that the Sabbath was made for the human being; consequently the Son of Man, having been given dominion in the human realm, is the Lord of the Sabbath. It is actually a necessary part of the argument that the Son of Man is Lord of the Sabbath, for if the Sabbath is (as one might very well claim on the basis of Genesis 1) in heaven, then the claim that the Son of Man who only has sovereignty on earth can abrogate its provisions would be very weak. Given the absence of verse 27 in both synoptic parallels, moreover, it might very well be a secondary addition in the Markan tradition, precisely to answer such an objection, while Matthew and Luke carry forward an earlier Markan tradition in which the Son of Man is declared Lord of the Sabbath without the Sabbath for Man logion. I think that this explanation of the connection between verses 27 and 28 answers many interpretative conundrums that arise when 27 is read as a weak sort-of human-istic statement.[25] We can now understand precisely what the entailment implied by ὥστε is. It is precisely *because* the Sabbath was created for the human and is therefore part of the human world that the Son of Man has sovereignty over it; it is not in heaven. In my view, this passage can only be understood if this manner, for, otherwise it leads us into interpretations, hardly plausible, that would would have Jesus claiming that any human being can abrogate the Sabbath at will or that he can abrogate the Sabbath because of his human nature and not because of his commission as ruler of the sublunar world. What may have been a traditional Jewish saying to justify breaking the Sabbath to preserve life is, in the Markan Jesus' hands, the justification for a messianic abrogation of the Sabbath. The

[25] Cf. R. H. Gundry, *Mark: A Commentary on His Apology for the Cross* (Grand Rapids, MI: Eerdmans, 2004, c1993), I: 144.

comparison to David is, of course, very pointed and does suggest that the Re-
deemer of Daniel 7:13–14 is indeed understood as the messianic King, son of
David, for just as David had ἐξουσίαν to violate the apparent provisions of the
Law when he and his disciples were in need, so too, the new David, the Son of
Man with respect to his disciples.[26]

Far from being anomalous in the Son of Man tradition, therefore, I would
conclude that these two verses strongly confirm the direct connection with
Daniel 7:13 and represent a Jesus who knows that he is the Son of Man and
precisely what this entails, as well.[27] Although other aspects of the messianic role
of the Son of Man are not emphasized in this pericope (at least partly since they
are not relevant to the context), there is nothing in them that suggests any
contradiction of the overall picture of the Son of Man as Messiah. Indeed, the
intimate connection between the claim of sovereignty and Daniel 7:13–14
certainly and strongly suggests that the term Son of Man is indeed a well–understood messianic title for the author and audience of Mark. I find it increasingly
difficult to even understand claims such as Morna Hooker's that "there is scanty
evidence to support the idea that it was a recognized messianic 'title.'"[28] I begin
to wonder what would count as evidence.[29] In these verses, so early in the
Gospel, we find Jesus, indeed, being proclaimed (by himself) as the Son of Man.
These verses have exactly the same plausibility as authentic words of Jesus as any
others in the Gospel. Or to put it into terms that I find more comfortable, they
are certainly plausibly read as growing from pre-Jesus speculation on the roles
and powers of the Son of Man. That Son of Man is not a heavenly *Anthropos* nor
a title for the human Redeemer but a name for a second divine person whose
role will be to be incarnated in a human being (however precisely that was
imagined in the first century) and redeem Israel and the world.

---

[26] This obviates the need for any corporate interpretation of the Son of Man. Cf. Hooker,
Son of Man in Mark, 99. Cf. Kim, *"The 'Son of Man'*," 4.

[27] Cf. the scholarly tradition cited (disapprovingly) by Morna Hooker that considers these
verses as late additions simply owing to the fact that they do not conform to preconceived
notions about what the Son of Man means; Hooker, *Son of Man in Mark*, 81–3.

[28] Hooker, *Son of Man in Mark*, 112.

[29] Indeed, startlingly enough, on the very next page, Hooker writes: "It is, indeed, only as
Messiah – i.e. as one who is leader and representative of his nation – that the one like a Son of
man in Daniel can be interpreted as an individual. Thus, when Enoch, retaining the Danielic
context, regards the Son of man as an individual, he concludes that he is none other than the
Elect and Anointed One. Later references in the gospel suggest that Jesus, too, had Daniel 7 in
mind, and that the Son of man, if he is an individual, must therefore also be Messiah. Mark's
portrait of the disciples, therefore, is entirely credible, for though they would never have
replied "You are the Son of man" in response to Jesus' question, they could nevertheless,
believing him to be Messiah, accept the term as his own self-designation without undue
surprise." Hooker, *Son of Man in Mark*, 113. I shall be coming back to discuss this passage in the
longer version of this paper.

Scripture and the Writer of Mark

Robert B. Coote

Great overview

1. The Scriptural Story and Markan Irony

The Jewish Scriptures' story of salvation runs like this: the Lord defeats the Empire in battle, leads Israel across the Sea and through the desert, where his law is revealed through Moses on the mountain. When Israel reaches their Land, Jesus (Joshua) leads them across the Jordan – the Sea again – and captures the Land. In time David becomes the Lord's anointed, the son of God, gathers a military following, as king marches to Jerusalem, captures the city, making it the city of David, and establishes the Temple of the Lord there, which his son builds and the Lord safeguards in David's name and for David's heirs. The story is the story of the way of the Lord; it begins with the crossing of the Sea and ends at Jerusalem with the building, and later the restoration, of the Temple.

This is the story of the Torah and Former Prophets. It is a story epitomized in one of the oldest compositions in the Bible, the song of Miriam in Exodus 15: the Lord throws Pharaoh into the Sea and leads Israel past stunned opponents to the mountain of his possession, the place of the Lord's abode, the sanctuary of the Lord's founding. And it is the story of the Latter Prophets. It is the story told by Isaiah of Israel's deliverance from Babylon, when the eyes of the blind shall be opened, the ears of the deaf unstopped, the lame shall leap like a deer, and the tongue of the mute sing for joy. The Lord will construct a highway through the dry land, and the ransomed of the Lord will return to Zion with singing. Israel, the suffering servant of the Lord, embodying the offices of king and prophet, will exult in the repossession of Jerusalem and the restoration and re-purification of the Temple. It is the story of the Twelve, from the desert of Hosea to the Temple of Haggai, Zechariah, and Malachi – with climactic arrivals at the Temple along the way: Hosea, Joel, Amos, Micah, Habakkuk, and Zephaniah all end with the restoration of the Temple, as do Jeremiah and Ezekiel. Nearly all the Prophets end with the restoration of the Temple – not surprisingly, since the theme of the Prophets, Former and Latter, is God's sanction of the house of David. And it is the story featured by Malachi: "I am sending my messenger to prepare the way before me, and the Lord whom you seek will suddenly come to his Temple," preceded by the return of Elijah.[1]

And it is Mark's story, the story in a Jewish form, told as true to Scripture, as all things Jewish must be. As a whole, the story follows Anne Wire's Jewish stories of prophets' signs and martyrdom and vindication; behind these lie the Torah, Prophets, and Psalms – Moses and David and their avatars – and their military subject.[2]

Mark of course adapts the story. The Scriptural story of salvation sets up expectations that in Mark are not fulfilled. Mark is saturated with irony – the discrepancy or incongruity between appearance or expectation and reality – in every part and at every level, with myriad instances; but its basic irony is the incongruity between it and its Scriptural template, the Scriptural story of salvation. With respect to the Scriptural story, Mark is an anti-story. The crossing of the Sea, Jesus' baptism, is a death. Jesus takes the place of Isaac and he really is sacrificed. The anointed, Jesus/Joshua, refuses to fight to recapture the land: he starts out in the desert waited on by the army of God, but resists Satan's temptation to storm the land and city straight away with such forces. The anointed's chosen lieutenants are obtuse, incompetent, insubordinate, and disloyal – they may look like the rebellious Israelites in the desert, but not like Moses' loyal henchmen. The first and longest of Jesus' few teachings in Mark, in Mark 4, regarding hearing and the seed, refers to hearing Mark itself and is an epitome and compounding of irony; it is based on Isaiah 6 and its blunt irony. In Mark, the blind receive their sight but stay blind: Bartimaeus hails the anointed, i.e. baptized, as the son of David, but the anointed himself, in an exegetical thunderbolt, reads Psalm 110 to prove him wrong. The anointed is not the son of David. He does not recapture Jerusalem. He shuts down the Temple's services and pronounces the Temple's destruction: he has come to Jerusalem not to restore the Temple but to see it thrown into the Sea. He is captured and executed – defeated, seemingly abandoned by God, forsaken by his closest followers who never grasped the nature of the campaign. He is raised, to go before them, as before, to Galilee where he started. There they can find him, presumably to wage the campaign, for trust in God, over again – if someone tells them.[3] No one tells them. Nevertheless the whole story *is* now told, by the writer of Mark, to be grasped by those with ears to hear, those "in on the irony."[4]

---

[1] See T. C. Gray, *The Temple in the Gospel of Mark: A Study in Its Narrative Role* (WUNT 242; Tübingen: Mohr Siebeck, 2008).

[2] A. C. Wire, *Holy Lives, Holy Deaths: A Close Hearing of Early Jewish Storytellers* (Atlanta: SBL, 2002).

[3] I.e. "the disciples including Peter." This makes the crux *epibalōn* in 14:72, the climax of Peter's story, all the more significant but no less uncertain. Does Peter's grief now prepare him to "hear"? Since the women did not tell and Peter never got the youth's message, the question stands, to engage Mark's hearers.

[4] Of the myriad ironies in Mark I will refer here to a mere few. See M. A. Tolbert, *Sowing the Gospel: Mark's World in Literary-Historical Perspective* (Minneapolis: Fortress Press, 1989),

I don't think there's any doubt that the writer of Mark painted himself into the picture, as many have proposed, as the _neaniskos,_ the naked then clothed youth, the only baptized person in the Gospel other than Jesus, who fled naked from the Passover skirmish on the Mount of Olives and reappeared in the tomb clothed in white knowing what happened. The scene of the skirmish, which begins with Jesus saying to the disciples, "You will all be scandalized, for it is written, 'I will strike the shepherd and the sheep will be scattered'" (Zech 13:7) and ends with the flight of the naked, of course reflects Zechariah (interpreting Amos): "I will gather all the nations against Jerusalem to battle, and the city shall be taken and the houses looted and the women raped [...] Then the Lord will go forth and fight against those nations. [...] On that day his feet shall stand on the Mount of Olives, and the Mount of Olives will be split in two [and the dead raised at this point, as tradition had it] [...] and you shall flee [...] you shall flee as you fled from the earthquake in the days of King Uzziah" (Zech 14:2–5; cf. Amos 1:1, 2:16[5]).

[handwritten margin note: Mk $14:27$ *]*

Also from Zechariah is this: "Rejoice greatly, Zion, your king comes to you, vindicated (*saddîq*) and victorious, humble and riding on a donkey..." (9:9). But in Mark's time it has not happened triumphantly as Zechariah announced, and will not yet. Moreover in the midst of Zechariah's drawn-out treatment of the restoration of the Temple, segueing into Malachi's treatment of the Temple cult, Zechariah refers repeatedly to the house of David, which Mark jettisons along with the Temple. Mark is not the conventional story. It is the Scriptural story, but suspended or in reverse, not from the Passover to the crossing of the Jordan, taking of the land, and restoration of the Temple, but from the Jordan to the Passover, when the Temple proves its injustice, on a night of defeat rather than victory, when the anointed is betrayed by his last follower, his first lieutenant, at the third cock crow, the very moment when on the first Passover the sun rose to reveal the Egyptian dead on the shore of the Sea. In Mark, embattled Israel dies and Egypt lives; hope lies elsewhere. Of course Mark is a story of apocalyptic hope – but first the story of Jesus.

98–103; H. C. Waetjen, *A Reordering of Power: A Socio-Political Reading of Mark's Gospel* (Minneapolis: Fortress, 1989); D. O. Via, "Irony as Hope in Mark's Gospel: A Reply to Werner Kelber," *Semeia* 43 (1988): 21–27; J. Camery-Hoggatt, *Irony in Mark's Gospel: Text and Subtext* (New York: Cambridge University Press, 1992), 92–177; J. Fenton, "Mark's Gospel – the Oldest and the Best?" *More About Mark* (London: SPCK, 2001), 44–58. See the comments of W. R. Telford, *The Theology of the Gospel of Mark* (New York: Cambridge University Press, 1999), 24–25. The articles by S. P. Ahearne-Kroll, R. Griffith-Jones, and E. S. Malbon in *Between Author and Audience in Mark: Narration, Characterization, Interpretation* (ed. E. S. Malbon; Sheffield: Sheffield Phoenix, 2009), while shying away from the term, deal latently with numerous ironies.

[5] This is one of the many instances where Mark appears to be interpreting a Hebrew rather than Greek text: "the naked one will be persecuted/driven out in that day."

2. Mark as Baptismal Polemic

Mark's story was not the early church's dominant or prevailing story of Jesus. Others too would have told Jesus' story as the story of salvation, including the irony of failure, but the failure was momentary, perhaps only apparent, and the irony short-lived, resolved by the triumphant finale, the resurrection. Mark cannot ignore the resurrection and Jesus' future war. But Mark does not merely downplay the resurrection and its triumphant aftermath, a commonplace of Markan interpretation. In Mark the resurrection and future war play no signifi-cant role in resolving the ironies of the story as a whole – a point to be empha-sized. Jesus' failure and shaming are resolved not by his resurrection, as in the prevailing account, but by his baptism – in ritual practice from the shame of nakedness to the honor of new birth clad in white – and this is the crucial difference between Mark as a Scriptural story of salvation and the story it was written against.

The church hierarchy's dominant story, we must suppose, played up not only the resurrection of the anointed Lord, but also the Jewish essentials, rather than playing them down or contradicting them as Mark does. God's law is revealed through Moses, who laid down the fundamentals of covenant obedience: the food laws, which are blood laws (Noah), male circumcision (Abraham), and the Sabbath (Moses). David is the founder of the Temple. In terms of the Jewish essentials, which were also largely the church's essentials, Mark makes outra-geous departures. Mark's story is based on baptism, beginning, middle, and end. This could scarcely be Peter's story. It treats Peter as shameful. Like the rest of the Twelve, Peter understands less than women and children; Peter is rebuffed by Jesus as Satan who tempted him to lead the angelic forces in a shock-and-awe campaign to take the land; and Peter throws away his allegiance in a craven threefold denial.[6] More importantly, the story is based on baptism to the ex-clusion of circumcision. Mark is the story of Jesus told in Pauline terms, a narrative Galatians, and if Galatians is scathingly partisan and polemical, so is Mark. Mark's polemical thrust matches Paul's, though it is more extreme. Mark takes the hierarchy's story of Jesus in terms of the Scriptural story of salvation and retells it in Pauline terms, and more radically than Paul himself.[7]

Recent years have seen a revival of Baur's contention, from a century and a half ago, that Paul was at the ideological fringe of the church, not its center, a maverick whose views represented not an early church consensus but marginal assertions.[8] If so, then Mark should be seen as fringe, too, contrary to Martin

---

[6] T. W. Jennings, Jr., *The Insurrection of the Crucified: The "Gospel of Mark" as Theological Manifesto* (Chicago: Exploration Press, 2003), 1.

[7] M. Nanos, *The Irony of Galatians* (Minneapolis: Fortress 2002). Cf. Gal 4:20: Paul would prefer not to use ironic rebuke, but must.

[8] J. Marcus, "Mark – Interpreter of Paul," *NTS* 46 (2000): 473–87; C. Roetzel, *Paul: A Jew on the Margin* (Louisville: Westminster John Knox, 2003), 1–7, 38, 50–65

Werner's classic first proposition against Baur that "where Mark agrees with Paul it is always a matter of *general* early Christian viewpoints."[9] In his recent discussion of Mark's Pauline character, Marcus lists more than a dozen similarities between Paul and Mark, many previously discussed by others, even without reference to the recent realization that Jesus could not have taught Paul's view of Moses. Marcus' main focus, though, was on Werner's second proposition, that "where in Paul's letters [...] characteristically Pauline viewpoints come to the fore, either Markan parallels are lacking or Mark represents contrary standpoints."[10] Marcus counters this by focusing on just one similarity between Paul and Mark out of many, showing, without difficulty, that "both Paul and Mark lay *extraordinary* stress on the death of Jesus," and quoting the Paul who wrote to the Corinthians that he had decided to "know" nothing in their midst except "Jesus Christ and him crucified" (1 Cor 2:2).

An equally important similarity between Paul and Mark is one that Marcus does not mention and that continues to be almost completely ignored in Markan studies, namely the priority of baptism over circumcision. Baptism in Mark should not be regarded simply as an incidental affirmation of a uniformly cherished rite. In the first century, baptism was not a neutral practice, but center ground in an intense battle of authority and ideas with respect to the significance of circumcision, the status of the covenant of Abraham, and the role of Moses for the Jewish sect that was the church. These were huge issues in Mark's context. Paul's position was not at all obvious to the heads of the church and many others in Mark's day.

Mark immediately establishes his agreement with Paul in partisan terms: Jesus became reborn as the son of God with his baptism, which nullified both his kinship ties and his covenantal bonds, prefigured his willing death, and laid the basis of his replacement of Moses. The latter point is made explicitly on the mountain equivalent of Sinai, where Jesus appears clad as the baptized initiate, Elijah and Moses disappear from view, and from the cloud the *bat qol* repeats the baptismal "This is my beloved son" and adds, referring to Deut 18:18–19, "obey *him!*" i. e. not Moses. If this had been the generally accepted understanding of baptism in the church, Galatians, Romans, and Mark would never have been written. Mark's position is clear not simply because circumcision is nowhere mentioned in the Gospel. At his baptism, Jesus crosses the Jordan from east to west, recapitulating the Passover like Israel under Joshua/Jesus and like Elisha following the ascension of Elijah, who now reappears to baptize Jesus.[11] But Moses made clear on the very day of Passover that to commemorate the Passover a man had to be circumcised[12]. Therefore the *first* thing that Jesus/Joshua

---

[9] Marcus, "Mark," 476.

[10] Marcus, "Mark," 476.

[11] Joshua 5–7, 2 Kings 2; this passage *through* the Jordan appears to be the meaning of *eis*, Mk 1:9, cf. 7:31.

[12] Exod 12:43–49.

did the instant all Israel reached the west bank of the Jordan on that Passover anniversary was to circumcise the entire new generation of men born during the 40 years in the desert – a half million circumcisions at once. And the allusion through the phrase *ho agapētos* to the sacrifice of Isaac, the first circumcised of all – a sacrifice that occurred on the very site of the future Temple – evokes the entire copious Jewish exegetical tradition regarding the connection between circumcision and the death and resurrection of the beloved son brilliantly laid out by J. Levenson.[13] This is what goes momentously unremarked in Mark's account of Jesus' baptism, and not because the hearer can take for granted that Jesus came from a good Jewish family who would have seen to his circumcision.[14]

Mark's story supported Paul and went beyond Paul, and in a context that Paul could conceptualize in theory but the writer of Mark knew in fact, the war for the salvation of Israel, against Rome as it turned out. In the midst of that war, Mark lays out the meaning of God's war, a dominant subject in Scripture and ubiquitous in the Prophets, interpreting exactly the same texts that all Israel in Mark's day, both inside and outside the church, were keenly searching to find out what the awful turmoil meant and where it was all headed. Mark's story was not the story – the narrative interpretation of Scripture – that many of the church's hierarchy wanted told in the midst of the war not only raging against Rome, but also pitting Jew against Jew, including within the church. Mark polemicizes by retelling the prophetic sign plot in part against the generic expectation of that plot. But that expectation, for the liberation of Israel, was *the* hope of the war, and there is no reason to think that the church hierarchy was not caught up in that hope, if not in the struggle itself. Mark told a story that could not help being viewed as disparaging the essentials of Jewish autonomy: Moses, David, and the Temple. Entering a visionary no-man's land, Mark embraced the likelihood of being branded a traitor to the cause. It is no accident that in Mark Jesus teaches that in the midst of the great war Jesus' loyal followers will end up before both Jewish and Roman magistrates because "brother will betray brother to death, a father his child, and children their parents; and you will be hated by all because of my name" (13:12–13). The crosses that peppered the landscape in Mark's world awaited not only the insurgents who fought for their freedom, but the followers of Jesus who did not.

Mark's context is a war of liberation. Mark's theology is not just of trust in God, like Paul, but of the cross per se, and not metaphorically for opposition and

---

[13] J. Levenson, *The Death and Resurrection of the Beloved Son: The Transformation of Child Sacrifice in Judaism and Christianity* (New Haven: Yale University Press, 1995).

[14] It would be difficult to exhaust the Scriptural exegetical resonances in the baptismal scenes in Mark. Beyond at least fifteen direct references to Scripture in the first eleven verses of Mark, with the exegetical complexes entailed, there is an entire tradition of interpretation regarding Adam that awaits full treatment; cf. Marcus, "Mark," 475, n. 11.

incarceration as in Paul. Mark applies Paul's "theology of the cross" to the war. In the midst of this war, Mark opposes what the teller took to be the prevailing view of a church hierarchy and its narrative of resurrection as the church's version of the narrative of national liberation: Jesus as the son of David, led by Yahweh, is about to return to his Temple, dispel the empire and its lackeys, restore the Temple to its rightful heir, and establish his kingdom in justice defined by the law of Moses, just as the prophets foretold. It is the quintessential Prophetic narrative of hope: the restoration of the house of David in Jerusalem. Narrative of apocalyptic hope though Mark is, to be fulfilled before the passing of the writer's generation, Mark squarely opposes the hierarchy's narrative of liberation on every significant score: the military, exodus way of Jesus entails no Israel delimited by Moses, indeed no Moses, no royal hierarchy, no return of Jesus in the midst of the liberation struggle, no military victory, no Passover triumph, no restored Temple, no son of David or Davidic inheritance, and, given the importance of the resurrection in the early church, a notoriously deflected resurrection.

3. Markan Irony and the Latter Prophets

Mark did not get his irony from the Scriptural salvation story as such, which in Scripture is told with little or no irony. But he did find irony in the Latter Prophets, and in abundance.[15] In countless passages, the Prophets target the irony of the complacency and self-righteousness of the elite, of which the elite are oblivious, and counter it with a corresponding irony. Take for example the passage in Malachi just before the passage quoted at the beginning of Mark: you have wearied the Lord by saying, "All who do evil are good in the sight of the Lord," i. e. "bad is good and good is bad." God's response: you are more right than you realize. The Prophets' counter-irony appears in numerous guises. An archetypal instance occurs in Amos' opening denunciation of the Israelite war-making creditor class: I will not be mollified, God rules, "because they have sold the *saddîq* for the (borrowed) silver, and the indigent for the pledged harvest, they who trample on the head of the poor, who shunt the case of the afflicted, who lie down on garments taken in pledge, and drink the wine of those they mulct." Here are four terms for the borrowing class, of which the last three are descriptive – indigent, poor, afflicted. The first, *saddîq*, is not descriptive ("righteous") but rather defines the status of the borrower vis-à-vis the creditor in the case of one vs. the other in the divine assize. The term *saddîq* signals God's verdict: the borrower is "innocent" and hence the creditor guilty, the reverse of

---

[15] C. J. Sharp, *Irony and Meaning in the Hebrew Bible* (Bloomington: Indiana University Press, 2009), 125–34.

what the creditor addressed by this oracle, in his judicial dealings with the penniless borrower, has every reason to assume.

Just as pervasive is the irony of the incomprehensible prophetic word. The prophet is commissioned as herald to announce God's judgment in plain Hebrew, but ironically the addressees cannot grasp the simplest points. This appears already in Samuel's catch–22 denunciations of Saul, who can't understand despite himself. It appears in commissioning scenes and related passages: Isaiah is commissioned to "make the minds of this people dull, stop up their ears, and shut their eyes." Later Isaiah complains that he might as well be talking baby talk, or speaking a foreign tongue (Isa 28:9–13). The prophet's words written are like a sealed document (Isa 8:16; 29:11–12). Jeremiah knows he'll be attacked for his message and begs off, but the Lord assures him that "I will be with you to deliver you." We look for Jeremiah's deliverance through his entire book, but it never comes. The Lord shuts up Ezekiel in his house, binds him hand and foot, and attaches his tongue to the roof of his mouth, then tells him to reprove the rebellious elite. Reduced to pantomime, Ezekiel remains speechless until the moment that word of Jerusalem's fall and the Temple's destruction reached Babylon: only the fulfillment of his message made it audible (33:21–22). Entire prophetic books are structured by such ironies.

In the Latter Prophets, all the prophets are spurned and persecuted by their powerful and privileged addressees; none is saved from this repression, none vindicated in his own person, even though on assignment from God. Instead, in Isaiah, Jeremiah, Amos, Micah, and Habakkuk, we find the most all-encompassing and perhaps most vital of Prophetic ironies, in which by an ironic reversal the prophet comes to represent the butt of his invective. This goes well beyond Horsley's "prophetic script" or Wire's story of "the prophet's sign." The prophets "are appointed [...] by God, spurned and sometimes oppressed by their addressees, including the Davidic court, and thus, as the weaker persecuted by the stronger, compelled to complain on their own behalf, only to have their complaint appropriated by the very court they have addressed once that court becomes, by the carrying out of God's judgment, the weaker in comparison with the stronger alien warriors and citadels" – a rhetorical device fundamental to the Prophetic corpus.[16]

There is also the irony of God painting himself into the corner of mercy, as in Amos. Later scribes might not all catch such ironies; but the numerous ironies of Jonah, through which they are epitomized, are unmistakable. Jonah is told to denounce Nineveh, but he knows that God will not follow through, and he never, as far as the story goes, recovers from his resentment at being sent on a

---

[16] R. B. Coote, "Proximity to the Central Davidic Citadel and the Greater and Lesser Prophets," in *"Every City Shall Be Forsaken": Urbanism and Prophecy in Ancient Israel and the Near East* (eds. L. L. Grabbe and R. D. Haak; Sheffield: Sheffield Academic Press, 2001), 62–70 [64–65].

fool's mission. This is the positive irony of God's grace in the prophetic corpus.[17] At the same time, the corpus is imbued with a negative irony, in which, though repentance turns away God's wrath, repentance is never finally accepted as adequate, but rebuffed as a prelude to further backsliding.

4. Mark, Empire, Judaism, and Church

Moreover Mark's story of salvation is no more a popular or peasant story than its Scriptural foil. As many peasants might have favored the war against Rome as opposed to it. A peasant perspective denouncing the Temple and foreseeing its destruction is rare in the Prophets. There is little like Micah's green prophecy – "Zion shall be plowed as a field, Jerusalem shall become a heap of ruins, and the mount of the Temple a wooded height" (3:12) – in which the spur where Jerusalem sits will revert to arable, without the original privately owned threshing floor, a vision of the fall of the house of David and hence the utter abandonment of its city, not just its Temple.

Mark opposes Temple heads. Many have made much of an anti-Roman polemic in Mark. I am skeptical about such an emphasis. Kelber's recent comment seems right: Mark "studiously evades any direct confrontational engagement with Rome [...] [Jesus] turns traditional concepts of political power inside out."[18] At the 2008 SBL meeting several speakers proposed to deconstruct Mark to show an unconscious acquiescence in Roman perspectives in the shaping of its supposed anti-Roman narrative. I found these papers illuminating but not entirely convincing because they chose not, or were unable, to take account of the main interest in a Mark that on the face of it exonerates Rome. That interest is not just the meaning of the Jewish Scriptures and Jewish essentials in the fragmented turmoil of the war as an inter-Jewish question, but as an interchurch question. In his stimulating article on Mark the storyteller as radical outsider, Pieter Botha rightly maintained that since we should assume a congruence between teller and teaching, the "lifestyle" of the writer of Mark must have stood "in opposition to society with regard to expression, attitude and even clothing," just as the writer must have opposed "keeping abuse of power and greed in its place."[19] In specifying what he means by "society," Botha says that

---

[17] R. B. Coote, *Amos Among the Prophets: Composition and Theology* (Philadelphia: Fortress, 1981).

[18] W. Kelber, "Roman Imperialism and Early Christian Scribality," *Orality, Literacy, and Colonialism in Antiquity* (ed. J. A. Draper ; SemStud 47; Atlanta: SBL, 2004), 135–153, esp. 137–142.

[19] P. J. J. Botha, "The Historical Setting of Mark's Gospel: Problems and Possibilities," *JSNT* 51 (1993): 27–55, esp. 48–49. The same perception, nearly ubiquitous, may be found in D. Rhoads, J. Dewey, and D. Michie, *Mark As Story: An Introduction to the Narrative of a Gospel*, (2nd ed.; Minneapolis: Fortress Press, 1999), who recognize the danger Mark runs but appear

"the story provides a cutting critique of the practices and authority structures of various institutions: Pharisees, Sabbath, temple and so forth." This is true as far as it goes; but it leaves unnamed Mark's main opponent, church authorities of his day and expectations they must have encouraged.

The article by A. Weissenrieder in this volume shows the emphasis in Mark with regard to Jewish essentials especially well. The fig tree standing for the Temple, she has shown, is not just a reflex of the fig tree in Jer 8:13, immediately following Mark's reference to Jeremiah's reproof of the Temple heads in Jeremiah 7 and their treatment of the Temple as a den of (*scil.* anti-Roman) insurgents, but also a Roman symbol. But as a Roman symbol, the withering of the fig does not signify a direct attack on Rome, as though the reference to Jeremiah were irrelevant. The fig tree, as a "cultural commemoration of Rome's founding fathers," evokes the issue of the founder of the city and Temple, in the first instance a Jewish issue, and in terms of the Markan story the whole reason Jesus has marched on Jerusalem and been hailed, ironically, as the one to refound the kingdom of David. The Temple is both a Jewish and a Roman institution. The Herods were beholden to Rome, of course, although Mark makes no reference to that connection other than the collusion of the Jewish Temple heads and the Roman governor, in a story however that shrinks that collusion to the single phrase "they handed him over to Pilate" and that places the entire responsibility for Jesus' death in Jewish hands. There is no reason for the intertextual and iconographic interpretations of the fig tree to be mutually exclusive. The story of the fig tree draws attention not simply to the destruction of the Herodian Temple by the Romans, but in the context of the whole story of Mark to what will be the disruptive surprise that Jesus comes not as the son of the Temple's founder David. Thus the fig tree joins the array of Roman symbols in Mark – legion, Vespasian-like healing, Roman royal insignia, etc. – contributing to inter-Jewish ironies.

---

to locate the danger outside the church: "To the Judeans, the followers of Jesus who renounced violence and who opposed the war would have been viewed as traitors" (p. 145). Morna Hooker has a pertinent discussion of Mk 4:12 in relation to Isaiah 6, in "Isaiah in Mark's Gospel," *Isaiah in the New Testament* (eds. S. Moyise and M. J. J. Menken; New York: T&T Clark, 2005), 35–49, esp. 38–39, on the irony of not hearing; but she does not call it irony, and she thinks the target is the non-hearing of the Jews, as in Romans 9–11. At present perhaps the sharpest social contrast drawn may be Horsley's view of "the conflict between rulers and ruled, between the Jerusalem high priestly families, on the one hand, and the Judean and Galilean peasants, on the other" over control of the "Israelite cultural memory": R. A. Horsley, "A Prophet Like Moses and Elijah: Popular Memory and Cultural Patterns in Mark," *Performing the Gospel: Orality, Memory, and Mark – Essays Dedicated to Werner Kelber* (eds. R. A. Horsley, J. A. Draper, and J. M. Foley; Minneapolis: Fortress Press, 2006), 174. This seems to lead to some odd irony-free readings of Mark, like the notion that Jesus was acting "like Moses and Elijah" intently to spearhead the renewal of Israel, which passes over the offense, the outrage even in the church, of Jesus' *replacing* Moses in fulfillment of Deut 18:15, as made clear in Mk 9:7–8.

5. Mark as Writer

What does all of this suggest about the writer of Mark and why he wrote Mark rather than just continuing orally to tell it? We start with the writer of Mark as writer.

In light of the preceding, I am inclined to regard the writer of Mark as a scribe, like the scribes who appear in his Gospel, adjunct to a Jewish magistracy steeped in the interpretation of Torah, Prophets, and Psalms essential to more or less self-governing Jewish communities everywhere.[20] Mark begins his work with these words: "The basis of the gospel [war report] of Jesus Christ son of God is as written in Isaiah the prophet."[21] The Scriptural amalgam of Exodus, Isaiah, and Malachi that follows is not merely the proof text for the appearance of John, but the Scriptural basis of Mark's whole story, a story composed as the exegesis of specific passages of Scripture, starting with Exodus and the *mal'āk* to be obeyed. (An aside here. To state the obvious, which with regard to a text like Mark can easily be lost sight of, the Exodus was central for Greco-Roman Jewish identity and essential in Jewish exegesis not only as a story of salvation, but also as a story of revealed law.[22] This is what makes the Torah Moses' Torah. This is the reason that Mark's account of Jesus *en tē erēmō* in the Galilean first structural third of Mark features the construal of the primary covenant laws of circumcision, Sabbath, and food taboos.) Mark then follows with a dozen more specific references to the Torah and Prophets, not incidental or gratuitous but in every instance meaning–laden and further unpacked as the story proceeds. Mark referred to, directly or indirectly, not only specific texts, but also typical exegetical problems presented by those texts and their juxtaposition. And many of them.[23] The writer of Mark knew Scripture the way Paul did: immersed in prolific detail, ready and able to bend passages to his narrative purposes. Paul handled Scripture, and as a separate matter he could probably read and write to some extent. We can wonder whether Paul's fluency with texts matched that of

---

[20] If in Palestine, see C. Hezser, *Jewish Literacy in Roman Palestine* (TSAJ 81; Tübingen: Mohr Siebeck, 2001).

[21] R. B. Coote, "Mark 1:1: *archē*, 'Scriptural Lemma,'" *Text as Pretext: Essays in Honour of Robert Davidson* (ed. R. P. Carroll; Sheffield: JSOT Press, 1992), 86–90.

[22] E. S. Gruen, *Heritage and Hellenism: The Reinvention of Jewish Tradition* (Berkeley: University of California Press, 1998), chap. 2, encapsulates the centrality of the Exodus for Jewish identity in the Hellenistic and Roman periods as well as the fluidity with which it was interpreted. Gruen's discussion also shows again that neither the text nor the interpretation of Scripture was fixed.

[23] R. B. Coote and M. P. Coote, "Homer and Scripture in the Gospel of Mark," *Distant Voices Drawing Near: Essays in Honor of Antoinette Clark Wire* (ed. Holly E. Hearon; Collegeville: Liturgical Press, 2004), 189–201. In addition to works cited there, see J. Marcus, "The Old Testament and the Death of Jesus: The Role of Scripture in the Gospel Passion Narratives," in *The Death of Jesus in Early Christianity* (eds. J. T. Carroll and J. B. Green; Peabody: Hendrickson, 1995), 205–233.

scribes. But Paul's or Mark's level of literacy does not much matter. They both worked largely from memory and achieved their virtuosity as interpreters of Scripture not in the scriptorium, but in the give-and-take of the synagogue, i. e. the assembly of the Jewish magistracy, in the arena of casuistry, exhortation, and debate.[24] Mark's distinct style and diction point as much as Paul's in the direction of someone steeped in the Semitic rhythms and cadences of the Hebrew Scriptures and their Aramaic interpretations.[25] The sole or even main source of Mark's Semitisms is not LXX Greek.[26]

The identity of the storyteller Mark as a scribe brings prevalent features of the gospel into focus. The writer may have been itinerant, as Botha has suggested, but if so he was an itinerant Jewish scribe, who once journeyed to town or village assemblies which were without benefit of Scripture texts, and now to comparable assemblies of followers of Jesus. Mark knew the Scriptures and he knew their interpretation. This is the knowledge of the synagogue. He might have acquired this knowledge partly in oral/aural disquisition. But since he was able to write, and since he (1) placed great value on rooting his story in Scripture, (2) made pervasive reference to Scripture and scriptural exegesis through citation and allusion throughout his story, (3) knew the Torah and Prophets – Torah and prophetic counterpart – intimately, (4) explicitly directs "the reader" regarding an interpretation of a passage of Scripture (Mk 13:14), and (5) framed Jesus' sparring with the Temple officials in Scriptural dispute with above all the Temple scribes both early and late in the Gospel[27] – for these reasons I think that the storytelling writer of Mark was a Jewish scribe, not a raconteur or rhapsode.[28]

---

[24] Cf. R. A. Horsley, "The Origins of the Hebrew Scriptures in Imperial Relations," in *Orality, Literacy, and Colonialism in Antiquity* (ed. J. A. Draper; Atlanta: SBL, 2004), 107–134, esp. 107–8.

[25] I am well aware of the indeterminacy of "the text" of Scripture in Mark's context described by Horsley ("A Prophet Like Moses," 170), but I cannot agree that "most of the references and allusions to Israelite tradition do not make explicit connection with a particular passage in a nascent scriptural text."

[26] E. C. Maloney, *Semitic Interference in Marcan Syntax* (Atlanta: Scholars Press, 1981), 243–52. Still there are many who continue to find no evidence at all of Semitic influence in Mark's Greek.

[27] Cf. e. g. Mk 2:6, 16, 18 (implied subject of *erxontai*), 25 ("have you never read […]" cf. 12:10, etc.).

[28] Horsley takes these reasons as evidence of exactly the opposite, of Mark's oral rather than written culture: R. A. Horsley, *Hearing the Whole Story: The Politics of Plot in Mark's Gospel* (Louisville: Westminster John Knox, 2001); Horsley, "A Prophet Like Moses," 168–69, cf. "proto-scriptural […] texts," 171, "proto-scriptural books," 178. Horsley minimizes Mark's relationship to Scripture: "Only in explaining the events that were difficult to accept and understand, such as the betrayal, arrest, and crucifixion of Jesus and the desertion of the disciples, does Mark appeal to the general and particular authority of the scripture" (*Hearing the Whole Story*, 264, n. 26). But that's a lot, and there's much more: the theme of the way, the baptismal basis of the whole, its pervasive irony, its studied structure, and more. Contrast V. K.

Mark's relationship to storytelling tradition appears to have been twofold. On the one hand, as a literate scribe Mark knew the Hebrew Scriptures intimately enough to tell the Scriptural story in a new mode, the story of Jesus Christ as a Scriptural story. As such he was a virtuoso performer, whose performance went well beyond the Scriptural story. In addition, Mark had not only the knowledge to tap into the complex exegetical tradition associated with the passages in Scripture of most concern to him, as to many Jews, but also the Scriptural know-how to transform the conventional affirmations of the Scriptural story through large-scale ironies, incongruities, and turnarounds, all rooted in the same Scriptures. Mark's exegetical tradition was informed by Paul's teaching, but went beyond Paul in its extremist views and radical impatience with the hierarchy's Jerusalem-centered liberation project.

On the other hand, as a teller of one ironic episode after another, Mark belonged, we might suppose, to a church tradition of ironic storytelling, possibly mainly by women, when they were allowed to talk, aimed against a male hierarchy seen as self-important and out of touch with divine strategy. This oral tradition in the church gave him not just stories to tell but also a way of telling, in the paratactic style of extended Scriptural narrative and stand-up comic, episode by episode.

Regarding language, Mark's mother tongue was probably Aramaic, possibly Hebrew. His Greek both shows Semitic influence – "syntactical Semitic interference permeates every page of the gospel" – and it is unsophisticated; neither feature is an indication of a rustic background.[29] Mark was a trained scribe, and as such an elite adjunct. He was probably fluent in Aramaic, Hebrew, and Greek, and probably knew some Latin. His linguistic abilities do not imply necessarily an elite background. Mark's Greek is not everyday speech. Like most ancient literature, Mark is written in a high language, even if faulty, in Mark's case in a Scriptural style.

With respect to the form of Mark, as a student of Albert Lord I have a healthy respect for the complexity and sophistication not only possible but to be expected in an oral storytelling tradition. It is conceivable that Mark as the expression of the intricacies of a complex and masterfully nuanced exegetical theme set conveyed through an overarching narrative development precipitated whole out of an oral matrix that produced countless stories of roughly the same nature and scope. But I doubt it. Instead, I suppose that, beyond the contributing oral influences of synagogue argument and Jewish storytelling which the

---

Robbins' statement of the view that oral and written tradition were completely intertwined in the early church: when people "spoke, they were interacting with written traditions; whenever they wrote, they were interacting with oral traditions" ("Interfaces of Orality and Literature in the Gospel of Mark," in *Performing the Gospel* 125–46, esp. 126). Cf. the apposite comments of Tolbert, *Sowing the Gospel*, 43–46.

[29] Maloney, *Semitic Interference*, 245.

writer of Mark must have participated in – unless he was simply the amanuensis of the teller I'm describing – Mark as a story orally rehearsed bore the same relationship to the oral performance of Mark the storyteller as that of Romans to the eccentric stump speech of Paul the disputatious envoy. That is, there wasn't much of an oral story tradition of which Mark is simply an exemplar. I am led to this supposition not only because of the function of irony in Mark, but also because of a well-known feature of Markan form, the chiastic or sandwich structure, and the related "episodes in concentric patterns," as Rhoads, Dewey, and Michie call them.[30] Horsley, citing Ong, regards this feature as a mark of orality, and he is not alone.[31] Since the structure of Mark is one of those subjects which everyone thinks is important but on which few agree, I know that I can't use it to convince anyone; but I can't ignore its influence on the way I read Mark. I belong to a minority who think that far from being a sporadic presence in Mark, these chiastic or concentric passages, like Mark's use of irony, are pervasive. They are more than episodic and are not limited to the more or less obvious instances, but are used throughout to organize Mark on three or four levels, from the patent nesting of episodes such as the raising of Jairus' daughter Talitha and the bleeding woman, to Mark as a whole, from Galilee to Jerusalem via the Jordan in between. With respect to orality, what strikes me most about this feature of Mark is the systematic, calculated way it is carried through ubiquitously. And, contrary to what one might expect and some have argued, that such concentric episodes offer a convenient opportunity to structure irony, I find only sporadic examples at most of irony being conveyed by them in Mark.[32] Ironically, Mark does use what Rhoads, Dewey, and Michie call "framing episodes," which are usually distinguishable from the concentric patterns, for ironic effect.[33] I say ironically, because Rhoads, Dewey, and Michie give as their example of this framing device the well-known connection between the healing of the blind man at Bethsaida (Mk 8:22–26 "I see people, but they look like trees out for a stroll") and of the blind man at Jericho (Bartimaeus), which frames the entire middle part of Mark, and say this about it: "The first healing of sight is difficult, done in two stages, indicating the difficult teaching to follow; the second healing of sight is instantaneous, indicating that the intervening teaching has been grasped" – which with regard to the disciples is not true, and with regard to Bartimaeus is not true since Jesus is not the son of David.[34]

---

[30] *Mark As Story*, 52–54.

[31] *Hearing the Whole Story*, 72.

[32] By contrast see G. van Oyen, "Intercalation and Irony in the Gospel of Mark," *The Four Gospels: Festschrift Frans Neirynck* (eds. F. van Segbroeck et al.; Leuven: Peeters, 1992), 949–974.

[33] The examples given of "paired episodes" (p. 52) fit better this category of structure in Mark.

[34] *Mark As Story*, 52.

For explaining the purpose of Mark's irony, perhaps we should begin with the situation that gave us the word. In Greek drama, the *eiron*, the dissembler, defeated his stronger opponent, the *alazon*, or braggard, imposter, by feigning in some way. Mark used irony because he was the weaker *eirōn* facing off against more powerful opponents. Mark also used irony to engage his hearers by getting them involved in the reality behind its irony, in a bid to alienate some from the hierarchy's story and to confirm others in their resistance to it, because irony subverts.[35] But for the source and main purpose of Mark's irony, we need look no further than the Latter Prophets, which document, with an intense urgency, poignancy, and nuance, the surprising turns of God's judgment and mercy, which are simultaneously just and incongruous. A scribe would not have to proceed far in the Prophets to realize that the Scriptural story of salvation is by itself incomplete, that the happy ending is not the end. It is not hard to imagine that someone as immersed in Scripture as Mark might be compelled to retell the story of Jesus to make this point. One would not have to read Scripture to recognize the ironies of arrogant power. But for Mark the scribe Scripture was where he knew these ironies best.[36]

Mark was a storyteller who presumably could tell his story orally. Whether he belonged to a tradition that produced such stories is less clear. Regardless, we can ask, why did he write his story? Partly he wrote it because that's what he did, write, and because there was a status, a power, in texts as such, a "formidable object," as Botha expressed it during the conference.[37] But I think the main answer is: to *fix* his story as an ironic story. In this he was still following the model of the main inspiration for his irony, the corpus of Prophets, which originated in a tradition of writing as oracle and law.[38] The Prophet books, incorporating the ironies of God's judgment and mercy, presented themselves as prophecy written to be preserved until fulfilled – most clearly in Isaiah 8, the follow-on to Isaiah 6. The prophets were misunderstood, unheeded, silenced, and suppressed in their own time, but their words were written and preserved and updated against not so much oblivion as the distortion of their message by ignoring the irony of self-righteousness, until their fulfillment, which for the corpus falls in the future. This is what the writer of Mark has done: put his version in writing in an attempt to keep it from slipping into the hierarchy's

---

[35] "The challenge of irony is a very nearly irresistible invitation to play the author's game on the author's field with the author's rules": R. M. Fowler, "Irony and the Messianic Secret in the Gospel of Mark," *Proceedings, Eastern Great Lakes Biblical Society* 1 (1981): 26–35.

[36] For a theory of irony in relation to Mark, see Camery-Hoggatt, *Irony in Mark's Gospel*, 15–89, 178–81.

[37] Cf. H. E. Hearon, "The Implications of Orality for Studies of the Biblical Text," in *Performing the Gospel*, 3–20, esp. 18–20.

[38] J. Ben-Dov, "Writing As Oracle and As Law: New Contexts for the Book-Find of King Josiah," *JBL* 127 (2008): 223–239; cf. Horsley, "Origins of the Hebrew Scriptures," 113–114.

default story of Jesus Christ and God's triumphant rule, the presumptuous – and popular – version.[39]

In sum, Mark *told* his story because he knew the Prophets and his immediate hearers did too. And he *wrote* the story because its irony, like that of the Prophets, tended to be lost, and thus like the Prophets the story was written to preserve an elusive truth until this truth became evident to all.

One could reply with Socrates and Plato that writing to preserve is a futile endeavor: "a written work is a child without father – it cannot protect itself" from revision and misunderstanding (Socrates), and for a man to write would be "to lay his thought open to the misunderstanding of the crowd" (Plato).[40] This presumably is why Isaiah describes the written words of prophecy as witness as a *sealed* document.

The point is not to be gainsaid: Mark was indeed a child without a protector, and was soon revised by Matthew, who rejected most of Mark's Pauline innovations, dissolved Mark's irony (probably he was never aware of it), and restored Moses and David.[41] Matthew's use of Scripture focused especially on Moses, as is well known, in a way very different from Mark.[42] Matthew did not envision a restored Temple, accepting the Temple as a lost cause. Nevertheless Matthew should not be thought of as marginal or retrograde, but closer to what had been the central position of the pre–70 church.

[handwritten margin notes: "I note", "Mat verse Mark"]

[handwritten note: Mark as unfinished prophet p377]

---

[39] See the discussion of the ambiguous position of the Jewish scribe in imperial relations in Horsley, "Origins of the Hebrew Scriptures," 117–124, and now more thoroughly R. A. Horsley, *Revolt of the Scribes: Resistance and Apocalyptic Origins* (Minneapolis: Fortress, 2009).

[40] J.-L. Solère, "Why Did Plato Write?" in Draper, *Orality, Literacy, and Colonialism*, 83–91, esp. 83.

[41] E. g. J. L. Houlden, *The Strange Story of the Gospels: Finding Doctrine through Narrative* (London: SPCK, 2002): Matthew and Luke were written because they disagreed with Mark.

[42] D. C. Allison, *The New Moses: A Matthean Typology* (Minneapolis: Fortress Press, 1994).

Mapping Written and Spoken Word in the Gospel of Mark

Holly Hearon

Written and spoken word come together in a variety of ways in the Gospel of Mark. This is illustrated by the many different studies that have been produced in relation to this subject. For example, a number of studies engage the Gospel as a written text that records stories which have been gleaned from oral tradition.[1] Others describe ways in which the composer of Mark's written Gospel employs narrative techniques associated with spoken word.[2] Whitney Shiner has mined the text of Mark for cues that signal how the Gospel may have been performed in the presence of an audience.[3] In this study, I chart another course, driven by the question: "How would a written text such as the Gospel of Mark been perceived, encountered, and engaged in a movement where the majority of members could not read?"[4] I attempt to answer this question by mapping out how written and spoken word are perceived, encountered, and engaged within the narrative world of Mark's Gospel. On the basis of this literary analysis I propose that the Gospel of Mark is a written text that self-consciously represents itself not as a written word but as spoken proclamation.

---

[1] E. g. R. Bultmann, *History of the Synoptic Tradition* (trans. John Marsh; New York: Harper & Row, 1963); R. A. Guelich, *Mark* (WBC 34a; Dallas: Word, 1989), xxxii–xxxv; W. Kelber, *The Oral and the Written Gospel* (Bloomington: Indiana University Press, 1983); B. L. Mack, *A Myth of Innocence: Mark and Christian Origins* (Philadelphia: Fortress, 1988).

[2] E. g. P. J. J. Botha, "Mark's story as oral traditional literature: Rethinking the transmission of some traditions about Jesus," *HvTSt* 47 (1991): 204–31; J. Dewey, "Oral Methods of Structuring Narrative in Mark," *Int* 43 (1989): 32–44; eadem, "Mark as Aural Narrative: Structures as Clues to Understanding," *Sawanee Theological Review* 36 (1992): 45–56. See also Kelber, *Oral and Written*.

[3] W. Shiner, *Proclaiming the Gospel: First-Century Performance of Mark* (Harrisburg, PA: Trinity Press International, 2003).

[4] It is estimated that between five to ten percent of the general population could read (W. V. Harris, *Ancient Literacy* [Cambridge, MA: Harvard University Press, 1989], 272).

1. Reading Written Words

In Mark 13:14, the writer of the Gospel startles the nodding reader into consciousness with the words "let the reader understand."[5] In the world of theater, this would be described as 'crossing the proscenium arch': a moment in which the divide that separates the stage from the audience is eliminated and the audience finds itself engaged as a character in the drama. In the Gospel of Mark, the words 'let the reader understand' cross the divide between written and spoken word and remind us that what is written on the page is encountered as spoken word through vocalized reading. To put it another way, these words are a self-conscious declaration that the Gospel of Mark is understood by its composer to be both written word (something that is read) and spoken word (something that is vocalized by a reader).[6]

In addition to the citation in chapter 13, there are three additional references to reading in the Gospel of Mark. Each of these refers specifically to the reading of Scripture and occurs in a question posed by Jesus to religious leaders, "have you not read?" (2:25; 12:10; 12:26). Since reading is almost always done aloud, often by a designated reader because so few people could read, it is possible that this phrase could also mean "have you not heard read," thus introducing a glimpse at the complexity of the relationship between written and spoken word.[7] In either case, the question "have you not read?" may not necessarily point to the act of reading or hearing the written word; in the context of Mark's narrative, it appears to be a way of holding the religious leaders accountable for the *content* of the written word. This is suggested by the rhetorical force of Jesus' question. It is further underscored by following the question, in each instance, with either a direct quote from Scripture (12:10; 12:26) or description of the Scripture's content (2:25).[8] Consequently, whether or not they are in fact

---

[5] All translations are from the NRSV unless otherwise indicated.

[6] For an overview of various ways this phrase has been interpreted see A. Yarbro Collins, *Mark* (Hermeneia; Minneapolis: Augsburg Fortress, 2002), 594–98. She concludes that the evidence points to the "reader" being "the one who actually reads the text to the audience [...]" (598).

[7] See P. Achtemeier, "Omne Verbum Sonat: The New Testament and the Oral Environment of Late Western Antiquity," *JBL* 109 (1990): 15–17.

[8] The description in v. 26 identifies Abiathar as high priest rather than Ahimelech (1 Sam 21:1–6). The two are confused also in the text of 2 Samuel (8:17). If Mark is relying on memory rather than a written text (as Richard Horsley proposes), this may reflect a similar confusion of names ("Oral Performance and Mark: Some Implications of *The Oral and the Written Gospel*, Twenty-Five Years Later," *Jesus, the Voice and the Text: Beyond the Oral and the Written Gospel* [ed. T. Thatcher; Waco, TX: Baylor University Press, 2008], 61–63). Robert Gundry proposes that Mark names Abiathar deliberately in order to create a link with Jerusalem, the narrative context of Mark 2 (*Mark* [Grand Rapids, MI: Eerdmans, 1993], 141). If Gundry is right, this demonstrates that the composer of Mark feels free to take certain liberties

able to read the written word, we are to understand that the religious leaders are expected to know the content of the written word. This suggests that they have access to the written word in a way that others do not.

It is worth noting that, within the scope of these three references, Mark manages to name the primary groups that are identified with leadership roles in Temple and synagogue: Pharisees (2:25), chief priests, scribes, elders (11:27), and Sadducees (11:26); in other words, members of the retainer class. Thus, within the narrative world of Mark's Gospel, reading is identified as a circumscribed activity in terms of who reads (religious leaders), what is read (scriptures), and the context in which reading occurs (here marked by institutional affiliation).[9] What these few references to reading reveal is that Mark does not construct a world of readers, but a world in which only a very few read or have direct access to written word.

The lack of direct access to written word is underscored by the paucity of references to written words found in the narrative world of the Gospel of Mark. In addition to scripture, the Gospel contains three additional references to words that have been written. All three are related to the regulation of civic life: a bill of divorce (10:4 βιβλίον ἀποστασίου),[10] a coin (ἐπιγραφή.) and a sign on which is written a criminal charge (15:26 ἐπιγραφὴ τῆς αἰτίας[...] ἐπιγεγραμμένη).[11] I would argue that what these written words say is less important than the power that these words represent. This is most evident in the discussion of the coin (12:13–17): here, the inscription is shown to be a sign that the coin belongs to Caesar. In this example, one does not need to be able to read in order to understand what the words mean. These are words that are perceived, encountered, and engaged as symbols of the power or action they represent. Thus, although they are written words, they do not alter the assertion that Mark's narrative world is not a world of readers.

---

with 'what is written' for the sake of proclamation. This may offer insight into how the composer views the written text of the Gospel.

[9] In 10:19, Jesus addresses a rich young ruler. Notably, he does not say "it is written" nor "have you not read"; rather "you know the commandments." In contrast to the religious leaders who are depicted as having access to written texts, there is no assumption that the rich young ruler has similar access.

[10] Although Mark 10:4 states that "Moses permitted [a man] to write a bill of divorce [...]" the vast majority of men exercising this right would have had such a bill written for them by a scribe. Writing is almost always a mediated encounter, either through hearing a text read aloud, or having a spoken word inscribed in writing by another.

[11] Only in John (19:19–22) is an objection to the sign raised by Judeans who read the inscription. This suggests that the relationship between written and spoken word is distinctive in each Gospel.

2. Scripture: Perceived, Encountered, Engaged

Nonetheless, it is a world in which one written word plays a significant role: the Scriptures. How, then, is this written word perceived, encountered, and employed? We can gain access to this by examining the various words that are used in the Gospel to refer to the scriptures.

Texts associated with the prophetic writings are referred to by the phrase "it is written", using the divine passive: γέγραπται (1:2–3; 7:6; 9:12, 13; 11:17; 14:21, 27).[12] When we think of something that has been written, we are most likely to perceive and encounter it as something to be seen and read. An examination of the phrase 'it is written' in the context of Mark's narrative world reveals that within that world it is perceived and encountered differently.

In four of the seven instances, the phrase "it is written" is followed by a quote from scripture (1:2–3; 7:6; 11:17; 14:27). Yet in none of these instances is the physical text present; rather, what 'is written' is encountered as direct discourse, a word spoken from memory.[13] In the three remaining instances the phrase "it is written" is used in reference to someone about whom something is said to be written: specifically the Son of Man (9:12; 14:21) and Elijah (9:13). In these latter instances no text is quoted, but a statement is made suggestive of what "it is written" says: i.e., that the Son of Man must suffer while Elijah would be mistreated. However, it should be noted that the unidentified Scriptures that appear to provide the content for these allusions to the Son of Man (e.g., Mal 3:22–23 LXX; Isa 52:13–53:12; Ps 22:1–18) and Elijah (1 Kgs 19:2–10) require an interpretive move in order to be linked to the figure named.[14] This introduces a step between what is written and what is represented as written (i.e. Scripture). Something similar is found in Mark 1:2–3, where a creative conflation of Exod 23:20, Mal 3:1 and Isa 40:3 occurs. Although these verses all belong to Scripture, the particular formula found in Mark 1:2–3 occurs nowhere in scripture. Thus what is 'written' in Mark 1:2–3 is the result of an interpretive move, either on the part of Mark's composer, earlier interpreters, or community reflection.[15]

Mark 12:26 contains the single reference in the Gospel to the Scriptures as a 'book' or scroll, where Jesus responds to the Sadducees with the query, "[...]

---

[12] Fitzmyer notes that this same language is found in the Qumran texts, indicating that by this time it functioned formulaically ("The use of explicit Old Testament quotations in Qumran literature and in the New Testament," in *Essays on the Semitic Background of the New Testament* [London: Geoffrey Chapman,1971], 7–10)

[13] A possible exception is Mark 1:2, although it could be argued that this is a case of direct discourse involving the voice of the narrator.

[14] See Marcus, *The Way of the Lord*, 94–110, 153–96.

[15] For different views on how these verses come to be conflated see Fitzmyer, "'4 Q Tesimonia' and the New Testament," *Essays on the Semitic Background of the New Testament* (London: Geoffrey Chapman,1971), 62–63; J. Marcus, *The Way of the Lord: Christological Exegesis of the Old Testament in The Gospel of Mark* (Edinburgh: T&T Clark, 1992), 12–17.

have you not read in the book of Moses [...]" (τῇ βίβλῳ Μωϋσέως).[16] Earlier in the same passage, the Sadducees have introduced a question to Jesus with the statement "Moses wrote for us" (12:19: ἔγραψεν. In this one passage, then, we find the close proximity of the words 'wrote', 'read', and 'book'. This is the closest we come to the idea of reading words inscribed on a page. Context, however, places the emphasis not on the physical text, but on authorship (i. e. "*Moses* wrote") and the authority embedded in the author, expressed by the words "for us" (an idea also found in 10:5, "[...] because of your hardness of heart he wrote this commandment *for you*;" cf. 1:44; 10:3). Once again, then, the perception is not of a text or βίβλος read, but of an authoritative word comprehended (cf. 10:19 "You know the commandments;" 12:28: "which commandment is the first of all?"). This perception of the written word as an authoritative word comprehended is born out by the way in which Jesus employs a verse from the book of Moses, quoted from memory, to counter the Sadducees' earlier quote (12:26: "have you not read in the book of Moses, in the story about the bush, how God said [...]"). It is not the act of reading the book that is called to our attention but knowledge of what is contained in the book, and its right meaning demonstrated in oral debate.

In summary, we find that in every instance of the phrase "it is written", the physical aspect of "what is written" is, in fact, absent. Rather, what is identified as "written" is encountered exclusively as a spoken word. This suggests that we should not assume that "that which is written" is perceived of as a sheet of papyrus inscribed with words, or encountered as words on a scroll to be read. Rather the "written" aspect of the text appears to evoke the perception of the text as an authoritative verbal expression voiced by God.[17] Moreover, this authority is shown to extend beyond the written text (i. e. Scripture) to include certain interpretive moves involving Scripture. In both instances, this 'written word', as represented in the narrative world of Mark, is perceived and encountered as a spoken word called forth from memory.

3. The Scriptures as Spoken Word

This description of how the Scriptures – as written word – are perceived and encountered points to ways in which this particular written word is engaged as a spoken word within the narrative world of the Gospel. The commandments

---

[16] In the Gospel of Mark, Moses is associated specifically with commandments (ἐντολαί): 1:44; 7:9–10; 10:3; 10:5.

[17] Richard Horsley draws a similar conclusion in "Oral Performance and Mark: Some Implications of The Oral and the Written Gospel, Twenty-Five Years Later," *Jesus, the Voice and the Text: Beyond the Oral and the Written Gospel* (ed. T. Thatcher; Waco, TX: Baylor University Press, 2008), 61–63.

(ἐντολαί) are the focus of public, oral disputes between Jesus and various religious leaders. In 7:1–23, for example, the Pharisees ask Jesus (ἐπερωτάω) why his disciples do not wash their hands before eating. Jesus makes a counter-charge to the Pharisees, pointing to commandments (recited from memory) that he says they ignore. Jesus then calls the crowds to himself (προσκαλέομαι) and tells them to "Listen up!" (ἀκούσατε) and "understand" (συνίετε) as he tells them a parable intended to up-end the 'human tradition' of the religious leaders. This leads to a question (ἐπερωτάω) from his disciples which results in further explanation. The language of this written narrative describes a thoroughly oral context in which actions are disputed, parables told and heard, and understanding arises from the posing of further questions.

An examination of the three remaining disputes over the commandments reveals a pattern of repetition: In 10:2, a question is raised by the Pharisees (ἐπερωτάω) regarding divorce while Jesus is teaching the crowds; in 12:18, the Sadducees ask a question (ἐπερωτάω) regarding levirate marriage; this last leads to a question (ἐπερωτάω) regarding which is the greatest commandment of all (12:28). The distinctiveness of this language to Mark is suggested by the omission of ἐπερωτάω in the parallel versions of 7:1–23 and 10:1–10 found in Matthew and Luke,[18] and by the trajectory of question-asking Mark builds, leading to the conclusion in 12:34 that "no one dared ask him (ἐπερωτάω) any question." Thus the commandments are most often engaged within the narrative world of the Gospel in contexts of oral discussion and dispute.

The other primary use of the Scriptures within the narrative world of the Gospel is as commentary. Here, again, the written word is encountered and engaged as a spoken word. The first time this happens, it is the voice of the narrator that speaks in 1:1–3: "The beginning of the good news of Jesus Christ, the Son of God. As it is written in the prophet Isaiah [...]" This initial quotation sets the narrative to follow within the context of prophetic anticipation of God's messiah. Thereafter, however, the scriptural commentary is spoken by Jesus. In 4:12 Jesus tells the twelve that they have been "granted the mystery of the kingdom of God" but "to those outside everything comes in parables in order that 'they may indeed look, but not perceive [...]'" (quoting Isa 6:9–10).

---

[18] Mark 7:5 (ἐπερωτάω omitted in Matt 15:1 and Luke 11:38); 10:2 (ἐπερωτάω omitted in Matt 19:3; the pericope is absent in Luke). Only in Mark 12:18 is ἐπερωτάω omitted in both Matthew (22:23) and Luke (20:27). The distinctiveness of this language is further underscored by the observation that it is not only the religious leaders who ask questions in the Gospel. The disciples, too, regularly engage Jesus with questions and, once again, we find that the parallel versions in Matthew and Luke regularly omit the word: Mark 7:17 (ἐπερωτάω omitted in Matt 15:12; no parallel verse in); 9:11 (ἐπερωτάω employed in Matt 1:10; pericope omitted in Luke); 9:32 (no parallel in Matt 17:22–23; ἐπερωτάω employed in Luke 9:45); 10:10 (no parallel verse in Matt 19:3–12; pericope omitted in Luke); 13:3 (ἐπερωτάω omitted in Matt 24:3; ἐπερωτάω employed Luke 21:7). It is interesting to note that the disciples ask Jesus one final question, in 13:3, after the religious leaders no longer dare.

Similarly, in 7:6 Jesus announces to the Pharisees and scribes that "Isaiah prophesied rightly about you hypocrites, as it is written, 'This people honors me with
their lips, but their hearts are far from me. [...]'" (quoting Isa 29:13). The
pattern is repeated in 11:17, when Jesus casts out those selling and buying in the
temple; in 12:10–11, following the parable of the vineyard, and 14:26, when
Jesus declares that the disciples will all become deserters. In each instance the
words of the prophets are used to describe or explain what is happening within
the narrative – but, with the exception of the words in 1:2–3, this is not done
through the narrator, but through the voice of Jesus. Thus this scriptural commentary is encountered as a word spoken in and to specific contexts.[19] In several
instances (e. g., 4:12; 14:62; 15:32) the Scriptures are not introduced by a formulaic phrase, but are simply an extension of Jesus' own speech. Here any
distinction between written and spoken word is completely collapsed.[20]

To summarize, the written word that dominates the narrative world of the
Gospel is the scriptures, variously identified as that which is written, the commandments, or the book of Moses. While the Scriptures are described by terms
that identify them as written (i. e. a book, Moses wrote, as it is written) they are
consistently perceived, encountered, and engaged as spoken word. Their status
as spoken word is underscored by the absence of readers in the text, and by the
rhetorical use of the language of reading to convey knowledge or comprehension of that which is written, rather than the act of reading itself. Thus, although
the Scriptures as written word are everywhere present in the narrative world of
the Gospel, they are not present as written word, but as a word spoken.

4. The Gospel as Written and Spoken Word

Can this brief analysis of written word in the Gospel of Mark tell us anything
about the Gospel of Mark as written word? I think it can, and for the following
reasons: First, it can be assumed that whoever composed Mark is creating a
narrative world that is recognizable to his audience. In other words, if the

---

[19] Vernon Robbins has similarly observed that, "There is no instance in Mark in which the
narrator appeals to the writings for external support for an event or for an assertion in the
narration. [...] the interface between orality and literature is internal to the narrational voices in
the text" ("Interfaces of Orality and Literature in the Gospel of Mark," *Performing the Gospel:
Orality, Memory, and Mark* [eds. R. A. Horsley, J. A. Draper, and J. M. Foley; Minneapolis:
Fortress, 2006], 145).

[20] There are, of course, many allusions to scripture within the Gospel narrative (e. g. the
dress of John the Baptist in 1:6 echoes that of Elijah in 1 Kgs 1:8). These are so tightly woven in
the fabric of the narrative world that they cannot be distinguished from it. While recognition
of these allusions is dependent upon familiarity with scripture, they are in no way dependent
on access to the written text. Indeed, their effectiveness depends on the images being embedded in the memories of readers and hearers.

written word – the Scriptures – were represented in a peculiar or unfamiliar way, it would disaffect the audience or risk having Mark's narrative cast off as bizarre. Consequently, how the scriptures are perceived, encountered, and engaged can tell us something about the relationship of Mark's audience to written word. Granted, it does not tell us how that audience relates to *all* written words. However, the narrative world represents an audience that has limited engagement with written words of any kind, and the primary word that they do engage is Scripture. Second the composer of the Gospel of Mark uses the Scriptures both to establish the context for the Gospel narrative and as a commentary on events within the narrative. This indicates that the composer of the Gospel of Mark expects readers and hearers to perceive a dynamic relationship between the Gospel narrative and the Scriptures, the one emerging out of the other. Thus how the Scriptures as written word are perceived, encountered and engaged should provide a warrantable analogy for consideration of how the Gospel of Mark as written word might be perceived, encountered and engaged.

What, then, does this analogy suggest? To begin, it suggests that, although the Gospel is self-consciously a written word, there is an expectation that it will be encountered as a spoken word. At the very least, it will be encountered as a written word that is read or spoken aloud, as suggested by the notice, "let the reader understand" in 13:14. Yet since the narrative world of the Gospel describes a context in which the written word (i. e. the Scriptures) is encountered *not* as words inscribed on a page, but, rather, as words remembered, it is possible that that the composer of the Gospel of Mark expects that the written Gospel also will be perceived and encountered, like the Scriptures, primarily as a word that is spoken from memory and heard.

This expectation is suggested by the way in which the composer of Mark employs the language of hearing. The verb ἀκούω is first used not in reference to Jesus' words, but in reference to Jesus (2:1–2): "[...] it was heard that he was at home. And many gathered [...]" (my translation). In the Gospel, people are continually drawn to Jesus because they have heard about him: crowds (3:8; 6:55); Jesus' family (3:21); a woman with a flow of blood (5:27); a Syrophoenician woman (7:25); a blind man (10:47). The distinctiveness of this language to Mark is signaled by the absence of the language of hearing in parallel passages in Matthew or Luke (excepting only Mark 10:47). In the Gospel of Mark, the language of hearing conveys first of all that the figure of Jesus makes an indelible mark on people's memory, giving rise to reports and rumors that, in turn, draw people to Jesus (cf. 6:14; 7:32; 822).[21] Thus words about Jesus are words that have been heard and held in memory.

---

[21] They are not always drawn for positive reasons. In 3:21, Jesus' family thinks he has lost his mind.

The language of hearing is also used in reference to Jesus' words. It is first encountered in the telling of the parable of the sower. Jesus begins with a call to "listen!" (4:3), twice punctuates the parable and its interpretation with the words "Let anyone with ears to hear listen!" (4:9; 4:23), and concludes with the admonition to "Pay attention to what you hear" (4:24). Again, the distinctiveness of Mark's emphasis on hearing is underscored by the absence of this language in three of the four parallel verses in Matthew and Luke.[22] The parable itself calls direct attention to hearing the word (4:15, 16, 18, 20), which earlier in the Gospel has been identified as the word spoken by Jesus (2:2: "he was speaking the word to them," cf. 1:45). The word that Jesus speaks arouses astonishment in those who hear him (6:2), and crowds listen to him with delight (12:37; cf. 11:18).[23] The authority of Jesus' word is signaled when a voice from heaven charges the disciples to "listen to him" (9:7; see also 13:31: "Heaven and earth will pass away, but my words will not pass away"). Ironically, it is the words that people say they have heard Jesus speak that become the justification for his condemnation (14:58; 14:64).[24]

The word represented by Jesus in Mark's Gospel, then, is a word that is embodied in Jesus, manifested by his actions, and proclaimed in his words. It is a word that is encountered wholly as a word that is heard and subsequently held in memory. This is conveyed most forcefully in Mark 8:17–18 where Jesus queries of the disciples, "Do you still not perceive or understand? [...] Do you have eyes and fail to see? Do you have ears, and fail to hear? And do you not remember?"[25] The parallel passage in Matthew (16:8–9) omits the reference to eyes and ears, and ties the language of remembrance to the feeding of the five thousand. By retaining the language of seeing and hearing in connection with memory the composer of Mark's Gospel points beyond the immediate context to the whole of Jesus' ministry.

The authority of Jesus' word in Mark's Gospel provides additional insight into how the composer of Mark perceives the nature of the written text of the

---

[22] The language of hearing is echoed only in Matthew 13:9 and Luke 8:8 (cf. Mark 4:9). Luke 8:18 reads "Take head then *how* you hear" in contrast to Mark's "Pay attention to *what* you hear" (4:24).

[23] Matthew and Luke continue the pattern of omitting the language of 'hearing' in parallel verses (compare Mark 6:2 with Matt 13:54 and Luke 4:22, and Mark 12:37 with Matt 23:1 and Luke 20:45).

[24] Matthew and Luke omit the language of 'hearing' found in Mark 14:58. The motif of judgment associated with the word spoken is found also in 6:11 (Matt 10:14) where Jesus says to the disciples, "If any place will not welcome you and they refuse to hear you, as you leave, shake off the dust that is on your feet as a testimony against them."

[25] The idea of remembrance occurs only two times in the Gospel of Mark: in 8:18 (μνημο-νεύω) and in 14:9 where it is said of the woman who anointed Jesus that "wherever the good news is proclaimed in the whole world, what she has done will be told in remembrance (μνημοσύνη) of her." This last underscores the link between memory and spoken word.

Gospel. I have proposed that the Scriptures – as written word – are perceived within the narrative world of Mark's Gospel not as a words inscribed on a page, but as an authoritative word. In the case of the Scriptures, this authority arises from the recognition of these written words, over the course of centuries and through multiple generations, as an expression of the voice of God. In the case of the Gospel of Mark, there can be no expectation that the text of Mark's Gospel will immediately acquire this kind of authority. Instead, I propose that Mark claims authority for "that which is written" in the Gospel through the figure of Jesus.

This authority is signaled in the opening verses of the Gospel (1:1–3), by locating Jesus in reference to Scripture, and in John the Baptist's assertion that "One who is more powerful than I is coming after me [...]" (1:7). The first major action performed by Jesus in the Gospel – the healing in a synagogue of a man possessed by a demon – is framed by references to Jesus authority (ἐξουσία). This authority causes wonder and amazement among those present for two reasons: First, it causes amazement because Jesus teaches as one who has author- ity. This authority is contrasted with that of the scribes who (along with the other religious leaders in the Gospel narrative) read and interpret the scriptures, but, as Jesus will claim in 12:24, do not know the scriptures. Towards the end of the Gospel, when the chief priests, scribes and elders challenge Jesus, asking him by what authority he acts (11:27–33), he answers them with a question, sending them into confusion as they try to weigh the potential consequences of their possible answers. Their inability to ultimately reach a conclusion re-enforces Jesus' authority.

The second reason the crowd in the synagogue is amazed is because Jesus shows authority even over unclean spirits. This power that accompanies Jesus' authority is highlighted in other narratives: in 5:30 when a woman touches Jesus and he feels power go out of him, and in 6:2 when Jesus teaches in a synagogue and those present are "astounded at what deeds of power" are done by his hand. In 12:24, the same text where Jesus' accuses the religious leaders of not knowing the scriptures, Jesus also accuses them of not knowing the power of God. The immediate reference is to God's power in relation to raising the dead, but there is an implication that they also do not recognize the power of God that is present in Jesus and which has been manifested in their midst. There are other texts that could be cited in addition, but these are sufficient to establish a pattern in Mark's Gospel of words and deeds that point to the authority of Jesus and, by extension, claim authority for what is written in Mark's Gospel.[26]

This authority, however, is not ultimately an authority that rests in the words inscribed on the page. Rather, I propose that it is an authority which is under- stood to reside in the written word when and as it is encountered and engaged as

---

[26] See, e.g., 2:10; 3:22–27; 4:41; 9:7; 14:62.

a spoken word. This is suggested, in part, by the way in which the written word which is Scripture is encountered and engaged in the narrative world of the Gospel, with one interpreter or teacher demonstrating true understanding of the text in oral debate (7:1–16; 12:18–27; 12:28–34; 12:35–37). However, I think it is signaled most distinctly by the way in which the language of proclamation is employed in the Gospel. The Gospel begins with the declaration that "this is the good news (εὐαγγέλιον) of Jesus Christ"—that is the proclamation of or about Jesus Christ.[27] The second time we encounter the noun εὐαγγέλιον it is linked with the verb "to proclaim" (κηρύσσειν [1:14]): "Jesus came proclaiming the good news of God." The verb κηρύσσω references a specifically oral context in which a public declaration is made by a herald.[28] The use of the verb κηρύσσω in conjunction with εὐαγγέλιον suggests that the composer of Mark's Gospel perceives the written text of the Gospel, i. e. the "good news," as principally a spoken rather than a written word.

This is born out by a pattern that emerges when the verb κηρύσσω is traced through the course of the Gospel (see diagram below). It is first used in 1:4 when John the Baptist appears proclaiming a baptism of repentance, and again in 1:7 when John proclaims that one is coming who is more powerful than he. Both of these verses are tied to the appearance of Jesus, who is the more powerful one anticipated by John and who, like John, brings a proclamation requiring repentance, because the kingdom of God has come near. Passing references to Jesus' proclamation occur in 1:38, 39 and then end. However, in 1:45 the act of proclamation is picked up by the leper whom Jesus heals, despite Jesus' instructions to remain silent. This begins a brief pattern of alternation. In 3:14 Jesus calls to himself twelve so that they might be sent out to proclaim (although they are not actually sent out at that time). In 5:20 we return to a context of healing when Jesus exorcises a demoniac whom Jesus then instructs to tell "how much the Lord has done" for him, and "what mercy God has shown" to him. The man then goes away proclaiming all that Jesus has done for him. In 6:12 the twelve, now sent by Jesus, go out and proclaim that all should repent. In 7:36 we again return to a context of healing. This time, however, it is the crowds who witness the healing who begin to proclaim. The healing itself also proves significant: it is the healing of a man who is not only deaf, but also has a speech impediment. Healed, his ears are opened and his tongue released so that he can speak plainly (7:35). This story is found only in Mark. A little later the disciples will encounter

---

[27] The genitive may be read as either subjective or objective: i. e. either the good news about Jesus or the good news proclaimed by Jesus. The noun, εὐαγγέλιον, is distinctive to Mark where it occurs seven times (1:1, 14, 15; 8:35; 10:29; 13:10; 14:9). Matthew employs the noun four times, but only once in a passage shared with Mark (Mark 14:9//Matt 26:13). Luke employs only the verb, while John employs neither the noun nor the verb.

[28] F. W. Danker, *A Greek-English Lexicon of the New Testament and Other Early Christian Literature* (3rd ed.; Chicago: University of Chicago Press, 2000), 543.

a boy with a spirit who keeps him from speaking (ἄλαλος) (9:14–29).[29] Significantly, the disciples are unable to heal him, perhaps anticipating their own silence at the end Gospel. The last two references to proclamation reveal that, collectively, all of these references form a wedge shape, moving out from John the Baptist, through Jesus, to selected individuals, and into the world: in 13:10 Jesus declares that before the end can come, "the good news must first be proclaimed (κηρύσσω) to all the nations" and in 14:9, the final reference to proclamation in the Gospel, Jesus declares that what the woman who has anointed him has done will be told in memory of her, "wherever the good news is proclaimed (κηρύσσω)."[30]

Diagram 1   *proclaim*

John the Baptist initiates the proclamation of/about Jesus Christ 1:4, 7
    Jesus proclaims the good news of God 1:38, 39
        A leper proclaims good news, but is admonished to remain silent 1:45
          The twelve are called to proclaim 13:14
          A demoniac is instructed to proclaim good news and does so 5:20
            The twelve go out and proclaim that all should repent 6:12
            The crowds who witness the healing of the deaf/mute proclaim 7:36
              Jesus declares that the good news must be preached to all the nations before the end can come 13:10
              What the woman who anoints Jesus has done will be told "wherever the good news is proclaimed" 14:9

The end of the Gospel re-enforces the pattern established by the verb κηρύσσω. The Gospel concludes with the disciples having fled and the women who come to the tomb going away in silence, saying nothing to anyone. Mary Ann Tolbert proposes that the composer of Mark's Gospel is passing on the task of proclamation to those who hear (and comprehend) the good news of Jesus Christ as proclaimed by the Gospel.[31] I think this is exactly right. If we look at the endings of the other Gospels, we find that each of them, through the post-resurrection appearances by Jesus, point to ways in which the now risen Jesus continues to be present in the community of believers: In Matthew, it is through the disciples teaching all that Jesus has commanded them; in Luke, it is through study of the scriptures and in the breaking of bread; in John, it is through the disciples sent into the world. In Mark, Jesus continues to be present through the proclamation

---

[29] In the versions of this story found in Matthew (17:14–21) and Luke (9:37–43a), references to the boy being unable to speak are omitted.

[30] It is perhaps significant that the final two occurrences of the verb κηρύσσω reunite it with the noun εὐαγγέλιον. In addition, these last two references provide a temporal reference ("before the end can come") and a spatial reference ("wherever the gospel is proclaimed") for the proclamation of the Gospel.

[31] M. A. Tolbert, *Sowing the Gospel: Mark's World in Literary-Historical Perspective* (Minneapolis: Fortress Press, 1989), 299

of the good news, but this is not a task that can be carried out by a written word; it is a task that falls on the believer and which requires a word that is spoken aloud. A corollary for this is found in Acts 15:21 where it is reported "For Moses, from generations of old in every city, has had those who proclaim him in the synagogues for/because he is read aloud." Here, it is the vocalization of what is written that transforms the written word into proclamation. Thus, I propose that the composer of the Gospel of Mark ultimately perceives this written word that is the Gospel not as words inscribed on the page, but as a spoken word, encountered and engaged as a word that is heard, understood, remembered, and proclaimed.[32]

5. Implications

This proposal presents at least two significant challenges to students of the Gospel of Mark.[33] The first is in relation to methodology. If the written text of the Gospel was heard more than it was read, then literary studies are no longer adequate in and of themselves for gaining insight into how the Gospel conveys meaning. They must be accompanied by studies that are attentive to oral and aural dimensions of the Gospel, including sound patterns, cues within the text to performance, and examination of the varieties of ways audiences (as opposed to individuals) might hear and engage the Gospel in performance. This, additionally, invites consideration of how texts in performance shape social memory and identity, and how these shift in relation to differing performances. The second is in relation to our understanding of the nature of the Gospel and how it was engaged by early Christian communities. Literary analysis requires that we focus on the text as it has been handed down to us. Yet, if Mark's treatment of the Scriptures provides any kind of an analogy for our understanding of how the Gospel was perceived, encountered and engaged, then we are challenged to focus not only on the text as we have inherited it, but to look for evidence of how memorial recall has shaped and reshaped the received text in contexts of discussion and debate and in relation to the changing experiences of Jesus' followers. The creative combination of prophetic voices in Mark 1:2–3 further suggests that portions of the Gospel may have been similarly combined with other narratives not necessarily a part of this particular Gospel, but which became associated with it through the minds, memories, and experiences of hear-

---

[32] Joanna Dewey has proposed that Mark's version of the Gospel continued to be performed after it was written, always with variations ("The Survival of Mark's Gospel: A Good Story?" *JBL* 123 (2004): 502.

[33] I do not assume that what has been proposed regarding the Gospel of Mark can be applied to the other Gospels. An expanded version of the research begun in this chapter will explore how each of the Gospels describes the relationship between written and spoken word.

ers, resulting in retellings that constituted a new text. This has implications both for the emergence of the Gospel as we have received it and for how the Gospel was encountered and engaged once it was constituted as a written word. Evidence of such retellings needs to be explored more vigorously. All of this points to a text that was not fixed in content, or static in meaning, but fluid. This, in turn, invites us to give greater weight to variant readings of the text, to examine how diverse communities may have engaged the Gospel in subsequent centuries, and to view the Gospel not so much as an end in itself than as an expression of an on-going process of proclaiming the good news in an ever changing world.

Writing in Character:
Claudius Lysias to Felix as a Double-Pseudepigraphon
(Acts 23:26–30)

Trevor W. Thompson

In a recent essay on the written record among early Christians, M. M. Mitchell calls attention to "the conspicuous literary skills of some key leaders in the first generations."[1] The earliest extant Christian documents, the letters of Paul, reveal a "skilled thinker and memorable personality"[2] who possessed the ability to create new texts as well as interpret the scriptures of Israel for other early Christ-believers. Yet, the rich, full spectrum of early Christian literary culture demonstrated in Paul's letters is not completely represented within Luke-Acts. Written in the late first or early second century, Luke-Acts portrays Jesus (e. g., Luke 4:16–30; 24:44) and his followers (e. g., Acts 2:14–36; 4:8–22; 7:2–53; 13:16–41; 15:13–21; 28:25–28) as skilled literate interpreters of Israel's scriptures. However, despite the expressed recognition of earlier Christian literature in the rhetorically rich periodic preface (Luke 1:1–4), the author largely ignores the production of texts by Paul and other early Christ-believers.[3] The narrative of Acts records only two instances of literary composition by Christians: Acts 15:23–29 and 18:27.[4] The former is an embedded letter that contains the so-called "Apostolic Decree." The latter refers to a non-embedded letter written

---

[1] M. M. Mitchell, "The Emergence of the Written Record," in *Origins to Constantine* (ed. M. M. Mitchell and F. M. Young; The Cambridge History of Christianity 1; Cambridge: Cambridge University Press, 2006), 177–94 (181).

[2] Ibid., 182.

[3] R. I. Pervo writes, "Far from being elevated to an active role in the postal service, Paul and Barnabas did no more than to *accompany* the letter carriers. The Paul of Acts not only fails to write letters, he is scarcely allowed to touch one" (*Dating Acts: Between the Evangelists and the Apologists* [Santa Rosa, Calif.; Polebridge Press, 2006], 54.

[4] The content of the letter to the Gentiles is summarized earlier in Acts 15:20 and again later at 21:25. Apart from the various references to what is written in the Psalms or the prophets (e. g., Acts 1:20; 7:42; 13:29, 33; 15:15; 23:5; 24:14), the remaining references to literary composition and literary material in Acts are limited to the mention of Saul's request and reception of letters from the chief-priest and council as part of his persecution/prosecution of Christians in Acts 9:2 (mentioned again in 22:5), the letter of the tribune in Acts 23:26–30, Festus' "writer's block" in Acts 25:23–27, and the denial of received letters from Judea by the Jewish leaders at Rome in Acts 28:21.

by the Ephesian believers to those in Achaia concerning Apollos (18:24–28). Given the preference for direct speech and the general avoidance of letters,[5] it is curious that the author of Acts embeds the text of a letter from Claudius Lysias to Felix within the narrative (23:26–30).

(26) Claudius Lysias to the most excellent governor, Felix, greetings. (27) This man was seized by the Jews and was about to be killed by them but I arrived with a military detachment and rescued (him) after learning that he is a Roman. (28) Since I wanted to know the charge on account of which they were accusing him, I led (him) down to their council. (29) I found he was being accused concerning disputes of their law with no accusation worthy of death or chains. (30) After it was revealed to me that there was a plot against this man, I sent[6] (him) to you immediately commanding his accusers also to speak against him before you.[7]

According to Acts, Claudius Lysias's opportune discovery of a plot to kill Paul (23:12–22) results in the hasty assembly of a sizable force for Paul's extradition to Caesarea and the composition of a letter to Felix (23:12–25). A military escort then successfully moves Paul by way of Antipatris (Acts 23:31) to Caesarea and delivers the letter (23:33). Felix reads the letter in the narrative and does not question the veracity of its contents. For the reader of Acts, however, the letter of Claudius Lysias to Felix contains numerous tensions with the prior narrative of Paul's arrest and detention (Acts 21:27–23:25). The inclusion of a letter from a Roman military tribune that both repeats and conflicts with the narrator's prior account of the same events warrants closer examination. In this brief essay, I first catalogue the notable (1) conflicts and (2) omissions in Claudius Lysias's recounting of the events recorded in Acts 21:27–23:25. Second, I take up the question of the letter's authenticity arguing on both historical and literary grounds that the letter of Claudius Lysias is a literary fiction by the author of Acts. Third, drawing upon the instruction provided by Aelius Theon in his *Progymnasmata* for successful refutation (ἀνασκευή) of a narrative (διήγησις Luke 1:1), I seek to demonstrate that the author of Acts deliberately refutes the narrative of Claudius Lysias with the preceding narrative of events in Acts 21:27–23:25, thus portraying Claudius Lysias as a duplicitous character.

---

[5] R. I. Pervo, "Direct Speech in Acts and the Question of Genre," *JSNT* 28, no. 3 (2006): 285–307. See also, among others, M. L. Soards, *The Speeches in Acts: Their Content, Context, and Concerns* (Louisville, Ky.: Westminster/John Knox Press, 1994).

[6] ἔπεμψα is an epistolary aorist anticipating the perspective of the reader. Cf. H.-J. Klauck, *Ancient Letters and the New Testament: A Guide to Context and Exegesis* (trans. by and in coll. with D. P. Bailey; Waco, Tex.: Baylor University Press, 2006), 433.

[7] On the grammar of μηνυθείσης δέ μοι ἐπιβουλῆς εἰς τὸν ἄνδρα ἔσεσθαι (23:30) see F. Blass and A. Debrunner, *A Greek Grammar of the New Testament and Other Early Christian Literature* (trans. and rev. by R. W. Funk; Chicago: University of Chicago Press, 1961), § 24.

1. Conflicts and Omissions in Claudius Lysias's "Revised" Narration

Interpreters have long noted the presence of both conflicts and omissions in Claudius Lysias's version of the events in comparison to the record of the same events in Acts 21:27–23:25.[8] With regard to the conflicts, four stand out. First, Claudius Lysias reports that he *rescued* Paul (23:27; ἐξαιρεῖν)[9] while the earlier Acts narrative indicates that he *arrested* Paul (21:33; ἐπιλαμβάνεσθαι). Second, the letter to Felix records that Claudius Lysias intervened on Paul's behalf *after* learning that he was a Roman citizen (23:27).[10] Yet, within the narrative of Acts,

---

[8] See the discussions in R. J. Cassidy, *Society and Politics in the Acts of the Apostles* (Maryknoll, N. Y.: Orbis Books, 1987), 96–100; H. W. Tajra, *The Trial of St. Paul: A Juridical Exegesis of the Second Half of the Acts of the Apostles* (WUNT 2.25; Tübingen: Mohr Siebeck, 1989), 106–8; R. C. Tannehill, *The Acts of the Apostles* (The Narrative Unity of Luke-Acts: A Literary Interpretation, Vol. 2; Minneapolis: Fortress Press, 1990), 293–6; G. Lüdemann, *Early Christianity According to the Traditions in Acts: A Commentary* (trans. by J. Bowden; Minneapolis: Fortress Press, 1989), 242–47; Klauck, *Ancient Letters and the New Testament*, 429–34; R. I. Pervo, *Acts: A Commentary* (Hermeneia; Minneapolis: Fortress Press, 2009), 577–88.

[9] P48 records ἐρυσάμην instead of ἐξειλάμην.

[10] Τὸν ἄνδρα τοῦτον συλλημφθέντα ὑπὸ τῶν Ἰουδαίων καὶ μέλλοντα ἀναιρεῖσθαι ὑπ' αὐτῶν ἐπιστὰς σὺν τῷ στρατεύματι ἐξειλάμην μαθὼν ὅτι Ῥωμαῖός ἐστιν: The aorist participle, μαθών, is here read as a causal circumstantial participle of antecedent action. For this use of the aorist participle with an aorist main verb see H. W. Smyth, *Greek Grammar* (rev. by G. M. Messing; Cambridge: Harvard University Press, 1984), § 1872; W. W. Goodwin, *Syntax of the Moods and Tenses of the Greek Verb* (rev. ed.; Boston: Ginn and Co., 1893), § 43–52; Blass, Debrunner, and Funk, *A Greek Grammar of the New Testament and Other Early Christian Literature*, § 39. However, there is a long tradition of scholars who read μαθών as an aorist participle of subsequent action with the resulting translation: "I rescued him, learning (subsequently) that he was a Roman." E. g., K. Lake and H. J. Cadbury maintain "aorist participles in this context appear to apply to coincident or even subsequent action" (*The Acts of the Apostles, Vol. 4* [ed. F. J. Foakes–Jackson and K. Lake; The Beginnings of Christianity, Pt. 1; London: Macmillan and Co., 1933], 294). Cf. R. B. Rackham, *The Acts of the Apostles: An Exposition* (13th ed.; London: Methuen & Co., 1947), 439–40; E. Haenchen, *Acts of the Apostles: A Commentary* (trans. by B. Noble et al. Wilson; Philadelphia: Westminster Press, 1971), 648; S. E. Porter, *Verbal Aspect in the Greek of the New Testament with Reference to Tense and Mood* (Studies in Biblical Greek 1; New York et al.: Peter Lang, 1989), 385–88. The texts most often cited as providing evidence for an aorist participle of subsequent action (Luke 1:9; Acts 16:6; 17:26; 23:35; 25:13) can be explained with equal plausibility as expressing coincident action with the main verb and/or as part of a single episode without emphasis on a strict sequence of individual events (e. g., in Acts 25:13, "King Agrippa and Bernice arrived in Caesarea with greetings for Festus"). With regard to Acts 23:27, Claudius Lysias's remarks might be a convenient "telescoping" of multiple events into one single episode (cf. J. A. Fitzmyer, *The Acts of the Apostles: A New Translation with Introduction and Commentary* (AB 31; New York: Doubleday, 1998), 728). However, note the similar constructions in Acts 16:38 and 22:29 where the aorist participle occurs after the main aorist verb but indicates *prior* action to that of the main verb. As an alternative, L. T. Johnson changes the punctuation by placing a period after ἐξειλάμην and taking μαθών with the content of 23:28 (*The Acts of the Apostles* [SP 5; Collegeville, Minn.: Liturgical Press, 1992], 405). Johnson's translation: "Having learned that he was a Roman citizen, I wanted to discover the reason they had a complaint against him." One would, however, expect a particle or conjunction signaling the break proposed by Johnson (cf. C. K. Barrett, *A Critical and Exegetical Com-*

con........ 3-4

Claudius Lysias learns of Paul's citizenship after the arrest (22:25–29). Third, Claudius Lysias presents his initial action in the letter as a deliberate, forceful response to a threat on Paul's life (23:27). The earlier narrative in Acts, however, portrays Claudius Lysias's initial action as an impromptu response to confusion and near riot around the temple in Jerusalem (21:30–31). Fourth, the concluding phrase of the letter παραγγείλας καὶ τοῖς κατηγόροις λέγειν [τὰ] πρὸς αὐτὸν ἐπὶ σοῦ (23:30) indicates that Claudius Lysias ordered Paul's accusers to appear before Felix. According to the earlier narrative in Acts, the disclosure by Paul's nephew to Claudius Lysias of a plot to kill Paul prompts Claudius Lysias to extradite him immediately with a sizable escort during the middle of the night (23:16–35) with no mention of accusers.[11] Notification of Paul's accusers prior to or concurrent with Paul's emergency extradition is contrary to the logic of the surrounding narrative.

Turning to the omissions, Claudius Lysias's account leaves out eight important items from the prior narrative of the same events in Acts 21:27–23:25. First, no mention is made of the confusion, tumult, and near riot around the temple in Jerusalem (21:30–22:23). Second, the letter lacks any reference to the binding of Paul in ignorance (21:33; 22:29). Third, Claudius Lysias does not mention his lack of understanding (21:34). Fourth, Claudius Lysias's inaccurate identification of Paul as "the Egyptian" is omitted (21:38). Fifth, the near flogging of Paul is noticeably absent (22:24–29). Sixth, the role of Claudius Lysias in convening the Jewish council is also omitted (22:30).[12] Seventh, Paul's home in Tarsus of Cilicia is not included (21:39) with the result that Felix – consistent with the logic of the narrative – later inquires of Paul concerning his home province (23:34). Eighth, the letter also omits the sequence of events which resulted in the disclosure to Claudius Lysias of a plot to kill Paul (23:12–22).

In addition to these oft-noted omissions in the letter of Claudius Lysias, a more subtle omission is often overlooked: the reported fear of Claudius Lysias (22:29; 23:10).[13] The prior narrative in Acts twice notes fear as a motivating

---

mentary on the Acts of the Apostles [ICC 33; Edinburgh: T & T Clark, 1998], 2:1083). The syntactical problems of Acts 23:27 are completely removed in P48[vid] by replacing μαθὼν ὅτι Ῥωμαῖός ἐστιν with the introduction of indirect discourse, κράζοντα καὶ λέγοντα εἶναι Ῥωμαῖον.

[11] Note the prominence of temporal references in the surrounding narrative: Τῇ δὲ ἐπιούσῃ νυκτί (Acts 23:11); Γενομένης δὲ ἡμέρας(23:12); αὔριον (23:20); ἀπὸ τρίτης ὥρας τῆς νυκτός (23:23); διὰ νυκτός (23:31); τῇ δὲ ἐπαύριον (23:32).

[12] Claudius Lysias simply leads Paul to the council (Acts 23:28; κατήγαγον εἰς τὸ συνέδριον αὐτῶν).

[13] Felix exhibits a similar response in Acts 24:25 (διαλεγομένου δὲ αὐτοῦ περὶ δικαιοσύνης καὶ ἐγκρατείας καὶ τοῦ κρίματος τοῦ μέλλοντος, ἔμφοβος γενόμενος ὁ Φῆλιξ ἀπεκρίθη· τὸ νῦν ἔχον πορεύου, καιρὸν δὲ μεταλαβὼν μετακαλέσομαί σε). Note also the fearful response from the captain of the temple in Acts 5:26 and the chief magistrates of Philippi in Acts 16:38. In the case of the latter, the chief magistrates – like Claudius Lysias – react with fear upon learning that

factor in Claudius Lysias's actions. First, Claudius Lysias "became afraid upon discovering that he (Paul) was a Roman citizen and that he (Claudius Lysias) had bound him" (22:29).[14] Second, following the escalation of tensions in the Sanhedrin,[15] Claudius Lysias "feared that Paul would be torn apart by them."[16] as a result, he orders the army to seize Paul and bring him to the barracks (23:10).[17]

The significance of the tensions between Claudius Lysias's account and the preceding narrative of Acts 21:27–23:25 merits explanation. The inclusion of the letter is at least partially explained by the role of the letter in introducing new, supplementary information to the narrative of Acts.[18] Thus, for example, Claudius Lysias is first identified by name in the epistolary prescript (23:26); prior to the letter he is simply referred to as a "military tribune" (χιλίαρχος).[19] Further, the letter reveals Claudius Lysias's assessment of the situation: Paul was under "no accusation worthy of death or imprisonment" (23:29). The formality of an indictment/accusation (ἔγκλημα) against Paul is also new. The reader of Acts learns for the first time that Claudius Lysias has ordered Paul's accusers to appear before Felix (23:30). The text of the dispatch thus effectively bridges the sequence of events on either side of the letter's narrated composition and delivery. It supplies information that was missing in the preceding narrative (e. g., the name of the military tribune) and anticipates the subsequent events and outcome of the proceedings (e. g., command for the accusers to appear before Felix and the declaration of innocence).[20]

However, recognition of the narrative function of the letter from Claudius Lysias to Felix does not provide a full explanation for the tensions between the events recorded in the letter and the preceding narrative or the letter's omission of notable events. One wonders why the author did not provide an account in the letter more consistent with Acts 21:27–23:25 or, as noted by Barrett, summarize the content of Acts 23:12–35 by writing, "The tribune, hearing of a plot

---

Paul and Silas are Roman citizens. In Acts 9:26 Paul is the object of fear from disciples who do not believe that Paul too is a disciple.

[14] ἐφοβήθη ἐπιγνοὺς ὅτι Ῥωμαῖός ἐστιν καὶ ὅτι αὐτὸν ἦν δεδεκώς.

[15] τοῦτο δὲ αὐτοῦ εἰπόντος ἐγένετο στάσις τῶν Φαρισαίων καὶ Σαδδουκαίων, καὶ ἐσχίσθη τὸ πλῆθος (Acts 23:7); Πολλῆς δὲ γινομένης στάσεως (Acts 23:10).

[16] φοβηθεὶς ὁ χιλίαρχος μὴ διασπασθῇ ὁ Παῦλος ὑπ' αὐτῶν.

[17] Compare also the reading of P48 at Acts 23:25 ἐφοβήθη γὰρ μήποτε ἐξαρπάσαντες αὐτὸν οἱ Ἰουδαῖοι ἀποκτείνωσιν καὶ αὐτὸς μεταξὺ ἔγκλημα ἔχῃ ὡς εἰληφὼς ἀργύρια γράψας δὲ αὐτοῖς ἐπιστολὴν ἐν ᾗ ἐγέγραπτο.

[18] B. R. Gaventa, *The Acts of the Apostles* (ANTC; Nashville: Abingdon Press, 2003), 321. For a brief discussion of the letter as an example of repetition in Acts see C. K. Rothschild, *Luke-Acts and the Rhetoric of History: An Investigation of Early Christian Historiography* (WUNT 2. 175; Tübingen: Mohr Siebeck, 2004), 139.

[19] Acts 21:31, 32, 33, 37; 22:24, 26, 27, 28, 29; 23:10, 15, 17, 18, 19, 22.

[20] See the discussion below. With regard to v. 30, Haenchen observes, "This detail is intended for the reader, who now knows how the action continues. Luke adds it in the letter for the sake of simplicity" (*Acts*, 648). Cf. R. Pesch, *Die Apostelgeschichte* (EKK 5; Zürich: Benziger; Neukirchen-Vluyn: Neukirchener Verlag, [2]2003), 251.

against Paul's life, sent him by night and under guard to Caesarea."²¹ The author
of Acts is doing more with the letter than simply bridging pieces of the narrative.

Despite these tensions, the version of events recorded in the letter serves the
interest of Claudius Lysias by allowing him to present his handling of the situation in the best possible light.²² Among those who maintain the authenticity of
the letter, the "spinning" of events is seen as confirmation of its genuineness²³
and/or as a reflection of "the hilarious and memorable manner of Paul's telling
the story."²⁴ Others, who regard the missive as a literary product from the author
of Acts, read the text as a plausible letter-in-character in which the author
records what a military tribune would have written to his superior (e. g., τίνας ἂν
γράψειε λόγους Κλαύδιος Λυσίας τῷ ἡγεμόνι Φήλικι).²⁵ Among the latter group,
some pass over the conflicts with the prior narrative of Acts and the notable
omissions in the letter of Claudius Lysias,²⁶ others downplay them in order to

---

²¹ Cf. Barrett concludes, "That Luke did not effect the transference in this way leads to the
probable inference that he found in the tradition the story of the nephew and some account of
the surprisingly powerful force that escorted Paul to Caesarea" (_Acts_, 2:1071). Acquisition of
the ability to compose a narrative in a "concise" manner was part of Greco–Roman rhetorical
training. E. g., the first–century C. E. rhetorician Aelius Theon in his _Progymnasmata_ regards
clarity (σαφήνεια), conciseness (συντομία), and credibility (πιθανότης) as the three virtues
(ἀρεταί) of a narrative (διήγησις 79. 20–21). He further notes that a narrative is concise from
the events (πράγματα) and style (λέξις). Concise narration both avoids the addition of unnecessary things (προστιθεὶς τὸ μὴ ἀναγκαῖον) and the removal of necessary things (83.15–19;
μήτε ἀφαιρῶν τὸ ἀναγκαῖον) (83. 15).

²² C. K. Rowe, _World Upside Down: Reading Acts in the Graeco-Roman Age_ (Oxford: Oxford
University Press, 2009), 70–1.

²³ E. g., D. G. Peterson notes, "If the letter is totally Luke's invention, it is hard to explain a
discrepancy between this report and Luke's account of the same events. The letter reveals a
Roman official needing to present himself in the best possible light (v. 27)." (_The Acts of the
Apostles_ [PNTC; Grand Rapids: Eerdmans, 2009], 624).

²⁴ C. J. Hemer, _The Book of Acts in the Setting of Hellenistic History_ (ed. C. H. Gempf;
WUNT 49; Tübingen: Mohr Siebeck, 1989), 207.

²⁵ H. Conzelmann, _Acts of the Apostles: A Commentary on the Acts of the Apostles_ (trans. James
Limburg, et al.; Hermeneia; Philadelphia: Fortress Press, 1987), 195; G. A. Krodel, _Acts_
(ACNT; Minneapolis: Augsburg Publishing House, 1986), 432; J. D. G. Dunn, _The Acts of the
Apostles_ (Narrative Commentaries; Valley Forge, Pa.: Trinity Press International, 1996),
308–9; Barrett, _Acts_, 2:1071; Fitzmyer, _Acts_, 726; Rowe, _World Upside Down_, 66. Contrast
Pervo who remarks, "The last idea in the author's mind was that the letter gave a general
purport of what Lysias wrote" (_Acts_, 584). Pervo thus seems to regard the letter as a transparent
literary fiction that is devoid of any plausible verisimilitude.

²⁶ In a recent essay, J. R. Howell rightly calls attention to the rhetorical act of amplification
(αὔξησις) and the skill of speech–in–character (προσωποποιία) in the analysis of Claudius's
Lysias letter ("Embedded Letters and Rhetorical αὔξησις in Sallust, Chariton, and Luke," in
Contemporary Studies in Acts [ed. T. E. Phillips; Macon, Ga.: Mercer University Press, 2009],
154–80). He effectively demonstrates that the letter of Claudius Lysias functions as "a proof"
that contains a statement of Paul's innocence amplified in the subsequent narrative of Acts
(178–79). His general avoidance (note the brief mention on page 164, note 32) of the tensions
is perhaps the result of his methodological axiom: "Therefore, I propose that answering that
latter question [i. e., _why_ an author might have composed a letter] is logically prior to providing

emphasize key themes, ideas, or narrative threads within the letter,[27] and still others regard some of the tensions as editorial slips by the author of Acts.[28] R. C. Tannehill and H.-J. Klauck observe, without detailed explanation, that the tensions between Acts 21:27–23:25 and the brief narrative in Claudius Lysias's letter cast doubt on the character of Claudius Lysias.[29] This final observation is pursued further in the following analysis.

2. Letter Citation or Literary Letter-in-Character

The author of Acts introduces the letter of Claudius Lysias to Felix with the phrase γράψας ἐπιστολὴν ἔχουσαν τὸν τύπον τοῦτον.[30] The precise meaning of the final four words is a matter of debate as evident in different translations: "to this effect,"[31] "in these terms,"[32] "as follows,"[33] "with this character,"[34] and "having this form."[35] At issue in interpreting ἔχουσαν τὸν τύπον τοῦτον is the

---

an answer to the former [i. e., *whether* an ancient author composed a letter contained in his or her respective text]." While I am sympathetic with his turn toward the question of *why* an author composes in character, I would argue that the *why* question is logically and temporally *concurrent* with the *whether* question; both questions informing and shaping each other.

[27] E. g., Haenchen writes, "Luke had no reason to depict the tribune handling the truth rather freely; that would have devalued his testimony. Luke rather in this recapitulation of events provides the reader with the image which he is to retain: the general impression that the Roman State respected Paul's Roman's citizenship from the beginning" (*Acts*, 648). Similarly, J. Roloff identifies four key points communicated in the letter: 1) Paul is a Roman citizen and under the jurisdiction of the Roman governor; 2) Paul's rescue from the Jews is thanks to Roman power; 3) No offence was committed from the Roman perspective; 4) The charges concern internal Jewish conflicts that lie outside Roman jurisdiction (*Die Apostelgeschichte* [NTD 5; Göttingen: Vandenhoeck & Ruprecht, 1988], 332–33). Cf. Conzelmann, *Acts*, 195; Rowe, *World Upside Down*, 66.

[28] With particular reference to παραγγείλας καὶ τοῖς κατηγόροις λέγειν [τὰ] πρὸς αὐτὸν ἐπὶ σοῦ (Acts 23:30), Pervo notes, "This slip is most likely due to the author" (*Acts*, 585).

[29] Cf. Tannehill, *The Acts of the Apostles*, 295; Klauck, *Ancient Letters and the New Testament*, 434.

[30] Cf. *EpistleArist* 34 (Δηλώσομεν δέ σοι περὶ τῆς κατασκευῆς, ὡς ἂν τὰ τῶν ἐπιστολῶν ἀντίγραφα διέλθωμεν. Ἦν δὲ ἡ τοῦ βασιλέως ἐπιστολὴ τὸν τύπον ἔχουσα τοῦτον: quoted in Josephus, *Ant* 12. 40–51 and Eusebius *Prep Evang* 8. 4) and 3 Macc 3:30 (Καὶ ὁ μὲν τῆς ἐπιστολῆς τύπος οὕτως ἐγέγραπτο). Similar expressions include περιέχειν τὸν τρόπον τοῦτον (1 Macc 15:2; 2 Macc 11:16; Josephus, *Ant* 11. 215–16) and the related ἔχειν τὸν τρόπον τοῦτον (1 Macc 11:29; 2 Macc 1:24). Note that P48 offers an alternative reading: γράψας δὲ αὐτοῖς ἐπιστολὴν ἐν ᾗ ἐγέγραπτο.

[31] Conzelmann, *Acts*, 193; Fitzmyer, *Acts*, 36, 725.

[32] F. F. Bruce, *The Acts of the Apostles: The Greek Text with Introduction and Commentary* (NICNT; 3rd rev. and enl. ed.; Grand Rapids: Eerdmans, 1988), 434.

[33] Haenchen, *Acts*, 644. Cf. Barrett who translates, "as follows" (*Acts*, 2:1069). Pervo renders it loosely as, "He prepared the following letter" (*Acts*, 578).

[34] Johnson, *Acts*, 403.

[35] Klauck, *Ancient Letters and the New Testament*, 431.

nature of the assertion made by the author of Acts. Do these words represent (1) a claim to accurate reproduction of an exact copy of an authentic letter from Claudius Lysias to Felix, (2) a historically plausible guess by the author of Acts concerning what Claudius Lysias would have written had he actually written a letter to Felix, or (3) some other option? Prior to analyzing the lexical and contextual data for the precise meaning of ἔχουσαν τὸν τύπον τοῦτον in Acts 23:25 two brief methodological points should be clarified. First, the determination that the author of Acts intends to *present* the letter recorded in Acts 23:26–30 as a genuine missive from Claudius Lysias to Felix does not demonstrate that the letter is in fact genuine. The author of Acts may have composed a letter and attempted to pass it off to the reader as a genuine document by embedding it in the narrative. Second, the determination that the letter of Claudius Lysias to Felix preserved in Acts is a literary product invented by the author does not prove that Claudius Lysias did not write a letter to Felix. It simply denies that the letter in Acts 23:26–30 is an actual letter between the two parties named in the prescript.[36]

The lexical debate – reflected in the different translations noted above ("to this effect," "in these terms," "as follows," "with this character," and "having this form") – revolves around the meaning of τύπος. E. A. Judge has argued influentially, based upon the use of τύπος in P. Oxy. 3366. 28, 32,[37] for a meaning of "text/copy" and concludes that one must ask, "whether the author of Acts did not mean his readers to take them [the letter of Lysias and the decision of the Jerusalem council] as the direct citation of transcripts available to him."[38] After raising the question, Judge claims that τύπος "ought always to refer to replication in some form or other (e. g. a seal impression, an image, an archetype, an outline, a set form – for the diversity of particular uses see LSJ), and one should not expect it to mean 'roughly as follows.'"[39]

The lexical argument of Judge has problems. His conclusion regarding the semantic range of τύπος is inconsistent. Near the beginning of the sentence he notes "replication in some form or other" – a broad generalization that can encompass different types and modes of replication (e. g., abbreviation or summary) – while later in the sentence he denies the meaning "roughly as follows" that seems perfectly consistent with the broad earlier statement. Few would

---

[36] In regard to the second point see Klauck, *Ancient Letters and the New Testament*, 434, note 17.

[37] P. Oxy. 3366, a third-century CE papyrus, preserves petitions to the Emperor along with a letter.

[38] E. A. Judge, "A State Schoolteacher Makes a Salary Bid," in *A Review of the Greek Inscriptions and Papyri Published in 1976* (New Documents Illustrating Early Christianity 1; ed. G. H. R. Horsley; North Ryde, NSW: The Ancient History Documentary Research Centre, Macquarie University, 1981), 72–78.

[39] Ibid., 77–78.

argue with Judge that τύπος *can* in certain contexts mean something like "exact/ verbatim copy." However, τύπος does not – as indicated by his own broader definition – always carry that specific meaning.[40] In addition to the inconsistency in definition, the argument of Judge relies upon a false dilemma that only entertains two possibilities. As presented by Judge, the letter in Acts 23:26–30 is either a "rhetorical approximation" of a letter written by Claudius Lysias or a copy "made verbatim" from an actual letter sent from Claudius Lysias to Felix. As recently noted by J. R. Howell, Judge's false either-or logical dilemma presupposes "the existence of an actual letter written by Lysias."[41] The presumed existence of this letter must be demonstrated rather than assumed. Cumulatively, the assertion that the author of Acts intended ἔχουσαν τὸν τύπον τοῦτον to signify accurate reproduction of an exact copy of an authentic letter is, at best, unproven.

In the absence of any historical evidence for the existence of such a letter from Claudius Lysias to Felix outside of Acts, arguments for or against the authenticity of the letter rest upon the letter itself. An analysis of the letter on historical and literary grounds weighs heavily against the acceptance of the embedded letter of Claudius Lysias as an exact copy of an actual letter sent to Felix.[42] With regard to historical problems,[43] four items stand against authenticity. First, the prisoner being transferred, Paul, is never named in the letter.[44] The letter thus depends upon the narrative context of Acts for this informa-

---

[40] For the semantic range of τύπος see W. Bauer, F. W. Danker, W. F. Arndt, and F. W. Gingrich, *Greek-English Lexicon of the New Testament and Other Early Christian Literature* (3d ed.; Chicago: University of Chicago Press, 2000), 1019–20.

[41] Howell, "Embedded Letters and Rhetorical αὔξησις in Sallust, Chariton, and Luke," 156.

[42] The argument presented here against the authenticity of Claudius Lysias's letter draws upon, amplifies, and combines prior observations with new comments in order to produce a focused argument. For prior arguments, see especially, among others, Pervo, *Acts*, 577–88. Howell rightly draws attention to important parallels between the characterization of Paul in the letter and the characterization of Jesus in Luke-Acts as part of his argument to contextualize the letter of Claudius Lysias in the narrative ("Embedded Letters and Rhetorical αὔξησις in Sallust, Chariton, and Luke," 162–64).

[43] The argument against authenticity based upon the title of the addressee (τῷ κρατίστῳ ἡγεμόνι) is not here included. For the historical plausibility of this address see Barrett, *Acts*, 2:1082; Pervo, *Acts*, 587, note 584. Three additional historical problems – not mentioned in the text above – emerge when the letter is examined within the narrative context of Acts. First, Claudius Lysias's judgment about Paul (μηδὲν δὲ ἄξιον θανάτου ἢ δεσμῶν ἔχοντα ἔγκλημα; Acts 23:29) is premature and seems to anticipate a later judgment. Second, the concluding phrase παραγγείλας καὶ τοῖς κατηγόροις λέγειν [τὰ] πρὸς αὐτὸν ἐπὶ σοῦ (Acts 23:30) seems to suggest that Claudius Lysias ordered Paul's accusers to appear before Felix either prior to or at the same time as the sending of Paul to Caesarea. Third, it is astonishing, given the language barrier, that Claudius Lysias understood the nature of the controversy surrounding Paul (cf. Acts 21:40; 22:2; τῇ Ἑβραΐδι διαλέκτῳ).

[44] Paul is the elided antecedent of τὸν ἄνδρα τοῦτον at the beginning of the letter (Acts 23:27).

tion.[45] Second, the letter lacks typical epistolary components: a proem (thanks-giving and wish for well-being) and a closing (farewell). The absence of these and other epistolary components is very common in the fictive embedded letters of ancient novels.[46] Third, the letter is in Greek and not, as one might expect, in Latin.[47] Fourth, it is difficult to understand how the author of Acts would have gained access to the letter between Claudius Lysias, a military tribune, and Felix, procurator of Judea.[48] Reconstructions of path of access for the author of Acts are unpersuasive.[49]

Turning to the literary problems, the embedded letter of Claudius Lysias to Felix resounds with common vocabulary, phrases, and important themes of Luke-Acts.[50] First, the language used of Paul's arrest (Acts 23:27; συλλαμβάνειν)

---

[45] Pervo highlights an interesting parallel in Heliodorus' *Aethiopica*. The embedded letter of Mitranes, a commander (φρούραρχος), to Oroondates, a satrap (σατράπης), records the trans-fer of the book's hero, Theagenes, as a prisoner (5.9). Within the letter, Theagenes is anony-mous and simply identified as the young Greek ("Ελληνα νεανίσκον). The reader of Heli-odorus's *Aethiopica* – like the reader of Acts – easily infers the prisoner's identity from the immediate context (*Acts*, 584).

[46] Pervo cites *Ephesian Tale* 2.12 as an example for the paring of formalities (*Acts*, 584, note 37). Note also, Chariton, *Chaer.* 4.4.7; 4.6.3–4; 4.6.8 (two letters); 8.4.4; 8.4.5. The two letters in 4.6.8 are reduced to simple instruction. The letter in 8.4.5, although lacking an epistolary proem and a body opening, does contain a developed epistolary closing.

[47] The letter does not read as a Latin translation. Latin letters from members of the Roman military who were stationed at Vindolanda, south of Hadrian's wall, are available at http://vindolanda.csad.ox.ac.uk/.

[48] This seems to be the primary ground for Barrett's rejection of the letter's genuineness (*Acts*, 2:1071, 1083).

[49] Judge maintains, "Written speeches will often have arisen only as retrospective stockta-king by their authors, their text remaining within their own discretion, while letters passed at once into the possession of their recipients and would be preserved by them as proof of the point they documented ("A State Schoolteacher Makes A Salary Bid," 77). B. W. Winter cites Judge in affirming, "Such a document [the letter of Claudius Lysias] would have been available to the defendant." He then appeals to the recorded action of Festus in gathering "the requisite documentation" for Rome ("Official Proceedings and the Forensic Speeches in Acts 24–26," in *The Book of Acts in its Ancient Literary Setting* [eds. B. W. Winter and A. D. Clarke; The Book of Acts in Its First Century Setting, Vol. 1; ed. B. W. Winter; Grand Rapids: Eerdmans, 1993], 309). Also appealing to Judge, Witherington argues, "This letter surely would have been read out loud upon Paul's arrival at the initial meeting between the prefect and Paul, in which case Paul heard what it said and could have conveyed its contents to Luke, if Luke himself did not accompany Paul on this journey [...] Precisely because it was an official report, it was the sort of document that would be preserved for the trial of Paul as an important reference work for Felix (and others?) to use. That Felix did indeed think the evaluation of Claudius Lysias was important is shown by 24:22" (*Acts of the Apostles*, 698–99). Cf. Peterson, *Acts of the Apostles*, 624. The logical problem with this line of reasoning as a deductive argument is that it affirms the consequent (e.g., an official document would have been read in a Roman court) in order to affirm the antecedent (e.g., there was a genuine, real letter from Claudius Lysias to Felix). The demonstration of Roman forensic practice with respect to legal documents does not, in and of itself, increase the probability that Acts here records a genuine, real letter from Claudius Lysias to Felix.

echoes that of Jesus' arrest (Luke 22:54; Acts 1:16) and the arrest of Peter (Acts 12:3).[51] Second, the superlative address κράτιστος is unique to Luke-Acts in the New Testament (Luke 1:3; Acts 23:26; 24:3; 26:25). Third, the report that Paul "was about to be killed" (Acts 23:27) uses a verb familiar to the reader of Luke-Acts, ἀναιρεῖν.[52] Fourth, Claudius Lysias's affirmation that Paul was about to be killed "by the Jews" (ὑπὸ τῶν Ἰουδαίων) is consistent with the portrayal of some Jews in Acts as agents of civil disturbance and violence (e. g., 9:23; 14:2–5; 17:5–9; 17:13; 18:12–17; 20:3, 19; 21:11).[53] Fifth, the occurrence of ἐπιστάς (Acts 23:27) creates an interesting lexical and narrative connection between the action of Ananias (Acts 22:13; ἐπιστάς), the action of the Lord (Acts 23:11; ἐπιστάς), and the action of Claudius Lysias toward Paul.[54] Sixth, the phrase βουλόμενός τε ἐπιγνῶναι τὴν αἰτίαν δι' ἣν (Acts 23:28) is similar to the earlier expressions ἐπιγνῷ δι' ἣν αἰτίαν (Acts 22:24) and βουλόμενος γνῶναι τὸ ἀσφαλές (Acts 22:30).[55] Seventh, ζήτημα (Acts 23:29; "controversy") only occurs in Acts in the New Testament.[56] Eighth, Claudius Lysias's statement affirming Paul's innocence (Acts 23:29; μηδὲν δὲ ἄξιον θανάτου ἢ δεσμῶν ἔχοντα ἔγκλημα) echoes Pilate's declarations about the innocence of Jesus (Luke 23:4; Οὐδὲν εὑρίσκω αἴτιον ἐν τῷ ἀνθρώπῳ τούτῳ)[57] and Gallio's remarks about Paul (Acts

[50] Scholars have long made this *observation.* E. g., Cadbury observes with regard to the "Apostolic Decree" and the letter of Claudius Lysias that they "are so characteristic of the author's style as to support the presumption that he is responsible for them (*The Making of Luke–Acts* [2nd edition; London: S. P. C. K., 1958)], 191). More recently, Howell reaches the same conclusion, "[Acts 23:26] is clearly a Lukan composition based upon the common themes, vocabulary, and phraseology shared by the letter and larger narrative of Luke–Acts ("Embedded Letters and Rhetorical αὔξησις in Sallust, Chariton, and Luke," 168). Unfortunately, a survey of the secondary literature did not discover a *thorough demonstration* of this point.

[51] Eleven of the sixteen occurrences of συλλαμβάνειν in the NT are in Luke-Acts (Luke 1:24, 31, 36; 2:21; 5:7, 9; 22:54; Acts 1:16; 12:3; 23:27; 26:21). For the "juristic terminology" in this passage see Conzelmann, *Acts*, 195. See also the helpful chart of parallels in Rothschild, *Luke-Acts and the Rhetoric of History*, 115–16.

[52] Twenty-one of the twenty-four occurrences of ἀναιρεῖν in the NT are in Luke-Acts (Luke 22:2; 23:32; Acts 2:23; 5:33, 36; 7:21, 28; 9:23, 24, 29; 10:39; 12:2; 13:28; 16:27; 22:20; 23:15, 21, 27; 25:3; 26:10).

[53] The expression ὑπὸ τῶν Ἰουδαίων occurs elsewhere in the New Testament only at Acts 20:3; 22:30; 1 Thess 2:14.

[54] ἐφιστάναι in Luke-Acts: Luke 2:9, 38; 4:39; 10:40; 20:1; 21:34; 24:4; Acts 4:1; 6:12; 10:17; 11:11; 12:7; 17:5; 22:13, 20; 23:11, 27; 28:2.

[55] Note also the lexical and contextual similarities between καὶ ἐκέλευσεν συνελθεῖν τοὺς ἀρχιερεῖς καὶ πᾶν τὸ συνέδριον, καὶ καταγαγὼν τὸν Παῦλον ἔστησεν εἰς αὐτούς (Acts 22:30) and κατήγαγον εἰς τὸ συνέδριον αὐτῶν (Acts 23:28).

[56] Acts 15:2; 18:15; 25:19; 26:3. Note in particular the close parallel with the statement of Gallio in Acts 18:15 (εἰ δὲ ζητήματά ἐστιν περὶ λόγου καὶ ὀνομάτων καὶ νόμου τοῦ καθ' ὑμᾶς, ὄψεσθε αὐτοί· κριτὴς ἐγὼ τούτων οὐ βούλομαι εἶναι) and the summary statement of Festus in Acts 25:19 (ζητήματα δέ τινα περὶ τῆς ἰδίας δεισιδαιμονίας εἶχον πρὸς αὐτὸν καὶ περί τινος Ἰησοῦ τεθνηκότος, ὃν ἔφασκεν ὁ Παῦλος ζῆν).

[57] Cf. Luke 23:14 (καὶ ἰδοὺ ἐγὼ ἐνώπιον ὑμῶν ἀνακρίνας οὐθὲν εὗρον ἐν τῷ ἀνθρώπῳ τούτῳ

18:14–15). It also anticipates the declaration of Festus (Acts 25:25; ἐγὼ δὲ κατελαβόμην μηδὲν ἄξιον αὐτὸν θανάτου πεπραχέναι) and that of Agrippa, Bernice, and their entourage with regard to Paul (Acts 26:31; Οὐδὲν θανάτου ἢ δεσμῶν ἄξιον [τι] πράσσει ὁ ἄνθρωπος οὗτος). Ninth, the verb "to accuse" (Acts 23:28, 29; ἐγκαλεῖν) is – with the exception of a single occurrence in Rom 8:38 – only found in Acts within the New Testament.[58] Tenth, the reported command given to Paul's accusers at the end of the letter uses a verb well-attested in Luke-Acts, παραγγέλλειν.[59] Cumulatively, the letter of Claudius Lysias bears the hallmarks of the vocabulary and themes of Luke-Acts. If this letter is an authentic missive from Claudius Lysias to Felix then Claudius Lysias thinks and writes in ways that are remarkably similar to the author of Acts.

The historical and literary arguments provide a compelling case for regarding the letter of Claudius Lysias to Felix as a literary fiction by the author of Acts.[60] It should be regarded as a double-pseudepigraphon, a letter *neither* from Claudius Lysias *nor* to Felix. However, the identification of this letter as a double-pseudepigraphon heightens the curiosity of its inclusion. The comments of Aelius Theon, a first-century rhetorician, concerning the composition and refutation of a narrative provide an explanation for the letter's inclusion as well as a fresh reading of the letter.

3. Intentional Narratives in Conflict

3. 1 Aelius Theon and the Refutation of a Narrative

Aelius Theon discusses narrative (διήγημα) immediately after the treatment of myth (μῦθος) in his *Progymnasmata*.[61] According to Theon (78. 16–25), a narrative has six elements (στοιχεῖα): person (πρόσωπον), action (πρᾶγμα), place (τόπος), time (χρόνος), manner (τρόπος), and cause (αἰτία).[62] Theon further

αἴτιον ὧν κατηγορεῖτε κατ' αὐτοῦ); Luke 23:22 (οὐδὲν αἴτιον θανάτου εὗρον ἐν αὐτῷ); Luke 23:41 (οὗτος δὲ οὐδὲν ἄτοπον ἔπραξεν); Luke 23:47 (Ὄντως ὁ ἄνθρωπος οὗτος δίκαιος ἦν).

[58] Acts 19:38, 40; 26:2, 7. The related noun ἔγκλημα is also only found in Acts (Acts 23:29; 25:16).

[59] Fifteen of the thirty-two occurrences of παραγγέλλειν in the NT are in Luke–Acts (Luke 5:14; 8:29, 56; 9:21; Acts 1:4, 4:18, 5:28, 40; 10:42; 15:5; 16:18, 23; 17:30; 23:22, 30). Note in particular the close parallel with Acts 23:22 (ὁ μὲν οὖν χιλίαρχος ἀπέλυσε τὸν νεανίσκον παραγγείλας μηδενὶ ἐκλαλῆσαι ὅτι ταῦτα ἐνεφάνισας πρός με). Conzelmann, observes, "With παραγγείλας κτλ., "ordering, etc.," the redactional character is especially clear (*Acts of the Apostles*, 195)." In addition, the noun κατήγορος (23:30) only occurs in Acts (23:35; 25:16, 18) in the New Testament. The same is true for the future form ἔσεσθαι (Acts 11:28; 23:30; 24:15; 27:10).

[60] On letter-writing as προσωποποιΐα see Aelius Theon, *Progymnasmata*, 115. 22.

[61] Aelius Theon, *Progymnasmata* (ed. M. Patillon; Budé; Paris: Belles Lettres, 1997).

[62] Cf. Pseudo-Plutarch, *Essay on the Life and Poetry of Homer*, 74. The "starting points"

describes what "belongs" (παρακαλουθεῖν) to each of the six elements (78.25–79.19). To the first element, "person" (πρόσωπον), belongs age, speech, fortune, etc. To the second element, "action" (πρᾶγμα) belongs, among other items, what is dangerous or not dangerous (κινδυνῶδες ἢ ἀκίνδυνον; 78.28), what is just or unjust (δίκαιον ἢ ἄδικον; 78.30–31), what is honorable or dishonorable (ἔνδοξον ἢ ἄδοξον; 78.31). In regard to "place" (τόπος) Theon's list includes size, near a city or town, and whether the act occurred in a sacred (ἱερός) or profane (βέβηλος; 79.8–9) location. "Time" (χρόνος) includes, for example, past, present, future; what is first, second and so on (τὸ παρεληλυθός, τὸ ἐνεστός, τὸ μέλλον, τί πρῶτον ἢ δεύτερον καὶ τὰ ἑξῆς; 78.31–34). Theon divides manner (τρόπος) into the sub-categories of unwilling or willing. The former includes things done by ignorance, accident, or necessity; the latter encompasses acts done by force, in secret, or by deceit. To cause (αἰτία), Theon assigns what happens "because of the passions" (διὰ τὰ πάθη): anger (θυμός), love (ἔρως), hate (μῖσος), envy (φθόνον), pity (ἔλεος), drunkenness (μέθη), and things similar to these (τὰ τούτοις ὅμοια; 79.18–19).[63] Theon later identifies fear as a cause in Thucydides's narrative of the Plataeans and Thebans (85.23). A narrative has, according to Theon, three virtues (ἀρεταί): clarity (σαφήνεια), conciseness (συντομία), and credibility (πιθανότης; 79.20–21), the last of which is the most important of the three (79.28–29).

After his instruction on the composition of narrative, Theon turns to refutation (ἀνασκευή) and confirmation (κατασκευή). He outlines a sequence of topics (τόποι; 93:15) one should employ: unclear (ἀσαφής), impossible (ἀδύνατος), if possible (δυνατός) then improbable (ἀπίθανος), if probable (πιθανός) then false (ψευδής), omission (ἔλλειψις), excess (πλεόνασμα), contradiction (μάχεται κατὰ τὴν διήγησιν), order (τάξις), inappropriate (ἀπρεπές), and not beneficial (ἀσύμφορον; 93.27–30). Exemplifying the topic (τόπος) of improbable (ἀπίθανος), Theon refutes Medea's murder of her children as dramatized by Euripides.[64] The refutation proceeds according to the prescribed elements of a narrative. Euripides, according to Theon, attributed the action to the wrong person (πρόσωπον) since it is improbable (ἀπίθανος) for a mother,

---

(ἀφορμαί) of every historical narrative are person (πρόσωπον), place (τόπος), time (χρόνος), cause (αἰτία), instrument (ὄργανον), act (πρᾶξις), impact (πάθος), manner (τρόπος). Text and translation available in J. J. Keaney and R. Lamberton, *[Plutarch] Essay on the Life and Poetry of Homer* (ACS 40; Atlanta: Scholars Press, 1996). Cf. also Lucian, *How to Write History*, 58, on the appropriate speech of an introduced character: Ἦν δέ ποτε καὶ λόγους ἐροῦντά τινα δεήσῃ εἰσάγειν, μάλιστα μὲν ἐοικότα τῷ προσώπῳ καὶ τῷ πράγματι οἰκεῖα λεγέσθω, ἔπειτα ὡς σαφέστατα καὶ ταῦτα.

[63] Theon regards fear as the cause behind the action of Plataean women who gave an axe to Theban intruders (Thucydides, *Histories*, 2.2.4).

[64] For different versions of the Medea story and its chronological development see Paul Dräger, "Medea" *Brill's New Pauly: Encyclopedia of the Ancient World* (2009), 8:546–49.

Medea, to harm her children (94.18–19). Theon regards the cutting of the children's throats as not probable (οὐκ εἰκός; 94.20). He further rejects the place (τόπος). Medea "would not have killed them in Corinth, where Jason – the father of the children – lived" (94.21–23). The timing (χρόνος) of the action is likewise improbable (ἀπίθανος) in light of the fact that Medea, a foreign woman, had been thrown out of the city by Jason, her former husband, who had recently acquired more power through marriage to the daughter of Creon, king of Corinth (94.22–26). As to manner (τρόπος), Medea would have tried to escape notice and would not have used a sword. Rather, since she was a sorceress (φαρμακὶς οὖσα), Medea would have used a drug (94.26–28). Finally, the cause (αἰτία) of anger (ὀργή) directed toward her husband is improbable (ἀπίθανος) because she, like Jason, would share in the misfortune of her action (94.28–31).

3.2 The Refutation of Claudius Lysias's Epistolary Narrative

Returning to Acts, the narrative in Acts 21:27–23:25 and Claudius Lysias's letter preserve different records of the same events. The instructions of Theon for the composition and refutation of a narrative offer new insight into the tensions of the accounts.[65] The earlier and longer record of Paul's arrest and detention in Acts 21:27–23:25 functions as a partial refutation of Claudius Lysias's account of the same events.[66] Comparison with Theon's six elements of a narrative (person [πρόσωπον], action [πρᾶγμα], place [τόπος], time [χρόνος], manner [τρόπος], and cause [αἰτία]) reveals that Acts 21:27–23:25 and Claudius Lysias's letter only agree in one of the six elements, person (πρόσωπον). Claudius Lysias, the military tribune, is the central actor. The dueling narratives of Acts disagree on the remaining five elements. The preceding narrative of Acts 21:27–23:25 refutes Claudius Lysias's accounts on the grounds of it being improbable (ἀπίθανος) and for omitting important details ("omission" [ἔλλειψις]). With regard to the improbable, Claudius Lysias arrests Paul (Acts 21:33); he did not rescue him (Acts 23:27). Claudius Lysias also rearranges the sequence of events ("time" [χρόνος]). Claudius Lysias learns of Paul's citizenship after (Acts 22:24–29) not before (Acts 23:27) he detains Paul. Turning to omission, the author of Acts, as Claudius Lysias, conveniently omits the binding and near torture of Paul (Acts 22:24–29) carried out in ignorance ("manner" [τρόπος]). Mention of the temple and its environs are excluded ("place" [τόπος]). The reported cause (αἰτία) of Claudius Lysias's action, fear (Acts 22:29; 23:10), is also not included.

---

[65] For a more general discussion of Greco-Roman preliminary rhetorical training and Luke-Acts see M. C. Parsons, "Luke and the *Progymnasmata*: A Preliminary Investigation into the Preliminary Exercises," in *Contextualizing Acts: Lukan Narrative and Greco-Roman Discourse* (ed. T. Penner and C. V. Stichele; SBLSymS 20; Atlanta: Society of Biblical Literature, 2003), 43–63.

[66] One could argue that the author of Acts is guilty of contradiction. However, the number and nature of the tensions listed above merit another explanation.

On this reading, the tensions between the narrative of events in Acts 21:27–23:25 and the record of the same events in Claudius Lysias's letter are intentional. The shorter narrative in the letter is refuted by the longer, preceding narrative of Paul's arrest and detention. While the author certainly wants to affirm and develop Claudius Lysias's affirmation of Paul's innocence,[67] the narration of events in Claudius Lysias's letter is challenged at every turn. The author of Acts skillfully uses the embedded letter-in-character of Claudius Lysias in order to demonstrate the duplicitous character of Claudius Lysias. On some occasions, the military tribune tells the truth (e. g., Paul is innocent) but on other occasions he distorts the truth for his own purposes (e. g., narration of events to a superior). The embedded letter of Claudius Lysias to Felix is then a plausible letter-in-character of a military figure who deceives a superior (e. g., τίνας ἂν ψευδῶς γράψειε λόγους Κλαύδιος Λυσίας τῷ ἡγεμόνι Φήλικι).[68]

4. Conclusion

The author of Acts was among those early Christian leaders who, in the words of Mitchell, possessed "conspicuous literary skills." The analysis of Claudius Lysias's letter to Felix above demonstrates the author's sophisticated participation in the broader Greco-Roman literary culture. Despite the author's portrayal of early Christians as speakers and the general exclusion of Christian text production from the narrative, the text of Acts evidences the author's ability to work proficiently in either medium. The letter of Claudius Lysias, a literary fiction carefully crafted by the author of Acts, requires the same rhetorical skill, speech-in-character (προσωποποιΐα), as the speeches. Through the characters of Acts, the author is both a skilled speaker and letter-writer. Recognition of the ability to write in character and thereby cast doubt upon the character of Claudius Lysias opens up new possibilities for thinking about the nature and complexity of the author's interaction with Rome and Roman agents in Luke-Acts.

---

[67] See especially Howell, "Embedded Letters and Rhetorical αὔξησις in Sallust, Chariton, and Luke," 154–80.

[68] Cf. Festus's speech to King Agrippa and Bernice in Acts 25:13–22. The conclusions reached here about the characterization of Claudius Lysias in the letter largely agree with those of Tannehill's narrative reading of this text. He notes, "The differences among versions encourage exploration of the reasons for departure from the authorized reference point. There are many possible reasons for differences, including appropriate shift in point of view and abbreviation or expansion in light of relevance, but biblical narrative provides ample illustration of the craft and deception of the human heart, as well as the need to bend others to one's will and deal with the powerful by flattery, through a slanted accounts of events." (Tannehill, *The Acts of the Apostles*, 296).

List of Authors

David L. Balch (1942), Professor of New Testament, Pacific Lutheran Theological Seminary/ Graduate Theological Union; M. A., B. D., Ph. D. Yale University; main areas of research: Roman domestic art, early house churches, Paul, Luke-Acts, Greco-Roman philosophy and politics.

Daniel Boyarin, Taubmann Professor of Talmudic Culture, UC Berkeley, PhD Jewish Theological Seminary of America; main areas of research: History of early Judaism as a complex religious poly-system, including the Jesus movement; rhetoric as a critical intellectual tradition; Talmudic philology.

Pieter J. J. Botha (1957), Professor of New Testament, Department of New Testament and Early Christian Studies, University of South Africa, PhD University of Pretoria; main areas of research: Graeco-Roman background of the NT; historical Jesus; anthropological history of early Christianity.

Robert B. Coote (1944), Nathaniel Gray Professor of Hebrew Exegesis and Old Testament, San Francisco Theological Seminary/ Graduate Theological Union; Ph. D. Harvard; main areas of research: Hebrew Scriptures (Torah, Prophets), history of early Israel.

Kristina Dronsch (1971); Postdoctoral Research Assistant, Johann von Goethe University of Frankfurt; Dr. theol. (Frankfurt, Germany); main areas of research: Gospel of Mark, Parables, Semiotics, Pneumatology in the Gospel of John.

John Miles Foley (1947), W. H. Byler Endowed Chair in the Humanities, Curators' Professor of Classical Studies and English, University of Missouri; M. A. (University of Massachusetts, Amherst; English), Ph. D. (University of Massachusetts, Amherst; English and Comparative Literature); main areas of research: Oral Tradition, ancient Greek, medieval English, South Slavic.

Holly E. Hearon (1956), Associate of New Testament, Christian Theological Seminary, B. A. D. Min. Union Theological Seminary/ Presbyterian School of Christian Education, Ph. D. Graduate Theological Union; main areas of research: Written and spoken word in antiquity; Women and Christian origins; the emergence of Christianity within Formative Judaism.

Catherine Hezser (1960), Professor of Jewish Studies in the School of Oriental and African Studies (SOAS), University of London, UK, Dr. theol. (University of Heidelberg), Ph. D. in Jewish Studies (Jewish Theological Seminary, New York), Habilitation (Free University Berlin); main areas of research: social history of Jews in Hellenistic and Roman Palestine; rabbinic literature, esp. Talmud Yerushalmi; ancient Judaism within the context of Graeco-Roman and early Christian society; daily life of Jews in antiquity.

Richard A. Horsley (1939), Professor Emeritus of Liberal Arts and the Study of Religion (but now emeritus) of the University of Massachusetts Boston, Ph. D. Harvard University; main areas of research: Gospels; historical Jesus; social and political history on ancient Roman Palestine; religion and politics in Paul, the Gospels, and Roman Empire; orality, writing, and oral performance.

Werner H. Kelber (1935), Isla Carroll and Percy E. Turner Professor Emeritus of Biblical Studies at Rice University, Comprehensive Theological Exam, Erlangen University, Th. M., Princeton Theological Seminary, 1963 M. A., University of Chicago, Ph. D. University of Chicago; main areas of research: the search for the historical Jesus, gospel narrativity, biblical hermeneutics, orality-scribality studies, the history of the Bible, memory, rhetoric, text criticism, and the Western receptionist history of the Bible.

Roger S. Nam (1970), Assistant Professor of Biblical Studies, George Fox University, Portland, Ph. D. University of California Los Angeles; main areas of research: comparative semitics, social scientific approaches to the Hebrew Bible.

Susan Niditch (1950), Samuel Green Professor of Religion, Amherst College Massachusetts; AB Radcliffe College 1972; Ph.D. Harvard University 1977; main areas of research: Hebrew Bible and Early Judaism with methodological interests in oral literature, folklore studies, and comparative religious ethics.

David Rhoads (1941), Professor of New Testament at the Lutheran School of Theology in Chicago, MDiv (Lutheran Theological Seminary at Gettyburg); Ph.D. (Duke University); main areas of research: Gospel of Mark; The Letters to the Galatians; The Letter of James; Narrative Criticism; Biblical performance Criticism.

Annette Schellenberg (1971), Associate Professor of Old Testament, San Francisco Theological Seminary and Graduate Theological Union, Ph. D. (Zürich); main areas of research: Old Testament wisdom literature, anthropology, reception history.

Andreas Schuele, Aubrey Lee Brooks Professor of Biblical Theology at Union Theological Seminary & Presbyterian School of Christian Education; Dr. phil. (University of Heidelberg), Dr. theol. habil. (University of Zürich); main areas of research: religious history and theology of the Hebrew Bible, Pentateuch, Isaiah.

Teun L. Tieleman (1960), Associate Professor of Ancient Philosophy at the Department of Philosophy, Utrecht University; Ph. D. obtained in Utrecht University; main areas of research: Stoicism, ancient medicine (Galen), later ancient philosophy, the sociology of ancient philosophy.

Trevor Thompson (1975), Instructor of New Testament at Abilene Christian University, Ph. D. Candidate, New Testament & Early Christian Literature, University of Chicago; main areas of Research: Greco-Roman education & rhetoric, Pseudepigraphy.

David Trobisch (1958), Magister theol., Dr. theol., Dr. habil. theol (University of Heidelberg); main areas of research: Letters of Paul, formation of New Testament, Biblical manuscripts.

Annette Weissenrieder (1967), Associate Professor of New Testament at San Francisco Theological Seminary and the Graduate Theological Union, Berkeley; Dr. theol. (University of Heidelberg); main areas of research: Theology of Paul and the Synoptic Gos-

pels, Greco-roman medicine and philosophy, New Testament anthropology, pneumatology, theories of the history of religion, Roman domestic art, numismatic, and architecture.

Antoinette Clark Wire (1934), Professor of New Testament Emerita at San Francisco
Theological Seminary and the Graduate Theological Union; main areas of research:
Gospel oral traditions, Pauline theology, women in early Christianity, and Chinese
Christian oral songs.

Ruben Zimmermann (1968), Professor of New Testament at Johannes Gutenberg University, Mainz, Germany; Dr. theol. University of Heidelberg; Dr. theol. habil. (University of Munich); main areas of research: ethics, gender-studies, hermeneutics of New
Testament, Jesus parables.

Index of Sources

Index of Names

Achtemeier, P. 121
Alberti, L.B. 92
Alexander, L. 229, 345
Alkier, S. 234
Alter, R. 6, 10, 17–18
Arav, R. 278–279
Assmann, J. 20, 83, 131, 211

Baeck, L. 358
Bakker, E. 53
Balch, D.L. 244, 249
Bar-Ilan, M. 51–52
Barabási, A.L. 46
Barlett, F.C. 131
Barr, J. 78
Barrett, C.K. 397
Bauckham, R. 231
Baum, A.D. 138
Baur, F.C. 366–367
Becker, H.-J. 48, 51
Begrich, J. 324–325, 330
Belo, F. 57
Ben Zvi, E. 294, 321
Bennema, C. 233
Bennett, D.J. 47
Bergmann, B. 239
Beyen, H.G. 236–37, 246, 258
Black, M. 355
Bookidis, N. 238
Botha, P.J.J. 57, 157, 181, 371, 377
Boudieú, P. 120
Bredekamp, H. 260
Brown, P. 87–88
Brown, R.E. 233
Buber, M. 13, 217
Bultmann, R. 54, 207
Burkert, W. 23, 249
Burrows, M. 76

Capurro, R. 208
Carr, D. 7, 8, 72–73, 80, 146
Carruthers, M. 173
Cassidy, R.J. 395
Cavallo, G. 350
Chafe, W. 53
Conzelmann, H. 398
Crawford, M.H. 268
Cross, F.M. 12
Culley, R.C. 5

Dettwiler, A. 231
Dewey, J. 56, 127, 157–158, 376
Dibelius, M. 54, 137
Doan, A.N 67
Dodd, C.H. 54
Doeve, J.W. 263
Draper, J. 139
Duffy, E. 87
Dundes, Alan 4

Eco, U. 120, 129
Eisenstein, J.D. 92, 94–96
Epp, E. 155, 211
Erll, A. 131

Finnegan, R. 6, 104
Fischer, J. 218
Fishbane, M. 67
Fitzmyer, J.A. 395
Fleddermann, H.T. 141
Floyd, M. 310
Flusser, D. 262
Foley, J.M. 4, 7, 8, 17, 56, 68, 103–118, 293
Foucault, M. ix
Fox, E. 13–14, 17
France, R.T. 128
Frazer, J.G. 265
Frei, H. 169

Index of Subjects

Errata and Corrigenda

Preface

ix, line 13 from bottom: correct subtitle: *Speaking, Seeing, Writing in the Shaping of New Genres* . . .

xii, line 11 from bottom: correct subtitle

xiii, line 1: "and" for "und"

Niditch

3, embedded quote, last line: delete first "of"

8, line 6: "Jaffee" for "Jaffe"

9, line 23: ". . . Abiezer?"

Tieleman

22, line 15: ". . . the revelation of a divine figure who clearly fulfills . . ."

24, line 10: ". . . basis of the interlocutor's . . ."

24, fn 18, line 3: ". . . 'aporetic'. . ."

26, line 25: "Some of the ideas . . ."

28, line 25: "citations" for "citation."

31, line 20: ". . . Western Greece): . . ."

32, line 14: "chance" for "change"; "others" for "other"

32, line 5 from bottom: delete second "with"

34, line 10: delete "the"

Hezser

42, line 9: "desserts" for "deserts"
55, line 4 from bottom: "thirty-one" for "thirty one"
58, line 2 from bottom: delete extraneous "?"
62, fn 38, line 1: "twenty-four" for "twenty four"

Kelber

72: . . . last BUT not least . . .
75, line 18: delete first comma
75, line 2 from bottom: "realities" for "realties"
86, line 13: insert comma after "Tables"
90, line 12: delete closed quotation mark
91, line 2: "explored" for "exploring"
97, line 5: "recklessly" for "reckless"
99, Line 7: delete close quote

Foley

108, Table, 4th (Reception) Column: "A/W" for "O/W"
110, line 19: *"Performance"* for "performance"
115, line 18: . . ."*Oral tradition*" for "*Oraltradition*"
115, line 22 *"Performance"* for "performance"

Dronsch

125, line 14 insert "between": ". . . no break between what . . ."
125, line 8 from bottom: "a" for "an"
126, line 5: " that is, a written medium, the written Gospel . . ."

Zimmermann

136, fn 25: "German" for "german"
139, fn 43: "and" for "und"
139, fn 43, line 3: . . . derived text,"
140, line 12: insert comma after "topic"
143, line 9: "semanticization" for "semantization"

Horsley

144, line 15: delete first "the"
160, line 4: delete hyphens
162, line 13: delete redundant "can be"
162, line 8 from bottom: delete hyphens

Rhoads

167, fn 5: "Omne" for "Omni"
175, line 8: "rhapsodes" for "rapsodes"
176, line 19: " . . . *performance*"
180, line 21: ". . . contexts"
185, line 3: delete hyphen
190, line 13: "Performances" for "performances"
191, line 8: capitalize "World Trade Center"

Trobisch

194, line 7 from bottom: "'a creature . . .'"
197, line 9: "Performance" for "performance"
198, line 5 from bottom: "Performance" for "performance"

Dronsch/Weissenrieder

205, line 11f: "indebted" for "undebted"
206, line 10: "inseparable" for "unseparable"
207, line 6: delete apostrophe
207, line 23: delete "the" before "Kelber's concept"
207, line 24: "with regard" for "regarding" the use of language . . .
207, line 5 from bottom: "two premises of" for "two premises"
208, line 7: insert comma after "Krämer"
212, section 2, lines 7-8: delete sentence: "Besides . . . swallows."
214, line 3: delete "both"
214, fn 40, line 2: delete commas; delete "is"
214, line 20: "guises" for "figure"
214, line 3 from bottom: "and" for "und"
215, fn 44, line 1: "Hermes" for "Hermes' "

215, fn 44, line 3: "of" for "to"
220, bottom line: "Thanatos" for "Thanathos"
228. fn 81: "Schniedewind" for "Schniewind"
229, line 4: "word." for "word:".
229, line 5 from bottom: "of" for "if"
233, line 19: insert "is" following "He"
235, line 19: "is" for "ist."
235, line 2 from bottom: "and" for "und"

Balch

238, lines 21, 22: "frescoes" for "frescos"
240, line 17: "poplar" for "popular"
241, line 3 from bottom: insert period
244, line 18-19: "Dionysus" for "Dionysius"
259, line 3: ." for . " and transpose period to end of line

Weissenrieder

261, fn 3 line 4: "issuance" for "issuancing'
261, fn 4: "Hezser" for "Heszer"
261, fn 5: "propaganda" for 'propaganda"
263, line 19: "other Gospels?" for "other Gospels."
263, line 22: "an" for "a"
264, fn 14 line 4: insert "in" before "which"
266, line 7 from bottom: "had" for "has"
266, last line: "image" for "images"
268, fn 24: "a connection can be made with" for "is to be expelled"
269, line 16: insert "with" after "minted"
276, line 1: "and altars," for "altars"
278, line 6: delete comma
279, caption: "by" for "from"
280, line 4: delete comma
281, line 5 from bottom: insert dash after "material"

Schellenberg

299, fn 53: "in" for "into"
308, fn 79 last line: delete comma

Nam

312, line 12: "on" for "of"
315, line 9: "gave" for "game"
316, line 16: I Chr 16 in parentheses
317, last line: "literacy" for "literary"
318, line 14: insert "the" before "deities"
319, line 20: insert "the" before "mode"
320, line 15: insert comma after Asaph
320, line 17: "participants' " for "participants,"
320, line 6 from bottom: "Levitical" for "levitical"
321, line 10: insert comma after "genealogy"
321, line 11: "replaced" for "replaces"
321, line 26: delete first "in"

Schuele

325, fn 11 line 2: "and" for "und"
333, fn 30 lin 3: "gods" for "God's"
333, *I lament*, line 1: "ships" for "shops"
333, *Enemy lament* line 1: " belongs with quote
334, line13 from bottom: "to" for "so"

Botha

335, line 3: "hundred and fifty"
336, line 2 from bottom: "Oxyrhynchus" for "Oxyrynchus"
338, last line: insert comma after "here"
345, line 15: "Performance" for "performance"

Boyarin

356, line 6: insert " following colon
358, fn 18 line 17: "holes" for "holds"
360, fn 21: "Cf." for "cf."
361, line 6 from bottom: delete final "would"

Hearon

381, line 18: delete period
382, line 6: written," for written", etc.
382, fn 15: "Testimonia" for "Tesimonia"
383, line 3: parenthesis before period
387, fn 22 line 2: "8:8" for "8:18"
390, line 3: insert "of the" before "Gospel"

Thompson

397, line 4: "As" for "as"

Index of Names

427: insert F. D. Gilliard   121

CPSIA information can be obtained
at www.ICGtesting.com
Printed in the USA
LVHW110229161220
674309LV00006B/130